Beyond the Horizons

BEYOND

THE

HORIZONS

The Lockheed Story
· · ·

Walter J. Boyne

THOMAS
DUNNE
BOOKS

ST. MARTIN'S PRESS 🙰 NEW YORK

THOMAS DUNNE BOOKS.
An imprint of St. Martin's Press.

Library of Congress Cataloging-in-Publication Data

Boyne, Walter J.
    Beyond the horizons : the Lockheed story / by Walter J. Boyne.
        p.   cm.
    Includes bibliographical references and index.
    ISBN 0-312-19237-1
    1. Lockheed Aircraft Corporation—History.   2. Aircraft industry—United   States—History.   3. Aerospace   industries—United States—History.   I. Title.
    HD9711.U63L595   1998   98-19397
    338.7'6291334'0973—dc21   CIP

Book design: Richard Oriolo

First Edition: October 1998

10 9 8 7 6 5 4 3 2 1

This book is respectfully dedicated

to all the men and women of the Lockheed family,

including all those who have flown or used

the products of that historic company.

Contents

. . .

Foreword

. . .

Lockheed. The name first entered my consciousness in the late 1930s, when I was a boy interested in model airplanes. Then, so many years ago, for reasons I can't explain, the name stood out for me from those of all the other aircraft companies. Whether it was Lockheed's airplanes, its image, or simply the distinctive name, I can't say. I just knew with the assurance of an eight-year-old that Lockheed was special. (Today, with equal assurance, I know that countless thousands feel the same.)

In later years I was hired by Lockheed, and began to learn its history and appreciate its products, people, and leaders. Now, some forty years after I first pinned a badge with the winged star to my lapel, there is no longer a Lockheed in the sense there was when its airplanes set records which still endure and its missiles and space systems deterred devastating conflict during the cold war. Instead, the New York

Stock Exchange lists a successor company, Lockheed Martin, a product of the dramatic reshaping of the U.S. aerospace industry in the 1990s.

Much of what Lockheed was about—its culture, reputation for cutting-edge technology, head-turning products, and global presence—remains as a rich vein in Lockheed Martin, yet a threshold has been crossed. It is a threshold that calls for a fresh, comprehensive Lockheed history, the final chapter.

In the pages which follow, Walter Boyne tackles the daunting task of chronicling Lockheed's history from the days when the Loughead brothers' Model G biplane graced the waters of San Francisco Bay through the merger which created (at the time) the world's largest aerospace and defense company. The story defies completeness in the span of just a few hundred pages, and some will find their favorite person, event, airplane, missile, or satellite accorded less attention than they would like. It defies completeness because for over sixty years Lockheed touched the lives of hundreds of thousands of employees and their families, creating an infinite reservoir of stories and memories.

The company supported our nation's defense of democracy through five wars, adapting to wrenching downturns in defense spending following each conflict. It flourished in the early days of commercial aviation, but ultimately left the market, skirting bankruptcy before closing the production line of the superb L-1011 in 1983. It branched from its aviation roots, anticipating the boom in missiles and space that followed *Sputnik*, and ultimately saw these new activities grow larger than the heritage aircraft business. Though the products were different, Lockheed's stature as a technology leader was enhanced.

The history of Lockheed is an immense canvas painted with bold strokes and vibrant colors. In a sense the original palette and composition trace to the founder of the modern Lockheed, Robert E. Gross. His impact was towering, his legacy enduring. Gross's vision, dignity, and ethical values defined the company during his tenure and—despite rare and isolated departures—long after he had departed.

Some say that Gross created a technology company. Viewed externally this appears true, but what of the source of the technology and the products for which Lockheed was so well recognized? They sprang from the minds and the hands and the dedication of countless men and women who, drawn by Gross's vision, affiliated themselves with the company, some for years, many for decades. This is their history, one written day by day over more than sixty years, in times good and bad, through wars, economic cycles, technology upheavals, and globalization of trade. It is a history worth recalling, a profile of achievement, a triumph worthy of Gross's vision to "Look ahead where the horizons are absolutely unlimited."

Daniel M. Tellep
Chairman and CEO
Lockheed Corporation
1989–1995

Preface:
Leaders, Timing, and
Technology

. . .

The twentieth century will be remembered for many things, and among the best of these are the truly remarkable achievements in air and space technology. From the Wright brothers' first flights on December 17, 1903, to the eve of the next millennium, aviation's incredible journey has carried over the windswept sands of Kitty Hawk, beyond the still beauty of space, to the roaring turbulence of newborn stars. A box camera's lens caught the first moment of Orville's 120-foot flight, preserving it for us forever in black and white. Today, only ninety-plus years later, the optics of the Hubble telescope reach out not only in distance but in time to the very beginning of the universe. No one knew it at the time, but Orville's flight was just the first tentative step toward the stars as aviation carried all science forward.

In that royal progress, as many as ten thousand companies around the world, with hope, passion, and full-page advertisements, have brought their skills and money to the world of aviation. Most of these firms disappeared swiftly, sometimes within weeks of their brave announcements, very often within a year. Only a few were able to prosper for an extended period before the intense competition that defines the world of aerospace business forced them to shut down or to be absorbed by another company.

Heroic names abound even among those that eventually succumbed to events, including such important foreign entities as Sopwith, Hawker, Bleriot, Breguet, Handley Page, and Fokker. In the United States, even some of the most famous aviation firms closed their doors or were absorbed, companies such as Curtiss, which dominated the industry for so long, North American, that great builder of fighters and bombers (and recently reborn as Boeing North American), and Consolidated, Reuben Fleet's famous creation. When they were in their prime, selling the top aircraft in their field, it seemed that they would prevail against all odds.

But the aviation world is cruel, and aging companies are subject to ills not unlike those of aging humans: hardening of managerial arteries, loss of corporate memory, and most insidious of all, too strong a tendency to conservatism. These contribute to the single most important factor in company failures: a lack of financial success. The ultimate success of the Lockheed Corporation revolved around its bold decisions coupled with wise and farseeing financial management.

A very few companies not only have survived the hard combats of the twentieth century, but renewed themselves in the struggle so that another one hundred years of increasingly scientific endeavor is a bright and pleasing prospect. One of the most successful of these began in 1913 when two brothers—the Lougheads—designed and built an aircraft in San Francisco. That first aircraft, and the small crew that built it, contained in microcosm the elements that, despite setbacks, would persevere to become the familiar Lockheed Aircraft Corporation.

Times were tough in those very early days of aviation, and despite the technical excellence of the Loughead brothers' aircraft, the firm was forced to go under. The brothers would return to aviation again and again, and one of them, Allan, would become a founder of the original Lockheed Aircraft Company in 1926, its name spelled to reflect its pronunciation. That organization would also build superb aircraft, record setters that were internationally recognized for their excellence and flown by the most famous pilots in the world. But it would not be able to survive the twin effects of its sale to a larger firm and the Great Depression of the 1930s.

Unlike most companies that met the same depressing fate, Lockheed would rise again with a resilience that would come to characterize it in the future, when beset by events even more threatening than the depression. Over the next six decades, it would achieve an unprecedented record of success, leading to a merger in 1995 with an equal, complementary partner, Martin Marietta, to become the Lockheed Martin Corporation, a dominant aerospace firm in the world today.

Its growth in the intervening years between its rebirth in 1932 and its present preeminent position were possible only because of a unique corporate culture, a legacy of Bob Gross, one embraced by the term "the Lockheed family." This culture, while difficult to define as it changed to meet new needs, nonetheless maintained certain consistent, identifiable traits. The Lockheed corporate culture involved brilliant people working together at all levels, strong individuals who were willing to sacrifice their time, and in some cases, their lives, to the ideals of the company. For most of them, company loyalty was a simple metaphor for their loyalty to their country, for they knew that the United States depended upon Lockheed products to a critical degree. From the early days of the production of the famous P-38 fighter to the remarkable success of its submarine-launched ballistic missiles to the great intelligence triumphs of its spy aircraft, spy satellites, and stealth planes, Lockheed has been absolutely vital to the security of the United States. Meeting the endless crises involved in producing advanced weapons meant working twelve-hour days and seven-day weeks for months on end as a matter of course. It was a strenuous but fulfilling regimen that became an accepted, even addictive, way of life for everyone from the shop floor to the boardroom.

An invaluable, indeed defining, result of Lockheed's unique corporate culture has been the almost unerring selection of the right leaders at the right time, who in their turn, in most instances selected the right technologies to pursue. In a manner unusual for an air and space company, Lockheed has for most of its existence had a nonengineer as its chief executive officer. A former president of the Lockheed California Company, Willis Hawkins, was one of aviation's greatest engineers, a Lockheed stalwart, and a keen rival of the world-renowned Clarence "Kelly" Johnson, perhaps the most highly regarded engineer in the history of aviation. (It speaks to both Lockheed's wealth of talent and its unique culture that two such towering geniuses could have worked together so well for so long.) Hawkins believed having a non-engineer as the top man to be a valuable company characteristic. He has commented that although Lockheed often had engineers to head divisions of the corporation, the top executive came from a different, usually financial or operational, environment. The result was that the CEO was less personally aware of possible engineering hazards—the dreaded "unknown unknowns"—and was thus less conservative. Because the CEO assumed the ultimate responsibility for decisions, the engineers felt free to take more risks, and for all of the history of air and space, successful risk management has been the essential key to progress.

Since the rebirth of the present Lockheed company in 1932, only eight men have held the top executive position. Each of these has operated in a different manner, for each one faced different challenges with different resources, and provided solutions unique to the individual. The results for Lockheed have been remarkable, for it has managed not only to keep in the technological forefront of aviation, but also to lead all competitors around the world by as much as two decades in fields such as reconnaissance and stealth. It has created aircraft such as the SR-71, one of the few aircraft to become almost a cult object in terms of popular following, and in the more than thirty years since its conception, one that has never had an aeronautical equivalent. With the exception of one doleful twelve-year period (1965–77), the Lockheed Corporation remained in the top echelon of its industry in profits, prestige, and influence.

Yet, over time, the general nature of its leadership style has manifested a distinct change, one that echoes a similar change not only in the general American population, but also within the U.S. military services. During the first half of the company's existence, from its first chairman, Robert Gross, down through the reign of board chairman Daniel J. Haughton, leadership was centralized and authoritarian. One, two, or three top managers made decisions, and merely informed a board of directors, mostly insiders, what those decisions were. Subsequent to Haughton's tenure, the influence of the board of directors has been considerably expanded, with many more outside directors involved. The result has been a less authoritarian, more decentralized management style for most of the organization, one more in tune with the changing national lifestyle. Fortunately, the right managers were chosen at each point.

Lockheed's good fortune in leadership has not been confined to its chief executive office, for it has also attracted and retained the top science and technology talent in the industry, year after year. There is both cause and effect in this. The top managers were wise enough to seek out, employ, and, most of all, endure their top engineers, for the latter were men of strong will and character, difficult to control and often painful to deal with. The engineers, tough, outspoken men including Clarence "Kelly" Johnson and Ben Rich, as well as many others, recognized their managers' tolerance—if not always their brilliance—and as a result, worked even harder, knowing that less-permissive managers at other firms would have inhibited their dazzling forays beyond contemporary engineering frontiers. One curious aspect of Lockheed's history is that it fielded a group of managers and engineers in its Missiles and Space Company who were in every respect equal to those of the aviation side, but were less well known because of the security requirements of their mission. These included men such as Eugene Root, Herschel Brown, Stanley Burriss, Louis Ridenour and James Plummer along with others who brought into being scientific systems and equipment that were thought to be impossible to create. Through their efforts, and the efforts of their teams, they placed the United States firmly in the lead in intelligence-gathering with incredible satellites, even as they created the most effective deterrent yet, the fleet ballistic missile system. Their contributions were often not even known to one another, much less to their academic peers. Even their closest family members were denied all knowledge of what they were doing. Yet they persisted, because they knew they were breaking new ground in the most important fields of military work in our nation's history.

The best engineers were attracted to Lockheed because they knew they would be allowed to work to their limits. In the early years, they were spared most of the bureaucratic digressions typical of the aviation industry; in later years things inevitably became more bureaucratic—and the complaints from older Lockheedians are loud about this—but still relatively less so than at other firms.

In simplest terms, Lockheed's leaders encouraged their outstanding engineers to go beyond the bounds of ordinary aeronautics and astronautics to achieve the great air and space milestones. These include the first American operational jet fighter, the P-80; the Mach 2 F-104; the great cargo planes like the C-130, C-141, and C-5; the U-2 and SR-71 spy planes; the Agena launch vehicle; the Discoverer (CORONA) and other spy satellites; the submarine-launched ballistic missiles; the F-117A stealth fighter; and the F-22 Raptor, plus other, still-classified programs. To quote Hawkins, who was influential on both the aircraft and the space side of the house, "Lockheed came up with irresistible products." Any one of these would have been the high point of the careers of ordinary engineers in an ordinary company; at Lockheed, they were but part of a continuum of technological excellence that extends from its first glimmerings in San Francisco Bay on out toward tomorrow's stars.

The style of leadership provided by top managers and first-rate engineers was contagious, permeating the Lockheed environment so that employees at every level felt a shared responsibility for the success of the firm. The fact that good morale was both wide and deep provided the company a flexibility it would need in meeting the challenges inherent in the new fields it elected to explore, and the strength to endure the financial and ethical storms that arose like back-to-back hurricanes in the 1970s.

For almost half its existence, Lockheed has been diversified into fields far from aviation, and has achieved the same degree of excellence in most of these. Some—like shipbuilding—were by nature more pedestrian, and thus paradoxically a reach too far. When it was apparent that they could not be managed in a satisfactory manner, they were given up. Nonetheless, one facet of the unique corporate culture has been the cross-fertilization of engineering and managerial talent among several varied fields. It is perhaps not extraordinary that the great Lockheed Georgia enterprise, which began with rebuilding B-29s for the Korean War and continues today as a production center for the venerable but ever-new C-130 transport and the F-22 fighter, began with a wholesale transfusion of people at all levels from California. Nor is it unusual that the boundless energy of the Lockheed Missile and Space Division was given its start from the parent company in a similar way. What is surprising is the way that each of these new companies has provided the training and the challenges to fashion its own cadre of leaders, who in many cases returned to top positions in the parent company. These transfusions of talent were sometimes as painless as a kiss, sometimes as painful as a bone marrow transplant, but have to date been so remarkably successful as to lead to the creation of one of the world's largest aerospace firms.

The author wants to state most emphatically that the people named in this book—executives, engineers, managers—are themselves metaphors for the teams they led. Many projects persisted for years, sometimes decades. In the course of a project, there are several people who lead it or make major contributions to it. Space limitations preclude naming each one, so the reader must see that when a chairman or a project engineer is mentioned in association with a project, he stands for all the many men and women who contributed to it.

In its long journey from a single-engine floatplane in San Francisco Bay to the creation of the X-33 VentureStar, potential successor to the space shuttle, the men and women of the Lockheed Corporation have worked with worthy counterparts in American and international industry and government. The cartoonists and the editorial writers who lampoon that easy target, the "military-industrial complex," have no idea how stringent the rules of military procurement can be; nor how difficult it is to meet demanding specifications with virtually impossible schedules and still make a profit. Proof of the rigor is easily found in the thousands of companies that have gone under. Lockheed was fortunate that while it did not always do well on its commercial aircraft, its contracts for military aircraft were for the most part profitable. The Lockheed Missile and Space Company proved to be highly profitable over the years.*

In the commercial world, outside the infamous but misunderstood "complex," one finds that the airlines are equally valuable, equally difficult partners, for each one naturally seeks to obtain the best economic advantage for itself in the purchase of a new airliner, as when Lockheed had to deal with the eternally eccentric but undeniably brilliant Howard Hughes. Even dealing with industry vendors is always conducted at the same level of stress and at surprising degrees of hazard, as Lockheed found out in its relationship with Rolls-Royce.

Despite these dangers, within the aviation community as a whole there exists a desire to progress and to succeed that makes the work exciting and fulfilling. A reciprocal trust was established among the people at Lockheed, in industry, and in the military services. It was this faith in their counterparts that enabled all three elements to advance further in air and space technology than anyone could have anticipated, and far beyond the best any competing system in the world has accomplished.

One unusual aspect of the first fifty years of Lockheed's progress was that much of its dynamism came from hard-driving workers who "came up the hard way." Most of these came from distinctly unprivileged backgrounds. Many not only lacked college degrees, but often even college or high-school attendance. They learned on the floor and in the air, and acquired confidence along with their hard-earned skills.

---

*The name of this element of the Lockheed Company changed continuously over the years. It is always shown as it was called at the time in question.

Yet these products of rough-and-tumble apprenticeships rallied to a more patrician executive group after 1932 to form a perfect combination to deal with the "eastern establishment" on one level while putting out products of creative western excellence at another. After World War II, this situation began to change, but for many years there was a leavening of old-timers who saw to it that the basic raw elegance of the Lockheed working style was not compromised. In time, far more advanced managerial methods became necessary, as a more cerebral approach was required to both the engineering and the financing necessary for dealing with advanced aeronautics and astronautics.

In the following pages, we will chart the progress of the Lockheed company from its very earliest days. We will examine how its leadership qualities adapted to the times, comparing the products of the evolving technology with those of contemporary competitors. We will look to the words of the men and women of Lockheed to explain just how its many successes as well as its occasional—but very painful— failures came about. The term "Lockheed family" will be seen again and again, to explain how the triumphs were achieved and, perhaps more important, how the bad times were endured.

Author's Note

. . .

The reader will find repeated references in the book to the "Lockheed family"—so many, in fact, that I have some concern that the phrase will be looked upon as merely an overworked literary device. However, in the course of several hundred interviews, telephone conversations, faxes, and E-mails with Lockheed alumni, it was impossible not to be impressed by the genuine familial sense that the various Lockheed corporations engendered in their employees at every level over the years.

The essence of this familial sense is difficult to convey. Lockheed veterans recall incidents and people with the greatest affection, and with a sense of nostalgia engendered by the long relationship they enjoyed. Often the most cherished events depend upon an intimate knowledge of the situations and the people involved. Some of these slices of the Lockheed fabric are difficult to reconstitute in a few paragraphs—they are too often a case of "you had to be there." But others bear retelling well, particularly when they involved some of the major Lockheed personalities.

It is more important to remember that this Lockheed family was in many ways responsible for the present security and prosperity of the United States. Lockheed, more than any other single commercial corporation, had responsibilities for the key offensive and defensive weapon systems of the cold war. Without fear of contradiction, it can be said that the combination of the Lockheed intelligence-gathering resources, including the U-2 and SR-71 spy planes and the CORONA— and subsequent—spy satellites provided information on a scale beyond the conception of the Soviet Union. This vast intelligence superiority enabled the United States to meter its defense expenditures at a rate that allowed the civilian economy to prosper as well. The Soviet Union did not have comparable systems, and its military expenditures were too much for the inherently faulty Communist economy to bear.

Lockheed also produced extremely effective offensive weapons, most notably the many generations of the Fleet Ballistic Missile system. There were others as well, great fighters and cargo planes, but the Polaris, Poseidon, and Trident series of submarine-launched ballistic missiles became the strongest—and most elusive—element of the United States' strategic triad.

The strength that Lockheed's formidable technological leadership imparted to the United States was vital to winning the cold war. Ironically, that cold war victory could have meant the end of Lockheed, geared as it was to defense production. However, the leaders at Lockheed had anticipated the problem and set in motion plans to accommodate to the post–cold war situation. Thanks to the spirit and capabilities of its employees, Lockheed was able to compete in the new commercial arena with equal success.

The eighty-five-year history of Lockheed was not without its failures, both technical and human. This book records those failures as well, but the reader will note that the company and its people succeeded far more often than they failed. It will also be evident that in every case of failure, no matter how difficult for Lockheed at the time, the firm came back rapidly, to greater achievements. That ability to perform well after adversity is, like the general pattern of Lockheed successes, attributable directly to the patriotism of employees at every level. Their complete devotion to their company was in large part because they felt their company was essential to the defense of the United States.

The recognition of this combination of familial loyalty and patriotic devotion to duty is absolutely fundamental to understanding the history of a corporation that grew from an awkward-looking flying boat tested on San Francisco Bay into one of the world's most successful corporations. The success of Lockheed far transcended commercial considerations, and the degree of this success may be found in the memories of its loyal alumni.

These memories, disclosed so freely in the interviews and replete with so much information, anecdotes, recollections, and insights, are a wonderful resource to draw upon—but there is a downside. There is absolutely no way that the history of Lockheed, extending from its origin in 1913 to the merger with Martin Marietta in 1995, can be compressed into a single volume. In those momentous years, there were literally thousands of projects—aircraft, missiles, satellites, and a vast array of other advanced equipment. Hundreds of thousands of people worked on these projects, some as managers, some as hands-on workers on the line. Each has his or her story to tell.

Thus the most difficult task was deciding what had to be told, and winnowing out, no matter how reluctantly, things that were in my perception slightly less important or interesting. Sometimes material which was equally important, and equally interesting, had to be left out for other reasons. I tried to obtain a reasonable balance between the various companies and divisions which composed Lockheed over the years. Security considerations also played a part, for much of the work undertaken by Lockheed Missiles and Space in all its many incarnations is still classified.

I have no doubt erred occasionally in my judgment; I am sure that some people of the Lockheed family will be bewildered that a particular project or a particular person was omitted. I ask both understanding and forgiveness, and can assure you that it was done only with great regret. There was material enough for a twenty-volume history, but my charter was to compress time, people, and events into a single volume.

Because of this, I would like to make it clear that the people and the projects that are named within are not only stories in themselves, but are metaphors for all of the team members who made important, thrilling events happen at Lockheed. Some programs—the Fleet Ballistic Missile program, for example—have been in existence for decades, under the leadership of many great managers, and succeeding only because there are and have been thousands of dedicated workers. It is impossible to track all of these in a single volume. Thus when a famous name like Kelly Johnson's is mentioned, no one would know better than he that his name is but a metaphor for the cracking good team that worked for him. In a similar way, the constraints of space force me to attribute to individual leaders—Robert and Courtland Gross, Dan Haughton, Roy Anderson, Larry Kitchen, Dan Tellep— many momentous events. Their names are symbols for the teams they led to Lockheed's triumphs.

And there were so many Lockheed triumphs that there is credit enough for all, mentioned or unmentioned. To have been a part of the Lockheed family is to have been a part of one of the most innovative, progressive, and successful aerospace firms in history.

Walter J. Boyne
Ashburn, Virginia

Acknowledgments

. . .

The almost joyous sense of family mentioned in the preface was characterized by the total cooperation of everyone at Lockheed, from the most senior executive down to the hardworking troops who ferreted out box after dusty box of information stored so well and so systematically at Rye Canyon.

There are so many people to thank for their cooperation that I am certain that I will omit someone's name. Let me begin with the senior management of Lockheed. I received enthusiastic support and information from Roy A. Anderson, Lawrence O. Kitchen, Daniel M. Tellep, Vincent N. Marafino, and Willis Hawkins. I also received their most thorough reviews, advice, and suggestions. It is worth noting here that Willis Hawkins, younger in his eighties than most are in their thirties, twice went through every page of the manuscript, initialing each page, and making voluminous suggestions and corrections in a handwritten print as precise as an IBM typewriter's. That Willis found time to do so between building his Glastar aircraft and flying his Beech Bonanza is remarkable. It should be noted that while the five men mentioned above reviewed the manuscript carefully several times, it was with the complete understanding that the author had the final say on what and how material would be presented.

Invaluable inputs and guidance were received from senior executives who took time from their busy schedules to be interviewed and to review my written material. They include Minoru "Sam" Araki, Norman R. Augustine, Mel Brashears, Kenneth D. Cannestra, Vance D. Coffman, Jack S. Gordon, Carl Haddon, Doug Kenyon, Carl Kotchian, John R. Kreick, John N. McMahon, Elsie Merrihew, Sherman N. Mullin, Fritz Oder, Susan M. Pearce, Val P. Peline, James W. Plummer, Jack Real, Derald Stuart, and Anthony G. "Jerry" Van Schaick. The volume of information resulting from these interviews was overwhelming. It complemented the marvelous Lockheed oral history program created and managed by William D. Perreault.

In addition, there were dozens of individual Lockheed employees whose help was invaluable, including Julius Alexander, Vince Arkangel, Ray Austin, Hugh Burns, Virnell Bruce, Robert Burgess, Robert Clayton, Marie Castillo, Steve Chaudet, David R. Corbeil, David Ferguson, Douglas Heydon, Peter Harrigan, Gaylen Hogan, Ralph Hurvitz, Bob Leeper, Ronald Lindeke, Michael W. DeNeal, Justin Murphy, Buddy Nelson, Alex Osorio, Don Parker, Ray Passon, M. W. "Marty" Phillips, Tom Pugh, Ross Reynolds, Jeff Rhodes, Lee Rogers, Yvonne Rossi, Lorraine Sadler, Cliff Schaefer, Eric Schulzinger, Eric Solinger, Garfield Thomas, Denny Thompson, John Turner, and Jan Wrather. Danielle DeSoto was always totally helpful and totally patient. Eric Schulzinger combined his photographic artistry with the marvelous digital filing and retrieving system that made photographic research a pleasure. He was ably assisted by Eric Solinger, Bo Edwards, and Denny Lombard.

It was my good fortune to know Clarence L. "Kelly" Johnson, Ben Rich, and Anthony "Tony" LeVier many long years before I began work on this book, and I called upon my memory in writing of them.

Ms. Marlaine Lockheed and John Lockheed gave me insight into the lives of Flora Haynes Loughead, Victor Lockhead, and Allan and Malcolm Lockheed. Their intimate knowledge was unavailable anywhere else.

I am grateful to others outside Lockheed, too, including historian and friend Gerry Balzer, historian Warren Bodie, noted attorney Brian

Freeman, Cargill Hall of the Office of Air Force History, Ann Hassinger of the United States Naval Institute, George S. McKenzie of the Goleta Air Museum in Santa Barbara, Wally Meeks for his usual good ideas, S. Katherine Schneider, National Reconnaissance Office, Henry Snelling for his always excellent editorial work, and Dr. George Watson of the Office of Air Force History.

My daughter Katherine Teague helped with research on Santa Barbara, while another daughter, Molly Boyne, assisted with the filing, bibliography, and most especially, transcribing the many hours of taped interviews. I owe sincere thanks also to Jacques de Spoelberch, a superb agent and friend, publicist Joe Rinaldi, and my editors, Thomas Dunne and Pete Wolverton, and their able assistant, Kristen Nardullo.

I must give special thanks to Susan Pearce for initiating this project, and for guiding me through it. Among the many nice things she did was to put me in touch with Trudy Sibley, who has worked long, hard, and with the greatest diligence to provide invaluable assistance and suggestions. Trudy was ably aided by Claire Bunnell. There was no request too difficult for these two women who epitomize the Lockheed spirit.

And the book would not have been possible without the diligent, intelligent research done by Birch Matthews. Birch, an accomplished author in his own right, dug deep and long for material, driving long hours to Rye Canyon, Burbank, Palmdale, and elsewhere. His knowledge of the subject, and his stubborn engineer's drive to get it right, enabled him to winnow the wheat from the chaff, so that I was presented with the richest material from the great quantity that he surveyed. Birch also conducted several valuable interviews. A great future by-product of his effort will be his own books based on his research.

Many people were helpful to my ace researcher, including Gerry Balzer, Vince Arkangle, Cliff Schneffer, Alex Osorio, Don Parker, Greg Austin, Elsie Merrihew, Carl Haddon, Jack Real, and Dave Kenyon.

To all of the above and more I am grateful beyond words. If I've forgotten someone, do not just forgive me—write me and tell me!

Beyond the Horizons

CHAPTER 1

In the Beginning, There
Were Two Brothers

California has always been the promised land of milk and honey, from the days of the first Spanish explorers to the unforgettable invasion of the gold rush miners to the present day. Its green fields and rebounding economy still beckon—some say too strongly—to people of every nationality.

But, now as then, California can be difficult, the land yielding its bounty only to those who work it hard, with a living wage from crops being as elusive as a living wage from the goldfields. One family that would give three men important to the aviation world would experience that hardness, be tempered by it, and wrest from California fame and a transient wealth that was savored to its fullest—while it lasted.

The three men were all sons of a remarkable woman, Flora Haines Loughead. Born on July 12, 1855, in Wisconsin, at least a century before her time, Flora was the daughter of John Penly and Mary Haines. Her father had a strong futuristic bent—as early as the 1860s, he predicted the future dominance of the automobile—and was probably the source of the mechanical genius later evidenced by the three Loughead boys. A brilliant individualist with an insatiable lust for life, Flora graduated from Lincoln University in Illinois at age seventeen. She was a journalist, married three times, had five children by two husbands, worked her own mining claims, farmed thirty-five acres, wrote many articles and more than a dozen books, taught her children at home, and in general behaved in a manner that would be widely applauded today but was unheard-of at the time.

She moved to Denver around 1875 and met the architect Charles E. Aponnyi. They were married in Sacramento that same year. He was an indifferent husband at best, and she supported herself as a journalist even as she bore Aponnyi a daughter, May Hope, and two sons, Victor Rudolph and John Haines, who died as an infant. The marriage ended acrimoniously in divorce in 1883, for Aponnyi had abused her physically and then deserted her; years later her diaries revealed how much she had come to loathe him. In 1886 she married John Loughead, who apparently adopted the children. Loughead was of Scots-Irish descent, the name indicating that his family lived at the head of a lake. John and Flora had two sons, Malcolm, born on November 15, 1886, and Allan, born on January 20, 1889. These children were born in Niles, California, near the Mission San Jose de Guadalupe, about twenty miles from Oakland. (Inexplicably, Victor chose to spell his name as Lougheed when, later in life, he followed in his mother's footsteps and became a writer. Both spellings were pronounced "Lockheed." To avoid confusion, the more familiar name Lockheed will be used from this point on, even with aircraft or company designations.)

Flora maintained her interest in mining into her eighties, camping out as she prospected for opals in mines near the Nevada-California border as late as the final decade of her long life. Fiercely independent, living alone, she made a living in her final years in part by sealing as many as three dozen opals in small, half-round glass paperweights that sold in department stores for up to five dollars each. Her fascination with prospecting was passed on to her sons and to her grandchildren. In the course of her life, rich in content and achievement if not material possessions, she had continued to prospect for husbands as well; her third was David A. Gutierrez, of whom little is known.

Members of the Lockheed family were and are reticent; while friendly, there is a familial tendency not to talk about themselves.

Perhaps for this reason, the story of May Hope's life is obscure, and the details of Flora's marriages are not well known—particularly their dissolutions. The Lockheeds lived in Santa Barbara, the scene of future successes, until about 1898, and then returned to the Oakland area for four years. In 1902, Flora moved the family—sans husband—to a thirty-five-acre ranch near Alma, California, only about ten miles from the Lockheed Martin Corporation's present Sunnyvale properties. There she raised grapes as a principal crop, supplemented by prunes and other fruit typical of the area.

At the turn of the century, making a living on a ranch of this size was difficult, but Flora was able to draw on her own considerable personal resources, writing feature articles for area newspapers, including the *San Francisco Chronicle*, and for magazines, including *Sunset*. She also began a successful book-writing career. In her lifetime she wrote both fiction and nonfiction, and among her novels were *The Man Who Was Guilty, The Black Curtain*, and *The Abandoned Claim*— the last one a children's book featuring a girl heroine named "Hope" after her daughter. She also wrote two standard library reference works, *The Libraries of California* and *The Dictionary of Given Names;* the latter remained in print at least until 1934. She had a scientific as well as a domestic bent, writing *The Natural Sciences* and *Quick Cooking*, the latter dedicated to "busy housewives." This indomitable mother of an aviation family died on January 27, 1943, the apparent victim of heart failure.

Malcolm went to San Francisco in 1904 to work for the local White Steamer Car distributor, for speed had a visceral appeal for the Lockheed boys. Malcolm's innate mechanical ability was recognized, and he was soon placed in charge of testing engines after they had been repaired, a weighty responsibility for such a young man. At the age of seventeen, Malcolm conceived of an invention that has affected the future of automobile design, the hydraulic four-wheel brake. It was a remarkable stroke of genius for someone who had never had any formal engineering training. Although it took him several years to perfect the concept, he eventually obtained a patent and created the Lockheed Hydraulic Brake Company to manufacture his invention. The first Lockheed four-wheel hydraulic brakes appeared as a seventy-five-dollar optional equipment item on Chalmers cars in the late fall of 1923 and were adopted as standard on the brand-new Chrysler line of cars, introduced in January 1924.

Malcolm, wealthy by the standards of the time, and certainly by the standards of the Lockheed family, sold his company and some fifty-six patents to the Bendix Corporation in 1932 for a "comfortable sum" said to be $1 million. Whatever the amount, it was not sufficient to maintain him in comfort all his life; Bendix extracted much more profit from the invention than he did. He returned to California, and, ever the optimist, began gold mining again at his Ilex mine. He lived the last twenty-nine years of his life at Mokelumne Hill, in Calaveras County, eventually forced to become a welfare recipient until his death on August 13, 1958. It was a sad end for a great—if stubbornly independent—inventor and entrepreneur.

His younger brother Allan was not strong as a boy, and Flora tutored him at home. He never finished grammar school, but received a well-rounded education from his mother and from reading that complemented his natural mechanical and engineering skills. It was an unusual upbringing, but one that stood him well in later life, when he would endure personal shocks as great as the San Francisco earthquake. At age seventeen, he was ready to follow in Malcolm's footsteps to seek his fortune.

When Allan arrived in San Francisco in 1906 he had to be content initially with a job in a hardware store, earning ten dollars a week. In a move that presaged many of his later business deals—in which love of the job outweighed monetary considerations—he took a four-dollar-a-week pay cut to work in an automobile repair shop. The pay cut probably did not bother Allan, whose frugal tastes reflected Scotch ancestry as his red hair did. A daredevil, he was hired by an automobile dealer to hurtle upward over the rough bricks in hill-climbing exhibitions, racing the jaunty "Full Jewel" Corbin automobile.

The three boys—Allan, Malcolm, and Victor—had the natural interest in aviation possessed by many mechanically inclined people during these early years of flight, but Victor was the first to participate. The oldest brother was an intelligent man—a founder member of the Society of Automotive Engineers and author of *Some Trends of Modern Automobile Design.* He wrote two seminal books on aviation. *Vehicles of the Air,* which appeared first in 1909, was in print for a number of years, and has been reprinted as recently as 1995. The second book, *Aeroplane Designing for Amateurs,* gave advice to the many budding aircraft builders around the country and was a harbinger of today's wildly successful Experimental Aircraft Association.

Victor worked for James E. Plew, a wealthy Chicago distributor of White cars and trucks, and was sent by Plew to San Francisco to obtain the rights for a tandem glider design of Professor James F.

Montgomery. His idea was to install an engine and create a salable powered aircraft. This proved not to be feasible, but Plew had also tasked him to acquire a Curtiss biplane. This was Curtiss's fourth production aircraft, and was shipped to Plew from the Curtiss factory in Hammondsport, New York, on November 30, 1909, for four thousand dollars.

Victor saw to it that Allan was hired to work on the two-aircraft fleet in Chicago. (Sadly, the previously cozy and supportive relationship of the three brothers came to an abrupt end in a bitter quarrel that pitted Allan and Malcolm against Victor. They never reconciled.)

Learning the Hard Way

It proved impossible even for Allan to put an engine in the Montgomery glider, however, and he instead concentrated on making the Curtiss pusher airworthy. In the process, Allan learned how to fly in the same manner that he later learned to design airplanes: just doing it. He joined a group of fellow enthusiasts who belonged to the Aero Club of Illinois and had a small flying field at the intersection of Fifty-second Avenue and Twenty-second Street, next to a railroad marshaling yard. This was a veritable hotbed of aviation, with several exotic designs along with the latest aircraft from Wright and Curtiss, despite the fact that there were no terminals, runways, radios, or landing lights—the principal piece of equipment was a mower to cut the tall marsh grass. As might be expected, James Plew was club president.

Allan's first opportunity to fly came when he met George Gates, who had cobbled together his own version of a Curtiss pusher, modified with a strange control system in which the midwing ailerons, the rudder, and the elevators involved separate control movements. Gates had been unable to get the aircraft off the ground; each time he tried, a wingtip dug in. He solicited Allan's assistance as copilot to handle the ailerons while he handled the rudder and elevators.

With rags wrapped around his hands so that the aileron control cables would not cut him, Allan sat behind the rudder/elevator man and in front of the pulsating four-cylinder fifty-horsepower engine that Gates had built from automobile engine parts. They made three or four straightaway hops, and both were vastly pleased with themselves. The unique control system was never used again, however.

Allan continued working on Plew's Curtiss biplane, installing a new engine in it. After Plew's regular pilots failed to get the Curtiss in the air, Allan spent two full days adjusting the rigging of the aircraft and preparing the engine to obtain its full thirty-five horsepower.

All the aircraft of this early period were extremely difficult to fly. The margin between top speed and stalling speed was very small—often as little as ten miles an hour—and this margin was reduced by a turn. Controls were relatively insensitive. To change direction or attitude, the pilot had to make large control movements and then be prepared immediately to return the controls to neutral to avoid over-correcting. The concept of stall recovery was largely unknown even to the most experienced pilots. And, although the aircraft did not go very high or very fast, a crash was often fatal because the pusher engine would rip forward from its strut mounting to crush the pilot.

None of this bothered Allan Lockheed, who was certain that his automobile-racing aptitude would be transferred to flying. On his second attempt he became fully airborne, and found himself circling tightly to stay within the confines of the racetrack from which he'd taken off. He landed successfully in the infield, and later said, "It was partly nerve, partly confidence and partly damn foolishness. I was now an aviator."

His new status, laden with both prestige and danger, inspired him to marry his longtime sweetheart from San Francisco, Dorothy Watts, in June 1911. They had two children, Flora Elizabeth, born in June 1913, and John Allan, born in May 1915. Dorothy passed away in 1922. As persistent in marriage as he would be in manufacturing, Allan married Evelyn Starr Leslie in 1924. This marriage ended in divorce. In 1939 he married Helen Kundert; one son was born to this union, Allan Haines Lockheed Jr. (the family named had been changed legally in 1926). For Allan, marriage and home life had to take a backseat to the battles involved in carving out a career in an entirely new, highly speculative, and terribly risky industry: aviation.

Plew now owned two Curtiss aircraft, and during the early months of 1911, Allan rebuilt them both. Plew hoped to recoup some of his money by a successful exhibition season. Allan successfully test-flew one aircraft, but the second crashed, killing its pilot. It was the last straw for Plew, who sold the surviving Curtiss and withdrew from flying.

With a total flying time of one and one-half hours, Allan was hired by an automobile dealer named Sam Dixon as an instructor pilot for the International Aeroplane Manufacturing Company of Chicago and to fly the "headless pusher Curtiss" (i.e., no forward elevator).

There he met a brilliant Czechoslovakian named Anthony Stadlman, who had just wielded a hacksaw to modify a standard pusher into the new configuration. Stadlman would later gain fame pioneering the concept of a "flying wing" aircraft.

Allan's $25-per-week salary was excellent for the time when a secondhand Curtiss could be purchased for $1,500. Allan next became an exhibition pilot at county fairs. This work was so dangerous that pilots received 25 percent of the gross, which was often guaranteed at $500 per day. To collect, pilots had to fly for at least five minutes, not an easy task if there was much wind or rain.

Young Lockheed proved to be a natural flier. On one occasion, he took a brand-new Curtiss up for its first flight. At its conclusion, the managers at the airfield suspended his flying rights for five days—not because he was careless, but because he flew too well, and they were afraid that less qualified people might try to imitate him.

Yet his wife was concerned about the danger, and her arguments prevailed: Allan quit exhibition flying, and decided to build his own aircraft. The couple returned to San Francisco, where they were joined by Malcolm.

A Significant Start

The Lockheeds had a no-nonsense approach to life and to engineering. They had to make a living while building their aircraft, and set to work in their old professions, Allan feeling no loss of status in changing from intrepid aviator to auto mechanic. Their concept of a new aircraft was equally pragmatic. Allan had already had close encounters of a near-fatal kind in pusher aircraft; he decided immediately that his aircraft would be of the more modern tractor type, with the engine up front. Both men knew that to make any money from the aircraft carrying passengers, it would have to carry two passengers plus the pilot.

In a manner that would be followed often in the later Lockheed Aircraft Corporation, the two brothers made sketches of several designs, labeling them from A to G. They selected the last design, and the Lockheed G was conceived as a very large three-place wood-and-fabric seaplane. Looking not unlike the later Curtiss JN-4 training planes, it was distinguished by midwing ailerons and the Breguet control system. The brothers purchased a seventy-horsepower Kirkham six-cylinder engine equipped with a handsome horseshoe-shaped

Although its structure appears crude by today's standards, the Lockheed Model G was
very advanced for its time, and had a most unusual characteristic for the period:
it made money.

radiator. Charles Kirkham would go on to design many excellent engines and a few delightful airplanes, but this engine was a lemon,
splitting its crankcase after a fifteen-minute run. It was replaced by an
eighty-horsepower Curtiss V-8.

The Lockheed G was the essence of simplicity, with wings of a
type that could be "built by the mile and cut off by the foot," simple
rectangular structures with no taper or dihedral. The fuselage used an
economical triangular section (i.e., one longeron and attendant bracing
eliminated) not unlike later Aeronca lightplanes. The single sled-type
pontoon was augmented by stabilizing floats under each wing.

It was the largest seaplane yet built in America, and marginally
larger than the two-place Curtiss Model F pusher flying boats being
manufactured in New York. In Europe, the Sopwith, Short, and A. V.
Roe Companies each constructed biplane seaplanes of similar size to
the Model G, but all were two-seaters designed for the military by far
larger, better-financed firms.

Finance loomed large with the Lockheeds, too—it always would.
Allan was the more outgoing of the two brothers, and he was largely
responsible for obtaining backing from the proprietor of the Alco Cab
Company, Max Mamlock, who helped them form the Alco Hydro-
Aeroplane Company with a $1,200 investment to supplement their

In 1919, the Loughead Aircraft Manufacturing Company of Santa Barbara built this Curtiss HS-2L for the Navy. Malcolm Loughead is in the gun turret, while Norman S. Hall, Anthony Stadlman, Berton R. Rodman, Allan Loughead, and John K. Northrop pose in front. (Loughead had not yet been transformed into Lockheed.)

own $1,800—and their sweat-equity. Other investors contributed an additional $1,000. Malcolm, more retiring than Allan, took the lead in the design effort. Neither brother had training as a designer or as a draftsman. The aircraft was built in a small wooden garage at the corner of Pacific and Polk Streets near the San Francisco waterfront. They had selected a seaplane for a number of reasons—a wider choice of landing fields, and, in San Francisco, proximity to a large, adventuresome boating community that would be tempted by a chance to fly. There were some disadvantages. A seaplane had to be strongly built to withstand the often choppy waters of San Francisco Bay, and this meant a heavier structure. A land plane could suffer a minor accident and be quietly gathered up for repairs, while a seaplane could have the same accident and sink beneath the waves.

Much was riding on the venture, for on June 1, 1913, Dorothy gave birth to Flora. Exactly two weeks later, on June 15, the Lockheeds trundled the Model G onto a ramp at the foot of Laguna Street, near Fort Mason. Allan ran the engine up, bounced down the ramp, taxied out into the bay, and took off—the first flight of a Lockheed aircraft.

Three flights were made, the second carrying Malcolm and the third with R. L. Coleman of the Alco Cab Company. The last two flights were twenty-minute tours of the bay, taking in Alcatraz and Sausalito and delighting the onlookers below in San Francisco. The Model G was not fast, with a top speed of 63 mph, but it cruised the bay at 51 mph and it was the only aircraft there to do it.

Later in the year, the Model G was damaged in a landing at a society gala in San Mateo. It was the last straw for Max Mamlock, who seized the aircraft and put it in storage. Allan resumed work as an auto mechanic, trying to drum up the $500 needed for repairs, until Malcolm dragged him off to the Yuba County goldfields for some more prospecting. With their quickly mined gold, they planned to redeem the Model G from Mamlock. Like most miners of the time, however, they made barely enough to live on, and Allan returned to turning wrenches for a living while Malcolm embarked on a series of adventures. In the last of these, he went to Mexico, where he served as an adviser to a one-plane air force. It belonged to General Venustiano Carranza, whose revolutionaries were fighting the *federales* of President Victoriano Huerta. Malcolm came back from Mexico with nothing to show for his efforts but a bullet-ridden Paige roadster that had served Carranza as a field car. The Paige would be literally the vehicle for Malcolm's greatest triumph—hydraulic brakes.

The Lockheed luck took a sharp turn for the better in 1915 at the Panama-Pacific Exposition. With help from Paul Meyer, an Alaskan pioneer who had made money out of the gold rush, not by mining, but by running a restaurant and bakery, the two brothers bought the Model G from the Alco Hydro-Aeroplane Company and refurbished it. Allan put his easygoing personality to work, talking up the joy of flying on the ramp and inducing people to fly. He was good. In just fifty days of flying passengers from the Yacht Harbor, they carried six hundred people at $10 a ride (and as Allan later expressed it "about an equal number of freeloaders"), grossing $6,000. They bought out their partner, Meyer, who had done well on his investment, and were able to place $4,000 in their account. The Model G had set a precedent for future Lockheed aircraft by earning money.

Back to Mom and Santa Barbara

Their mother now lived in Santa Barbara, where she worked for the *Santa Barbara Independent,* and her boys' preoccupation with aviation suited her own adventuresome soul to a T, as did her two grand-children.

It was a splendid time. Santa Barbara in 1916 was an idyllic California town of about sixteen thousand, complete with luxurious tourist magnets like the famous Hotel Potter, where room rates reached an astronomical $4 a day. The population was growing rapidly and there were many desirable neighborhoods where residential building lots could be purchased at prices ranging from $500 to $2,500. Making motion pictures was one of the primary industries, with two operating studios. Silent-film star Mary Miles Minter, of the Flying A Studio, was always available for publicity shots of activities at the factory. (Film fans will remember her performances in *Dimples* and *Anne of Green Gables*—or possibly her involvement in the still-unsolved murder of her lover, film director William Desmond Taylor.)

The one area of the city with which the Santa Barbara city fathers were not too pleased was State Street, which had become an ugly mishmash of small town architecture, much of it unsightly and dilapidated. Nonetheless, the Lockheed brothers found the neighborhood prices just right, and established the Loughead Aircraft Manufacturing Company in the rear of William L. Rust's garage at 101 State Street, only three blocks from the waterfront.

This time, their plans were a little more ambitious, and they sought both financial and engineering help. In both instances they found remarkable success. Alvin Oviatt, an "Akron oilcloth king" who lived in an estate in Montecito, one of the posher neighborhoods, provided most of the financing, along with a local physician, Dr. W. P. Lindley, and sales manager James A. Farra. Burton Robert Rodman, a successful machine-shop and auto-rental-service owner, also backed the brothers and became the president of the firm. Allan was vice president, while Malcolm was secretary-treasurer.

By now a faithful old soldier, the Model G set some records, including the first flight to Pelican Bay in the islands across the Santa Barbara Channel. More important, it continued to generate income, carrying passengers at five dollars each for a ride over the Channel Islands, and doing film work for the local motion picture studios. The Model G would continue to earn its keep through 1918, when it would be broken up and its engine sold. It was almost certainly the most profitable flying boat of the era, establishing a rate of return on investment that would be difficult to duplicate in the future.

Yet the Lockheed brothers had an even more ambitious aircraft in mind, a twin-engine flying boat capable of carrying ten people, including the pilot. Their reasoning was simple: if the three-seat Model G could make money, a ten-seat aircraft would be even more profitable.

One day, as the small group labored on their new project, they noticed a young man walking back and forth, hesitating as if summoning enough nerve to enter. He finally came in and was greeted warmly by the Lockheeds, whom he later recalled as "pleasant people, easy to contact and become acquainted with." Hired on the spot to begin one of the most fruitful aviation careers in history, he was John Knudsen Northrop, a fair-haired, reticent young man who, with excellent high school training, proved to be a superb engineer. In a 1974 interview with historian Gerald Balzer, Northrop said that he "drew up the wing truss structure, designed and stress analyzed it and did every bit of the drawing including three-view drawings and all the detail fitting drawings and parts that were necessary for the airplane." His stated ability to do one of the rarest, most difficult, and most necessary of aviation tasks at the time, stress analysis, is most unusual. Stress analysis was not then (and of course is not now) taught in high schools, and requires a knowledge of calculus, also not a high school subject.

Northrop would go on to a brilliant career with Douglas Aircraft and the later Lockheed Aircraft Corporation, and often did freelance work for other companies. He eventually headed his own company, and would become forever identified with the flying wing. In later years, Northrop's fame for what he accomplished with the flying wing would be of grievous concern to his colleague Stadlman, who had conceived of the flying-wing concept himself, and went to his grave believing that Northrop had gained the fame that was due him.

Northrop designed and helped build the hull and wings of the new aircraft, which was designated the F-1. With a seventy-four-foot-span upper and forty-seven-foot-span lower wing, the F-1 was equipped with two 150-horsepower Hall Scott A-5a engines, another California product. The F-1's design was distinctive, having twin booms and a triple tail.

Norman S. Hall, advertising and sales promotion manager for the firm, had a keen sense of the value of publicity. A news release was issued when the keel of the F-1 was laid in 1916. Before the United States entered the war, both Malcolm and Allan publicly volunteered their aircraft plant and personal services to the government "in event of trouble with any foreign power." They even threw in their secret new method of rustproofing the metal parts of seaplanes, probably the

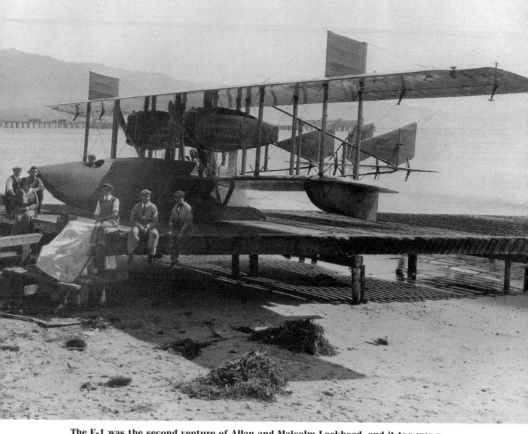

The F-1 was the second venture of Allan and Malcolm Lockheed, and it too was a success. Given their lack of experience, the choice of building a large twin-engine seaplane was daring, to say the least.

most valuable offer they could make. Hall saw that their offer got wide coverage. The war reached out to touch them in other ways—John Northrop became a private in the Signal Corps.

After the United States entered the war on April 6, 1917, Allan went to Washington to get a contract for the mass production of the F-1. He was able to impress the legendary Jerome Hunsaker, then a lieutenant commander running the Aircraft Engineering section, and managed to come home with a promise of a contract to build two single-engine Curtiss HS-2L flying boats and the agreement of the navy to test the F-1. It was the start of the always bittersweet relationship between industry and government. On the strength of the contract, Allan took two crucial personnel actions. He hired Tony Stadlman as factory superintendent and was able to secure Northrop's release from his $21-per-month job in the Signal Corps to return to Santa Barbara and a $1,800 annual salary.

The Lockheeds hoped to get big navy production contracts for their own aircraft, but work was slow, and the F-1 did not make its first flight until January 1918. Its performance was remarkable, being able to carry a useful load of 3,100 pounds. It seemed obvious to Allan and Malcolm that, once the F-1 was tested, the navy would buy it in quantity.

Norman Hall brought off a most sensational Lockheed public affairs triumph in the formal public "rollout" ceremony of the new aircraft. On March 28, 1918, a massive celebration was held at the launching ramp on West Beach between Bath and Castillo Streets as the F-1 was placed on view before a crowd of thousands lining the beach and boulevard, with speeches by Santa Barbara's mayor, H. T. Nielson, prayers by a minister, and a christening by the ubiquitous Mary Miles Minter (with a wine bottle filled with water in deference to the no-alcohol ruling of Josephus Daniels, the secretary of the navy). As a coup de théâtre, nine white pigeons were released; they circled the aircraft quickly and then landed on its nearly nine-foot-long propellers.

Despite the hoopla—perhaps campy now, but then touching in its patriotic sincerity—the F-1 was ready for action, proving it in a record-setting delivery flight to the navy in San Diego on April 12, 1918, flying the 211-mile distance nonstop in 181 minutes. Allan, Malcolm, and Carl E. Christoffersen were on board; the last named made sandwiches for the group on the flight down, and so rates a mention as perhaps the first flight attendant in history.

The Lockheeds demonstrated another probable industry first, and an exceedingly advanced technique for the time: an aerial test bed for flight controls. The F-1 was fitted with the Deperdussin control system, which the armed services had standardized in August 1916. (It is the type still used today, with pedals to operate the rudders and a central stick or wheel to control the ailerons and elevators.) Allan was by now most familiar with the Breguet system used on the Model G. To prepare himself for the F-1, he modified the controls on the Model G to conform to the Deperdussin system, and then practiced flying it.

While the navy tested the F-1, the company was humming, employing eighty-five men on a seven-day workweek. It did an excellent job turning out the two Curtiss flying boats, which were later praised by the navy for the quality of their fit and finish.

The average price for all 1,117 HS-2Ls delivered to the government was about $30,000; the larger firms like Curtiss, which produced 675 of the airplanes, naturally had a learning curve that permitted production economies. The Lockheed contract for 2 aircraft was for

$90,000, and they still lost about $5,000 on the cost-plus-12.5 percent contract, for they expended funds experimenting with ways to improve the aircraft, for which the government felt no need for reimbursement.

When they realized that no production contract for the F-1 would be forthcoming, the Lockheed brothers determined to convert the flying boat to a land plane and make a sensational transcontinental flight to Washington, D.C. Jack Northrop supervised the conversion, which cost almost $10,000. One of his engineering techniques was to place redesigned parts in a large glass tube, then have cigar smoke blown in at one end, so that he could determine the airflow patterns.

His results were good; the top speed of the modified aircraft, now called the F-1A, was increased by 10 mph. Two pilots, Aaron R. "Bob" Ferneau and Orvar S. T. "Swede" Meyerhoffer, were tasked for the trip, along with a mechanic, Leo G. Flint. Meyerhoffer was reputed to be able to swear in seven languages, and he had the opportunity to use them all. With flashguns popping, they took off from what is now a factory site in Goleta, California, on the morning of November 23, 1918, but were forced to land six hours and ten minutes later at Tacna, Arizona, when an engine rocker arm gave way. The part was replaced, but a precautionary landing was made at Gila Bend to refuel. On takeoff, the F-1A again lost an engine and crashed into a riverbed, severely injuring Meyerhoffer and Flint. Luckily the aircraft did not burn, but Flint's life hung in the balance for three days. The letter they had been carrying from Miss Minter to President Woodrow Wilson was never delivered.

The plane was brought back to California and rebuilt to its original flying-boat configuration, and was used for carrying passengers and film work again. The latter was especially profitable, as the Lockheeds charged $150 an hour for flight time and $50 an hour for standby time. The F-1 had a brief moment of fame in October, when the State Department chartered the aircraft to give King Albert and Queen Elizabeth of Belgium a flight to the Channel Islands. The flight was successful, and Allan and Malcolm were awarded the Belgian Order of the Golden Crown.

This was almost the end of the flight path for the F-1, which was sold to another group to start a charter service to Catalina Island. The venture never materialized, and the F-1, a remarkable aircraft, was left to rot on the beach at Santa Barbara.

Malcolm was beginning to tire of aviation, for he had perfected his four-wheel hydraulic brakes on the Paige car he'd brought back from Mexico and extensively rebuilt. He tested the Paige on Santa

Barbara's streets, boasting that he could "stop the car on a dime and have a nickel change left over." He proved it by roaring into a storage garage at 35 mph and screeching to a halt just before he crashed into the wall. His old fascination with automobiles had returned, but there would be one more venture with aircraft at Santa Barbara before he took his invention east.

The Lockheed S-1: A Look into the Future

Timing is everything. The F-1 came a little too late to find its way into the navy production scheme. The Loughead Aircraft Manufacturing Company's next—and last—airplane, the S-1, would come too soon after the war ended, with its merits submerged in the flood of war surplus aircraft that deluged the marketplace. Yet the S-1 was revolutionary in many ways, not least of which was the spirit in which its principals approached their task.

On July 28, 1919, Allan and Malcolm Lockheed, John Northrop, and Anthony Stadlman signed a lengthy formal agreement. They promised to share in all patents and inventions connected with aviation developed by any of them, and by majority vote, determine which patents and inventions would be developed. As the men involved had produced only four airplanes over a six-year period, the paper spoke volumes for their appreciation of one another and for their expectations of the future.

And for them, the future was the still undiscovered holy grail of aviation—"everyman's airplane." They wanted to create a safe, simple, inexpensive aircraft that would be the aeronautical equivalent of the Ford Model T. They arrived at a new method of construction that would produce a streamlined aircraft of great strength at low cost, *when manufactured in quantity.*

The Lockheeds developed a fuselage with monocoque (single-shell) construction, in which the structural strength stemmed from the outside skin rather than internal bracing. They used a concrete mold of the S-1 fuselage's desired size and shape, and laid up a shell using three layers of spruce plywood strips, all well laced with casein glue. Long discussions were held on the best way to apply a uniform pressure to the plywood so that it would cure properly, and without any weak spots caused by entrapped air. Stadlman was a proponent of applying pressure by means of an air bag, and his argument carried the day. The wood was pressed against the form by an air bag, which was held, in turn, by a cover bolted to the mold's framework. The rubber bag was inflated, placing a uniform pressure of fifteen to twenty pounds per square inch on the plywood strips for twenty-four hours, until the plywood shell had cured. Two such shells could then be assembled around a lightweight frame structure of formers and stringers to form a strong, lightweight, highly streamlined fuselage. The other three partners assisted in the development of Allan's idea, which would prove to be valuable only seven years later. Allan had preferred a circular fuselage, but Northrop held out for an elliptical shape as more efficient.

Northrop had turned to nature in the design of the wings, dumping bread near the waterfront, and studying the way gulls managed low-speed flight. The result was a lower wing designed so that it could be turned to a vertical position to act as an air brake. The lower wings were also differentially operated so that they eliminated the need for conventional ailerons. The rest of the S-1 was fairly conventional, with strut-braced biplane wings that could be folded parallel to the fuselage side, so that it could be easily towed or stored. The shape of the rudder and vertical surface would reappear, with the method of building the fuselage, on the later Lockheed Vega.

The depth of the group's talent was displayed in its reaction to the news that the S-1's planned Green engine from England was not going to be available. They simply designed and built a water-cooled, two-cylinder, horizontally opposed four-cycle, valve-in-head power plant of twenty-five horsepower. Called the XL-1 Aircraft Motor, it featured twin magnetos (unusual for the time) and two high-pressure oil pumps, yet weighed only 90 pounds. The compact engine fit within the S-1's streamlined fuselage, with only the cylinder heads protruding. The radiator was neatly faired into the bottom of the fuselage.

The aircraft's performance was exactly on the mark. With an upper wingspan of 28 feet and a lower wingspan of 24 feet, it weighed only 375 pounds empty, and 600 pounds fully loaded. Although the top speed was only 70 mph, it could cruise at 52 mph, and had a stall speed of 25 mph. Strongly built, it was stressed for 6 gs. Fuel consumption was only one gallon per hour, remarkable for the time.

Allan had grown wary of test-flying his own products, and hired a veteran airmail and test pilot, Gilbert George Budwig, to test the S-1. Budwig reported that the S-1 was exceptionally pleasant to fly. The tiny little aircraft landed so slowly that rotating the lower wing to be an air brake would rarely be required.

Yet it transpired that not only did "everyman" not want an airplane, but those who did could find plenty of war surplus JN-4s for

Like many other manufacturers of the period, the Lockheed brothers found that their product, the excellent S-1 biplane, could not compete against inexpensive war-surplus Jennies.

$350 or less. The S-1 was far more economical to operate but its initial price of $2,500 made it impossible to sell.

The firm had spent almost $30,000 in creating the S-1, and found absolutely no buyers. The lure of the four-wheel brake was too much for Malcolm, who took his invention east to Detroit, where he founded the Lockheed Hydraulic Brake Company. Allan worked as the California distributor for the brakes, and also sold real estate. Jack Northrop moved to Santa Monica, where he worked for Donald Douglas, and, among other things, designed the fuel system for the Douglas World Cruisers of 1924, the first airplanes to fly around the world. Stadlman found other work, biding his time for Allan to come up with a new venture.

The only tangible part of the S-1 that remains today is its engine, owned by Monte and Patricia Groves of Sunnyvale, California. The intangible remains of the S-1 are enormous. It led in just seven years to the formation of the Lockheed Aircraft Company. Its most important feature, the molded plywood fuselage, would be found on the record-breaking aircraft in one of the most exciting periods of aviation.

CHAPTER 2

The Vega:
First Star of a
Major Constellation

Timing Is Everything

The Lockheeds had been unfortunate in their timing both for the F-1, built too late in the war to receive a production order, and for the S-1, which could not compete in the postwar market. But Allan Lockheed was resilient, and would demonstrate once again his ability to work a full-time job to earn a living and at the same time labor to create a new aircraft. By 1926, his effort was about to pay off, for the timing for his new plane-building venture was exactly right on several counts. Like a surfer certain of his wave, the new Lockheed Aircraft Company would catch the surge in aviation precipitated by the New York-to-Paris flight of Charles Lindbergh on May 20–21, 1927.

Organizing for Success

Nineteen twenty-six was a year of incorrigible optimism. American automobile production led the world, and there were 9 million cars on the growing number of streets. Hollywood has survived the death of Rudolph Valentino, and was turning its eyes on new stars like Dick Arlen. The film spectacle *Ben Hur* was packing them in ($1.50 best seat in the evening, 50¢ balcony seat at the matinee), and Babe Ruth was hitting home runs with regularity. Allan organized his new company as a Nevada corporation in December 1926. The firm would produce the most sensational line of commercial aircraft of the decade as it grew in size and reputation, only to be absorbed by a larger corporation. Initially, timing was also propitious for finance, as the great boom of the 1920s was hurtling on its intoxicating upward curve and the October 1929 stock-market debacle was beyond imagination. And, equally important, the time was right to use the sensational new Wright Whirlwind J5 engine just coming onto the market after more than six years of development.

The air-cooled Whirlwind engine offered a new level of performance, in large part because it was not burdened with a heavy, drag-inducing, leak-prone radiator with all its associated hoses and clamps. The $6,000 J5 developed about 220 horsepower, weighed less than six hundred pounds with lubricants and accessories, and could run night and day without failing. The J5, its developments, and its so-similar competitors from Pratt & Whitney would revolutionize the commercial and military aircraft markets, having special effect on the design of carrier-based aircraft.

The term was not then in vogue, but networking played a great role in forming the new company, which came about almost directly as a result of the strong associations made by members of the old Santa Barbara firm. Gilbert George Budwig had instructed for the Air Service before doing some test work on the F-1. Another Air Service instructor, W. Kenneth Jay, had dropped by the plant in 1919, met with Malcolm Lockheed and Northrop, and inspected the F-1. Jay was an almost prototypical accountant, a slight, balding, soft-spoken man with an excellent eye for figures. He was a financial adviser to Fred S. Keeler, a well-to-do brick and tile manufacturer from the Midwest. Keeler owned stock in the Empire China Company, which had a factory in Burbank, where the Lockheed firm would eventually settle.

By 1926, Budwig had moved into the upper ranks of aviation,

becoming an assistant secretary with the Department of Commerce, which, empowered by new legislation, was just beginning to make its influence felt on aviation. Budwig introduced Jay to Allan Lockheed, who had been working with Northrop to develop a four-place passenger plane.

The energetic Northrop was doing a great deal of moonlighting from his regular job at the Douglas Aircraft Company, always with the permission of Donald Douglas. He had reengineered the wing of the M-1 monoplane for Claude Ryan, increasing its strength and reducing its weight by two hundred pounds, and directly preparing the way for Donald Hall's design of the *Spirit of St. Louis.* He also contributed heavily to the design of Vance Breese's series of monoplanes.

Northrop and Lockheed drew on their patented manufacturing technique of using a concrete mold and an inflatable rubber bag to build the fuselage of their new aircraft, knowing that it would lend itself to the creation of a roomy transport with a minimum of interior bracing. It would also reduce production costs—if more than one Vega could be sold. The two men had some disagreements; Allan was against using a cantilever wing, believing that the public would not accept a wing structure without obvious strut bracing. Northrop, who was familiar with Tony Fokker's designs, insisted that the aircraft be as clean as possible. The self-effacing Northrop won his point, as he often did. He was a rather short, slightly built, shy, soft-spoken individual, but when he was determined to have his way, the power of his intellect and a temper that could suddenly blaze up with the ferocity of an unmasked battery of guns lent force to his personality.

Northrop knew that a stoutly built plywood-covered wooden cantilever wing without the usual multiplicity of struts was essential to the clean lines he sought. The weight penalty over conventional wood-and-fabric construction was slight, and the reduction in drag was large. If one casually compared the external appearance of a wing from each manufacturer, one might be tempted to say that Northrop had borrowed his ideas liberally from Fokker. In fact, the taper, spar placement, and internal construction of the Northrop wing were significantly different from the Fokker's and in many ways forecast the construction of the all-metal wings he would later build. Northrop's confidence in his design was perhaps reinforced by his knowledge that his father, Charles Northrop, a master carpenter, would help build it.

It was the molded wooden fuselage that truly distinguished the new aircraft and that gave it an unprecedented manufacturing versatility. Like the S-1, the fuselage was made up of laminated spiral strips

The Vega production line was quite modern for its day. In less than a decade, Lockheed production was to soar into the thousands.

of vertical-grain spruce. The inner and outer layers were about ¹⁄₂₄ of an inch thick and ran longitudinally from nose to tail. The central ply was ¹⁄₁₆-inch spruce and ran at right angles to the other two plies. Each ply was liberally coated with the best-quality waterproof casein glue and bonded for eight hours under 150 tons of pressure, applied via the custom-shaped rubber bag, into a smooth shell of ⁵⁄₃₂–³⁄₁₆-inch thickness. The shells were then applied by means of cement-coated barbed brass nails to a series of circular laminated spruce diaphragms (formers) that provided great strength at a light weight. At points of concentrated loading, such as the engine mount and wing and tail surface attachments heavier stiffening diaphragms were used to distribute loads. (Years after the Vega was out of production, tests were run on the formers and they were found to be stronger than steel for their weight.) The strength of the semimonocoque construction permitted engines of as much as 650 horsepower to be installed in later variants of the basic design.

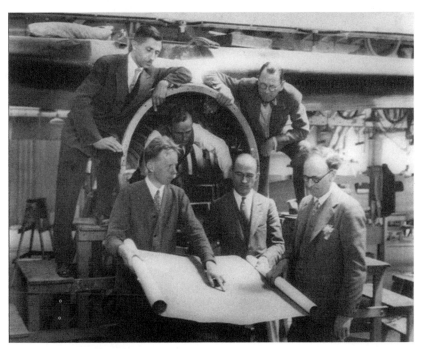

Another assembly of giants: from left, Allan Lockheed, John K. Northrop, Anthony Stadlman, and Gerard Vultee.

The resulting fuselage was clean, streamlined, and amazingly flexible, for holes could be cut into it almost anywhere for access hatches, navigation stations, and doors, thereby customizing it for any desired use. Repairs in the field were also easy, and crashes were less lethal because there were no longerons to crumple and pierce crew or passengers. In addition, the standard fuselage, whose length and diameter were fixed because of its method of construction, nonetheless lent itself to a variety of wing placements, cockpit positions, and undercarriage types. Performance increased over time, from the creditable 135-mph top speed of the original Vega to the 226-mph Orions. Range and altitude capabilities also varied widely, for the basic Lockheed could be configured as required for its mission.

One Fuselage Mold: Many Different Aircraft

Although out of chronological order, it will be helpful here to explain the various types of single-engine Lockheeds that will be referred to later. All of the wooden-body Lockheed shells were turned

A truly great pilot, Roscoe Turner
realized that flying an airplane
was no longer enough for the
American public. They demanded
showmanship, and he delivered.
Here he stands with the Bendix,
Harmon, and Thompson trophies.

out from the single concrete mold/pneumatic bag, which had a capacity of six shells (three fuselages) per week.

The traditional high-wing Vega was built in greatest numbers, with a total of 129 being manufactured. Northrop had almost immediately begun the design of the Explorer, a low-wing, single-float aircraft with a wing seven and one-half feet longer than that of the Vega. Its manufacture was delayed, however, and ultimately only 4 were built, none with a single float. Airmail pilots like to be placed in the rear of the fuselage, so that much of the energy of a crash would be absorbed before it reached them, and so it was with the Air Express, which carried its wing mounted parasol fashion above the fuselage on struts. Charles Lindbergh's requirement for a special aircraft led to the Sirius, which will be described in detail below. A total of 15 Sirius aircraft were built, and they led directly to the Altair, essentially a Sirius with a hydraulically operated retractable landing gear—the first of its kind. Only 6 Altairs were built, of which 5 were converted Siriuses; 1 Altair, in turn, was converted to an Orion.

The Orion, a swift and very modern-looking airliner, was the most successful of the low-wing wooden-body Lockheeds, and 35 were built. The Orion was to have an important effect upon the rebirth of

The Lockheed Explorer was an early Jack Northrop variation on the basic Vega design. This is the *City of Tacoma* flown by Albert H. Bromley.

the Lockheed firm, as we shall see. One final design was the end product of the original Lockheed formula, the XP-900 fighter, a remarkable airplane that looked ten years ahead of its time when it appeared in 1931. With the various conversions, a total of 198 single-engine Lockheeds were produced between 1927 and 1937; in that same time period, the Lockheed organization would undergo evolutionary changes internally while being subjected to revolutionary changes externally. Internal changes included engineering oversight, as Jack Northrop was succeeded by Gerard Vultee, who turned the reins over to Richard A. Von Hake, who was primarily responsible for the Orion design.

Keeler: A Good Judge of Airplanes— and the Stock Market

It was the basic original Lockheed Vega design that impressed Jay, however, and he prepared a prospectus intended to raise $25,000 for the new company. Jay's original intent was to bring four or five investors in, but when Fred Keeler saw the prospectus, he offered to put up the entire $25,000. As things developed, he put up $2,550 for 51 percent of the common stock and $20,000 for all of the preferred.

(Venture capitalists were not significantly more generous in 1926 than they are today.) Allan invested $2,450. Northrop became chief engineer (his salary was increased by $7.50 a week over the one he earned at Douglas), and Anthony Stadlman was recruited to be the factory superintendent. A pilot and a self-taught engineer, Stadlman was far more than that, but he excelled at the task assigned.

In an instance in which Northrop's wishes did not prevail, the name Lockheed Aircraft Company was adopted. Northrop felt that he was primarily responsible for the design of the aircraft; his own reputation was well established, and he would have liked to have the plant named for him. Keeler, the businessman, saw commercial value in the Lockheed name, in part because of the aircraft they had built previously, but primarily because Malcolm's Lockheed hydraulic brake business, in which Keeler was also an investor, was now universally known.

A Thumbs-up from Eddie Bellande

The fuselage of the first Lockheed Vega was rolled out of the tiny plant at 1001 North Orange Drive near the corner of Sycamore and Romaine Streets in Hollywood. The wings were placed on a truck and the fuselage was towed, tail first, to a vacant field near Inglewood. Known as Mines Field in honor of the real estate agent who handled its sale to the city, it subsequently became the location of Los Angeles International Airport.

While the sleek-looking Vega was being assembled and readied for flight, it was closely examined by Edward Antoine Bellande, one of the foremost test pilots of the day. Short and stocky, but with nerves of steel and the ability to infer what design improvements were needed from a test flight, Bellande had done his first test work at the Curtiss factory in Hammondsport, New York. He had served as an instructor pilot in the navy during World War I, and subsequently worked as a barnstormer, skywriter, crop duster, and itinerant test pilot. He was very prominent in California flying circles, not least because he flew Cecil B. DeMille's all-metal Junkers Larsen JL-6 monoplane. DeMille was an ardent aviation enthusiast, and Bellande worked for him at the Rogers Airport, located at the corner of Wilshire and Fairfax in Los Angeles. Unlike many of the early test pilots, Bellande survived flying's twin dangers—crashes and starvation—to become a successful corporate executive.

Despite a ready grin, the swarthy Bellande was a serious man who

Edward "Eddie" Bellande made
the first flight in the Vega; he
pronounced it a success.
Bellande was not only a famous
test pilot, he was part of
Hollywood's high society.

knew exactly how much was riding on the first flight of the new Vega. The fever for aviation had been building in the United States since the war, fueled in part by the speculative nature of the stock market, which looked to aviation as the next great growth industry, one that would rival the automobile. Lindbergh's epochal flight to Paris, followed by his winning the hearts of all Americans with his boyish, modest manner, had set off a virtual orgy of races, both in the air and in the stock market. If the flight test was successful, the new Lockheed Aircraft Company had an excellent chance to survive and grow. If the tests were unsuccessful—the airplane crashed, or performed so poorly that investors were frightened off—it would probably be the end of the line for the infant company.

With an eye on publicity, the test flight of the first Lockheed was scheduled for July 4, 1927. The Vega impressed Bellande, for its clean lines were a departure from every other aircraft in its category. Made entirely of wood, except for the engine mounts, the aircraft was beautifully finished, and carried a large Lockheed star insignia on its triangular-shaped vertical surface, the first instance of its use. The day was hot, and Bellande waited until 4:00 P.M. to make the first flight in an aircraft that he knew was faster and more demanding than any he had ever flown. The takeoff was uneventful, and in an hour's flight he put the Vega through a series of maneuvers that did not press its envelope, but nonetheless demonstrated its superb handling qualities.

The startling beauty of the prototype Vega seems commonplace today. At the time, its streamlined fuselage and cantilever, strutless wings were considered revolutionary. Left to right: Jack Frost, Eddie Bellande, Jack Northrop, Allan Lockheed, unknown.

When he landed, he climbed out of the aircraft and gave the endorsement expected of test pilots: "Boys, she's a dandy. A real joy to fly."

He had some other words for Jack Northrop, a pilot himself, and who flew the second flight as the first of the many passengers Vegas would carry over the years. Bellande told Northrop that the prototype Vega "had a bit of a wobble," and indicated that it needed less rudder and a larger vertical surface. Northrop would redesign the empennage (tail surfaces) of subsequent wooden-body Lockheeds to give them their distinctive curved vertical surface and rudder.

Lindbergh Fever

Lindbergh's famous flight to Paris simply ignited the flame of an aviation fire that had been smoldering for years. Many factors prepared, then stoked, the bonfire. The glut of war-surplus aircraft was almost exhausted. The life span of wood-and-fabric aircraft was limited, even if continually protected from the elements by a good hangar.

Those aircraft remaining in war-surplus storage were becoming severely deteriorated and increasingly expensive to bring to flying condition. They were also very old hat in a country determined to be modern in all things.

Lindbergh's flight was exploited by thousands of entrepreneurs, who flogged songs, books, sheet music, candy bars, painted plates, and every imaginable souvenir that would accept a photo or a painting of Lindbergh or his Ryan. The effect upon the aviation industry was dramatic. All over the country, backyard manufacturers built aircraft to cash in on the craze. Their efforts were often seized upon by promoters who sold stock to an enthusiastic (read greedy) public. Ninety-nine percent of the time the aircraft was capable of only indifferent performance and found no market. The new company usually folded quietly after the stock promoters had prudently removed their take from the endeavor.

The exploitation of Lindbergh's flight by others would continue on into the depression years. The madness reached its zenith early, with James D. Dole's May 25, 1927, announcement of an offer of $25,000 to the first flier and $10,000 to the second flier to cross from the North American continent to Honolulu within one year from the start date, August 12, 1927. (August 12 was a Hawaiian holiday, celebrating its becoming a U.S. territory in 1898.)

Coming only four days after Lindbergh's triumph, the announcement threw a barrel of gasoline upon the aviation bonfire. The prize money was a great inducement ($25,000 then being the equivalent perhaps of $250,000 or more now), but the real attraction was the possibility of metamorphosing from an unknown laborer in aviation's ill-paying vineyard into Lindbergh. It was an intoxicating prospect, and pilots from all walks of life examined the equipment available to them, discounted the odds, and entered the race, which was immediately labeled the Dole Derby, after the pineapple king himself.

Dole's announcement had an immediate effect upon the Lockheed Aircraft Company when William Randolph Hearst's son, George, agreed to buy a Vega for the bargain price of $12,500. The Vega had already cost $17,500, and preparing it to the elaborate Hearst specifications would cost even more. However, the entire Lockheed team understood that the prestige and positive coverage the Hearst newspaper organization would bring was worth many times the loss in revenue.

The Hearst team was looking for a crew to fly the Vega, and Jay recommended a former student of his from World War I pilot training, the exceedingly likable Jack W. Frost, as pilot, and the young but very capable Gordon Scott as navigator. Frost was a dapper gentleman, with a mustache and a smile not unlike that of the great racing pilot Roscoe Turner, and a similar penchant for flashy clothes. Unfailingly courteous, even under the stress of preparing for the race, Frost generated copy for newspaper stories like an ice machine makes ice, a continual bite-size flow of interesting items and events. Scott was only twenty-four, but was a respected engineer at Douglas who had practical experience on the route, having navigated the yawl *Jubilo* in a race to Honolulu the previous year.

Once they decided to take the plunge—a deliberately ominous phrase—the Hearst team called for some remarkable, farsighted modifications to the aircraft. An earth inductor compass generator, like the one Lindbergh had used, was installed, and the navigator's compartment was cramped, with seat, instrument panel, Pioneer speed and drift indicator, radio receiver, and chart table. Overhead, a hatch was cut into the Vega's fuselage so that Scott could use his sextant. As a nice touch, a small folding windshield raised automatically when the hatch was opened to make using the sextant easier. A life raft, complete with the usual food, water, and distress signals, was placed behind the navigator, as was the radio transmitter. It would be removed later to save weight—perhaps, in the light of later events, a fatal error.

Two main fuel tanks were placed in what had been intended as the passenger compartment, near the center of gravity and directly below the 160-gallon wing tank. Two flotation bags were installed, one forward and one aft. Northrop designed a mechanism to inflate the flotation bags in less than a minute with compressed carbon dioxide. Combined with empty fuel tanks (as they would presumably be if forced down at sea), the flotation chambers could support 8,500 pounds—almost 4,000 pounds more than the plane's gross weight. If a landing at sea was imminent, the landing gear could be jettisoned. The aircraft fuselage was packed with cork, and rubber caulking strips had been supplied to seal doors and windows in the unlikely event of a landing at sea. Taken together, the modifications were designed to keep the Vega afloat for at least thirty days—if it survived the impact of landing in the open ocean.

Yet the prospect of coming down at sea seemed remote. Lindbergh's engine had run flawlessly for more than thirty-three hours on the much-longer 3,600-mile flight to Paris. It was only 2,439 miles to Honolulu, which the Vega, with its 110-mph cruise speed, could make easily in less than twenty-four hours. There was one important difference, however. Lindbergh's navigation had brought him unerringly to Paris, but if he had made an error, he could not have missed landfall somewhere on the European continent. Hawaii was but a mere speck in the vast ocean, and a navigation mistake of as little as three and one-half degrees—scarcely more than a needle's width on the compasses of the day—would send an errant aircraft off into the endless void of the Pacific.

The *Golden Eagle* Glistens

Absolutely delighted with the performance of the Vega, the little Lockheed team worked hard to bring it up to Hearst specifications, which required that it be painted a bright orange with red trim. The name *Golden Eagle* was later painted in large letters on the fuselage sides. Frost's and Scott's full names were also neatly lettered on the fuselage near their stations, in smaller print. Eddie Bellande had tested the *Golden Eagle* as much as time would allow, checking fuel consumption and doing the inevitable trimming that a new aircraft requires. He set several point-to-point records, one a three-hour-and-twenty-minute flight from Rogers Airport to Oakland with Allan, Northrop, and Jay as passengers.

It was a splendid aircraft, clearly more modern than the other seven entrants in the Dole Derby, for which excitement continued to build even though it had been rendered so anticlimactic by two previous flights that it should have been a nonevent.

The first Oakland-to-Hawaii flight was made on June 28–29, 1927, by Lieutenants Lester J. Maitland and Albert F. Hegenberger in the Atlantic C-2A *Bird of Paradise,* essentially a Fokker F VIIa-3m built in the company's American plant. They landed at Wheeler Field after twenty-five hours and fifty minutes in the air. Far from being a stunt, the difficult flight had been planned for years, and called upon all of the Army Air Corps resources to make the attempt. The crew encountered both clouds and icing, and even with the modern equipment installed probably would not have been successful if Hegenberger had not been a master navigator. He was helped by directional beacons specially stationed at Crissy Field, California, and near Paia, Maui, which enabled him to check his course both outbound and inbound. The army stressed that the trip had long been planned, and had no connection with the Dole contest; Maitland and Hegenberger refused an offer of ten thousand dollars to tell their story to the press—quite a sacrifice, given that it was equivalent to about twice their combined annual salaries.

The *Bird of Paradise* had been an Army Air Corps aircraft, backed by the support of the War and Navy Departments. Two civilians, pilot Ernie Smith and ex–merchant ship navigator Emory Bronte, decided to be the first civilians to make the flight, and elected not to wait for the official Dole race, being willing to forgo the prize money for the honor of being first. In the beautiful silver prototype Travel Air 6000 *City of Oakland,* manufactured by the redoubtable Walter Beech, they took off on July 14, and crash-landed without injury on the island of Molokai the following day after a flight of twenty-five hours and thirty-six minutes. Their achievement never received the acclaim that it should have, being lost between the praise accorded the *Bird of Paradise* crew and the tragedy of the Dole race.

The Dole Derby mania continued unabated, even after three would-be entrants crashed en route to Oakland, two of them with fatal results. The race finally began on August 16, 1927, only forty-three days after the first flight of the Vega. Of the eight aircraft assembled for the race, one crashed on takeoff, two were forced to return, and one failed to start. Of the four who departed, only two reached Hawaii. Art Goebel and Bill Davis landed first in their blue-and-silver Travel Air 6000, after a twenty-six-hour, seventeen-minute, thirty-three-second flight. Martin Jensen and Paul Schluter, a ship captain turned navigator for this flight, were second in the bright yellow Breese *Aloha,* making the flight in twenty-eight hours and sixteen minutes.

No word was ever heard of the first Lockheed Vega, the *Golden Eagle,* which simply vanished from the face of the earth, as did the Buhl biplane *Miss Doran.* The latter had carried not only pilot John "Augie" Pedlar and navigator Vilas Knope, but also and quite irrationally a passenger, the beautiful young Mildred Doran, for whom the plane was named. She was twenty-two years old, and had made the flight to "be somebody." In a grisly epilogue, Major William Erwin and Alvin Eichwaldt were lost in the *Dallas Spirit,* a Swallow monoplane that set off to make the flight even after it was known that two aircraft had been successful and two were missing. It carried a radio, and Eichwaldt's poignant last transmission revealed that it was in a fatal spin into the sea.

The Vega Makes History

The loss of the *Golden Eagle* might well have destroyed the fledgling Lockheed Aircraft Company if, prior to the Dole race, it had not made such a tremendous impression upon the aviation community in general and upon an Australian explorer, Captain George Hubert Wilkins, in particular.

Wilkins was staring idly out of his San Francisco hotel room when he saw the *Golden Eagle* fly by on one of its test flights. He was accustomed to flying the conventional aircraft of the time, and the Vega looked to him like something from the next century. He recalled the incident with the words, "It gave me a thrill that another might experience if he saw his ideal woman in the flesh."

Wilkins ferreted out the identity of the aircraft and promptly drove to the Lockheed plant and decided on the spot that he wanted a Vega. He agreed to the purchase price of fifteen thousand dollars, for the power and performance of the Vega offered great possibilities for scientific research. Wilkins hired the first airmail pilot in Alaska, Ben Eielson, for whom Eielson Air Force Base was later named. Eielson shared Wilkins's vision of establishing Arctic air routes, a concept then as far out as contemporary talk about flights to Mars.

They took the aircraft to Barrow, Alaska (near where a later hybrid Lockheed would carry Wiley Post and comedian Will Rogers to their deaths), and the orange-and-blue Vega, christened *Detroit News,* made a colorful addition to the forty-eight-degree-below-zero weather. A hazardous takeoff was made on April 15, 1928. Wilkins and Eielson made scientific history in the first thirteen hours of their 2,200-mile flight when they confirmed that the so-called Atlantic Land Mass did not exist. Seven hours later, a blinding blizzard forced them to make a precautionary landing on a desolate windswept beach of Dead Man's Island off Spitsbergen, Norway. They were trapped by the blizzard for four days, and to the outside world it seemed that the *Detroit News* had suffered a fatal anonymous disaster as had the *Golden Eagle.* When the blizzard lifted, they had to dig the aircraft out and tramp down the snow to make a runway. After several nerve-wracking attempts, the Vega carried them on a five-minute flight across open water to reach the coal-mining settlement at Green Harbour, Spitsbergen.

The world went wild over the pair's achievement against such great navigational, meteorological, and geographical odds. King George V knighted Captain Wilkins, and Eielson received the Harmon

The combination of the Vega airframe and the Wright Whirlwind engine proved to be irresistible to explorers and record seekers. George Hubert Wilkinson and Carl Ben Eielson won fame with their epic flight across the frozen North, from Point Barrow to Spitsbergen, in April 1928.

Trophy for the most outstanding aeronautical achievement of 1928, along with a Distinguished Flying Cross from the United States Army. The Vega's speed, stamina, comfort, and versatility were extolled by the two explorers, the press, and Lockheed's advertisements. Orders for Vegas began pouring in.

Wilkins—Sir Hubert now—turned next to the exploration of the Antarctic, and with plenty of funding from backers bought a second Vega, this one on floats. The Lockheed Company was so grateful for the positive attention Wilkins had focused on the Vega that it sold the second aircraft to him at cost. A significant new personality, Gerard F. Vultee, had joined Lockheed after graduating from the California Institute of Technology. Vultee engineered the twin pontoons conversion of the Vega to a seaplane; later he would design many of the Lockheed low-wing aircraft which followed.

Wilkins hired the famed bush pilot Joe Crosson to fly the second Vega. They began their Antarctic operation in November 1928, and proceeded to make exploration history. On an initial flight of 1,300 miles in the original Vega, Wilkins was able to photograph and roughly map some 100,000 miles of previously unknown territory. It was a mammoth accomplishment, on a scale never achieved before, and done with the utmost economy. On this trip, Wilkins reciprocated Allan Lockheed's kindness by exercising his prerogative as an explorer to name unknown geographical points. Thus he gave the name Lockheed to a range of mountains, and Whirlwind (after his engine) to a huge glacier. With a glance at the Lockheed organizational chart, he created Cape Northrop and Cape Keeler, after the company president.

The High Tide of Wooden Lockheeds

It was a sunny time for the new firm, as Air Associates of New York placed a $250,000 order for twenty Vegas. The world now beat such a path to the corner of Sycamore and Romaine that a move to Burbank was made in 1928. There Keeler located twenty thousand square feet of factory space in a building partially occupied by the Mission Glass Works on San Fernando Road. Now surrounded by hundreds of square miles of streets and buildings, at the time it was a bucolic paradise where farmers coaxed a living from the soil by irrigating and tilling what had been desert. It was flat, and just a mile from the new factory was an area that became the United Airport in 1929; it was subsequently known as the Union Air Terminal, the Lockheed Air Terminal, and finally the Burbank-Glendale-Pasadena Airport.

Along with the shift in the manufacturing site came some key personnel changes. Northrop saw that the era of wood was over, and wished to execute his aerodynamic ideas in metal, with all its advantages of handling, durability, weather resistance, and strength. Northrop in later interviews indicated that his energies were being misdirected into lobbying for his ideas instead of designing aircraft, primarily because of internal disputes within the tiny Lockheed staff. With his typical forthrightness, he quit, and Ken Jay joined him. The new Northrop firm would have a long history of beautiful commercial and military aircraft that included the Alpha, Beta, Gamma, and Delta, and perhaps most important of all, the basic design of the Douglas SBD, which won the Battle of Midway. Gerry Vultee replaced Northrop as chief engineer in June 1928 and expanded upon Northrop's ideas for a line of aircraft structurally similar to the Vega.

Two Vegas were built in 1927, twenty-nine in 1928, and a peak of sixty in 1929, extraordinary production quantities for the time. The quantity of sales and the economical manufacturing techniques permitted the Wright-equipped Vegas to sell for as little as $14,750, while the Pratt & Whitney–engined versions cost about $19,000. (These were bargain prices; for comparison, a top-of-the-line Cadillac custom Imperial sedan cost $4,450 at the factory.)

Lockheed was held privately from its origin in December 1926 until July 1928, when it went public, its stock being listed on both the Los Angeles and San Francisco Curb Exchanges. At the time it went public, there were 17,500 shares of preferred and 21,250 shares of common stock outstanding. In November 1928, the shareholders authorized an increase in Class B common stock from 25,000 shares to 150,000 shares, and current shareholders had the opportunity to purchase 5 shares of the new common stock at $6 per share for every share of stock they then owned. All preferred stock was retired through the five-for-one purchase option.

Although the exact amount of stock that Keeler owned at this time is unknown, it is estimated that he may have held as many as 55,590 shares. This would undoubtedly influence his decisions in the months to come, for the stock market fever that had facilitated Lockheed's growth now intervened to change its direction. The desire to create a "General Motors of the Air" had set off several acquisition and merger binges. The Curtiss Wright Corporation, run by former *Wall Street Journal* editor Clement M. Keys, consisted of Curtiss Aeroplane and Motor, Wright Aeronautical, Curtiss-Wright Flying Service, Keystone, Curtiss-Caproni, Curtiss-Robertson, Moth, and Travel Air. The United Aircraft and Transport Company comprised Boeing, Boeing Air Transport, Stout Air Services, Chance Vought, Hamilton Metalplane, Hamilton Aero Manufacturing, Stearman, Sikorsky, Northrop, Pratt & Whitney, and many more. The Detroit Aircraft Corporation (D.A.C.) was by far the smallest, with assets in December 1929 of about $6.5 million. By comparison, United Aircraft and Transport had total assets of $41.3 million, and giant Curtiss-Wright had $78.4 million.

Anxious to catch up, D.A.C. made a quick series of moves, taking over established aircraft manufacturers and related industries, and making them divisions. These included the Lockheed Aircraft Corporation; Ryan; Eastman; Blackburn; Grosse Isle Airport, Detroit; Parks Air College, near East St. Louis; Gliders, Incorporated; the Aviation Tool company; the Marine Aircraft Company and the Winton Aviation Engine Company. Edward S. Evans was president of Detroit Aircraft, which planned a $20 million capitalization figure, based on the issuance of 2 million shares of stock. The directors of the firm included many notables, among them C. F. Kettering, inventor of the automobile self-starter and vice president of engineering for General Motors; Harold H. Emmons, who had led the development of the Liberty engine; Edsel Ford; Ransom E. Olds; Henry M. Leland, founder of Cadillac *and* Lincoln; and Roy D. Chapin of Hudson.

Evans promptly declared that the Detroit Aircraft Corporation would be an operating company in every sense of the word, and the heavy automobile experience reflected in the board would help D.A.C. apply Detroit industrial methods to building aircraft of every description, from "$3,000 training ships to $6,000,000 dirigibles." The latter example referred to the ZMC-2 metal-clad dirigible built for the U.S. Navy and flown at the 1929 Cleveland Air Races. All manufacturing and selling activities were to be directed from the Detroit headquarters. Plans were made to permit existing automobile distributors to become selling agencies for D.A.C. aircraft. D.A.C. was heavily into all-metal construction, not only with the ZMC-2 and the Marine "metalclad" flying boats, but also with the design of metal fabricating equipment, including automatic riveting machines for aircraft.

Detroit exchanged one and one-third shares of stock in the new corporation for each share of Lockheed stock. Allan Lockheed opposed the takeover, but Keeler was the majority stockholder and a keen-eyed businessman who may have perceived the coming crash. The D.A.C. stock had an initial capital value of $15; the one-and-one-third share exchange ratio would have meant that Lockheed stock was evaluated, for this deal, at $20 per share. The price of D.A.C. stock would plunge to twelve and one-half cents a share in the stock market debacle.

Much discomfited, Allan resigned, sold his holdings at $23 per share, and organized a new company, the Loughead Brothers Aircraft Corporation. (There is no little irony in the fact that after having changed his name to Lockheed, Allan could no longer use it, and had to revert to the original spelling for his company.) The formal takeover took place on July 23, 1929. Keeler was replaced by Evans as president, but was retained as a director. James Work took Lockheed's place as vice president. Work had formerly run the Naval Aircraft Factory in Philadelphia.

As unpalatable as the takeover must have been to the original Lockheed employees, Detroit Aircraft conferred a signal favor upon the company by sending one of its own employees, Carl B. Squier, to be general manager. Normally a new guy from the acquiring company is a hatchet man; Squier was anything but, and would eventually

A man of infectious good humor, Carl Squier became a formidable salesman of Lockheed products.

become one of the most beloved employees of the Lockheed Company. (On one occasion, funds were very tight with the new company. Squier won all hearts by selling his car and standing at the door of the plant, dispensing $10 to each of the employees leaving work for the day.)

Squier was born in Decatur, Michigan, on April 17, 1893; after two years at the University of Michigan, he entered the U.S. Army Air Service,* trained at Rockwell Field, and served with the 90th Observation Squadron in France. He had a wide variety of civil experience in aviation, working with Martin and Stinson and operating his own Squier Air Services. He joined the Eastman Aircraft Corporation as sales manager, to sell the sesquiplane seaplanes that Tom Towle (of Ford Tri-motor fame) designed. He came to Lockheed in 1929, and it was said of him that had there been no Carl Squier, there would have been no Lockheed Aircraft Company, for he was, indeed, one hell of a salesman, whose motto was said to be "Make a Friend, Sell a Plane."

Vultee remained as chief engineer, assisted by Von Hake and James Gershler, to help Squier expand an already celebrated product line. The name Lockheed, already distinguished by the Wilkins explo-

---

*In 1926, the U.S. Army Air Service changed its name to the U.S. Army Air Corps, then to the U.S. Army Air Forces in 1941, and finally to the U.S. Air Force in 1947.

A constellation of historic Lockheed products. From the left, Amelia Earhart's Vega, Charles Lindbergh's Sirius, Wiley Post's Vega, and an Orion in which Hal Roach flew a 16,500-mile round-trip from Los Angeles to Buenos Aires.

ration efforts and Art Goebel's record-breaking nonstop west-to-east transcontinental record of just under nineteen hours, became almost synonymous with record setting. Famous pilots—or pilots who wished to be famous—turned to Lockheed almost automatically. Records fell in a veritable cascade of daring flights. It was the fashion then (and to a surprising extent, still is) for pilots to set point-to-point records. Lockheeds set numerous nonstop records to and from many different cities. New York was a favorite jumping-off spot, and record flights were made to Los Angeles, Mexico City, Hungary, the Canal Zone, Berlin, Norway, and elsewhere.

The names of the fliers who knew "It takes a Lockheed to beat a Lockheed" (in Allan's famous phrase) included such luminaries as Frank Hawks, Jimmy Mattern, Laura Ingalls, Ruth Nichols, Lou Reichers, Sir Charles Kingsford-Smith, Michael Detroyat, Francisco Sarabia, and others. But the best-remembered records were those established by a few truly elite aviators, including Charles and Anne Lindbergh, Amelia Earhart and Wiley Post. Fortuitously, the three Lockheeds that these record breakers flew all survived and now belong to the National Air and Space Museum.

Lindbergh Gets Sirius

Charles and Anne Morrow Lindbergh took a different, more deliberate approach, not seeking to set records but to map the way for future commercial flights. Jack Northrop had already designed a low-wing version of the Vega, called the Explorer, and Vultee adapted this in 1929 to Charles Lindbergh's specifications for a low-wing-

Charles and Anne Lindbergh used their specially built Lockheed Sirius in a series of route-proving flights. In April 1930 they flew from Glendale to New York, setting an unofficial speed record in the process. From the left: Carl Squier, unidentified, Charles and Anne Lindbergh, Gerard Vultee.

monoplane. The same mold turned out the fuselage skins, but instead of the Vega cabin, two conventional cockpits were installed. (Later, at Mrs. Lindbergh's suggestion, a sliding canopy was designed by Vultee to give the cockpits protection from the elements. Lindbergh wanted the Sirius to be adaptable to engines of increased power and to the installation of twin pontoons. Already thinking of the future, he also asked that they design a wing that would incorporate a retractable landing gear, a feature that then appeared on the very successful Orion series.

Marshall "Babe" Headle conducted the test-flying, with Lindbergh's assistance. During the test period on the aircraft, a number of improvements were introduced, including handsome wheel pants, a hydraulically controlled adjustable propeller, and Mrs. Lindbergh's sliding canopy.

On April 20, 1930, Colonel and Mrs. Lindbergh, on what was basically a familiarization flight, set a transcontinental record of fourteen hours, forty-five minutes, and thirty-two seconds from Glendale to New York, with a brief refueling stop in Wichita. The following

Famous pilots naturally gravitated to Lockheed. Here Lindbergh sits
in the front cockpit of his Sirius.

year, a 575-horsepower Wright Cyclone engine was installed, along
with twin EDO floats.

Carrying almost the same registration number (NR-211) as the
now-retired *Spirit of St. Louis* (N-X-211) the Sirius would take the
Lindberghs on survey flights of future overwater routes for Pan American Airways. They made a hazardous trip from China via Alaska and
the North Pacific in the summer and early fall of 1931, only to have
the Sirius dropped by a crane into the Yangtze River near Hankow.
The Lindberghs jumped free into the very polluted Yangtze, on what
was just one of several hair-raising adventures they experienced.

Shipped back to the United States and rebuilt, the Sirius had a
710-horsepower Wright Cyclone engine and a controllable-pitch propeller installed, making the most advanced exploration aircraft in the
world in June 1933. Thus equipped, they began a thirty-thousand-
mile survey flight around the North and South Atlantic that was invaluable for Pan American. Anne Lindbergh supplemented her
fortitude and good humor with radio and navigational skills throughout the grueling flight. The Sirius, christened *Tingmissartoq* (the one
who flies like a big bird) in Greenland, eventually became a primary
exhibit in the National Air and Space Museum's Milestones of Flight
gallery.

More Than Lady Lindy

In 1928, Amelia Earhart had received what she felt was unearned fame by being a passenger on the transatlantic flight of the Fokker trimotor seaplane the *Friendship*. She was determined to make the flight on her own "for the fun of it," in the phrase she used to turn away inquiries about her motivation. Working with veteran pilot Bernt Balchen, she had the twenty-second Lockheed (and twentieth Vega) prepared for a transatlantic solo flight with the installation of a new 420-gallon fuel system and a supercharged Pratt & Whitney Wasp engine of 450 horsepower. Painted deep red with gold trim and registered NC 7952, Earhart's plane took off from Harbour Grace, Newfoundland, on May 20, 1932, the fifth anniversary of Lindbergh's flight, and landed in an Irish field near Culmore, after a flight of fifteen hours and eighteen minutes. Three months later, she made the first woman's solo transcontinental nonstop flight from Los Angeles to Newark, New Jersey, in just nineteen hours and five minutes. The following year, she sold the aircraft for $7,500 and it was placed on exhibit at the Franklin Institute in Philadelphia. It was later acquired and refurbished by the National Air & Space Museum, where it is currently exhibited, the oldest Lockheed in existence.

Earhart purchased a second Vega, a Hi-Speed Special 5C model, NC 965Y, installed the engine from her original ocean-spanning Vega in it, and had it painted in her favorite red-and-gold color scheme. With Paul Mantz as her mentor this time, she took off from Wheeler Field, Hawaii, and flew to Oakland in just eighteen hours and sixteen minutes, the first person to fly the route alone.

The story of Earhart's last flight in a Lockheed will be told in a following chapter, but it should be noted that in personal appearance, manner, and degree of adulation, she was very similar to Charles Lindbergh, and so inevitably was called "Lady Lindy" by the press. The nickname, while intended to be flattering, was unfair, for Earhart deserved to be honored on her own merits. She was less fortunate than Lindbergh in her choice of a spouse, George Putnam, for while Anne Lindbergh was always supportive, Putnam tended to be exploitative. Amelia Earhart was a feminist, and tirelessly labored to improve the lot of women by demonstrating that a woman could compete in what had been considered to be exclusively a man's world.

Amelia Earhart, with Carl Squier and Lloyd Stearman, with her Vega in front of the
Lockheed hangar in Burbank. The car is a Hudson Terraplane, for which
Amelia served as spokesperson.

Wily Wiley

One floor below Amelia's aircraft in the National Air & Space Museum is the most famous Vega, the glistening white, blue-trimmed *Winnie Mae*. Wiley Post, a grumpy one-eyed pilot of considerable skill, native intelligence, and latent scientific talent, flew the *Winnie Mae* into history with two record flights around the world followed by a series of innovative high-altitude flights that were years ahead of contemporary understanding.

The concept of global journeys had begun with Magellan and reached its first aeronautical height in Jules Verne's famous novel *Around the World in Eighty Days*. The first successful aerial

Wiley Post modified his globe-girdling Vega with a droppable landing gear to improve performance. A skid was built into the bottom of the fuselage for landing.

circumnavigation took place in 1924, when four American Douglas World Cruisers began and two completed an epic 175-day trip. The most successful German airship, the hydrogen-filled *Graf Zeppelin,* had flown in sedate majesty around the world in 21 days, covering twenty-one thousand miles, carrying twenty passengers at 70 mph for about three hundred airborne hours. Wiley Post knew that he could make the trip in much better time flying the Vega Model 5B powered by a Pratt & Whitney Wasp engine. Owned by his boss, Mr. Florence C. Hall, the aircraft was named *Winnie Mae* for Hall's daughter. (It was Hall's second Vega, both having borne the name *Winnie Mae.*)

Post teamed up with navigator Harold Gatty and did a thoroughly workmanlike job of preparing for the trip, including intensive physical preparation for the strain expected from long hours of flying and the changes induced by the time zones they had to traverse. They took off from Roosevelt Field on Long Island on June 23, 1931, and began a grueling journey that kept Post at the controls for hours, battling winds and weather, bad landing fields, hazardous takeoffs, and almost hysterical receptions everywhere they landed. They survived Russian mud, Pacific storms, and a bent propeller in Alaska. When they touched down again at Roosevelt Field on July 1, they had flown around the world in eight days, fifteen hours, and fifty-one minutes.

It was not enough for Post, who immediately began planning a solo trip. On July 15, 1933, he took off from Floyd Bennett Field in New York, and, aided by an early Sperry automatic pilot and a directional radio borrowed from the Air Corps, he set an incredible pace. Bone-weary, he set a solo nonstop record as he flashed across the Atlantic to Berlin. After facing almost continuous storms and the terrible landing facilities of the Soviet Union, he had another landing accident in Alaska, where once again his propeller was damaged. After quick repairs, he managed to complete the trip in the record time of seven days, eighteen hours, and forty-three minutes.

Post became fascinated with high-altitude flight, for he knew that with a supercharged engine, aircraft could fly faster where the air was less dense. He was also among the first to consider using what came to be known as jet-stream winds at altitude to enhance his ground speed.

He devised his own specially built pressurized suit, working with the B. F. Goodrich Company. He made two attempts to exceed the existing altitude record of 47,352 feet, then held by Italy. On the first, his propeller control froze, but on the second he reached an unofficial height of 55,000 feet. The record was not officially recognized because of a barograph failure. The *Winnie Mae* was then specially modified for an attempt on the nonstop transcontinental record, being fitted with a droppable landing gear, a metal skid to belly in on, and a highly supercharged engine. Shortly after his takeoff from Burbank, the *Winnie Mae*'s engine failed and he had to make a forced landing on Muroc Dry Lake, where his "man from Mars" pressure suit at first terrified his rescuers. The engine had been sabotaged. Someone, still unknown, had dumped two pounds of emery dust and filings into the intake manifold.

Post made three subsequent attempts for a coast-to-coast record, but fate was against him each time. In the process, Post had flown the *Winnie Mae* at speeds in excess of 340 mph—an incredible advance over the 135 mph of the first Vega, and an indication that the advances in aviation technology could yield improvements in performance beyond anything yet contemplated.

Wiley Post lost his life with comedian Will Rogers, who at that time was a celebrity of immense importance, a sort of combination of

Not formally trained, Wiley Post was an intuitive engineer who did pioneering work in a pressurized suit that presaged those worn later by astronauts.

Leno and Lehrer in the manner in which he mined the political scene for comedic content. Post had purchased a hybrid "Orion/Explorer" aircraft from the famed aircraft broker Charles Babb. The combination of an ex-TWA Orion passenger-plane fuselage and an Explorer wing was a shop lash-up, lacking any engineering basis, and which the Lockheed Aircraft Company disclaimed before and after the almost inevitable accident. Post also located some EDO J-5300 floats that had been first used by a Pacific Alaska Airways Fairchild 71, and were to be installed in Seattle. Pratt & Whitney furnished a free 550-horsepower Wasp, and a three-bladed controllable pitch propeller was installed.

Post hired Pacific Airmotive in Burbank to install the instruments and equipment, fit the ill-assorted parts together, and finish it in a Waco Red with silver trim paint scheme. The completed aircraft was attractive, but its beauty concealed a fatal flaw. It was so excessively nose-heavy that it could not be controlled at low speeds without power. Post must have realized this from the first test flight, and it must have been a burden to him all during the flight from Burbank to Alaska. He flew on, nonetheless, until late in the afternoon on August 15, 1935, he made a final takeoff, this time from Walakpa Lagoon, near

The aircraft Wiley Post lashed together for his last flight was made up of Lockheed Orion and Explorer components, but was definitely not a Lockheed design. Post must have known that it was fatally nose-heavy, but chose to fly it anyway. He and the famed humorist Will Rogers crashed to their deaths at Point Barrow, Alaska, on August 15, 1935.

Point Barrow, Alaska. The engine apparently failed at about two hundred feet, with the aircraft in a nose-high attitude. It immediately nosed down and crashed, killing both men instantly.

It was a sad and totally unnecessary end for two men, each great in his field. The accident would not have happened if the aircraft had been properly engineered, and the Lockheed Aircraft Company went to great lengths to point out that although components from Lockheed aircraft had been used, it was definitely not a Lockheed design. It was in fact, no one's design at all.

The Orion Legacy

Single-engine Lockheeds would be used by forty-eight domestic and eleven foreign airlines, including the predecessors of such famous names as United Air Lines, American Airlines, Pan American, and Swissair. Some were relatively simple "one-Vega" operations, while others employed Vegas, Orions, and Air Expresses to complement their larger Ford, Boeing, and Douglas airliners.

The Vega and Air Express had both been successful airline

Jimmy Doolittle and his famous Orion, the *Shellightning*. Used by him as an executive transport, the metal-bodied Orion eventually found a home in the Swiss Air Transport Museum.

aircraft, the former specializing in airmail and freight and the latter in charter work. The Vega, in particular, allowed pioneer airlines like the Alaska Washington Airways, Braniff Airways, Wedell Williams Air Service, Bowen Air Lines, and Nevada Airlines to survive, if not to prosper. (Nevada Airlines, with its Los Angeles–Reno route, quickly became known as the "the Alimony Special.")

It was the Orion, however, that made the most important contribution. First flown in early 1931, it featured the patented Lockheed flush-fitting retractable landing gear, an NACA cowling, and seats for six passengers. With a top speed of 226 mph and a sizzling for the time cruise speed of 175 mph, the Orion had no peer in the world.

As previously noted, a total of thirty-five Orions were manufactured, all with wooden bodies, and one metal-fuselage Altair was converted to an Orion. This aircraft later became Jimmy Doolittle's famous *Shellightning*, and is now in the Swiss Transport Museum at Lucerne, finished as Swissair's first Orion.

A total of twelve U.S. airlines operated the Orion, but it was Varney Speed Lanes Air Service that bridged the gap between the Lockheed Division of the fast-expiring Detroit Aircraft Company and the Lockheed Aircraft Corporation, which came into being in 1932.

Walter T. Varney was a colorful wheeler-dealer who had actually made money in the airline business, a rare feat for the time. In 1926, his original Varney Air Lines had carried mail on the routes no one else wanted—Elko, Nevada, to Pasco, Washington, via Boise, Idaho—and he sold his holdings to United Air Transport (later United Air Lines) for $2 million in 1930. He next formed Varney Speed Lines Air Service in California, operating Lockheed Orions, and setting the stage for Lockheed's life after bankruptcy, for it was in Varney's interest that a Lockheed plant be kept operating so that replacement aircraft and parts would be available to him. And, as the future owners of the new Lockheed Aircraft Corporation would be quick to understand, if Varney needed parts, so would the operators of the other 150-plus Lockheed aircraft still flying.

The First Lockheed Fighter

By 1930, the only element of the Detroit Aircraft Corporation, the would-be "General Motors of the Air," that was operating at a profit was the Lockheed Division. Funds from Lockheed were drained to sustain the corporation's other enterprises, but the collapse of the stock market, the depression, and the general demise of the aircraft market spelled doom for D.A.C.

In an effort to secure a military contract, D.A.C. used its own funds to develop an aircraft to meet the Army Air Corps requirement for a two-place fighter to replace its aging Berliner Joyce P-16s. Robert Woods, who would later gain fame with the Bell P-39, designed a slim fuselage housing an in-line, liquid-cooled Curtiss Conqueror engine of six hundred horsepower, and mated it to an Altair wing and tail. (D.A.C. had previously built metal fuselages for nine Vegas and one Sirius.)

Called the XP-900, it had a sensational top speed of 235 mph, 46 mph faster than the contemporary Boeing P-12E biplane fighters. The Air Corps agreed to buy the aircraft as the YP-24, and then awarded a contract for $250,000 for five YIP-24 fighters and four Y1A-9 attack aircraft. (The "YP-24" designation was an anomaly; normally the progression ran from XP to YIP to P.)

Unfortunately, on October 19, 1931, one landing gear of the YP-24 refused to come down, and the pilot, Lieutenant Harrison Crocker, was ordered to abandon the aircraft. Crocker could probably have made a safe landing on one gear, sustaining only minor damage, but

The XP-900, Lockheed's first fighter aircraft, used a standard Orion wing coupled to a metal fuselage. Despite an accident to the prototype, the advanced design was eventually modified and put into production by Consolidated.

Harvey Christen was the very first employee of the Lockheed Aircraft Corporation, which he served with distinction for many years.

the Air Corps was unfamiliar with retractable gears, and felt that it was more prudent to abandon the aircraft.

It did not really matter to Detroit Aircraft, for it could not fulfill the contract. It had lost more than $700,000 in 1929 and had seen the value of its $15 par value stock drop to 12½¢; there was no alternative but receivership. The Lockheed Aircraft Corporation came under the control of the Title Insurance and Trust Company of Los Angeles. During the receivership, Carl Squier would go on directing a skeleton work force, which managed to build two more Orions and an Altair. In addition, parts for two Vegas were acquired by two groups of former employees. Firman Gray directed a crew which completed one Vega in May 1932, while Dick Von Hake completed another in March of 1933. In between these dates, on June 16, 1932, the company was closed. Only one man was employed in the factory, Harvey Christen, who served as mechanic, supply clerk, sweeper, and night watchman. He would go on to do much more.

It was axiomatic that a firm with the potential to produce sensational designs like the Vega, Sirius, and Orion could not be kept closed. Only five days after the sad ceremony of shutting its doors, a new Lockheed Aircraft Corporation would be born.

CHAPTER 3

Rebirth and Resurgence

Although two of the men who did so much to launch a great aviation firm, Allan Lockheed and Robert Ellsworth Gross, came from totally different backgrounds, each managed to arrive at exactly the right time for the Lockheed company.

As previously noted, Allan came from a family poor in material goods but rich in mental resources. Robert, the man who would lead the rebirth of Lockheed in 1932, could trace his surname to English records as far back as 1273. The Ellsworth line of the family was no less distinguished, with Sir John Ellsworth's name being recorded during the life of Edward III (1312–77). The Ellsworths were in America by 1646, and the two lines came together early in the nineteenth century. Robert's father, Robert Haven Gross, was born in 1864 and married Mabel Bowman Bell. The two children born of this union,

One of the most beloved
executives in Lockheed history,
Robert E. Gross was known for
his dapper wardrobe, his interest
in art, and his business acumen.

Robert and his younger brother Courtlandt Sherrington Gross, would
lead Lockheed to ever greater heights.

Allan and Robert were similar in three respects. First, each was
taught by his mother at home. Allan never received any formal schooling, but after four years of home tutoring, Robert entered elementary
school. On his first day, he was started in the first grade, but was
rapidly moved up to the fifth by day's end. Second, they were both
fascinated by automobiles, with Allan racing Corbins, and Robert
owning a succession of exotic foreign cars including a Mercedes, a
Voison, and a Hispano Suiza—all automobile companies with strong
aviation associations. Later in their lives, each shared a third quality,
the ability to pick exactly the right kind of people to meet a current
organizational need.

Robert was graduated from the West Newton, Massachusetts,
high school, and went to the exclusive St. George's Preparatory School.
He was graduated from Harvard in 1919, having distinguished himself
athletically if not academically—the "gentleman's C" was very much
the mode. He captained both the baseball and hockey teams, and in
the innocent manner of the day, so far removed from today's com-
mercialized college sports, sometimes served as coach as well. Only five
feet seven and one-half inches tall, but strongly built, Robert had a

ruddy complexion and a quick smile, a persona that served him well in dramatics, where he no doubt picked up skills that were useful to him in negotiations in later years. Enlisting as a private during World War I, he rose to the rank of first lieutenant; the war ended before he could go overseas.

His father had been highly successful in the coal-mining business, and was president of the New River Company. As a boy, Robert traveled with his father through the West and the South, sometimes sitting on a suitcase in a tent, listening to his father handle management problems, picking up information that would prove to be useful to him when he launched his entrepreneurial career.

He won his first job on the baseball diamond at Harvard—a friend of his father, George Lee, watched him play, liked what he saw, and invited him to a job after graduation with Lee, Higginson & Company, an investment firm. Robert worked for them for eight years, in a variety of positions, and it was there that he first became exposed to aviation, traveling around the United States and Europe.

In 1927, he was sent by his firm to look at the Canon-Reliance Fuel Company of Canon City, Colorado, which had not been operating profitably. Gross examined the properties, and, based on the knowledge he had acquired of the business, he bought the company for $120,000. He managed to bring his coal company around to a very profitable state, primarily by selling coal to the Santa Fe Railroad, and without leaving Lee, Higginson. Informal reports indicate that he was a millionaire in his early thirties.

Later that year, one of his assignments for Lee, Higginson took him to the Stearman Aircraft Company, in Wichita, Kansas. There he made his first flight, in a Stearman biplane piloted by Lloyd Carlton Stearman and in company with Mac V. Short, two men whose lives would later mesh with his own. Stearman already had carved out a distinguished career, having been chief engineer for E. M. "Matty" Laird and then, in 1924, joining with Walter Beech and Clyde Cessna to create Travel Air. (The aviation world was a small one; Cessna had flown the first plane Stearman had ever seen, and Beech had taught him how to fly.)

Stearman left in 1926 to create his own company, Stearman Aircraft, at Venice, California, but returned to Wichita in 1927. There he built and sold no fewer than 249 of his rugged series of biplanes—a huge number for the time. Ironically, the most famous aircraft to bear his name, the Stearman Model 75, the famous "Kaydet," was manufactured after his departure from the firm by the Stearman Division

Robert E. Gross had headed the Viking Flying Boat Company prior to coming to Lockheed. The Viking was an adaptation of the French Schreck aircraft that had been built in large numbers.

of the Boeing Company. Although elements from Lloyd Stearman's previous designs were used, the Kaydet was designed by Harold Zipp and Jack Clark.

Gross not only bought a $20,000 interest in Stearman Aircraft, but also purchased an aircraft. Inoculated with aviation fever, in 1928 he and his younger brother Courtlandt formed the Viking Flying Boat Company, a Delaware corporation, to manufacture a licensed version of the French Shreck pusher biplane flying boat in New Haven, Connecticut. In 1931, he formed a second Viking Flying Boat Company, a Connecticut corporation, to finance building a hangar on New Haven Airport. The first company leased the second company's hangar, then acquired the Bourdon Aircraft Corporation, which built the delightful little Kitty Hawk biplane ("Flies Like a Hawk, Lands Like a Kitten").

With these investments, which by some accounts totaled more than $400,000 over time, Gross should have made more money than he had in coal mining. The Stearman company was acquired by United

Aircraft and Transport in a stock transaction that yielded a fine paper profit. The Kitty Hawk was well liked, its relatively small dimensions imparting a nimbleness that made it fun to fly. The well-proven four-place Viking flying boat should have been extremely successful, for the original firm, FBA (Franco-British Aviation), had built almost four thousand similar aircraft for a variety of air forces. A few were sold, including five to the U.S. Coast Guard in 1936 at a price of just under $5,000 each. Given serial numbers V-152 through 156, these were given the unusual designation 00–1. Some wags suggested that the hyphen was a minus sign, given the small size of the flying boats. The Coast Guard order, which had been facilitated by Franklin Kurt, a prototypical sportsman pilot of the period and expert on water flying, resulted in a net profit of $5,846.98, minus a $2,000 royalty fee to FBA. The accounting picture was not as satisfying, because the book value of the unfinished boats that had been used to satisfy the contract was $27,190, resulting in a net loss of more than $23,000 on their manufacture.

Gross was to experience on the East Coast and in Wichita what the Lockheed Division of Detroit Aircraft was experiencing in California: the Depression. The stock market crash wiped out Gross's investment in Stearman and reduced sales for Viking, although the latter firm stayed in business until the demands of an expanding Lockheed firm would draw Courtlandt west in 1940. The financial debacle did not alter Robert's faith in Stearman, nor did it diminish his fascination with aviation. Not a pilot, and definitely not an engineer, Gross had a love for aviation that enabled him to persevere in adversity. More importantly, that love gave him an intuitive sense of what the market required, and enabled him to make a series of correct decisions over the next thirty years that would bring him to the top of his industry. The word most frequently used by his contemporaries to describe Gross was "visionary," and he is remembered with deep affection by all who knew him.

Varney Speed Lanes

Walter Varney had purchased the last Lockheed aircraft to leave the plant before its doors were closed, a gleaming white, red-trimmed Orion. Varney Speed Lanes (he changed the name from Speed Lines) operated a fleet of six Orions between Los Angeles and San Francisco. The swift Orions made the trip in two hours and fifteen minutes at a speed that was 50 to 75 mph faster than the competing Fords and Fokkers. (Current airline timetables show that modern 500-mph jet airliners make the same trip in one hour and twenty-seven minutes—saving only forty-eight minutes. This relatively small difference in elapsed time can be attributed to the fact that the Orions had far less complex departure and control procedures—they simply took off, flew to their destinations at a low altitude, landed, and taxied up to the terminal.)

Varney invited Gross to come out and inspect his operation and provide financial advice, a high compliment given Varney's demonstrated record of buying and selling at opportune times. Gross's price was right—he received no salary, and his job was, in his words, "to sit around with no obligations and no title, making an occasional suggestion as to how the airline could be pulled out of the red." Varney also wanted Lloyd Stearman to design a slightly larger replacement for the Orion. On September 16, 1931, the three men formed the Stearman-Varney Corporation, intending to manufacture a single-engine all-metal aircraft of Stearman's design. The company had a tremendous asset: a young man named Hall Hibbard, who had worked for Stearman in Wichita, and would become one of Lockheed's engineering legends, fathering the Electra, the Hudson, the P-38—and the career of a young man named Clarence Johnson.

Back in Burbank

Back in Burbank, an unpaid Carl Squier was fighting desperately to keep his old company's assets together as an entity, and avoiding their being sold off one item at a time until there was nothing left to Lockheed but the name. Accounts differ as to how Squier and Gross met; some attribute the meeting to a telephone call from Squier, others to Gross's initiative. It doesn't matter, for Gross was immediately interested and flew down to "check the bricks." He found some repair work going on, including a $4,011 job on a Boeing Model 100 that was being modified for Howard Hughes—the first step toward his long and profitable, if sometimes turbulent, relationship with Lockheed.

Squier, who used the term "Cheer without interruption" as an upbeat catchphrase, had a complete inventory of every tool, spar, bolt, and chair that remained behind the Lockheed doors, plus a precise evaluation of material in stock and work in progress. A conservative

The Lockheed Orion demonstrated how far the basic design of the Vega could be stretched. Operated by Varney Speed Lanes, the Orion was well liked by both pilots and passengers.

Hall Hibbard, an extremely talented aeronautical engineer himself, had a gift for extracting the most from the people who worked for him.

tally indicated exactly $129,961 in assets, plus the potential of doing repair and replacement business with Varney and all the other Lockheed owners. Squier, who soon became known informally as the world's greatest airplane salesman, now undertook to sell Robert Gross on the idea of reviving Lockheed.

Gross was well aware that Lockheed had almost always made a profit on its own operations, and that only its debilitating relationship with Detroit Aircraft had forced it into receivership. In examining the Lockheed Aircraft operating statements for November and December 1931 and January 1932, he found that Lockheed had income of $191,159 for the period, and a net profit of $23,956. Further investigation revealed to him that Lockheed had about $63,000 in accounts payable, leading him to believe that the firm could be procured for about $60,000 or less. (It must be recalled that in 1932 bankruptcies were increasingly common, and creditors were often delighted to get ten cents on the dollar, for the alternative was often no repayment at all.)

Oddly enough, he was strongly counseled against buying Lockheed in an impassioned five-page letter from his brother Courtlandt. (The correspondence between the two brothers and the father reveals a deep affection and generosity. It was "Courtie" and "Bobbie," and they signed their letters with the terms "affectionately" or "best love." One can get a true picture of Robert Gross in many ways from his letters, for even when dealing with so persistently exasperating a person as George Putnam—Amelia Earhart's husband—he was unfailingly considerate and friendly.)

Courtlandt Gross argued that buying the Lockheed plant to make metal Stearman aircraft did not make sense. He also cautioned that Gerry Vultee was developing an aircraft for E. L. Cord (ultimately the Vultee V-1A) and that Boeing was surely going to develop something from its Monomail prototype. Courtlandt noted that with all due respect to Stearman and Hibbard, "the day is past when one or two men can design a successful airplane." He made an adverse comparison of their own Kitty Hawk with a Waco to drive his point home—the Kitty Hawk was a good airplane, but did not compare to the Waco in engineering detail. In the end, he advised his brother to stick with Varney in the airline business and let the manufacturing side go.

Yet Robert Gross had not sensed the aura of cooperation and vision that he had expected to find in the Varney Speed Lanes operation. He thus discounted Courtlandt's advice and was primed to be receptive to Squier's salesmanship. He recognized the implicit value of the company's name, and, although he believed that at least a few more of the wooden Lockheeds could be sold, he saw, as Northrop had, that the future of aviation lay in metal aircraft. (On March 31, 1931, a TWA Fokker F10A crashed in a violent storm, carrying Notre Dame football coach Knute Rockne to his death. The subsequent Bureau of Air Commerce inspection requirements for aircraft with wooden wing spars and ribs were so onerous that airliners so equipped became too expensive to operate.)

In a later interview, Robert Gross said, "I thought I would get Lockheed bought, get Stearman and Hibbard settled, and then go back East and resume my activities there." The Depression had been cruel, but Gross was able to form an investment group that included Walter Varney, who put up an initial $10,000, and then, when it looked as though the funding would be insufficient, another $10,000. Randolph C. "Bob" Walker, a mutual friend, introduced Gross to Cyril Chappellet. Walker would contribute $5,000 in his wife's name and Mr. and Mrs. Chappellet contributed $10,000. A final $5,000 was received from Thomas Fortune Ryan III.

An organizational structure was drawn up, with Lloyd Stearman, who wanted to keep his hand on the engineering tiller, as president and general manager. Squier was vice president and sales manager, Gross was treasurer, Chappellet was secretary, Richard Von Hake was chief engineer, and Hibbard was assistant chief engineer.

Other groups were interested in Lockheed, one of them being led by Allan Lockheed himself. Allan wanted to be sure that he had enough money to win the bidding and set his sights on what proved to be an impossible goal: raising $100,000. The irrepressible Roscoe Turner also sought to enlist Earl Gilmore's financial aid to buy the firm. Both failed.

Thus, on the morning of June 21, 1932, in the U.S. district court in Los Angeles, the thirty-five-year-old Gross would submit a bid of $40,000 on behalf of his investors for the defunct Lockheed Aircraft Company. There were no other bids, and Judge Harry Hollzer accepted the offer with the wry comment, "Young man, I hope you know what you are doing." The Lockheed Aircraft Corporation was reborn.

The exact method of its rebirth is interesting. The Title Insurance and Trust Company as receiver sold the property and assets of the Lockheed Aircraft Company to Walter Varney as trustee for the other investors for $40,000 cash. On June 20, 1932, after its incorporation, 4,000 of the authorized 50,000 shares of the new Lockheed Aircraft

Corporation's stock were exchanged for all the property and assets of the Lockheed Aircraft Company. (An ancillary agreement was made to the effect that Varney agreed to buy all the transports he needed from Lockheed, and Lockheed agreed not to sell any aircraft to his competitors.) The 4,000 shares were divided so that Varney received 2,000, Chappellet 1,000, Ryan 500, and Jacqueline Walker 500. On the same date, Gross, Stearman, and Varney agreed to purchase 800 shares of Lockheed Aircraft Corporation capital stock in exchange for all the property and assets (i.e., the design for the ten-passenger all-metal single-engine aircraft) of Stearman-Varney, Incorporated. The shares were to be issued to Robert Gross. (Stearman-Varney, Incorporated, was apparently then allowed to lapse, no formal action being taken to dissolve the corporation.)

Robert Gross's generous nature was revealed again in a letter written on the same day, giving half his Lockheed stock and half his Viking stock to Courtlandt. Such was the nature of their relationship that "Courtie," much touched, refused the offer "unconditionally." All brothers should get along so well.

On July 1, 1932, an official board meeting was held, with Stearman, R. C. Walker, and Cyril Chappellet named as directors and Gross as chairman of the board. He was to receive a minimum salary of $300 per month, and an option to buy 500 shares of stock at $10 per share. Stearman received a $400-per-month salary, and a similar stock option. Squier received $400 per month as well as a 1 percent commission on the gross amount of sales. It was also agreed that 5,000 shares of stock be authorized at a price of $10 per share, and that 2,000 shares be offered for immediate sale. This was quickly amended to authorize offering the entire 5,000 shares for sale.

An Investment Bonus

It was almost immediately apparent that in addition to $10,000, Chappellet would add a great deal to the firm, for he was that rare hybrid, the adventurer-businessman, who combined a strong drive to fly with an entrepreneurial bent. Like Gross, his father had been in the mining business, and later went into petroleum, where he became a close friend of Howard Hughes's father. This relationship aided both Cyril Chappellet and Lockheed later.

The young Chappellet was oriented to reality early in life, doing summer work as an oil-field roughneck when he was only fourteen. A

Lockheed was blessed through its history with excellent leaders. In 1934 they included, from left, Ronald King, assistant treasurer; Carl B. Squier, vice president-sales manager; Lloyd Stearman, president; Robert Gross, chairman of the board and treasurer; Cyril Chappellet, secretary, and Hall Hibbard, vice president and assistant chief engineer.

B student in high school, he went to Stanford and studied mining engineering briefly before switching over to economics. He flunked out in his first year because he had poor study habits, but returned to graduate in good standing in 1927.

Upon graduation, Cyril joined the U.S. Army Air Corps as a cadet and graduated in 1929—one of his classmates being an already taciturn Curtis LeMay. Chappellet elected to join the reserves rather than go on active duty, and immediately got a job with Western Air Express flying the trimotor Fokker F-10. (Western Air Express later merged with Transcontinental and Western to create Transcontinental and Western Air, Incorporated—TWA—potentially one of Lockheed's strongest customers.)

Chappellet enjoyed flying for TWA, but, deciding he wanted a career in business, he established a partnership and with a capital investment of $500 created the Airlines Consolidated Ticket Office, the world's first ticket agency dedicated exclusively to air travel. The agency prospered and a branch office was set up in San Francisco. There he made friends with Randolph Walker, who introduced him to Gross.

Deciding early on that he wanted to "hitch himself to Gross's rising star," Chappellet would prove to be the keel of the Lockheed ship, keeping it stable through its many rapid changes of course over the next several decades. Chappellet was a perfect complement to Gross, whose ebullient optimism sometimes needed a steadying influence. Together, they would create an unbeatable team, taking Lockheed through the worst depression in history as it grew in just eight years from a risky $40,000 venture in 1932 to a huge corporation with its stock valued at $40 million in 1940.

Gross Takes a Giant Step

One of the many great tributes paid to Robert Gross later in his life was that he "knew what kind of an airplane to build." This talent manifested itself early in the life of the Lockheed Corporation, when Gross resolutely put behind him the thought of further development of the wooden Lockheed models, even though four Vegas, one Altair, and seventeen Orions would be built between 1933 and 1937. (The Orions were the mainstay of the company during the early years, earning laurels in exploration, gathering news, and, oddly enough, in combat. As many as fourteen Orions went to Spain to serve with Spanish Republican (Loyalist) forces; only one survived the war. The very first Orion to enter Spain had been built for the racing pilot Michael Detroyat, and later placed at the disposal of author-diplomat André Malraux. On one of its trips to Madrid it carried Robert Capa, the photographer who would become world-renowned for his work in Spain. Other Lockheeds served the Loyalists, including a Vega, a Sirius, and two Electras.)

Back in the echoing empty bays of the Lockheed factory in 1932, Gross had to consider the advice of Varney, Stearman, and Hibbard, all of whom believed that their design for a single-engine all-metal aircraft was not only a good one, but economically feasible. Gross undoubtedly knew that Boeing's Monomail was, as Courtlandt had warned, leading to the debut of a new twin-engine airliner, the Model 247. Moreover, in a letter of September 12, 1932, to Courtlandt, Gross wrote, "We got the jump on TWA's ideas concerning a large transport plane some three weeks ago, and have been in receipt of a letter two or three days [sic] from Tommy Tomlinson along the same line." His reference is to TWA's solicitation to Lockheed and to Douglas for an airliner with a better performance than that of the Boeing 247.

As a result, Gross had decided to cancel the single-engine Stearman design and commit to a "bi-motor," in the phrase of the time. It was an inspired decision. The Boeing and Douglas airliners had made single-engine designs obsolete. The Bureau of Air Commerce issued a regulation, effective October 1, 1934, that forbade

In 1933, the Lockheed Aircraft Corporation was still small enough to have all its
employees gather together for a single group photograph.

single-engine transports operating in the United States to carry passengers on scheduled services at night or over terrain unsuitable for
emergency landings.

Corporate Growth

Immediately after the founding of the Lockheed Aircraft Corporation,
Thomas F. Ryan III had purchased an additional 500 shares of stock
at the $10 par value, and William L. Graves acquired 700 shares at
the same price. Six thousand shares were transferred to the Lockheed
Aircraft Corporation of Delaware, which later became known as the
Southern California Aviation Corporation. In 1933 an additional
500,000 shares were issued at par value of $1. (The 6,000 shares held
by the Southern California Aviation Corporation were exchanged for
90,000 of the new issue; thus, each holder of the original 6,000 shares
got a nominal 50 percent return in less than a year.)

By April 1934, 289,741 shares were on the market. Lockheed
had made a net profit of $25,962 during 1933. The value of getting
in early was revealed in a letter to Gross by Frederick M. Warburg in
July 1958. Warburg had invested $8,000 in the issue of $1 par value
stock. In his letter, he said, "I have, thanks to your work and that of
your great organization, been able to give a $25,000 Harvard schol-
arship in memory of Hank Flower's son; $5,000 to Lenox Hill Hos-
pital; $5,000 to Middlesex School, and a $250,000 gift to a program
for Harvard College." This might not be all that resulted from the
original investment, but earning $285,000 from $8,000 is not bad.

Enter the Electra

The Orion had officially been the Model 9; to preserve continuity, the first product of the Lockheed Aircraft Corporation was the Model 10. The name Electra also represented stellar continuity, being the name of one of the six visible stars in the cluster of heavenly bodies known as the Pleiades in the constellation Taurus.

Thanks to the breathtaking importance and almost unimaginable scope of his work, the image of Clarence "Kelly" Johnson in recent years has been so overwhelming that the design and success of the Model 10 is attributed primarily to him almost by default. Johnson certainly made important contributions, of which more later, but the aircraft that emerged really stemmed from Hall Hibbard and Richard Von Hake (primarily responsible for the wooden Lockheeds still being built and repaired, but designer of the Electra landing gear) and, to a lesser degree, Lloyd Stearman. Hibbard recalled Stearman as having a "fabulous, almost intuitive sense of proportion and design sense." Other famous names were also involved as Lockheed aircraft, for the first time, stopped being the product of an individual primary designer but instead were the products of highly qualified design teams. James Gerschler did much of the general design and stress work on the Electra. George Prudden designed the main spars and other important elements of the structure. C. F. "Carl" Beed worked with Prudden on the wing spars and designed the fuselage. Jack Infield worked on the Electra cockpit and instrument panel.

The ultimate success of the new Lockheed line stemmed in part from the fact that it became the home to many engineers who had tried their hand at manufacturing their own aircraft, and who had not found a Gross to guide them. Prudden had worked with Bill Stout and then went on to design his own all-metal aircraft. Morton Bach had built commercial aircraft of his own design. Henry Ogden built and tried to market a tiny trimotor, but would find his greatest satisfaction as a pivotal figure in Lockheed's first overseas operations. There were many others.

The Model 10 was a major departure from previous Lockheed practice, with the only important aerodynamic similarities being the NACA cowlings and the use of modified Clark Y airfoil, similar to that used on the wooden Lockheeds. The Electra was an all-metal, low-cantilever-wing monoplane, with seating for a crew of two and ten passengers. Hibbard imparted enormous integrity to the design by building the wing stubs integral with the fuselage, with a heavy truss to connect the wing spars. Although the truss took up cabin space, its strength permitted heavier loads, gave long life to the airframe, and permitted growth to larger designs. As an example of the aircraft's longevity, in 1937, a Lockheed 10A sold for $73,000 to Trans-Canada Airlines, a forerunner of Air Canada. After serving for the airline, the Royal Canadian Air Force, and a variety of civilian owners, it was repurchased in 1983 by Air Canada (price this time was $75,000—a $2,000 appreciation over forty-six years) refurbished, and flown with its original markings on goodwill flights. It was scheduled to retire again in 1997, after sixty years of service.

The Model 10 had placed itself in the forefront of airliner design by using every available engineering advance. Exceptional attention was paid to the integration of the NACA cowlings, nacelles, wing, and fuselage. The Pratt & Whitney Wasp Jr. radial engines were rated at 450 horsepower at takeoff and 400 at cruising altitude. Two bladed variable-pitch propellers were used. The internal structure was of 24 ST duralumin while 24 ST Alclad was used for the stressed-skin covering, including the control surfaces—an unusual—(and much advertised) feature for the time. The electrically operated landing gear retracted rearward to a position behind the streamlined engine nacelles. The wings were fitted with split trailing-edge flaps to reduce landing speed.

The original design had a single fin and rudder, large wing fillets (very modish at the time), and a windshield with a rearward rake. (Five production aircraft were equipped with the rather odd-looking forward rake, but these were subsequently modified to the standard shape.) A large fifty-five-inch wingspan model of the aircraft was tested in the University of Michigan eight-foot-diameter wind tunnel in March 1933, under the supervision of Professor Edwin A. Stalker. One of his assistants was twenty-three-year-old Clarence Leonard Johnson, who would become internationally renowned as "Kelly" Johnson.

Johnson had come to Lockheed in 1932, seeking employment. Dick Von Hake told him that nothing was available at the moment, but to return in a year. Johnson secured a fellowship and returned to the University of Michigan for a year of graduate study, studying such subjects—then esoteric—as supercharging, boundary layer control, and the airflow around an aircraft's fuselage wings and tail, all of which would stand him in good stead at Lockheed. His genius was already well recognized as he moonlighted doing wind-tunnel tests for major firms.

The first reports on the wind-tunnel testing received by Lockheed indicated that the original design was satisfactory and within the normal bounds of stability. When Johnson returned to Lockheed, he was hired as a tool designer at eighty-three dollars per month. Never shy, he almost immediately told Hall Hibbard that he disagreed with Stalker's wind-tunnel test reports, and that he was sure that the aircraft would be unstable.

Hibbard was beloved by his coworkers, one reason being his excellent control of his temper. Only thirty years old at the time himself, and with a master's degree in aeronautical engineering from MIT, he could have been forgiven a natural reaction to toss Johnson out on his ear. Instead, he listened to him, and over the ensuing decades, as Johnson's star rose and his reputation surpassed his own, Hibbard continued to manage him patiently, getting the best out of him for Lockheed.

Hibbard's patience may have stemmed from his upbringing. The son of a Presbyterian missionary, he spent the first thirteen years of his life in a remote section of the Philippine Islands, some six hundred miles south of Manila. He returned to his birthplace in Fredonia, Kansas, to go to school, completing both grammar school and high school. Always fascinated by things mechanical, he knew he had a natural engineering bent, and a chance flight in an airplane confirmed his desire to be an aeronautical engineer. He graduated from the College of Emporia, Kansas, with a bachelor's degree in mathematics and physics in 1925, and from MIT in 1927. He married Irene Curtiss on June 1, 1928, and ever after attributed all his important career decisions to her, including his decision to join Lockheed.

He began work at Stearman as a draftsman, his first job being cutting rolls of drafting paper into standard sizes, and in the course of the next three years rose to became project engineer. Part of this time he spent in New Haven, Connecticut, working as a consulting engineer on Bob Gross's Viking flying boat, which was found to require some redesign and needed to have a drawing system set up. He had driven to New Haven with his wife in their first new car, a Ford Model A. While there, Hibbard was impressed by Gross and infected with Gross's love of fine cars, being particularly smitten by his Rolls-Royce and custom-bodied Hispano Suiza. As his career progressed, Hibbard too began to indulge himself in cars; just before World War II, he had modified a maroon 1940 LaSalle so that it was three inches lower slung, and featured a cutout on its exhaust.

Wind-Tunnel Warriors

Johnson worked hard over the first few months of his employment. Impressed, Hibbard, who became chief engineer in 1933, sent him back to the University of Michigan for additional wind-tunnel tests. In the course of more than seventy runs in the wind tunnel, Johnson discovered that vertical surfaces placed near the tips of the horizontal tail increased tail efficiency remarkably. The tip fins, which were supplementary to the conventional vertical fin, modified the vortex created by the flow from the high-pressure side of the tail to the low-pressure side, improving longitudinal stability. Johnson then suggested making the tip surfaces act as the fin and rudder, removing the original center vertical surface. The removal of the central fin further improved flow over the horizontal stabilizer. The new fin and rudder placement also made the aircraft much easier to control during single-engine flight, for control effectiveness was increased. Placing each rudder directly behind an engine insured that the pilot could use the full effect of increased power on the "good" engine to maintain directional control—the physical manifestation of the "dead-foot, dead engine" rule. Johnson was also surprised to find that pitch stability was improved substantially, an unexpected but welcome result.

The Model 10's empennage had evolved into what would become a classic Lockheed signature, the oval-shaped twin fin and rudder that would appear on successive transports, bombers, and fighters. In Burbank, Hibbard was overjoyed with his solution, which was easy to engineer and inexpensive to manufacture. He wrote to Johnson, thanking him and noting that it was "an important discovery and I think it is a fine thing that you should be the one to find out the secret."

Johnson's analysis also took issue with the wing fillets, showing that they increased drag by as much as 20 percent at high angles of attack, and also with the forward rake of the cockpit windshield, but these were retained on the first prototype.

Construction of the prototype was pressed with enthusiasm and speed; drawings were kept to a minimum, with very close cooperation existing between the craftsmen in the shop and the engineering department. The lack of drawings would be troublesome later in the life of the Model 10, as much of the information needed for construction had been kept in "little black books" of the various foremen. A lesson was learned: subsequent Lockheed aircraft all had complete drawing coverage.

Truly a legend in his own time, Clarence L. "Kelly" Johnson is shown here in the University of Michigan wind tunnel. It was here that Johnson saw that a single-tail version of the Electra would have stability problems and suggested that a twin-tail design be adopted.

With the construction number 1001, registration number X233Y, the prototype Electra flew on February 23, 1934, with Marshall Headle at the controls. Flight tests were very satisfactory, with the exception of the wing fillets, which were subsequently deleted, and the forward-raked windshield, which was changed to a more conventional type on the fifth production aircraft.

Gross had known the risk he was taking, committing his new, untried, and still undercapitalized firm to building a sophisticated twin-engine airliner. He was aware that Boeing, long a leader in the military field, had built up considerable transport experience with its Model 40 and Model 80 aircraft. It had also developed the two Monomails, all-metal, low-cantilever-wing single-engine types, and the very advanced Y1B-9 bomber, a twin-engine aircraft with retractable landing gear. While the project was kept under tight wraps, it was known that Boeing was building the Model 247, which would be the first true modern airliner. Douglas had built a large number of military aircraft, including transports, and had assembled a superb team that

The twin-engine, all-metal Electra, with its retractable landing gear, was a remarkable departure from the wooden Lockheeds that had preceded it. This Model 10 is shown in the livery of an airline that became a good Lockheed customer, the Chicago & Southern.

was using Jack Northrop's ideas on metal structure to build the DC-1.

The 247 and the DC-1 were both larger than the projected Electra, which Gross saw as what would be called today a "niche-market" airliner. He wanted it to be used by the smaller airlines, which did not require an aircraft as large as either the Boeing or the Douglas. He hoped that the combination of lower initial price, lower total operating costs (if not necessarily seat-mile costs), and more than anything, *speed*, would appeal to smaller U.S. and foreign carriers.

Gross proved to be exactly on the money. A June 6, 1935, analysis of competing aircraft showed that at $.2756 per mile, the Electra was far cheaper to operate than the Douglas DC-2 ($.3860), Boeing 247D ($.3537), Curtiss Condor ($.4746), or Stinson A ($.3307). The seat-mile cost in the Electra was $.0276, lower than any but the much larger fourteen-passenger DC-2, which had a seat-mile cost of $.0272. But, as Gross was quick to point out in his correspondence, aircraft rarely flew with all their seats full; if the DC-2 had an empty seat, it was more expensive to operate than the Electra.

The DC-2 and the Electra were faster than all the others, with a

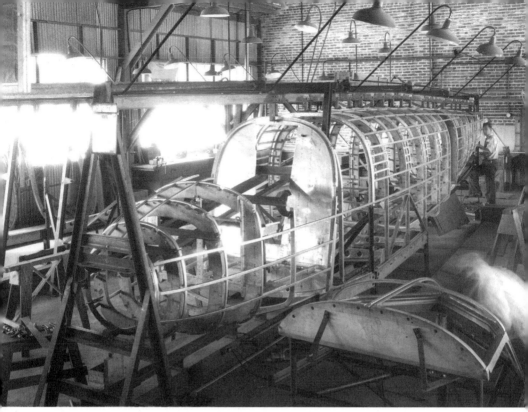

The Lockheed engineers and shop personnel became adept at building mockups. This talent would serve them well when it came to selling the British Purchasing Commission on the Hudson bomber.

block (i.e., takeoff to landing) speed of 170 mph. And when it came to cost, the Electra at $54,500 was more expensive only than the $42,000 Stinson, an eight-place, 145-mph, fabric-covered trimotor. The Electra cost $31,000 less than the DC-2, $19,000 less than a 247D, and $13,500 less than the antique-looking Curtiss Condor biplane.

Northwest Airways ordered the prototype with an option for two more Model 10s even before the Electra's first flight, and, as Northwest Airlines, the company would long be a good Lockheed customer. The first aircraft was delivered on June 29, 1934, even though the Department of Commerce's Approved Type Certificate No. 551 was not issued until the following August 11.

Despite a $25,692 profit in 1933 and advance sales of $335,900, the cost of producing the prototype and gearing up for production was draining Lockheed's resources, and it was forced to go to the new Reconstruction Finance Corporation to get a $200,000 line of revolving credit. Gross also had to manage some personnel changes. He wrote to his father on December 21, 1934, that "I had to slip the knot with

Lloyd Stearman. Although the ordeal was harrowing and quite a wrench, I had to do it." He went on to say that Stearman worked best in an organization devoted to experimental work, and that "the easy-going environment here in California is also perhaps not conducive to bringing out his best effort." Gross succeeded Stearman as president on December 15, 1934. Walter Varney had disposed of his stock in May 1933, and subsequently protested over the sale of Electras to other airlines, saying that such sales violated his agreement. Lockheed lawyers treated it as a bogus issue, and it did not deter Varney from buying Lockheed planes later on.

Perspective

The magnitude of Gross's achievement can scarcely be overestimated. He took over a bankrupt company with aging, inadequate facilities, at a time that many people consider the very depth of the depression. He then entered competition with two established rivals, both of whom had strong military contracts, large engineering departments, and comparatively easy access to financing. His competitive tool was a totally new aircraft, foreign to the experience of everyone on his staff in terms of material, size, and cost, and laden with all the risks implicit in an advanced new design.

By December 29, 1934, 11 Electras had been delivered, 6 to Northwest Airlines and 5 to Pan American Airways. Built as the Model 10-A, 10-B, 10-C, and 10-E, Electras were tailored to customer requirements for different or more powerful engines. When the last Model 10 had been delivered in July 1941, a total of 148 aircraft had been sold, 74 to domestic and 74 to foreign users, including thirteen airlines. (Used Electras tended to migrate to foreign owners.) Of the total, 101 were Model 10-As. Within the United States, the Electra was sold to eight airlines as well as to private owners and the U.S. military. Gross could not have hoped for more, nor could Lockheed's stockholders and customers.

Yet the times were not easy. In 1934, development costs of the Electra caused Lockheed to lose $190,891, despite sales of $562,759. Sales almost quadrupled in 1935, to almost $2.1 million, and a profit of more than $217,000 was realized. Against the backdrop of the relentless Depression, during which established companies were folding like flowers in the fall, such performance was remarkable.

Military Variants

Lockheed's prior experience with the military had been very limited, confined to the ill-fated YP-24 and a handful of Altairs and Vegas. Yet the Depression loomed like a cloud over all business activities, and it seemed prudent to solicit orders for military versions. Lockheed had proposed a military version of the original Electra to Anthony Fokker even before the Electra's first flight. Preliminary development was also under way for three light bombers and a multiplace fighter intended for ground attack equipped with a 37-mm cannon below the fuselage and "fully accessible and completely exposed to the flow of air for cooling." Although the U.S. military was the preferred customer, Lockheed would have been glad to sell these warplanes to any nation, if allowed to do so. They would have been good performers, for with 750-horsepower Pratt & Whitney Twin-Row Wasps, top speed would have approached 270 mph.

None of the proposals elicited any orders, but the U.S. military was quick to order standard transport versions plus a few unusual "one-off" types. The Air Corps ordered three Y1C-36's and one Y1C-37 as staff transports. The navy purchased two, the XR20-1 and XR30-1 (the latter for the Coast Guard). When war came, Lockheeds of many types were impressed into military service under a variety of designations.

The most unusual and important of the military variants was the Air Corps XC-35, a research aircraft for testing pressurized cabins and high-altitude operations. Project engineer Ferris Way designed an especially strengthened circular-cross-section fuselage, but used the standard Electra wing and empennage. Windows were not installed, and a ten-pound-per-square-inch pressure differential was sought. The innovations worked well, and the plane achieved ground speeds of up to 350 mph at an altitude of twenty thousand feet. The Army Air Corps was awarded the Collier Trophy in 1937 for sponsoring the development of the XC-35. The aircraft today is in storage awaiting restoration as part of the collection of the National Air and Space Museum.

Even though few military Electras were built, none as genuine combat aircraft, the company gained experience and confidence to permit it to embark upon further military proposals that would lead to the creation of the versatile Hudson just a few years later.

Amelia Earhart flew to further fame in her next Lockheed, a specially modified Electra. She disappeared in the aircraft in 1937 on an attempted flight around the world.

Private Owners

Unquestionably the most famous Electra—and one of the most famous aircraft of all time—was the Model 10-E purchased by the Purdue Research Foundation for Amelia Earhart. George Palmer Putnam was the driving force—and the check writer—behind the purchase, and he ceaselessly negotiated with the makers of engines, tires, instruments, and everything else to provide their equipment and services at actual cost, without profit, even as he lobbied Lockheed to reduce its price. He placed a ten-thousand-dollar check for down payment which promptly bounced; when presented again, it was paid.

Putnam had been a thorn in Lockheed's side for years, as he had a penchant for seeking commissions on sales with which he had little or nothing to do. In the course of the negotiations for "Miss Earhart's airplane," as he termed it, he placed an order for three Lockheed Model 14s, which were just coming down the production line. He would never fulfill the order, but allowed Lockheed to keep bumping his delivery date back.

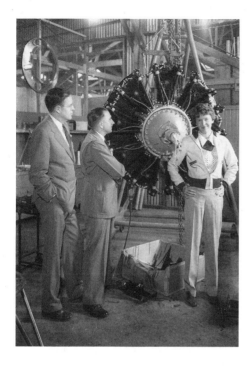

Paul Mantz, who would earn fame flying aircraft for the motion-picture industry, was Earhart's mentor and friend. From left, George Putnam (her husband), Mantz, and Earhart.

Earhart's 10-E was substantially modified with additional gasoline tanks, special cockpit soundproofing, insulation, and navigation equipment. Lockheed would guarantee a range of 4,000 miles with 1,050 gallons of fuel, and 4,500 miles with 1,200 gallons, with the aircraft cruising at four thousand feet at 145 mph for best range. With the heavier fuel load and additional equipment, gross weight was about 16,141 pounds, an astounding 5,641 pounds (a 54 percent increase!) more than the standard 10-E.

Gross had asked Putnam to communicate with Cyril Chappellet directly, and Putnam in turn had asked Chappellet to consider Paul Mantz as Putnam's primary representative at the factory. In one plaintive letter to Putnam, Chappellet listed the changes to the aircraft and their effect on weight. He said, "We wish to point out to you that the above gross weight of your Electra has reached the point where we would deem it highly inadvisable to add anything more to it." Gross indicated to Putnam that while Lockheed was not concerned about the flying qualities of the heavyweight Electra once airborne, the critical condition was takeoff, when heavy loads would be placed on the landing gear and center section. The point was amply demonstrated when Earhart crashed on her attempted takeoff in Honolulu.

Earhart flew the aircraft, NR 16020, with Helen Richey as copilot

Faced with strong competition from Douglas, Lockheed opted for a strategy of providing smaller but faster aircraft. This Super Electra was purchased by British Airways.

in the 1936 Bendix Race, placing last behind three old rivals. Louise Thaden and Blanche Noyes won in a Beech Staggerwing at 165 mph; Laura Ingalls was second in a Lockheed Orion at 157 mph. Richey, Earhart's copilot, had won fame as an endurance pilot; later she became a member of the British Women's Ferry Command during World War II. Sadly, she committed suicide in New York at the age of thirty-seven.

The controversy and myths surrounding the story of Amelia Earhart's last flight are both too well known and too complex to repeat here. It is sufficient to say that faced with a daunting navigation task, Amelia Earhart apparently did not exercise all the prudence that she might have, especially in terms of becoming proficient operating her radios. She and her navigator, Fred Noonan, disappeared on July 2, 1937, on their flight to tiny Howland Island, a dot in the vast Pacific.

A second commercial Electra, NC 16059, a sister ship to Earhart's, had a happier career. It was used by Eastern Airlines captain H. T. "Dick" Merrill and J. S. Lambie for a special round-trip crossing of the Atlantic in early May 1937. On the eastbound leg they carried newsreels of the crash of the German zeppelin *Hindenburg* to Great Britain; on the westbound leg, they brought the first photographs of the coronation of King George VI.

Upsizing and Downsizing

The Model 10 Electra, very fast and pleasant to fly, had a tonic effect upon Lockheed's balance sheet. It proved to be an immensely flexible basic design, capable of being reduced or expanded in scale with equal success. Scaling an aircraft down is generally more difficult than scaling it up. When scaled down, the Model 10 yielded the Electra Junior, the Model 12. When scaled up, and made considerably more sophisticated, it became the Model 14 Super Electra.

Independent research by supersalesman Squier indicated that an aircraft smaller than the Electra could be sold to feeder airlines. This was confirmed by an invitation from the Bureau of Air Commerce to manufacturers to submit designs for just such an aircraft. The by-now-proven team of Hibbard and Johnson quickly came up with the six-passenger Model 12, designated the Electra Junior. Wingspan was reduced and weight was pared down about 18 percent. The greatest difficulty in scaling down a design is encountered with the reduction of wing area, which goes down by the square. In this instance, wing area was reduced from 458 square feet to 352 square feet—a whopping 23 percent. Yet the Electra Junior, powered by the same engines as the Model-10A, retained its delightful handling characteristics, while delivering a top speed of 225 mph and a cruise of 213.

This was hot performance, but Lockheed was now competing against itself (and with other entries like the Beech Model 18), and only 130 Model 12s were delivered over the six years between its June 27, 1936, first flight to termination of production in 1942. Most were acquired by private operators or government agencies. Almost half went to military customers. The largest single procurement was from the government of the Netherland East Indies, which took delivery of 36 aircraft.

The United States Navy purchased 7 Electras, designated JO-1 and JO-2. Another standard Lockheed Model 12 was fitted with a non-retractable tricycle landing gear for test work; designated the XJO-3, it had a flyaway price of $67,500. It was tested aboard the

USS *Lexington,* but the routine use of tricycle-gear aircraft would not come until the jet age after the war.

Electra Junior: The Spiritual Father of the U-2

The most glamorous of all the Model 12s were the two aircraft purchased by British Airways for use by a legendary figure, Frederick Sidney Cotton. As a captain in the First World War, Cotton gained fame with his "Sidcot" flying suit, which was a well-padded mechanic's coverall. It was much warmer and far more comfortable than the leather jackets that had been the vogue. Bucking tradition, regulation, and RAF propriety with equal abandon, Cotton was directly responsible for the establishment of the Photographic Development Unit (later Photographic Reconnaissance Unit) of the Royal Air Force. As Wing Commander Cotton, he "charmed two Spitfires out of Dowding," then stripped and polished them so that they would cruise at thirty-five thousand feet with a range of 1,750 miles, immune from German interception.

Cotton's rogue behavior had the implicit backing of the chief of the Air Staff, Air Chief Marshal Sir Cyril Newall, who had enabled him to cut his photographic reconnaissance teeth on Lockheed 12s before the war. The British government, acting on behalf of the French intelligence service, used British Airways as a cover and Carr Brothers, Incorporated, of New York as an agent. They purchased the first Electra on November 16, 1938. A standard Lockheed 12 was modified with the installation of two additional forty-eight-gallon fuselage tanks and by placing a forty-centimeter-square opening in the bottom of the fuselage, equipped with a hatch that could be opened and closed in flight. A removable hatch was provided in the cabin floor. The price of the aircraft, including shipping via the SS *Britannic,* was $53,383.

Correspondence reveals that Lockheed relished the assignment. The firm readily accepted the cover story that "Mr. S. Cotton has a lot of oil interests in Iran (Persia) and expects to use this 12A in connection with his oil companies in that territory, and for the purposes of taking aerial photographs, mapping and so forth."

An order for an identical Model 12 was received by Lockheed's European sales representative, Ferris M. Smith, on January 11, 1938. The first Electra Junior was assigned the British registration letters

G-AFKR, while the second received G-AFPF. A third Electra Junior was subsequently acquired from a private source, and registered G-AFTL. (The first two Electras were subsequently turned over to France, as F-ARQA and F-ARPP, respectively.)

Cotton, who would have fit in quite well with the buccaneers of the Spanish Main, had three F-24 cameras mounted in the Lockheed, one pointing straight down, and two mounted at an angle to take obliques. (Later, additional Leica cameras were mounted in the leading edge.) He had the Lockheed painted an "exquisite duck-egg green," which made it almost invisible at the heights he flew.

Operating out of the airport at Heston, he then began a long series of important reconnaissance flights through the Mediterranean, on which he took photographs of Libya, Eritrea, Sardinia, and the Dodecanese. Later, he flew into Germany often, on some occasions giving curious Luftwaffe officers a treat by flying the Germans in "Der kolossal Lockheed," and covertly snapping photographs as they went sightseeing over German defense installations. He left on his last mission from Berlin on August 24, 1939.

It was a "kolossal" intelligence coup, and shook up an indifferent Royal Air Force bureaucracy with the requirement for advanced photo intelligence services. Cotton's work also presaged Lockheed's post–World War II future, when its name would become synonymous with covert intelligence-gathering.

New Projects Prepare Lockheed for Expansion

Looking beyond the Model 10 and Model 12, Lockheed was increasingly interested in expanding its horizons by dealing with the military. Sketches had been drawn of a proposed twin-engine fighter, tentatively called the XPW-1, circa May 1936. That same year, Lockheed's XFM-2 multiplace fighter lost a hotly contested competition to Bell's striking XFM-1 Airacuda by a fraction of a point. The loss was probably a benefit to Lockheed, for specifications were unrealistic and the Airacuda proved to be a resounding failure, as the multiplace fighter concept was an aeronautical dead end.

In 1937, however, Lockheed responded to an Air Corps invitation to participate in Design Competition X-608, for a twin-engine high-altitude interceptor. The term "interceptor" was new in Air

Corps procurement and differed markedly from the European concept of short-range, fast-climbing aircraft to intercept bombers (e.g., the Supermarine Spitfire). Twin engines were specified because the only available liquid-cooled engine, the Allison V-1710, could produce only about one thousand horsepower, which was inadequate for the range, speed, and armament the Air Corps planners had in mind. After studying a number of configurations, some very radical, Kelly Johnson created a twin-boom, twin-tail aircraft with the cockpit in a central nacelle as Lockheed Model 22. As the following chapter will show, after a long development period, it became the immortal P-38 Lightning.

Enter the Super Electra

Boeing had outsmarted itself in the airliner market by reserving the first sixty production 247s for United Airlines; other airlines, unwilling to let United become the only airline operating a modern airliner, turned to Douglas and to Lockheed. The Douglas DC-2 had been a smashing success, and by the fall of 1935, the firm was at work on the DST—Douglas Sleeper Transport—and the DC-3. Lockheed management knew that it had to respond with an airliner larger than the Electra or be edged out of the marketplace. New funding was required, and two stock issues raised $1.6 million in capital, some of which was used to purchase the factory facilities it had been renting.

Douglas had too great a head start for Lockheed to try to duplicate the twenty-one-passenger carrying capacity of the DC-3. Instead, Hibbard and Johnson opted for a scaled-up, more rotund version of the Model 10 that would carry fourteen passengers at a maximum speed of 247 mph and a cruise speed of 215 mph. The DC-3 cruise speed was officially listed at 180, but in practice it usually cruised at about 160–170 mph.

To gain the significant 45-mph speed advantage, the Lockheed engineers accepted a high-wing loading and a relatively short wing. The DC-3, with its ninety-five-foot wingspan, had almost twice the wing area of the Lockheed.

To reduce approach and landing speeds to a reasonable level, very sophisticated Fowler flaps were used, a feature that would appear in many subsequent Lockheeds. In an aircraft with conventional split flaps, the effective camber (airfoil curvature) of the wing is increased by moving the trailing edge of the flap down. With Fowler flaps, the flaps moved back, also increasing wing area, as they rotated down to change the camber of the wing. The Fowler flaps were perhaps too effective; flight trials quickly revealed that they should only be extended a maximum of 60 percent. Experience revealed that the Super Electra would benefit from the incorporation of slots in its highly tapered wings. The five openings just aft of the leading edge of the wing smoothed out the airflow and delayed tip stall.

Don Palmer was designated project engineer on the Model 14. Work proceeded slowly because money was tight, and the Model 12 program was still in process. Yet Lockheed's growing sophistication was evident. It was managing to produce and sell three airliners, plus develop what proved to be a contract-winning fighter. Construction of the prototype super Electra did not get under way until early 1937. Lockheed's chief test pilot, Marshall Headle, made the first flight of the Super Electra on July 29, 1937, in front of the customary crowd of cheering Lockheed employees.

Headle had graduated from Massachusetts State College in 1913. He served as a soldier with the French army during World War I, and learned to fly there. Subsequently he transferred to the U.S. Air Service and became an instructor pilot at Tours and Issoudon in France. After the war he flew with the U.S. Marines until becoming Lockheed's chief test pilot in 1929. Headle would ultimately log thousands of flying hours and fly hundreds of different types of aircraft. As Lockheed production built up, Headle would head a staff of seventy-five experimental and production test pilots.

The test program for the Super Electra was uneventful, although the aircraft was not as docile on takeoff or landing as its predecessors had been—it was not an aircraft for low-time pilots. An Approved Type Certificate No. 657 was awarded on November 15, 1937, the first of four ATCs given variants of the aircraft. Northwest Airlines was once again the first customer for the Super Electra, ultimately ordering eleven, eight of them before the first flight. (Things were simpler in those days; on July 13, 1937, Gross gave Northwest Airlines an option for the purchase of four more Super Electras for the sum of one hundred dollars.) By November 17, 1937, less than four months after its first flight, Lockheed had $5 million in orders for the Model 14, a heady sum for a firm started for less than 1 percent of that amount five years before.

Yet disaster would stalk the Super Electra, with ten crashes occurring between January 10, 1938, and January 3, 1939. Four of these were Northwest Airlines aircraft, and two were craft of the Polskie Linhje Lotnicze (LOT), the Polish airline. At least six of these were caused by pilot error, including one in which a British Airways pilot crashed while buzzing his son's school. But the tail-flutter problem that Kelly Johnson had worried about in the Model 10 manifested itself in the January 10, 1938, crash of a Northwest Super Electra at Bozeman, Montana. The flutter problem was solved by the installation of balanced control surfaces.

Even though at least two of its crashes were clearly caused by pilot error, Northwest withdrew the Super Electra from service, replacing it with the DC-3. Only one other U.S. carrier, tiny Santa Maria Airlines, would buy the aircraft new from Lockheed, and only Continental Airlines purchased used aircraft from Northwest, buying two. Yet the Super Electra would be transformed into a line of highly successful military aircraft. (It is a sad coincidence that a little over twenty years after the first flight of the Super Electra, the Model 188 turbo-prop Electra flew on December 6, 1957. It would also be so tarnished by mechanical difficulties that it too would be a commercial failure, but just like its namesake, it would lead to a very successful military aircraft, the P-3 Orion.)

Lockheed ultimately built 112 Super Electras, of which 81 were sold to foreign customers. Japan acquired 30 for airline use; these were given the code name "Toby" under the Allied designating system. Tachikawa acquired a manufacturing license, and built 64 examples. Kawasaki built an additional 55, these being designated Type LO, and called "Thelma" by the Allies. After complaints about the takeoff and landing characteristics, Kawasaki produced 121 of a redesigned version, the Ki-56 "Thalia," which incorporated many of the same design changes Lockheed would use later in its Lodestar. One final Japanese version of the Super Electra, the Tachikawa SS-1, featured a circular pressurized cabin, similar in concept to that used on the XC-35.

Fame and Infamy

Two Super Electras received worldwide notice. The first of these was a Model 14-N, powered by 1,100-horsepower Wright Cyclone engines, specially modified to Howard Hughes's requirements and christened *New York World's Fair 1939.*

At this stage of his life, Hughes had solidly established his reputation as motion picture maker, financier, and pilot. On September 13, 1934, he had established a world speed record for land planes of 352 mph in the H-1 racer, to the design of which he had contributed

After a careful survey of available aircraft, Howard Hughes purchased the Super Electra
for his record-setting flight around the world in 1938. Hughes had a long and
sometimes turbulent relationship with Lockheed, and his interest was influential
in the decision to produce the Constellation.

much. On January 19 of the following year, he set a transcontinental
record in the "long-wing" version of the aircraft, crossing the country
in just seven hours, twenty-eight minutes, and twenty-five seconds.

His next goal was to set a record for a round-the-world flight,
and, after considering many aircraft, settled on the Super Electra. He
placed a deposit of $12,287.60 on the number 19 Electra, which was
promptly pulled out of the production line to be worked on as a special
project. Hughes had extra tanks for 1,200 gallons of fuel installed,
along with the most advanced radio and navigation equipment. With
a crew of four, Hughes made the round-the-world flight in three days,
nineteen hours, and fourteen minutes. Taking off from Floyd Bennett
Field on July 10, 1938, Hughes flew a relatively short 14,672-mile
distance on a route that carried him from New York to Paris, Moscow,
Omsk, Yakutsk, Fairbanks (where he was met by Wiley Post's widow),
and Minneapolis, to land again in New York on July 14. His flight

time of seventy-one hours, eleven minutes, and ten seconds translated into an average speed of 206.1 mph, a tribute to the clean design of the Super Electra.

The second Super Electra to receive world acclaim did so on an ignominious assignment. The first of an initial purchase of four Model 14s by British Airways, G-AFGN, was used to carry British prime minister Sir Neville Chamberlain on the last two of his appeasement flights to Germany. (His first flight had been in a Lockheed Model 10, G-ABPR.) Chamberlain, who had never flown before and had to steel himself to make the attempt, was determined to find a way to halt Hitler's aggression. On September 13, 1938, he disembarked from his Super Electra on its return from the Munich conference that had so brutally sacrificed Czechoslovakia, carrying the infamous "scrap of paper" that, he said, promised "peace in our time."

Fortunately for Lockheed and the world, the basic design of the Super Electra was to gain immense importance in an airplane that would fly less than ninety days after Chamberlain's return from Munich. It was the Model B14L, named for the explorer Henry Hudson, which propelled Lockheed to a major position in the industry and enabled it to make its great contributions to winning World War II.

A Look Back at the Final
Lockheed Brothers Aircraft

Given the great contributions of Allan and Malcolm Lockheed to the organizations which preceded the Lockheed Aircraft Corporation, it is only fair to review their efforts within the aircraft industry after the formation of the new firm in 1932.

Allan was terribly disappointed when Robert Gross made his successful bid for the bankrupt Lockheed Aircraft Company. He was also understandably hurt that the new management did not find a place for him in the rejuvenated firm. But, with his usual energy and enthusiasm, he developed a new aircraft design, then hired some engineering consultants, including the famed Walter Diehl, to assist him. The degree of Malcolm's assistance is unknown, although there is speculation that he had a financial interest in the new enterprise. Gathering together a nucleus of key workers, he used his own funds to set up in 1929 a firm which was later called Alcor, for the Allan Lockheed Corporation.

Allan and Malcolm Lockheed made another attempt at the aviation business with their Olympic Duo-6. Basically a Vega fuselage adapted for an unusual close-set twin-engine installation, the aircraft crashed on a low-speed pass at Rosamund Dry Lake.

The first of his designs was similar to, but slightly larger than, the original Vega, using a circular cross section instead of the Vega's oval shape to gain the maximum cabin volume. In 1930, he decided to install two Menasco C-4 Pirate engines of 275 horsepower each. The engines were laid on their side and spaced just far enough apart to provide about twelve inches' clearance between the propellers. Lockheed's intent was the same as Hall Hibbard's some five years later with the Vega Starliner (see next chapter): to provide twin-engine reliability while minimizing the hazards of single-engine operation.

Lockheed named his new aircraft the Olympic Duo-4. He used the same construction techniques on it that had been so successful on the Vega—one-piece cantilever wooden wing and a fuselage built with the same concrete mold/vacuum bag technology used on the Vega. The aircraft was quite handsome, except for a rather stalky landing-gear arrangement, and flew for the first time on March 18, 1931, at Rosamund Dry Lake. Unfortunately, it collided with a photographic truck placed at the side of the runway and was turned over. It was rebuilt with two six-cylinder Menascos as the Duo-6, but failed to find a market.

Still undeterred, Allan formed the Alcor Aircraft Corporation again in February 1937 in Oakland, California. There he directed the construction of a very sleek six-passenger feeder airliner—again a parallel to the Starliner—and again brought Anthony Stadlman in as shop

The first product of the newly formed Vega Airplane Company, the Starliner was intended to be a feeder aircraft for smaller airlines. It was unusual in that it had two Menasco engines coupled to drive a single propeller.

superintendent, with Harold E. Webb as chief engineer. Designated the Alcor C.6.1 (commercial, six-passenger, first model) Junior Transport, it was a sleek all-wood aircraft constructed in the usual Vega method. The manner in which its slender Menasco engines were faired into the wings gave it a futuristic look, especially in flight with the gear retracted. The two engines were laid on their sides and positioned closely together, as on the Duo-6, with their propellers only twelve inches apart, placed only eighteen inches forward of the fuselage.

The first flight of the C.6.1 took place on March 6, 1938, with Mike Casserly at the controls. The aircraft proved to be thoroughly satisfactory, and the dean of test pilots, Eddie Allen, was hired for the final flight tests for Department of Commerce certification—ten hours at ten thousand dollars. Alan Lockheed actively marketed the aircraft, quoting a price of just under thirty thousand dollars, and a cruise speed of 200 mph. Single-engine performance was very impressive; the aircraft could maintain level flight at altitudes up to twelve thousand feet with either engine out.

Against Lockheed's express orders, test pilot Casserly and engineer Webb took the Junior Transport out for a test flight on June 27,

An extremely modern-looking aircraft for the time, the Alcor C.6.1 was Allan Lockheed's valiant last attempt to manufacture aircraft. The C.6.1 featured closely-set twin engines, to simplify "engine-out" conditions. It was lost on an unauthorized test flight on June 27, 1938.

1938. They took the aircraft to sixteen thousand feet and then dove it, reporting speeds of over 300 mph. The aircraft encountered aileron flutter and began to break up. Casserly managed to slow it down, but recognized that it was not controllable. Both men bailed out safely and the C.6.1 plunged into San Francisco Bay.

It was the final blow to Allan Lockheed's aviation career. Financially wiped out, he turned to selling real estate while doing aviation consulting on the side, a sad finale for a man who had devoted his life to aviation.

CHAPTER 4

Lockheed Builds to
Meet the Needs
of War

F ate intervenes with companies just as it does in the lives of individuals. It developed that the Lockheed Aircraft Corporation's
ability to initiate, then master, its huge wartime expansion was facilitated to a very great extent by an external circumstance, the failure of
British planning.

Because of its horrendous losses suffered at the hands of the relatively primitive German U-boats in World War I, Great Britain had
in the interwar years developed the antisubmarine warfare device
ASDIC, essentially a sound ranging system that permitted detection
of submarines underwater. So great was its faith in this system (and
in convoys) that it considered the U-boat problem solved, and so failed
to develop more effective antisubmarine measures. It possessed far too
few escort vessels and neglected to build up a modern long-range maritime reconnaissance aircraft force, even though it had used a huge

fleet of 685 planes and 103 airships in this role to help contain the submarine menace in 1918. When war came, the German U-boat fleet employed surface tactics that largely negated ASDIC's effectiveness, and the Royal Air Force Coastal Command had nothing with which to counter the new submarine threat, being forced to rely upon fewer than 200 tiny Avro Ansons for maritime reconnaissance and antisubmarine work, with just a handful of Short Sunderland flying boats in prospect. Although the Anson was considered modern when purchased, being the RAF's first monoplane to enter squadron service and the first aircraft with a retractable (albeit hand-cranked) landing gear, it had severe limitations. The "Faithful Annie," as it was affectionately termed, had a nominal top speed of 188 mph, but in service was forbidden to exceed the speed of 170 knots under any conditions. Violent maneuvers were also proscribed, making flak evasion difficult. The Sunderland was a wonderful aircraft, but for too long would be too few in number to be effective.

One of England's great—if largely controversial—patriots, Canadian-born William Maxwell Aitken, Lord Beaverbrook, who under Winston Churchill would head Great Britain's aircraft production effort, was already attempting to stimulate his nation's aviation effort. Beaverbrook was a doer. Having attained his goal of amassing £5 million by the age of thirty-one, not always by the most altruistic of methods, he moved to England and became a member of Parliament. Newspapers and aviation became the focus of his interest, and he had his chief pilot make inquiries to Lockheed about the Model 14 in February 1938.

Lockheed was also being courted by the usual wolf pack of entrepreneurs who wished to sell its planes abroad on a commission basis, and by a number of foreign countries. Connerton Triamerican Aviation dangled an order for "100 bombers for France. Also bombers for England, quantity unknown." J. H. Millar of Aviation Corporates, Ltd., pressed to represent Lockheed for unspecified sales. Bob Gross's longtime friend Jack Gillies, who was once principal in the Long Island Country Club of the Air, laid aside his responsibilities as sole distributor for the Grumman G-21 amphibian to try to sell Lord Beaverbrook three Super Electras at prices ranging from $89,425 to $93,325, depending on engine choice. (Beaverbrook already owned a G-21.) Japan's procurement of aircraft and license rights has already been mentioned. Sales were envisaged to nine British airlines, from British Airways to the Isle of Man Air Services. Czechoslovakia attempted to arrange a sale, predicated upon British financial support, and interest was expressed for some additional purchases by China, Romania, and Poland. (These matters were considered important enough that some wire traffic was conducted in code, in which five-digit blocks of letters were used for certain words and phrases, e.g., OKPYO being "stop," AIGIT "appears to have," and so on.) Italy's Ala Littoria S. A. sought a manufacturing license, initially for the radical Lockheed Model 27, a twin-engine, canard-surfaced (horizontal stabilizer on the nose) twenty-four-to thirty-five-passenger aircraft that was never built, and then for a four-engine pressurized aircraft of about thirty-passenger capacity. Lockheed had the four-engine Model 44 Excalibur in the works, but it was not pressurized, and so no orders resulted. (Willis Hawkins maintains that the Model 44 was almost purely camouflage to maintain the Constellation as a secret.)

Lockheed was already standing on tiptoe in anticipation of large orders from France and England, and early in 1938 issued an internal memo on the arrival of the British Air Commission in New York. Sir Henry Self headed both the Joint Anglo-French Air Commission and the British Air Commission, with Air Vice Marshall H. N. Cave-Browne-Cave as the British Air Ministry representative. The beginning of what became a traditional polish was put to the proceedings by Kenneth Smith of the Lockheed sales department. He had obtained photos of every member of the visiting British group; when they arrived, he introduced each one by name and title to the other Lockheed representatives.

The British Purchasing Commission's ostensible interest was a navigation trainer, but they were obviously open to suggestions, and Lockheed had several to make. Kelly Johnson had approved a lengthy report on a "Convertible Transport Bomber" version of the Super Electra almost a year earlier, on April 9, 1937. Other studies had followed, and Lockheed was so well prepared to respond to the British needs that it was able to create a wooden mock-up in a hectic five days of round-the-clock work. (As previously noted, Lockheed had already considered several military versions of its all-metal aircraft, including a proposal for a bomber version of the Model 10 to Anthony Fokker himself, apparently for resale to the Soviet Union. The Model 212s sold to the Netherlands East Indies incorporated single guns in a dorsal turret and fixed, firing-forward, and underwing bomb racks.) The mock-up would have to be revised to meet specific British requirements as the details of the contract were negotiated, but the fact that it was available and on hand for inspection impressed the British representatives, and raised Lockheed from its previous position in the

West Coast shadow of Douglas and Boeing to the rank of a principal contender for the flood of contracts about to be unleashed from Europe.

Throughout this period of truly heady excitement at the success of its products, Lockheed management was wary of taking on any additional commitments, pending word of a decision by the British Purchasing Commission (BPC). The original Lockheed proposal to the BPC for a bomber retained the wings, empennage, and powerplant installation of a standard Super Electra, with the fuselage modified to include a bomb bay (originally specified by the British to be large enough for two five-hundred-pound bombs, but later increased to make room for twelve one-hundred-pound bombs) and equipped with a modest armament of three machine guns. Single flexible guns were located in the nose and the tail and another was located in the navigator's compartment aft of the bomb bay.

The British didn't care for the crew placement, and asked that the navigator be placed close to the pilot so that they could work together on reconnaissance missions. The man who was later to command the RAF's Bomber Command, Sir Arthur Harris, was invited to return to see the changes a few days later. Harris demurred because he still had to visit the Consolidated and Boeing plants. Later he wrote, "To my astonishment, only twenty-four hours later a car arrived to fetch me out to the Lockheed works, and there I saw a mock-up of all our requirements in plywood, fitted complete in every detail, with two alternative noses hinged on to a real aircraft all ready for our inspection. . . . I was entirely convinced that anyone who could produce a mock-up in twenty-four hours would indeed make good all his promises—and this Lockheed most certainly did."

The skill and drive Hibbard and Johnson gave their team was manifested in Lockheed's willingness to subordinate all production efforts to the swift manufacture of Hudson aircraft for Great Britain. On May 25, 1938, top Lockheed managers were dispatched to England via the SS *Queen Mary* to negotiate the deal, including Courtlandt Gross, Carl Squier, Richard Von Hake, attorney Robert Proctor, and a Clarence L. Johnson so youthful in appearance that the British had to be reassured that he was actually qualified to render opinions on the discussions in progress. (Johnson, a twenty-eight-year-old farm boy of Swedish extraction whose acquaintance with luxury was minimal, suddenly found himself on board the *Queen Mary,* en route to posh quarters in the Mayfair Court Hotel in London. Far from being intimidated, he spent part of his time on board filling a notebook with his redesign of the *Queen Mary,* then the world's fastest liner. On a similar trip later, he remembered spending the time more enjoyably, dancing with his attractive young wife, Althea.)

In the jet age, we tend to forget how much longer it took to travel and how much more difficult communication was, and how each influenced the way business was conducted. Ocean-liner sailing schedules were the key, and the correspondence from the period shows how carefully they were considered for both mail and travel. Some business was conducted, ironically enough given Lockheed's pro-British mission, on the German liner *Bremen.* Costs were carefully monitored; when Lockheed's New York representative, George Swayne, made a transatlantic telephone call to Carl Squier, he followed it with a letter explaining why he had thought the matter so urgent as to incur the expense.

Lockheed was already assessing the full import of a large contract with Great Britain, and had begun planning the establishment of a facility in Liverpool where aircraft could be assembled, tested, and modified. This would become an important part of Lockheed's total business in the not-too-distant future, but for a firm formed but six years before on a scratched-up capital of $40,000, it was remarkably farseeing.

In the course of negotiations, the British had asked that a Boulton-Paul dorsal turret replace Lockheed's proposed installation and two fixed forward-firing Browning .303 machine guns be placed in the nose. Uprated Wright Cyclone engines of 1,100 horsepower were selected, and the performance, especially compared to "Faithful Annie," was excellent, as the following table shows:

	Avro Anson	Lockheed Hudson Mk. I
Max speed	188 mph	246 mph
Cruise speed	158 mph	220 mph
Range	660 miles	1,960 miles
Bomb load	360 pounds	1,200 pounds

Lockheed's position was undoubtedly strengthened by an increasingly bellicose Hitler. Finally, on June 23, 1938, a contract was signed for two hundred Model B14Ls at a price of $25 million. At the time, it was the largest contract ever secured for a foreign sale by an American company, and it included a remarkable incentive provision. The contract could be expanded to include as many more aircraft as could be delivered by December 1939, up to a maximum of fifty additional planes. Courtlandt Gross had led the Lockheed negotiating team, and he returned in triumph on the *Normandie,* his satisfaction with the deal heightened by the congratulatory telephone messages he received from both his brother Robert and their father.

It should be noted that the $25 million contract came at a time when Lockheed had only $334,000 in cash, and limited credit connections. The most important of these was Charles A. Barker Jr., a mild-mannered man whose neat suits and small mustache were perfect for his role as vice president of the California Bank. Already on the board of directors, Barker came over to Lockheed as treasurer, and with Gross, exploited the contract to gain more than $1 million in loans. He would prove to be invaluable in the years to come, one of the many executives at Lockheed who would be invisible to the public at large, but always to be found at the center of any important deal.

Sober Celebration

The absolute joy that attended the contract signing, with all that it presaged for the future, was tinged with the realization that there was an enormous amount of work to do and relatively limited resources with which to do it. The firm was still small; at the end of 1937, it had only 1,989 employees, and Robert Gross's almost relentless vision of the future had set it on an expansionary track that was already straining the available factory-floor area. It took great efforts on the part of Cyril Chappellet and others to keep employment down to levels that could be managed within the current cash flow, while still responding to Gross's calls for expansion.

Meanwhile, the prototype XP-38 was in the process of construction and would be rolled out in December 1938; the brilliance of Hibbard and Kelly's twin-boomed design was already apparent, and it seemed inevitable that large orders would result. Work was continuing on large four-engine transport designs, one of which would ultimately evolve as the immortal Constellation. And, influenced by Hibbard and perhaps by memories of the success of the Orion, Gross was still enamored of the idea of a small feeder airliner. During the previous year, on August 17, a wholly owned subsidiary, the AiRover

Company, had been formed with Mac V. F. Short as its president, to create the plane Gross had in mind.

AiRover becomes Vega

Lockheed had enjoyed a long, almost familial, relationship with Al Menasco, whose Burbank Menasco Manufacturing Company produced powerful but expensive engines for many of the smaller racing aircraft and for high-performance private planes. Two years prior to the formation of AiRover, Hall Hibbard had talked with Menasco about the feasibility of coupling two of his six-cylinder inline engines to a single propeller. The object was to reduce drag, provide twin-engine reliability, and eliminate the problem of asymmetric thrust if one engine failed. Menasco developed the idea and became the principal patent holder, but he shared one patent with Hibbard on the multiple-motor drive for airplane propellers. After a great deal of work overcoming design flaws in the clutches that engaged and disengaged the engine to and from the propeller, the Unitwin reached a high level of reliability. (This was not an easy accomplishment. Other countries approached the problem with mixed success, the most notorious failure being that of the Daimler Benz DB 606 coupled engine employed on the Heinkel He 177 bomber. The difficulties associated with the engine earned the He 177 the nickname "Luftwaffe's lighter" for its many in-flight fires.) In late 1937, a Lockheed Altair, rather unimaginatively named *Flying Test Stand*, was assembled from parts on hand, and the first of the Menasco Unitwin engines was installed. More than one hundred hours of test-flying proved the unit was successful, and a decision was made to proceed with the new feeder liner design. The *Flying Test Stand* was later modified with a Wasp radial engine and sold as a standard Altair D.

Lockheed's relationship with Menasco took a more direct turn in the summer of 1938, when in Bob Gross's words the engine company "practically blew up in our faces." Gross would have purchased Menasco Manufacturing, but Lockheed finances did not permit this at the time, despite the fact that the company was on its way to record profits of $442,111 on net sales of more than $10 million. (Lockheed had posted positive net income every year since 1933 with the exception of 1934, when the development costs of the Electra resulted in a $190,891 loss.) Instead, two of Lockheed's original investors, Mr. and Mrs. Randolph C. Walker from San Francisco, with some friends put up $75,000 and obtained warrants to purchase additional shares in the floundering Menasco Company. The Walkers made a condition that Cyril Chappellet and Gross be elected to the board of directors and be responsible for the management of the company. They selected Gardner W. Carr to be president, while Al Menasco became vice president, sales. A friendly arrangement, one that assured a supply of engines to Vega, it had a salutary effect upon Menasco stock, lifting it from $.85 a share to $2.00. As Gross and Chappellet had been compensated jointly with an option to buy twenty-five thousand shares of stock at $1.00, it was also quite profitable.

By 1938, the rather tricky name AiRover (bad aircraft from the company would undoubtedly have been called "airdogs") had fallen out of favor, and the subsidiary was renamed the Vega Airplane Company as a tribute to the original Lockheed monoplane. Hibbard created a very modern low-wing, tricycle-gear monoplane, with the by-now signature Lockheed twin-fin empennage. It was powered by a 520-horsepower Unitwin engine and was given the felicitous name "Starliner." A propeller malfunction on takeoff caused test pilot Vern Dorrell to make a forced landing just off the edge of the runway on its first flight on April 22, 1939. The aircraft suffered minimum damage, and flight testing continued. During July, the aircraft was reworked extensively. Flight testing had revealed that with the twin fins outside the propeller slipstream, directional control could be maintained only by the application of the right brake as takeoff power was reached, hardly a desirable situation, especially on a short runway. A single vertical surface, with a small dorsal fin, was fitted, and the cabin and cowling contours were reworked. The Starliner suffered one more minor accident before successfully completing an eighty-five-hour test program. A handsome aircraft, looking somewhat like a modern Bonanza on steroids and endowed with an excellent performance, the Starliner ran into two insuperable obstacles and was canceled. The first was a lack of interest on the part of airliners—with only four or five passenger seats, the aircraft was too small for the booming airline traffic of the late 1930s. The second was more important: every square inch of the new 750,000-square-foot plant being built just one mile from the main Lockheed plant in Burbank would soon be required for the production of military aircraft. The Starliner ended its days as a prop for motion picture studios, the fate of more than one California prototype.

Courtlandt Gross was finally brought west and in June of 1940 was made president of the Vega Aircraft Corporation. As will be noted

Developed from a design purchased from North American, the Vega 35 was attractive, but did not possess the flying qualities desired for a trainer.

later, Vega would build Venturas, Harpoons, and Flying Fortresses, and would initiate the Neptune. Before becoming fully engaged in these programs, however, the Vega Aircraft Corporation would engage in some individual projects, including four Vega 35s, a sleek-looking low-wing trainer designed by North American. The Vega 35 was evaluated by the USAAF as a trainer, and rejected on a number of accounts, including being underpowered, having too-small cockpits, and being spirally unstable. Vega later built the XB-40, a B-17 converted with additional armament, and the XB-38, a B-17E converted to have in-line Allison engines. It also built five Model 40 target drones.

The name Vega outlived its corporate existence by less than two years. By December 31, 1941, the pressures of war had removed the requirement for a subsidiary to develop new civilian products, so Vega was merged with Lockheed by trading three shares of Vega for one share of Lockheed stock. By November 30, 1943, it seemed meaningless to continue the fiction of the Vega Aircraft Corporation as an independent entity, and it was simply reabsorbed into the Lockheed Aircraft Corporation to simplify bookkeeping.

The Lockheed workforce had expanded from its low point of 334 people in 1934 to nearly 3,000 by December 1938. The expansion would have an implicit long-term benefit for the firm, unrecognizable at first, but palpably evident in later years. During this period of growth, some of Lockheed's most brilliant leaders entered the firm's employment, worked hard, succeeded, survived the postwar reductions, and went on to key positions. It is salutary to look at just a sampling of this influx of genius to gain an impression of how deep Lockheed's roots reached out to all America, and how, in the midst of the most terrible foreign war in our nation's history, the rapidly growing company was able to sustain its sense of family relationship between management and labor, and, perhaps even more difficult, among members of management.

Nascent Management Stars

The almost obsessively loyal nature of Lockheed employees may well have stemmed from the egalitarian selection process that came about as the World War II expansion began. For almost a decade, the country had been gripped by a depression, and jobs had been difficult to obtain. Young men—for women were not yet entering the aviation industry in significant numbers—who might ordinarily have gone to college, given their intelligence and their family background, found themselves working at relatively menial jobs, and were glad to have them.

The buildup at Lockheed thus served to attract the best and brightest young people available. Among them were individuals who would rise to the top management jobs in the company. For most of them, the trajectory of their rise would be constant, but their career paths would often swing widely from one discipline to another in what would prove to be the Lockheed system of natural selection.

A. Carl Kotchian was from tiny Kermit, North Dakota, a town so small that it disappeared completely when the railroad passed it by, the wood and brick from its buildings being carried away to build new homes where the track ran. Kotchian symbolizes in many ways how Lockheed cast a wide but fine net for its talent. He worked his way through the Graduate School of Business at Stanford—a long reach from Kermit—and then, in his industrious fashion, took the requisite courses to become a certified public accountant. Many top Lockheed people would come from Stanford, including Chappellet, Barker, Ted Rathman, and others, but few came to Lockheed as Kotchian did— thinking it was another aircraft firm entirely. In January 1941,

Rathman asked Kotchian if he would like to come to work for Vega. Somehow Kotchian, a big, hearty man then and now, understood him to mean "Vultee," and started out for Downey, but following Rathman's driving instructions. He wound up in Burbank, nonplussed to find out that "Vultee" was actually Vega. He applied nonetheless and was hired at the then-princely sum of two hundred dollars a month, going on to a stellar, if ultimately controversial, career, acting as future chairman Dan Haughton's balance wheel much as Chappellet had performed that role for Gross.

The University of Michigan was another rich source of Lockheed talent, providing those premier engineers Kelly Johnson and Willis Hawkins, and also Ken Cannestra and Carl Haddon. Haddon graduated in 1931 with a bachelor of science degree in aeronautical engineering. In the depth of the Depression, when unemployment was at its peak, Haddon got a job with the Keystone Aircraft Company, of Bristol, Pennsylvania, then the sole purveyor of bombers to the Army Air Corps. The Keystones were ponderous twin-engine biplanes, not much improved in performance over World War I Gothas, but they represented two important things to Haddon: airplanes and a meal ticket. He worked his way through a number of companies, including Consolidated and Stearman-Hammond, and then went to Sweden in 1938 to help establish a modern aircraft industry, which then included Svenska Aeroplan AB, which subsequently became SAAB, and is now Saab. Haddon came back to the United States in early 1940, and chose Lockheed as his next place of employment. The employment process was far different than today's with its tailored résumés, interview process, and background checks. Then, he recalls, the "biggest obstacle was the receptionist, who was also the telephone operator and general handy girl." She was Vera Doan, who married the man who at the former Lockheed Company's nadir was its sole paid employee, Harvey Christen. Haddon told her, "I've got ten years' design experience in airplanes, and I want to see the chief engineer about a job." She sent him right in to see Hall Hibbard, who hired him on the spot—no interviews, no reference checks, no waiting. His career path to the presidency of the Lockheed Aircraft Corporation would involve running programs as varied as the Excalibur, the Constellation, the F-104, the SST, and the L-1011.

Kotchian and Haddon were both supportive of another newcomer to Lockheed, Dan Haughton, who worked his way from chopping wood for mine-shaft supports at the age of nine, graduating to coal-mine "wood-chuting" crews before entering the University of Alabama, to the Lockheed Aircraft Corporation in February 1939. There, the almost unbridled power of his personality and his rigorous operating methods would hurtle him to the top as he expanded the company, brought great successes, and, under the pressure of events (many of his own doing), staved off imminent bankruptcy. The boy who had cut trees into mine ties at three cents apiece wound up his career in successful direct negotiations with the prime minister of Great Britain, the Congress of the United States, the banking industry, and the airline world. His time at Lockheed, which will be covered in depth later, had an almost operatic quality in terms of its high drama, hubris, triumphs, and defeats.

Not everyone who got to the top at Lockheed came from Stanford, Michigan, or indeed, any college at all, and there is no doubt that the company was enriched by the influx of talented people who battled to overcome the problems of the Depression to reach high management levels without the benefit of a college education. One of these, a man inevitably remembered kindly by his colleagues, is Frank Frain, who graduated from high school in 1930 to take a job as bank messenger. He worked his way up learning the banking business and came to Lockheed in 1942 as a financial analyst. Frain went on to become one of Lockheed's masters of finance, supervising the company's various forays into diversification, and helping Haughton stave off the financial disasters of the 1970s.

Thousands more came to Lockheed as it expanded, some to stay only for the war years, other for full careers. As they percolated to many levels throughout the company, they conferred upon it a distinctive culture of cooperation and friendliness that was nurtured during the tumultuous process that began with the Lockheed Hudson.

The Impact of the Hudson

The Hudson was the right plane at the right time, benefiting first from the funds of the British Purchasing Commission, and then from the lavish largesse of the lend-lease program, described by Winston Churchill as the "most unsordid act." Lockheed was also the beneficiary of having the right management already engaged in the correct process of expansion. Robert Gross believed that another great war was imminent, but he could not know the exact timing, and despite the success of the Electra, the late years of the 1930s were not a totally convincing basis for expanding the firm. Just 91 aircraft had

The Hudson bomber was a huge success, and it inspired many variants like these AT-18 gunnery trainers. The Hudson established Lockheed as a top manufacturer of quality combat aircraft.

been delivered in 1937, and 101 in 1938. The difficulties with the Super Electra would probably have rendered it unmarketable in another year or two. Yet all of these problems evaporated with the Hudson. In 1939, Lockheed delivered 287 Hudsons, along with 65 other aircraft, for a total of 352. These were numbers that could, quite literally, be taken to the bank and to the stock market.

Studies for the expansion were under way even before the arrival of the British Purchasing Commission. One of these was brought to fruition in 1940, when Lockheed purchased the Union Air Terminal in Burbank from United Airlines for $1.5 million, and established Lockheed Air Terminal, with Chappellet as President. It would be a profitable operation over the years, and ultimately was sold to the Hollywood-Burbank Airport Authority for $51 million in 1978.

The signing of the British contract launched a furious effort by Lockheed to meet and exceed the contractual requirements. (It also caused furious resentment in Great Britain, where it was deemed unpatriotic to purchase any aircraft not designed at home.) Lockheed expanded its workforce, which would reach 7,000 by the end of 1939, climb to almost 17,000 in 1940, and go on to peak at 90,853 in 1943. During this period the company was forced to begin doing what would formerly have been anathema: farming out substantial elements of work to subcontractors such as Rohr Aircraft.

All the efforts were successful. The prototype Hudson, fitted with a mock dorsal turret, first flew on December 10, 1938, with deliveries of production aircraft beginning in February 1939. Tooling problems caused a slow buildup, with only 50 aircraft completed by June 1939. Eventually, however, the production rhythm accelerated so that the 250th Hudson rolled out the door by mid-November 1939, and Lockheed not only collected handsomely on the British contract's incentive provisions but received a second order for an additional 350 aircraft. It was but the beginning of a flood of 2,941 Hudsons that would pour from Burbank. The British Commonwealth purchased 1,338, and, in addition, 1,302 were supplied by lend-lease. Three hundred were built specifically for the USAAF, and one was built for U.S. civil use by the Sperry Corporation.

As with all aircraft in volume production, improvements, additional armament, new equipment, and more powerful engines were introduced as time passed. Thus, while the Hudson I weighed 17,500 pounds fully loaded, had a maximum speed of 246 mph, and a range of 1,960 miles, the Hudson IV weighed in at 22,360 pounds, had a top speed of 284 mph, and a range of 2,160 miles. All Hudsons retained their passenger windows—Lockheed elected not to bother to remove them.

Although the Super Electra's teething problems in airline service had marred Lockheed's reputation, the Hudson, so modern and so desperately needed, was welcomed by the British with open arms. Its high wing loading made takeoffs and landing more demanding than with aircraft such as the Anson, but this was a small price to pay for the vastly improved performance.

The Hudson had enormous organizational consequences. Lockheed had established a tentative field-support organization to support overseas customers of the Lockheed Models 10, 12, and 14. This concept had blossomed from the original handwritten notes and in-the-hall conversations to a tiny office near the final assembly line to a huge facility at Liverpool to reassemble Hudsons as they arrived in England. (A similar plant was created in Australia.) Additional bases were set up in Scotland at Abbotsfinch and Renfrew, while an enormous maintenance and overhaul base was established in Ireland at Langford Lodge, near Belfast, which grew swiftly into a huge organization. In the next three years the six thousand workers at that facility would assemble, modify, or repair battle damage on 22,500 aircraft of more than thirty different types. The Lockheed Overseas Corporation was formed to operate the establishment under the direction of the supersalesman Carl Squier. (Squier had fought for years to obtain orders for aircraft

The Lockheed Hudson performed an invaluable role in anti–submarine warfare for the United Kingdom. It did much to blunt the effectiveness of German U-boat attacks.

by the ones, twos, and threes; it must have seemed incredible to him to have orders for thousands of aircraft flocking in faster than they could be built.) The Lockheed Overseas Corporation provided great depth and breadth of experience in overhaul and modification work, and was essential to the later establishment of the very successful Lockheed Aircraft Service Company.

A classic bit of Lockheed management style was demonstrated when difficulties arose with the management of the overseas venture. The facility manager, while efficient, was proving to be too hard on personnel, and morale was bad. Courtlandt Gross (who became president of the Vega Aircraft Corporation in 1940) surveyed the situation and summarily replaced the man with Gene Ogden (designer of the trimotor Ogden Osprey). It was all done with a minimum of fuss, but a delicate situation was saved by Gross's prompt intervention. Ogden quickly got things smoothed out, the original manager was released with two months' pay, and morale shot up.

The experience would prove of immense postwar benefit to Lockheed when the Lockheed Aircraft Service Company was established as a wholly owned subsidiary. It proved to be extremely profitable, providing services that ranged from airport operation to airline management. It led directly to Lockheed's involvement with foreign contractors in joint ventures that resulted in a technology transfer that enabled countries that had been prostrated by the war to develop indigenous aviation industries. A company originally formed with the intention of supporting a handful of foreign Model 10s and 14s was transformed in time into a high-tech service provider for customers worldwide.

The Hudson in Combat

There are hundreds of stories about the Hudson in combat, some apocryphal, but most based on real events. It was rugged, and earned the nickname "Old Boomerang" for its ability to take punishment and return from missions. It was the first aircraft of American design to destroy an enemy aircraft. On October 8, 1939, a Hudson of the RAF's No. 224 Squadron shot down a Dornier Do 18D patrol plane off Jutland.

Other Hudsons participated almost anonymously in some of the opening acts of the war. A No. 220 Squadron Hudson spotted the *Altmark*, the German oiler that was attempting to bring home to Germany the British sailors captured by the *Admiral Graf Spee*. It directed HMS *Cossack* to the *Altmark*, and the British sailors were rescued. Hudsons were reportedly used to strafe and bomb the encircling German troops at Dunkirk. On August 27, 1941, the versatile Lockheed bomber became the first aircraft to capture a submarine when a Hudson of No. 269 Squadron under the command of squadron leader J. H. Thompson forced U-570, commanded by Lieutenant Hans Rahmlow, to surrender. The Hudson, supported by a Consolidated Catalina from No. 209 Squadron, circled over the slightly damaged submarine until surface ships arrived to take off the crew and tow the U-570 to port. Less than a month later, U-570 was put into service by the English navy as HMS *Graph*.

Another antisubmarine-warfare first was scored by a Hudson of No. 608 Squadron, which fired rockets from its underwing racks to sink a submarine off North Africa. And the first Army aircraft to sink a U-boat was a Hudson; an A-29 from the 396th Bomb Squadron sank U-701 (captained by Lieutenant Commander Degen, who had just sunk two ships and damaged a destroyer and two tankers) on July 7, 1942.

The Hudson was excellent at antisubmarine warfare for the same reasons that it was attractive as an airliner. It had the same power as the much larger DC-3, but was ten thousand pounds lighter, and, unlike the Anson, could be thrown around with fighterlike abandon, enabling it to make more than one pass before a submarine could submerge. Single-engine performance was excellent. If the plane had a drawback it was the precision required on landing, but pilots quickly adapted to this.

The most significant event in Hudson antisubmarine-warfare work occurred early in its career and went almost unnoticed because of tight security. By January 1940, twelve Hudsons were equipped with airborne radar, ASV-1 (Air to Surface Vessel Mark I). Despite the primitive nature of the equipment, which forced the Hudsons to fly as low as two hundred feet, it heralded a revolution in antisubmarine warfare that eventually would overcome the threat of U-boats.

Hudsons even joined the Wellingtons, Hampdens, and Whitleys on the RAF's first thousand-aircraft raids against Hitler's *Festung Europa*. But brilliant acts of war were not the normal Hudson role. Most often it soldiered under difficult conditions doing routine antisubmarine patrol, ground-attack work, photoreconnaissance, and ordinary passenger and cargo transport. It took a beating in the early months of the war in the Far East, when it was thrown into battle against the onrushing Japanese. When the tide of the Pacific war shifted, the Hudson did well in reconnaissance, bombing, and supply roles.

As the war progressed, the Hudson became relatively obsolete, and was relegated to crew training, air-sea rescue, weather reconnaissance, and occasional clandestine operations. Besides Great Britain, it was used with pride by the air forces of Australia, Brazil, Canada, China, New Zealand, and the United States. Toward the end of its active service with the RAF, many Hudsons were stripped of their armament and reequipped as transports, the role for which they had originally been designed.

In many ways, the war dealt the Hudson a similar role to the Curtiss P-40. Both airplanes had the great advantage of being in quantity production, and thus available, so that they were used in many theaters even though their opponents were operating aircraft with superior performance. There was a great difference in one respect, however. The P-40 represented the apogee of the fortunes of the Curtiss Company, which was never able to get a follow-on fighter into production, and after the war soon removed itself from the aircraft business. In contrast, the Hudson proved to be a starting point for

Lockheed, teaching the firm how to build quality military aircraft in quantity, manage change, expand, and, more important, create new products that would meet emerging market needs.

Lockheed's much-honored engineer, Willis Hawkins, made a thoughtful summary of the Hudson in his 1983 Wings Club lecture. He said the Hudson was a success because Lockheed had taken a risk with its technology in introducing the Fowler flaps to permit a high wing loading. (Hawkins knew this well, as he was the designer of the conspicuous flap tracks that were a trademark of the Hudsons and later Lockheed aircraft.) But more than that, Hawkins noted, the Hudson taught Lockheed true systems management, not the paperwork science of the 1960s, but the hands-on type, getting to the right guy who is in charge and can make decisions. He cited an example. At one point, a failure of the government to deliver the correct government-furnished equipment—in this instance, generators—had undeliverable Hudsons parked all over Burbank. The failure to deliver had halted government payments, and Lockheed was fast exhausting its cash and its credit. Lockheed's management went to the Army Air Forces with the concept of progress payments to allay the financial crisis, and agreed to pick up responsibility for insuring that all GFE arrived on time. Hudsons began to be delivered again, even as the tempo increased on the most well remembered Lockheed product of the war. Hawkins thus put his finger on Lockheed's simple but effective formula for success: taking risks backed by technological and scientific capability and an aggressive management that could lead its personnel to make things happen in a difficult marketplace, whether government or civilian. The formula would be used often in the future.

The P-38

Few aircraft have captured the public imagination more swiftly or held it longer than the beautiful twin-engine, twin-boom airplane with which Lockheed began its long and successful history of fighter production. The utterly distinctive shape of the Lightning bristled with innovations, including tricycle landing gear, heavy firepower concentrated in the nose, turbo-superchargers, Fowler flaps (the first on a fighter), and a blistering performance. P-38s were demanded by leaders in all theaters of war, and earned the respect of both the Germans and the Japanese. It functioned in a wide variety of roles, some far beyond the imagination of either Johnson or Hibbard, and its traditional

Lockheed quality and rugged construction enabled it to return home over long distances despite heavy battle damage. The two top American aces of the war both flew P-38s exclusively. Even today, the elegant Lightning still draws cheers at its increasingly rare air-show appearances.

The unusual nature of the XP-38 is not so obvious now, but when the design was submitted to the Air Corps as Lockheed Model 22-64-01 in April 1937, it was so radical that many of those assessing it regarded it as impractical to build or use, and incapable of achieving its predicted performance figure of 400 mph.

Working as a team, Hibbard and Johnson had selected the unusual configuration from a variety of even more radical choices (including such exotica as buried engines, push-pull engine placement, and so on). Yet the unique twin-boom, center-nacelle concept was perhaps the least sophisticated element of the carefully thought-out design, many components of which—such as the distinctive wing planform, inspired by that of the Electra—would find their way into later Lockheed products.

The requirement for two engines was straightforward enough. To reach the desired Air Corps specification of 360 mph at twenty thousand feet, about 2,000 horsepower would be required, and there were not yet engines of that power in production or even in test programs. The available engine was the Allison V-1710, which had begun its development in 1930 as a potential replacement for the Maybach engines used in dirigibles. On February 12, 1935, the very day that the first Allison engine was available for delivery, the giant airship *Macon* crashed into the Pacific, ending the navy's infatuation with dirigibles and forcing a cancellation of its contracts with Allison. The company was then sold to General Motors, where engineer Ronald M. Hazen (another University of Michigan graduate) had the V-1710 turning out one thousand horsepower by 1937. The great Donavon Berlin tried the new Allison in the Curtiss XP-37 (it had previously been tested in a Consolidated A-11) and again in the P-40, thus launching the primary American-designed liquid-cooled engine of the Second World War. Some forty-seven thousand would be built by war's end, and many are in use today.

When Hibbard and Johnson selected the Allison for use in the P-38, it had a horsepower potential of 1,150. They coupled it to an exhaust-driven turbo-supercharger, so that its power could be maintained at altitude. (The turbo-supercharger was GFE and was not a good match for the P-38 at altitude, where the turbocharger tended to malfunction. Takeoffs would be made in humid conditions; at high altitude, the moisture condensed and froze, leading to false pressure-sensor readings. This resulted in excessive manifold pressure when the aircraft descended. The excess manifold pressure could damage an engine, and caused many a P-38 to fly home on one engine. The turbo-supercharger worked well for the airplane at low and medium altitudes, where the engines could be left at high power settings for long periods of time without damage.)

Despite its long development period, which stretched back to the bewhiskered Sandford Moss's experiments at General Electric after World War I, the turbo-supercharger (which was also the key to the success of the B-17 and B-24) was an extraordinarily risky choice at the time, given the turbine blade materials available and the very limited experience with the device, of which fewer than one hundred had been built. Yet the P-38's twin-boom design was perfect for the installation of the turbo-superchargers and their elaborate ducting, and offered other advantages as well. The booms provided room for the engines, main undercarriage members, and radiators, and the long moment arm resulting from their length made it possible to have smaller fin and rudder assemblies. The greater length also resulted in the P-38 being a very stable gun platform, an important but often overlooked design element for fighters. The propellers rotated in opposite directions, thus canceling their torque effect and also contributing to the stability of the gun platform, as well as making takeoffs easier to handle.

The slender, tapered wings had a very high aspect ratio (wing length-to-width ratio) for a fighter, and their distinctive shape would later be found on the much larger Constellation. While efficient, the fifty-two-foot wingspan naturally inhibited the rate of roll of the heaviest fighter yet proposed to the Air Corps. At its maximum gross weight of 15,164 pounds, the XP-38 was more than twice as heavy as the then first-line fighter, the Curtiss P-36, which weighed in at 6,010 pounds. In later production aircraft, beginning with the P-38J series, the roll rate was facilitated by ailerons assisted by a hydraulic boost mechanism that required only 17 percent of the manual effort needed previously.

The unique center nacelle not only provided maximum visibility for the pilot and protection on two sides from enemy fire, it also allowed installation of a 20-mm cannon and four .50-caliber machine guns. (A 37-mm cannon had been proposed for the XP-38.) Not required to fire through the propellers, these were unhampered by

One of the most distinctive, and arguably the most beautiful, of World War II fighters, the Lockheed P-38's elegant lines were derived from functional requirements.

The American aircraft industry was revolutionized by the influx of women workers, who proved to not only be equal to the men they replaced, but in many instances rendered a performance superior to them.

synchronizing gear and provided parallel streams of fire up to a thousand yards' distance. The P-38 would prove to be the only twin-engine single-seat fighter to be produced in quantity, only 112 being built of its nearest competitor, the Royal Air Force's Westland Whirlwind. Ultimately, 9,925 Lightnings would be built by Lockheed, with another 113 delivered by Consolidated-Vultee's Nashville operation, for a total of 10,038.

The full force of Johnson and Hibbard's genius was not confined to the external details, but also addressed production and performance considerations. Flush riveting and precisely butted joints made for the smooth external surfaces, which became a Johnson trademark. The metal skin sections that cover an aircraft are of varying thickness to suit the strength required of them. To compensate for this variance, the internal structure of the P-38 was adjusted so that whatever the thickness of the skin, the external surfaces retained a smooth contour. Like the transports, but unlike other fighters of the period, all control surfaces were metal-covered. This seemingly innocuous detail is an indication of how farseeing Johnson was; one has only to read Pierre Closterman's account of the incredible increase in the maneuverability of the Spitfire with the introduction of the metal-covered surfaces to appreciate Johnson's vision, far in advance of any reports of combat experience.

Such considerations were important, for despite the success with the twin-engine transports, the new fighter was a much more difficult production challenge. When the contract was awarded for one prototype XP-38 on June 23, 1937, James M. Gerschler began the detail design process, integrating many elements that were foreign to past Lockheed experience, including the General Electric turbo-superchargers, heavy armament, tricycle landing gear, and the incorporation of much standard military equipment. Nonetheless, by December 1938, the XP-38 was completed and transported in deepest secrecy to March Field in San Bernardino, where one of America's great unsung heroes, and a tremendously important advocate for the Lightning, Lieutenant Benjamin S. Kelsey, was standing by to conduct the initial tests.

An MIT graduate like Jimmy Doolittle, Kelsey was one of the men so devoted to the Air Corps that he stayed in despite the low pay, lack of promotion opportunity, and genuine hazard. He had entered the Air Corps in 1929, flew as Doolittle's safety pilot on the famous "blind flying" experiments, and became head of the fighter projects branch at Wright Field. Despite many offers of outside employment, he was totally undismayed by the fact that he was still a first lieutenant after ten years of distinguished service. Kelsey was fully absorbed in a job he believed in, exercising authority that exceeded that of many of the country's top executives even as he subsisted on the hardscrabble pay. When war began his rise would be swift, and he would retire as a brigadier general in 1955, ironically at a time when brigadier generals typically had less responsibility than he had exercised as a first lieutenant. He was a thoughtful man, with a big grin and the devout belief in his own abilities, which ranged from building his own airplanes to tailoring his own suits from wool taken personally from his own flock of sheep. (The airplanes were exquisitely crafted and beautifully finished, and were relatively better in appearance than the heavy tweed suits he wore. These had the cut and fit of outfits worn by vaudeville comedians, a fact of which he was either totally unaware, or chose to ignore, for he wore them proudly.)

Kelsey supervised the assembly of the hot-looking fighter, and initiated taxi tests that revealed serious deficiencies in the aircraft's wheels and brakes. Preliminary fixes were made and Kelsey took off on the first flight on January 27, 1939—and promptly encountered a second problem, violent vibration of the flaps. Kelsey elected to make a long, low approach that ended safely in a spectacular "four-point landing" that sent a cascade of sparks flying. Keeping the nose high to provide drag for braking, he had touched down on the two main wheels and the bumpers fitted to the bottom of the twin fins.

The flap problem was solved quickly in a manner that Kelsey later said followed the precepts of the famous designer William B. Stout, which was "Simplicate and add more lightness." Problems continued with the brake system, and a marginal longitudinal stability problem was cured in later production aircraft by a 7 percent increase in the area of the horizontal stabilizer. The clean design and heavy weight of the P-38 would yield further problems later in the test regime, when the aircraft dive speeds would build up to the point of compressibility, a condition predicted in a 1937 report by Kelly Johnson. In a dive, the P-38 was flirting with the sound barrier; as it approached its limiting Mach number, severe buffeting would cause loss of control. The brakes and flap difficulties were relatively easy to solve; overcoming the compressibility problems would take months of tests before a solution was discovered by Ward Beman, who devised a small electrically operated dive flap under each wing to counteract a strong nose-down pitching moment at high speed.

Despite the obvious hazards, a political decision was made that the XP-38 would gain much-needed public visibility if Kelsey would make a record run to Dayton. General Hap Arnold approved, specifying that if all went well, the airplane was to be refueled for a trip to New York in an attempt to break Howard Hughes's transcontinental speed record. It was an extraordinarily risky proposition, given that the complex XP-38 had logged less than five hours of test time.

On February 11, 1939, Kelsey took off, refueling at Amarillo, Texas, and landing at Dayton, recording ground speeds in excess of 400 mph en route. Approval was given to proceed to New York in the record attempt. Routine traffic at Mitchel Field required him to make an extended approach during which he had to add power to reach the field. When he advanced the throttles, there was no response on the right engine and only a partial response on the left. Slow, with flaps and gear down, he knew that applying full power to the good engine would cause an uncontrollable roll. He was forced to crash-land on the Cold Stream Golf Course at Hempstead, Long Island. Unhurt but terribly dejected, he climbed out to survey the wreckage. The damaged plane was totally destroyed when it was cut up to be transported in a closed truck. The elapsed time of seven hours, forty-three minutes failed to beat Hughes's record of seven hours and twenty-eight minutes; the flying time, however, had been only seven hours and two minutes.

Despite an exhaustive investigation, no absolute cause for the crash was ever established; Kelsey believed it to be either vapor lock or carburetor icing. Curiously, the crash had no lasting adverse effect on P-38 production, for the Air Corps had proved that Lockheed had built a 400-mph airplane in response to a requirement for only 360 mph. The loss of the sole prototype did of course inhibit the test program.

The first concrete evidence of Air Corps approval came on April 27, 1939, with the award of a $2,180,275 contract for 13 YP-38s (fondly called "Yippees" by Lockheed employees). This conformed to standard Air Corps practice of buying 13 service test aircraft before committing to production. The YP-38 was completely redesigned in preparation for a production run that Robert Gross estimated would not exceed 80 aircraft. But as the situation in Europe grew ever more serious, U.S. production orders of 66 and then 410 followed. In April 1940, the indispensable Anglo-French Purchasing Committee awarded a contract for 667 aircraft for France and Great Britain. Two months later, following France's defeat, the entire order was assumed by the British. The export models differed in numerous respects, but principally in their use of unsupercharged Allison engines, which reduced performance at altitude. In addition, the size, weight, and complexity of the Lightning were foreign to British experience, and after testing, all but 3 of the order were canceled. The canceled aircraft were readily accepted by the USAAF as P-322s (and because they lacked superchargers were referred to as "castrated P-38s"), some for operational use, and some being used only for training.

The nineteen long months before the YP-38's first flight on September 17, 1940, saw many changes at Lockheed. "Dick" Pulver replaced Gerschler as project engineer, as the latter was having some difficult personal problems. Haddon became Pulver's assistant. Lockheed suffered a significant loss when longtime chief test pilot Marshall Headle was injured in Lockheed's own low-pressure altitude chamber in a decompression accident. The disaster so fatally impaired his health that he died in 1945 at the age of fifty-two.

Lightning Strikes the Lockheed Aircraft Corporation

The impact of the series of contracts for first the Hudson and then the Lightning launched Lockheed Aircraft into a frenzy of activity. By the end of 1940, the firm that had begun life with its offices in a shabby ranch house and its factory in a failed pottery factory had 1.6 million square feet of floor space under cover; that area would peak in mid-1943 at an incredible 7.7 million square feet. One acquisition was colorful—Robert Gross secured the purchase of the rambling G.G.G. distillery, just north of the airport on San Fernando Road, where the first P-38s would be built. The number of personnel increased in a corresponding fashion, rising from almost seventeen thousand at the end of 1940 to a peak of almost ninety-one thousand in mid-1943.

Ninety-one thousand people meant ninety-one thousand paychecks, and despite the accelerating sales (almost $700 million in 1943) and profits (a wartime peak of over $8 million in 1942), it took all the efforts of Chappellet and Barker to maintain an adequate cash flow. Lockheed had to compete for engineers and skilled personnel in the booming aviation market. The expanded workforce brought an entirely new set of problems involving training, promotions, security, and the like. The trained workforce had long since been absorbed;

Despite massive construction efforts, Lockheed manufacturing floor space could not keep up with the demand for aircraft, and production lines spilled outside into the California sunshine.

most of the people entering the workforce were doing so for the first time. Barriers were broken as women and minorities were hired to do jobs that had always been in the white-male province.

As much pressure was exerted on the engineering staff as on the production people, for the initiation of Lockheed aircraft first to service and then to combat use brought about a requirement for continuous changes and improvements. As the pace of production grew, a supplier's failure to provide a critical part could mean that huge numbers of incomplete aircraft would be stashed in every available spot on the airfield. Engineering changes had to be grouped and executed in blocks so that control of drawings and technical orders could be maintained. At Lockheed (as elsewhere) a system evolved in which aircraft would emerge from the production line only to enter a modification line and receive the latest updates prior to being released for service.

After the stunning attack on Pearl Harbor, the fear of a similar strike on the West Coast was very real. Aircraft factories were camouflaged with netting that was replete with trees, houses, and so on to make the area look like a rural countryside from the air.

Lightning in Combat

Flight test and production of the first P-38s occurred almost simultaneously as World War II unfolded with its long series of disasters to the Allied cause. Although the European war had gone on for more than two years by the time of Pearl Harbor, the USAAF, like all the American armed services, was woefully unprepared. A massive expansion had occurred since 1939, when the Air Corps had only about eight hundred airplanes in first-line service, and was training pilots at the rate of three hundred per year. By Pearl Harbor, the training goal had been lifted to thirty thousand pilots per year—one hundred times the peacetime total—and although there were more than fifty combat groups, most were mere cadres around which a fighting unit was to be formed, and even these were spread out around the United States

Despite having far greater manpower reserves, the United States employed women in factories earlier and on a far greater scale than did totalitarian Nazi Germany. Women workers were immortalized as "Rosie the Riveter" in story and song.

and its possessions. None was equipped with first-rate combat aircraft. Even the very best American aircraft in service, Boeing B-17s and Curtiss P-40s, were still not up to European standards of armor and armament.

But changes were in the wind, and combat commanders demanded priority on receiving the Lockheed P-38 long before any were ready for combat. In the first years of the war Major General Ira Eaker insisted that P-38s be sent to the Eighth Air Force in Europe, where their long range made them desirable as escort fighters, while in the Pacific, Major General George Kenney was adamant that they be sent to the Fifth Air Force, where he could use them on long-range fighter sweeps.

Deliveries were slow in both the European and Pacific theaters. Only 266 had been delivered by the end of 1941; another 1,421 would be delivered in 1942 as problems of production and parts were overcome. Lockheed deliveries would rise to 2,497 in 1943, peak at an incredible 4,186 in 1944, and taper off to 1,553 in 1945. Success in combat would also come gradually, as the complex P-38s required care in assembly and expert maintenance and logistic support. In the end, as is so often the case in war, the role of the P-38 was far different from that for which it was originally designed. The success or failure of the aircraft depended on the operation of the engine/turbo-supercharger combination, which took time to mature.

Engine problems sometimes mitigated the effectiveness of the P-38. Fortunately, the basic design created by Hibbard and Johnson was so strong, and so capable of growth, that it was able to prevail over the inadequacies of its power plant and prove its mettle in dozens of roles far beyond anyone's original concepts.

Combat against the Japanese

The P-38 would see action against the Japanese first. In the following three years of war it would demonstrate its prowess in every part of the gigantic Pacific theater, which ranged from Alaska in the north to China and Indochina in the far west to Australia and the myriad islands of the South Pacific.

The few P-38s were distributed equally at first, a handful going to the South Pacific, some as reconnaissance types. In Australia, the greatest American reconnaissance pilot, Captain Karl Polifka, led A-Flight of the 8th Photographic Squadron in long-range sorties from April 16, 1942, on. (Polifka fought in both the Pacific and European theaters during World War II and would ultimately be lost over North Korea in 1951.) The 8th Photographic Squadron used Lockheed F-4s, essentially P-38Es stripped of armament and fitted with four K-17 cameras and two additional seventy-five-gallon fuel tanks. The F-4s also had a drift sight and an auto pilot and were painted a beautiful cerulean blue. Polifka set a pattern that would be followed in every theater of war. The F-4s and F-5s would penetrate deep into enemy territory "unarmed and unafraid" to bring back millions of photographs that paved the way for future bombing raids, invasions, and defensive preparations.

A few early P-38s were sent to the 11th Air Force in Umnak, Alaska, where their first try at combat came on June 6, 1942, when they—in error—attacked a Soviet freighter. The first Lightning kills took place in the Alaskan theater on August 4, 1942, when Second Lieutenants Kenneth W. Ambrose and Stanley A. Long of the 54th Fighter Squadron destroyed two Kawanishi H6K "Mavis" four-engine Japanese flying boats near Atka.

The 39th Fighter Squadron of the 35th FG began receiving its aircraft in Australia in the late summer of 1942. Operational missions began in October, and by December, the P-38s were able to intervene over New Guinea. Second Lieutenant Richard Bong, a high spirited, cheerful young man from Poplar, Wisconsin, was on loan to the 39th from the 9th FS. He scored the first two of his forty victories on December 27, knocking down an Aichi D3A Val and a Misubishi A6M5 Zero. A colleague, First Lieutenant Thomas Lynch, also scored two victories, shooting down two Najajima Ki 43 Oscars. Lynch rose to the rank of lieutenant colonel and scored twenty victories before crashing to his death on March 9, 1944.

The Lightning proved to be particularly suitable to combat in the South Pacific for a number of reasons. It had a remarkable range, and at low altitudes, where most combats took place, its supercharger-engine matchup worked well. It was very rugged, able to sustain major damage and return to base. The complex Lightning was relatively difficult to maintain, but its ground crews took pride in their work, knowing that the twin-engine layout gave their pilots confidence. They knew that if they lost one engine, the other could be depended upon to get them home across the long, cruel stretches of the Pacific, the tangled jungle masses, or the rugged mountains of the China-Burma-India theater, where the Tenth and Fourteenth Air Forces operated.

It was the Lightning's long-range capability that earned its role in the most daring mission of the war, one for which drama, intrigue, and élan rivaled the Doolittle raid on Tokyo. Made aware by code breakers that the inevitably punctual Admiral Isoroku Yamamoto, the man who had devised the attack on Pearl Harbor, was planning a routine inspection trip to Bougainville, a top-level decision was made to assassinate him. The task fell to Thirteenth Air Force P-38s because no other aircraft in the theater, Army or Navy, had the combination of range, speed, and firepower to fly low over the ocean for 435 miles from Guadalcanal to intercept Yamamoto's Mitsubishi G4M1 Betty as it flew to Ballale, a tiny island off the coast of the southern tip of Bougainville. Major John W. Mitchell, commander of the 339th Fighter Squadron, was given the responsibility for the attack. He led sixteen P-38Gs, equipped with long-range drop tanks, on a five-leg, two-hour-and-forty-five-minute flight over the ocean. The Lightnings arrived thirty-five miles off Ballale, just in time to intercept Yamamoto's flight, which consisted of two Bettys and six Zero escort planes. Both Bettys were shot down, Yamamoto's plane crashing in the jungle. (After the battle, a total of three Bettys and three Zeros were claimed. Japanese records indicate the loss only of the two Bettys.) The attack finished off Yamamoto without alerting the Japanese to the fact that their code was broken. But it also started another fight, still going on today, as to who shot him down. Captain Thomas G. Lanphier made the first claim and was for a long time assumed to be the victor; Lieutenant Rex Barber always believed that he had scored the victory, and in later years compelling evidence was amassed to support his case. (In 1960, the United States Air Force historians assigned one-half credit to Lanphier and to Barber, thus displeasing everyone.) One thing is certain: Yamamoto was shot down by a pilot flying a Lightning.

The P-38 became the backbone of the Army Air Force's fighter groups in the brutal campaigns that forced the Japanese back from their easy conquests. The Lightnings had to take off from primitive, dust-laden fields with heavy loads that would allow them to fly long distances to engage the enemy. Initially, the Lightning squadrons were distributed among three groups in General George Kenney's Fifth Air Force.

One of these, the 475th, was commanded by Colonel Charles McDonald, the third-ranking P-38 ace of the war, with twenty-seven victories. McDonald had the pressure and the privilege of initiating Charles Lindbergh into combat. Lindbergh, delighted to be employed in meaningful war work after his ill-favored attempt at pacifist politics before the war, had a long acquaintance with Lockheed products. His cruise-control methods of low rpm and high manifold pressure were widely adopted, extending the range of the Lightning to seven hundred miles. Lindbergh was flying with McDonald's flight of eight P-38s on July 28, 1944. They encountered two Japanese Ki 51 Sonia reconnaissance planes; in a long, confusing dogfight, Lindbergh found himself firing at one Sonia that kept turning into him, finally passing under him by less than ten feet. His shots had gone home, however, and the Sonia crashed into the water below.

Kenney ultimately had five groups fully equipped with Lightnings (the 8th, 18th, 49th, 347th and 475th). More than one hundred pilots became aces in the P-38 in the Pacific, where the Lightning claimed 1,358 victories, more than any other fighter. Among those aces was Major Bong, far more mature now than before the war, when his joyful exuberance had led him to fly under the Golden Gate Bridge and earn a reprimand from General Kenney. Bong was deadly serious in combat, doing three tours and scoring forty victories to rank him as the highest-scoring American ace of all time. Among his many decorations was the Medal of Honor, but he remained unaffected by them, retaining his ebullient good nature and pleasant manner. In August 1945, after he took off in a new P-80, a fuel-pump failure caused him to crash fatally at Burbank, California.

His strongest rival was Major Thomas B. McGuire. McGuire,

Major Richard Bong was America's leading ace in World War II, with 40 victories, all achieved in the P-38. He is shown here with famous long-distance flyer Jimmy Mattern, a Lockheed test pilot.

who with thirty-eight victories was second only to Bong in victories, was from Ridgewood, New Jersey. In his first combat he shot down three enemy aircraft, and became an ace three days later with two more kills. Determined to outscore Bong, the irascible, talkative McGuire flew with reckless abandon, and on December 26, 1944, scored seven victories in one day over the Philippines. McGuire lost his life on January 7, 1945, when he crashed while attempting to assist a comrade who was being attacked by an Oscar.

The Lightning was progressively developed during its service in the Pacific, and late in the war the P-38M two-seat night fighter evolved. Equipped with an ASH-type radar mounted under the nose, the P-38M's performance was almost as good as the single-seater's. Beloved by pilots and by its ground crewmen, the Lightning distinguished itself under conditions far different from those for which it had been conceived.

The range of the Lightning proved as valuable against Japan as it would be over Europe, and allowed the plane to take its toll of enemy aircraft and installations from Indochina to Okinawa. Its range also conferred upon it the distinction of being the first Allied aircraft to land in Japan after its surrender; on August 25, 1945, Colonel Clay Tice and his wingman landed at Nittagahara, Japan, supposedly due to "engine problems," but more probably out of sheer curiosity.

Combat against the European Axis Powers

The P-38 suffered not only from slow deliveries but also from being the pawn in the political wars that flared up between the Eighth Air Force and USAAF headquarters. General Eaker wanted P-38s as long-range fighters to escort his bombers into Germany, but he was forced to relinquish them for Operation Torch, the invasion of North Africa. This delay, coupled with engine-supercharger problems encountered in the moist, cold air found in Europe for so much of the year, protracted the Lightning's development as a premier fighter plane. Yet the brilliance of the aircraft's design made it suitable for missions that had never been envisioned and were often totally different from those of the Pacific theater.

The first Lightning victory in the West came on August 14, 1942, when Second Lieutenant Elza Shahan, based in Iceland with the 27th FS, attacked a Focke Wulf Fw 200, the aircraft that Churchill had termed "the Scourge of the Atlantic." Shahan shared the victory with Second Lieutenant Joseph D. R. Shaffer, who was flying a Curtiss P-40C for the 33rd FS. It was the first of many kills of German and Italian aircraft.

Shipping was still a critical problem in 1942, and the long range of the P-38s enabled them to be ferried to England via a hazardous 2,965-mile route that led from Presque Isle, Maine, through Goose Bay, Labrador; Bluie West 1, Greenland; and Reykjavík, Iceland, to Prestwick, Scotland. For the movement, aircraft were organized into squadrons of three flights each, each flight to have two elements, and each element consisting of a B-17 and 4 P-38s. Out of a total of 186 P-38s dispatched during 1942, only 7 were lost, far fewer than the 10 percent rate expected. Of these, 6 were forced to land, along with 2 B-17s, on the ice cap on the eastern coast of Greenland. (Some of those were found again two hundred feet below Greenland's ice and snow in a well-publicized aircraft archaeology attempt). Although the long trip was later made thousands of times, the implicit hazards kept it from ever being routine.

The 1st and 14th Fighter Groups carried the Lightning to war

The P-38s fought in every theater, but were at their best advantage in the Pacific, where combat took place at altitudes and weather for which they were best suited.

in North Africa in mid-November 1942, doing long-range bomber escort, ground attack, and reconnaissance work. As green units, still working out the difficulties encountered in moving to a new theater of combat, initial results were not entirely satisfactory. The German Messerschmitt Bf 109G and Focke Wulf Fw 190 fighters they met were flown by seasoned veterans whose tactics dictated combat at fifteen thousand feet and below, where the Lightning's size put it at a disadvantage in maneuvering.

The Lightnings were to score their greatest successes in North Africa over the sea, decimating incoming formations of German transports, and it was in this venue that they earned their German sobriquet *der Gableschwanz Teufel*—"the fork-tailed devil." And the photo-recce Lightnings of the 3rd Photographic Group did patient, dangerous work preparing for the invasions of Sicily and Italy, mapping huge areas of enemy territory in more than three hundred sorties.

No one—not even Hibbard, Johnson, or Kelsey—could have ever imagined in 1937 that seven years later their P-38 "interceptor" would be doing long-range combat, level bombing, dive-bombing, and reconnaissance on such a scale, or that ultimately, Lightnings would be able to range all the way across the German Reich in shuttle missions to the Soviet Union.

Operations from England

P-38 operations over Europe had been curtailed when the aircraft were diverted to participate in the fighting in North Africa. It was not until October 15, 1943, that the 55th FG became operational with the VIII Fighter Command; it was followed in short order by the 20th FG. The P-38H's range now permitted it to penetrate a hundred miles farther into Germany than the Republic P-47s could, and there were continuous attempts to improve on that figure. The 55th got off to a good start by scoring three victories with no losses on its first mission to Wilhemshaven on November 3. Ultimately, the range of the P-38 was extended to the point that it could escort bombers all the way to Berlin.

Meanwhile, fighter operations in Europe were still encumbered by the strict injunction to "stay with the bombers," which meant that attacks could not be initiated against enemy fighters that were not attacking, nor could enemy fighters be followed once they'd been engaged. In addition, the Lightning pilots suffered from inadequate cockpit heating (the engines' being in the booms instead of just in front of the cockpit's firewall, as in single-engine aircraft, reduced the transfer of heat) and had to wear so many layers of clothing that their movements were inhibited. The Allison engines also suffered problems with the turbo-superchargers, and there were difficulties with the operation of the intercooler controls.

The P-38 also became an extremely effective ground-attack aircraft in the 20th FG, particularly suited to beating up German airfields. The Lightning was soon given additional tasks. In the 55th, some P-38Js and subsequent models had their standard nose replaced by an extra crew position with a Norden bomb sight to use through a Plexiglas nose enclosure. Called "Droop Snoot" Lightnings, they led formations of P-38s, each one of which carried two two-thousand-pound bombs—the same standard bomb load as a B-17! This was further developed with the introduction of radar into the lead aircraft.

For reasons of range, standardization, and economy, the North American P-51 was selected as the standard long-range escort fighter, replacing the P-38 in July 1944. Although many pilots welcomed the change, many others, having lost the only engine the Mustang had, devoutly wished they were back in the Lightning.

The Ninth Air Force used the P-38 in a tactical role, beginning in April 1944, with the 474th FG and then soon after with the 367th

Engines, always critical to aircraft design, take longer to develop than airframes do. The Lockheed XP-49 was to have had Continental engines; they did not materialize and the project was dropped.

and 370th. The 474th used the Lightning until war's end, the other two groups converting to P-47s in March 1945. Two things contributed to the relatively greater success of the Lightning with the Ninth. Combat usually took place at lower altitudes and hence warmer temperatures, where the Allison engines worked better and the pilots did not suffer so much. The second factor was the decline in the quality of German pilot training. The P-38s were thus generally able to hold their own in fighter-versus-fighter combat, even as they concentrated on ground-attack work that included strafing airfields, pillboxes and other fortifications, and trains and trucks.

In Europe, as in all theaters, Lockheed reconnaissance planes would be the workhorses to the last day of the war and beyond.

In the course of its development through many models and modification into many variants, the P-38's performance was continuously improved. Maximum speed did not go up very much over time, but range was greatly extended to the P-38L's 2,600 miles. Maximum weight increased by a third to 21,600 pounds in the L model. More important, reliability was greatly improved as the aircraft matured.

Follow-on models to the P-38 included the XP-49 and XP-58; neither of these aircraft had a fair chance at development because the engines intended for them failed to materialize. Joe Towle made the first flights in both aircraft—the XP-49 on November 14, 1942, and the XP-58 on June 6, 1944—but in each case, both time and requirements had passed the aircraft by and no production ensued.

Continually changing mission requirements and the failure of the Wright Tornado engine resulted in the two-seat, pressurized cabin XP-58 Chain Lightning not being placed into production. Only one was built.

Back in Burbank

The next part of the Burbank story requires a slight retrogression to 1940. Then Lockheed was faced with the comparative failure of the Lockheed Model 14. As previously noted, Northwest Airlines had disposed of its fleet, and sales were slow, in part because the Super Electra had a high seat-mile cost compared to the competing Douglas airliners.

A team led by engineer Jay Cowling redesigned the Model 14 by increasing its length by five and one-half feet, which provided space for fifteen or eighteen passengers, depending on whether or not the airline elected to have a galley installed. The alteration required a number of modifications to secure the desired flying characteristics; these included raising the horizontal stabilizer by one foot and altering the

The Lodestar was a logical extension of the Electra. Passengers are boarding a
National Airlines plane to fly "the Buccaneer Route."

trailing edge of the wing. The resulting aircraft was designated the
Model 18 and called the Lodestar, to disassociate it from the Super
Electra's reputation.

The redesign succeeded in reducing the seat-mile operating cost
to be competitive with the DC-3, although it caused a reduction in
both top and cruising speeds of about 25 mph compared with the
Super Electra with the same engines. Even so, domestic sales were
slight, only 33 going to U.S. airlines and 10 to private customers.
Foreign governments and airlines, many cut off from their normal
sources of supply, bought a total of 96 Model 18s. The remainder of
the 625 Lodestars that were manufactured during its three-year production run went to the military services under a variety of designations. Some of these were transferred under lend-lease to Great Britain.

But just as the Hudson bonanza grew out of the Model 14, so
did the Ventura and Harpoon series arise from the Model 18, with
3,028 being produced, just 87 more than the Hudson. Robert Gross's
vision in establishing the Vega Airplane Company and funding its
seven-hundred-thousand-square-foot factory was amply repaid when
first the Ventura and then the Harpoon rolled from its lines, along
with 2,750 Boeing B-17Fs and Gs built as a part of the Boeing-Vega-
Douglas pool. Vega achieved the lowest man-hours per aircraft in the

Stretch is an implicit indication of the quality of the design, and Lockheed always built planes with "stretch." The Ventura was a development of the Lodestar. It had a substantially better performance than the Hudson and became a mainstay of the Royal Air Force, the USAAF and Navy, and several foreign air forces.

pool, and old-time Lockheed employees swear that the USAAF preferred Vega-built B-17s above all others.

The Ventura was offered to the British Air Ministry as either a replacement for the Hudson in the general reconnaissance role, using the same engines that powered the civilian Lodestar, or as a light/medium bomber with engines of up to two thousand horsepower.

The Ventura proved to be not very well liked by the Royal Air Force, which received its first deliveries in September 1941, and began using it as a medium bomber. Although it had an overall attrition rate of about 3.6 percent, which was average for Bomber Command at the time, a large percentage of the total Venturas lost was incurred in just two or three disastrous raids, where the extent and quality of German opposition proved to be too much. Venturas in the European theater were withdrawn from Bomber Command in the autumn of 1943 and allocated to Coastal Command, charged with the no-less-demanding tasks of reconnaissance and maritime patrol. Ironically, Allied Venturas in the Mediterranean theater were initially intended for convoy coverage and reconnaissance but proved to be very successful when op-

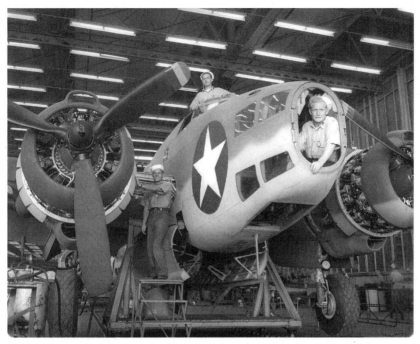

As the war progressed, the Lockheed workforce became increasingly proficient at adapting new designs to production standard. Here Navy personnel look over a Ventura emerging from the production line.

erated as medium bombers. The Ventura was also used by the Australian, Brazilian, Canadian, Free French, New Zealand, and South African air forces.

The USAAF made only limited use of the Ventura as B-34s as trainers for a variety of schools. It was much more attractive to the United States Navy, which found that the speed of the Ventura offered an element of surprise invaluable in attacking surfaced submarines. The U-boat lookouts were skilled in aircraft detection, and having sighted an enemy aircraft, could submerge in what seemed like mere seconds. A fast reconnaissance plane like the PV-1, as the navy designated it, gave a tremendous advantage. A Ventura made its first U-boat kill off the coast of Newfoundland, when Lieutenant Thomas Kinaszczuk and his crew from VP-82 (later VP-125) sank the U-174. The submarine, captained by Commander Ulrich Thilo, had sunk four vessels in its seventeen-month career.

The Ventura also performed well as a bomber. A PV-1 from VB-136 made the first American offensive sweep over Japan since the April 18, 1942, Doolittle raid when it flew a patrol over Paramushir, in the

The Harpoon was a Ventura with new outboard wing panels, revised vertical tail surfaces, and other modifications, including increased fuel capacity for increased range. It was a powerful weapon.

Kuril Islands. Harassing raids were flown by VB-135, VB-136, and VB-139 until the end of the war. Radar-equipped Aleutian PV-1s also acted as pathfinders for USAAF B-24 operations.

The Venturas were as adaptable as the P-38s, and were used as patrol planes, bombers, and ground-attack aircraft using rockets. The marines adapted several as night fighters using the SCR-5217A radar. Rushed into action by the fall of 1943, the all-black Ventura scored its first victory on November 13, shooting down a Japanese Betty fifty miles south of Empress Augusta Bay.

The navy expressed interest in a development of the Ventura, and in the course of time the Vega Model 15, the Harpoon, materialized. The new aircraft featured a seventy-five-foot wingspan, nine and one-half feet greater than the Ventura's, and larger vertical surfaces. Fuel load was increased by 20 percent, and armament was greatly increased—the PV-2 had eight forward firing guns. The bomb load was upped to four thousand pounds.

The Harpoon made its first flight on December 3, 1943, with Bud Martin, Frank Osberg, and Jim Kendrick as its crew. Production was slowed by labor difficulties and it was not until March 1945 that it went into combat, going to the Aleutians with VPB-139. Both combat and engineering tests revealed some weaknesses in the wing, which caused further production delays. A rebuild of the wing solved the problem.

Although it did not see a great deal of combat, the Harpoon proved to be very well liked, and was continued in production after the war's end, a total of 535 being built. It was used extensively by reserve units in the postwar U.S. Navy, as well as by Italy, Japan, the Netherlands, Peru, and Portugal.

But the PV-2's importance went far beyond a 535-aircraft production run. With its four-thousand-pound bomb load and two-thousand-mile range, it solidified the navy's thinking about land-based aircraft replacing flying boats as the principal type of reconnaissance and antisubmarine aircraft. The Harpoon was part of a wartime continuum that led directly to the P2V Neptune, which put Lockheed in the leading position in the postwar marketplace as the primary producer of patrol aircraft.

The Neptune would form one leg of a brilliant postwar marketing triad for Lockheed, with the Constellation and the P-80 Shooting Star being the other two legs. All three aircraft were begun during the war, and all three would not only prove to be extremely successful in their respective classes, but would lead to future developments. One, the P-80, would bring into formal existence the most unique, productive, and inventive engineering departments of all time, an assemblage of free-spirited geniuses who would be known formally as "Advanced Development" but colloquially would be referred to as the "Skunk Works."

These three aircraft, and the follow-on designs they would generate, would enable Lockheed to prosper in the highly competitive postwar years, enabling it to take its first tentative steps leading not only to new products, but to whole new divisions that would create truly amazing triumphs in aircraft, missiles, and satellites.

Remolding for the
Postwar World

The end of World War II presented the American aircraft industry with problems of incredible magnitude. It had grown beyond all imagination in the numbers and types of aircraft being produced. Before the war began in 1939, the U.S. aviation industry was straining to produce 3,000 aircraft a year, all of a relatively small size, powered by engines of moderate horsepower and equipped in the most Spartan manner. By 1944, the industry was producing at a rate of 100,000 aircraft a year. For the most part, these were larger and far more sophisticated designs, equipped with some of the most powerful reciprocating engines that would ever be built. In 1939 a simple aircraft radio was considered exotic; by war's end planes were equipped with a formidable array of radios, radar sets, radar altimeters, and a host of other gear that required the backing of a huge industry to create and support it.

From its production run of 5 aircraft in 1932, Lockheed had expanded more than a thousandfold to a wartime peak of 5,864 aircraft delivered in 1944; the firm would deliver a total 19,077 aircraft between July 1, 1940, and August 31, 1945. Employment peaked at more than ninety-four thousand in mid-1943, but improvements in productivity and a rational reduction in production effort as the needs of the services were met allowed Lockheed to reduce employment selectively by the end of 1944 to less than sixty-three thousand.

The end of the war brought the abrupt cancellations of contracts. Aircraft deliveries fell to 2,828 in 1945, and then to 465 in 1946, less than 10 percent of 1943 deliveries. Employment fell correspondingly, from just over thirty thousand in 1945 to just over seventeen thousand in 1946.

The vast change of scale was a tremendous challenge to Lockheed management, particularly to Robert Gross, whose letters of the period reflect his anguish at having to address the decisions to be made about whom to keep employed, and how to reconcile the decisions with the twenty-four thousand Lockheed employees who had been in the armed forces and who were entitled to first consideration for reemployment upon their return. Few companies have had a chief executive like Gross, whose undoubted competitive nature and willingness to risk all on a company project were matched by his genuine concern for his people and their well-being.

As a direct result of Gross's compassion, Lockheed was not as ruthless as it could—and probably should—have been in the reduction of its personnel in the uncertain climate that faced it. Despite the huge volume of business from 1941 through 1945, rising wages, inflated costs of goods, taxes, and wartime regulations kept profits low. Lockheed earned about $32 million on $2.4 billion in net sales, a miserly 1.3 percent return over the entire period of the war. In the immediate postwar years, Lockheed management had to negotiate canceled contracts, close down but still maintain unused factory and office areas, and begin the investment in new products for the postwar marketplace.

The year 1946 was brutal from a financial standpoint. Even after a federal income tax credit of $11.2 million, Lockheed still posted a loss of $10.7 million. The company had anticipated the problems and set up a $15 million reserve fund; $13.8 million of this was transferred to report a $3.1 million net income, a purely illusory figure given the circumstances. The reserve fund having been depleted, Lockheed was unable to perform the same bookkeeping operation the following year, and had to post a $2.5 million loss, the first since 1934. A net income of more than $6.2 million was reported in 1948, but Lockheed was still in trouble with excessive loans, high inventory, and disproportionate costs in sales and administration.

Gross also faced acute personal problems during the period, highlighted by the death of the vice president of engineering, Mac V. Short, who collapsed and died from a heart attack only forty minutes after leaving a meeting with Gross in August 1949. Short, only fifty-one was very well liked in the aviation community, and his death came as a shock.

Gross also had to contend with major business decisions. Curtiss-Wright had made earnest attempts to merge during 1943, with Gross promised control, but the deal did not go through. There was no loss of goodwill, however, for in 1946, Curtiss-Wright, delighted to have Lockheed as a customer for its R-3350 engines, aided in financing TWA's purchase of Constellations. Very serious negotiations were undertaken for an advantageous purchase of the aircraft operations of Consolidated-Vultee, a company approximately equal to Lockheed in terms of both assets and backlog of orders. In a September 1946 letter to Randolph Walker—asking him to be prepared to resign as a director in the event the deal went through—Gross indicated that a deal would be consummated that fall, and that Lockheed would be the surviving firm. (A similar deal was consummated decades later, when Lockheed purchased the aircraft division of Convair's successor firm, General Dynamics.) Some preliminary discussions on merger were also held with Vought. Neither of these came to fruition, but it is interesting to speculate on what might have been, given the fortunes of each of the companies in the years to come.

All of Charlie Barker's banking skills were called upon, and an increasingly reluctant banking industry continued to supply loans to keep operations going. There were few benefits from all the financial problems, but the downsizing in personnel had an unforeseen bright side. By very close management, the reduction in force permitted a refined selection process to retain the very best personnel. Few could be retained in their former positions, but these were the children of the depression, and they understood the necessity for economy. They accepted positions lower in rank and pay with grace, and then worked hard to go back up the ladder when conditions improved.

The process of refining the personnel ore at Lockheed had one very curious aspect, extremely desirable in some respects, but fraught with hazard if not managed properly. This was the inescapable fact that Lockheed had within its ranks several men for whom the term "genius" was not an exaggeration; further, it would acquire others of the same order in the next few years. Thus, Lockheed would enjoy the services of extraordinary and extraordinarily diverse people such as Hall Hibbard, Kelly Johnson, Willis Hawkins, Ben Rich, Nathan Price, Irving Culver, Dan Tellep, and many others. Any one of these would have been a star on his own at any other company—and any one of them might have had trouble in a corporate environment other than Lockheed's. The personality so influenced Lockheed's management style and corporate culture that a genuine sense of family was created, enabling everyone to work to his full capacity side by side on a wide spectrum of products. This is not to say that there was not an occasional dustup when their strong personalities clashed, nor that there were not occasional manifestations of ego-based rancor, but on the whole, they managed to find the space within Lockheed to work to the maximum of their own abilities—and thus carry the firm forward further and faster than anyone might have imagined.

The term "Lockheed family" has the ring of a public-relations ploy, a saccharine description of ordinary good morale, but this is not the case. In interview after interview, the term emerged spontaneously from people employed at every level who echoed the importance of the sense of belonging that Bob Gross had instilled. An undeniable, close-knit sense of family held the company together, allowing it to excel in good times, and, as will be shown subsequently, ensuring that it stayed together in bad times. And today, even among people who did not know him personally, this sense of identity is attributed to Bob Gross.

The result of Lockheed's precipitate drawdown was totally different from the wartime demobilization of the armed forces, which was done with such reckless abandon that the military strength of the nation was reduced to a negligible quantity. Lockheed emerged from the force-reduction era as an efficient, highly competitive organization, lean, taut, and staffed with men and women who had earned their spurs in the war and were now committed to making Lockheed a leader in peace. They were aided by a management wise enough to allow itself to be energized by its rich concentration of men of engineering genius yet strong enough to control the direction of their effort. Yet it is fair to say that even Lockheed's management had no idea of how far and how high the resources thus employed would ultimately reach.

Despite the phenomenal wartime growth, Lockheed's top leadership team had remained fairly small, the only significant addition being Courtlandt Gross's move to the West Coast to become president of the Vega Airplane Company in 1940. The Gross brothers were to maintain tight control during the expansion because of their policy of delegating authority and identifying promising young talent. The postwar success of the firm resulted from some chance situations as well, for as events transpired, Lockheed would be tasked to produce three aircraft that would be vital in the immediate postwar period.

The Right Products at the Right Time

Circumstances had worked greatly to Lockheed's favor in that three of its major product lines—the Constellation transport, the Neptune patrol plane, and the P-80 jet fighter—all filled definite postwar needs. Each of these had come into being during the war, and each one would reach maturity in the postwar years, giving Lockheed the boost it would need to sustain itself in a vastly different environment. Each one would also have lasting psychological effects within the company, for the Constellation would inspire a lingering—and costly—hunger to remain in the commercial air-transport business and the Neptune would make Lockheed premier in the antisubmarine-warfare business, while the P-80 would not only lead to a host of derivative aircraft, it would be the beginning of the most distinguished aeronautical engineering group in history, the justly fabled Skunk Works. Known early on and more prosaically as the Advanced Developments Project Group, the Skunk Works would provide the United States with a series of aircraft so advanced that there was literally no competition for them anywhere in the world.

The first studies on what would become the best-known of the three aircraft upon which Lockheed would base its postwar recovery, the Constellation, began in 1938. Douglas had dominated the twin-engine airliner market, to the detriment of Lockheed products, and now threatened to do the same by introducing the DC-4 (later designated the DC-4E), a large forty-two-passenger aircraft that featured a triple tail design to meet the height limitations imposed by existing maintenance hangars. The DC-4E proved to be a failure, and was never put into production. (It was purchased by the Japanese, and ultimately used as the basis for the design of one of their few four-engine bomber prototypes, the Nakajima G5N Shinzan, also a complete failure.)

The first Lockheed four-engine transport project was the Model 44 Excalibur, the initial model of which would have carried twenty-one passengers at a top speed of 262 mph at 15,500 feet. Airline reaction was negative to this first offering—the aircraft was an insufficient advance over the DC-3. Subsequent design studies eventually led to an advanced version of the Model 44 which was to have had the capability to carry forty passengers at a speed of 300 mph. Pan American Airways then became very interested in the Excalibur, and contract negotiations were progressing when competition once again intervened. Boeing introduced the Model 307 Stratocruiser, a thirty-three-seat, 246-mph transport with a moderately pressurized passenger cabin that allowed it to cruise at 18,000 feet, with an internal cabin pressure altitude of only 8,000 feet. Boeing had created the 307 by adapting the wings and empennage of a B-17C to a circular fuselage, the first of the wide-bodies.

The famed Daniel Webb "Tommy" Tomlinson had done extensive experimental high-altitude work for TWA, and convinced his boss, Jack Frye, that the next generation of airliners had to be pressurized for reasons of speed, fuel economy, passenger comfort, and weather avoidance. Frye turned to Lockheed for the competition, bringing Howard Hughes, a major stockholder in TWA, with him in the summer of 1939. They wanted Lockheed to go far beyond its Excalibur design, specifying a pressurized transport with a nonstop coast-to-coast capability, a speed of at least 250 mph, and a six-thousand-pound cargo capacity. (For a period of time Hughes sought to get a super-luxurious, twenty-seven-passenger transport that would provide the rich and famous with exclusive transportation. Lockheed played along, knowing that the pounds Hughes allocated for luxury items for the twenty-seven passengers could be translated eventually into seats for forty or more.)

Work on the Excalibur, which had reached the wind-tunnel model and mock-up stage, was deferred, but as late as August 22, 1940, an interdepartmental memo indicated that the project was going to be revived in six months. This suited Hughes, who insisted on secrecy and regarded the Excalibur as a cover for the Constellation. The Excalibur's designation was transferred to the new aircraft as the Model 49 Excalibur A. Hall Hibbard and Kelly Johnson were assigned as chief engineer and chief research engineer, respectively, while Don Palmer later assumed the role of project engineer. (Hawkins maintains that the main function of the Excalibur Model 44 was to serve as a decoy and divert attention from the secret work being done on the Constellation.)

Hughes has through the years been given credit for much of the

Howard Hughes followed the development of the Constellation closely, and is shown here with TWA's Jack Frye. The two men flew a Lockheed C-69 to a new Los Angeles–Washington record of 7 hours and 3 minutes on April 17, 1944.

design of the Constellation, particularly its unusual S-shaped fuselage, usually reported as having been "scrawled on the back of an envelope." It is a great story, but, like most such stories, untrue. Although Hughes already had unorthodox working habits, being given to nocturnal phone calls and meetings in out-of-the-way places, he was still far from being the eccentric that he would later become. He was influential in determining the performance specifications, and did make suggestions about details of the cockpit design, but otherwise did not interfere with the process. People who worked with Hughes invariably report that he was pleasant, highly focused on the business at hand, and able to understand fully engineering discussions and decisions.

The Model 49 naturally drew heavily on past Lockheed experience, using the basic Excalibur layout, and essentially scaling up the wing of the P-38, using the same airfoils and incorporating Fowler flaps. The controls were hydraulically boosted, another legacy from the P-38. The hydraulic controls were intended to get the maximum effect from the minimum-size control surfaces. A tricycle landing gear was adopted, as was a triple vertical tail surface, the latter (as with the

The Connie, as it was inevitably known, provided high speed, reliability, passenger comfort, good operating economics, and tremendous popular appeal.

DC-4E) so that the aircraft could fit in existing hangars. The eccentric elliptical shape of the Model 14's vertical surfaces was adapted to facilitate identity as a Lockheed product.

The single greatest visual difference between the Constellation and all other transports, before or since, was in the delicate curve of its fuselage. Ordinarily, the horizontal centerline of a transport-aircraft fuselage is a simple straight line from nose to tail. The Constellation's nose dips down, and the fuselage flows in a very lazy S to the rear, where it turns up. An intense young engineer named Ward Beman was responsible for the design. His goal was to have the fuselage shape accurately match the flow of air along the body of the aircraft, so as to avoid disrupting lift over the wing. When he made his first calculations, it was apparent that a fuselage so designed would require a nose gear of inordinate length. As a result, Beman swept the nose down. At the other end of the ninety-five-foot-long fuselage there was a requirement to lift the tail surfaces to avoid the unfavorable effect of slipstream on the horizontal surfaces, and to keep the tail of the fuselage and the bottoms of the outboard fins from scraping the runway on landing.

The net result was an aesthetic triumph. The aircraft, with its unusual fuselage, slim, high-aspect-ratio wing, and triple tail touched a receptive chord in the aviation community. The overall image was enhanced by the name Constellation, which was instantly shortened to the affectionate "Connie."

Yet the fuselage was not as easy to build as a conventional design, making the standardization of parts like access panels and hatches more difficult. Hall Hibbard told of an embarrassing trip he made as an airline passenger on an early Constellation. Somehow, before takeoff, an escape hatch fell off into his lap. Takeoff was delayed so that a replacement could be installed; the first three parts that were brought out to be installed did not fit. (Hibbard was careful not to reveal his position at Lockheed to the other exasperated passengers.)

Lockheed had pioneered cabin pressurization with the XC-35 of 1937, and on the Constellation used a four-pound-per-square-inch differential to provide a six-thousand-foot cabin altitude while cruising at eighteen thousand feet.

The design effort proceeded swiftly and the performance potential grew. By the fall of 1939, Lockheed was ready to offer the airlines two versions of the Model 49, each with a forty-four passenger capacity, a top speed of 360 mph, and a cruise altitude of twenty thousand feet, which was then described charitably as being "over the weather." Passenger capacity was expanded over time to as many as sixty, but there were many variations to meet specific airline requests.

A choice of either Pratt & Whitney Double Wasp or Wright Double Cyclone engines was offered, both types providing two thousand horsepower. After obtaining permission from TWA to offer the aircraft to other airlines, 84 orders came in, 40 each from Pan American and TWA, plus 4 more from a still-unidentified source; this was deemed sufficient to launch the program.

Creating the Model 49 took time, and although the threat of war intervened, Lockheed was authorized to proceed with the construction of three prototypes on May 4, 1941. For the next year, considerable confusion ensued, as initially Lockheed was going to be allowed to deliver the 80 aircraft on order to Pan Am and TWA. These were to be government-owned and airline-operated, and were to be followed by an additional 180 C-69 transports for the USAAF. In May 1942, a decision was made to procure the aircraft for the USAAF, the first 50 versions to be essentially like the original civilian Model 49 Constellation, while the next 180 were to be C-69B "Airborne Task Force" cargo planes.

A series of further changes ensued; ultimately the USAAF ordered a total of 313 Constellations. After all the chaos, postwar cancellations resulted in only 15 of these being delivered to the USAAF, but the commercial airline market would be ready and waiting.

The first flight of the Constellation was made on January 9, 1943, from the Lockheed Air Terminal. The test-flight crew was truly distinguished, with Edward T. Allen on loan from Boeing. Allen was the most sought-after "large airplane" test pilot in the business; sadly, he would lose his life in the crash of the second Boeing XB-29 only thirty-seven days later. He was accompanied by copilot Milo Burcham, Lockheed's chief test pilot, but a man with little four-engine experience. R. L. "Rudy" Thoren (also a Michigan man) was flight engineer and Richard Stanton was the crew chief. Thoren was invaluable for his work in designing and installing the test equipment with which the airplane was so liberally equipped. He also set the precedent for the careful in-flight handling of the Wright R-3350 engines, which were extremely sensitive and prone to prompt failure if the correct operating procedures were not used. The versatile Kelly Johnson was also on board, performing a role he liked, that of flight-test engineer. Landing at Muroc Dry Lake (now Edwards Air Force Base) after a fifty-minute flight, Allen thought the airplane performed so well that he was no longer needed, and returned to Seattle.

After an extensive test program, Hughes and Frye took a leaf out of the publicity flights of the previous decade on April 19, 1944, by flying the number two Connie from Burbank to Washington's National Airport nonstop in six hours, fifty-seven minutes, and fifty-one seconds, a new transcontinental speed record. They averaged 331 mph at a 65 percent power setting. The import of the flight was not lost on airline operators. It was in this airplane (serialed AF 43-10310) that Orville Wright made his last flight, handling the controls for a brief period of time. The wingspan of the Connie was three feet longer than Orville's 120-foot first flight in 1903.

A total of 233 of the early Model 049 Constellations would be built through 1951; of these, 28 would be purchased by the military. Among these were VIP transports for Generals of the Army Douglas MacArthur and Dwight Eisenhower. As president, Eisenhower used VC-121A *Columbine II* and VC-121E *Columbine III;* the latter is on exhibit at the USAF Museum in Dayton, Ohio. Putting the converted military version of the Connie into the field gave Lockheed a lead over Douglas, whose pressurized DC-6 would make its first flight in 1946, with deliveries to airlines beginning in November of that year.

The Constellation entered commercial service on February 3, 1946, flying Pan American's New York-to-Bermuda route. TWA

Intended as a revolutionary commercial transport, the Constellation was pressed into military service as the C-69. The military Connies served well and helped to prove the aircraft for civilian service.

On April 26, 1944, Orville Wright took the controls of a Lockheed C-69 after its take off from Wright Field. It was his last flight, made more than four decades after he and Wilbur had their success at Kitty Hawk.

encroached on what had been Pan Am's turf by inaugurating transatlantic service between New York and Paris on February 6, 1946. Other carriers using Connies would soon follow suit. On March 1, TWA began transcontinental service with the Constellations. Their

TWA featured Constellation service, and promoted it extensively as with the
staged photo of passengers boarding.

greater speed enabled them to cut two to three hours off the en-route
time offered by the Douglas DC-4s of American and United.

Airlines using the Constellation lost some of their initial advantage when the Civil Aeronautics Board grounded the Constellations
from July 12 to September 20, 1946, because of crashes. The first
occurred on June 18, 1946, when a Pan Am Constellation on a New
York-to-London flight was forced to make an emergency landing at
Willimantic, Connecticut. A severed supercharger drive shaft had
flailed around, shearing the engine mounts so that the number four
engine dropped completely off the airplane. (The crew showed its
aplomb and made headlines after the precautionary landing by serving
the passengers a light lunch along with tea and coffee.) There were as
yet no repair facilities for the Constellation in the East, so the lightly
loaded aircraft was flown back to Burbank on three engines. Less than
a month later, on July 11, an electrical fire occurred on a TWA training
flight. Smoke filled the cockpit, and five of the six people on board
were killed in the crash landing. (The next year, the DC-6 was to
suffer a similar grounding after a fire caused by a fuel leak into the
cabin heater system.)

Despite the Constellation's
higher speed, sleeper comfort
was still desirable on very long
flights. This configuration
was intended for long
overseas routes.

The delay in production had an adverse effect on Lockheed's financial position, and was a significant factor in making the civil Constellation program a financial failure.

The first purely civil Constellation was the Model 649, which featured improved passenger comfort items and was nicknamed "Gold Plate." As with each of the successive Constellation improvements, the maximum gross takeoff weight was increased. The original Model 049 had a maximum gross takeoff weight of 85,000 pounds; this rose ultimately to 160,000 pounds in the Model 1649.

Competition from the DC-6 induced Lockheed to create the Model 1049 Super Constellation, of which 579 military and civil versions would be built. The fuselage was stretched by eighteen feet five inches to gain a ninety-two passenger capacity, the small round windows gave way to a larger rectangular type, and maximum takeoff weight went up to 120,000 pounds, some 35,000 pounds greater than the original. Higher speeds were not the primary objective; the numerous design refinements were intended to provide a higher degree of passenger comfort and, ultimately, "brand loyalty"—repeat customers were good for the airlines and for Lockheed.

The initial series of 1049s were underpowered, as the intended turbo-compound version of the Wright R-3500 Turbo-Cyclone engine was not yet available, and the stretched Connie did not fare well

At a time before the concept of political correctness had intervened in advertising,
Lockheed and its customers—in this instance KLM—liked to use pretty women
to introduce new aircraft. Here women in Dutch costumes line up before the
new Model 1049 Super Constellation.

in the competition with the Douglas DC-6B, only twenty-four being
sold. The complex turbo-compound engines became available on the
Model 1049C and imparted greatly enhanced performance, at the cost
of reliability. Each engine had three turbines to recover power from
the exhausts; these drove fluid couplings to feed power back to the
engine, increasing output by 20 percent. The 1049C's cruising speed
was increased to 330 mph, and its performance eclipsed that of the
DC-6B.

Despite the threat of the jet airliner looming on the horizon,
successive models of the Constellation introduced further refinements,
even as Douglas introduced the DC-7B on June 13, 1955. Lockheed
was ready with the 1049G "Super G," which entered service on November 1, 1955, with TWA, while Pan American raised the ante with
the Douglas DC-7C (inevitably the "Seven Seas") on June 1, 1956.
The DC-7C's wings had an extra 10-foot span, which placed the engines five feet farther out from the passengers. The plane became immensely popular, even though it was slightly slower than its

Even the installation of a huge radar dome did not mar the beautiful lines of the
Lockheed RC-121D Warning Star airborne early-warning aircraft. The radar permitted
the aircraft to function as an airborne combat information center.

predecessor. Lockheed responded by putting a brand-new 150-foot-span wing on its Super Constellation to create the ultimate aircraft in its line, the L1649A Starliner.

The Wright Turbo-Compound engine continued to be used by both Douglas and Lockheed, despite engine failures so numerous that they led to the generic nickname "the world's fastest trimotors" for the products of both manufacturers.

Although Douglas won the commercial market race by selling 878 examples of the DC-6/7, compared with only 510 versions of the Constellation, the latter exercised the greater hold on people's minds and hearts. There was something about its magic lines and triple tail that made it the most glamorous and best-remembered of the piston-engine transports.

As noted previously, the Constellation would not have been a profitable program for Lockheed had it not been for the 346 aircraft sold to the military and used over a twenty-six-year period. They were employed by the navy and the air force for personnel and cargo transport, reconnaissance (photographic, electronic, and weather), airborne early warning, VIP transport, electronic relay, electronic countermeasures, and a variety of special duties including mapping the earth's magnetic field.

The versatility and endurance of the Constellation was put to its most productive military use in Southeast Asia, where air force

EC-121s of the College Eye (originally Big Eye) task force flew 13,391 sorties and amassed 98,777 hours of combat time. In their primary College Eye mission, the EC-121s would station themselves in an elliptical orbit about fifty miles from Haiphong over the Gulf of Tonkin, passing on information on enemy air activity, with the goal of preventing surprise MiG attacks on F-105 and F-4 formations. The leading USAF pilot ace, then Captain Steve Ritchie, has commented that every one of his five victories over MiG-21s was the direct result of information furnished by College Eye aircraft.

Other EC-121s would fly similar pattern over Laos near the Plain of Jars. Besides directing air operations over North Vietnam and Laos, they acted as airborne communications relay stations through which combat aircraft could transmit strike results. They directed the operations of fighter escorts on strikes, as well as the MiG combat air patrols. Other duties included assisting in rescue efforts for downed crews and directing fuel-hungry aircraft to waiting tankers. It was hot, grueling work for the eighteen-member crews, who would spend as many as sixteen hours on a mission, unable to leave their crew positions for most of that time. And it was far from the original, posh role envisaged for the Connie; intended to transport only the elite in an atmosphere of luxury, a job it did well, the graceful Constellation also turned to and did a warrior's work when called upon.

A Longtime Lock on the Market

The second aircraft in Lockheed's stellar postwar stable was the P2V Neptune, upon which work had begun as a private venture, Design V-135, at the Vega Aircraft Corporation on December 6, 1941. This was to be a clean-sheet departure from the ongoing evolutionary development of the Hudson and Ventura series of aircraft. The vice president of engineering, Mac V. Short, was determined that the new patrol plane would have a much longer range, carry a larger ordnance load, and be much faster, yet have a lower approach and landing speed than its predecessors, and he gave the assignment to Jack Wassall, then chief engineer at Vega. R. A. Bailey and Lou Height became codesigners of the aircraft. The Neptune, as it was called, broke all precedent by being planned as a land-based patrol plane from the start, although during its long gestation period, other land-based aircraft would assume such duties. And as long as its gestation period was—it did not make its first flight until May 17, 1945, with Joe Towle at the controls,

Two men who had managed Lockheed's growth from a 40,000-dollar speculation into a multimillion dollar empire, Hall Hibbard, left, and Robert Gross.

The Hudson got Lockheed into the anti–submarine business, and the P2V Neptune would confirm its hold on the discipline. The P2V became the anti–submarine weapon of choice for many U.S. allies.

some forty-one months after Short's go-ahead—it would have a far longer production run. It was manufactured at Lockheed through 1962, and the last example of the derivative model built in Japan, the P2J, did not come off the production line until 1979, more than a third of a century from the start date.

The Neptune thus signaled a new era in which aircraft became regarded as platforms for other technology, and as such, had a far greater longevity than ever before. Unlike the Hudson, which had served in the front line for about five years, the Neptune and legendary aircraft like the Boeing B-52, Lockheed C-130, and Grumman A-6 achieved a life span far longer than their designers had dreamed. This long-lived utility came about because the performance of the basic aircraft design was excellent, and the airframe was susceptible to modification. Such a basic change was bound to have a tremendous impact on the industry, and would foster a change in the thinking of Lockheed's management, causing them to look further afield for new business. The expansion of interest would come slowly, but when it came, it would prove to be the salvation of the company both fiscally and in terms of its future management.

The Neptune's development had been delayed because of the priority accorded to the Hudson, Ventura, and Harpoon aircraft. All of these were developments of civil designs, but the Neptune broke new ground. Its clean lines remained almost unchanged over its history, despite the addition of much equipment.

The performance growth possibilities of the Neptune were demonstrated brilliantly in a flight that began on September 29, 1946, from Perth, Australia. The very first production P2V-1, heavily modified to carry more than fifty thousand pounds of gasoline and weighing an astounding eighty-five thousand pounds, was boosted off the ground by four rocket-assisted takeoff (RATO) bottles. It then flew nonstop to Columbus, Ohio, to set an absolute world's distance record of 11,235.6 miles. Named *The Turtle,* but forever remembered by its press-generated nickname *Truculent Turtle,* the Neptune took only fifty-five hours and seventeen minutes for the trip.

Given that the war ended only four months after the Neptune's first flight, the design might well have died aborning. The initial production order for 116 P2Vs was slashed to 51 in anticipation of the postwar drawdown. Yet the navy was in a time of trial. The budgetary threat of a newly independent United States Air Force made it absolutely essential for the navy to have an aircraft capable of carrying a nuclear weapon for long-distance strikes. The Neptune was the only possible candidate—if it could be flown off carriers. A careful study indicated that this could just be done—wingtip clearance on takeoff was only a few feet—and the decks of three *Midway*-class carriers were strengthened to handle the weight of an extensively modified P2V-2. Carrier trials were conducted off the USS *Coral Sea.* On April 28, 1948, Commander Thomas D. Davies (who had also flown *The Turtle* on its record-breaking flight) made a RATO with deck to spare, the first carrier launch of an aircraft of the Neptune's size and weight, and setting a pattern for several generations of aircraft to follow.

The Neptunes were also used for electronic reconnaissance, cruising up and down off the coast of China, then turning directly inbound so that their sensors could pick up Chinese radar. When they approached the coast they'd do a quick 180-degree turn and head out to sea.

These and other similar demonstrations of the aircraft's capability kept it in production, although in relatively small numbers. Five were delivered in 1946, 47 in 1947, 74 in 1948, and 34 in 1949. The advent of the Korean War on June 25, 1950, brought new tasks— Neptune squadrons flew thirteen tours of duty during the war—and new production orders. Eventually, a total of 1,051 Neptunes were produced by Lockheed, plus another 130 by Kawasaki in Japan.

The soundness of the design was reflected in the increase of its performance over time, and in its adaptability. The final U.S. version, the P2V-7 (later the P2-H) had a maximum gross weight of 79,895 pounds, a top speed of 403 mph, and a maximum range of 5,930 miles. Its power had been vastly increased as it became a four-engine aircraft. The two Wright R-3350 reciprocating engines were continuously upgraded, with the R-3350-32W Turbo-Compounds of 3,500 horsepower eventually being installed. These were augmented on the P2V-5 and following aircraft by two 3,250-pound static-thrust Westinghouse J34 jet engines mounted in underslung wing pods. These were used for takeoff and landing, and for dash speeds in combat.

The adaptability was demonstrated in its multiple missions, which included long-range nuclear attack, antisubmarine warfare, polar exploration (equipped with skis), combat support, VIP transport, cruise-missile launch, drone-vehicle launch and control, target tow, and electronic surveillance. Few aircraft have succeeded so well in doing so many tasks over such a long period of time.

The Neptune was doubly important to Lockheed. Not only did the influx of cash from its contracts permit Lockheed to maintain a workforce in a time of recession, it also established a long-lasting relationship with the United States Navy. This was enhanced when the Neptune was replaced for patrol duties by another Lockheed product, the P3V (later P3) Orion. The patrol planes thus put Lockheed on solid ground with the navy, establishing a long and cordial relationship that would continue during the course of work on the three famously successful submarine-launched missiles, the Polaris, Poseidon, and Trident.

The replacement of P2Vs by P3s was phased over time so that

The Neptune and its natural quarry, the submarine. The P2V became a platform into which ever-more sophisticated anti–submarine warfare equipment could be fitted.

the Neptune was returned to combat in Southeast Asia. The last Neptune left navy service in April 1978, after thirty-one years of operations.

The versatility of the Neptune permitted it to be a four-service aircraft, being used by the U.S. Army as the AP-2E for special missions, by the USAF as the RB-69A, and by the Marine Corps as the P2V-2. The RB-69A was essentially a Neptune extensively modified by the Lockheed's Skunk Works so that it could be used for a wide variety of clandestine operations, including deep penetrations of Red China by Taiwanese crews. The Neptune was also used by ten other nations for patrol and antisubmarine duty. When the P2Vs were at last retired, many found work in Canada and the United States as forest-fire fighters. About two dozen survivors are on display in museums around the world and a few are in the hands of private collectors.

The Shooting Star: The Key to R and D

There have been dozens of key fighter planes in aviation history, from the Fokker Eindecker and the North American Mustang to the MiG 15. Only one aircraft, however, was not only distinguished in its own right, siring a host of derivative aircraft that were also great, but also established the basic foundation for the most innovative, most successful, and most important aircraft-development facility in history. That fighter is the Lockheed P-80 Shooting Star, and the facility is the fabled Skunk Works, now officially the Lockheed Martin Skunk Works.

Both the P-80 and the Skunk Works came about as a direct result of two phenomena. The first was the often mentioned Bob Gross's establishment of the Lockheed corporate culture, which had the confidence and the vision to permit the existence of a concept group that not only contravened normal in-house organizational mores, but ran counter to those of the customer as well. The other was the titanic genius of Kelly Johnson, who combined in one forceful personality the abilities of an incredibly brilliant engineer, a farseeing production expert, a hands-on expert, and a charismatic workforce leader who could drive as he inspired and inspire as he drove. He will be prominent in the following pages.

Too Much, Too Soon

On August 27, 1939, Flight Captain Erich Warsitz lifted off the ground at the Marienehe Airfield in a Heinkel He 178, for the first jet flight in history. The little plane was powered by a Heinkel HeS 3 engine of 838 pounds of thrust and designed by the young Dr. Hans Joachim Pabst von Ohain. One year and one day later, on August 28, 1940, the famed racing pilot Mario de Bernardi flew the Italian Caproni-Campini, a two-seat all-metal monoplane with a 900-horsepower Isotta-Fraschini radial engine driving a variable-pitch ducted-fan compressor. Fuel injectors forced fuel into the compressed airflow, where it was ignited, and provided the thrust for what may have been the slowest jet in aviation history. On May 15, 1941, the Gloster E.28/39 took off from the airfield at Cranwell to provide the Royal Air Force with its first jet aircraft. Gloster's chief test pilot, P. E. G. "Gerry" Sayer, was at the controls, and the British inventor of the 850-pound-thrust Power Jet engine which powered it, Squadron Leader Frank Whittle, was on hand to watch. General Henry H. Arnold became interested in jet propulsion, and a forced-draft effort resulted in test pilot Robert Stanley flying the first American jet, the Bell XP-59, from Muroc Dry Lake on October 1, 1942. It was powered by two General Electric 1-A engines of 1,400 pounds of thrust and derived directly from Whittle's design. Unfortunately, the basic airframe was totally inadequate for a fighter and the fifty production P-59A and B aircraft were relegated to trainer status.

The promise of the Heinkel engine was not realized because of engineering and political problems. Despite its many contributions to the war effort, the Heinkel firm was out of favor with the Nazis, and was overtaken by other manufacturers in the German jet industry. The Caproni-Campini was simply an engineering dead end. Only the English jet engine would lead to further developments in England and also in the United States, where the failure of the Bell P-59 design would bode well for Lockheed.

At the time Warsitz made the first flight in the Heinkel He 178 in 1939, the key personnel at Lockheed were already evincing an interest in jet propulsion, and within months were working not only on a jet engine, but on the aircraft to use it. It was Robert Gross's custom and prerogative occasionally to hire people whose ideas he liked, and give them free rein. Such was the case with Nathan "Nate" Price, in Willis Hawkins's words "a big tall Airedale" of a man, an amiable genius who was an expert in turbo-superchargers. (Price was an amazing visionary; in the 1950s, he had designed a ballistic-missile passenger-transport system, complete in every detail including a system for rapid baggage retrieval after a half-hour transcontinental trip.)

In 1941, Price was well into the design of an extremely advanced jet engine, one that was in all respects years ahead of any of those mentioned above. It had a thirty-seven-stage low-pressure compressor, a twenty-five-stage high-pressure compressor, an intercooler, a four-stage turbine, stator blades cooled by fuel, and with only a two-foot diameter, was to be capable initially of 3,500 pounds of thrust with a potential for development to 5,500 pounds of thrust. Johnson was impressed by the engine design (designated L-1000 at the time, and later in its development as the XJ37) and led Hawkins, Phil Colman, Gene Frost, and others in the creation of the Model L-133, which was designed to have two of Price's engines—a total of 7,000 pounds of static thrust. The aircraft was extraordinarily advanced, made largely of stainless steel and equipped with a canard surface (horizontal surfaces on the nose), boundary layer control, and a blended wing and body reminiscent of the present-day F-16 fighter. A 600-mph top speed was projected.

Johnson and Hibbard, with some other Lockheed team members, took the L-133 fighter design to Wright Field to sell it to the USAAF,

Hall Hibbard examines a circa 1940 Lockheed L-1000 turbojet engine designed by the brilliant engineer Nathan Price. The engine was promising, but the pressures of war forced Lockheed to work with General Electric for an engine for its first jet plane. Price later invented an intercontinental-ballistic passenger-carrying missile system.

and met with no interest—the project was considered too advanced to be realized in time to help the war effort.

Nonetheless, components of the L-1000 were built and tested by the Menasco Company. Lockheed realized it could not afford to build the facilities to test and manufacture such an advanced engine, and the government was opposed to having airplanes and engines manufactured within the same corporate structure. An auction was held for the design rights. These were picked up by the Curtiss-Wright Corporation, but little was done with them, and the project was allowed to lapse in 1952.

The growing evidence of German success in developing jet aircraft forced a USAAF decision to seek a countermeasure. Lockheed's interest in jet aircraft was recalled, and the chief of the Engineering Division of the Materiel Command, and one of the great unsung heroes of the American military, then Brigadier General Franklin O. Carroll, met once again with Johnson and Hibbard on May 17, 1943. The USAAF tendered Lockheed an opportunity to build a jet fighter of its own design around the de Havilland Halford H.1B Goblin jet engine of a nominal rating of 3,000 pounds of thrust.

The Goblin was the product of Major Frank Bernard Halford, who was the designer of the long series of de Havilland Cirrus and Gypsy engines, as well as the far more powerful Napier Rapier, Dagger, and Sabre power plants. The British government had given him access to Whittle's work, and the result was the Halford H.1, which went from drawings in April 1941 to successful runs at 3,010 pounds of thrust a year later, and flight in the Gloster Meteor prototype on March 5, 1943. The freehanded use of Whittle's work was undoubtedly the result of the pressures of war, but it was financially unfair to Whittle.

Lockheed accepted the challenge to build an airframe immediately, and less than a month later submitted a proposal for the Lockheed Model L-140. The project received the Wright Field designation of MX409 and the aircraft was subsequently designated XP-80. Official approval was given on June 17, and work was under way immediately. In these days of $2 billion bombers, the XP-80's contractual cost of $642,404 has a certain poignancy. This amount was to include building a prototype aircraft, wind-tunnel models, flight testing, and a fixed fee of $22,584. The aircraft was to be delivered in 150 days.

The urgency of the contract played into Kelly Johnson's hands. He had long been advocating establishing an experimental group under his direct supervision. His goal was to have the designers and expert workmen work in close association, with a minimum of paperwork and no outside interference. Ordinary bureaucratic problems stemming from support functions like purchasing or administration were to be eliminated. In effect, he wanted to be able to translate drawings into metal directly by the close cooperation of designers and workers, with a minimum of interference from the company or the customer. With Gross's go-ahead, he now established the prototype organization for what would become known first as the "Skonk Works" and later the "Skunk Works." In Johnson's mind, the ideal situation would arise from the customer telling Johnson what was desired and when it was needed, and agreeing to keep his hands off until it was done. The Skunk Works would then work with a free hand at providing the customer's needs or better, on time, and on the negotiated budget.

The facetious name "Skonk Works" derived from Johnson's necessarily obsessive need for secrecy and the most influential comic strip of the era, Al Capp's *Li'l Abner,* which had a political point of view and an intellectual following corresponding to those of Garry Trudeau's *Doonesbury* today. Johnson insisted that his small band of 123 engineers and workers not tell anyone what they were doing, or even where they were working. Capp's comic strip featured an Ozark-like locale called Dogpatch, where the main industry was the "Skonk Works," headed by Big Barnsmell, the "inside man at the Skonk

Works." (Other Capp characters included Hairless Joe and Lonesome Polecat, but they did not have the security clearance necessary for employment at the Skonk Works.) Yet another Lockheed engineering genius, Irving Culver, about whom much will be said later, observed Johnson's requirement for secrecy by jokingly answering the telephone with the salutation "Skonk Works, inside man Culver." A principal player in the design of the XP-80 structure, Culver later reported that Kelly Johnson was not amused, but eventually came to accept the name. (In the 1960s, Capp's lawyers objected to Lockheed's use of the term, and the phrase was changed to "Skunk Works," a name that was copyrighted by Lockheed in 1973.)

The new experimental group reported directly to Hall Hibbard, who was now vice president and chief engineer, but Johnson was the guiding figure. He established the ground rules for the organization: the prototype was to be completed in 150 days; the workforce, which was never to exceed a total of 123 men, was sworn to secrecy. It would work ten hours a day, six days a week, with no work on Sundays. Working conditions were abysmal, for the team was forced to use a scrap-wood and canvas-roofed temporary building near the wind tunnel at Plant B-1.

As important as the new project obviously was, it represented but a small part of Lockheed's total annual sales of almost $700 million and 1943 production of 5,223 aircraft. Fortunately, the USAAF regarded the program as having the highest priority, and followed through by delivering all government-furnished equipment (instruments, control stick, tires, guns, and so on) immediately. Only one government employee was permitted into the Skunk Works facility—a condition of the contract negotiated by Johnson.

Work on the XP-80 proceeded swiftly, despite delays in the delivery of a suitable engine. In the meantime, Lockheed and the USAAF were looking to the future. An agreement was reached that the production aircraft would use the General Electric I-40 engine. (The I-40 drew heavily on the experience GE had gained building advanced versions of the Whittle engine. The result was a four-thousand-pound-thrust centrifugal-flow engine of a quite sophisticated design for the period.) Production aircraft were also going to be larger and heavier than the XP-80, with pressurized cockpits and an armament package to be defined after tests with the prototype. Routine considerations for production aircraft, including ease of production and maintainability, inevitably called for what amounted to an entirely new aircraft, the

Lockheed Model L-141; the USAAF referred to the next prototype as the XP-80A.

With Johnson following every step in the process, the XP-80 came together quickly; it was completed and accepted 143 days after the contract had been signed, exactly 7 days ahead of schedule. Persistent engine troubles were being encountered, and flight-testing was delayed when the air ducts leading to the Halford engine collapsed during run-up. The engine had to be replaced, but chief test pilot Milo Burcham was able to make the first flight on January 8, 1944, at 9:10 A.M.

It was a crucially important date for Lockheed and the USAAF, and both were represented by their top people, including Robert Gross and Cyril Chappellet, each of whom must have been thinking what progress the sleek fighter represented for their almost twelve years of labor.

Burcham's first flight was successful but was only six minutes long because he could not get the gear to retract. The failure has been attributed to a safety switch that Burcham forgot about, while the log entry for his flight attributes it to a maladjustment of the scissors-switch. The fuel tank was topped off, and Gross broke the tension with his usual sense of humor. He commented on the short flight followed by a refueling by calling out to Kelly Johnson, "Great range, Kelly." It's not recorded whether or not Johnson laughed.

Burcham took off for a second flight, this time for twenty minutes, and showed the appreciative crowd the amazing maneuverability and speed of the XP-80. Subsequent flight-testing proved the general suitability of the design, although some minor fixes were required to correct poor stall and spin characteristics, high-stick forces, and other important but not intractable difficulties. The XP-80, painted an unusual spinach green, went on for some thirty-four months of service before being retired. It was restored and placed in the National Air and Space Museum in 1976.

The XP-80A as developed had wings two feet longer in span, but slightly narrower in chord. Gross weight went up by about 50 percent, to 13,780 pounds. Internal fuel tankage was increased, and wingtip tanks were fitted on the second aircraft. Thirteen service test YP-80As were ordered, also powered by the GE I-40 engine.

As was inevitable, accidents marred the XP/YP-80 test program. The first YP-80A was lost on October 20, 1944. Lockheed's chief test pilot, Milo Burcham, had a flameout just after taking off from the

The first product of the Skunk Works, the Lockheed P-80 put the company in the forefront of the jet age. Seen here (left to right) are Kelly Johnson, Tony LeVier, and Milo Burcham, who made the first flight.

Burbank Airport; he crashed into a gravel pit and was killed instantly. The fuel pump had failed and there was no emergency backup. On March 20, 1945, ace racing pilot Tony LeVier was flying the beautifully finished first XP-80A—known as the Gray Ghost because of its light gray color—when a turbine failed; the disintegrating engine literally chopped the tail off the aircraft. LeVier bailed out but broke his back when he hit the ground. Later in the year, on August 6, the P-38 expert and leading ace, Major Richard Bong, was killed in a P-80A. As was the case with Burcham, the accident was attributed to a sheared fuel-pump driveshaft. An electric backup pump had been installed as result of Burcham's accident, but Bong had failed to turn on the switch.

The trend was alarming; by the time of Bongs's death, eight aircraft had been destroyed and seven damaged, and six pilots had been killed. By September 1946, more than sixty accidents had occurred, primarily due to pilot error. The new aircraft, while deceptively simple to fly when all was going well, was demanding on takeoff and landing and in the event of a malfunction. It was evident that a transition trainer was required, and this would be fulfilled in TP-80C,

Clarence "Kelly" Johnson shakes test pilot Milo Burcham's hand after first flight of XP-80 on January 8, 1944. The aircraft was completed only 143 days after contract award.

which Tony LeVier first flew on March 22, 1948. It would become the immortal T-33.

Nonetheless, accidents were regarded as a way of life. The engines were new and untried, as was the airframe, and the speed, altitude, and handling qualities of the Shooting Star all made demands upon the pilot. It should be remembered that there were only token safety programs available in the Air Force at the time, and training standards were low compared to the stringent requirements of later years.

The production P-80As were powered by the 3,850-pound static-thrust GE J33 engines (also built by Allison). General Hap Arnold wanted to wrest the world's speed record away from the British and allocated funds to prepare the XP-80R. On June 19, 1947, Colonel Alvin Boyd put the XP-80R through the speed traps at Muroc to set a new world's speed record of 623.8 mph—the first time the United States had held the record since 1923, when Al Williams had flown a Curtiss R2C-1 at 267 mph. Boyd's speed translated into 1003.6 kilometers per hour, making him the first to break the "1,000-kilometer barrier."

The P-80 production program had been kicked off with initial

The hot-performing Shooting Star gave the United States a firm foundation upon which to build its jet fighter force. Exhibiting the same growth potential of the Lockheed transports, it was modified to serve many roles.

contracts for 500, 500, and 2,500 aircraft. When V-J Day came on August 15, 1945, these orders were reduced to a total of 917 aircraft. Over time, additional contracts were let, and in its seven-year production life, 1,742 Shooting Stars would be built in a wide variety of variants. Power and weight both went up, as did performance.

The Air Force changed the designation from P-80 to F-80 in 1948. Both F-80s and RF-80s did stellar work in Korea; 75 percent of enemy losses due to air attack were attributed to F-80s in the first months of the war. A Shooting Star flown by Lieutenant Russell Brown shot down a MiG-15 in the first jet-versus-jet battle in aviation history. Lockheed F-80s would shoot down thirty-seven enemy aircraft in combat while losing only fourteen, but time and swept wings had passed them by, making them better suited to ground-support work than dogfighting. All told, the F-80s flew 98,515 sorties in Korea.

The Navy and Marines acquired F-80s from the Air Force to facilitate their conversion to the jet age. Six South American nations (Brazil, Peru, Chile, Colombia, Ecuador, and Uruguay) obtained surplus F-80s for their air forces; the last ones were phased out of oper-

Because it was so revolutionary, the P-80 allowed Lockheed to maintain viable production lines after the war, when many other firms were forced to shut down. These P-80s are shown at the Burbank plant, waiting for their engines to be installed.

ation in Uruguay in 1975, to cap a distinguished thirty-one-year career.

Kelly Johnson's experimental group had phased out as the P-80 had entered full-scale production, but the Skunk Works concept would remain ingrained in Lockheed's consciousness, and would emerge, fully formed, a few years later when required.

As previously noted, the accident rate of the P-80 called for a transition trainer, and this became the TP-80C. (The designation was changed first to TF-80C and then T-33A.) The T-33 had a longer fuselage to provide room for the student's cockpit, and a reduced fuel-tank capacity. It was an immediate success and a financial bonanza for Lockheed, with 5,691 being produced. Variants were built in Canada (656) and Japan (210). The T-33 became the jet trainer of the free world, with Lockheed delivering 1,058 aircraft to a number of countries as a part of the Military Assistance Program. It was used as an attack (AT-33) and reconnaissance (RT-33) aircraft by several smaller air forces. The last T-33 in USAF service was retired in 1997.

An improved version, the T2V-1, was built for the navy as a result of a private venture instigated by Lockheed as the Model L-245. Basically an improved T-33 with a raised rear cockpit to provide the instructor with a better view and a larger vertical surface to compensate for the increased canopy area, the aircraft incorporated significant aerodynamic improvements. These came in the form of leading edge slats

The P-80 was stretched into the two-seat T-33 trainer, which proved to be slightly faster than the original Shooting Star. The T-Bird became the standard jet trainer of the West. More than 6,500 T-33s were built, including those produced in Japan and Canada.

and a boundary-layer control system (the very thing Johnson had studied in his advanced program at the University of Michigan) that reduced landing and takeoff speeds. The improved visibility and lower approach speeds interested the navy, and, suitably strengthened for carrier landings and takeoffs, 150 T2V-1s were purchased. Unfortunately, the boundary-layer control system was difficult to maintain, and no follow-on contracts ensued.

Affectionately called the "T-Bird," the T-33 was a delight to fly, its only drawback a rather uncomfortable seat that grew harder as the flight grew longer. Many T-Birds are flying still, and there have been occasional attempts by outside firms to revamp the basic design with new engines.

All-Weather Fighters

In November 1948, Russell Daniel, then chief engineer of the Skunk Works, was given what seemed to be a relatively straightforward

The T2V-1 SeaStar was a more sophisticated version of the Navy's TV-2 version of the T-33. A total of 150 were built.

problem, the development of the basic two-seat TF-80C airframe into an all-weather fighter equipped with radar and carrying a radar observer. Daniel's task was fraught with difficulty. The increased weight of the aircraft, designated the YF-94 Starfire, required the installation of an after-burning version of the Allison J33 engine, which increased power to 6,000 pounds of thrust, but upset the structure, aerodynamics, and center of gravity of the TF-80C ancestor. A modest armament package of four Browning M-3 .50-caliber machine guns was installed, along with the Hughes E-1 fire control system.

Daniel and his team resolved the major problems, and ultimately 854 Starfires were built, including 387 of the fundamentally redesigned F-94C. Virtually a new airplane, the F-94C had the more powerful Pratt & Whitney J48 engine, which generated 8,750 pounds of thrust with afterburner, and could drive the aircraft to supersonic speeds—in a dive. Top speed in level flight was 640 mph. The laminar flow wing was much thinner, and the advanced Hughes E-5 fire control system was installed.

Perhaps the most radical change was the armament. Twenty-four "Mighty Mouse" 2.75-inch Folding Fin Aircraft Rockets were placed

The F-94 Starfire evolved from the T-33 and was the USAF's first all-weather jet fighter. A total of 854 Starfires of all types were built.

in the nose. These were unguided, and had a disconcerting tendency to flame out the engine when salvoed, but they were a step along the missile highway. Later, wing pods were developed that carried twelve rockets each, for a total of forty-eight. The new armament completely altered fighter-versus-bomber tactics, which were never really resolved until the advent of more sophisticated missiles.

The F-94 was an interim aircraft, pressed into service with available electronic gear while later interceptors such as the Convair F-102 and F-106 were in the process of development. Nonetheless, it served for ten years, not being phased out until 1959. F-94As and Bs served during the Korean War, downing three enemy aircraft by gunfire and one by an unfortunate midair collision that also destroyed the F-94.

Other Early Postwar Projects

The three major aircraft series covered above—the Constellation, the Neptune, and the F-80 and its derivatives—strengthened Lockheed immeasurably as it recovered from the immediate postwar slump. Sales rose to over $820 million by 1953, employment had grown back to more than fifty thousand, and net income reached a record $15.4 million. But not all the projects of the postwar years were successes. Space limitations prohibit an in-depth discussion, but each one deserves a capsule summary.

Little Dipper A single-place aircraft designed by John Thorp (later well known for his home-built designs) caught the eye of Mac Short, and with Gross's permission a prototype was built as the Lockheed Model 33 in April 1944, when it was fairly evident that the war was well on its way to being won. Although the aircraft was being built at Lockheed expense, approval was obtained from the army to build the prototype as a single-place, twenty-five-foot-wingspan "aerial flying motorcycle" called the *Airtrooper* for army use. The Little Dipper was flown in August 1944, and proved to be pleasant to fly, gaining a 100-mph top speed from its specially built two-cylinder Franklin engine. At the war's end, the army lost all interest in the project, and in the ensuing months, Lockheed found there was no civil market for the aircraft.

Big Dipper Faced with the certainty of contract cancellations, many aircraft manufacturers wished to break into what seemed certain to be the boom in postwar civil aviation. The two-place "Big Dipper," also designed by John Thorp, was equipped with a tail-mounted propeller driven by a 100-horsepower engine. A vicious stall was encountered during testing, and a wing fillet was designed to eliminate this. Unfortunately, on February 6, 1946, a careless takeoff accident in which the stall played a part destroyed the prototype, and injured the crew, pilot Prentice Cleaves and project engineer Frank Johnson. The project was dropped.

Saturn The civil airline market had an irresistible appeal to Lockheed management, despite the difficulties of earning a profit therein. With the Constellation well situated for the major airlines, Lockheed saw a market for an aircraft that would do what the original Electra and Lodestar had done: serve the smaller airlines so that they could feed the large airlines. Don Palmer was project engineer, and his team created the workmanlike twin-engine high-wing monoplane Saturn, which was first offered in the fall of 1944 at eighty-five thousand dollars to an apparently receptive market. Conditional orders for no

The desire for postwar civilian business led to the development of the "Little Dipper" and the "Big Dipper." Both aircraft performed fairly well, but the civilian market for light planes did not develop as expected, and both projects were cancelled.

fewer than five hundred of the aircraft were placed, and Tony LeVier made the first flight on June 17, 1946. Fourteen months later, in August 1947, all testing problems of the two prototypes had been overcome and Lockheed had a 228-mph, fourteen-seat airliner ready to sell for one hundred thousand dollars. Unfortunately, the postwar market was deluged with thousands of Douglas C-47s, many virtually new, that were only slightly slower and sold for a quarter of the price. Despite being a good airplane, the Saturn was canceled, with a loss of $6 million.

Constitution One of the most beautiful large aircraft ever built, the Model 89 shows the artful hand of Willis Hawkins in every line. Built under a navy contract as the XR60-1, and named the Constitution by Robert Gross himself, the aircraft was to have been powered by 5,500 shaft-horsepower Wright Typhoon turbine engines. W. A. "Dick" Pulver was project engineer, and his team created an excellent aircraft, but the Wright engines were never developed. When equipped with four of the most powerful piston engines available, the Pratt & Whitney R-4360 "corncob" radial of 3,500 horsepower, there was insuffi-

Despite intensive market surveys that indicated otherwise, Lockheed found that surplus military aircraft filled the feeder airliner market for which the handsome Saturn was intended. Only two were built.

cient power to deliver the performance implicit in the airframe. Joe Towle and Tony LeVier made the first flight on November 9, 1946, with Rudy Thoren as flight engineer. The huge aircraft, designed to seat 180 passengers, took off in less than two thousand feet, and after a two-hour-and-seventeen-minute test flight, landed at Muroc, demonstrating its 80-mph landing speed. If the Typhoon turboprop engine had materialized, the Constitution would have been transformed and almost certainly been bought in reasonable quantity by both the military services and the airlines. Two Constitutions were built, and they served the navy for a few years before being declared surplus. Both were purchased by civil owners for under one hundred thousand dollars and were ultimately scrapped.

XF-90 The bloody skies over Regensburg and Schweinfurt had convinced the USAAF that long-range escort fighters were absolutely necessary in the jet age. In June 1946, at a time when P-80s were still new in squadron service, the USAAF awarded Lockheed a contract for two XP-90 prototypes.

Kelly Johnson had examined a twin-engine jet and proposed it to the USAAF in late 1945, initially with Nathan Price's L-1000

Test pilot Tony LeVier and flight engineer Rudy Thoren stand in
front of the Model 75 Saturn.

engines and subsequently with GE and Westinghouse engines. Working with Hawkins and most of the key players of the Skunk Works
team, Johnson was distressed to find that the close relationships and
efficient (if unorthodox) working methods of the Skunk Works were
difficult to maintain. This would have an impact on later programs,
but would be resolved to Lockheed's ultimate advantage.

A series of designs evolved, including variable geometry (swing-
wing) and delta configurations, with the latter being preferred by the
USAAF. Extensive wind-tunnel tests led them to decide that a conventional fixed, swept wing was most able to meet the desired specifications, which were so altered over time that the competition became
more oriented to a ground-attack plane rather than a long-range penetration fighter. The contradiction in missions could not have been
more marked. A penetration fighter needs lots of fuel, meaning a bigger
airframe designed to obtain maximum range. A close-support aircraft
needs to be agile, able to carry large loads of ordnance externally, and
able to operate out of fields near the front for a quick turnaround. As
a result it has less need for range and can be smaller in size.

The beautiful XR60-1 Constitution required more powerful engines than were available at the time. The Constitution was the largest Lockheed aircraft until the advent of the C-5 Galaxy.

Once underway the P-90 project was beset by a variety of problems, internal and external, that hurt morale and spun the first flight date out to June 3, 1949—nearly four years after Johnson's initial design proposals had been tendered. A long, confusing competition was held against the McDonnell XF-88 and the North American XF-93, a development of the F-86. All three aircraft had difficulties during the competition, but the XF-88 was ultimately declared the winner on September 11, 1950. In time, it too was canceled, but it led directly to the successful F-101.

The XF-90 proved to be a handsome aircraft, superbly built, but overweight, 50 percent heavier than the XF-88. It was thus comparatively underpowered and, most important, conceived for one mission and evaluated against another. It was with more relief than sadness that Lockheed put it to bed. One of the prototypes survived three atomic blasts during testing in 1952 in Nevada, while the other was used as a structural test specimen by NACA.*

XFV-1 Since the days of Leonardo da Vinci, the prospect of a vertical-rising aircraft has had a gut appeal, and to no one more than the United States Navy, which in the postwar years envisioned vertical-takeoff

*The National Advisory Committee for Aeronautics (NACA) was the predecessor to the National Aeronautics and Space Administration (NASA).

The desire for a fighter that could take off and land vertically led to the development of the XFV-1 "Pogo Stick." Insufficient power required that the aircraft be tested with a fixed undercarriage for conventional takeoffs and landings.

fighters rising from small platforms to defend the fleet. The advent of jet engines made a vertical-takeoff fighter possible, and when awarded a development contract, Lockheed assigned the task to Art Flock as project engineer in August 1950. Termed a "tail-sitter," the XFV-1 was distinguished by a portly fuselage, stub trapezoidal wings, two huge contrarotating propellers, and a large cruciform tail upon which it rested. The terminally ill-starred Allison XT40 engine of 5,800 shaft horsepower, upon which so many companies forlornly pinned their hopes, provided a 1.2:1 power-to-weight ratio. The contract called for two prototypes.

The basic unsolvable problem was that while it was not especially demanding for the pilot to take off vertically, it was virtually impossible for him to land vertically, particularly onto a pitching deck.

The famous Lockheed test pilot Herman "Fish" Salmon made a first flight on June 16, 1954, the XFV-1 being equipped with a stalky temporary fixed undercarriage to permit a conventional takeoff. No vertical takeoffs or landings were ever attempted at ground level, though these were simulated at altitude. Many transitions from horizontal to hovering flight were made.

The excessively long development program, the failure of the Allison engine to mature to its projected 7,100-shaft horsepower rating, and the inherent landing difficulties caused the program to be canceled on June 16, 1955, to everyone's relief.

Poised for a Noble Future

Lockheed's successes far exceeded the few failures mentioned above, and the strong Lockheed engineering and managerial staff now was poised for the last half of the twentieth century. The importance of the tight security of the original "Skonk Works" was newly appreciated, and would be asserted in the future. Long before the era of very-high-speed flight was signaled to all by the October 14, 1947, breaking of the sound barrier by the Bell XS-1, Lockheed was examining the possibilities of hypersonic flight in a test vehicle for a ramjet engine. The end result would be the X-7, a ramjet test vehicle that would be the small beginning that would lead Lockheed into its tremendous accomplishments in missile manufacture and space flight. The firm would continue to pioneer with aircraft, and some of the very greatest of them were but a short distance into the future. Perhaps most important of all, Lockheed's management was able to mold the synergy of the company's potential, the needs of the cold war, and the unfolding advances in technology into new, virtually unlimited horizons beyond anything that even the great visionary Robert Gross could ever have imagined.

CHAPTER 6

The Skunk Works

The special nature of the fabled Skunk Works requires a digression from the general chronological approach of this book. Conceived, and long desired, by Clarence Johnson, it was brought into being to create the USAAF's first operational jet fighter, the P-80 Shooting Star. Originally termed simply "the experimental group," the organization in time was given the more formal designation Advanced Projects Development, which became a division before being named the Advanced Projects Development Company in 1990.

But in the postwar period, as the P-80 turned from a secret project into a mass-production effort, the physical manifestation of the Skunk Works was allowed to lapse as the inevitable reductions occurred in Lockheed's size and scope. Yet the efficiency—and indeed the conceptual beauty—of the Skunk Works persisted, in large part because of Kelly Johnson's native initiative and penchant for secrecy.

The Skunk Works' philosophy and methodology were applied to other Lockheed projects, including the F-104 fighter, but blossomed in 1954 with the advent of the U-2 program and its concomitant requirement for a secret production line. It has remained in existence ever since, producing the most important and sophisticated aircraft weapon systems in history. All of the major Skunk Works products (those that are not still classified) will be discussed in later chapters.

The impact of the Skunk Works upon Lockheed, the military services, our country, and the world has been so great that it is desirable to look at it in a special way, including an appreciation of several of the top Skunk Works engineers and managers. In many ways, the fortunes and the maturation of the entire Lockheed Company may be found in microcosm in the manner in which these successive managers led the Skunk Works. They created its mystique and they governed both the demands made upon its workers and the rewards that were provided them.

A major difficulty to overcome in this analysis is to give insight into just how towering a personality Kelly Johnson was, without diminishing in any way the large number of extraordinarily talented people who worked with him. Although Kelly Johnson retired in 1975, his presence lingered on, first as a two-day-a-week consultant and then as an almost deified memory after his death in 1990. It is present even today in the thoughts and minds and especially the consciences of current Skunk Works employees.

All of the elements relating to Kelly—his genius, his size, his strength, his personality, his managerial methods—are so much larger than life that it is difficult to relate just how accomplished were other members of the Skunk Works, without seeming to poach on Kelly Johnson's mythic turf. Yet, indisputably, no other aeronautical-engineering organization in the world possessed such a wealth of diverse talent over so extended a period. Hall Hibbard, enormously talented himself, hired Johnson and was his mentor; he recalls that he induced Kelly to lead rather than drive the people who worked for him. Hibbard always said that Johnson could spot trouble better than anyone, that he could "see the air" to determine if the airflow was bad or if there was a flutter problem. But Hibbard gave yet another dimension to Johnson when pressed to state the man's single finest characteristic. Hibbard, the brilliant engineer, was well acquainted with leading industrial, military, and political figures; he had observed Johnson for forty years, and had perhaps as great a knowledge of and appreciation for Johnson's engineering genius as anyone. Yet Hibbard saw in Johnson a noble characteristic that transcended his abilities as an engineer. Choosing his words carefully, Hibbard responded that Johnson "was intensely patriotic . . . a magnificent American." No praise could have pleased Johnson more.

Another great engineer, Willis Hawkins, was Johnson's contemporary, and a fourth leading figure, Ben Rich, worked for Johnson for twenty-five years. Both men were as qualified as Johnson in many ways and excelled him in certain areas—yet both men always made their deference to and appreciation for Johnson very evident.

Hawkins said that Johnson developed a culture of getting things done, in part by swift decision making. When asked if Johnson was stubborn, Hawkins replied he was "stubborn cum laude," but hastened to add that when convinced that he was wrong, Johnson bore no animus and gladly adopted a better suggestion. Hawkins stated that Johnson seized the creative leadership role from Hibbard, who then functioned as the middleman between Johnson and Robert Gross, whose lack of technical background might well have excited Johnson's temper. It was Johnson's failing that he, in Hawkins's words, "was not necessarily a gentleman in all conversations with somebody he felt intellectually impaired, if you will." Gross had the greatest admiration for Hibbard, who became the conduit for matters passing between Johnson and Gross. And, as great as Hawkins's admiration for Johnson is, he always points out that Johnson recognized that he had many good designers working for him. Hawkins considers him to have been the world's all-time-great program manager, who knew when and where to take technical shortcuts to keep a program moving on schedule.

There were many other engineers at Lockheed whose light was contained under the bushel of Kelly Johnson's personality, and who understood and accepted that fact, feeling privileged to work for him. Perhaps the most fortunate (but least noted) aspect of Johnson's ability, personality, and demeanor was their halo effect upon other engineers at the Skunk Works who may have been less gifted than he, or Hawkins or Rich, but were nonetheless capable. (They would not have been there at all had they not been capable, as Johnson would have seen to it personally.) Inspired by Johnson, and given the opportunity to achieve under the projects he conceived, they rose to far greater heights of engineering excellence than they might have done elsewhere under more benign, but less rigorous, leadership.

The degree of security that Johnson insisted on was incredible. Men worked their entire careers at the Skunk Works without ever once telling their wives anything about what they were doing. People who were good friends at the factory, ate lunch together, and shared hobbies like bowling or fishing after work nonetheless maintained an absolute silence on what they were doing at work, even if they worked in adjacent spaces. Security became more than a way of life, it was a code of ethics and honor, and even a trivial breach was not only unacceptable, it was outrageous in the mores of the "Skunks," as they called themselves. Even today, when the demise of the cold war has permitted some of the older stories to be told, veteran Skunks are still obviously uncomfortable discussing things that were once top secret and are now declassified.

In the final analysis, it was psychologically beneficial that this code of silence was preserved so well. It may have been the only thing that prevented such a critical mass of intellectual brilliance—and often larger-than-average human egos—from exploding under the pressure of working for Johnson. Looking back, it is now obvious that the broad spectrum of the Skunk Works' achievements provided more than enough credit to go around for everyone who worked there. For this reason, Kelly Johnson's well-deserved reputation can retain every bit of its sheen, even while the great innovative engineering work done by others is brought to light and praised.

Kelly

Clarence L. "Kelly" Johnson was born in Ishpeming, Michigan, on February 27, 1910, the seventh of the nine children his Swedish immigrant parents would bring into the world. His father, Peter, had come to the United States in about 1890, at the age of twenty-eight; he was an expert carpenter and bricklayer, and from him Kelly gained his appreciation for tools and precision craftsmanship.

Johnson always did well at school, getting excellent grades in everything but gym. His first schoolyard fight came about when a larger boy persisted in calling him "Clara" rather than Clarence, and finally bullied him into a fight. It was a mistake; the smaller Johnson broke the bully's leg, promptly earning the respect of his classmates, who, in the fine logic of the schoolyard, then bestowed the nickname "Kelly" upon him, taking it from a popular song of the time, "Kelly with the Green Necktie."

Johnson's early life was Spartan but rewarding; he worked hard at a variety of tasks, from cutting wood to picking berries, while expanding his horizons at the local library. In that rather cozy pretelevision era, library shelves were filled with the exploits of Tom Swift and other young fictional heroes whose plots centered upon the latest inventions. Kelly devoured these and became fascinated with airplanes, drawing them and subsequently building hundreds of models. He decided at the age of twelve that he would design aircraft, and promptly created his first design—the Merlin I battle plane, placing it in a scrapbook on aviation he created. It was a good effort, rather like a streamlined Bristol fighter of World War I, well proportioned, and, had it been built, it would undoubtedly have flown. He later built a wooden model of it that won him a twenty-five-dollar prize—a huge amount in those days. Some forty years later, his last design, the Lockheed SR-71, would be unlike any aircraft in history, with a performance that surpassed all others—and has yet to be surpassed.

After graduating from Flint Central High School in Flint, Michigan, Johnson attended Flint Junior College and the University of Michigan, graduating from the latter in 1932. He worked hard, and he expected top grades. On the few occasions when he didn't get them, he would argue his case for higher marks—and usually win. It speaks well of his family's industry and prudence—and his own frugal habits—that an immigrant carpenter's son could be allowed to go away to work his way through college. He managed to live a Spartan but interesting life by working a combination of jobs that ranged from washing dishes to subcontracting out the university's wind tunnel for moneymaking projects of his own.

He and his longtime friend and colleague, Donald Palmer, contracted with the then-powerful Studebaker Corporation to test the air resistance of car bodies. The classic Pierce Silver Arrow design was one product of his consulting, while another was the streamlined bodies placed on five 85-percent-stock Studebaker racers for the 1933 Indianapolis 500. Kelly and Palmer had used wooden bodies for their wind-tunnel work, carefully sculpting streamlined shapes to smooth out the airflow. Their design was very successful, reducing air resistance and raising the racers' average speeds about 10 mph (about 10 percent) over the previous year's. One small glitch occurred, however, when the full-sized cars were raced. In the standard racing-car bodies of the time, the wind whistled through the cockpit, blowing away the buildup of engine heat. In Kelly's design, the airflow was so smooth over the bodies that it swept around the open cockpits even as the big Studebaker engine pumped in heat. As a result, the drivers and their mechanics (who rode with them in those days) had to pull into the pits, where slits were hacked into the sides of the bodies to provide ventilation. Nonetheless, all five of the Studebaker racers finished the race, placing seventh, ninth, tenth, eleventh, and twelfth—a good showing for any stable of cars, and particularly fine for semistock racers.

The University of Michigan was good to him (and to Lockheed), and he learned basic skills there that carried him far. He attributed the techniques he devised to use titanium as a basic structural metal in the Blackbird series of aircraft to practices he had picked up while in school.

As previously noted, young Johnson interviewed with Lockheed in 1932, and was told that although there were no current job openings, he should try again. He returned to the University of Michigan and obtained his master of science degree in aeronautical engineering, along with sufficient confidence to go back to Lockheed and not only get a position, but question the first design of its chief engineer, Hall Hibbard.

He was able to get away with this in part because Hibbard was a tolerant, patient man who recognized the fierce integrity and intelligence that emanated from Johnson even as a youth. He had hired Johnson on the basis of his scholastic record and his recommendations, and, as he laughingly recalled later, because they needed another player for their ball team. Kelly Johnson became the sixth engineer on the Lockheed engineering staff.

Physically prepossessing, he seemed much taller than his five-foot-eleven-inch height and much heavier than his two-hundred-plus-pounds weight (in his prime). His posture, walking or sitting behind a desk, was aggressive, leaning forward as if battling a wind—and winning. In his biography, his friend and protégé Ben Rich attributes Johnson's great physical strength to his years of construction work, carrying bricks. Johnson himself said that his ability to win almost every arm-wrestling match came from strength acquired making and putting up laths—the thin narrow boards used to support plaster in the days before drywall. Johnson recalled that he could earn ten dollars by putting up two thousand laths. Inasmuch as putting up each lath involved four to six nails, a tremendous amount of muscle was required.

Kelly Johnson the Husband

Johnson was totally obsessed by his work, and dedicated himself to it almost without respite. It was fortunate that he found in his family life a strength and inspiration that recharged him. It is fair to say that Johnson was coddled at home—he needed to be taken care of, and he was.

His first wife, Althea Louise Young, was the assistant treasurer at Lockheed when they met in 1933. They shared an interest in horseback riding, dancing, and eating well, and made up their minds to marry as soon as Kelly earned enough to support her—he did not want her to work. After a four-year courtship, they were married in 1937.

It was well she did not work, for life with Johnson was a full-time job, given his penchant for overwork, and, later in his life, some health problems. Yet they had a happy life together, first in a home Johnson designed and later on the ranch properties they purchased. The first was the 226-acre Lindero Ranch, about twenty miles from Encino, California, which was ultimately overtaken by suburban creep. They then bought a 2,000-acre spread about thirty miles north of Santa Barbara.

Althea became ill in 1964, and passed away in December 1969, a victim of cancer. Before her death, she had urged Johnson to re-marry—she knew how he needed to have someone smooth out life's ordinary perturbations. He married Maryellen Elberta Meade in May 1971, only to suffer another tragedy. After a year of truly happy companionship, she too became unwell from a preexisting diabetes condition. In a long ordeal, she became progressively more infirm, losing her sight and being confined to a wheelchair after an amputation. She died on October 13, 1980.

During Maryellen's long illness, the Johnsons had been be-friended by Nancy Powers Horrigan, who often took care of her when Kelly was away at work, or when he, too, was ill, for he had suffered from chronic stomach problems as well as having to endure a triple bypass heart operation. In the course of time, Nancy and Kelly had grown close, and they both realized that he needed her companionship to carry on. Despite some concern about the appearance of haste, they decided to marry in November 1980.

The Peers of a Man Who Had No Peers

Johnson's accomplishments during his forty-two years at Lockheed are so formidable that even the simplest recounting of them inevitably seems like gross exaggeration. Therefore, before citing examples

Perhaps the best-known
aeronautical engineer in history,
Kelly Johnson was truly a legend
in his own time.

of his genius, it might be prudent to humanize him by noting that he
was not without fault, and that he was not universally beloved—although he was universally respected. Johnson did not suffer fools at
all, much less gladly; he was often imperious and sometimes rude. He
had a hair-trigger temper and it is said that on occasion he came close
to taking physical action against a response he did not like, and he
certainly threatened to do so many times. He was solicitous of, rather
than averse to, publicity and recognition. Over time, as his long list
of highly distinguished awards grew, he became impatient, and there
was some degree of hubris in his dealings with others. Later in his
career, he sometimes alienated potential customers by telling them
what he knew they needed instead of providing them what they
wanted. He was often correct in his views, but the net result was
detrimental to the corporation he loved. Given the immense pressures
of his job, and the social mores of the time, it should be no surprise
that Johnson occasionally had a bit too much to drink.

Yet there was no one like Kelly Johnson for seeing solutions to
impossible demands and for motivating a workforce to accomplish
otherwise unattainable goals. He was adept at selecting other geniuses
and near geniuses to work with him. Most important, he excelled in
giving the United States weapon systems that were in advance of those

of competitors, sometimes by an incredible margin of *thirty or forty years,* a degree of ascendancy unparalleled in any other scientific discipline.

He possessed an intuitive engineering sense of great precision. He would, and often did, analyze a project and make a preliminary estimate of the work hours involved, and was almost always exactly correct. His intuitive expertise worked even in esoteric areas; he could estimate the temperatures that a leading edge might reach under certain conditions of flight, or the number of cycles that a structure could endure before failure, and almost always he was proved to be correct by later empirical evidence. This certitude would give him the confidence to embark upon seemingly impossible tasks (such as those set for him by the Central Intelligence Agency and the USAF later in his career) and carry them out. It also made him inclined to reject suggestions from others if he did not see their merit at once. He was difficult to convince that he was wrong, but if so convinced, he adopted a better solution with enthusiasm and no rancor. He drove himself harder than anyone, and quite literally lived for his work.

He recorded his work in a daily log that outlines in brilliant simplicity the difficulties and the triumphs implicit in each day's work. It is startling to examine the logbooks and see, for example, how he could visualize a concept for an entirely new aircraft such as the radical A-12 progenitor of the Blackbird family in the most comprehensive detail. He would record his ideas and mathematical calculations in clear, regular handwriting without striking out or overwriting any entries. He would lay out the planform, dimensions, weight, materials, manufacturing times, performance, even the probable problems, in clear, succinct language; his estimates would later prove to be almost exactly on the mark. He did, as Hibbard suggested, "see the air," but he also saw the heat, the strength, the heft, the fatigue, and even elements as esoteric as how the shape would appear on radar.

The proud pantheon of aviation-engineering genius is filled with men and women of great ability. Yet there is a general consensus that one man is without peer, and that man is Kelly Johnson, the only individual ever to win the prestigious Collier Trophy twice—in 1959 for the Lockheed F-104 fighter and in 1964 for the Lockheed YF-12, the predecessor of the SR-71. Such was the force of his personality that he not only imposed it upon the small advanced development group known as the Skunk Works, he extended it throughout the corporation. Further, the culture he created became self-sustaining; after his retirement in 1975 the Skunk Works continued to function in the style that he demanded, even though led by men of very different personalities.

That style was simple, direct, and rigorous; it required the best, most diligent unflagging effort from a small crew of men—it was before the days of equal opportunity—who were carefully selected as the best possible candidates from the general pool of Lockheed engineers. Over time, he evolved a system of fourteen operating rules that have been recounted many times in the past, but never better than in an August 1992 paper prepared by the Lockheed Advanced Development Company, entitled *The Skunk Works Approach to Aircraft Development and Support.*

The report has an almost ingenuous air, noting that Johnson's language might not be entirely applicable to a modern environment, and providing a parenthetical explanation for his straight-from-the-shoulder maxims. As important as these rules are from a program manager's viewpoint, they are even more important from a societal viewpoint, for these are the rules of a company that is part of the military-industrial complex. Further, the rules are those of a company that operates "in the black," i.e., its books are not open to the public or to any but a limited circle in Congress and government. And yet far from exploiting these circumstances to the advantage of the firm, the rules place the greatest demands upon the contractor to deliver the finest product at the lowest cost on the swiftest schedule. Following his rules enabled the Skunk Works to produce results that are the exact opposite of the typical political cartoon showing the bloated capitalist and highly decorated general gorging at the public trough. As a simple example, when the U-2 program was completed, the surprising reliability of the aircraft had resulted in an accumulation of sufficient spare parts to build six additional aircraft. This was done and Kelly was still able to refund $2 million on a $22 million program.

The fourteen points that work so well to the advantage of the nation also work well for Lockheed, for the Skunk Works has always earned a higher rate of return on investment than its other divisions, despite the greater challenges it has faced.

The Fourteen Points

The famous "fourteen points" of Kelly Johnson were not formally set down until the 1950s. They were an amalgamation of his own credo of "Be quick, be quiet, be on time" and a series of rules that he and Don Palmer, his friend from the wind tunnel at the University of Michigan, created for the rapid execution of the P-80 project. These provided for the close interrelationship of the project engineer, the men cutting metal and building the aircraft, purchasing, and the customer. They also emphasized a minimum amount of drawings and paperwork. The drawings and memoranda that were created, however, had to be clear, concise, and comprehensive.

In typical Johnson fashion, these fourteen rules are short and concise, yet embrace all aspects of Skunk Works effort, including program management, organization, contractor-customer relationships, documentation, customer reporting, specifications, engineering drawings, funding, cost control, subcontractor inspection, testing, security, and management compensation. Reading the rules easily evokes the image of Johnson the visionary at his best—creative, responsible, determined, frugal, comprehensive, and, unquestionably, autocratic. Johnson's basic rules follow, with the later 1992 Lockheed expansion of their meaning in italics. The author will occasionally insert his own comments in parentheses after Lockheed's statements.

1. The Skunk Works' manager must be delegated practically complete control of his program in all aspects. *It is essential that the program manager have authority to make decisions quickly regarding technical, finance, schedule, or operations matters.*

2. Strong *but small* project offices must be provided both by the customer and contractor. *The customer program manager must have similar authority to that of the contractor.* (The proviso on the size of the customer's project office was difficult to enforce, and totally opposite to the prevailing trend in military and/or intelligence organizations. In some instances, the size of the customer's project grew so rapidly—and turned over so often—that the essential magic of the Skunk Works was diluted.)

3. The number of people having any connection with the project must be restricted in an almost vicious manner. Use a small number of good people (10 to 26 percent compared to the so-called normal systems. *Bureaucracy makes unnecessary work and must be controlled brutally.* (Following this rule carefully was one of the prime reasons that the Skunk Works so often returned a higher return on investment than other divisions.)

4. A very simple drawing and drawing release system with great flexibility for making changes must be provided. *This permits early work by manufacturing organizations and schedule recovery if technical risks involve failures.* (The value of this rule is indisputable, but counter to the massive issue of Air Force regulations [375 series]. These sought to establish an absolute configuration control system, and were ascendant just at the time that Kelly Johnson began having difficulties selling his concepts to the Air Force.)

5. There must be a minimum of reports required, but important work must be recorded thoroughly. *Responsible management does not require massive technical and information systems.* (This rule, in its turn, flew in the face of the massive reporting made possible by the advent of computers. Given that perhaps 90 percent of all computer-generated reports proceed from computer to wastebasket without being read, rule 5 is more important today than in the carefree precomputer days when it was created. Unfortunately, myriad government requirements make adherence to the rule increasingly difficult.)

6. There must be a monthly cost review covering not only what has been spent and committed, but also projected costs to the conclusion of the program. Don't have the books ninety days late and don't surprise the customer with sudden overruns. *Responsible management does require operation within the resources available.*

7. The contractor must be delegated and must assume more than normal responsibility to get good vendor bids for the subcontract on the project. Commercial bid procedures are very often better than military ones. *Essential freedom to use the best talent available and operate within the resources available.* (The italicized comment seems to be a non sequitur. This was indeed a pioneering insight, one that preceded a revolution in quality-control concepts.)

8. The inspection system as currently used by the Skunk Works, which has been approved by both the Air Force and Navy, meets the intent of existing military requirements and should be used on new projects. Push more basic inspection responsibility back to subcontractors and vendors. Don't duplicate so much inspection. *Even the commercial world recognizes that quality is in design and responsible operations—not inspections.*

9. The contractor *must* be delegated the authority to test his final product in flight; he can and must test it in the initial stages. If he doesn't he rapidly loses his competency to design other vehicles. *Critical, if new technology and the attendant risks are to be rationally accommodated.* (This is another area that provoked Kelly's rage when his Air Force customer stipulated that flight tests would be done by Air Force pilots.)

10. The specification applying to the hardware must be agreed to in *advance* of contracting. The Skunk Works practice of having a specification section stating clearly which important military specifications will not knowingly be complied with and reasons therefore is highly recommended. *Standard specifications inhibit new technology and innovation and are frequently obsolete.* (Military project offices are staffed by human beings with their own agendas and priorities; the desire to "hobby-shop" a new aircraft with changes is ever present, and rule 10 provides a means for inhibiting this. One of the greatest achievements of the Skunk Works has been the reduction in specification size. Whereas the C-5 and the F-15 required literal carloads of paperwork to convey the specifications, the Skunk Works tailored specifications on the 1954 U-2 to 35 pages; the more complex SR-71 of 1962 required 54 pages. The Have Blue prototypes of 1975 got by with 25 pages; the F-117 required 77 pages in 1977; and the TR-1 [an advanced version of the U-2] needed 91 pages in 1979.)

11. Funding a program must be timely so that the contractor doesn't have to keep running to the bank to support government projects. *Rational management requires knowledge of, and freedom to use, the resources originally committed.* (An almost wistful rule, and one violated most often because controlling funds not only controls the project, it controls the people and the organization. Management is not always rational outside of the Skunk Works.)

12. There must be a mutual trust between the customer project organization and the contractor with very close cooperation and liaison on a day-to-day basis. This cuts down misunderstanding and correspondence to an absolute minimum. *The goals of the customer and producer should be the same—get the job done well.* (As things transpired over time, the Skunk Works under Kelly began to lose the mutual trust between contractor and customer. Part of the problem was that the customer [particularly the USAF] changed its representatives too frequently, so that a working rapport was difficult to establish. But another part of the problem was what only can be called hubris on the part of Kelly, who often did know better than his customers what they really needed, but was unable to convince them of the fact diplomatically. Later Skunk Works managers would be charged to work more closely with the customers.)

13. Access by outsiders to the project and its personnel must be strictly controlled by appropriate security measures. *This is a program manager's responsibility even if no program security demands are made—a cost avoidance measure.* (There is almost a naive, plaintive quality to this rule, given the monstrously difficult security regulations that external bureaucratic forces later caused to be imposed, and which cost so much in time, money, and morale.)

14. Because only a few people will be used in engineering and most other areas, ways must be provided to reward good performance by pay *not based on the number of personnel supervised.* (Kelly's italics.) *Responsible management must be rewarded and responsible management does not permit the growth of bureaucracies.* (The almost pious italicized addition overlooks the stark truth of rule 14: people build empires to get more pay. Lockheed's management wisely saw to it that Skunk Works personnel received higher compensation than their colleagues in similar jobs in other divisions of the corporation.)

The success of the rules has been demonstrated over the years, but it goes without saying that the rules themselves would be meaningless if the production process they governed were not driven by the burning genius of Kelly Johnson and his successors. And while succinct and simply stated, the rules embraced all of the myriad elements that made up the functioning Skunk Works.

Less Is More

The typical Skunk Works program office is kept small. Even for so sophisticated a program as the F-117A stealth fighter, the Lockheed management team never exceeded thirty people. In this instance, the corresponding Air Force System Program Office (SPO) was of about the same size. When, as was the case with the F-117A, the Skunk Works is also a production facility, the number of employees might reach four thousand—all carefully selected from the best resources the parent company has to offer. The support that is typically organic to a program office—health and safety, legal, environmental, etc.—is provided to the Skunk Works program managers from centralized company sources.

Kelly Johnson was a master of many disciplines, and the Skunk Works' engineering practice still requires its engineers to be a cut above mere specialists in their fields. Although engineering design is crucial, it is equally important to take production and maintenance factors into consideration early on. Engineering drawings are required to have all necessary information included, from procurement through manufacture, test, inspection, acceptance, and maintenance. The process is swift, with drawings released within a day, because engineers have direct interface with their manufacturing and supply counterparts, and can alter drawings on the spot to meet needed changes.

In some respects, the Skunk Works' manufacturing process anticipated by forty years the situation that currently prevails in the world, that is, the extensive use of technology demonstrators, low rates of procurement for new systems, and extensive upgrading of existing systems. The use of elaborate mock-ups was almost always avoided; with today's computer-aided design and manufacturing systems, they are rendered almost unnecessary.

The Skunk Works tests the components of its system often and early, and in an integrated fashion, to determine how they are mutually affected in operation. A standard feature of Skunk Works operations that is being adopted widely throughout the industry is the integrated laboratory testing of system avionics, including sensors, core avionics, cockpit controls and displays, and software, to uncover problems early.

Because the products of the Skunk Works, such as the U-2 or the SR-71, are produced in relatively small numbers, it is often more cost-effective for the customer to contract with Lockheed for field service support. In the case of the F-117A, the Air Force elected to create its own maintenance and support organization. Like all the armed services, however, the Air Force has a relatively high turnover rate in personnel, and getting F-117A maintenance and support up to the desired standard required extra effort and periodic assistance from Lockheed.

The Payoff

A simple chart reveals with startling clarity the speed with which the Skunk Works incorporated outstanding examples of advancing aviation technology.

Aircraft	Year	Months from Go-ahead to First Flight	Technological Advances
XP-80	1944	4 (143 days)	Jet propulsion
XF-104	1954	13	Mach 2 aerodynamics; sophisticated engine inlets; Gatling gun
U-2	1955	8	Ultrahigh altitude; lightweight structure
A-12	1962	32	Titanium structure; advanced propulsion; Mach 3 speed
SR-71	1964	24	Same as A-12 with sophisticated guidance and sensor packages
Have Blue	1977	18	Stealth
F-117A	1981	30	Stealth; precision guided munitions; passive fire control
YF-22	1990	46	Stealth; supersonic cruise, agility; multiple weapons capability

In assessing these figures, it might be remembered that it typically takes sixty months for General Motors or Ford to develop and introduce a new-model automobile.

Those Who Came After

Kelly reached the age of sixty-five in 1975, and, under Lockheed rules, had to retire. The man he personally picked to succeed him was Ben Rich, with whom he had worked for twenty-five years. The men could not have been more unlike in personality. Where Johnson was aloof, withdrawn, and forbidding, Rich was gregarious, outgoing, and inviting of friendly visits. Kelly's progress down the hallway to his office was followed by a wave of silence as people scuttled to the side; Ben's progress was followed by growing echoes of laughter from each office door as he improved on the current bawdy story he was telling. Kelly liked to dictate exactly how work was to proceed; Rich preferred to outline the goal and leave the methods to the engineer. Kelly rarely admitted that he could learn from his engineers; Rich made their teaching him a condition of their employment.

Yet Rich had other qualities, and, as we shall see, they were qualities needed by the Skunk Works and by Lockheed when he succeeded Kelly. Most important of all, Rich maintained the Skunk Works tradition of excellence in advanced projects, as would his successors, Sherman Mullin and Jack Gordon, both of whom we'll meet later.

The environment in which the Skunk Works did business changed drastically after Johnson's departure, and Rich found that some of his predecesor's rules were obsolete. In Rich's opinion, the advent of computer-aided design and production programs stifled creativity and forced many engineers to change from being system engineers to specialists. It also mitigated the utility of Kelly's rule 4. In a similar way, rule 11 was made obsolete by the sheer number of government agencies, bureaucrats, and regulations, which forced cost sharing for program development and required potential competitors to work together on joint programs.

Rich also developed his own management philosophy that was in some ways diametrically opposed to Johnson's. He believed in one strong leader (himself) but one who relies on a dependable staff to develop alternatives to solve problems. That leader must also concentrate on developing teamwork, and have the right to pick his own personnel. Rich believed strongly in delegation—he preferred to give a task to a trusted subordinate, and leave him to get on with it. He avoided directing every detail of a project, realizing the enormous psychic and moral value obtained by an engineer creating his own solution to a problem.

Far more interpersonally aware than Johnson, Rich systematically praised people for their efforts, and publicly gave credit for successes. Yet he could be stern; any ethical or professional lapse was swiftly dealt with.

Johnson and Rich were very much alike in one respect: they thoroughly enjoyed their work, but they registered their pleasure differently. Johnson internalized the joy he felt in working, maintaining an external cold intensity that ceaselessly bore down on the objective. Rich was a more gregarious man, with a happy, joking manner that served to lighten everyone's spirits. Both men served the Skunk Works well.

The Skunk Works Today

Many elements have combined that might have changed the very nature of the Skunk Works. The end of the cold war removed the single enemy, the Soviet Union, against whom most of its efforts had been directed. The consequent downsizing of the armed services and the reduction in defense spending also had effect. The fact that it became a separate company, rather than a division, in 1992 also altered some of its method of operation. And, in 1995, the merger of equals resulting in the creation of the Lockheed Martin Corporation brought about further changes, including, for the first time, the pursuit of a commercial, nonsecret program, the X-33 prototype for the space shuttle replacement.

Yet the heart and soul of the Skunk Works remain the same, as do the attitudes of its people. The same desire for undiluted excellence at a reasonable price is still there, as is the pride in being part of an aeronautical tradition. And, although no one can admit it, there must be, just as in the past, secret programs going on, still in the black, ahead of all others, and bearing the proud logo of the Skunk Works.

In the course of the following chapters, we'll pick up the story of the people and the products of the Skunk Works as they evolved over time.

CHAPTER 7

Progress at Burbank

Lockheed had grown up in Burbank. Allan Lockheed moved the firm from rented quarters in Hollywood to Empire Avenue in Burbank in 1928, where it shared a building with the Mission Glass Works. There the first airstrip, all of 1,500 feet long, was graded. When Robert Gross and his backers took over the moribund Lockheed firm in 1932, they occupied the same site. By 1936, Gross was able to buy the plant he had been leasing; in 1939, he built a 750,000-square-foot plant for its subsidiary, the Vega Airplane Company, about one mile away and adjacent to the Union Air Terminal. It would become known as Plant A-1.

A continual process of expansion followed for many years to meet wartime demands. In 1940, Lockheed purchased the Union Air Terminal (previously owned by United Air Lines) for $1.5 million, an amazing figure in terms of a forty-thousand-dollar start-up company being able to swing such a deal almost off the back of its hand. The field was renamed Lockheed Air Terminal, and operated as a subsidiary. Cy Chappellet was named president, following the pattern set at Vega, and underlining the need for a corporate umbrella to manage the expansion of companies. The purchase was a true real estate success story; in 1978, Lockheed sold the facility to the Hollywood-Burbank Airport Authority for $51 million. Even when discounted for inflation, it was a very nice profit.

Wartime expansion has been discussed previously; Lockheed reached a peak of 7.7 million square feet by 1943, a 65-fold increase! One of the unique facets of the wartime plant planning was the creation of an enormous camouflage system in which a miniature suburban/rural area was created on a chicken-wire-and-canvas structure above the plant. Had any Japanese bombers appeared, they would not have seen the Lockheed plant, but instead, houses, trees, and cows. At least, that was the hope.

It was accepted as routine at the time that Lockheed would own, rather than lease, these massive facilities, accepting the attendant maintenance costs. This point, innocuous then, would loom large later in major decisions on Lockheed's operations when it operated large leased facilities.

As the Lockheed Corporation grew, expanding to, for example, Marietta, Georgia, and Sunnyvale, California, the corporate headquarters grew more powerful. A clear distinction had to be drawn between the Lockheed Aircraft Corporation (CALAC), which was in the business of making aircraft, and the Lockheed Corporation (CORLAC), the umbrella for all its operating companies. Being located on the same field, and even in the same building, CALAC would get more than it felt was its share of top management attention. The main offices of the two organizations, CALAC and CORLAC, were separated by two massive swinging doors, and the phrase "smashing through the swinging doors" came to indicate a visit—usually unpleasant—by corporate management. Because of their distance, plants in Georgia and Sunnyvale, California, were not similarly afflicted.

There was another reason besides proximity that caused Lockheed's top management to lavish attention on LAC. The Burbank plant was building the kind of airplanes that Lockheed loved to build—advanced fighters, exotic Skunk Works products, and airliners. The firm had an almost unreasoning fondness for the latter, given that it had never made a profit on its civil airliners, although they traditionally became moneymakers when adapted to a military role. Not

As Kelly Johnson was to engineering at Lockheed, so also was Lockheed's founder, Robert Ellsworth Gross, to management. Gross was beloved by his employees and highly respected in the industry.

even the company's pride-and-joy airliner, the Constellation, made money—until military production orders came along.

The story of Lockheed necessarily revolves around its people and their products—planes, missiles, satellites, and more. And, as its leaders determined its products, it is instructive to match the leaders and the products they chose to back with the progress of the company.

At Burbank, the Lockheed tradition was to build airplanes that were technically advanced and endowed with performance that outstripped those of competitors. It was implicitly a risky policy, for the chances of failure with a very advanced aircraft are naturally greater than with a more conservative design. Some of the risk was minimized because Lockheed's management had remained amazingly stable over the years, with Robert Gross staying firmly in control. Gross, while not an obsessive workaholic like Haughton, nonetheless remained fully focused, eschewing hobbies and travel, divining what the next generation of aircraft should be, and, always, concentrating on the well-being of the Lockheed family. Gross was chairman of the board of directors from December 1933 until he died, much beloved by family, friends, and industry colleagues, on September 3, 1961, a victim of pancreatic cancer.

His brother Courtlandt remained his able number two from June 26, 1940, on, when Courtie became president of the old Vega Airplane

Company. When that firm was absorbed in 1943, he became a corporate vice president and general manager. He was promoted to executive vice president of the corporation in 1952 and then to president in 1956. He succeeded his brother as chairman on September 13, 1961. Courtlandt Gross would serve as chairman until May 2, 1967, when Haughton succeeded him.

During the twenty-two postwar years of the Gross brothers' reign as top management, the Lockheed Corporation blossomed. As will be shown in subsequent chapters, the corporate character would be diversified and refined by its expansion in Georgia, Sunnyvale, and elsewhere. All the while, Lockheed-California, as the "home plant" in Burbank was termed, would continue to make history with advanced designs, troubled airliners, and outstanding military aircraft. The design, testing, and production of some of these, such as the F-80, Constellation, and Neptune, have been previously discussed, but as the 1950s arrived, new and more exotic aircraft were in the works.

These aircraft would have a crucial importance and be utterly different in their impact than previous planes from Lockheed. In the past, Lockheeds had often affected aviation history; in the future, certain Lockheeds would affect world history.

The Skunk Works Rides Again:
The Lockheed F-104

Although Lockheed possessed a host of excellent engineers and designers who were assigned to important duties, there is no question that the Skunk Works, as led, driven, inspired, cajoled, and cuffed by Kelly Johnson, was the paramount force in creating new and advanced aircraft products. Like a booming bass drum in a marching band, Johnson set a fast pace for others to keep up with or be left behind in the dust. The men who worked for him picked up his tempo and passed it on. There was a resonance to the energy and thrust of the Skunk Works that permeated the Burbank plant. Fortunately, the top managers at Lockheed—the Gross brothers, Haughton, and Kotchian—were protected in large part by Hall Hibbard's ability to handle the raw energy Johnson radiated, and so they supported Johnson's efforts with the necessary equipment, finances, and marketing. In another, less understanding environment, Kelly Johnson might never have achieved what he did. For example, it is hard to imagine his reaching the same peaks at Boeing, where his contemporaries would have been brilliant engineers like Edward C. Wells, George Schairer, George Martin, and Jack Steiner, among others. At Boeing, people characteristically worked in a calm, collegial atmosphere, no less demanding, but lacking the freewheeling flamboyance of the Skunk Works.

Johnson had noted the excellent performance of the MiG-15 fighter in Korea, and saw it generate a groundswell of interest in the lightweight fighter all around the world. The arguments for a lightweight fighter were appealing—then and now. A lightweight fighter would be less expensive to buy, build, and maintain *only* if the designer chose to cut back on certain features of larger fighters, e.g., less fuel, less armament, and less radar, in order to meet the reduced weight goals.

Johnson intended to design an air-superiority fighter, one that would secure dominance over the enemy in the classic dogfights that had characterized both World War II and the Korean War. Initially, his concept was difficult to sell to the United States Air Force, which traditionally preferred larger fighters with longer range, redundant systems, and multiple missions—in short, a heavyweight fighter.

Johnson understood the counterargument. There were certain fixed elements of design that would always be proportionately larger in a small aircraft than in a large one, and thus impair the performance of a smaller fighter. These included the percentage relationship of the weight of certain specified equipment (radar, radios, guns, etc.) to the total weight of the airplane. The size of the pilot, and for good visibility, the size of the canopy, were also a "given" that could not be reduced. Jet engines were still in a relatively new state of development, and more thrust was usually obtained with a bigger engine, which in turn meant larger size, more weight, and increased fuel consumption— meaning more fuel, more fuel tanks, more plumbing, and so on.

Yet Johnson believed these obstacles could be overcome, not least because test data from the Douglas X-3 Stiletto research plane had been provided by the USAF. The X-3 had been a failure because of its engine installation, but the program clearly demonstrated that short, very thin, straight wings were appropriate for the supersonic regime. These data had been corroborated by Lockheed's own experience with the X-7 test vehicle. Johnson intended to apply this information to a new jet-fighter design, the CL-246, using razor-thin (and razor-sharp!) wings which were only 3 percent as thick as their chord (roughly, the width of the wing).

Johnson was not only a brilliant engineer, but also a brilliant salesman. In November 1952, he sent an unsolicited proposal to Lieutenant General Donald L. Putt in the Pentagon, where unsolicited proposals are often given short shrift. The subject of such proposals is usually not covered by an existing requirement, and existing requirements are almost always in excess of available funds. Unsolicited proposals carry a hazard to the issuing company as well; if successful, they can generate a competition with other contractors, the outcome of which is uncertain.

Yet Putt was a brilliant thinker who would do well in the military and in his subsequent civilian career. He was well versed in research and development, and he was willing to take risks—particularly when Kelly Johnson was involved. A General Operational Requirement was created, and three other manufacturers—North American, Northrop, and Republic—submitted entries. Lockheed won the competition, and a letter contract was issued on March 12, 1953, for two prototype XF-104 aircraft.

The Lockheed team's design was breathtaking, calling for a Mach 2 capability at combat altitudes over sixty thousand feet. Dogfights were foreseen to be of short duration at Mach 2, and so a new gun was installed, the six-barrel, 20-mm Vulcan cannon, popularly termed the "Gatling gun." It was a first step in the right direction, but F-104 armament would require a new fire control system and missiles to be fully effective.

Johnson and Hibbard had created the initial proposal, receiving support from a strong team that included Willis Hawkins and Gene Frost as deputy design managers. Other members included the veterans Irv Culver, Dick Heppe, and Philip Colman. Work on the engine installation was assigned to a relative newcomer who was in the process of making a name for himself, Ben Rich. William Ralston was named chief project engineer. A formal Skunk Works modus operandi was instituted with the same ground rules that had been used on the P-80 program.

The stunning single-engine XF-104 prototype appeared to be a simple aircraft, but appearances were deceiving. Johnson selected a midwing configuration, which was rarely used on fighters because of structural considerations. He attached the tiny thin wings (which extended only seven feet on each side of the fuselage!) to the XF-104's rather slender engine inlet ducts, which in turn were attached to the fuselage. The midwing position gave 12 percent less drag than an otherwise similar low-wing installation. The vertical surfaces were very tall, with the horizontal stabilizer mounted almost at the top. To offset the adverse roll anticipated with rudder deflection, the wings were given cathedral (angled down) rather than the normal dihedral (angled up).

The F-104 was put through an intensive wind-tunnel program, using both Lockheed and the National Advisory Committee for Aeronautics (NACA) facilities. Flutter became a dreaded engineering complication almost as soon as aircraft speeds exceeded 150 mph, and the supersonic F-104 promised to have its share of problems. Extensive studies helped determine the relative placement of wing and tail surfaces, as well as the positive effects of using tip tanks, so that production F-104s were almost exempt from flutter.

Johnson envisioned the use of Gerhard Neumann's advanced General Electric J79 engine in production models of the F-104, but was forced to install the less powerful 10,500-pound-thrust Wright J65-B-6 turbojet in the first prototype. The first XF-104 flew on March 4, 1954, with the veteran test pilot Tony LeVier at the controls.

The aircraft's performance, even with the less powerful engine, was exceptional. Testing proceeded swiftly, despite the loss of the second prototype on April 18, when test pilot Herman "Fish" Salmon became the first to use the F-104's controversial downward-ejection seat. The occasion arose when firing the gun shook the latches for the fuselage panel under the ejection seat, blowing it out. Salmon was wearing a pressure suit; his face mask fogged and his head was immobilized. He could see the left horizon, and keep the aircraft relatively level, but could not determine his direction. A hurried conversation with Tony LeVier resulted in a decision to eject.

Seventeen YF-104s were ordered as service test aircraft. These were substantially redesigned to accommodate the General Electric J79 engine of 9,380 pounds of thrust dry and 14,800 pounds with afterburner. A special air intake with half-cone center bodies was created to accommodate the new engine's voracious appetite for air (and fuel), and the cockpit was redesigned to accommodate an upward-firing ejection seat. These aircraft established many new records, including an altitude record of 91,249 feet, set by Major Howard C. Johnson on May 7, 1958, and a closed-course speed record of 1,404.19 mph set by Captain Walter W. Irwin on May 16.

The USAF production orders that followed successful tests soon mounted to a total of 722 Starfighters, as the aircraft was called. The first order was for 17 YF-104 service trial aircraft. Despite the F-104's sizzling Mach 2 performance, the Tactical Air Command was in the process of changing its requirements, having a new charter to carry tactical nuclear missiles. As a result, Air Force orders were cut back to a total of 296, including 153 F-104As, 26 F-104Bs, 77 F-104Cs, and 21 F-104Ds.

The USAF had in fact held true to its heavy-fighter bias, and with reason. It was the nature of the USAF mission to have to penetrate deep within an enemy country, engage in air battle, and return. The F-104 did not have the range for this mission, and it was not adaptable to the heavy bomb loads carried by rival aircraft such as the Republic F-105, whose empty weight was more than twice that of the Starfighter.

Fortunately for Lockheed and NATO, European countries did need a fighter with the F-104's characteristics. The aircraft was eased into European service under the Military Assistance Program and in buys for the German Air Force. Eventually, the aircraft was built under license in Belgium, Canada, Germany, Italy, Japan, and the Netherlands. A substantial coproduction effort was undertaken for two-seat versions with Belgium, Germany, and the Netherlands. The F-104 had a long series of accidents in Germany until adequate training was provided to the pilots and adequate training programs were established.

The most important version of the Starfighter was the F-104G, of which 1,127 were built, including those manufactured in Europe and Canada. The first F-104G built by Lockheed and first flown on June 7, 1960, featured a more powerful engine and a different mission. Instead of being a lightweight air-superiority fighter, the F-104G was conceived as a multirole, all-weather fighter, the latter capability conferred by a far more capable electronics suite.

The F-104G's empty weight had climbed only about 600 pounds over the initial-production F-104As, but its gross weight had risen by 3,200 pounds, primarily because of an increased weapons capability. The F-104 was now in the same weight category as the Republic F-84F Thunderjet.

Yet the design still had growth potential. The Italian Air Force worked with Lockheed to create the F-104S, which had capability both as an interceptor and as a ground-attack aircraft, with an added reconnaissance role. The last of 246 F-104Ss was delivered in 1980— twenty-seven years after the Lockheed design had been selected for production.

The Starfighter saw limited combat in Vietnam. Fourteen foreign nations operated the F-104: Belgium, Canada, Denmark, Germany,

The highly advanced Lockheed F-104G was used effectively by the new German Luftwaffe.

Greece, Italy, Japan, Jordan, the Netherlands, Norway, Pakistan, Spain, Taiwan, and Turkey. In every air force in which the Starfighters were operated, their pilots were considered to have the "hottest" airplane.

Curiously enough, it might be said that the two greatest contributions that the F-104 design made to the USAF were entirely derivative. The first was to institutionalize the methods of the Skunk Works as a permanent feature at Lockheed. The second was to serve as a departure point for what would become the first of the two most significant reconnaissance planes in history, the Lockheed U-2.

The U-2 would bring changes that seemed to contradict the Skunk Works' experimental nature: the requirement for full-scale production of an aircraft with unprecedented—and what many considered unachievable—performance.

The U-2

Gathering intelligence on the Soviet Union proved to be far more difficult for the United States than it had been to gather intelligence on Japan during World War II. The vast size of the country, the traditional Russian mind-set, and Soviet counterintelligence efforts left the United States virtually void of information at the most critical period of its history. Numerous efforts were made to probe the borders of the gigantic country with various types of intelligence-gathering planes, and several losses occurred. But the heart of the country was still a mystery. John McMahon, of whom we'll learn more later, was the former deputy director of the Central Intelligence Agency as well as president of the Lockheed Missiles and Space Company. McMahon recalls that much of the anxiety generated by the cold war stemmed from this lack of visibility into the Soviet Union. Our clandestine intelligence amounted to nothing, and the best information we had from defectors was always stale. The concern about the bomber and missile gap was real, and there was an imperative need to obtain hard intelligence on Communist activities.

The Soviet Union had exploded its first hydrogen bomb on August 12, 1953, years in advance of the time that the United States thought it possible. A new heavy bomber, the Myasishchev M-4 (code-named Bison in NATO, called Molot [hammer] by the Soviets) made its debut to the world over Red Square on May 1, 1954. It was an extraordinary effort even, as was discovered much later, if it did not fully meet its design requirements. The rapid rate of Soviet rocket experiments resulted in the launch of *Sputnik* in October 1957, an event that would shock the world.

Thus it seemed evident that, for the first time since 1812, a foreign power would soon possess the means to attack the homeland of the United States. And such an attack would not be a raiding party, with the burning of the White House as its most heinous offense. Popular magazine and newspaper accounts superimposed the postblast image of Hiroshima on aerial photos of New York, Washington, and other cities to give an approximation of the devastating damage to be expected from such an attack.

It became absolutely necessary to create an aircraft that could fly over the Soviet Union on strategic photoreconnaissance missions to determine how close the enemy was to launching an attack. The risk was great, for the ever-distrustful Soviet leaders remembered that Germany had done exactly the same thing prior to its June 22, 1941, invasion.

Fortunately, at the same time that such reconnaissance became an inevitable military requirement, technology had evolved to make it just possible, and Major John Seaberg, working at Wright-Patterson

Air Force Base, began advocating such a design. He saw that the potential for jet-engine operation at high altitude was becoming better understood, and the basic airframe design necessary was clearly within the state of the art. The aircraft potential was matched by three simultaneous developments in the requisite on-board equipment: Dr. Edwin Land (of Polaroid fame) had developed high-resolution cameras able to use new Hycon Corporation lenses, and Eastman Kodak had created the necessary Mylar-based film.

In March 1953, Seaberg helped the Air Force establish design requirements for a weapon system that would have the capability to undertake missions of a 1,500-mile radius, at an altitude of at least seventy thousand feet, carrying up to seven hundred pounds of payload, that is, sophisticated cameras for photoreconnaissance. Weight considerations dictated a single-place aircraft, although this placed inordinate demands on the pilot.

It was assumed that the aircraft would be difficult to detect and impossible to intercept. Three companies were invited to bid on Weapon System MX-2147, code-named Bald Eagle: Bell, Fairchild, and Martin. Larger companies such as Boeing and Lockheed were excluded on the basis that the smaller firms would give the project a higher priority. By early 1954, the Martin entry, a highly modified version of the Canberra bomber with a much larger wing and using Pratt & Whitney J57 engines, was accepted as an interim measure, twenty RB-57Ds being ordered. The rather ungainly-looking Fairchild entry was dropped.

The winning Bell entry was designated the X-16; when the contract was subsequently signed in September 1954, twenty-eight were ordered. Construction got under way immediately upon signing. The X-16 (the designation was selected for security reasons) was a very advanced aircraft with a fragile, foreign appearance, not unlike a very refined Bison. Its long wings seemed disproportionately wide for its sailplane heritage, while its fuselage seemed to be at once too short and too slender. J57 engines were planned, and it was to have an in-flight refueling capability. The contract meant a great deal to Bell, which had no conventional aircraft in production and was moving steadily toward becoming a specialist manufacturer of experimental research planes and helicopters.

But the Air Force had not reckoned with Kelly Johnson.

A Private Offering

Johnson was often intuitively aware of the military's requirements, often before the military was. He had begun design work in 1953 to see if the existing F-104 configuration could be modified to the high-altitude, long-range reconnaissance role, assigning Phil Colman and Gene Frost of the preliminary design department to the task.

Under the company designation CL-282, the Skunk Works team developed an aircraft with a very long, high-aspect-ratio wing (ten to one) mated to a fuselage and empennage essentially similar to those of the XF-104. Like the earlier Messerschmitt Me 163 Komet rocket plane (and the French Sud Est S.E. 5000 Baroudeur), the CL-282 was to use a jettisonable wheeled dolly for takeoff, and skids for landing, saving the weight and space required for a conventional landing gear. Unlike the X-16, the cockpit was to be unpressurized, the pilot relying on a full-pressure suit and helmet. The CL-282 was not yet the U-2— but it was an attention getter.

At this stage of his career Johnson was still warmly received by his Air Force colleagues, and he made preliminary contacts with the movers and shakers, including then–brigadier general Bernard Schriever. With their encouragement, he prepared a detailed proposal that was as advanced in its business sense as in its engineering, for he offered to have Lockheed take complete maintenance and servicing responsibilities for the aircraft in the field. This was a new concept and one that would later prove invaluable in other programs.

Johnson's proposal arrived on May 18, 1954, two months after the X-16 had been selected. Not surprisingly, it was rejected, in part because a selection had already been made, but also because Johnson had picked the General Electric J73 engine as the power plant. Other men might have been discouraged. Kelly Johnson persisted, going, as he so often did, to people at the very top.

Among these were Dr. Joseph V. Charyk (then in charge of the Central Intelligence Agency's research programs and later undersecretary of the Air Force) and Trevor Gardner, the brilliant, acerbic assistant secretary of the Air Force for research and development. Gardner, with Schriever, would mastermind the USAF intercontinental ballistic missile (ICBM) programs.

The president of Massachusetts Institute of Technology, James R. Killian, chaired the President's Science Advisory Committee, called, naturally enough, the Killian committee. That group, with its absolutely first-rate scientists, voiced its concern about North America's vulnerability to a surprise Soviet ICBM attack. It advocated an immediate acceleration of American ICBM and IRBM (intermediate range ballistic missile) programs and put forward a requirement to obtain hard intelligence on Soviet capabilities and targets. The concept of a high-altitude reconnaissance aircraft that would traverse the Soviet Union received approval from both President Eisenhower and CIA Director Allen Dulles. Their participation in a program of this nature meant that the security requirements would be extraordinary.

In a subsequent series of top-level meetings, analysis of the competing aircraft showed that the Lockheed CL-282 would be competitive if redesigned to accommodate the J57 engine. The decisive factor was Kelly Johnson's pledge to have an aircraft in the air eight months after go-ahead, a reflection both of the urgency of the situation and Johnson's unbridled confidence in his team. Richard Bissell, an economist, was nominated as Dulles's special assistant to direct the CIA's program, code-named Aquatone. Bissell's Air Force counterpart was to be Colonel Osmond J. "Ozzie" Ritland. (Later, Brigadier General Leo P. Geary would become the USAF point man.) These men would work with Lockheed on even more crucial programs in the not-too-distant future. Trevor Gardner visited Lockheed on December 9, 1954, to give formal authorization to proceed.

In his memoirs, Kelly recalls lunching with a large group that included Air Force Secretary Harold Talbott and CIA Director Dulles. Asked bluntly why he thought Lockheed could build twenty airplanes for about $22 million and have the first one flying in eight months, he was about to answer when General Putt intervened with, "He has proven it three times already—on the F-80, F-80A, and F-104." The statement reflected Putt's integrity, for he could not have been happy about a rival high-altitude aircraft being introduced that, as things turned out, killed the Air Force's X-16 program.

The U-2 Program

The U-2 program was begun under a cloak of secrecy that characterized the Skunk Works and its products. The designation U-2 was given to convey that this was a utility aircraft like the Air Force version of the Cessna 310, which in Air Force service was designated the U-3. Ed "Baldy" Baldwin sketched out the basic configuration. The CL-282 was redesigned with a longer fuselage, to allow additional space for fuel, accommodate the larger J57 engine, and provide a more commodious equipment bay for the cameras and other intelligence-gathering devices. In the process, it received a bicycle-style landing gear with two main wheels and twin tail wheels—still unusual, but less radical than the takeoff dolly/skid combination. The main gear was supplemented by outrigger gear. These dropped on takeoff and were reinserted by the ground crew upon landing.

The long, tapered, high-aspect-ratio (10.2 to 1) wing looked as if it had been lifted from a sailplane. The combination of 565 square feet of wing area and excess power endowed the U-2 with a remarkably swift and steep climb capability.

Weight control, a science that would elude Lockheed in some later aircraft, was carried to—and as some accidents revealed, beyond—the bounds of safety. The fragile U-2 wing weighed only three pounds per square foot—about one-third the weight of a conventional jet-aircraft wing. The fragility imposed severe g-load limits upon the aircraft, just 2.5 g positive and 1.5 g negative—less than commercial airline practice at the time. The "Angel," as the U-2 became known, would have to be flown with delicate hands.

Kelly carefully chose his engineering team, which initially numbered about fifty, and ultimately reached just over eighty. They worked in darkest secrecy in a room in Plant B-6, next to the experimental manufacturing area. The usual Johnson whip was cracked to solve the inevitable problems inherent in so radical a flying machine.

First Flight

The development of the U-2 aircraft was done in parallel with the test and installation of mission equipment along with the acquisition of a secret test area northwest of Las Vegas, Nevada. The location had been scouted by Tony LeVier flying the company Bonanza, and promised good security.

The first flight of the U-2 was made quite by accident on July 29, 1955, when the aircraft casually leaped into the air during a high-speed taxi trial. The official first flight took place on August 1, 1955. LeVier was the pilot, with Johnson and Bob Mayte flying chase in a T-33.

LeVier and Johnson had had heated discussions over the proposed technique for landing the U-2. Johnson asked that the aircraft be landed on its main wheels first, although this was exactly the opposite of the technique learned the hard way on the bicycle-gear Boeing B-47, where it was essential to touch down on the rear gear first to avoid porpoising. LeVier disagreed, but followed Johnson's instructions.

The forty-five-minute test flight went off without incident, except for the landing, when the light weight and large wing area conferred an extreme amount of "float"—even at idle power, the aircraft simply did not wish to stop flying. When touching down on the main wheels first, the aircraft bounced into the air, and LeVier took it around. A second try had the same results; on the third try, LeVier did it his way, bleeding airspeed close to the stall and flying with a nose-up attitude so that the aircraft settled to the ground, tail wheels first, followed by a light bounce and then a smooth rollout.

Kelly Johnson had not quite made his prediction of eight months from contract signing to first flight, but he was close—only one month off.

Testing proceeded rapidly as construction of the first batch of twenty aircraft continued. The U-2 was demanding to fly and to land, and the criteria for becoming a U-2 pilot were high. The missions were long and the required full-pressure suit was not only uncomfortable, but also a potential source of danger. The first U-2 casualty occurred when test pilot Robert Sieker, flying the prototype aircraft, had the faceplate of his helmet blow out at high altitude. He lost consciousness and the aircraft crashed, killing him.

Despite the obvious hazards, the challenge of the mission was irresistible to military pilots, who had to drop out of their own service and pretend to be employees of Lockheed to disguise their CIA relationship. The process was called "sheep-dipping," and the pilots retained their seniority and promotion possibilities. One of them, Gary Powers, would gain international attention.

CIA Operational Use

The potential use of the U-2 induced President Eisenhower to propose his famous "Open Skies" plan at the July 1955 Geneva summit meeting. He suggested that the Soviet Union and the United States and their allies put forward their existing force structures, which could then be verified by a specified number of reconnaissance flights each year.

The Soviet Union had more to lose than gain—it had relatively unfettered access to U.S. information, while it retained an iron curtain of secrecy over its own. In the past, it had handled Western reconnaissance attempts roughly, shooting first and refusing to answer questions later. It downed almost fifty intruding aircraft in the decade after the war, some of which had simply strayed off course. Eisenhower's offer was ignored, and the president was virtually forced into a position in which he had to sanction U-2 operations, as fraught with risk and uncertainty as they were. The Soviets could easily consider them a *causa belli*, for the thin veneer of "civilian operation" postulated by the CIA could have been exposed or ignored.

Appropriately enough, the first U-2 mission was flown on Independence Day, 1956; it was not known that the final overflight mission would be flown on an equivalent Soviet holiday, May 1, just four years later. The first sortie was made from Weisbaden, Germany, on a route that took it over Moscow and Leningrad. The results were all that could have been hoped for—photographs that revealed otherwise unobtainable secrets about Soviet defenses and industrial capability.

The hopes that the U-2's mission profile would elude Soviet radar proved to be unfounded, for after a second overflight, the Soviet foreign ministry protested vehemently. The United States was prepared for the protest, and anticipated that the Soviets would be able to prevent future U-2 operations within two years. Fortunately, the U-2 would be able to traverse the Soviet Union for four years, making at least thirty overflights as well as many flights on the periphery of the country. Electronic sensors became as important as cameras on these missions, as the United States moved further into the electronic-warfare age.

The operation gathered immense amounts of information, including some that, ironically enough, would prove a burden to the Republican administration. The U-2 flights revealed that the Soviet bomber fleet was not as impressive as had been thought. It also showed that while the potential enemy ICBM threat was very real, and demanded that the United States accelerate its own programs, the tremendous "gap" claimed by the Democratic presidential candidate, John F. Kennedy, did not exist. Eisenhower could not refute the charges for security reasons, and Kennedy hammered on the subject throughout his ultimately victorious campaign.

The United States stonewalled Soviet protests even as it frustrated enemy countermeasures, which included rigorous diplomatic efforts and the threat of military reprisals if the flights did not cease. Prestige

The fate of the Lockheed U-2 seemed sealed with that of Gary Powers when the latter was shot down over the Soviet Union. The U-2 went on to become one of the longest-lived reconnaissance aircraft in history. Powers was returned to the United States, only to lose his life while flying a helicopter.

prevented the Soviet Union from going public with its protests, so the United States was able to contain them within ordinary diplomatic exchanges. The Soviets were outraged that an enemy aircraft could gather intelligence with impunity, and terribly embarrassed that their vaunted missile and interceptor force could not operate effectively at the heights at which the U-2 flew. It was difficult for a man as volatile as Premier Khrushchev to keep his emotions contained within the pressure cooker of the Kremlin, and the Soviet military desperately sought countermeasures.

May 1, 1960

Francis Gary Powers was a USAF pilot, temporarily transferred to the CIA. He enjoyed the clandestine work and had flown many U-2 missions, including several overflights of the Soviet Union. Soviet ICBM activity had accelerated, and a mission was approved for the great May 1 holiday, when it was hoped that the defense systems might be less vigilant.

Powers took off from his Pakistan base of operations at Peshawar to begin a flight of almost four thousand miles; his planned recovery point was Bodø, Norway. En route, he was to photograph Soviet ICBM installations, including those at Piesetsk and Sverdlovsk.

At the latter site, (also known as Yekaterinburg, where the czar and his family were executed), at an altitude of about seventy thousand feet, Powers's U-2 was broken up by the blast effect of no fewer than fourteen surface-to-air missiles, the telephone-pole-sized and-shaped SA-2s that would become so familiar in Vietnam. Powers was almost trapped in the cockpit, managing to escape after a harrowing fall of more than fifty thousand feet. He was captured and later placed on trial by the jubilant Soviet government. Khrushchev, with typical histrionics, used the news to vilify President Eisenhower with demands for an apology. Eisenhower refused, and the Paris summit broke up in disarray on June 17.

Powers was formally charged with espionage and given a typical Soviet show trial. On August 17, he was sentenced to ten years in a labor camp for espionage. After two years of covert negotiations, he was released in an exchange for the notorious Soviet spy Rudolf Abel. Powers was accompanied on his release by John McMahon, then with the CIA and later a top executive at Lockheed.

Although overflights of the Soviet Union were brought to a halt, the U-2 continued operations elsewhere and the aircraft was continuously developed over time. Control of the aircraft, after the usual jurisdictional disputes, was eventually passed to the Air Force, with the last (known) CIA missions taking place in October 1974.

Despite the restrictions on overflying the Soviet Union (which led in turn to other, even more important developments at Lockheed) the U-2 remained at the center of intelligence activities and continues in that role to the present time. It distinguished itself over Red China in operations from Taiwan, including missions that were flown by specially trained pilots of the Nationalist Chinese air force.

The most important missions of the U-2 took place over Cuba in August of 1962. These provided clear photographic evidence of the installation of Soviet IRBM sites and led to the historic confrontation between John F. Kennedy and Nikita Khrushchev during which the Soviets "blinked." On October 27, the pilot of one on these missions, Major Rudolph Anderson, was shot down and killed by a SAM missile.

U-2s served with distinction throughout the Vietnam War, flying hundreds of hours per month under difficult conditions. Constantly modified, they would serve both the military and scientific communities over the next twenty years, including excellent service in the Gulf War.

The U-2's Incredible Versatility

For an aircraft designed with one specific mission in mind, ultrahigh-altitude long-range reconnaissance, the basic U-2 design proved to be extraordinarily adaptable for military and civil use. It was qualified aboard U.S. aircraft carriers, from which operational missions were flown. Modified for in-flight refueling, its already prodigious range (2,800 to 3,500 miles) was limited only by pilot endurance. It became the world's premier "sniffer," sampling air at high altitudes to determine how and when and what kind of nuclear explosions had taken place. Later it was equipped for launching missiles and ejecting capsules for later recovery. A wide array of sensors was fitted for everything from electronic snooping to ocean reconnaissance. NASA (and its predecessor, NACA) used it for an equally broad spectrum of civilian tasks, ranging from weather reconnaissance to experiments in atmospheric physics.

Although the modifications varied the external appearance of the U-2 over the years, the basic size and shape of the airplane remained intact, the most obvious change being the addition of a second cockpit for the U-2CT, the two-seat trainer version. Aircraft power was significantly upgraded when the Pratt & Whitney J75 engine was installed in the U-2B series.

A virtual redesign occurred with the U-2R, when the wingspan was increased to 103 feet and the fuselage lengthened to 63 feet. The larger dimensions resulted in an aircraft more closely matched to the power output of the J75 engines, and provided much greater space for equipment. This was augmented by the addition of wing attachment points that could support large equipment pods. The USAF ordered twenty-five U-2Rs in 1968; these routinely would have been the last production versions of the aircraft.

Fortunately, Johnson and his team had the foresight to store rather than destroy the U-2 tooling, for in 1979, the USAF ordered that an advanced version, the TR-1A, be placed back into production. This marked the first time ever that a USAF aircraft had been placed back into production after the line had been closed.

The many model designations include the U-2, U-2A, B, C, D, E, F, G, J, R, and EP-X, as well as the ER-2, TR-1A, and TR-1B. In

December 1991, the air force renamed the TR-1A the U-2R and the TR-1B the U-2RT. The designation for NASA's ER-2 did not change. The color of the U-2 series did not change quite as often as designations, and ranged from plain aluminum to the more familiar dark matte black to gloss black to white to a simple camouflage.

Time, deliberate security subterfuges, the use of the same serial number by different aircraft, and the general high security of the program obscure exactly how many of the type were built. A "best-guess" estimate ranges from 114 to 120, the latter figure including those built up from spares. More than 40 have been lost in accidents, a record that reflects the dangerous nature of their missions and the structural compromises necessary to achieve the desired performance. Most of all, it underlines the bravery of the U-2 pilots, who endure great hardship and expose themselves to constant danger under conditions of anonymity.

It is fitting that an aircraft that came into being to fly as high as possible over enemy territory would find its useful life extended by its ability to interface between specialized equipment on the ground and satellites based in space. The TR-1A and U-2R distinguished themselves in the Gulf War, where they provided high-altitude surveillance. The matte-black-painted aircraft flew out of Taif in Saudi Arabia, and, using their ASARS-2 nose-mounted radar, searched deep within enemy territory to detect enemy vehicles, much in the manner of the more well publicized J-STARS aircraft, but gathering intelligence rather than controlling the battlefield. The TR-1As and U-2Rs were also used to intercept Iraqi military communications and for photo-reconnaissance.

When Tony Le Vier first flew the U-2 in 1955, its operational life was optimistically estimated to be about two years. The demonstrated capabilities of the U-2 platform and the inevitable advances in electronics equipment will keep it in front-line service well into the twenty-first century. Even Kelly would be surprised.

A Lockheed Commentary

The top executives at Lockheed at the time the U-2 was initiated in 1955 were Bob and Courtlandt Gross. The U-2 program represented a substantial risk, in that it was charting new territories and might well not have succeeded. Lockheed's leadership elected to allow its top engineering talent, as represented by Kelly Johnson and his staff, to commit themselves fully to a program that had an initial contract value of about $22 million, at a time when Lockheed's net U.S. sales amounted to just under $674 million. In other words, the Gross brothers chose to place the corporation's most powerful engineering talent on a program that represented only 3 percent of its total business.

The reason they did so, of course, was sheer patriotism. The investment in talent and facilities at the Skunk Works could have been far more profitably used in commercial ventures, the best example of which might have been a jet passenger liner competitive with Boeing's 707. The issue simply did not arise. The United States had a military requirement that Lockheed felt it was best suited to fill, and Robert Gross saw to it that his company responded to the need.

A Retrograde Step

Lockheed has had a lifelong infatuation with commercial airliners despite its long and losing battles with Douglas. Just as the DC-2 and DC-3 preempted the prewar piston-engine transport market, so did the DC-6 and DC-7 dominate the postwar market. The last and finest of the Lockheed piston-engine airliners was the Model 1649 Starliner, which was the most beautiful of all the innately attractive Constellation series.

The 1649 was intended to compete with the highly successful Douglas DC-7C, but didn't enter the marketplace until a year after its rival—and only fifteen months before Boeing's 707 would sweep the board clean.

The Starliner had an entirely new 150-foot-span wing with the capacity for 50 percent more fuel, but retained the previous series Constellation fuselage and empennage. Despite their maintenance-troubled history, Wright R-3350 Turbo Cyclone engines were installed because a suitable turboprop engine was not yet available.

Failing in the competition with Douglas, and falling behind de Havilland and Boeing in the race for a jet airliner, Lockheed turned to the turboprop. It sought to buy time by gaining experience with turboprops via the installation of Pratt & Whitney YT-34 turboprop engines on two navy R7V-2 and two air force YC-121Fs, both military versions of the Constellation.

The conversions were successful, and the four military turboprops were the fastest propeller-driven transports in the world at the time.

Using the data from these programs, Lockheed attempted to market a civil version that would have had both speed and range, but there were no takers: the jet age was imminent, and the last variation of the venerable Constellation was not able to compete.

An internal Lockheed memorandum analyzed the market problems with the later-model Constellations. The conclusion was that the basic airplane had been priced too low and that the Douglas competition was stronger than had been anticipated. In addition, the Wright turbo-compound engines had not performed as well as they should have. The most important finding, however, was that market research had been inadequate, particularly in regard to customer appreciation of pure jet aircraft. This latter miscalculation would influence Lockheed's next project as well.

Robert Gross and the Electra: Integrity under Duress

Lockheed found itself without an entry in the first-generation jet airliner sweepstakes to compete with either Boeing's 707 or Douglas's DC-8. However, it did have successful experience with the C-130 turboprop, and at least two airlines, American and Eastern, had expressed interest in a turboprop airliner. Capital Airlines had ordered the Vickers Viscount, a four-engine turboprop, and had been notably successful with it. It was hoped that a turboprop airliner would be profitable on short-haul sectors where it would be difficult to operate the first-generation jets. Gross was convinced that the 150- to 200-mph speed differential of jets over turboprops would not be important on the 75 percent of airline runs which were under three hundred miles, and the 87 percent which were under five hundred miles. The savings of the turboprop on the shorter runs were significant (even in the days when fuel prices were low), and Gross said, "The airlines cannot afford—and I really mean *afford*—to pass up the economical turboprop to concentrate exclusively on the glamour of speed."

The first rendition of a turboprop transport for American Airlines drew directly on the C-130. It was rejected by American's vice president for engineering, Bill Littlewood, because he didn't approve of the ditching characteristics of high-wing aircraft. (It did not matter that at the time the largest body of water crossed by American Airlines routes was the Mississippi.)

The turboprop Model L-188 Electra was intended to provide airlines with a short-to-medium range transport. An unfortunate design problem with the engines led to an early termination of the airliner version of the aircraft. The problem was remedied, and the aircraft was modified to become the stalwart P-3 Orion patrol plane.

The Electra was created by virtually the same group that had done the C-130, including Willis Hawkins, Gene Frost, and Bill Statler. The next series of design studies resulted in what would be called the Model L-188, a low-wing, four-engine aircraft with a portly fuselage. Willis Ward did the three-view layouts, as he had been doing for almost all of the new Lockheed aircraft. The new plane was substantially larger than the Viscount and elicited orders for thirty-five planes from American and forty from Eastern. The turboprop engines and the latest wing designs produced an aircraft that lacked all the elegance and grace of the Constellations.

Robert Gross named it the Electra, in honor of the first aircraft designed by his firm, and bestowed his direct creative input on it. Statler tells a story of Gross coming around, as was his habit, to look over the engineers' shoulders. Statler had a three view of the Electra on his board; at that time the vertical surface of the aircraft was squared off.

Gross looked at it and said, "It looks too much like a DC-7. Do you have one of those curvy things?" Statler opened his desk drawer and took out a French curve, which Gross then used to change the tip of the vertical surface to an elliptical shape. When he'd gone, Statler put a note on the drawing that read, "This vertical tail contour drawn by Robert Gross. Don't anybody ever change."

The Electra's appearance needed all the help it could get. With a rotund fuselage reminiscent of the C-130, it was twelve feet shorter than the 1649, with normal seating for sixty to eighty. The wing seemed disproportionately short, particularly with the Allison T56 engines mounted well outboard, their long, lean nacelles thrusting forward and supporting a huge four-blade propeller.

Yet the Electra was a straightforward design and was first flown on December 6, 1957, eight weeks ahead of schedule, by test pilot Herman "Fish" Salmon, copilot Roy Wimmer, flight engineer Louis Holland, and flight test engineer William Spreuer. The Electra used only 1,800 feet of runway on takeoff and made a virtually flawless flight of one hour and twenty-seven minutes. Four aircraft were put into a test program which resulted in the award of a Federal Aviation Administration type certificate on August 22, 1958. The first production aircraft was delivered to American Airlines on December 5, 1958, just one day less than a year after its first flight. The celerity with which the aircraft had been designed, built, certified, and delivered amazed rival companies. An extensive sales effort had been moderately successful, with four more airlines buying 54 more aircraft, to bring the total on order to 129 by the time of the first flight. As events unfolded, only 170 would be built.

Trouble stalked the Electra almost from the beginning, with three crashes occurring by March 17, 1960. The first crash occurred on American Airlines only a week after the Electra had entered service, and was attributed to pilot error. The second was a Braniff aircraft, on September 28, near Waco, Texas, while the third was a Northwest plane on March 17, 1960, in Indiana. The second and third crashes were clearly the result of massive in-flight structural failures that tore the aircraft apart in the air.

The media focused on the Electra, which almost instantly became so unpopular that further orders dried up. Veteran aviator and former Lockheed executive Elwood Quesada was the administrator of the Federal Aviation Administration. He courageously resisted enormous media and congressional pressure to ground the aircraft. Instead, he imposed a 295-mph limit on the aircraft's cruising speed while the accidents were investigated.

It was a good solution; at the lower airspeed, accidents were far less likely to happen, and the airlines were still able to use the aircraft. Lockheed was at first utterly mystified, because they knew that they had investigated the problems associated with the relatively light, long engine with the propellers mounted well out from the wing, and designed the wing structure to handle all expected loads.

Investigation revealed that under certain conditions of engine nacelle or power-plant damage, a phenomenon known as "whirl mode" could occur. "Whirl mode" refers to the results of the application of a force to gyroscopic characteristics of a rotating propeller. When such a force is applied, precession occurs; that is, like a gyroscope, the propeller reacts ninety degrees out of phase to the applied force. This causes the structural resistance of the engine mounting system to apply a nose-down pitching moment. This forces the propeller disc (as viewed from the rear) to turn to the left due to precession. This in turn causes a nose-down propeller disc yawing to the right, which causes a nose-up pitch, completing the cycle. This combination of effects is termed the "whirl mode," and its direction of rotation is opposite to that of the propeller.

In a normal aircraft, the whirl mode could operate only within the limits of the flexibility of the engine mounts. If, however, some structural element of the power plant, the power-plant mounting system, or the nacelle was in a damaged or weakened condition, the whirl mode would not damp out, but could become more violent, increasing damage to the structure, and could approach the natural frequency of the wing. This would perpetuate the whirl mode in a form of induced flutter and lead to catastrophic failure.

John Margwarth, another University of Michigan man, was director of safety for Lockheed, and it was his insight that led to an investigation revealing that the Electra's fatal flaw was in the three-member structure connecting the gearbox and the engine, a part supplied by the engine manufacturers. When one member of that structure failed, the engine mount became flexible. On an outboard engine, at the Electra's original cruise speed, failure of the strut induced immediate, violent flutter that tore the wing off.

Technically, Lockheed could have passed the problem off to the engine manufacturer, disclaiming responsibility. Instead, it redesigned the wing structure so that it would not flutter when such a failure occurred. (Allison also redesigned the strut so that it would not fail.) Additional mounts were added to stabilize the propeller in the event that any mount failed, or if breakage occurred between the gearbox and the power section. The nacelle structure was also strengthened by the addition of reinforcements and diagonal braces.

Lockheed was rocked by the three crashes and their adverse publicity. For weeks there was one meeting after another to handle the latest problem. It was soon evident that engineering the wing modification was not going to be as difficult as finding a way to pay for it. Carl Kotchian recalled coming out of a meeting with Robert Gross, the latter sunk deep in thought. (Gross had been under considerable strain for some time; he would die less than two years later.) In the garage, Gross asked, "How much do you think the modification is going to cost?" Kotchian hesitated and said, "Well, I think it's going to cost maybe $25 million." Gross turned white, then replied, "Well, we've got to do it."

And Lockheed did, instituting the Lockheed Electra Action Program (LEAP) and modifying all Electras at its own expense, whether they were within warranty or not. The LEAP program came in just under Kotchian's $25 million estimate.

Kotchian further recalled that Gross's forthright decision to take responsibility paid dividends later, when they were selling the L-1011 TriStar wide-body jet. Customers who had benefited from Gross's forthright decision on the Electra were convinced of Lockheed's integrity and thus more inclined to buy the L-1011.

By December 31, 1960, the FAA had lifted its speed restrictions, and all aircraft, now called Electra IIs, returned to service. The window of opportunity for the Electra had been small to begin with, given the imminent success of jet airliners, and the accidents effectively foreclosed any further sales. Nonetheless, the Electras that were in service proved themselves as safe, capable performers. On shorter routes, jets did not have a significant speed advantage, and the Electras were far more economical to fly as they used so much less fuel.

Just as misfortunes with the Model 14 Lodestar had been salvaged by military orders, so would the troubles with the Electra be more than offset by large U.S. Navy orders for its development, the P3V-1 Orion patrol plane.

The Orion

The manner in which Lockheed manufactured and serviced its aircraft induced strong customer loyalty, and this was nowhere more evident than in sales of patrol and antisubmarine aircraft to naval air forces around the world. Services that had begun to learn the maritime patrol business with the Hudson had been brought to greater heights of efficiency with the Ventura, Harpoon, and Neptune.

The Orion became the free world's definitive anti–submarine patrol aircraft, serving in dozen of countries. It provided both detection equipment and offensive weaponry on a scale never before possible in a patrol aircraft.

The problems with the Electra airliner had not surfaced in 1957, when Lockheed responded to a navy specification for a modern maritime patrol aircraft with a modified version of the L-188. Lockheed was in the very satisfactory position of having eliminated its traditional competitors, Martin and Consolidated, from the field.

The first Orion flew on November 25, 1959, and an initial production contract was let for seven P3V-1s in October 1960. The Electra crashes provided the press and Congress with an argument for canceling Orion procurement on the basis that it was not safe. The Navy, fully informed on the nature of Lockheed's proposed fixes, held its ground, and Orion production went forward.

The first Orion was actually the third Electra prototype, modified by a seven-foot section being removed from the forward fuselage. Much of the proposed navy avionics equipment was installed, along with the fourteen-foot magnetic anomaly detector (MAD) boom protruding from the rear of the fuselage. When the first Orions entered U.S. Navy squadron service on August 13, 1962, they were redesignated P-3A, in line with the new Department of Defense system.

The Orion was a perfect platform for the swiftly evolving electronic equipment used in antisubmarine warfare. Its performance with the 4,500-shaft-horsepower Allison T56 engines was excellent, having a top speed of 405 mph and a range of 5,570 miles. More important for its mission, however, was its ability to fly at low altitudes and relatively low speeds for long periods of time, with ample room for spare crew members.

Over the more than thirty years of its production, the Orion has had more than sixteen designations to reflect changes in equipment and mission. The most radical change occurred with the Canadian version, the CP-140 Aurora, which used the avionics systems and the data-processing capability of Lockheed's later aircraft, the S-3A Viking.

The adaptability of the Orion made it invaluable during the cold war, when the threat of Soviet submarines was at its peak. Fourteen nations operated the P-3, and developed a remarkable portfolio of missions that proved to be useful in the post–cold war period.

New equipment, including special imaging radar, infrared, low-light-level long-range video cameras, and extensive radio equipment to relay communications permit the Orion to do its work at a distance, out of range of hostile forces. The aircraft is an extremely flexible platform, with its long range, long duration, large payload, and ability to fly economically at both high and low altitudes. The P-3C version of the Orion was in fact a major Lockheed turning point, in that it had the first digital, computer-based, software-controlled avionics system developed by Lockheed. This would lead to a long series of future advanced digital systems in the S-3A Viking, F-117 Nighthawk, and F-22 Raptor.

During Desert Shield and Desert Storm in 1991, a multinational Orion force monitored compliance with United Nations' shipping restrictions in the region, then provided surveillance and battle-damage assessment during the air and ground war. More than half the Iraqi ships sunk by allied warplanes resulted from P-3 detection and identification. The Orions flew more than 1,200 combat sorties, logging twelve thousand flight hours during the campaign.

Tension in the Balkans provided another opportunity for the Orions to expand their role. The Orions monitored movements of troops and equipment in Bosnia, while using electronic emission sensors to keep watch on missile and artillery sites. Special Orions have been fitted with long-range video cameras to provide real-time intelligence to senior U.S. and NATO leaders. Pilots fly a W-shaped flight path to get them over their targeted areas with minimum exposure to possible hostile actions. The sight of a P-3C streaking through trouble-laden Bosnia skies, its self-defense package spitting out flares and chaff to spoof possible surface-to-air missiles, was a welcome pat on the back for the aircraft designers and system engineers.

The Orion's varied equipment is effective in combating drug-smuggling operations along the southern U.S. border. The on-board sensors can detect not only illegal air traffic, but also such ground activities as drug production and shipping.

Despite these additional missions, undersea warfare remains an important task for the Orion, as the ultimate sub hunter for both nuclear and diesel-electric boats. Improved submarine equipment and tactics have made undersea warfare an even more demanding task, one that requires the hunter aircraft to stay aloft for long hours at a time. The Orion, with its wide variety of sensors and weapons, is hunter and killer in one.

The One That Got Away—Fortunately

When, in August 1963, the Federal Aviation Administration issued a request for proposal for a supersonic transport, Lockheed was well prepared to respond, having studied the concept for more than seven years. Its initial offering, the CL-283, was for a 218-passenger transport with a 450,000-pound gross weight. It, with an entry from Boeing, was selected for the second phase of the competition.

A new, larger version, the Lockheed L-2000-7, emerged as a 266-passenger, 590,000-pound double-delta-wing design. The double-delta wing was chosen for a wide variety of reasons, including its combination of swift-transonic acceleration and excellent low-speed handling characteristics. In 1965 dollars, Lockheed expected the aircraft to have direct operating expenses of about one cent per seat mile, when operating at its four-thousand-mile range. This was competitive with contemporary subsonic jet airliners. The aircraft would have earned a profit with a 55 percent passenger load factor. The total market for supersonic airliners was estimated to be about nine hundred aircraft—which would have just recouped the investment of the government and the company in the project.

Boeing's entry used a variable-geometry (swing-wing) design, and

Although it did not seem so at the time, it proved to be fortunate that Lockheed did not win the contract for developing a supersonic transport, as it was not the time to do so technically, economically, or environmentally. The Lockheed L-2000 design was elegant. A similar configuration was later adopted by Boeing, the contest winner.

despite the opinion of many that Lockheed's design was superior, won the competition. Further along in the development process, Boeing switched to a double-delta design not unlike Lockheed's.

Losing the competition was ultimately beneficial to Lockheed, for the supersonic transport program was canceled for a variety of reasons, including environmental and economic concerns. Given that only sixteen of the Anglo-French Concorde supersonic transports were purchased, the nine-hundred-aircraft requirement was probably a vast overestimate, and a lower number would have caused significant losses to Lockheed.

A Management Review

By 1961, when Courtlandt Gross became chairman and Dan Haughton president of the Lockheed Corporation, the company had more than seventy thousand employees, net sales of $1.4 billion, and a net income of $26 million. In terms of product, the Neptune was still in production, with the Orion just getting under way. The F-104 production line was continuing at a healthy rate of four per month. The Electra problems had been met, the LEAP program contributing a substantial portion of 1960's $42 million loss. A new venture into the helicopter business looked promising, and the Skunk Works was occupied with, among other things, the U-2 and its supersecret successor, of which, more later.

There were also a variety of subsidiary businesses that will be addressed in an appendix, including the ill-fated Lockheed Shipbuilding and Construction Company, the Lockheed Electronics Company, the Lockheed Engineering and Management Services Company, and others.

In addition, there were two other major elements of the company, which will be dealt with in succeeding chapters, and which were spawned almost simultaneously by the mother organization in Burbank. The first of these was Lockheed Georgia, where the C-130, one of the greatest aircraft of all time, in terms of its performance and its profitability, would be manufactured. The second of these was in Sunnyvale, California, where the Lockheed Missiles and Space Company (LMSC) would develop highly classified products that would include fleet ballistic missile systems and a wide variety of satellites. LMSC would not only generate an unending stream of profit, but would mold a whole new corps of Lockheed executive talent which would guide the destiny of the company for much of the twentieth century, and probably much of the twenty-first.

CHAPTER 8

Expanding Horizons

A company's character is shaped by many things, including leadership, management style, product, public appreciation, clientele, media relations, and, not least, the cultural makeup of the workforce.

At Burbank, Lockheed would be subject to all of these influences as it tentatively—almost accidentally—expanded its horizons at its new plants in Marietta, Georgia, Sunnyvale, California, and elsewhere. The new plants would begin with a strong Burbank influence, but this would be moderated over time by the factors indicated above to create totally distinct—and in some respects, totally different—industrial personalities. Yet each would retain an absolutely fierce sense of being part of the Lockheed family. This tenacious loyalty also often encompassed a pride of place, an abiding sense that each one was the most important element of the company.

This was only a first step in a continuing evolution, for there was a continual interchange of executives among the Burbank, Marietta, and Sunnyvale sites (and other locations as well). This free exchange of talent would shape Lockheed's corporate destiny in a manner that would exactly suit the vision of Robert Gross, who sought and fostered talent as a master gardener might seek and foster exotic plants.

Inevitably (because humans were involved), this interplay of managerial style, talent, energy, and vision was spiced by occasional arrogance and hubris. This resulted in occasional turbulence for Lockheed as it reached new heights, encountered difficulties that caused it to drop to unaccustomed depths, and then, tempered by the battering of fate, soared again to its present lofty position in the industry.

The causes of these rises and falls were many, including the type of contracts being pursued, the nature of the product, the quality of competition, the degree of cooperation from the customer, the excellence—or lack thereof—of the management, and the response of the workforce. Just as a ship's captain is awarded credit for a record crossing but held accountable for running aground, so are the top executives of a company accorded the praise or the blame for the company's fortunes under their leadership. In the following pages, we'll see many magnificent achievements accented with infrequent but sometimes appalling failures. Both successes and failures will be attributed to the top managers of the time in question, but with full recognition that many more factors than just managerial leadership are involved. The need for clarity and the demands of space make it necessary to resort to an iron law of fame: whoever is in charge is awarded the credit or the blame for the events that happen on his or her watch.

In 1951, fortune and a demonstrated track record would dictate that Lockheed would expand its aircraft business to Georgia. This new business was closely allied to its experience, and represented a relatively straightforward expansion of its existing base. Lockheed would again be building big airplanes for a familiar customer, the United States Air Force.

A corporate decision was made to establish a separate Missile Systems Division to "expand our current operations in the design and building of *pilotless aircraft* and their systems." The italics are the author's and reflect the naive, almost innocent lack of awareness of exactly what it was starting. The firm that would become the Lockheed Missiles and Space Company (LMSC) in Sunnyvale had its grounding in "pilotless" aircraft, but from 1951 would grow into an infinitely more sophisticated company whose scientific successes were more than an order of magnitude greater than any previously developed by Lockheed or any other aerospace firm, and whose history will be dealt with in the following chapters. Most of LMSC's assignments would be totally foreign to all of Lockheed's past experience, and the magnificent triumphs it achieved—only a few of which can be related even today, for reasons of security—are a tribute to the managers, engineers, and scientists who took on unprecedented challenges. Unlike the Georgia company, where there was the normal tight security of a defense plant, LMSC would be plunged into the "black" world of supersecurity as ironclad as that of the Skunk Works. Its programs would not just be secret—their very existence would be denied. The urgent demand for accomplishment of tasks absolutely vital to the national interest and the availability of virtually unlimited funds would be reminiscent of the Skunk Works approach, with a similar beneficial managerial fallout.

Both the new organizations would have profound economic, political, and cultural impact on their respective communities. The Georgia plant spurred the southern industrial revolution that continues to this day, while the Sunnyvale plant was the seed corn for what is now Silicon Valley, the heart of America's strength in the world of computers, software, and the other exotica that will shape the twenty-first century. And from the ferment of these two organizations, both growing to formidable size in a very brief period, would be distilled the future leadership of the Lockheed Corporation. Both firms would become, in effect, campuses of "Lockheed University" for grooming managers for higher positions within the corporation.

And, most important of all, both companies would allow the Lockheed Corporation to make what many consider to be the greatest of all industrial contributions to winning the cold war, by providing multiple means to enforce the U.S. policy of deterrence and containment of the Soviet Union.

Lockheed's products were vital in many areas, but four—spy planes, satellites, fleet ballistic missiles, and airlift aircraft—were especially so. Deterrence would be furthered by its famous spy planes, the U-2 and the SR-71, which provided otherwise unavailable information on the Soviet Union. The fantastic results of the spy planes would be vastly exceeded by the information provided by Lockheed's incredible spy satellites, beginning with Corona, and then going far beyond even that formidable achievement. These would lay bare most of the major secrets of the Soviet Union, enabling the United States not only to evaluate the potential threat, but also to meter its reaction to that threat economically. While the planes and the satellites differed vastly in their technology, they shared one common feature: most people believed these modern instruments could not be built to perform as intended.

A further and perhaps decisive deterrent came from the revolutionary submarine-launched ballistic missiles (SLBMs), Lockheed-designed and-built, from the first Polaris to the latest Trident. Again, nothing similar had ever been achieved, and there were many who said the task was impossible, that a ballistic missile could not be launched from a submarine. Yet the Lockheed/navy team, working with other companies, solved the problems to create the stealthiest and most invulnerable element of the American strategic triad of SLBMs, ICBMs, and bombers, and did so in an amazingly short time. Perhaps the most important benefit of the triad was that it deterred the Soviets from exercising the first-strike doctrine, in which their military leaders believed and which they would have executed if not kept in check by the threat of massive retaliation from the United States.

The policy of containment was furthered by Lockheed transports, including the C-130, C-141, and C-5. Their unmatched global reach permitted the United States to confront and contain Soviet-sponsored initiatives by transferring troops and arms to critical areas, as when Lockheed transports brought the tanks and guns that enabled Israel to survive in 1973. Compassionate missions flown to disaster areas around the globe were an equally important element of containment. The world watched in awe as an endless procession of huge Lockheed transports brought in food, water, and medical supplies to areas struck by earthquakes or suffering the results of civil wars.

Operations continued at the "home" plant in Burbank, where vital contributions to both civil and military aviation were made. Inevitably, however, the benefits of the expanded horizons in Georgia and Sunnyvale would redound to the greater benefit of the mother firm.

The Gross Brothers: Looking Ahead for Lockheed

In the 1940s, the greatest single accolade a businessman could receive was to be on the cover of *Time* magazine. This honor was accorded to Robert Gross on January 14, 1946. His brother Courtlandt would be paid a similar tribute just over twenty years later, on February 11,

1966. The two-decade interval would see Lockheed's continuing growth under the guidance of the Gross brothers, but would also see its future shaped by the men they chose for upper management.

The article accompanying the 1946 cover captured the essence of Robert Gross and foresaw the future of Lockheed in a few pithy paragraphs. It began by detailing the wide public acceptance of the Constellation, and then commented on the "star-shooting career of the Lockheed Corporation." It noted that in 13 years, Lockheed had grown from a $40,000, fifteen-employee gamble to a giant with $50 million in working capital, thirty-two thousand employees, and a backlog of $215 million, unprecedented for the time.

Time stated that among "plane-making tycoons, predominantly an inbred and individualistic group of onetime designers and pilots, Bob Gross is a sport. He is not a pilot. He knows little about aerodynamics. As a production man and administrator he is just so-so. Yet he has one talent which more than balances these apparent deficiencies. He has a seemingly intuitive salesman's sense of knowing what planes will be wanted a few years hence, and then being ready to deliver them. On top of this, he has a knack for getting his ideas across, and a flair for picking men who can translate them into planes."

Gross, of course, was doing far more than that, for with his brother he was establishing a culture that would continue to pick the right men who could translate even more advanced ideas than his own into even more sophisticated equipment than aircraft.

When the younger Gross appeared on the *Time* cover in 1966, he was chairman of the board. He presided over an even more impressive increase in the growth of the Lockheed Corporation, a growth that was fed in part by the cold war and in part by the hot war building in Vietnam. His principal instrument in managing what was now the Defense Department's biggest single contractor was a man he had personally picked for the job, Daniel J. Haughton.

Haughton would be closely monitored by the Gross brothers. Both men wanted to be sure that the management of the company would be left in good hands after they retired, and to them good hands meant a person totally devoted to every aspect of Lockheed's expanding business, and one who would take care of the "Lockheed family." Haughton clearly filled that bill.

Revolution in Georgia

World War II found Marietta, Georgia, still a sleepy town. Located just a few miles north of Atlanta, Marietta was locked in the traditions of the Old South, the prospect of more "Yankees" arriving to build an aircraft factory in their midst raising the image of General Sherman and his invaders. Fortunately, the inveterate patriotism of the population for the World War II effort—and the prospect of thousands of high-paying jobs—quickly brought public sentiment into line. There was general acceptance of a decision by the Defense Plant Corporation to build a government-owned plant in Marietta, where the Bell Aircraft Corporation would build Boeing B-29s. Air Force Plant No. 6 opened on March 15, 1943, when its first five hundred employees came to work. The main production building was huge: 1,000 feet wide and 2,000 feet long and standing four and one-half stories high, it was at the time the largest aircraft assembly building under a single roof. Ultimately, the facility would cover more than 4.5 million square feet. The main buildings were air-conditioned, an incredible innovation at a time when such comfort could be found only in premier motion picture theaters. One can imagine how the feature was appreciated by the new workforce, many of whom had previously spent the hot summers sweltering in the fields of local farms.

After the plant was in production, a young attorney from Atlanta, James V. Carmichael, was selected to head the operation. The production rate built up slowly toward its goal of 40 aircraft per month, and by war's end, 368 B-29s had been built. Many in the workforce had come to the new plant completely untrained, never having seen an aircraft factory, a machine tool, or even sheet aluminum before. Their skill grew so rapidly that Bell executives elected to change from the standard industry cost-plus-fixed-fee (CPFF) contract to contracts setting a flat price for an aircraft. The Bell gamble paid off; production efficiency soared, and Bell made almost 10 percent of the contract price versus the 2 percent generally earned on a CPFF contract.

With the end of World War II, the factory was closed, but the advent of the Korean conflict in June 1950 caused it to be reopened. Found wanting because of the U.S. postwar demobilization frenzy, the Air Force did not have enough bombers on hand to maintain the deterrent force of the Strategic Air Command and fight the Korean War. Aircraft had to be scavenged from the desert boneyards, and reservists had to be recalled to fly them.

The Air Force tasked Lockheed to reopen the Marietta plant in January 1951, to refurbish 120 B-29s that had been languishing in plastic cocoons at Pyote, Texas. Lockheed was chosen because the Air Force had bigger plans for it—the production of the Boeing B-47 bomber under license. Lockheed's Vega unit had participated with Douglas in building B-17s during the war in the so-called B-V-D (Boeing-Vega-Douglas) committee (the acronym was slyly funny in 1944, when BVDs were an old-fashioned brand of long underwear). Carmichael was brought back initially to supervise operations as general manager. He was first assisted and then replaced by a rising star in the Lockheed family of "high-potential" executives, the energetic Dan Haughton.

A southerner himself, Alabama-born Haughton had entered the aircraft industry working as an accountant at Consolidated Aircraft. He must have done well, for when his boss, P. E. Ryker, left Consolidated to work for Dick Von Hake, Lockheed's vice president of manufacturing, he invited Haughton to come along. The younger man did so about a year later, just as the production tempo on Hudson bombers was building up. There, he initiated two of his many long-lasting relationships, for Haughton was a man who inspired loyalty and admiration. The first was with his secretary, Monte Orman, who stayed with him for the next thirty-five years, and the second was with Courtlandt Gross. Monte would become his virtual alter ego, scheduling his busy days and shielding him from less-important demands on his precious time. Courtlandt would see him to be the perfect man to whom to pass the reins still held so tightly by the Gross brothers.

Their first meeting set the tone for what became a very sympathetic relationship. Haughton recalled in an interview that the first time he met Courtlandt was in the office next to his own. Gross was sitting in an office swivel chair talking on the telephone. He leaned back too far, catapulting himself to the floor, but without interrupting his telephone call, and blithely ignoring Haughton's amused reaction. Notwithstanding this unique introduction, Gross would become one of Haughton's most important mentors.

It was Haughton's style to learn more than the nuts and bolts of the organization—he learned the cut of the thread, the pounds of torque, how many drops of oil were needed, and always, the most economical usage of every part and every man-hour. He never attempted to pass himself off as a machine operator or an assembler, but he could observe a manufacturing process and optimize it. He became expert at systematizing production at the lowest level, and, as he rose

Daniel Haughton was selected by Robert and Courtlandt Gross to succeed them. Haughton was a gifted manager, totally devoted to Lockheed.

in rank, he practiced his talent on an increasingly wide basis at each new rung on his steeply inclined ladder to the top. Ultimately, he would run the entire corporation in a similar manner, insisting on knowing all the details, spotting irregularities and deficiencies, and categorically demanding improvement. What he did once by roaming the factory floor he did later by roaming across the country from plant to plant, holding in one day early-morning meetings in Georgia and late-evening meetings in Burbank, each meeting revolving around scores of information-laden charts. His managers had to know their jobs as he knew his, and that meant in depth and breadth and with passion.

Despite his rigor, Haughton was considered by many to be at heart a charming Southern gentleman who retained the potential, in the words of Lockheed group vice president Carl Haddon, to "get out his blowtorch" when the situation demanded it. The feeling of affection for Haughton, mixed with recognition of his sometimes blistering tactics, is characteristic of most of those who worked with him. Many were touched by how obviously Haughton was devoted to his wife. In the later years, when she was stricken with an incapacitating disease, he attended to her tenderly and personally, arranging his otherwise relentless schedule to be with her at the evening meal.

Allan and Malcolm Lockheed in the capacious cockpit of their Model F-1, one of the largest seaplanes in the world at the time of its construction.

The Aquila remotely piloted vehicle, a forerunner of an ever-more important discipline.

Flares designed to spoof infrared
missiles trail behind a Hercules.

The C-130, designed as a warplane, has functioned
in many more humanitarian roles than had ever been envisaged
for it. It is ideally suited for many Coast Guard uses.

Born in a swirl of controversy, the Galaxy has proved itself to be equally indispensable to combat or compassionate missions.

"Of all sad words…" The Cheyenne was a magnificent helicopter, innovative and in advance of its time. It fell victim to a protracted development and rising costs.

The performance of the prototype CL-475 helicopter encouraged
Lockheed to increase its efforts to establish a
foothold in the industry.

The versatile Constellation lent itself
to a wide variety of tasks.

The D-21 drone was a high-risk attempt to extend
the utility of the SR-71A; it proved to be too dangerous to
use in the manner shown. D-21s were subsequently
used successfully by B-52 mother planes.

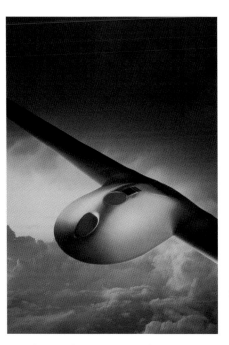

The Darkstar points the way to
what may be
the future of reconnaissance,
the uninhabited aircraft.

The enormous success
of the U-2 in a military role was
equalled by the success of its sister ship
ER-2, operated by NASA for
peacetime missions.

The great success of the original Electra led to the development
of a slightly smaller, more affordable Electra, Junior.

The F-104 Starfighter became an integral part of the new German Luftwaffe, operating in a variety of roles.

The disconcerting angularity of the F-117A Nighthawk is part of the reason for its stealth characteristics. The F-117A's complex computer system manages to endow it with excellent flying characteristics.

The acquisition of General Dynamic's Fort Worth Division went smoothly and the F-16 Fighting Falcon became a stalwart addition to the stable of Lockheed fighters.

Three very different shapes, each with distinct capabilities. Together they form a formidable arsenal of fighter aircraft. From the left, the F-16, the YF-22, and the F-117A.

The incredible stealth characteristics of the diamond-shaped F-117A model were proven in this sculptural setting.

The immortal Hudson bomber was vital to Great Britain in its war against Germany's submarines. It was the key instrument in transforming Lockheed into a major manufacturer of combat aircraft.

Of all the great leaps forward in astronomy, the Hubble Space Telescope remains the most astonishing.

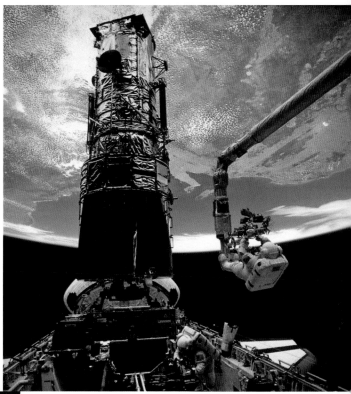

The photographs from the Hubble combine art, philosophy, science, and the very basis for religion in a single composition. For each answer they provide, they raise a thousand more questions.

It is almost impossible to comprehend the enormous distances, the vast sizes, and the incredible duration of times involved in photographs like these.

The beautiful Lockheed L-1011 was beloved by
pilots and passengers. An unquestionable success as an
aircraft, it encountered insurmountable marketing
problems that doomed it to economic failure.

Lockheed always managed to "stretch" its aircraft so that the
maximum performance was extracted from the basic design. The
Lodestar carried the original Electra's configuration to its limits.

The Agena spacecraft was one of the unsung heroes
of the space age. Reliable, versatile, and used in hundreds of
applications, the Agena did for the exploration of space what
the Douglas DC-3 did for commercial air transportation.

At once the most mysterious and most recognizable
of aircraft, the SR-71's beauty is accented by the power
implicit in the flame of its engines.

Almost every Lockheed transport ultimately saw military duty,
and none served better than the Constellation.

The Navy's T2V-1 SeaStar was a carrier–based
development of the Air Force's T-33.

Time seems to stop at the beginning of a Space Shuttle launch. Then, in a burst of flame and vapor, the beautiful spacecraft launches from earth.

The Space Shuttle poised on the Earth's horizon like a gigantic monument to human imagination.

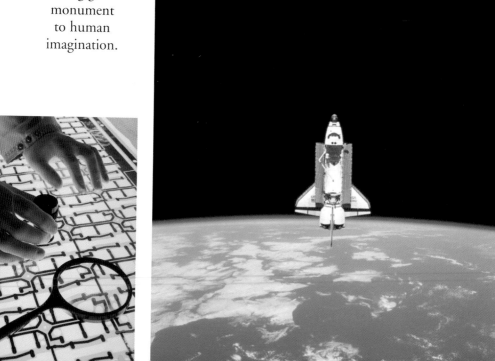

Fast, powerful and versatile, the S-3 Viking became the most capable carrier-based anti–submarine warfare aircraft in history.

The Sea Shadow represented not only a revolution in ship design, with its stealth characteristics, but also in ship construction techniques.

The products of the Skunk Works arranged in a star outline: from the twelve o'clock position: SR-71A; F-94C; U-2; F-104, F-117A, and the F-80.

The MILSTAR satellite system provides military communication capability.

The hazards implicit in a totally new engine design did not deter Kelly Johnson and his Skunk Work engineers. When presented with the brand-new jet engine, they designed a classic airframe to use it, the P-80 Shooting Star.

Antisubmarine warfare assumed an unparalleled importance with the advent of nuclear submarines capable of launching nuclear weapons. The P-3 Orion established itself as the world's premier anti–submarine aircraft.

The immortal Lockheed Vega began its career setting records and ended it serving as a difficult target for radar to track.

The Trident submarine– launched ballistic missile reached a level of sophistication that even the most ardent proponent of Fleet Ballistic Missiles would not have dreamed of even a decade before.

The X-17 was a pioneer not only for the new and untried world of missiles, but also for Lockheed engineering and management techniques. It did well in both tasks.

The YF-22 won one of the most demanding fighter competitions in history, emerging as the USAF's premier fighter for the 21st century.

The YF-22 prototype's beauty lent itself to dramatic photographs; this seems to be as much a sculpture as an aircraft.

Haughton Marches to Georgia

About 150 people were detailed with Haughton from the Burbank operation to initiate the reopening of the former Bell plant. Among the most important of them was A. Carl Kotchian, who brought about twenty people with him as assistant director of financial operations. He would succeed Haughton as general manager in 1956. The two men would work closely together over the years and would together rise (and, sadly, fall) with Lockheed's fortunes, with Kotchian succeeding Haughton as president of the Lockheed Corporation when the latter became chairman of the board. They were recognized and respected by their co-workers as an extraordinarily effective, if sometimes rough, team.

Employment soon soared to about ten thousand, once again breathing life into the local economy. The original charter of Lockheed's Georgia Division[1] operation specifically ruled out a separate engineering or marketing organization; these were to remain in California. Yet the distance from Burbank provided the Georgia management with a moderate degree of independence, which it enhanced by an outstanding performance.

The production of the B-47 was phased in just as the refurbishment of the B-29 was being completed. Boeing had provided parts to assemble 8 B-47Bs, and Lockheed went on to produce 386 B-47Es. In an unusually benevolent gesture, given the normally cutthroat competition of the industry, Boeing had shared its cost-of-production information with Kotchian, who promptly put it to good use. Lockheed was able to price its bid on the B-47s low enough for the Air Force to agree to it, but high enough to earn a substantial profit when Haughton's managerial talents envoked high performance from the new workforce. It was an auspicious beginning for Lockheed Georgia and for Haughton.

The B-47 contract was structured as a Cost Plus Incentive Fee (CPIF), one of the first of this nature with Lockheed. In a CPIF contract, if you bettered your contractual estimates, your profits went up—and if you overran them, profits went down. Just as it had been in World War II, the Georgia plant proved to be exceptionally productive, making the contract highly profitable for Lockheed. Haughton recalled that about $200 million of the total estimated contractual amount of $750 million was returned to the Air Force, and he believed

1. Like Lockheed Missile and Space, the name of the Lockheed operation in Georgia changed as it grew.

that success of this magnitude was the principal reason that Robert and Courtlandt Gross agreed to allow production of the C-130 transport in Georgia. The allocation of C-130 production to Georgia made it necessary to build up an engineering and sales staff, and thus establish a completely integrated airplane division of the company. This in turn would serve as the platform from which to launch a dynasty of Air Force transport aircraft.

Haughton's style was impressed upon the Georgia Company early with the first Lockheed management incentive plan. The initial portion of the B-47 contract called for about 25 million man-hours of work at an average of $5 per hour. Haughton was convinced that this time could be reduced if managers could share in the resulting profit. It was a revolutionary idea at Lockheed, and took some persuasion to get in place—part of the persuasion being Haughton's excluding himself from participation.

In the fall of 1956, Courtlandt Gross paid a three-day visit to the Georgia Division. In his usual quiet, gentlemanly style, he went over the entire operation carefully with Haughton, including the ongoing transfer of C-130 manufacture from Burbank to Georgia. Then, only fifteen minutes before he was to depart in his plane back to California, he said, "Dan, I'd like to have you come back to the corporation as executive vice president, and run all the divisions for us." Haughton agreed immediately, leaving for the West Coast on October 1, 1956. There he would oversee Lockheed's general expansion and impose his management methods on most—but not all—of the organization.

Despite the whirlwind sixteen-hour-per-day, seven-day-per-week style by which he exercised iron control over the aircraft side of Lockheed, Haughton, as we will see, could never impose on what ultimately became the Lockheed Missiles and Space Company the same degree of micromanagement control that he did on other divisions. This was in part because of the intense security of LMSC's operation, where "need to know" was rigorously enforced, and in part because of the nature of LMSC scientists and engineers, whose culture was so different from that of the people on the manufacturing floor of an aircraft plant. Some say that Haughton did not entirely grasp the breadth of LMSC's systems, which extended far beyond finished hardware. As things happened, Haughton's "benign neglect" vastly benefited first LMSC and then the corporation as a whole. Despite his personal inclination to micromanage, Haughton seemed to understand that Sunnyvale personnel might not respond to the methods that had worked so well for him in Georgia.

Georgia's Hercules:
The Beginning of a Noble Transport Dynasty

During the Korean War, the operations of the USAF's Far Eastern Air Forces Combat Cargo Command had been heroic, and in some instances absolutely crucial, but were for most of the war terribly handicapped by inadequate equipment. Its most modern operational aircraft, the Fairchild C-119, proved to be only marginally more effective (and much less reliable) than World War II Douglas C-47s and Curtiss C-46s.

The Air Force sought to remedy the situation on February 2, 1951, with a request for proposal for a medium-weight transport issued to Lockheed, Boeing, Douglas, and Fairchild. In broad terms, the Air Force's General Operational Requirement (GOR) called for a transport able to

1. carry ninety-two infantrymen or sixty-four paratroopers on a mission with a combat radius of 1,100 nautical miles, or, alternatively, a thirty-thousand-pound cargo over 960 miles;

2. operate from short, unprepared airstrips of clay, sand, or humus soil;

3. slow down to 125 knots for paradrops and even slower for assault landings;

4. have both a rear ramp operable in flight for heavy-equipment drops and side doors for paratroop drops;

5. handle bulky and heavy equipment including bulldozers, artillery pieces, and trucks; and

6. fly even with one engine out.

This last requirement was critical. Previous transport aircraft, operating with heavy loads out of the short fields in the forward area, often could not survive the loss of an engine on takeoff—there was not enough power to keep them airborne.

Willis Hawkins, then head of preliminary design, acted as general supervisor for Lockheed's proposal, Kelly Johnson being preoccupied with what would become the F-104 fighter. Eugene Frost was Hawkins's deputy for Temporary Design Designation L-206, later called

One of the most brilliant aeronautical engineers of all time, and an excellent manager as well, Willis Hawkins has received innumerable awards for his many contributions to Lockheed and to the aerospace industry. Hawkins rose to prominence in both the aeronautical and the missile sides of Lockheed.

the Model 82. Art Flock and Dick Pulver were tasked to lead the project into the development stage for prototypes. Ultimately, the patent for the C-130 would be assigned to Bill Statler and Gene Frost. As was the case with most Lockheed projects—and decades before the modern "integrated product team" concept—most of the men were specialists in their field who had worked together closely before (e.g., Pulver and Flock on the huge Constitution four-engine transport, or Frost and Hawkins on Nate Price's L-133 jet project).

Johnson's penchant for high-speed, high-performance aircraft was so great that he always argued against research aircraft such as the Bell X-1 or the North American X-15, believing that aircraft should be designed both to have outstanding performance *and* to perform an operational mission. Thus, it is not surprising that the prospect of a strictly utilitarian transport did not excite him. As it was Johnson's tendency to be totally focused on his own work, the development of the Model 82 progressed rapidly without his oversight.

Like everyone else, Johnson was unaware that the fate of the Georgia operation, and indeed, the fate of Lockheed itself, rode on the sturdy if unprepossessing wings of what was to become the C-130 Hercules. And it transpired that the fate of the C-130 rode in turn upon the judgment and courage of Hall T. Hibbard.

Hibbard was vitally important to Lockheed because of his engineering talent and his strong relationship with Robert and Courtlandt

Gross. It was said of Hibbard that he was "their arbiter of risks, their source of judgment on the value and probable success of new ventures."

Less than four months after the Air Force's RFP, Hawkins brought the Model 82 proposal to Hibbard for approval. Hall asked, "Has Kelly seen this?" When told no, Hibbard sent for Johnson. Kelly, perhaps not entirely immune to the "not-invented-here" syndrome, examined the drawings and the model, turned to his boss, and said, "Hibbard, if you send that in, you'll destroy the Lockheed Company." He then walked out. Always the gentleman, the embarrassed Hibbard hemmed and hawed and finally said, "Well, the model certainly has a nice finish on it."

But Hawkins persisted, and in the end, Hibbard signed off—a courageous thing to do, given the powerful influence of Johnson's opinion. (The Lockheed response to the Air Force's request for a proposal was less than three-quarters of an inch thick. Only fourteen years later, the Lockheed proposal for a proposed Air Force transport would weigh six thousand pounds.) The Air Force evaluated the competing proposals swiftly and awarded a contract to Lockheed on July 2, 1951, for two YC-130 prototypes.

A "classic" design usually refers to an object of an earlier era—perhaps an automobile such as the 1937 Cord 812 or an aircraft such as the P-38—that was so handsome, so correct in its time, that it still looks "right" even after it has been superseded by more modern designs. The simple, workmanlike appearance of the new Lockheed C-130 transport militated against its ever being considered a classic solely by this definition. But the career of the C-130 made the term "classic" irrelevant as it redefined the concept of aircraft beauty by the faithful service it rendered. With very little change in shape—a nose job here, a tail tuck there—and no significant change in dimension, the Lockheed C-130 has never been superseded at its task, even as it reaches toward a half century of production life. (Some examples underline how remarkable this is. It is as if Rickenbacker's 1918 Spad would still have been performing duty in Vietnam in 1968 or Lindbergh's 1927 *Spirit of St. Louis* was still crossing oceans in 1977.) With more than 2,150 aircraft produced, almost a hundred design and mission variants built, and service performed for scores of nations, the Hercules still has no genuine competitor. It has had imitations, aircraft such as the Transall C.160, which borrowed its general shape in a twin-engine version, and the C-130 is still used as a model for aircraft projected for the future, such as the European Future Large Aircraft

The prototype YC-130 Hercules turboprop transport first flew at Burbank on August 23, 1954. Developed continuously, the type has remained in production ever since, becoming the Western world's most important cargo aircraft.

(FLA). But no other aircraft has ever come close to being able to do what the C-130 does so well and so economically. Not even the generally similar appearing but less capable Antonov An-12 "Cub," some 900 of which were built for the Soviet bloc before its production run ended in 1973, equaled the C-130. The only prospective replacement for the C-130 is the new C-130J, a highly refined but still clearly related descendant of the original YC-130. The Royal Air Force, much to the distress of its European neighbors, has already expressed preference for the here-and-now C-130J over the yet-to-come FLA.

As with many great designs, form had followed function. The air force had demanded, among other things, a large, easily accessible cargo area. The proposed concept began with a square-shaped 4,500-cubic-foot box that had almost exactly the dimensions of a standard railroad boxcar. Structural and volumetric considerations and the need to operate from rough fields dictated the use of a high wing. The requirement to avoid impinging on available cargo space, plus the hazard of rough-field operation, led to the adoption of an extremely simple but rugged dual-tandem-wheel landing-gear system mounted in streamlined stub-housings at the bottom of the fuselage. Even though a relatively narrow gear, the low center of gravity of the aircraft precluded the crosswind handling problems that dogged previous similar installations.

Despite the utilitarian function, the external form of the C-130 was, if not sleek, attractive. From the tip of the tail fin to the sleek greenhouse nose, with its twenty-three windows to give great visibility for steep approaches to short fields, the lines of the Hercules are smooth and straight.

Rear-loading cargo gliders appeared during World War II, and the air force had experience with rear-loading cargo planes such as the Fairchild C-119 and C-123, but the C-130 design improved on all previous attempts.

Kelly Johnson, despite his initial reservations, was very proud of the rugged C-130. He told a story of how he and Hall Hibbard were being shown through a newly built four-story engineering building at Lockheed by the building's architect. The man was particularly proud of the strength of the building, telling them, "The floor is designed for 250 pounds per square foot." He went on to note that the floor had twelve inches of concrete with ⅜-inch reinforcing rods spaced every twelve inches. Johnson and Hibbard looked at each other and smiled—they knew that the floor of the C-130, made out of thin dural structures, was designed to withstand 300-pound-per-square-foot loads. The cargo compartment tie-downs had to be able to restrain a 25,000-pound bulldozer from driving on forward through the cockpit in the event of a crash landing. And it all had to be built at the lowest possible weight. They praised the architect for his work—and didn't tell him about the C-130's floor loading.

The choice of four Allison T56-A-1 turboprop engines was particularly fortunate, for they provided more than adequate power for the initial requirements, especially those for one-engine-out operation. The turboprops demonstrated good fuel economy even as they endowed the aircraft with the potential for a 360-mph top speed, almost double that of its World War II predecessors. The surplus power of the four turboprop engines permitted the entire fuselage, including the cavernous cargo compartment, to be pressurized. The pressurized cargo compartment was necessary to obtain the advantages that accrue to a turboprop engine at higher altitudes, while maintaining a safe cabin environment for passengers or paratroopers. The rugged structure that pressurization required also gave the C-130 an exceptionally tough airframe, able to withstand the rough-and-tumble of operation in the field over several decades.

The first YC-130 aircraft were built in Burbank. As with the Boeing B-52, it was the second prototype that made the first flight, a sixty-one-minute trip from Burbank's Lockheed Air Terminal to

Edwards Air Force Base on August 23, 1954. Stanley Beltz was pilot, Roy Wimmer copilot, Jack Real (later for many years a close confidant of Howard Hughes) flight test engineer, and Dick Stanton flight engineer. Kelly Johnson, no doubt repenting his earlier doubts about the aircraft, flew in the accompanying Neptune chase plane. The number one YC-130 would serve as a static test article before making its first flight on January 21, 1955.

Tests quickly proved that flight characteristics were excellent, and performance was much better than had been projected in all parameters—cruising speed, takeoff distance, climb rates, service ceiling, and landing distance. The maximum payload of 40,000 pounds exceeded air force requirements. Lockheed had estimated that the aircraft would have a gross weight of 113,000 pounds, but brought the airplane in at 108,000 pounds, a 5,000-pound saving. The aircraft that would in due course be named the Hercules was, in short, a winner.

While flight testing proceeded, a whirl of activity surrounded the transfer of manufacture to the Marietta plant, where a team led by the new project engineer, Al Brown, prepared to tackle the first air force contract for seven production aircraft. The Marietta workforce had almost doubled, to just less than twenty thousand, and C-130s began to take shape at the height of B-47 production in 1954, when 143 of the six-jet bombers were built. It was an ideal production situation, for, as the B-47s phased down, C-130 production built up.

The rollout of the first production model on March 10, 1955, was graced by the presence of Governor Marvin Griffin, who made three futile attempts to christen the aircraft with a bottle of water from the nearby Chattahoochee River, succeeding only on the fourth try. The first flight took place on April 7, 1955. This aircraft was severely damaged a week later on its third flight when a loose quick-disconnect fuel-hose coupling started a fire in the number two engine; it was ultimately repaired and subsequently gave long service.

Other difficulties occurred with the Curtiss-Wright electric propellers, which were changed first to an Aeroproducts design and finally, on the C-130B series, to a Hamilton Standard. One near disaster occurred when an aft ramp blew out while undergoing ground pressurization tests, an incident that led to performing pressurization tests underwater in huge specially built tanks.

The initial series of Air Force contacts called for 204 C-130As, and the first aircraft was delivered to the 463rd Troop Carrier Wing at Ardmore, Oklahoma, on December 9, 1954. The initial C-130As had a plain "Roman nose," that is, the outline of the nose was an unbroken forward-slanting line. This was soon changed to the "Pinocchio nose" with the addition of the AN/APN-59 radar dome.

There was some concern that, in Haughton's words, "the string would run out" and the Air Force would not order any more C-130s. (Australia bought 12 C-130As, the first of many foreign sales.) He and Carl Kotchian advocated the development of a follow-on and invested several million dollars in the preparation of the C-130B, which had more internal fuel and more powerful Allison T56-A-7 engines of 4,050-shaft horsepower. The landing gear and the general structure were strengthened and takeoff weight was increased to 135,000 pounds. The USAF bought 123 B models, and 33 were sold to foreign countries, sustaining an international trend which continues to this day.

Over time, the availability of more powerful versions of the trusty Allison T56, plus the need for longer range, led to more powerful variants with increased internal and external fuel capacity. Thus, the C-130E's internal fuel was increased to almost 7,000 gallons, supplemented by the two 1,360-gallon external underwing tanks. (Pilots still debate the net results of the external wing tanks; some claim the extra weight and drag detract from performance enough to negate their value.) The Allison T56-A-7 engines were retained. The first C-130E flew on August 15, 1961. A total of 490 E models were built, including 377 for the USAF, four (as C-130Gs) for the navy, and 109 for foreign customers.

The utility of the aircraft was vastly increased with the introduction of the low-altitude parachute extraction system (LAPES) for the delivery of cargo. Later aircraft received the AWADS (adverse weather aerial delivery system), which permitted pinpoint navigation for airdrops under difficult conditions, as occurred in the relief efforts for Bosnia.

Another increase in power, this time to 4,508-shaft horsepower, distinguished the C-130H, which was unusual in that it was delivered first to a foreign service, the Royal New Zealand Air Force. The C-130H first flew on November 19, 1964, and has been delivered to more than fifty air forces. It remains in production today, and will continue to be so for many years to come.

Space limitations preclude more than the briefest account of the seventy-plus variations of the C-130. Its duties include those originally programmed for it as a medium transport, plus those of gunship, electronic warfare, search and rescue, tanker, airborne command post, Antarctic delivery system, battlefield illumination, bomber, forest-fire air tanker, weather reconnaissance, airborne early warning, airborne battlefield command and control, airborne radio and television relay, special forces operations, special operations, airborne emergency hospital, drone launch and control, and many more. It is used by the USAF, the U.S. Navy, the U.S. Coast Guard, and the U.S. Marines, and at present count, sixty-four foreign countries.

In addition to its military uses, more than one hundred civilian versions have been built. The L-100 was essentially a demilitarized C-130E, the designation change serving to make its sale to foreign countries more palatable. Two stretched versions, the L-100-20 and L-100-30, were built, and some of the early L-100s have been modified to L-100-20 standard. These civilian versions are in use by eight foreign air forces and thirty civil operators, including five in the United States. At the time this is written, more than 2,150 C-130s have been sold.

The C-130 Hercules was the subject of numerous development programs, including extensive experiments with boundary layer control. Two additional Allison T56 engines were installed in place of the external tanks; these blew air through a ducting system over the flaps and all control surfaces. The rest of the aircraft was standard, with the exception of an enlarged rudder to maintain control at low speeds. The modified Hercules achieved true STOL (Short Takeoff and Landing) performance, getting off the ground in 750 feet and landing in 700. On June 19, 1984, flight tests began on an independent Lockheed project, the High Technology Test Bed (HTTB).

The HTTB aircraft was a converted Lockheed L-100-20, and was equipped with extensive telemetry equipment. Over an eight-year period, the aircraft was modified in many different ways, including drooped wing leading edges (to maintain aileron control with the planned very steep, low-speed approaches), double-slotted, fast-acting flaps (to increase lift coefficient), new engines, new propellers, and a host of other variations. The HTTB was lost on February 3, 1993, when during a high-speed taxi test it inadvertently became airborne, swerved to the left, and crashed.

The most radical of all the C-130 modifications was made under the Credible Sport program. Three standard C-130H aircraft were selected for modification for use in rescuing the hostages from the American embassy still being held by Iran in 1980. The modification included installation of no fewer than thirty rocket motors: eight for assisting takeoff, eight for reducing sink rate, eight to reduce the landing distance, and six for pitch and yaw control at low speeds. Minor aerodynamic changes were made, including extending the leading edge, the flaps, and the ailerons. Exotic radar and navigation equipment was added, as was an in-flight refueling capability. The task of the C-130 apparently was to land within a football stadium area, so that a rescue could be effected. Unfortunately, the test aircraft crashed on October 29, 1980. After Iran released the hostages in time for President Reagan's inauguration, the Credible Sport program was canceled. Given the extraordinary demands placed on aircraft and crew, the program would have been better named "Incredibly Sporty."

Now the future for the Hercules lies with its C-130J military and L-100J commercial improvements. The new aircraft is fifteen feet longer than the standard C-130, and has new propulsion and avionics systems. The J model offers a 40 percent greater range, 40 percent higher cruising ceiling, 50 percent improvement in time to climb, 21 percent increase in maximum speed, and 20 percent decrease in the maximum takeoff run. New Allison AE2100D3 engines, rated at 4,591 shaft horsepower, are 15 percent more fuel-efficient. An all-composite six-blade Dowty-Aerospace R391 propeller system is lighter in weight and has fewer moving parts than previous C-130 propellers. The modern flight station has liquid crystal display (LCD) instrumentation, holographic heads-up instrument displays, and multifunctional heads-down LCD displays that are compatible with special night-vision devices, enabling operation in areas of total darkness when conditions so dictate.

The C-130J made its first flight on April 5, 1996, and is currently in production for the Royal Air Force, U.S. Air Force, and Royal Australian Air Force.

The Hercules as Warrior

The Hercules went to war in Vietnam as a troop transport, and was soon found wherever there was fighting. It was engaged in action in a bewildering variety of roles, including clandestine operations, all over Southeast Asia. The United States would benefit enormously as it transpired that the incredible bravery of the aircrews was matched by the rugged adaptability of the aircraft. Pressed into one perilous situation after another, operating under the worst weather conditions and always, even when at rest, subject to enemy attack, both aircraft and crews distinguished themselves throughout the long years of the war.

In the Vietnam "war without a front," the C-130s were tasked to supply isolated outposts where short, rough landing strips had been hacked from the surrounding jungles. Landings and takeoffs were routinely made under enemy fire, the pilots sometimes sneaking out for takeoff between incoming mortar rounds. When runways were closed, the C-130s went in at low level to do parachute extraction drops amid a hail of antiaircraft fire. The Hercules often took hits that would have downed a less-rugged aircraft, flying back to base with gaping holes in the airframe, engines knocked out, fuel streaming from punctured tanks, and tires hanging in shreds. A few got caught by direct hits from heavy weapons and didn't come back.

A few specific examples will indicate the variety and the strength of the C-130s' achievements. In Operation Birmingham, on April 24, 1966, C-130s flew 56 sorties on the first day into a 4,600-foot dirt strip that seemed to be the size of a postage stamp when contrasted with the enveloping green of the surrounding jungle. The 130s would not only bring in troops, but supply them as well, as during Operation Junction City. On February 22, 1967, the only full battalion-sized drop of American paratroops took place from Hercules transports. Once on the ground and engaged in desperate fighting, cut off from any resupply from the ground, the troopers of the 173rd Brigade were sustained by more than fifty C-130s dropping equipment and supplies.

Later that year, in November, 250 C-130 sorties were flown into Dak To, where the asphalt strip was torn into shreds by enemy fire, and takeoffs and landings had to be steered around jagged holes like a skier slicing through a slalom run. There, on November 15, enemy shelling blew up an ammunition dump, destroying two parked C-130s and turning the entire area into a roaring furnace that spewed forth one explosion after another. It seemed inevitable that a third Hercules, parked within the firestorm, would go up in flames as well. Without regard for their own safety, Captain Joseph K. Glenn and Sergeant Joseph F. Mack leaped in the aircraft and taxied it from the inferno to safety, an act for which they were each awarded the Silver Star and the Distinguished Flying Cross.

Early the next year, North Vietnamese general Vo Nguyen Giap hoped to repeat his 1954 victory over the French at Dien Bien Phu. His forces had surrounded American and South Vietnamese troops at Khe Sanh on January 21, 1968. The Americans were determined to resist at whatever cost, and dug in as the North Vietnamese sappers pushed their trench lines ever closer. The Americans called in B-52s as flying artillery, and placed their dependence upon airlift aircraft for resupply.

The C-130s reached a peak effort at Khe Sanh, landing to off-load troops and supplies and take on wounded as long as conditions permitted, and then going on to make bulk deliveries by parachute extraction methods when the North Vietnamese troops had advanced so close that landings were no longer possible. Ground radar was used to guide the C-130s to their precise drop points, which the Hercules crews flew with precision, ignoring that the entire run-in was awash in sheets of antiaircraft fire from below and from both sides of the course line. C-130s accounted for 90 percent of the total supplies that were brought in to sustain the defenders at Khe Sanh, enabling them to withstand Giap's assault and eventually break the siege.

Elsewhere in Vietnam, some C-130s were delivering troops, food, and munitions to the troops on the ground, while others acted as airborne battlefield command-and-control posts, covert-operations transports, tankers, rescue aircraft, and even as bombers. In that un-likely role, never envisioned by the air force or Lockheed, C-130s were used to drop the fifteen-thousand-pound BLU-82 blast bombs that decimated enemy troop concentrations or created instant helicopter landing pads in the jungle. The Hercules also dropped BLU-82s in the Persian Gulf War, this time to clear minefields.

In a feat of brilliant engineering, the HC-130s of the Air Rescue Service were modified into tankers that could service the Sikorsky HH-3E and HH-53B and C rescue helicopters. (The prospect of helicopters conducting aerial refueling had never previously been given serious consideration. The difficulties were enormous in terms of the hazard of the hose or boom to the rotor disc, the incompatibility of speeds between tanker and helicopter, and the placement of the receiving receptacle. The HC-130 and the HH-3s were sufficiently advanced to develop the technique and equipment for refueling in flight.) The "Herks" and the "Jolly Greens" became a team that flew missions far behind enemy lines to rescue downed aircrew members.

As a part of the Vietnamization process, by which American forces were systematically withdrawn as South Vietnamese forces were built up, thirty-five C-130As were provided to the South Vietnamese Air Force. Nineteen of these were used to carry refugees from South Vietnam to Thailand when the collapse came in 1975, but thirteen were captured by North Vietnam and introduced into its air force. Thus in Vietnam, the Hercules was pushed full circle, from sustaining an ally to reinforcing the erstwhile enemy.

The fighting qualities of the C-130, so well proven in Vietnam, were demonstrated again on July 4, 1976, in the superbly executed

Operation Thunderbolt. On the previous June 27, an Air France Airbus A300B2 on a flight from Tel Aviv to Paris landed at Athens. There it was boarded by four terrorists, who hijacked the aircraft after takeoff and ordered it to Benghazi to refuel, before taking it to Entebbe, Uganda, where the terrorists knew they would receive support from President Idi Amin. The 12 crew members and 256 passengers were taken off the aircraft and housed in an old airport terminal building. After 12 more persons had joined the terrorist group, they demanded the release of 53 convicted terrorists detained in Israel, in exchange for the hostages.

The Israeli government refused to bargain with the terrorists. Instead, the Israeli Air Force used four C-130s, accompanied by a Boeing 707 electronic-countermeasures aircraft, in an elaborate rescue effort that succeeded beyond all expectations. The Hercules aircraft swept in to land, and in a brilliant forty-minute foray, 245 commandos killed the hijackers and about 20 of the cooperating Ugandan troops, and rescued the hostages. Sadly, 3 of the hostages had been killed in the initial firefight. The commandos then destroyed seven MiG fighters—to prevent pursuit—and the C-130s carried the Israeli forces and the erstwhile hostages back to Tel Aviv. It was a stunning achievement, made possible only by the C-130s' range, speed, and carrying capability.

Over the years, the C-130s have since proved themselves in many other conflicts, large and small. These include the ongoing battles in Lebanon; in Africa, including South Africa, Rhodesia, Angola, and elsewhere; in the Middle East, in the long, bitter conflict between Iran and Iraq; in the Indian subcontinent in wars between India and Pakistan; and elsewhere.

In the brief, furious 1982 Falklands campaign, the Hercules served both the British Royal Air Force (RAF) and the Fuerza Aerea Argentina (FAA). The RAF's Hercules flew more than thirteen thousand hours, including forty-four refueled airdrops to British ships and ground forces. The Argentine C-130s flew in a surveillance radar station in the first wave of the attack and then took on a standoff reconnaissance role during which one of their number was shot down.

The United States employed the C-130 in Operation Urgent Fury in Grenada in 1983, and again in Operation Just Cause, in Panama, in 1989. It served with great distinction in the Persian Gulf War, flying in thousands of tons of equipment and supplies, and operating with a departure reliability rating of more than 96 percent.

Against this backdrop of military operations, it must not be forgotten that the work of the Hercules has resulted in far more lives saved than killed. It has flown thousands of humanitarian missions carrying heavy equipment for disaster relief, fuel, clothing, food, and medical supplies to Somalia, Bosnia, Rwanda, the former Soviet Union, Paraguay, Haiti, and scores of other destinations. It did not matter whether the catastrophe was man-made or natural, the result of earthquakes, famines, floods, or fire—the Hercules could be counted on to drop in and unload whatever was needed, from "instant hospitals" to water purification plants to simple sacks of staples such as rice or flour. For much of its life, the C-130s could have borne the Red Cross sign of mercy as appropriately as they wore the star-and-bar insignia of the USAF.

The C-130 has also saved more lives and hundreds of millions of dollars of property in its fire-fighting efforts. Air National Guard and air force reserve units operate C-130s equipped with a special aerial fire-fighting apparatus called the Modular Airborne Fire Fighting System (MAFFS). The MAFFS can be loaded on any standard C-130 in two hours. The units disperse a fire-retardant chemical called Phos-Chek D-75, a dry powder composed of fertilizer salts and a coloring agent manufactured by Monsanto. Mixed with water, it forms a gum-like solution that has an excellent drop pattern and adheres to trees and brush. In effect, the Phos-Chek inhibits the combustion potential of trees and shrubs by providing a chemical barrier. It is a stirring sight to see a formation of two C-130s, slowed down to 140 mph and only 150 feet off the ground, fly into the heart of a raging forest fire. The two aircraft can spray fifteen tons of Phos-Chek over an area the size of five football fields in less than six seconds.

Ski-equipped C-130s served well in the polar regions, and, in civil use, helped build the Alaskan pipeline. Thus, the C-130 became an unending source of revenue for Lockheed Georgia, and of course for the corporation as a whole. There were some other concurrent projects that, despite their promise, did not quite yield the same results. It was only when Georgia stuck to its military transport guns that fortune smiled.

The Incomparable C-141 StarLifter

One of the happiest, most fondly remembered programs in Lockheed Georgia history was the C-141 StarLifter program, which required the transfer of additional personnel from Burbank. The

The Hercules is extremely versatile, and has served as a rescue aircraft, gun ship, drone launcher, and airborne command post.

StarLifter rescued the air force's Military Airlift Command (as the former Military Air Transport Service was redesignated in January 1966) from terminal obsolescence and would then demonstrate its efficiency for more than three decades. The Military Airlift Command (MAC) had been doing a yeoman's work with its slow, high-maintenance fleet of Boeing C-97s, Lockheed C-121s, Douglas C-118s, and Douglas C-124s. The C-124—"Old Shaky," as it was fondly called—was perhaps the most versatile, with its ability to haul outsized cargo, but the growing crisis in Vietnam dictated the acquisition of modern jet transports. The C-124 took ninety-five flying hours and perhaps three times that many maintenance hours to go from Travis Air Force Base, California, to Saigon and back, with 20,000 pounds of fuel. It made the trip at low altitudes, pounding through all the massive weather problems that could erupt along the long route. The C-141, flying in relative comfort above most of the weather, could carry the same cargo the same distance in thirty-four hours, with far less maintenance effort. The C-124 had to be unloaded by the traditional railroad methods of hand trucks and muscle power, but the C-141 incorporated the new 463L materials-handling system,

One of the best-liked cargo aircraft in Air Force history, the Lockheed C-141 was almost trouble-free during development and production. Later, its capacity was expanded by stretching the fuselage to raise internal volume.

which permitted the aircraft to off-load as much as 68,500 pounds of cargo within the hour it took to refuel.

The C-141 was one of the few military procurement programs to receive full backing and assistance from then secretary of defense Robert S. McNamara. This would be only temporary, however, for by the latter part of the program, he had reversed his field and pressed for the termination of the C-141 in favor of the larger C-5A Galaxy.

The C-141 and Desegregation

The C-141 program was noteworthy for another, less well known, reason: it was the vehicle by which Lockheed desegregated the Georgia operation, a difficult task given the state laws then obtaining. Robert Gross had given Dan Haughton his marching orders to see that the plant complied with new federal laws promoting integration. Haughton passed on the instructions and Dick Pulver and his crew brought desegregation about indirectly and with subtlety. The signs that had indicated segregated rest rooms and drinking fountains were quietly removed. Paper cups by the thousands were placed by all drinking fountains, and no one challenged the change. The segregated lunchrooms were simply abandoned, and carts were placed in hallways to provide the food. The indirect approach worked, not immediately but over time and without any upheaval. The percentage of black employees steadily increased, and black supervisors became increasingly common. The process of change did not take place overnight, but it was sustained, and the efforts were successful.

The Men behind the Winning Airplane

In May 1960, the USAF issued a Specific Operational Requirement (SOR) for an aircraft capable of carrying a maximum load of over sixty thousand pounds over a 3,500-nautical-mile distance. This was followed in December of the same year by a RFP for the Logistics Transport System 476L. Lockheed entered a hard-fought competition with Boeing, Convair, and Douglas, and was declared the winner on March 13, 1961.

F. A. "Al" Cleveland, chief advanced design engineer, had made significant contributions to the winning proposal. As a result, he was first made assistant chief engineer, and then C-141 engineering program manager. His longtime colleague Chuck Wagner would become the program manager.

The story of Chuck Wagner is worth telling at some length because it is typical of the lives of many of the people who subsequently made Lockheed, and especially Lockheed-Georgia, great. It also reflects the care with which Lockheed management, even very early on, nurtured high-potential employees. Like so many of his colleagues, Wagner would follow a classic Horatio Alger career path. In his case, his progress led to his becoming program manager of the C-141, the most advanced jet transport in the world at the time.

Born in San Antonio on August 10, 1909, Wagner received his high-school education in California. From his earliest years, he followed the practice of working and going to school simultaneously, working at night while in high school, going to school at night in his college years. He worked at a wide variety of jobs, including grunt labor in the Bakersfield oil fields, all the while picking up junior college credits. Wagner became a machinist in 1928, and then took courses from a cultural gem of the Depression, one that rescued many an industrious lad from the ranks of the unemployed, the International Correspondence School. (ICS advertisements may still be found in many magazines, their style virtually unchanged from the Depression years, but their course content upgraded to computers and electronics.) This training would be invaluable to him in the aircraft industry, and in particular, in the C-141 program.

While continuing his dual track of daytime work and nighttime school, he learned to fly at John Nagle's famous East Side Airport in Los Angeles, taught by the man who would become Lockheed's premier test pilot, Tony LeVier. Wagner joined Lockheed in 1936 as employee number 400, making 69¢ per hour, working on the tooling used for the Model 10. He paid for his flying by commuting to work by plane, then giving as many as three fellow employees short flights around the airport at lunchtime for $2 a flight. Wagner would eat his own sandwich as he flew. He later joked that he made $5.52 for eight hours' work and $6 for one hour of flying at lunch.

Wagner worked on each of the Lockheed aircraft as it appeared, moving up in the organization as he did so. He gained the confidence of management to the degree that he was sent, with Dan Haughton, to the Harvard Business School in 1946—quite a step up from International Correspondence courses.

But it was at Georgia, on the C-141, that all of Wagner's expertise came to the fore, for there he persuaded the USAF that the aircraft's manufacture could be engineered to use numerically controlled machinery—if the service could put the machine tools in place. The Air Force agreed, and millions of dollars' worth of the then-new numerically controlled machine tools were installed in the plant. The results, in terms of efficiency and precision, were seen in all subsequent Lockheed production in Georgia. It was Wagner's greatest personal triumph as a program manager for Lockheed, for the C-141 was produced on time and under budget.

Engineering the C-141

The two previous American jet transports, the Boeing 707 and Douglas DC-8, were sleek low-wing aircraft with thirty-five and thirty degrees of wing sweep, respectively. Instead of following this pattern, the C-141 adopted engineering cues from the C-130, resulting in a high wing with twenty-five degrees of sweep and a low aircraft floor with a large hydraulically operated clamshell door in the rear and a ramp to permit vehicles to drive on board. Unlike the C-130, these external doors were not designed for cabin pressure loads; an internal pressure door was hinged so that it could retract into a recess overhead.

The C-141's wing featured a new airfoil section that was in fact a forerunner of the supercritical airfoil. The plane also incorporated load-canceling wing spoilers that extended all the way from the fuselage to the ailerons, and would be useful in relieving stress loads in flight.

At about ten feet wide and nine feet high, its cross section was not much different from that of the C-130. However, the cargo compartment was seventy feet long, thirty feet longer than that of the Hercules. For power, the C-141 had the benefit of the newly developed Pratt & Whitney TF33-P-7 turbojets of twenty-one thousand pounds of thrust. The engines, developed from those used on the B-52H, were a vast improvement over previous practice, with greater power, rapid throttle response, and lower specific fuel consumption. Cleveland was particularly proud of the innovative design of the nacelles, which housed long ducts from the fan of the engine all the way back to the exhaust nozzle, an installation that worked well on the relatively low-bypass-ratio TF33.

The C-141 took the first step toward today's glass cockpit by including a digital computer as a standard part of its avionics. It also incorporated an all-weather landing system.

Under Cleveland's direction, the Georgia team used systems analysis to choose the optimum cruise speed of about .767 Mach and the relatively modest twenty-five-degree wing sweep of the new transport. Secretary McNamara and his band of whiz kids at the Department of Defense were no longer seeking top performance in terms of speed or range, but rather were demanding designs with improved cost-effectiveness over the life cycle of the aircraft. In the case of the StarLifter, it was fortunate that they did, for so much would be demanded of the C-141 over so long a period of time that its extended life would have been difficult to achieve with more rigorous performance requirements.

Perhaps the most radical element of the C-141 was its use of the T-tail, as advocated by Frank Wilson and his aerodynamics division at Lockheed-Georgia. Aircraft with T-tails have the potential problem of the so-called deep stall, when airflow over the tail gets blanketed by the wing, eliminates elevator effectiveness, and makes stall recovery impossible. Wilson and his group were aware of the hazard, and their design incorporated vortex generators and a stick-shaker to warn the pilot not to exceed certain critical angles of attack.

The first C-141A flew at Marietta on December 17, 1963, celebrating the sixtieth anniversary of the Wright brothers' first flight. The 160-foot span of the C-141 was 40 feet longer than the original flight, and while the Wright Flyer weighed some 600 pounds and flew at less than 40 mph, the StarLifter had a maximum takeoff weight of 323,100 pounds and a top speed of 565 mph. The C-141A epitomized the incredible progress of six decades of flight.

Service Use

The StarLifter entered operational service with the Military Airlift Command on April 23, 1965, and was immediately put to good use carrying troops and equipment to Vietnam. There, the demands of the war had accelerated a growth from 33,779 passengers and 9,123 tons of cargo per month in 1965 to 65,350 passengers and 42,296 tons of cargo by 1967.

The C-141 was plunged into combat operations from the start, airlifting men and equipment directly from Hawaii to hot spots in Vietnam. New tactics were developed to maximize the utility of the aircraft. In Operation Eagle Thrust, in November 1967, C-141s flew 10,365 troops of the 101st Airborne Division, with all their equipment, direct from Fort Campbell, Kentucky, to Bien Hoa Air Base, South Vietnam. An expedited off-loading process reduced the average C-141 ground time at Bien Hoa to an incredible 7.4 minutes.

The C-141s soldiered all through the Vietnam War, flying vitally needed equipment in and frequently being used as aeromedical evacuation aircraft on the return trip. They also served to bring back the saddest cargo, the bodies of U.S. servicemen killed in combat.

When the war was over, they distinguished themselves again, first with the return of 588 American prisoners of war released from their years of confinement in Vietnamese prison camps in February and March 1973. The second was during Operation Frequent Wind in April 1975, the evacuation from Saigon of American and Vietnamese personnel to avoid their capture by the victorious Communist forces.

The StarLifter continued to distinguish itself in combat situations. During the 1973 Yom Kippur War, when the Israeli forces had been decimated and desperately needed resupply, C-141As delivered more than ten thousand tons of supplies in 421 missions. As would happen often in crisis situations, "friendly" European nations denied the USAF staging points for refueling. It was evident that the Air Force needed additional transport capacity, fitted with in-flight refueling equipment.

An unusual solution ameliorated the problem, and was brought into being through an inspired sales campaign to both the Department of Defense and to Congress. Lockheed managers showed how the basic C-141A design could be improved by the insertion of a thirteen-foot four-inch fuselage plug forward of the wing and a ten-foot plug aft, increasing the usable volume of the fuselage by almost 33 percent. An in-flight refueling boom receptacle was installed to vastly enhance the aircraft's range characteristics. Although both the Congress and DOD were initially reluctant to spend more money on the program, it soon became apparent that this was an efficient way to increase USAF airlift capacity.

The aircraft modified for test first flew on March 24, 1977, and the results were so successful that the 270 existing C-141As were modified in a similar manner to C-141B status. The result was equivalent to the addition of 90 of the original C-141As to the fleet, at a fraction of the cost of purchasing new airplanes.

The utilization of C-141s remained high, and the USAF, concerned about exceeding the operational life of the aircraft before it could be replaced, began a number of conservation programs to limit its flying hours and reduce the gross weights carried. A series of crises worked against this program, beginning with the operations in Grenada and Panama. All conservation plans were thrown to the winds with the advent of Operations Desert Shield and Desert Storm, in which the hardy StarLifters once again distinguished themselves.

The scope of the resupply effort in the Persian Gulf was enormous. When Saddam Hussein swept through Kuwait on August 2, 1990, there were no U.S. forces in the region. Six months later, 525,000 Americans and their attendant—sometimes luxurious—equipment were ready to begin Desert Storm.

The mission was extraordinarily demanding, for the flight path took the C-141Bs from the United States to a European staging point before flying into Saudi Arabia. The average round-trip took thirty-eight hours. The Military Airlift Command's entire fleet of 265 C-141s and 85 C-5s was thrown into the fray, and at the peak of the round-the-clock operations, one of these giant aircraft was landing at Dhahran every seven minutes.

The Lockheed giants were supplemented by C-130s, Douglas KC-10s, airliners from the Civil Reserve Air Fleet to deliver almost 5 billion ton-miles of personnel and cargo during the six months of intense operations, dwarfing the almost 700 million ton-miles flown during the fifteen-month-long Berlin Airlift.

As successful as the C-141 program was, for both the Air Force and Lockheed, the airplane specifications had not considered the requirement to carry large pieces of equipment for the Army, such as main battle tanks or dismantled helicopters. Even as the C-141 he had sought was being produced, Secretary of Defense McNamara intervened again, demanding a new transport. This time he insisted on procurement requirements so rigorous that it would impact the design of the new aircraft, the economic future of Lockheed, and the Air Force's airlift capability.

The C-5 Galaxy

Many aircraft have been controversial; few have ever suffered the intensity and duration of the controversy that surrounded the C-5 program from the start. Fortunately, the Galaxy survived the turmoil and was able to prove by decades of truly distinguished service that its design was inherently correct. The problems in the program, as will be seen below, stemmed from a wide variety of sources, some governmental, some from Lockheed, but many from the media, which found the Galaxy an evergreen source of sensational stories. It is to Lockheed's credit, and, to a lesser degree, to the credit of the Air Force, that the program was continued to its ultimate success when on so many occasions it seemed that cancellation would have been an easier alternative.

All of the problems, and even the need for the aircraft itself, could have been avoided if all Army requirements had been factored into the original design process for the C-141, and it had been produced with a greater volumetric capacity. This did not happen, and Vietnam made it painfully clear that a gargantuan new transport was required, one capable of carrying the largest and heaviest equipment possessed by the Army.

President John F. Kennedy had, for reasons of economy and the changing world political situation, begun a policy of reducing U.S. forces overseas. American military presence was to be exchanged for military flexibility, in which U.S.-based forces could be transported to overseas destinations in sufficient quantity quickly enough to deter conflict.

Design efforts for this very large aircraft, initially designated CX-4, but later called the CX-HLS (Cargo, Experimental—Heavy Logistics System) began in 1963 with a daunting requirement to carry 125,000 pounds of cargo eight thousand miles, with a maximum payload capability of 250,000 pounds over a shorter distance. At maximum gross weight, the aircraft had to be capable of taking off from an eight-thousand-foot runway, and to land on a four-thousand-foot-long semiprepared airfield in the combat area. (The last requirement was not adequately considered, for it should have been obvious from the start that the air force would be reluctant to bring so valuable—and so vulnerable—an aircraft into a forward combat zone.) A key requirement, one that would be undone by a host of other factors, was a design life of thirty thousand flying hours.

Once again, Boeing, Douglas, and Lockheed competed, but there was an additional aspect to the competition, one that would be seen again in the future. This was a competition for the engine between Pratt & Whitney and General Electric. As events transpired, Lockheed and General Electric were selected as winners, with the C-5 becoming the beneficiary of the General Electric TF39-GE-1, a 40,000-pound-thrust high-bypass-ratio turbofan engine.

The C-5A resembled the C-141 in general configuration, but was almost twice as big, with a maximum takeoff weight of 769,000 pounds. Like the StarLifter, the wing had a twenty-five-degree sweep and, initially, no leading-edge high-lift devices. Later, leading-edge slats were fitted and an Active Lift Distribution Control System (ALDCS) was installed. The ALDCS is a computer system that takes inputs from accelerometers mounted in various strategic locations, analyzes the data, and in response to airplane maneuvers or gust air loads, commands symmetrical deflection of the ailerons to reduce wing bending. This reduces fatigue and extends the life of the aircraft even as it provides a better ride.

The Galaxy was considerably faster than the StarLifter, having a top speed of 564 mph and a cruise speed of 506 mph. The need to transport heavy army equipment was met in part by the huge cargo compartment, 19 feet wide, 121 feet long, and ranging in height from 9 feet 6 inches beneath the wing-box structure to 13 feet 6 inches in the aft section. It could handle an M1 Abrams main battle tank, four M551 Sheridan light tanks, or a CH-47 Chinook helicopter. The upper deck of the fuselage houses the flight crew of five (pilot, copilot, flight engineer, and two loadmasters), a fifteen-man relief crew compartment with bunks, and, in a separate compartment behind the wing carry-through section, rearward-facing seats for 73 passengers. (The author has flown as a passenger in the C-5 and can report it is the most comfortable airliner in the air, bar none.) The lower fuselage section normally carries cargo, but can be equipped with palletized seats to carry 290 passengers.

In addition to the by-now traditional Lockheed aft fuselage/cargo door configuration, the C-5 incorporated a forward cargo door distinguished by its ability to swing up like a visor. This permitted cargo to be loaded from either end, and allowed easy on- and off-loading of

In contrast to the C-141, the C-5A Galaxy was plagued during development and production by problems. Over time, however, the design matured and it became one of the most efficient cargo aircraft in history.

heavy equipment. It has more than five times the cargo capacity of the C-141.

Although not usually assigned such duties, the Galaxy can be employed to drop airborne troopers and their equipment. In an exercise at Pope AFB, North Carolina, on June 7, 1989, a C-5B dropped four Sheridan tanks (each lowered to earth by eight G-11 parachutes) and seventy-three paratroopers for a world record of 190,346 pounds.

The elaborate landing gear of the C-5A, which included a crosswind landing feature and kneeling, was dictated by the need to land on semiprepared fields. After more than 2,600 variants of 660 basic undercarriage configurations had been reviewed, the final design consisted of four six-wheel main bogies that retract into the familiar fuselage side sponsons, and a four-wheel nose gear.

Wing Fixes and New Orders

The considerable difficulties with the execution of the C-5 contract will be covered in a later chapter. It is sufficient to say here that Lockheed asked the Air Force if it would accept an increase in weight, if the required performance was maintained by an increase in engine thrust, which could have been done for about $5 million. The Air Force adamantly held to the weight requirements, telling Lockheed that it could increase the engine thrust at its own expense if it wished, but that the weight goals would have to be met.

The result was a weight-reduction program that significantly reduced the strength of the wing, and consequently, the service life of the aircraft. Later this had to be compensated for by a modification. In 1980, Lockheed was given a contract to build completely new wing torsion boxes for the entire fleet of C-5s. Fleet retrofit began in 1982 and was completed by 1987.

By then the sterling performance of the Galaxy in the unremitting hard service of the Military Airlift Command proved that the aircraft was not only indispensable but, against all arguments to the contrary, in short supply.

To offset this, the Air Force favored procurement of forty-four McDonnell Douglas KC-10s and fifty Lockheed C-5B aircraft, while continuing research efforts on the proposed C-17 transport.

Boeing naturally opposed this idea, proposing a modification of the 747 transport for the task. The proposal was rejected by the Department of Defense. Despite this, under Senator Henry "Scoop" Jackson's leadership, the Senate adopted an amendment to the fiscal year 1983 authorization bill to substitute 747s for C-5Bs.

Future chairman Larry Kitchen recognized that an immediate effort had to be made to persuade the House to recommend the C-5Bs in its own version of the authorization bill, and to do so by a large majority. He felt that in the subsequent committee negotiations, the C-5B would be selected for the final authorization bill. Kitchen then worked tirelessly to direct a massive campaign to visit every congressman and the principal staff personnel to educate them on the comparative values of the C-5B and the modified 747. These efforts were successful, for the House was overwhelmingly in favor of the C-5B, and this view prevailed in the joint committee hearings.

Thus it was that fifty C-5Bs were ordered and delivered by 1986. The C-5B had a considerably improved performance, with more powerful engines and a maximum gross weight of 837,000 pounds and a maximum payload of 291,000 pounds over a 3,400-mile range. It dispensed with the C-5A's complex crosswind landing gear, and introduced an improved automatic flight control system (AFCS) and a malfunction detection and analysis and recording system (MADAR II).

The C-5 in Service—The Miracle of the Immense Planes

The first C-5A flew, amid considerable pomp and ceremony, on June 30, 1968. There was equal ceremony attending the first delivery of a C-5A to MAC, made on December 17, 1969, and embellished with the slight embarrassment of having one of the twenty-eight wheels fall off on landing. The aircraft became operational in September 1970, with the delivery of eight aircraft to Charleston Air Force Base, and was soon flying with its "little" brother, the C-141, on both European and Asian routes.

Seventeen years and forty-one days after the first flight of the original C-5, the C-5B took to the air on September 10, 1985, with first deliveries to MAC beginning on January 8, 1986. At the time this is written, 126 C-5s (76 C-5As and 50 C-5Bs) are still flying, serving in eleven squadrons: six active, four reserve, and one National Guard. With proposed updating, they will undoubtedly be serving until well into the twenty-first century. After the wing fix, the C-5s did not encounter the fatigue problem that has beset the C-141, and which dictates the latter's retirement in the not-too-distant future.

The utility of the Galaxy was proven for all time during the Vietnam War. It made the first of many trips on June 5, 1970, when it landed at Cam Ranh Bay. It served with distinction for the remainder of the war, and afterward in support of the South Vietnamese, being particularly effective reacting to the Communist Easter offensive in the spring of 1972. Its career was marred by one of the saddest events of the entire Southeast Asian conflict. On April 4, 1975, a C-5A took off from Tan Son Nhut Air Base as a part of Operation Baby Lift, a maneuver in which 250 Vietnamese infants were to be airlifted to the United States. Just after climbing to twenty-three thousand feet, the C-5A suffered a massive structural failure in the area of the rear cargo door. The pilot, Captain Dennis Taylor, by extraordinarily skillful airmanship, managed to crash-land the crippled aircraft near the Saigon River. Two hundred six people, including most of the infants and their escorts, were killed.

Half a world away, the C-5s had distinguished themselves in the Israeli airlift of October 1973. Egyptian and Syrian forces surprised the Israelis with a massive joint attack. It was soon evident that the Israelis had miscalculated the military consumables it needed to resist the dual assault, and a cry for help went out to Washington. There the Air Force Chief of Staff, General George Brown, made a unilateral decision to send two squadrons of McDonnell F-4 Phantom fighters, and provide the airlift necessary to send ammunition and other supplies.

The operation, called "Nickel Grass," routed MAC aircraft through the Azores directly to Lod Airport in Israel. (A "competing airline" operated by the Soviet Union funneled supplies to the Arab invaders.)

The C-5 completely vindicated itself in Nickel Grass, carrying in M-48 and M-60 tanks as well as major sections of aircraft. When the normally stoic Israeli prime minister Golda Meir saw the first tank being delivered by a C-5A, she was overcome with emotion and said, "For generations to come, all will be told of the miracle of the immense planes from the United States."

The effectiveness of the American airlift during the Gulf War was noted previously in the discussion of the C-141. The C-5 fleet flew 42 percent of the cargo and 18.6 percent of the passenger missions. The ability of the C-5 to carry entire helicopters ready for operation as soon as they were rolled off the ramp and serviced was vitally important to the U.S. Army.

In proving themselves again, the C-5s also proved the validity of the USAF "Total Force" concept, for the huge aircraft were operated with distinction by both Air National Guard and Air Force Reserve units. One C-5A flown by reservists of the 433rd Military Airlift Wing (MAW) from Kelly Air Force Base crashed at Ramstein, Germany, on August 29, 1990—the only transport lost in the airlift, and the fifth Galaxy to be lost in its history.

A Step Back in Time: Other Georgia Products

As he was to do often later, Carl Kotchian succeeded Haughton at Georgia, becoming general manager. (Over the years, the names of companies and divisions within Lockheed have been altered many times to suit the expansion or contraction of business; the same is true of titles. A few years later, for example, Kotchian would have been president of the Georgia Company, rather than general manager of the Georgia Division.)

As previously noted, under the combined B-47/C-130 production effort, employment at the Georgia plant had climbed to almost

Carl Kotchian worked well with the demanding Daniel Haughton to expand Lockheed's influence. Kotchian was a great salesman, and one of the prime movers behind the L-1011 project.

twenty thousand. A slight decline had begun in 1956, the year Haughton left, and this continued through 1960, when employment dropped back to just over ten thousand. Aircraft deliveries had fallen as well, from a spike of 149 in 1957 down to 55 in 1960.

It is understandable, then, that the Georgia plant, newly endowed with its own engineering and marketing capability, would wish to have some new product lines to bolster production and profit. And, while Kotchian had begun his career as an accountant and learned manufacturing under Haughton's guidance, he was at heart a salesman who enjoyed traveling, making contacts, and most of all, making sales. This talent would reach its peak with his championing of the later L-1011 TriStar airliner, a magnificent, if star-crossed, aircraft.

The C-140 JetStar

W. A. "Dick" Pulver succeeded Kotchian as vice president and general manager in August 1959, with C. S. "Chuck" Wagner as his assistant. Pulver had been chief engineer; when he moved up, he nominated Art Flock to replace him. Flock was always remembered as a man who had a lot of feeling for the human interests of his people, while at the same time being a top engineer. These executives would lead GELAC (as Lockheed Georgia was called) through both major and minor programs for almost a decade.

Lockheed Georgia's initial foray into another product line followed the pattern of the C-130, in that the first two examples of what became the JetStar executive jet transport were built in Burbank with the usual Skunk Works style and enthusiasm. The patent for the JetStar was assigned to Bill Statler and Kelly Johnson. Production was subsequently turned over to Georgia.

There is still a lingering sense of hurt at Lockheed—"betrayal" is the term often used in interviews—over the JetStar project. The firm had been led by the Air Force to believe that substantial orders of up to 300 aircraft would be given to the winner of a competition for the UCX, or utility transport, experimental. As events transpired, the Air Force would buy only 16 of the very advanced aircraft. Lockheed had opted not to enter a similar competition being held for the UTX, or utility trainer, experimental, an aircraft about one-half the size of the proposed UCX. This proved to be a mistake, for the smaller aircraft would be "more affordable." North American won the UTX contest with what became the T-39 Sabreliner, and ultimately sold 211 military versions of the aircraft.

Although the Air Force dragged its heels on C-140 procurement, initially buying only 5, with the Navy purchasing 2 more, the Lockheed sales force brought in orders for 29 more from civil corporations and the Canadian government, enough to begin production. Lockheed management could not foresee that the production rate was to be strung out over a long twenty-three-year period during which 204 JetStars would be built. It was a shame, for it was an excellent aircraft, well ahead of its time, but caught in the combined grip of a decline in military budgets and a niche market where few aircraft of its size were required.

The history of the C-140 program is somewhat controversial, for it was considered by its Skunk Work creators to be a total success, while the staff at Georgia who inherited the program found it to be riddled with problems. Chuck Wagner recalled in an interview that the aircraft did not have the cross-country capability it claimed, and the Georgia engineers could not get their hands on the prototype for further testing because it was being used for other purposes by the Skunk Works.

A jet transport was not a new concept at Lockheed, which had done many studies on jet-powered airliners. By 1950, drawings and models of the L-193, a sixty-four-passenger swept-wing jet with four engines mounted under the fuselage, were shown to several airlines, but elicited little interest. Work on the L-193 was not wasted, however, for it provided data from which would be derived the CL-329, as the UCX entry would be designated by Lockheed, and in which it would invest $6 million to bring it to production.

Kelly Johnson imposed the Skunk Works' methods and pace upon the CL-329, scheduling a first flight for the completed prototype in only eight months. He maintained his usual constant pressure upon the engineering personnel and the workforce right up to the morning of the first flight on September 4, 1957. The effectiveness of Kelly's efforts might be measured against the competition, McDonnell, whose four-engine entry did not fly until nineteen months later. The Mc-Donnell Model 119 looked like a miniature version of a Douglas DC-8. The lack of a suitable power plant delayed its development, and its pylon-mounted engines were so close to the ground that foreign-object ingestion was a major problem.

Kelly's task had not been easy. The layout chosen for the JetStar was very advanced and quite reminiscent of the newly introduced French airliner, the Sud Est S.E. 210 Caravelle. Like the French aircraft, its clean swept wings were unencumbered by engines, which were mounted aft on the fuselage. Its horizontal surfaces were mounted directly to the oversize (in appearance) vertical stabilizer. Kelly favored the aft-mounted engines for a number of reasons, including their relative immunity from foreign-object damage while taxiing, the ease with which pilots could manage engine-out operations, even at low speeds, and the reduction of noise in the passenger cabin. Johnson also had some private concerns about what the effect of a wheels-up landing might be on pylon-mounted engines on a low-wing aircraft.

As with McDonnell, engine selection was a major design problem. The lightweight engines from General Electric and other manufacturers that would come to be the engines of choice for many later executive jet aircraft were not yet available. Johnson cut the Gordian design knot by choosing Bristol Orpheus turbojets of 4,850 pounds of thrust. These were to be manufactured under license by the Wright Aeronautical Division of the Curtiss-Wright Corporation. The licensing agreement fell through, and while both prototypes were flown with two Bristol Orpheus engines, later aircraft were fitted with four of the smaller engines that had become available by then.

In terms of performance, the C-140/Orpheus engine combination was a good one. In February 1958, the prototype flew nonstop

Lockheed did not have as much luck marketing its smaller aircraft as it did with its larger cargo aircraft. The Jetstar was one of the first executive jet transports, and the Jetstar II shown here was an improved version.

from California to Marietta, Georgia, in just three hours and twenty-nine minutes.

The second prototype was the first to have four engines, flying for the first time in January 1960, with Pratt & Whitney JT12-A-6s of 3,000 pounds of thrust. In Georgia, Lockheed engineers pioneered a complete wind-tunnel surface-pressure model that revealed that the four-engine-nacelle configuration presented severe aerodynamic problems. After extensively redesigning the nacelles, most of the mutual interference and transsonic buffet was eliminated. The subsequent excellent results with the JT-12s led to their installation on subsequent production aircraft. The range of the aircraft was extended by the installation of 565-gallon slipper tanks over the wings.

A total of 164 JetStars were built, including the two prototypes. These were followed by 40 JetStar IIs, which had more powerful 3,700-pound-thrust Garrett turbojets and a modified wing tank.

The JetStars were much beloved by their civil and military customers, who found them fast, dependable, and very versatile. However, the only person believed to have made money selling the JetStar was Howard Hughes, whose last-minute midnight negotiations enabled him to buy aircraft early in the program, when their price was lowest. He then later resold them to customers for a profit. Hughes had a special hangar built in Georgia for his airplanes. He would have them

The LASA-60 Santa Maria was the first aircraft to originate out of the Lockheed-Georgia facility. A six-place single-engine light utility transport, it was first flown on September 15, 1959.

parked inside, and never flown. A twenty-four-hour guard kept everyone out, even Lockheed executives. When Hughes died, Jack Real, one of the few men who had Hughes's complete trust, had the aircraft removed from the hangar, refurbished, and sold at a profit. In keeping with his character, Hughes, despite his plethora of JetStars, always borrowed Lockheed's aircraft when he wanted to make a trip.

It is a shame that JetStar sales did not match its performance, for the aircraft would go on to set scores of records, including a nonstop ten-hour and twenty-six-minute flight from New Orleans to Bonn, Germany, by Jacqueline Cochran—a distance of 4,938 miles.

LASA-60 Santa Maria

Lockheed-Georgia's first original aircraft was the LASA-60, a high-wing, six-passenger, fixed-gear aircraft that resembled a Cessna 185 on steroids. The aircraft would not substantially improve Lockheed's profit picture, but it did diversify Georgia's interest in manufacturing, and pioneered the concept of foreign manufacturing agreements that would become very important only a few years later.

The Santa Maria was a product of the Mooney brothers, Al and Art. Their design efforts extended all the way back to 1922 and included such sterling aircraft as the Monocoupe. The Santa Maria was intended to meet a specification prepared by General Juan Azcarate of Mexico, who also sought to have the aircraft produced in his country.

Design work began in January 1959. Anticipating by thirty years the concept of outsourcing to reduce production costs, Lockheed management knew that the company's overhead would make the LASA-60 too expensive, and not only acceded to Azcarate's request, but sought other licensees elsewhere where labor costs were low.

The aircraft was first flown at Marietta on September 15, 1959, powered by a 250-horsepower Continental engine and capable of a top speed of 167 mph. The second Marietta prototype was delivered to the foreign company in Mexico in which Lockheed had invested, Lockheed-Azcarate, where it was used as a pattern aircraft for the eighteen production versions that followed.

The basic design met with more success in Lockheed's partnership with Aeronautica Macchi of Italy. The firm, a descendant of the great company that had made the famous Schneider Trophy racers and the fighters of Mussolini's air force, developed the design with a series of more powerful engines. A much-modified version of the Aermacchi-Lockheed AL60B-1, as it was called in Italy, became the Aeritalia-Aermacchi AM.3C forward-air-control aircraft. The AMC.3 was subsequently built under license in South Africa, where it was also redesigned and enlarged for other work. The combined production of all LASA-type aircraft was approximately 170, a reasonable number for a large transport perhaps, but unprofitable for smaller designs.

And Now for Something Completely Different

Georgia's independence from the Burbank operations can be inferred from its 1961 proposal to the U.S. Army for a midwing VTOL (Vertical Takeoff and Landing) research aircraft. The Lockheed VZ-10 (XV-4) Hummingbird would ordinarily have derived from the Skunk Works. The aircraft was intended as a prototype for a battlefield surveillance aircraft that could be stationed forward with the front-line forces.

The Hummingbird was an attractive, if unusual-looking, two-place aircraft, with a thick, bulky fuselage, rather small, narrow-chord wings, and a tall T-tail. It originally used the principle of jet augmentation developed by Clemson graduate Frank Sutton, an expert in thermodynamics, to increase the static thrust of its two Pratt & Whitney JT-12 jet engines. The idea was that an ejector system could

The United States Army was very interested in vertical-lift aircraft in the late 1950s, and Lockheed-Georgia responded with the VZ-10 Hummingbird. First flight was on July 7, 1962. A second version, the XV-4B, was tested by the USAF in 1968, but no orders ensued.

be built so that the exhaust from an engine, if ejected vertically through a large number of nozzles, would entrain additional air from outside the aircraft, augmenting the total lifting capacity by as much as 50 percent. In laboratory tests, gains in power of as much as 230 percent were achieved, but in actual tests of the VZ-10, the net augmentation proved to be only about 15 percent, and vertical takeoff was impossible. A much modified second version, the XV-4A, achieved vertical takeoff on May 28, 1963. The two prototypes were delivered to the U.S. Army. One suffered a fatal crash on June 10, 1964, and the other was relegated to test work before being stored. The Hummingbird, somewhat surprisingly given its unorthodox configuration and the high drag of its bulky fuselage, was expected to have a top speed of 518 mph and a range of six hundred miles.

The Air Force expressed interest in the concept, and the surviving prototype was modified with an even larger fuselage into the XV-4B, the Hummingbird II. With the advent of more powerful smaller engines, the concept of jet augmentation was abandoned, and no less than six General Electric J85 engines for a total thrust of eighteen thousand pounds were installed. Four of these were lift-jet engines (i.e., they were mounted vertically in the fuselage and pointed straight down) while two were used for either lift, by diversion downward by a valve, or propulsion. The engines were smaller than the jet-augmentation mixing chambers had been, so there was room for additional fuel. The bulkier fuselage degraded performance, and the expected maximum speed dropped to 463 mph.

Flight trials of the modified XV-4B began in August 1968, but the aircraft was lost in an accident on March 14, 1969, bringing about program termination.

The Nuclear Airplane

Lockheed-Georgia spent over three years on Weapon System 125A, a proposed nuclear-powered supersonic bomber, working with Pratt & Whitney. The nuclear reactor would have been mounted in the aft fuselage, behind the bomb bay. The program, which had started in the California Company preliminary design department under Al Cleveland, and was transferred with him to Georgia, was ultimately canceled. Lockheed would continue to conduct design studies, and in 1958 responded to an Air Force request for proposal for a continuously airborne missile launch and low level system (CAMAL) that was also canceled.

The Future of Lockheed-Georgia

The future of Lockheed-Georgia rests primarily on two programs. The first is the evergreen C-130, now being offered as the C-130J, and, barring some still unknown revolution in aerodynamics or engine technology, destined perhaps for another half century of production in ever-modified form. This forecast might seem optimistic were it not for the fact that an expanding world economy will bring many more nations to the point where they will require military and civil transports with the C-130's utility. As each of these nations emerges, the potential for new orders increases.

The second program is the Lockheed Martin F-22. Destined to

be the standard air superiority fighter of the United States Air Force, the YF-22 made its first flight on September 29, 1990. The history of the YF-22 and its successful test program will be dealt with later, but the current production program will not be completed until the second decade of the twenty-first century.

The Lockheed-Georgia facility will also continue to modify the P-3 Orion and S-3 Viking aircraft, and there is every possibility that new production of follow-on aircraft will be required in the future.

CHAPTER 9

The Golden Opportunity: Missiles and Space

Rarely has an industrial giant, so vital to our national security for so many decades, had such a tentative start. The great Lockheed Missiles and Space Company, which has served as sword and shield for the defense of the free world, was launched after the war in an offhand manner. Robert Gross, very much aware of the potential shown by German V-1 and V-2 weapons, expressed an opinion that Lockheed had better look into the "pilotless aircraft business." In discussions with Hall Hibbard it became apparent that Lockheed did not have the experience to do the target-seeking and weapons guidance side of the missile business. The company instead opted to begin by building the test vehicles—what later became known as "platforms." Whether by chance or foresight, this brilliant move would pay dividends for decades. (Gross was always careful to validate his ideas, particularly the more far-reaching ones, with what became known as the Corporate Policy Committee. In addition to Gross, it was composed of his brother Courtlandt, Hall Hibbard, financier Charles Barker, and longtime investor and counselor Cyril Chappellet. These men knew when to rein Bob Gross in—but more importantly, they also knew when to let him run with an idea.)

Research began almost immediately, but the first major opportunity for business occurred in early 1947, when Willis Hawkins led an effort to respond to an air force request for a pilotless flying test bed for a series of ramjet engines, one that would be capable of supersonic speeds. (At this early period of the jet age, the ramjet engine was appealing because of its potential for enormous power and its relative simplicity—it operated like a turbojet, but without the need for a compressor or turbine. Its principal drawback was the requirement for it to be accelerated to a relatively high speed, approximately 300 mph, before it would run.)

The scope of the air force request was remarkable, given that many people still considered supersonic flight to be impossible, and would continue to do so until Captain Charles Yeager put the myth of the "sound barrier" forever to rest on October 14, 1947. The test vehicle was to be able to reach speed of Mach 3—three times the speed of sound—and sustain this speed for at least three minutes of operation at an altitude of fifty thousand feet. It also had to be immensely strong, able to withstand an 8-g turn at top speed. To realize full value from the tests, the engine and test instruments had to be recoverable.

Pilotless or not, Lockheed was tasking itself to design a Mach 3 airplane, one able to sustain temperatures up to nine hundred degrees Fahrenheit and be safely returned to earth. It was the sort of challenge Hawkins liked, and he once again assembled a team of key people. These included the brilliant Irv Culver, a man who was said to have invented his own system of mathematics; Al Cleveland, a superb aerodynamicist whose efforts with giant transports and a proposed nuclear airplane have already been noted; and Fred Jenks, a retired Air Force colonel with a doctorate in mathematics, who flew a P-38 during drop tests of one-third-scale models of the project and who became program manager. E. O. "Rick" Richter, a wind-tunnel expert and fine instrumentation engineer who greatly expanded the science of telemetry in the course of the program, was also a key man. (Among Richter's patents was one for the Rotodome, the antecedent of the rotating antenna used later on the Airborne Warning and Control System

[AWACS]). Curiously, although this select team had the insight to be able to meet the overwhelming technical challenges of the project, none of its members then saw much development potential in it.

Progress on the full-size missile was not swift. Some of the early experimentation was almost laughably primitive, as when Al Cleveland launched small aluminum models of the X-7 by a bungee cord from a ditch at the Burbank airport. The aircraft was built in the Advanced Development Projects facilities, and was shipped to White Sands for the test program. Hawkins recalls with great good humor their early tests of models for the X-7. Two-by-fours were knocked into a crude launch platform, and a Jeep was used as a blast shield. The first time they tried to fire it, they did a countdown—because they had seen this done in other launches at White Sands. When the button to launch was pressed—nothing happened. They were afraid to approach it because it might blow up. The Air Force offered to post a guard around the missile, and the Lockheed representatives spent the night considering what to do. Finally Tom Dudley, an engineer, figured out that the booster could be disengaged, because there was an external line that went from the battery to the booster igniter. Dudley brought a rifle, and at one hundred yards' range, he cut the external line with a bullet. Encouraged, they approached the missile to find that the missile timer had been stopped when its hands were held up by an oversized screw protruding through the case. Things were simpler in those days.

Production was undertaken at Plant B-6 in Burbank, and it was not until April 26, 1951, that the first full-scale test flight took place. Like so many missile first flights, it was a failure. Lockheed persisted, and eventually the X-7 became a workhorse.

The basic airframe that emerged was simple and slender—a needlelike fuselage fitted with short, thin, tapered wings, not unlike those that would appear on the later F-104, and simple, squared-off tail surfaces. However, when the test engine and the necessary booster rocket were attached, the X-7 ensemble assumed an almost grotesque appearance because of the huge aerodynamic surfaces required by the booster. Launching the X-7 from the ground was feasible, but at the cost of reduced top speeds. Maximum performance was obtained by dropping the X-7 from a Boeing B-29 carrier aircraft. The booster's disproportionately large aerodynamic surfaces made it impossible to launch from the bomb bay, à la Yeager's Bell X-1. Instead, a pylon was placed between the numbers three and four engines on the left wing, to which the X-7 was attached, its needle nose lancing forward between the arc of the propellers.

The rather innocuous looking X-7 research missile became the basis for the formation
of what became the extraordinarily successful Lockheed Missiles and
Space Systems organization.

Launch took place from the mother ship at altitudes up to 40,000
feet. The aft-mounted rocket booster generated 100,000 pounds of
thrust, which took the X-7 to speeds at which the ramjet could operate
for the remainder of the test. It flew in a racetrack pattern around the
White Sands Missile Range. Later models had twin boosters with a
combined thrust of 105,000 pounds.

Of all its radical aspects, the recovery procedure was perhaps the
most unusual, and as might be expected, proceeded from Irv Culver's
radical thinking. Protruding from the X-7's nose was a long spike,
which also served to mount the instruments for speed and altitude and
as an antenna. At the end of a flight, a series of parachutes deployed
at prescribed altitudes, and the X-7 floated down to nose-spike itself
in the ground. With the parachutes draped over it, the spiked X-7 was
said to resemble the famous Joshua cactus. Ground impact, while minimized by the parachutes, was severe, but the recovery system worked
so well that some X-7s flew many missions; the record was thirteen.

One of the most important but least recognized aspects of the
X-7 program was the testing and imagination required to build components able to withstand the colossal stress of rocket launches,
atmospheric heating, high-g turns, and rugged recoveries. Tests standards were primitive—one engineer fired .22 rifle bullets at a shielded

capacitor, while Irv Culver used a jackhammer to validate the toughness of a booster socket.

The X-7 platform was designed to be adaptable to an ever-larger series of Marquardt ramjet engines, and was a key element in making the long-lived Boeing Bomarc interceptor missile possible. A redesigned version, the X-7-3A, was equipped with a new wing and fitted with twin boosters mounted under the wing roots. These dispensed with the huge aerodynamic surfaces required for the single-booster system, and enabled launches to be made from the bomb bay of a new mother ship, a Boeing B-50.

The X-7 series repeatedly set new speed and altitude records in a test program unmatched anywhere in the world, reaching a top speed of 2,881 mph and altitudes over 106,000 feet. (It must be emphasized that this was all terra incognita for Lockheed—and everyone else— before Hawkins launched the program. It is one thing to develop a new transport that is perhaps moderately more efficient than its competitors, and quite another to leap into an entirely new, unknown scientific world, and to do so with extreme success.)

They were unaware of it at the time, but the X-7 engineers were already demonstrating the philosophical approach that would make the company great. They recognized that nothing had been done in the past to compare with their new challenges, so there were no precedents to stifle their imaginations. If a test article needed to be "bulletproof" they tested it by firing a bullet, real or metaphorical. And although the X-7 program did have follow-ons, including the Q-5 and Kingfisher target drones (which had the drawback of being faster than the missiles for which they were targets), its real importance was in being the lead horse for Lockheed in a totally new, utterly demanding environment. What became LMSC, there emerged a free-thinking, open, innovative system of doing business that was a complete departure from the codified methods that the rapid expansion of the aviation sector of the business had required. It is perhaps all the more remarkable that this system developed under organizational rules of secrecy that rivaled those of the Skunk Works. The new methods that were generated almost spontaneously by eager scientists and engineers working on extremely demanding projects would first bring LMSC to the fore in the corporate structure, and then, through a series of leaders grounded in this "school," go on to permeate the entire corporation.

A Rising Star

As important as the X-7 program was to the Air Force, it was absolutely critical to the development of Lockheed's burgeoning expertise. It fostered a tolerant mind-set on the part of Lockheed's admittedly airplane-oriented top management to esoteric projects. Once again, a formidable intellect would materialize to help shape Lockheed's destiny. In 1953, an engaging, good-humored, recently arrived but already rising star, L. Eugene Root, suggested that Lockheed form a separate division to pursue work on ballistic missiles and even satellites—then so revolutionary an idea as to be tinged with a touch of science fiction.

Root came from farming stock; born in 1910 in Lewiston, Idaho, he moved with his family to California, and graduated from Stockton High, where he played on the football team for four years. After high school, he helped his father on a huge one-hundred-thousand-acre peat farm and, in classic Horatio Alger fashion, ran a newspaper route on the side. One of his customers admired his industry and agreed to loan him money to supplement his scholarships, enabling him to enroll in the College of the Pacific, where he also played football and engaged in campus politics. For the latter, he once had himself flown low over the campus to drop campaign literature directly on the student body.

He did so well at the College of the Pacific that he was urged by no less a sponsor than Dr. Robert A. Millikan to transfer to the California Institute of Technology just as it was beginning its great leap forward in the world of aerodynamics. Millikan, Cal Tech's president, had induced Dr. Theodore van Karman to head the Guggenheim Aeronautical Laboratory, where a new ten-foot wind tunnel, huge for its time, was built. It was heady company for a farm boy from Stockton, but Root relished it. He excelled again at Cal Tech, graduating in 1934 with two master's degrees, one in mechanical engineering and a second in aeronautical engineering. He went directly to the Douglas Aircraft Company, where he worked happily for $24.48 a week with stellar engineers such as Arthur E. Raymond, the man primarily responsible for the design of the Douglas DC-1, -2, and -3 airliners. There, Root overcame a tendency to be airsick to act as flight test engineer on the DC-2, helping the company resolve some instability problems. His solution, applying aerodynamic balance to moving control surfaces, was granted a patent—not bad for a twenty-five-year-old newcomer, and certainly a portent for his future.

Root had a brilliant career with Douglas, culminating in an immediate postwar tour of Germany to recover scientific data. He was particularly taken with information on the German rocket programs, which he would soon put to good use, first with the Rand Project, and later the RAND Corporation, where he also became a strong proponent of in-flight refueling. RAND was an independent nonprofit organization designed to study defense security problems for the benefit of industry and government. Root served as RAND's representative in the Pentagon, working with then-Colonel Bernard A. Schriever, the father of American intercontinental ballistic missile programs. He became a special assistant to the U.S. Air Force deputy chief of staff, development, and also served on the Air Force's Scientific Advisory Board.

Root was at the Pentagon when he caught the eye of Robert Gross, who invited him to come to Lockheed as corporate development planner, a typical example of Gross's vision. (In some respects, Robert Gross and General of the Air Force Henry H. "Hap" Arnold were very much alike. Neither man was technically adept, but both could see what was required for the future, and pick the key personnel to fulfill those requirements.) Root was to head a group of specialists who would advise management on industrial and economic trends, along with the best opportunities for the future.

Upon arrival at Lockheed, Root went through the normal processing, and was asked, "What's your department number?" With typical ebullience, he responded, "There isn't any—but let's call it the Root de toot department." The name stuck with the department over the years. His advent at Lockheed would, through an involved set of circumstances, put him in a position to have a tremendous influence over not only an important sector of the company, but over the development of executive talent. The standards of management, leadership, and ethics that Root established would enable Lockheed to become a premier contractor in missiles and satellites. Those standards would also train the personnel who would lead Lockheed's recovery from the disastrous situation in which it became embroiled in the late 1960s to its present position of eminence.

LMSD

Gross announced the formation of the Lockheed Missile Systems Division (LMSD) in January 1954. The new division had a

$400,000 backlog of work on the X-7 project, and sixty-five people were employed in an old engineering loft in Building B-1 at Burbank. Only a year later, the division had recorded sales of $7.2 million, almost all of it in the previously nonexistent ramjet missile technology business. By August of 1955, the backlog of work had soared to $29 million, all in a field in which Lockheed had little previous experience. An interim move was made in May 1954, to a seventy-seven-acre facility in Van Nuys, but it was apparent that much larger quarters were needed. As the company grew, so did it generate new operating elements, including a base at Cape Canaveral, Florida, to augment its test facility at Alamogordo, New Mexico.

Unfortunately, all was not well in LMSD's initial administrative arrangement. Gross's normally prescient management vision had been cloudy when he selected retired Air Force Lieutenant General Elwood P. "Pete" Quesada to head the new organization as vice president and general manager. While personally popular, Quesada created an explosive management situation by his unusual, and to some, eccentric, hiring and management methods. He was intent on acquiring a large staff of scientists, and the rapid growth of business required hiring an equally large staff of engineers. Quesada was perceived to have a preference for scientists over engineers in the work process. He was maladroit in assigning projects, sometimes assigning similar tasks to more than one individual, and in other instances not making any assignments at all, leaving large numbers of high-paid professionals without anything to do but collect their paychecks—probably the worst thing possible for their morale. The resulting confusion caused a rift between scientists and engineers that culminated in many of the scientists leaving in a body. (Many veterans of LMSC consider this to have been a blessing in disguise. They believe the initial projects at the facility demanded a degree of hardheaded common sense that was often more readily found in engineers than in pure scientists.)

The situation was exacerbated because Quesada did not communicate with the Gross brothers, nor did he get along with that keystone of Lockheed engineering, Willis Hawkins, who nominally was his assistant, along with Herschel Brown. (Retired chairman Roy Anderson would say of Herschel Brown that he had the genius of Gene Root and the steady industry of Stan Burriss combined—a formidable combination.) Eventually, the courtly Courtlandt Gross asked Quesada to leave, and his place was taken temporarily by Hall Hibbard. Hibbard would later select Root to become the general manager of LMSD, with the profound results alluded to above. (Quesada went

Willis Hawkins excelled in every field of endeavor, and was as important to the innovative new missiles and space side of Lockheed's business as he had been to the aircraft side. He read and initialed every page of the manuscript for this book twice, offering innumerable valid suggestions and corrections, all hand printed as precisely as an IBM typewriter.

on to become the first head of the Federal Aviation Administration, where, as has been shown, he treated Lockheed fairly when the Electra problems surfaced.)

X-17: Hypersonic Key to Reentry

The creation of an intercontinental ballistic missile required solving thousands of problems, and of these, one of the most difficult was that of the warhead's reentry into the earth's atmosphere. The tremendous heat and turbulence generated by a body reentering the atmosphere would turn a warhead into a self-consuming falling star unless the correct shape and materials were used to protect it. In November 1954, the USAF awarded Lockheed a sole-source contract to help solve this problem, and once again Hawkins, still LMSD's director of engineering picked Frank Bednarz for the project.

The Lockheed team followed Irv Culver's concept and fashioned a relatively simple vehicle consisting of three sets of solid rockets. The first stage of the rocket boosted the vehicle to about five hundred thousand feet, but was not separated from the second and third stages. The vehicle, stabilized by the booster, then fell back into the atmosphere pointing straight down. At a designated altitude, usually between seventy thousand and ninety thousand feet, the first stage was

The X-17 as a three-stage solid-fuel test vehicle that played an important role in solving the problem of reentry to the atmosphere.

jettisoned and the other two stages were fired in succession in what Hawkins termed a "pile-driver technique." Previously unimaginable speeds of Mach 11 to Mach 20 were achieved. In effect, the missile traded the high density of low altitude for the high velocity of reentry, so that the same conditions of airflow temperature and heat rate were attained, but much less expensively, and much closer to the earth. As a result more information could be obtained from telemetry.

Lockheed undertook a series of tests with quarter- and half-scale vehicles, and the first full-scale missile was launched on August 26, 1955. Designated the X-17, the vehicle was in general appearance not unlike later surface-to-air missiles such as the Soviet SA-2, although the three stages of its rockets provided a tapered shape. The first stage of the rocket generated 48,000 pounds of thrust; the second stage had three rockets each generating 33,900 pounds of thrust; while the third stage had a single rocket of 35,950 pounds of thrust. All three rockets were manufactured by the Thiokol Company. Just over forty feet long, fitted with four stabilizing fins at their base and weighing about 12,000 pounds, the X-17s were launched from Cape Canaveral, Florida and from Vandenburg AFB and Point Magu, California. The X-17 was carried on a transport trailer, not unlike a modern mobile missile launcher. Twenty-six X-17s were launched; of these, nineteen made successful flights that generated the information used by the air force to design the warheads for its ICBMs. Additional X-17s were successfully launched for the navy to help design warheads for the Polaris SLBM. The data would also be crucial in the design of recovery capsules from spacecraft.

The concept of the X-17 came from Irv Culver, who had been

in the first group of Lockheed engineers to move from aircraft to missiles. The scientist who directed and analyzed the reentry body data was Dan Tellep.

Later in their life, the X-17s demonstrated an unusual versatility; instead of their climb-and-dive trip-hammer mode, they simply blasted upward as high as three hundred miles, there to explode a nuclear warhead in an experiment to determine if nuclear explosion by-products would be trapped in the earth's magnetic field.

On to Sunnyvale

On November 4, 1955, less than two years after LMSD's tentative launch, Lockheed announced the purchase of a 275-acre tract of land near the bucolic hamlet of Sunnyvale, and close to the great airship hangars at Moffett Field. Palo Alto was only seven miles away, and the proximity of Stanford University was a real attraction, given that many top Lockheed managers were alumni. Twenty-two additional acres were acquired in the Stanford Industrial Park. The location and the geography of the acquisition permitted Lockheed to build a series of research laboratories with separate adjacent manufacturing and test facilities which would be virtually self-contained, and thus able to operate under the stringent requirements of secrecy that a flood of defense contracts would bring. Lockheed had embarked upon a program of supplying high-speed, high-altitude vehicles of unprecedented performance, and it needed the laboratories and the people to re-create the physical forces and atmospheric conditions under which these weapons would operate. Implicit in their creation was an unprecedented requirement for new electronic and optical testing equipment. This new test equipment was to be created on a scale so large and so sophisticated that entirely new disciplines had to be developed to meet the task. (One incredible by-product of this demand for intellectual resources was the growth of what is now called Silicon Valley.)

The challenge was daunting, but the Gross brothers and Dan Haughton, the latter now engaged in managing all of the businesses, plunged ahead with tremendous courage. They knew better than anyone how political events could suddenly dry up a well of contracts, and that the huge investment being made in LMSD (by 1958, the acronym stood for Lockheed Missiles & Space [not Systems] Division) could never be recouped by anything but defense business.

The traditional shovel was pushed aside at Sunnyvale on May 17, 1956; instead, ground was broken by a scientifically detonated charge of powder, one that symbolized the fiery rocket trails of Lockheed's future. During the ceremonies, Lockheed's president, Courtlandt Gross, announced that the plant was going to be three times larger than originally announced, to accommodate the accelerating growth of business. (LMSD's backlog reached $60 million in sales by the end of 1956 and $160 million by the end of 1957. By 1959, it became Lockheed's largest division in terms of sales [$362 million] and employment [18,966].) Robert Gross's "pilotless aircraft" venture was destined to prosper, for the Cold War, in all its fury and duration, would insure that Lockheed's investment was repaid many times over.

Two Directions: Both Correct

Lockheed Missiles and Space Division's developing scientific capability was noted with approval by the Department of Defense, and rewarded by a seemingly endless series of new challenges. The scope and nature of these challenges was staggering, and they would place Lockheed in the unique position of being an active partner in the official national policies of first, deterring the Soviet Union from open warfare, and second, containing it within its current sphere of political influence.

Herschel Brown, who would later become the division's general manager, succinctly stated LMSD's task: "One challenge was to build a missile that could be launched from a submerged submarine; the other was to build a satellite from which we could recover a capsule." Given that Lockheed had just entered the space and missile business, these were sobering assignments.

The Fleet Ballistic Missile (FBM) had the potential of being the most effective deterrent weapon in history. When the Air Force was made an independent service in 1947, the questions of roles and missions were paramount. An attempt was made to address this question by the new secretary of defense and former secretary of the navy, James Forrestal, at a conference (participants likened it more to a knife fight than a meeting) of the service chiefs in Key West, Florida, in 1948. There, the development of the ICBM was assigned to the Air Force, while the development of the intermediate range ballistic missile (IRBM) was assigned to both the Army (Jupiter) and the Air Force (Thor). The Navy was left out, and it was furious. A key to alleviating the situation came in 1955, when the National Security Council recommended that at least part of the IRBM force be sea-based.

The second challenge was even more daunting, for it was the foundation of a space-based intelligence-gathering system of almost unimaginable complexity, under the auspices first of the Air Force and subsequently also the Central Intelligence Agency. Although the initial requirements were primitive by today's standards, they were light-years beyond the state of the art at the time. The successful fulfillment of these, and of subsequent ever more rigorous requirements, was perhaps the most important element of the American policy of containment. They gave the United States unparalleled insight into Soviet activities, and enabled it to fashion the most economical, cost-effective responses. Had the United States not possessed this capability, it might have bankrupted itself on military spending, as the Soviet Union ultimately did.

LMSD became the Lockheed Missiles and Space Company (LMSC) in June 1961, to reflect the twin paths fate had thrust upon it. LMSC would have a Missile Systems Division (MSD) and a Space Systems Division (SSD), and while there would always be a strong economic, moderate managerial, and limited technical cross-fertilization between the two entities, the absolute need for the strongest security requirements resulted in their growing up as distinct entities. Only the very top managers of one division knew anything about the work of their counterparts in the other division; everyone else was isolated on the strictest "need-to-know" basis. And because security was so rigorous, even top management at corporate headquarters had only a limited insight into the mechanics of the programs. That limited insight came to be regarded as sufficient, for LMSC quickly proved to be a great cash cow that would sustain the company during tough economic times. Lockheed's senior management could comfortably let LMSC's inner workings remain a closed book as long as the profits continued to flow.

Missile Systems Division and the Fleet Ballistic Missile

The story of the creation, development, test, and deployment of the submarine-launched ballistic missile is without question the story of how well the military-industrial complex can work. The term gained notoriety when it was taken out of context from President Eisenhower's speech, and is glibly used as a code word for the way in which the military and industry are supposed to conspire to bilk the public of their hard-earned tax money. The U.S. Navy/contractor cooperation on the development of the fleet ballistic missile system proved conclusively how false a perception this is.

Over the years, there have undoubtedly been abuses of the defense procurement system, but for the most part, the defense industry has not been kind to manufacturers, a condition witnessed by the thousands of firms that have gone bankrupt trying to supply military needs. A much smaller number of firms have prospered over the years, but objective investigation reveals that the average return on investment is significantly lower than for nondefense counterparts.

The military-industrial complex's existence is not based on the profit motive, but rather on the fact that modern weapon systems could not be produced without extremely close cooperation between the military and industry. It would be impossible for the military services to communicate their needs without a deep understanding of industrial capability, and it would be equally impossible for industry to respond to those needs without a broad understanding of military requirements.

The very best illustration of both the need for and the positive results of the military-industrial complex is the Fleet Ballistic Missile system. The FBM system resulted in five generations of submarine-launched ballistic missiles, and was derived from an intimate, enduring relationship between the U.S. Navy, Lockheed, and its many subcontractors. These programs were delivered almost without exception on time and within the budget. This outstanding mutual effort brought about the SLBM as the third leg of the strategic triad upon which the United States depended for the deterrence of the Soviet Union. The Soviet Union was not only deterred, it ultimately collapsed—primarily because its own military-industrial system failed to function correctly. The Soviet government was unable to continue flogging its corrupt, chaotic economic system to sustain the necessary military development to oppose that of the United States. Deterrence worked, and it worked because of the strategic triad. In the final analysis, the fact that it worked also made it relatively inexpensive, for if it had failed, the cost would have been incalculable.

The Beginning: From Jupiter to Polaris

In 1955, the Navy was assigned the task of providing a sea-based support system for the Jupiter IRBM developed by the Army. Despite its subsidiary nature, it was nonetheless a point of entry into the missile business. On November 17, the Secretary of the Navy created a Special Projects Office (SPO) to handle the task, and, not incidentally, to be responsible for a new high-priority program: a sea-based IRBM. Admiral Arleigh "Thirty-knot" Burke assigned the detail to the newly frocked Rear Admiral William Francis "Red" Raborn. Burke, a leader in the "Revolt of the Admirals" in the B-36/carrier controversy, later said, "I did not want a technical expert, because a technical expert would be too narrow-minded. I wanted an aviator because if this missile were successful, it would jeopardize the aviation branch. . . . I chose Red Raborn because he was a hard-working man."

Raborn, a 1928 Naval Academy graduate, had won his wings at Pensacola in 1934. He became an aerial gunnery expert, and participated in fast carrier operations aboard the USS *Hancock* in battles against the Japanese throughout the war zone. After a tour of combat in Korean waters, he served in a series of staff positions that led to his promotion to rear admiral in 1955. Later in life, he was deputy chief of naval operations, and after his retirement, served as director of the Central Intelligence Agency from 1965 to 1966. He died in 1990 at the age of eighty-four.

The degree of Burke's backing for the IRBM project may be inferred from the way he allocated Navy resources. When money was tight, he cut back the Navy by fifteen thousand personnel, killed the Martin Seamaster jet-flying boat program, and terminated the Regulus missile program. He spelled out his intentions in a December 2, 1955, letter, which is quoted in part below:

> 3. If Rear Admiral Raborn runs into any difficulty with which I can help, I will want to know about it at once along with his recommended course of action for me to take. If more money is needed, we will get it. If he needs more people, those people will be ordered in. If there is anything that slows this project up beyond the capacity of the Navy Department we will immediately take it to the highest level and not work our way up through several days.

Burke's paragraph 5 is equally illuminating:

> The next report on this should be made by somebody who is enthusiastic, who gives evidence of his enthusiasm, and whose knowledge demonstrates that he has a thorough grasp of the problem and is pushing ahead faster than anybody else could.

It would soon be evident that Burke had found his man in Raborn, who was red-haired, barrel-chested, quick with a quip, and able to get along with people even under conditions of great stress. His stature enabled him to endure tough congressional inquiries and win crucial votes of confidence with his candor and the credibility of his promises. Raborn was granted a "hunting license" to pick forty civilian and military people for his team. These were the first strands in the industry-government team Raborn knitted together, using management methods not found in any books. He did not believe in giving rewards for saving money—he gave rewards for things that advanced the in-commission date. He expected people to work seven days a week if necessary—when he heard complaints that people wanted to spend time with their families, he suggested that they bring their wives into work on Saturdays.

One of Raborn's great gifts was to make decisions on the spot, and let the chips fall where they may. Gene Root characterized Raborn's methods as demanding, but satisfying, because they "required complete intellectual honesty." Stan Burriss was so imbued with the team concept that he made the decision to give up a $45 million contract Lockheed had signed for a general-purpose computer to another company, simply because he knew it was best for the program. In other circumstances, a manager making such a decision would have been fired on the spot—at LMSD it was greeted with roars of approval because it made sense.

Admiral Burke had equally stringent requirements for contractors, and Raborn began the process of selection as soon as he took over on December 5, 1955. Within twenty days he had selected the major FBM contractors on the basis of their one-day presentations, and LMSD was selected as the prime contractor/system integrator. Undeterred by their absolute lack of experience in the area, on December 13, 1955, Robert Gross, Hawkins, and Hibbard offered the United States Navy a plan to manage the fleet ballistic missile weapon system.

They were authorized to do so on December 17, and ten days later, Lockheed, with other contractors, attended a briefing by Raborn in Washington. Wishing to infuse some excitement, Raborn asked the companies that were going to join his project to come forward and write their company name on his briefing blackboard. Gene Root made it to the blackboard first, wrote "Lockheed" in large letters, then turned and said, "We're ready. Who's next?" It was the attitude Raborn wanted.

Raborn's team's initial task was to develop the Jupiter into a 1,500-mile-range missile that could be fired from shipboard and be operational five years later, on January 1, 1960. A submarine-launched version was to be ready in another five years, on January 1, 1965. This schedule would soon seem laughably lenient.

The Jupiter required cryogenic liquid fuels that would be extraordinarily hazardous on shipboard and almost certainly lethal on a submarine. Another important factor was the stability of the launch platform—when a rocket was launched, the initial acceleration was so slow that a rough sea might cause the ship to slam up into the departing missile.

In the next few months, fortune would smile often on the program. The first instance was its acquisition of Captain Levering Smith, who was to direct the development of the missile and its solid-propellant boost system, to be supplied by the Aerojet-General Company. Then a series of technical developments intervened to permit a far better alternative than the Jupiter.

The first, and perhaps most important, technical development was the assurance from Dr. Edward Teller of the Atomic Energy Commission that future nuclear warheads could be made far lighter than previously thought, only some 30 percent of the weight of the Jupiter missile's payload. (The same breakthrough enabled Colonel Bernard Schriever to accelerate the Atlas intercontinental ballistic missile.) The second was Dr. Charles Stark Draper's development of a small inertial guidance system for use in missiles, only 15 percent of the weight of the Jupiter's guidance system. The third was an advance in the power to be derived in solid-propellant fuel by the addition of metallic aluminum.

Dr. Derald A. Stuart, one of the most brilliant men ever to work at LMSC, made a crucial observation. While the energy per *pound* of liquid rocket systems was much greater than that of solid systems, the energy per *cubic foot* was comparable, and in shipborne missiles, it was energy per cubic foot that counted.

Captain Smith was tasked to design a new missile that would take advantage of these developments. Working with Lockheed and the other contractors, he produced in one week's time the essential details of a two-stage solid-propellant nuclear missile with a 1,500-mile range. The missile was approved by the secretary of defense on December 8, 1956, and Admiral Raborn gave it the name Polaris.

The Polaris concept's apparent simplification of the program brought about an accelerated schedule calling for an interim submarine capability by January 1, 1963. The major concession to the schedule change was a reduction in required range to 1,200 miles; Admiral Burke was in effect trading range for time.

Recent generations of Americans cannot begin to grasp the cultural shock that the revolutionary arrival of *Sputnik I* on October 4, 1957, had upon our nation. The country was quite literally stunned, and while comedians joked that the Soviet Union succeeded only because "their German scientists were better than our German scientists," there was a sense of national shame and urgency that had never been felt before, and has never been felt since.

This urgency was immediately incorporated in the schedule for the Polaris. The interim capability was to be achieved by January 1, 1961, and the full operational Polaris Model B was to be ready by June 1963.

While Lockheed was focused on the development of the missile itself, the Navy had to address the creation of the SSBN (Ship-Submersible-Ballistic–Nuclear powered). The new submarine would have the capacity to cruise submerged for sixty days to points from which the missiles could be launched against specific targets upon the receipt of the order to fire. The Navy provided an interim solution for the SSBN by taking a submarine already on the Electric Boat ways, the *George Washington,* splitting it just aft of the conning tower, and inserting a 130-foot-long midsection that contained room for two rows of eight missiles. The area became known as "Sherwood Forest" aboard ship for the tall tree-trunk-like appearance of the launch tubes. The number of missiles was arrived at by a sort of "Kentucky windage" analysis, trading off technical and operational factors to arrive at a reasonable solution. The *George Washington* and its four sister ships of the 598 class were 380 feet long and 33 feet wide, displacing 6,700 tons when submerged. They carried a crew of ten officers and one hundred men, and were driven by steam turbines powered by a water-cooled nuclear reactor.

There were numerous other challenges associated with creating this new class of submarines, but these were well within the grasp of naval designers and did not approach the problems facing the Raborn-Root team. Three inertial navigation systems were installed to provide navigation capability for the submarine and to enable the missile to be launched from a specific spot. One of the most important decisions was to use gas to eject the missile and allow the rocket motor to be ignited in the air, well clear of the submarine. Compressed air was used for the first ten boats, but this was replaced later by a gas-generating propellant. Curiously, underwater launch turned out to be better—and far safer—than surface launch, for the submarine was a steady platform and the fluid dynamics of the launch were not so troublesome as had been imagined.

The Polaris Series

The dimensions of the missile section of the submarine hull had to conform to the hull's original size, and this in turn dictated the limits on missile size. It was agreed that the missile diameter would be fixed at 54 inches, length at 28.5 feet, and weight at (ultimately) 28,500 pounds. The launch tube was 3 feet longer than the missile, to accommodate ancillary equipment and potential growth.

These were the only limitations on the imagination of the planners who met for the first time on January 7, 1957, as the Special Task Group. LMSD sent a "Polaris Master Development Plan," accompanied by Hawkins, burr-cut Stan Burriss, Frank Bednarz, Dr. Louis Ridenour (head of Lockheed's Research Laboratories), Sid Brown, and Willy Fiedler, one of "our German scientists," who had managed the V-1 pilotless bomb program in World War II. A decision was made early on to make the missile performance requirements flexible, so that increases could be achieved as improved components became available.

LMSD expanded once again, this time with a huge 4,400-acre test facility at Santa Cruz. Managed by Art Hubbard, the facility tested the Polaris in more than three hundred captive firings. The problems encountered in ballistic missile development from the very first V-2 included nozzles, thrust and vector control, terminating thrust, and general missile configuration. Submarine deployment added to these with problems of storage, maintenance, underwater launch, and first-stage ignition.

As more than one veteran of the program has remarked, if all the

The Soviet Union constantly increased the numbers and the accuracy of its intercontinental ballistic missiles, to the point that U.S. land-based missiles and bombers were in jeopardy. The incredible response was the Polaris, a submarine-launched ballistic missile that revolutionized the strategy of deterrence. The first Polaris was launched from the submerged USS *George Washington* on July 20, 1960.

problems had been known at the beginning, no one would have started.

By September 24, 1958, the flight test of the Polaris AX-series of prototypes began at Cape Canaveral with the usual initial failures. Yet these failures were essential to pinpoint problems that never could have been imagined, much less simulated, in a laboratory setting. For example, it was found that the expanding exhaust gases from the rocket behaved differently at low altitudes and speeds than they did at high altitudes and high Mach numbers. At upper elevations and higher speeds, a backflow of hot gases caused a concentration of heat that disrupted the airflow around the missile and damaged equipment.

In a similar way, it was determined that the rocket could be controlled by thrust vectoring, using Willy Fiedler–designed "jetevators," metal quadrants activated in the rocket exhaust. The crucial timing of thrust termination, absolutely essential for accuracy, was effected by simple blow-out ports on the front of the rocket.

These and other problems were solved by the first truly successful flight of the AX-6 on April 20, 1959. By August 27, the Polaris was successfully launched at sea from the test ship *Observation Island.*

The second series of prototypes was tested on a large scale through the next year; out of forty flights, only twenty-eight were completely successful; eleven were partly successful and one was a failure. Prudence might have demanded more testing to insure success, but the schedule was running out, and a decision was made to launch the first operational Polaris A1 missile from the *George Washington* on July 20, 1960. The 1,000-mile flight down the range was a success, and in what some called bravado but was really well-earned confidence, a second successful missile was launched three hours later.

Raborn sent "success" messages from the submarine to the president and to Navy officials. One paragraph of his message reflected the national attitude toward the use of a nuclear deterrent. It said: "God grant that we will never have to use this new and powerful sea star in anger, but will be allowed to keep it below the oceanic curtain in the world's greatest hiding place, on a silent peace patrol for free men." There was a bit of a poet in the admiral.

Thus, in just under four and one-half years, the program had gone from conception to reality, for on November 15, 1960, the *George Washington* sailed from Charleston, South Carolina, for the first FBM patrol in history.

By the January 1, 1961, deployment date, the Polaris A1 had met all the interim requirements, including a 1,200-nautical-mile range. The impact of the deployment of an SSBM on the strategic scene was equivalent to that of *Sputnik* on the scientific scene. The international strategic equation was altered forever, as an invisible, almost invulnerable deterrent was deployed, one that provided an unassailable second-strike capability to guarantee "assured destruction" of the enemy.

The Soviet Union reacted with the skill and intensity it mustered at the time, and diverted vast resources to creating and sustaining a similar fleet. The later breakup of the Soviet Union caused an interim decline in submarine activity, but Russia, in the face of its diminished defense spending, has recently decided to give priority to its fleet of nuclear missile launchers as being its most sustainable, most effective strategic weapon.

Subsequent Developments

The by now experienced Navy-Lockheed team was able to bring the Polaris A2 swiftly into service. The principal changes were lengthening the first-stage motor by thirty inches, and enhancing the performance of the second stage by reducing its inert weight through the use of glass filament–wound chambers, increasing its power and introducing a rotatable nozzle for control. These improvements combined to give the Polaris A2 a 1,500-mile range.

The first submarines designed from the keel up to handle ballistic missiles came into service with the 608 class, of which the USS *Ethan Allen* was the first of five. These had a length of 410 feet and a submerged displacement of 7,900 tons, and retained the 33-foot beam width. Both the 598 and 608 class used the compressed-air eject system for launch. Work was immediately begun on the 616 class, of which 31 would be built. These were 15 feet longer than the 608 class boats, and displaced 8,250 tons, submerged. The crew was increased to 14 officers and 126 enlisted personnel, and the missiles used a gas-steam generator eject system.

The Polaris A3 was approximately an 85 percent new design, intended to achieve a 60 percent increase in range without any increase in overall size. Implicit in the greater range was a requirement for greater accuracy as well. Advanced engineering introduced new thrust-vector controls, revised reentry-body materials, the use of a nylon-phenolic ablative shield, and more powerful propellants. The single warhead was replaced by three reentry bodies. These covered the target area more effectively and reduced the possibility of interception.

After a somewhat troubled test period, the A3 missile became operational on September 28, 1964. The A3 was delivered a year ahead of the original schedule and its 2,500-mile range covered the entire Eurasian landmass, and opened up vast new areas of the ocean for purposes of concealment.

If Lockheed's LMSC and the navy had done no more than bring the A3 into service, that fact would have been considered an extraordinary example of industrial proficiency. It was in fact just a starting point for the continued development of fleet ballistic missiles that would tip the balance in world power.

The Fleet Ballistic Missile program was one of the most successful defense programs in history. It resulted in a succession of SLBM that included the Poseidon, a major improvement on the Polaris, and first sea-launched in 1970.

The Poseidon C3

The Soviet Union was adept at countermeasures, and despite the potent capability of Polaris missiles, it was necessary for the navy to look to the future. It had been determined that the requirements for shock-mitigation of the missiles within the launch tubes could be reduced. This permitted missile diameter to be increased from the Polaris's fifty-four inches to as much as seventy-four inches, and made possible improvements in range, payload, and accuracy.

It soon became apparent that the most efficient new missile would be a multiple independently targeted reentry vehicle (MIRV). Called the Poseidon C3, the new missile used the full seventy-four inches available for diameter, was thirty-four feet long, and weighed a massive sixty-four thousand pounds—well over twice as much as the original Polaris. Efficiency was gained by a Post Boost Control system that accurately metered reentry-vehicle separation and deployment. The C3 could carry up to fourteen small Mk 3 reentry bodies, each of which could be independently targeted. Independent analysis indicated that the Poseidon would be eight times as effective as its Polaris predecessors.

The first Poseidon launch from a submarine took place on August 3, 1970, from the USS *James Madison*. Thirty-one 616-class subma-

The Trident represents the fifth generation of SLBMs, and is carried on the huge *Ohio* class nuclear submarines.

rines were modified to carry the Poseidons, whose effectiveness was a force multiplier, easing patrol and maintenance schedules while imposing far greater challenges on the defenses of the Soviet Union.

The Trident System

While the improved missiles offered a much greater strategic capability, the submarines carrying them had not received a similar degree of improvement. Soviet anti-submarine warfare efforts had intensified, and it was necessary to counter them. The proposed answer was the Undersea Long-Range Missile System (ULMS), which would consist of new submarines, much quieter because of improved hull and propulsion designs, and a new missile. In early 1972, the ULMS was redesignated Trident 1 (C4). The Trident test program, based on the great experience of the past, went smoothly, and first went to sea in October 1974, on the USS *Francis Scott Key*.

The USS *Ohio* was the first of the new Trident-class submarines, which were stealthy, required less manpower, and were endowed with a thirty-year service life that required overhauls only every nine years. The Trident-class submarine is 560 feet long, 42 feet wide, has a submerged displacement of 18,700 tons, and can carry twenty-four of the larger Trident missiles.

The Trident is a much more sophisticated missile than the

Poseidon, with a more powerful three-stage engine, decreased inert weight, and more efficient energy management. The latter was achieved by generalized energy management steering, which involves shaping the trajectory by burning all boost propulsion stages to burn-out, rather than using thrust termination with blow-out panels. Additional range was achieved in part by increasing propellant volume by adding the third-stage rocket motor within the nose fairing. The range was almost doubled, to nearly five thousand miles, yet the Trident carried the same payload with equal accuracy. The additional range removed the requirement for the expensive and politically volatile forward-basing policy.

The Trident missile was also the beneficiary of the general gain in missile electronics. This permitted the installation of additional equipment, including a stellar-inertial guidance system, and improved navigation and fire-control systems. Similar improvements in materials technology allowed the substitution of composite graphite-epoxy materials to build structures at 40 percent of their weight if done in aluminum. The science of aerodynamics contributed an unusual and unexpected improvement with the invention of a deployable aerospike, a needlelike extension extended shortly after launch that reduced the frontal drag of the missile by 50 percent.

The Trident (C4) was thirty-four feet long and seventy-four inches in diameter; it weighed 65,000 pounds. It had achieved twice the range of the Poseidon, and was brought in on schedule, within 6 percent of the original cost estimates.

No matter how successful the last program, progress demands change, and it came in the form of the Trident II (D5), on which Lockheed began advance design work in 1978. The navy issued a letter contract on October 21, 1983, and a formal contract was signed on March 12, 1984, for a total amount in excess of $5.7 billion for eighty-two test and production missiles.

The Trident II is significantly larger, weighing in excess of 120,000 pounds, and having a length of just over forty-four feet and a diameter of eighty-three inches. Performance details are classified, but equal or exceed those of the original Trident. The structure of the Trident II has been lightened by the extensive use of graphite-epoxy structures in the first and second stages.

Perhaps the greatest, and hardest-earned, tribute for the Trident II came from Representative Les Aspin, then chairman of the House Armed Services Committee, and a man noted for his vigilant oversight of defense programs. Aspin stated, "Of all the strategic weapon systems that we have looked at, we've given this one the highest marks." He attributed the Trident II's success to five factors, which were:

1. The navy program management created a no-cover-up culture.

2. The program had continuity of management.

3. The Strategic Systems Project Office (SSPO) had authority commensurate with its responsibility.

4. The SSPO had responsibility not only for the production of the Trident, but for its reliability and logistics as well.

5. The D5 program avoided novelty for its own sake.

Reflections

The Fleet Ballistic Missile program was an almost miraculous accomplishment, squeezed into a timetable that any sensible manager would have deemed impossible. And it was due to the incredible cooperation—and ability—of the Navy-Lockheed team, who had not addressed but assaulted problems to insure their solution.

The author, as a retired Air Force officer, must reluctantly admit that the system used by the Navy in staffing the FBM project office was superior to the corresponding system management efforts by the Air Force. The difference was in tenure. The Navy would assign personnel for an average of six years on the project, while a typical project officer would average only twenty-seven months on a comparable Air Force program. The Navy often placed its officers in deputy positions, then advanced them to program officer when the incumbent left, giving even more experience. The longer tenure enabled strong relationships to develop between Navy and contractor personnel. Put baldly, Naval officers could embrace a single program for a substantial portion of their career without fear that their career progress would be inhibited; Air Force officers did not have the same assurance.

Raborn served in the most admirable style from December 5, 1955, through March 8, 1962, carrying him through the Polaris A1 and A2 programs and most of the way through the Polaris A3. He was succeeded by Vice Admiral I. J. "Pete" Galantin, who had sunk 23,820 tons of enemy shipping as commander of the submarine *Halibut* in World War II. Galantin, the only submariner to direct the program, served for three crucial years, during which the Poseidon C3 was well launched.

Galantin was succeeded by Raborn's right-hand man, Captain Levering Smith, among whose decorations was one for transforming research on solid rocket propellants into reality. He came to the SPO in April 1956 and became director of the Strategic Systems Project Office (as the SPO was later renamed) in February, 1965. He retired from the Navy as a vice admiral on April 1, 1972, but agreed to be recalled and remained on active duty in the same position until November 15, 1977. His twenty-one-year tenure is probably unmatched in any weapon system in U.S. history, and covered the entire Polaris, Poseidon, and Trident missile programs.

There were many other naval officers who influenced the fleet ballistic missile program, but two stand out for both their accomplishments and their long stewardship of the program. Rear Admiral Robert H. Wertheim worked on the program from 1956 to 1961, and again from 1965 until his retirement in 1980. He was "the warhead man," coordinating efforts with the Atomic Energy Commission. Rear Admiral Glenwood Clark, a nuclear physicist, was involved in fleet ballistic missile work from 1966 to 1985. The continuity and focus that such longevity in leadership positions confers is of incalculable value.

It was more customary for contractor personnel to be with programs longer, and the fleet ballistic missile program was blessed by having people from Lockheed who were fully equal in ability and dedication to Raborn and his colleagues. Dan Tellep, who would rise to the very top of Lockheed and then the Lockheed Martin Corporation, began work on X-17 missile reentry flight experiments in 1955, and developed high-temperature insulation materials that were later used on the Space Shuttle. He made great contributions to the FBM and continued through with LMSC until 1986, and of course maintained his interest from his subsequent corporate positions. Stan Burriss had also had a prominent position in the X-17 program, as flight test director, and became director of the Fleet Ballistic Missile system in 1956. Bob Fuhrman joined the Polaris program in 1958 and rose to the position of general manager of the Missile Systems Division in 1969, before going on to other senior positions. Derald Stuart was a tenured professor at Cornell, consulting on solid rocket propulsion, and it was he who helped persuade Admiral Raborn of the potential efficacy of solid-fuel rockets. Stuart joined Lockheed in February 1958 as Propulsion Staff Manager, and continued with the FBM program until his retirement in 1987.

Other strong managers and bold personalities left their imprints on the FBM program. Typical of this breed were men like Lloyd Wilson, Ray Munson, Ken Smith, Art Hubbard, Howie Burnett and Dave Montague.

The tremendous success of the FBM program may fairly be attributed to the fact that the oft-derided military-industrial complex was composed of brilliant, dedicated men and women on both sides. They worked without regard to clock, paycheck, and in some instances, their health, to assure that the weapon systems the nation needed were provided in the shortest possible time.

The achievements of the Missile Systems Division were so great, so swift, and so profitable that it would ordinarily seem unlikely that its organizational counterpart, the Space Systems Division, would be able to do equally well under the demanding circumstances of space flight—but such was the case.

Space Systems Division (SSD)

Security considerations make it impossible even in today's post–cold war world to tell more than the smallest percentage of the many contributions the Space Systems Division has made to the defense of the free world. Only the very first achievements, those that began in the early 1950s, have been cleared for discussion. There are many people from Lockheed who participated in what was unquestionably the most important and decisive intelligence campaign in history, one that effectively opened the Soviet Union to complete inspection. Unfortunately, for reasons of security, they are still unable to tell exactly what they did or how they did it. Even when a program has been declassified, its participants remain unwilling to divulge information as a matter of habit, and because of concern that they might inadvertently stray outside the bounds of declassified material.

Lockheed's involvement in the black world of gathering intelligence from space began in the immediate postwar years. An early RAND Corporation study entitled *Feasibility and Utility of Satellite Vehicles* had induced a tepid level of interest at Lockheed. The plaintive beeps of *Sputnik I* brought about a superheated atmosphere in which Lockheed would more than rise to the occasion—it would rise beyond all known boundaries in space with exotic equipment that had never before been conceived of, and most of which remains top secret today.

Opening Closed Skies

President Eisenhower understood that Premier Khrushchev's rebuff of the Open Skies proposal meant that more information had to be obtained on Soviet intentions. One alternative, exercised hundreds of times but kept a closely guarded secret for decades, was the presidentially authorized overflights of the Soviet Union and its allies by North American RB-45s, Boeing RB-47s, and Lockheed Neptunes. These were supplemented by Project GENETRIX, with methods that harkened back to World War II and the Japanese efforts to bomb the United States with incendiary-laden balloons. Beginning on January 22, 1956, camera-carrying balloons, launched from bases in Turkey and flying at altitudes up to forty-thousand feet, drifted across the Soviet Union, taking photographs. They were recovered in midair over the Pacific. More than four hundred balloons were launched and forty-five were recovered. The photographs were useful primarily for mapping. (In 1957, a single attempt was made to use the jet streams to launch balloons from the Pacific, to fly west over the Soviet Union and be recovered in Western Europe. The initial balloon came down just inside the East German border and immediately was placed on exhibit in Red Square as an example of an American provocation.)

The U-2 provided an interim capability, but the advances in Soviet technology demonstrated by *Sputnik I* and *Sputnik II* pointed the way to the future. The latter, besides being a stunning scientific achievement, was also a masterstroke of public relations because it carried a dog, Laika, the first animal to travel in space. These orbital flights caused the secretary of defense, Neil H. McElroy, to accelerate a program begun even before the first *Sputnik*, in October 1956. At that time, the Air Force's Ballistic Missile Division had given Lockheed a contract to develop an advanced military satellite system (WS-117L).

WS-117L had three programs: Discoverer, about which more later, SAMOS (still classified), and MIDAS, a satellite communication system. To its chagrin, Lockheed lost the MIDAS contract to TRW & Hughes in the early 1960s. It worked very hard to win the contract back for many years, and finally succeeded with the award of the Space Based Infrared System (SBIRS), to be discussed in the next chapter.

The WS-117L upper-stage vehicle weighed several thousand pounds and was capable of in-orbit propulsion and control. This became the workhorse satellite of the space age, named for the star Agena, otherwise known as Beta Centauri, and perpetuating the Lockheed custom of using stellar phenomena for names.

A Lockheed technical paper succinctly describes the system. It says:

> Mated to a rocket booster, Agena consisted of a three-axis gyro guidance and control system with correction inputs from horizon sensors that enabled precise cold-gas valve firings; an electrical system with six one-hour batteries; a telemetry, command and tracking system; a recovery system of a thermally protected reentry capsule with a retro-rocket, cold-gas spin-stabilized attitude control system, power supply, telemetry link and acquisition beacon, sequence timer and parachute; and a propulsion system using a Bell rocket engine delivering 16,000 pounds of thrust for orbital injection. A vertical looking, reciprocating, 70-degree panoramic Itek camera exposed the Eastman Kodak film by scanning at right angles to the line of flight. The first camera used a 24-inch focal-length, f/5.0 Tessar lens, with image motion compensation. The imagery was retrieved by air catch following ejection by a sequence timer of the General Electric reentry capsule containing the film.

The three-axis stabilization created a thermal problem, for the upper surface was exposed continuously to direct sunlight during part of each orbit, while the entire vehicle would be cloaked in freezing temperatures during other parts. A passive cooling system was installed that used conduction and radiation techniques to control temperatures. The technique was subsequently adapted for all U.S. satellites and space probes. In marked contrast, the Soviet Union used an active thermal system, which was far less reliable.

Agena made its first trip into orbit in 1959, and subsequently achieved scores of spectacular firsts, including the following:

1. first spacecraft to achieve a circular orbit;

2. first spacecraft to achieve a polar orbit;

3. first to be stabilized in all three axes in orbit;

4. first to be controlled in orbit by ground command;

5. first to return a man-made object from space;

6. first to propel itself from one orbit to another;

7. first to propel a spacecraft on successful Mars flyby;

8. first to propel a spacecraft on a successful Venus flyby;

9. first rendezvous and docking of two spacecraft;

10. first spacecraft to provide propulsive power for another.

These astounding feats were achieved by a company with no previous experience in the field, and upon its first venture into the discipline. The Agena was used in dozens of programs in the course of hundreds of missions, carrying out the majority of space missions for both the Air Force and the National Aeronautics and Space Administration (NASA). It has carried on more diversified experiments and been used on more different boosters than any other satellite, yet its name is only moderately familiar to the public today. There are two reasons for this. One is security, which cloaked many of the missions in secrecy, so that no publicity was given. The other is that most of the Agena missions (with the exception of its role as a target docking device in Gemini-Agena missions) had no obvious relationship to manned space flight, and thus failed to capture widespread interest.

The Agena was a remarkable technical success, serving as the upper stage of many standard launch vehicles (Atlas, Thor, and Titan) and as the satellite platform for many primary and secondary payloads. The rocket motor of the Agena had begun life as the Bell Model LR81-BA-1 rocket engine and had been intended to give a stand-off capability to a bomb pod planned for use with the Convair B-58 Hustler supersonic bomber.

The Agena's success was achieved at a time when its components were still based on pretransistor technology. Minoru "Sam" Araki worked his way through the ranks as a systems engineer to become president of LMSC and a vice president of the Lockheed Martin Corporation. Sam laughingly recalled in a 1997 interview that the orbital sequence of early Agena spacecraft was controlled by mylar punch tapes not unlike the paper tapes used in a player piano! Curiously, in the light of all the successes of the Agena program, Araki expressed a common Lockheed feeling that the repeated success of the Agena had actually been detrimental to the firm, in that it induced a "standard production model" mentality that inhibited thinking on some later

The AGENA orbital vehicle became the workhorse of the space program, used as the upper stage on standard launch vehicles like the Atlas, Thor, and Titan. It was the satellite platform for many primary and secondary payloads in both civil and military applications.

proposals. There was in fact a "Standard Agena," the Agena-D, which was twenty-three feet three inches long, five feet in diameter, weighed 674 pounds empty, and had a thrust of 17,000 pounds from its Bell rocket engine. Agenas would launch 362 times, with a 90 percent success rate. (Fred O'Green, a man who many predicted would become chairman of Lockheed, but who instead became chairman of Litton Industries, was project engineer for the Standard Agena.)

The Agena is as important for its effect on Lockheed as for its achievements in space. Araki recalls, "In the late 1950s and early 1960s, we were in a pioneering stage, because nobody had gone into space before, and nobody even had the basic scientific and physics knowledge to go into space. So in a sense, we had to invent science, invent engineering methods and invent management methods to build and develop systems for space." The process of "inventing science" would become a way of life for SSD, a mental set that permitted bidding on contracts that demanded achievements that ordinarily would have been deemed impossible.

Of all the vital missions the Agena accomplished in its lifetime, none was more important or ambitious than that undertaken under the code name Discoverer, but was actually a derivative of the original Weapon System 117L, with its own code name, CORONA.

Five earlier achievements made it practical to proceed with CORONA. These were:

1. the availability of the proven Thor booster;

2. the successful development of the Agena spacecraft;

3. the technology available from ballistic missiles to provide re-entry vehicles to shield the payload on its return to earth;

4. improved cameras derived from the GENETRIX program; and

5. equipment and techniques for aerial retrieval of payloads, also derived from the GENETRIX program.

WS-117L had envisioned a series of separate systems using satellites to collect photographic, infrared, and other, still classified, forms of intelligence. An extensive test program was planned, with WS-117L being transferred to the Strategic Air Command for operation in 1960. World events moved more swiftly than the test program had envisioned, and the very size of the program had brought a great deal of public attention, including apt media speculation that WS-117L was to be a true "spy in the sky." Because of this, the Discoverer "cover" for the CORONA program later had to be substantially enhanced by announcements that the test launches would include biomedical experiments, including recovering live animals from space.

By March 21, 1958, a decision had been made at the presidential level to transfer the photographic element of WS-117L to a separate program, Project CORONA. A new agency, the Advanced Research Projects Agency (ARPA), was established on February 7, 1958, to exercise authority over all military space projects. CORONA was to be carried out under the authority of ARPA and the CIA, with the support and participation of the Air Force. (As a result of this, the CORONA program lacked the clear lines of management authority that the U-2 program enjoyed, and there was bureaucratic friction later between the Air Force and the CIA.) The object was to create a photo-reconnaissance satellite, the first in history. In essence, the ARPA/CIA/Air Force team would task Lockheed and its subcontractors to achieve what had never been attempted before with a space booster, a spacecraft, a reentry vehicle, a camera, film, and a control network—none of which had ever been tested. The permutational chances of failure were astronomical if you simply multiplied the known chances of failure against each other. If you then multiplied the resultant number by the chances of failure from some totally unknown event, it might have seemed obvious that the objectives of the CORONA program could never be achieved.

Fortunately, both government and industry were endowed with strong, supportive leaders who believed—in fact insisted—that the program could and would be done, because it was absolutely vital to the nation's security. The CIA leader, Richard Bissell (who kept his mind sharp by memorizing railroad timetables), had been instrumental in the U-2 program, as had air force major general Osmond "Ozzie" Ritland. (John McMahon, who was a top man at both the CIA and then Lockheed, characterized Ritland as "an imaginative general who didn't worry about who got credit. . . . He was really a team player.") Both men knew how to get things done on the government side, without intruding unnecessarily on the contractor side. The simplicity of the approach was characterized by the April 25, 1958, CORONA work statement, a one-page document.

As an indication of the exotic, occasionally eccentric nature of the program, Bissell later recalled that he had first learned of the program and his future role in it informally from Dr. Edwin Land. Land—the developer of the Polaroid process—was deeply committed to the concept of reconnaissance. Land was involved in the U-2 and later in the A-12/SR-71 programs, and thus knew of the program before its director.

At Lockheed, James W. Plummer was CORONA program manager, with overall responsibility for the project. McMahon stated that "what Kelly Johnson was to the U-2 program, Jim Plummer was to the CORONA program." The respect with which Plummer was held by his Lockheed and government colleagues is remarkable; he had the gift of a management style which elicited the best from everyone by a process of example. In interview after interview the author conducted at all levels of management, Plummer was referred to with admiration that borders on awe.

Born in Idaho Springs, Colorado, in 1920, Plummer moved with his family to California when he was a young boy. He graduated from the University of California in 1942 with a bachelor's degree in electrical engineering, just in time to be commissioned in the navy. After being sent to Harvard for advanced electronics, and then to MIT for secret training in radar, he put his theoretical knowledge to use flying with then–Lieutenant Commander, later Admiral, Bill Martin, a pioneer in naval air night-fighting tactics. Plummer flew in Grumman torpedo planes, training personnel on the use of radar for night low-level bombing. After the war, Plummer gained his master's degree in electrical engineering and went to work for Lockheed, where his first program was the X-17. He was then given responsibility for the payload section of the WS-117L program, but was soon pulled off and assigned to what was described to him as an "underground" program. He was required to tell his friends that he was leaving Lockheed and then to avoid any contact with his "former" Lockheed associates. A cover story was floated that he had been assigned to a nuclear project. Plummer was assigned a new office—in the Flamingo Motel on Palo Alto's famous main drag, El Camino Real—and there started the process of designing the payload for CORONA.

His original criteria led to a spinning satellite, a football-shaped device about six feet long and two and one-half feet in diameter; it had a reentry body in the nose and a camera in the middle. Plummer's original concept was replaced when a proposal was received from the Itek Corporation, a Boston University spin-off. Itek proposed a longer-focal-length camera than the original Fairchild camera, carried within an earth-center stabilized pod. This was a significant scientific challenge, happily met by Agena's three-axis stabilization. It became the standard for subsequent photo-reconnaissance systems.

Plummer's staff grew to four engineers, two administrators, and a shop crew of ten, and they moved to quarters leased from Hiller Aircraft in Palo Alto. During this period, he was allowed to have contact with only person at Lockheed, Gene Root. Root was president of LMSC and committed the total resources of the company to the CORONA program. He was the only top Lockheed executive to be fully briefed on the program objectives.

Plummer is a slender, very athletic man with a strong presence: when he walks into a room, people take notice. He is modest, and it is difficult to get him to talk about his own contributions—he insists that it was a total team effort in which he played but a part. His reticence stems in part from the heavy security under which the program was conducted, and which was not lifted until the project was declassified on February 24, 1995, twenty-three years after the last CORONA mission. However, Plummer is quick to credit his colleagues, including Willis Hawkins, who won plaudits for his common-sense approach to esoteric engineering, and particularly Fred O'Green, who, as previously noted, managed the design, manufacture, and test of the Agena vehicle for CORONA. O'Green was famous (perhaps infamous) for calling people in during the early-morning hours to work on a technical problem. But he was there at all hours himself, and no one complained.

Plummer gives enormous credit to Dr. Frederic C. E. "Fritz" Oder, whose background was perfect for CORONA and subsequent programs. Oder had entered the Air Force in 1941, serving in the Pacific theater. After the war, the Air Force sent him to UCLA, where he completed his Ph.D. As assistant to the commander, Air Force Western Development Division, he had figured prominently in the development of the Atlas, Thor, Titan, and Minuteman missile systems, and was the first director of the Air Force Advanced Reconnaissance System (WS-117L). After retiring from the Air Force as a colonel in 1960, he worked for six years at Eastman Kodak before joining LMSC in 1966 as vice president, Space Systems Programs and Engineering. His coworkers place him on the same sort of pedestal as Plummer, and note that he had an uncanny knack for picking talent, both to work on his own projects, and to be nominated for swift progression at Lockheed.

Lockheed's principal government contacts in the CIA were Bissell and John Parangosky, who was first deputy, then chief of the CORONA Program Office Development Staff. Within the Air Force, Plummer worked primarily with Ritland and Colonel Clarence L. "Lee" Battle, who guided day-to-day management of the program. He also created "Battle's Laws," a set of ten management principles designed to achieve the same work result as Kelly Johnson's rules.

Although Plummer may not be forthcoming about his own role, his colleagues are quick to point out that it was his leadership qualities that kept morale high during the almost endless interval when things did not go well, and his intellectual qualities that kept the program on course. Plummer is also always very complimentary about the contributions of the major subcontractors. These include Itek (which under the leadership of Walter J. Levison developed the twelve-inch, f/5 panoramic camera known as HYAC); General Electric (which created the satellite recovery vehicle [SRV]); and Eastman Kodak (which provided the technical solutions required when it was found that low temperatures and vacuum of space caused the water in the camera film to evaporate, making it brittle and easy to tear).

Plummer's reputation was such that he was called to head the top secret National Reconnaissance Office in 1973; he left Lockheed reluctantly, and did so only because he felt it was in the national interest.

It is difficult to remember now, but there was neither real-world nor academic experience upon which to draw for this pioneering endeavor, except for the basic principles of physics and engineering. Plummer and his Lockheed engineers had to learn how to analyze, design, build, test, and operate in space literally from scratch. There were no computers; the design tools were slide rules and mechanical calculators. The state of the art of components consisted of vacuum tubes and electric-driven motor timers.

Many Failures—Then Success

As the photoreconnaissance mission of the CORONA had to be conducted in a near polar orbit, there were few suitable launch sites. It was decided to use Vandenberg Air Force Base, eight miles northwest of Lompoc, California, where the major drawback was that launches had to be timed to occur between the regular passage of Southern Pacific Railroad trains.

The CORONA mission called for a launch of the missile, which was at first the Thor/Agena, from Vandenberg to orbit, where the reconnaissance would be undertaken. When the information had been gathered, the recovery sequence began. The Agena vehicle (which had been yawed 180 degrees immediately after it had been inserted in orbit) would be pitched down through 60 degrees to position the satellite recovery vehicle (SRV) for retrofiring. The satellite recovery vehicle would be separated from the Agena and spin-stabilized. The retrorocket would then be fired, slowing down the SRV into a descent trajectory. The spin of the SRV would be slowed, and its retro-rocket thrust cone, heat shield, and parachute cover would be jettisoned. The deceleration parachute would be deployed, and then a main parachute would open.

Then the second part of a profoundly Rube Goldbergian recovery operation began. Prepositioned recovery aircraft, initially Fairchild C-119s and later Lockheed C-130s, would catch the parachute with a trapezelike collection of cables between two long poles hanging down from the open aft cargo door. The cables had hooks with which to snag the parachute. Once caught, the parachute and recovery vehicle would be winched on board. Not surprisingly, it took an enormous amount of practice and the development of specialized equipment to make this recovery system work.

The first launch, on January 21, 1959, retroactively designated

DISCOVERER 0, was a failure as small solid propellant ullage rockets fired. (The ullage rockets were intended to insure that liquid Agena propellants were pushed against the bottom of the tanks so that proper flow to the pumps would occur.) The damage was not catastrophic, and the problem was easily identified and solved. President Eisenhower called Bissell in for a personal report on the situation.

On February 28, *DISCOVERER I* was launched with partial success. The *DISCOVERER I* is believed to have landed somewhere near the South Pole.

Eleven straight failures followed. *DISCOVERER II* ejected its capsule prematurely, and it fell to earth near Spitsbergen. *DISCOVERER III* was the only one to carry live animals, four black mice. The Agena misfired, driving the vehicle into the Pacific Ocean; no mouse survived, and, as might be expected, there was an outcry from the British Society Against Cruel Sports.

The first to carry a camera was *DISCOVERER IV*, launched on June 25, 1959, but its payload did not go into orbit. *DISCOVERER V* attained orbit, but low temperatures caused the camera to fail. The recovery capsule did eject at the correct time, but disappeared, only to be discovered, still in orbit, more than a year later. *DISCOVERER VI* had both a camera and a retro-rocket failure. *DISCOVERER VII* failed to go into orbit, while *DISCOVERER VIII* went into an eccentric orbit, the camera failed, and the recovery parachute failed to open.

As might be expected, pressure began to build on all concerned, for failures had occurred in every element of the vehicle. Plummer recalls today that there was no doubt in anyone's mind that they would ultimately succeed; they also knew they would have their bosses' backing, for the requirement for intelligence that could be obtained from a working CORONA system was overwhelming. No one in the West knew for sure how many Bison and Bear bombers the Soviets possessed, where they were based, or how many ICBMs were operational.

The eight failures caused a stand-down from November 20, 1959, to February 1960, to analyze the causes of failure. On February 4, *DISCOVERER IX* was launched and failed to achieve orbit.

DISCOVERER X was flown on February 19, and for the first time, film was recovered from a CORONA vehicle, but under miserable circumstances. The Thor rocket booster had to be destroyed by the range safety officer fifty-two seconds after liftoff; the payload came down a mile away.

On April 15, *DISCOVERER XI* was launched; the orbit was

Perhaps one of the greatest intelligence coups in all history, the CORONA reconnaissance satellite system provided invaluable intelligence on a scale never before considered possible—and in the deepest secrecy. President Dwight D. Eisenhower was a primary moving force behind the CORONA program.

The CORONA capsule containing the intelligence data, was captured by this improbable method—snatched out of the sky by a C-130 transport.

perfect, the camera worked, and the film was exposed and then transferred to the recovery capsule. Unfortunately, the spin rockets exploded, and the payload was lost.

The urgency surrounding the program was reinforced on May 1, 1960, when Gary Powers's U-2 was shot down. Another stand-down was called, and a decision was made to launch *DISCOVERER XII* purely as a diagnostic flight, carrying instrumentation instead of a camera. Unfortunately, it failed to go into orbit. The concept was repeated with *DISCOVERER XIII,* launched on August 10, 1960, without film and camera. The vehicle completed seventeen orbits, and capsule ejection was normal. The capsule came down about eighty miles from the predicted impact point, but floated and was recovered.

The successful recovery was given massive publicity, with many shots of President Eisenhower beaming at the capsule prior to its being given to the Smithsonian Institution.

The next mission justified the faith that had been placed in Plummer and his crew. *DISCOVERER XIV,* launched on August 18, 1960, was a complete success, making seventeen orbits around the earth, then ejecting 20 pounds of film in its capsule, to be snatched out of the air at 8,500 feet on the third pass by a C-119 of the 6593rd Test Squadron, flown by Captain Harold E. Mitchell.

The film was analyzed, and while it lacked the resolution of U-2 photos, it covered areas of the USSR never previously photographed. The single mission had produced photo coverage of a greater area than all the U-2 missions combined. It was an outstanding accomplishment, and it boded well for the future as equipment, launch techniques, and film were refined. A twenty-four-inch camera with a new Petzval lens was installed, and resolution was improved from forty feet to twelve feet.

Sam Araki commented later that "failure by itself is not necessarily bad, if you are disciplined to learn from it, and implement what is needed to fix the problem. The Corona program pioneered many concepts, and the launch pad was actually our factory."

The 145th and final CORONA launch took place on May 25, 1972, with recovery on May 31 of two reentry vehicles carrying 160 pounds of film. The resolution was such that a print seven feet wide by one hundred feet long was sharp from end to end. CORONA had provided photographic coverage of 750 million square nautical miles of the earth's surface. The cameras had improved from a single camera with a forty-foot resolution to twin-camera panoramic system with a ground resolution of six to ten feet. By June of 1964, CORONA had photographed all twenty-five Soviet ICBM complexes, and had thoroughly debunked the bomber and the missile gap. It is not too much to say that CORONA provided military intelligence that may have precluded the United States from making a fatal miscalculation about Soviet intentions. It was thus of almost equal benefit to the United States and the Soviet Union.

Unfortunately for the purposes of this book, the successors to CORONA are all still classified, even though some of them have been superseded in operation by later equipment.

The Lockheed/Air Force/CIA team that had worked together so well in the CORONA program hit a rocky spot during the Bay of Pigs fiasco in 1961, in the aftermath of which Bissell was fired. President Kennedy appointed John McCone to run the CIA, and he elected to get out of the reconnaissance business, giving the reconnaissance budget (which roughly equaled all the rest of the CIA budget) to the Air Force, along with the responsibility. An unusual situation followed: both the Air Force and the CIA gave Lockheed contracts for the CORONA program. Lockheed management sent both contracts back and said, "We will run the program at our expense until you decide who is going to be in charge." And they did so, for several months, until the Air Force finally issued the contract.

After thirteen years, the program ended, but recently released National Intelligence Estimates reveal that CORONA

1. imaged all Soviet medium-range, intermediate-range, and ICBM complexes;

2. imaged each Soviet submarine class from deployment to operational bases;

3. provided inventories of Soviet bombers and fighters;

4. revealed the presence of Soviet missiles protecting the Suez Canal in Egypt;

5. identified Soviet nuclear assistance to the People's Republic of China;

6. monitored the SALT I Treaty;

7. Uncovered the Soviet antiballistic missile program;

8. identified Soviet atomic-weapon storage installations;

9. identified People's Republic of China missile-launching sites;

10. determined precise locations of Soviet air defense missile batteries;

11. observed construction and deployment of the Soviet ocean surface fleet;

12. identified Soviet command and control installations and networks;

13. provided mapping for Strategic Air Command targeting and bomber routes;

14. Identified the Piesetsk Missile Test Range, north of Moscow.

CORONA and later efforts made Lockheed into a world aerospace leader, with unparalleled expertise in the collection, relay, processing, fusion, dissemination, analysis, and control of space and ground information systems.

Innovation and Diversity: LMSC's Key Strengths

During the period in which the Fleet Ballistic Missile and the reconnaissance satellites were successfully developed, LMSC was involved in hundreds of other projects of great importance, each one of which is worthy of a book of its own. Space limitations (and, often, security considerations) prohibit even naming all of them. In each case, formidable problems were posed, and Lockheed/government/ subcontractor teams overcame them. Just the merest sampling of these include the use of Agena on many NASA launches, including Ranger and Mariner; the development of techniques of undersea mining; studies on the Manned Orbiting Laboratory, an early attempt at a space station; the development of nuclear-powered generators for use in space; the launch of the Lunar Orbiter; the creation of a prototype Deep Submergence Search Vehicle (DSSV); the launch of the Nimbus-D weather satellite; the Clean Sweep system for removing oil spills; the insulation to be used on the Space Shuttle; the Hughes *Glomar Explorer*, ostensibly a bottom-mining vessel, but in reality designed to recover a sunken Soviet nuclear submarine; the creation of military and commercial satellite systems; antiballistic missile defense; and the list goes on and on.

All the programs were notable in many distinctive ways, but one bears mention because it illustrates LMSC's ability to pioneer new technologies. On June 10, 1984, the Missiles and Space Company conducted a watershed test in which its experimental ground-based interceptor (called the Homing Overlay Experiment) was launched from a remote atoll in the Pacific. It successfully intercepted a dummy warhead launched on an ICBM booster from Vandenberg Air Force Base. Described as a bullet hitting a bullet, the debris from the 20,000 mile-per-hour impact (which occurred nearly 100 miles above the earth) fell to a swath on the ocean some forty miles wide and eighty miles long. This dramatic demonstration was pivotal in our country's commitment to the development of ballistic missile defenses.

LMSC's success was in great measure directly responsible for the victorious outcome of the cold war. While other elements of the firm provided strong weapons in the form of both aircraft surveillance and antisubmarine-warfare aircraft, LMSC had gone to the heart of the matter. It had designed, built, and launched the satellite systems that gathered the information with which to determine the capabilities and intentions of the Soviet Union. LMSC had backed up its reconnaissance efforts with the strong fleet ballistic missile force that the Soviet Union found difficult, if not impossible, to counter.

The irony of Lockheed's great achievements in helping to win the cold war lay in the fact that the end of the cold war meant a sharply diminished military requirement for Lockheed products. Diminished requirements meant more than just diminished profits; the very existence of LMSC and Lockheed was suddenly at stake. A downsizing was inevitable; the great question was whether Lockheed could compete in the new marketplace when the downsizing had run its course.

Lockheed management realized that Lockheed would have to reinvent itself. It would have to adopt entirely new ways of doing business to survive in the commercial marketplace. More than that, it would have to develop new products, new customers, and ever more efficient ways of doing business. Many observers felt that it would be difficult, if not impossible, for a longtime defense contractor, one whose work was conducted primarily "in the black" with very little scrutiny, to compete in the cruel world of commercial business.

LMSC led the way for Lockheed to prove them wrong.

CHAPTER 10

LMSC: Scientific Breakthroughs and the Challenge of Peace

Over the years, Lockheed's management continually tried to buttress its defense business with contracts with other government agencies—federal, state, and local—and with commercial companies. LMSC was always most diligent at this task and the purpose of this chapter is to illustrate how far its efforts led the company, and how well it prepared not only LMSC but Lockheed as a whole for the merger with Martin Marietta. That preparation included the simultaneous extension of LMSC's capabilities into new civil and military programs, both before and after the date of the merger.

The Cosmic Time Machine

One of the most technically significant—and philosophically satisfying—steps toward the goal of securing contracts other than for defense has been the Hubble space telescope, which became a symbol of Lockheed's ability to adapt the experience gained in its defense efforts to worthy civil projects.

Called "a Cosmic Time Machine," the Hubble Space Telescope has captured the imagination of the world, at first because of the sheer audacity of the concept and then because of the drama attendant on its launch. The initial difficulties and subsequent repair efforts heightened the excitement. Finally, both scientists and the man in the street were staggered by its mind-expanding penetration of the universe. Developed under the leadership of Val Peline, Bill Wright, and Bill Bulkin, the Hubble Space Telescope continues to amaze and confound the world with its glimpses of infinity.

The Hubble Space Telescope was first proposed by the late Lyman Spitzer Jr., a Princeton astronomer, who suggested in 1947 that scientific instruments of all sorts be placed in orbit. In 1954, he suggested that a telescope be so placed, an idea as radical as any then appearing in contemporary Buck Rogers or Flash Gordon comic strips. Planning began in the 1960s, and work began in the 1970s and 1980s. The Space Telescope became operational in the 1990s, after its launch by the crew of the space shuttle *Discovery* on STS-31, April 25, 1991.

The new space telescope was named for Edwin Powell Hubble, the astronomer who first identified galaxies outside of our own Milky Way in the 1920s, and determined that they are speeding away from us. This work provided the basis for the "big bang" theory of an expanding universe moving away from the primal event of 15 billion to 20 billion years ago.

Approximately the size of a railroad tank car, the Hubble is 43.5 feet long, 14 feet in diameter, and weighs 25,500 pounds. In orbit, unimpeded by the distortion of the earth's atmosphere, the space telescope gave astronomers the opportunity to look back 14 billion light years to the very beginning of the universe. It would, in a single stroke, expand the observable universe 350-fold, an unimaginable bonanza to astronomers. Lockheed was responsible for building the unit and integrating the sophisticated scientific instrumentation that made it function. The physical demands on the Space Telescope, with all its intricate equipment, were astounding; it orbits the earth every ninety-five minutes, encoun-

The Hubble Space Telescope continues to awe the world with the beauty of its photos and the almost imponderable importance of the information they render.

tering temperatures ranging from over 150 degrees Fahrenheit to minus 150 degrees. The telescope's electronic sensors were designed to collect light at incredibly low levels; the images captured were to be converted and sent by radio waves to the Goddard Space Flight Station.

Designed as a permanent, space-based observatory, the Hubble was equipped to be serviced and refurbished in orbit. Its equipment includes a Wide Field/Planetary Camera, a Faint Object Camera built by the European Space Agency, a Faint Object Spectrograph and a High Resolution Spectrograph.

Following the telescope's launch, scientists were dismayed to find an aberration in its main 2.4-meter (94-inch) mirror. A tiny distortion—the mirror (manufactured by the Perkin-Elmer Corporation) was too flat near the edge by about one-fiftieth the width of a human hair—resulted in the light collected by the mirror being spread into a fuzzy halo.

After initial problems were rectified, the Hubble Space Telescope has provided an
endless stream of data that has revolutionized scientific thought.

The Space Shuttle *Endeavour*, on STS-61, launched from Cape
Canaveral on December 2, 1993. Its crew of seven carried out the
repairs. To correct the Hubble's vision, a large device called the Corrective Optics Space Telescope Axial Replacement (COSTAR) was
installed. COSTAR used ten corrective mirrors to rectify the error.
While the repairs were under way, a new Wide Field/Planetary camera
was installed and other repairs were made. (Sam Araki changed the
popular repair analogy from correcting astigmatism to a heart-bypass
operation: the repairs put in a new, correct, optical path to correct the
problem, bypassing the old optical system.)

At the time of this writing, the Hubble Space Telescope has
circled the earth more than thirty-seven thousand times, in a path that
totals more than 800 million miles; its data are stored on hundreds of
optical disks, and it has observed eight thousand celestial objects. Every
observation from the Hubble has expanded scientific knowledge. It
has been learned that massive black holes are real, and are commonly

Lockheed's involvement in space include its shuttle processing activities.

found in the cores of galaxies; that planet formation is common among stars; that there is a thin oxygen atmosphere on Jupiter's icy moon, Europa; and that a belt of hundreds of millions of comets encircles the solar system. It is, in short, a cornucopia of scientific data, and LMSC's role in the project is one of Lockheed's proudest achievements.

The Hubble program also readied the company for a major shift in its operating methods.

The Cold War Ends and the Changes Begin

The Missiles and Space element of Lockheed had long been tremendously important for its contribution to the firm's profit. In the ten-year period from 1983 through 1992, LMSC accounted for 46 percent of total corporate sales of $96.1 billion, and for 72 percent of the total earnings for the period of $2.8 billion.

These excellent earnings had been justified by the nature of LMSC's work in both the missile and space sides of the house. It should be underscored that the defense contracts had not been golden handshakes. LMSC had to perform to contract specifications that were probably beyond the capability of any other defense firm and still submit to the same type of rigorous review of profits that other, less technologically premier, firms did. LMSC had achieved profitability by being highly productive, delivering on time, and paying close attention to incentive clauses for performance.

Lockheed was comfortable with its earnings from government contracts, but never stopped trying to develop commercial interests as well, even though previous efforts by aviation companies to undertake both commercial and military work in the same facility almost always failed. Most defense firms found that the demands of commercial work were too disparate, not only in terms of quality-control methods and record keeping, but in competitive pressures. As a result, commercial endeavors usually encountered cost overruns that made them unprofitable. LMSC, faced with the same challenges that had undermined other companies, would overcome them.

Victory in the Gulf: What Now?

The successful conclusion of the Persian Gulf War was a major factor in the ultimate dissolution of the Soviet Union. The Soviet military realized that the impressive power demonstrated by the United States in the Gulf War amounted to nothing less than space-based warfare. The leaders of the Soviet Union knew that their nation's wretched economy could no longer support the military apparatus necessary to compete with the United States at the new, higher standards that had been invoked. World War II had been won by attrition and the application of overwhelming industrial might, and this was the premise for U.S. success for much of the Cold War. In vivid contrast, the Gulf War was won as an "information age war," and all future wars in which the United States participates will probably be fought on this basis.

The end of the Cold War thus presented Lockheed with an entirely new situation. As patriots, members of management were delighted that the long period of struggle had been resolved without a nuclear exchange, and were proud of Lockheed's major—one could almost say dominant—role in achieving that happy outcome. But as businessmen, the same leaders realized that the new political era brought with it a new business era, one that meant a complete change in thinking, methods, and products.

As Sam Araki said, "We spent the years from 1991 to the present to reinvent the company, to have a new strategy, a new way of doing business, and more importantly, to capture markets we never sought before." To do this, LMSC had to create standards of quality control and production of such a high level that they could be used for both commercial and military contracts.

During the cold war, Lockheed products had been concerned with treaty monitoring, the verification of national capabilities of the Soviet bloc, and enabling the U.S. Navy to deliver an overwhelming nuclear strike by submarine-launched missiles. Space-based systems had been oriented to gathering information and providing the requisite support for a retaliatory nuclear attack. With the victory in the Gulf War, the focus shifted, and the primary value of space-based systems became their ability to gather and control information and to provide the means for the use of precision guided munitions.

Yet the Cold War victory meant that defense spending was going to be reduced by as much as 40 percent. LMSC, recognizing that it had to both remain competitive in military contracts and obtain new commercial business, reacted with a cost-cutting program that reduced its personnel strength by more than 50 percent. The painful downsizing was complicated by a third factor. To obtain commercial business, LMSC had to make drastic changes in its method of operation, particularly in the ways that it designed and built systems.

Well before then—undersecretary of defense William Perry and the new DOD director of acquisition, Paul Kaminski, had issued their call for the adoption of commercial standards in lieu of adherence to the ever more complicated "Mil-Spec" (military specification) standards for procurement, Araki had insisted on introducing commercial practice into LMSC. The effects upon LMSC were traumatic at first, and then acted like a tonic, making the entire Missiles and Space Group much more competitive.

The previous work Lockheed had done as prime contractor for the Strategic Defense Initiative placed it in an excellent position to win the vitally important $1 billion contract from the USAF for the MILSTAR Military Strategic And Tactical Relay program. That experience, in turn, prepared Lockheed for the intense competition of the commercial marketplace, for it used MILSTAR as a pilot program for acquisitions reform. This would be the pattern for the company's future success. Each new program would be technically more demanding than any in the past, but the cumulative learning from past programs served as an adequate launch vehicle to achieve new technical and system management heights.

Araki is given credit by many for the successful acquisition and execution of the MILSTAR program. The venerated Fritz Oder has called Araki the best systems engineer in the space business, and one of the few who became a very able manager. Araki, a man with an infectious sense of humor, tells with great relish the story of the revolution within LMSC that was necessary to win the MILSTAR contract.

Lockheed had attempted to get into the communications satellite business for a number of years, but had failed miserably in many competitions. Araki attributes the failures to Lockheed's having become so comfortable doing business with its military customers on classified contracts that it forgot how to bid on new products. Top LMSC management recognized the situation, and to offset it, created a new internal organization called Advanced Programs and Development (APD). The purpose of APD was to break out of the habits of the past and capture new customers with new products.

The MILSTAR competition promised to be exceptionally difficult because the two companies that had done virtually all previous communication satellite programs, TRW and Hughes, had decided to team for it. On the advice of the APD organization, Lockheed informed the Air Force Systems Command that it was not going to bid, because the TRW/Hughes team was too strong. Other companies followed suit, and, to secure competition, the Air Force decided that TRW and Hughes would have to furnish the payload of electronics for all competing teams. It was a crucial blow to TRW and Hughes, who were suffering from the same problem of intellectual arrogance that had prompted Lockheed's creation of APD. They had won so many competitions in the past that they were not able to respond adequately under the new ground rules. Lockheed took the payload, redesigned it, and won the competition hands down.

In the MILSTAR program, Lockheed was to design, develop, and produce a highly sophisticated, jam-resistant global satellite communications system for use by all three military services for command and control. MILSTAR will also be the first communication system to allow all branches of the U.S. armed forces to communicate with one another on the same secure network. Given the current mandate for joint operations by the services, such interoperability is essential. MILSTAR is also the first system to provide satellite-to-satellite communications without the need for costly—and vulnerable—overseas ground relay stations. This feature, termed "crosslinking," lets users connect directly at any spot around the world without time-consuming ground relays. The crosslinks also improve security, ensuring that the intersatellite communications will not be jammed. This feature enables theater commanders to establish and control their own customized networks from a single location, using one or more satellites as the network's processing hub.

MILSTAR is essentially a "switchboard in the sky," providing U.S. joint forces around the world with voice, data, imagery, facsimile, and video communications. MILSTAR meets the essential command, control, and communications (C³) mission by using a six-satellite constellation placed in near equatorial geosynchronous orbit at an altitude of 22,500 miles, with the satellites equally spaced to provide uniform coverage. The network of satellites was designed to be reconfigured to accommodate specific communication needs. While earlier military communication satellites were vulnerable to jamming, MILSTAR was designed to maintain secure and survivable communications, even in wartime. MILSTAR is also resistant to natural and man-made scintillation.

The first MILSTAR satellite was boosted into orbit by a Titan IV rocket with a Centaur upper stage in early 1993. Follow-on satellites (MILSTAR II) were modified to incorporate some of the lessons learned during Desert Storm. Surprisingly, as complex as the system of satellites, service terminals, and associated equipment is, it can be operated as easily as an ordinary telephone.

Deployed in space, a MILSTAR satellite is a sculptural work of art, with a grace that belies its ten-thousand-pound weight. In orbit, with antennae and solar arrays extended, the satellite measures 52 feet across. The flexible solar arrays are a miracle of space utilization, folding out from tiny five-inch-thick boxes to extend to a 108-foot-long structure when fully deployed.

The System of Systems Concept

The proliferation and continual growth of military satellite systems occurred before and after the 1995 Lockheed Martin merger. Both Lockheed and Martin Marietta had been successful in satellite operations; it transpired that their product lines, including various weapon, communications, navigation, weather, and other systems could be combined into a single architecture. This meant that every system could operate as a part of an overall system of systems, with immense advantages accruing in terms of reliability, redundancy, colocation of program offices, and the ability to foster growth in later developments.

For example, the preexisting Defense Satellite Communications System (DSCS), used so successfully in the Persian Gulf War, can be

A MILSTAR satellite weighs some 10,000 pounds, is deployed in a geosynchronous orbit at 22,500 miles above the earth, and provides unprecedented military communications capability.

managed and operated in conjunction with the new MILSTAR system. (The DSCS satellites were a product of the Martin Marietta Valley Forge plant.) In a parallel manner, the Theater High Altitude Area Defense (THAAD) system being developed for defense against theater ballistic missiles both inside and outside the earth's atmosphere also can be operated within the overall satellite system.

THAAD is intended to engage enemy missiles at long range and at high altitudes, and to give the United States and its allies multiple opportunities to intercept incoming missiles. The approximately 1,900-pound missile is over eighteen feet long, and uses an infrared terminal guidance seeker to make its precision "hit-to-kill" collision with the incoming missile.

THAAD is the first system developed to defend against theater ballistic missiles. It is designed to intercept incoming ballistic missiles at the periphery of the earth's atmosphere, to protect the defended area against missile debris. The THAAD system involves the missile itself, the launcher, battle management command, control, communications, and intelligence (BM/C³I), and radar system. Contractor responsibility for the system extends through its entire life cycle, from initial concept to final disposition. Integrated Product Teams (IPTs)

Defense against ballistic missiles is more important than ever, given the proliferation of weapons of mass destruction. The THAAD (Theater High Altitude Defense System) is an advanced system for the destruction of incoming missiles.

are formed with each of the more than sixty other firms involved in creating the system.

THAAD was undertaken deliberately as a high-risk development effort because of the urgent requirement for its deployment.

Over time, the THAAD missile has not performed flawlessly, and fourteen years after the original Homing Overlay Experiment demonstration of exoatmospheric intercept, Lockheed still worked to develop the miniaturized technology to make feasible the deployment of effective theater nuclear defense.

An even more demanding requirement exists for national missile defense, and Lockheed Martin joined with Raytheon and TRW to form the United Missile Defense Company, dedicated exclusively to developing an effective defense against ballistic missile attack on the United States. The company did not win the competition.

The experience with THAAD development helped furnish the expertise which enabled Lockheed Martin to win in 1996 the contract for the development of an essential component of the Space-Based Infrared System (SBIRS), the next-generation missile warning and tracking system. SBIRS will meet the four basic needs of space and missile warfare: missile warning, missile defense, technical intelligence, and defining the character of the battle area in terms of launch point, trajectory, predicted impact point, and the active and passive defenses available. It is intended to provide the initial detection of a ballistic missile attack on the United States, its deployed forces, or its allies, an increasingly important mission as ballistic missiles and weapons of mass destruction continue to proliferate. Whatever shortcomings the leaders of the former Soviet Union might have had, they were at least rational, and knew better than to initiate a nuclear war. In today's world, the possibility of an unauthorized nuclear launch by a terrorist group or by a rogue nation is much greater than ever before.

The SBIRS program is both evolutionary and revolutionary. In its initial stages, it will use existing satellite systems and their associated infrastructure. Subsequently, new satellite systems will be deployed, and these will be able to use existing commercial ground stations for processing communications. The five geosynchronous satellites will incorporate many commercially proven components to reduce both cost and risk. Ultimately the system will consist of satellites deployed in highly elliptical orbits (HEOs) and low earth orbits (LEOs), using relay ground stations and ground terminals. Like MILSTAR, SBIRS will be able to be used by all the military services, to facilitate joint operations. The new A2100 commercial satellite bus will be used for the first time for a military requirement.

In Pentagonese, SBIRS is the first major program to apply acquisition streamlining to Defense Acquisition Board documentation. It used the Single Acquisition and Management Plan (SAMP), a single thirty-nine-page document which replaced seventeen documents that usually totaled over one thousand pages. In real-time terms, it took only three months to reach the first significant management milestone; previous practice would have required twelve months for the same task.

As with every modern weapon system, SBIRS calls upon the full strength of U.S. industry to meet its goals. Lockheed Martin Missiles & Space is the prime contractor, systems engineer, and integrator, and provides the payload. The Aerojet Corporation of California and Northrop Grumman of New York supply the primary infrared sensor payload. The Honeywell Corporation's Clearwater, Florida, division manufactures the onboard spacecraft and payload processors, while

Lockheed Martin and Aerojet team to provide ground systems, satellite telemetry, tracking and control, and mobile ground elements.

And, again like MILSTAR, the experience gained in SBIRS will be useful in commercial satellite operations, which are proliferating at an amazing rate. When *Sputnik* made its first beeping sounds, the world was impressed, but not even the most farseeing visionary of the time could have foreseen that within fifty years the heavens would be so filled with satellites that priorities for orbital positions would become hotly contested.

Moving from Defense to Commerce

As the MILSTAR system moved from concept to fruition, a revolution occurred in personal communication: the advent of the cellular telephone. The success of acquisition reform in the MILSTAR program had engendered sufficient confidence for LMSC to undertake a high-risk commercial venture. It became a subcontractor to the Motorola Corporation to build 125 buses to carry the Iridium global telecommunications payloads—the biggest satellite production job in Lockheed's history—for the Iridium system. Previously, building as many as six identical satellites was considered a most unusual production run.

The motto "One World—One Telephone" captures the Iridium concept. The system is intended to make conversation on handheld telephones possible anyplace in the world by means of a constellation of sixty-six satellites in a low orbit only 420 miles above the earth's surface. The relatively small satellites (only about 1,500 pounds) will be electronically interconnected to provide users with instantaneous global telephone transmissions of all types, including voice, data, fax, and paging. Iridium is intended to revolutionize communications for business professionals, residents of rural areas, travelers, disaster relief teams, or anyone who needs a wireless handheld telephone with a single worldwide number. One can visualize troops in combat in some distant foreign land putting down their rifles to take a call from home in their foxhole, for the location of the subscriber does not have to be known—the satellite-based system will track the location of the telephone continuously. The Iridium telephones will also interface with computers and other communications equipment.

While there were many technical innovations, the most radical

The phrase "one world—one telephone" encapsulates the essence of IRIDIUM, a satellite-based wireless personal communications network for any type of transmission—voice, paging, fax, or data.

change for LMSC was in the contract: it was fixed price, not cost plus fixed fee. The two terms—fixed price versus cost plus fixed fee—sound somewhat alike, but differ greatly in risk involved. In the former, the product is delivered with much more regard to the cost of its manu-facture, for if the contractor spends too much, he has to absorb the loss. In the latter, costs can go up, but they are still covered, and a fixed fee will be earned.

The new satellites were to be produced for less than $7 million per bus, including nonrecurring costs, a unit cost substantially below any comparable satellite built in the past. Lockheed's solution, under Araki's leadership, was to meld all of the knowledge and best practices to be gained from previous classified programs and combine them with Motorola's "Six-Sigma" quality assurance program. A major effort was to reduce the cycle time by half by cutting the schedule for milestones such as preliminary design review, critical design review, and test pro-grams. Integrated product teams were given authority to "get things done" using commercial practices instead of time-honored—and time-wasting—government practices.

The new methods shaped a new culture, one that was easily adapted from Iridium to other programs.

Trading with the (Former) Enemy

Dr. Mel Brashears recalls a staff meeting the morning after the Berlin Wall had fallen. In it he speculated with what he calls today a naive projection: "The world is going to be different! It wouldn't surprise me if Germany was reunited in three to five years, and that there wouldn't be any Soviet Union by the end of the century!" He laughs now that his projection was off by so much, for Germany was reunited that same year, and the Soviet Union collapsed on Christmas Day, 1991.

The sudden interest in Russia was prompted by a Lockheed board member, Dr. James Gibbons, dean of the School of Engineering at Stanford University. During a board meeting in which Tellep was reviewing Lockheed's strategic direction in broadening its commercial business, Gibbons asked "Have you considered doing business in Russia?" The answer was a prompt "no." Gibbons went on to explain that Dr. William Perry—at the meeting as a consultant to Lockheed—had been traveling frequently in Russia and believed that under proper circumstances there could be worthwhile business relationships. Within hours the group had concluded that the Russian Proton rocket would fit precisely within the strategic direction Lockheed was heading. The Proton's reliability was outstanding, and the projected number of satellite launches was so great that there was a gap that the Proton could fill.

Lockheed was mindful of the great success of the French firm Arianespace, which had gone in a decade from a zero share of the world's commercial launch market to periods where they possessed 100 percent of the market. The United States had adopted the Space Shuttle as its primary shuttle launching technique, and the *Challenger* accident of 1986 put the United States at a real disadvantage in the commercial launch world.

By 1992, Lockheed's forecasts indicated a huge market growth in telecommunications, remote sensing, and global positioning, just three of the many types of systems that would be needed. A business proposal was prepared and Brashears and Perry went to Moscow in September 1992. The Russians did not know the precise reason for Lockheed's visit, but welcomed them with open arms anyway.

On the first day's meeting, Brashears outlined Lockheed's concept of cooperation with Energia, the firm building the Proton. The general idea was that a joint venture would be created in which Lockheed would invest capital and resources in exchange for the right to the Proton rocket. The goal of the new venture was to market the very successful and reliable Proton launch vehicle in a market that is demanding more and more launch capacity. The Proton has the capability to launch a twenty-ton payload into low earth orbit.

The first sentence of the Russian response was to the effect that "We can sign this deal today." This was the start of what became an outstanding partnership, Lockheed-Khrunichev-Energia-International (LKEI), which in just five years has generated more than $2 billion of business in the commercial market.

Lockheed continued to develop and market its own launch vehicles, including the Atlas, which had been pioneered by General Dynamics. All these, combined with the Proton, have generated $4 billion of business. This is equivalent to a 50 percent share of the world market, a marked and welcome increase from the zero percent of 1992.

Brashears pays tribute to Gibbons and Perry for fostering the early instincts for cooperation with Russia. Perry (who had also inspired the acquisitions reform process) believed that the best way to stabilize U.S.-Russian relations was to embroil the two countries in mutually profitable business arrangements. Lockheed Martin has continued to expand the relationship with Russian enterprises to the point that the partnership includes the Russian government as well as Russian factories.

Brashears recalls that on the very first day of their first Moscow meeting, they were entertained in the typical lavish Russian fashion at dinner. It developed that there were remarkable similarities in the history of Lockheed and Khrunichev. Both firms had concentrated primarily on aircraft at first, and both became involved in space as a part of the defense effort. Brashears said that Lockheed had been aware of Khrunichev's defense activities and always admired the quality of their product. The Russians responded that in 1960, when Gary Powers's U-2 was shot down, the Soviet defense ministry distributed pieces of the wreckage to a number of industries. Khrunichev received many of the samples and was amazed at the advanced state of the U-2's materials and the processes by which they must have been made. The mutual revelations boded well for the future.

Lockheed extended the partnership by signing an agreement with Energia Scientific and Industrial Corporation to cooperate on future space programs. The new consortium was called Lockheed-Khrunichev-Energia International (LKEI). In June 1997 a new joint venture was formed with an organization with the intriguing, nostalgic nation name of Intersputnik. A consortium of twenty-two nations, led by Russia, Intersputnik corresponds to the Western Instelsat system.

The new firm, Lockheed Martin–Intersputnik, has access to many orbital slots. There will be more such ventures in the future, not least because the joint ventures have been massively significant in transforming the Russian economy. At the time of Brashears's and Perry's first visit to Moscow, the streets were drab and the stores empty of merchandise. All that has changed, and the ancient city is teeming with activity, due in no small part to the new joint ventures.

The Full Spectrum

As LMSC was transformed into LMMS (Lockheed Martin Missiles & Space) over the course of the merger it became apparent that the new company had experience and expertise in every area of space operations. LMSC, and then LMMS, had created and operated launch sites, conducted shuttle operations, developed a family of launch vehicles, and created a wide variety of satellites. It also possessed the necessary ground equipment and personnel to manage the systems and utilize the information derived from them.

The process was unquestionably synergistic; each new contract won brought new experiences and enabled the company to raise its technology to an ever higher level. Perhaps the most obvious example lies in the Commercial Remote Sensing System (CRSS), which was sustained after Lockheed's original $150 million investment. CRSS is actually three programs in one. The first is the space segment, in which LMSS will develop two satellites and launch them on a Lockheed Martin Launch Vehicle (LMLV-2) Athena. The second is the ground segment, in which three ground stations will be developed. The third is one of the most important services provided by LMSS, the system design and integration. LMMS is building the system for Space Imaging, EOSAT, a firm in Thornton, Colorado, in which Lockheed Martin has a major investment.

With a digital camera from Eastman Kodak, the *IKONOS I* satellite will provide one-meter-resolution black-and-white (panchromatic) and four-meter-resolution color (multispectral) digital imagery for commercial and government contractors worldwide. The digital camera (or scanner) passes over the target at a precise, controlled speed and reads out electronic charges at specified intervals of time. In just two seconds, the camera scans an area eleven kilometers square— about the size of San Francisco—and produces 2 billion bits of information. This information is compressed to 600 million bits and transmitted via an X-band antenna to the ground station in two seconds, thus delivering digital images from space in "near real time."

The system will have application to the mapping required for civil engineering, construction, real estate, land management, agriculture, mining, environmental monitoring, tax assessment, transportation, and infrastructure planning. As a simple example of its utility, Space Imaging EOSAT will offer real estate and insurance agencies a CD-ROM which covers the San Francisco Bay Area. The imagery will let users discern objects on the earth's surface as small as one meter in size; cars, boats, sidewalks, swimming pools, and other features will be clearly depicted. The use of such imagery is especially valuable in a before-and-after situation, when damage assessment has to be made after a natural disaster.

Insiders at LMMS believe that the high-resolution satellite imagery market is just getting started, and is, relatively, where the cellular phone market was ten years ago.

A Thousand New Frontiers

A schematic drawing of the progress from the early days of the X-7 to the present would be similar to an inverted pyramid tree, for each new venture served as the basis for the launch of several others, and these, in turn, launched still more. There were several elements in LMSC's physical makeup that facilitated this ever-expanding progress. Leadership was paramount, of course, and will be addressed in the following section. The physical layout of LMSC, with its large, conveniently located campus of buildings that could each be segregated for security reasons, lent itself to a variety of programs. LMSC also created specialized facilities at a variety of other sites to meet emerging program needs. These included plants at Austin, Texas, (for the Air Forces Precision Location/Strike System and subsequent systems such as the Remotely Piloted Vehicle); the research laboratories in Palo Alto; the Huntsville Research and Engineering Center in Alabama; and the Lockheed Ocean Laboratory in San Diego.

These efforts permitted many bold ventures into commercial space, with IRIDIUM, Commercial Remote Sensing Satellite (CRSS) and the relationship with the Russians to market Proton rockets as examples. It had also moved forward with a family of new small launch vehicles, and was well-positioned in upcoming military satellite competitions. The question was whether or not these new ventures would pay off in time to offset continuing declines in its traditional programs. This issue disappeared with the merger with Martin Marietta.

Intercontinental ballistic missiles continued to present an unparalleled threat, especially as their numbers grew. The credibility of massive retaliation as a deterrent was dependent upon the ability of the United States to detect a missile attack in sufficient time to launch a response. The best—the only—way to do this was from space, and this led to the MIDAS system, the nation's first-generation surveillance system, which was introduced in the mid-1960s. For MIDAS, surveillance meant maintaining a vigilant watch over every square inch of the earth's surface twenty-four hours a day, 365 days a year. The task was made possible by the introduction of new technology that permitted infrared cameras to be placed on satellites in low earth (two hundred–plus miles) orbit. The infrared cameras, rudimentary by today's standards, were sensitive to heat and capable of detecting the launch of an ICBM.

Complete coverage of the earth's surface was necessary because missiles could readily be concealed in the vast expanse of the Soviet Union and its satellite countries. The introduction of the submarine-launched ballistic missile meant that oceans had to be monitored as well.

Cameras in low earth orbit passed over the surface of the earth about every ninety minutes, and made adequate surveillance more difficult to achieve. By the late 1960s it became evident that the ideal solution was to place advanced infrared cameras over the earth at a geostationary altitude—a point in the sky that rotates precisely with the earth, so that the satellite is always in place. From the approximately twenty-two-thousand-mile altitude at which it is placed, a single satellite can cover about 43 percent of the earth's surface.

The Defense Support Program (DSP) was deployed in the 1970s to achieve this mode of surveillance. TRW has built twenty-four of the five-thousand-pound satellites, which are designed to detect and track all ICBM, IRBM, space launches, and nuclear explosions, as well as the launch of small tactical missiles. The system worked well during the Gulf War. DSP is operated by the Twenty-first Space Wing, located at Peterson Air Force Base, Colorado, and its warnings are relayed to the North American Air Defense Command (NORAD) and U.S. Space Command.

Even as DSP was being placed into operation in the 1970s, effort was already under way to create a third-generation system with even greater capability. It was recognized that while DSP had detected Scud launches during the Gulf War, tactical missiles in general have a smaller plume, and so are "less observable," in the jargon of the industry.

The quest for a new system gained momentum in 1983, with President Reagan's Strategic Defense Initiative, with the start-up of the Boost Surveillance and Tracking Systems (BSTS) program. Lockheed had been involved at every step of the way, but in 1985, Dan Tellep called Dr. Mel Brashears and told him that he was assigned to BSTS.

Budgets and requirements kept changing, and Brashears, now president, space and strategic missiles for Lockheed Martin, recalls that by 1991, the BSTS program was transferred from the Strategic Defense Initiative Office back to the Air Force. The program was reconstituted in 1991 as the Advance Warning System (AWS), which fortuitously became one of the first systems to benefit from the acquisition-reform tidal wave that was sweeping the defense industry.

Over the next two years the program was redefined for the third time. AWS was dropped and the Space-Based Infrared System (SBIRS) was born. The process of moving from BSTS to AWS to SBIRS took almost a decade, and during that period, Lockheed worked closely with other manufacturers, particularly Hughes, with whom it was teamed to produce the infrared camera. When the Lockheed Martin merger occurred in 1995, Hughes withdrew from the team, and a new competition to manufacture the infrared camera was required. The Lockheed Martin team won this competition, and then went on to win the SBIRS contract, which is estimated to have a value of $17 billion to $20 billion over the next twenty years. Under the new contract, Lockheed Martin will provide the satellites, ground stations, and system integration needed for a total systems solution against the threat of either ICBM or theater ballistic missiles. The contract award was strongly influenced by the excellent results of Lockheed's acquisition-reform experience with AWS and with MILSTAR.

SBIRS is a collection of satellites that are judiciously placed around the equator at geostationary altitudes. Four satellites cover all the pertinent areas of the globe. The cameras on board the satellites take pictures every few seconds. The pictures are immediately translated into digital images of the earth, and the information is transmitted to the ground station in Denver, Colorado, for processing and display.

If there is a rocket launch of any kind, anything from the takeoff of the Space Shuttle to a test of an intermediate range ballistic missile, the cameras immediately pick it up. It is displayed with warnings and indications to the Commander in Chief of Space Command, who has the responsibility to decide what is occurring and what the national response should be. The information includes precisely locating the missile launch, determining its trajectory, and predicting where it will impact, all within sixty seconds of the launch.

SBIRS is so designed that it can readily incorporate any defensive system against missiles if a decision is made to deploy it. Its design is entirely treaty compliant as it stands, because it is a passive system, but it has the inherent accuracy to be the eyes and brains of a defensive system if required.

There are many other programs with great portent for the future, such as the Airborne Laser, an aircraft-mounted laser capable of destroying enemy missiles almost immediately after launch; the International Space Station Centrifuge and Globebox, to provide on-orbit research capability; SOFIA, the Stratospheric Observatory for Infrared Astronomy—the list is long and varied.

This necessarily succinct catalog of space-based projects only touches the surface of LMSC activity, but illustrates another phenomenon. Where for decades individual projects had dominated Lockheed thinking, from the first Electra to the Fleet Ballistic Missile program, the Lockheed (and of course, now Lockheed Martin) mind-set is now devoted to whole families of scientific disciplines within which individual projects can be pursued. Perhaps reasonably enough, the individual projects that are now pursued invariably involve a large portion of the previously mentioned family of scientific disciplines themselves.

LMSC's Management Pool

The task of managing these multifaceted programs was and is daunting, but LMSC has proved to be an endless source of profit, of innovative new disciplines, and most important, of systems concept and engineering, the core of successful management for space systems.

Lockheed has been in an almost constant process of growth and evolution since the 1960s, with some divisions of the company prospering, while others went through periodic difficulties. The result was that positions varied in their importance over time; for example, it was possible for a vice presidency at one company to be a more important position than a presidency at another. As a result, Lockheed has had to redesignate positions and titles of top managers to reflect those changes.

Thus, there has been a migration from general managers to presidents to group president to corporate president as the organizations grew in size and complexity. Most of the future leaders of the Lockheed

Robert A. Fuhrman began with
Lockheed in 1948 as a member
of the Polaris team. His
managerial and engineering
skills saw his rapid rise to the
top of LMSC.

Corporation would gain experience and exposure working their way up the LMSC ladder, sometimes becoming a corporate officer, also, on the way. In some instances they would move to positions of responsibility (and not always in their own field) at Lockheed-Georgia, or some other center. Some topped out very comfortably as president of LMSC or elsewhere, for the management pyramid always narrows toward the top, and there could be only so many chairmen, presidents, and vice presidents of the Lockheed Corporation over the years.

A few stellar performers from LMSC would follow this path, but with the position of president or chairman of the Lockheed Corporation as their final achievement. Among them would be Bob Fuhrman, Roy Anderson, Larry Kitchen, and Dan Tellep. Each of these men would be quick to point out that his success was possible only because of the excellence of his colleagues' performance.

Space limitations prevent telling the full corporate progression of each of the four men named in the previous paragraph, but Bob Fuhrman's career can serve as a quick illustration of the sometimes labyrinthine path to the top at Lockheed.

Fuhrman was born in Michigan on February 23, 1925, and graduated from that spawning ground of Lockheed engineers, the University of Michigan, in 1945 with a bachelor's degree in aeronautical engineering. He served in the U.S. Navy as a pilot, then earned a master's degree in fluid mechanics and dynamics from the University of Maryland in 1952. He joined the Ryan Aeronautical Company, where he helped develop the X-13 jet-propelled vertical takeoff aircraft. Fuhrman joined LMSC in 1958 as a member of the Polaris systems development staff. He became chief engineer of the Missile Systems Division in 1964 and was elected vice president and assistant general manager of the Missile Systems Division in 1966. Three years later, he was elected a Lockheed corporate vice president and named general manager of the Missile Systems Division.

Then, in what would become a typical Lockheed method of encouraging personal growth, he was named president of the Lockheed-Georgia Company in 1970. The following year he became president of the Lockheed-California Company, while two years later he became executive vice president at LMSC. He became president of LMSC in 1976, serving until 1984; at the same time, he was senior vice president of the corporation. In 1979 he became chairman of the board of LMSC, and was elected a member of the Lockheed Corporation's board of directors in May 1980. He became group president, missiles and space systems, in 1983, then served as Lockheed's president and chief operating officer in 1986. In 1988, he was elected vice chairman of the board and chief operating officer of the Lockheed Corporation. He retired in 1990, but continued to serve as adviser.

The Basis for Premier Technology:
Research Laboratories

It would be roughly correct to state that the research laboratories established in Palo Alto in 1956 are for LMSC what the Skunk Works were for Lockheed's aeronautics business. The laboratories, like other Lockheed units, have had a series of name changes over the years, but the heart of their mission has always been to maintain Lockheed not on, but beyond, the very cutting edge of technology.

Located in the Stanford Industrial Park in Palo Alto, the laboratories grew from a relatively small, but strong, technical staff into what later became known as the Advanced Systems Divisions (ASD). In 1962, the organization consisted of four major laboratories and five engineering directorates whose primary missions were to support the major missile and space programs. In the Electronic Sciences Laboratory, research led to a successful information retrieval system, DIALOG, which by 1981 had become the largest on-line information retrieval system in the world. Other experiments pioneered the use of laser communications and digital image-processing techniques. The Material Sciences Laboratory conducted research in a number of disciplines, including electrochemistry, metallurgy, and fluid mechanics. Experiments led to the development of the thermal insulating material selected for use on the Space Shuttle. The Physical Sciences Laboratory investigates nuclear physics, astronomy, and space physics, and a further reorganization created the Research and Development Division under E. P. Wheaton, who directed efforts to find new market opportunities and new product lines. In 1963, the labs were supplemented in Alabama by the Huntsville Research and Engineering Center (HREC), which gave direct support to both DOD and NASA programs.

By the 1970s, the laboratories were engaged in a wide spectrum of exotic activities, including manned space systems, silent aircraft, information systems, ballistic missile defense, and many more.

The events selected in this chapter are but a few of the thousands that occurred in more than four creative decades of LMSC history. The personalities mentioned are but a few of the thousands of important people who made LMSC great as they created complex, and often highly classified, systems.

It is necessary now to retrace our steps through a very difficult period for Lockheed during the 1960s and 1970s. Then it seemed to many that the grand old firm would not survive, when its equity would be driven to perilously low levels and when it seemed certain that the aircraft divisions of the firm would have to be sold off. Lockheed did survive, and then prospered in phenomenal style, but only because of the tremendous depth of managerial talent that was developed at LMSC.

CHAPTER 11

Family Strength
Overcomes Adversity

Although the period began with what seemed to be an exceptionally favorable combination of circumstances, the years from 1965
to 1977 marked the most troubled time the Lockheed Corporation
would ever experience. The company was clearly at the very forefront
of aircraft technology, with the U-2 in operation, the brilliant SR-71
in production, the F-104 reaching its proper station in life in foreign
markets, the C-130 the mainstay of airlift units, the C-141 becoming
operational, and the Orion in steady production. We've just examined
the incredible achievements of LMSC, with its regal procession of Fleet
Ballistic Missiles in the works on one side of the house and an endless
series of highly classified—and highly profitable—satellites—satellites
coming from the other. With other operating units doing well, 1965
sales reached a comfortable $1.8 billion level, though profits were typ-
ically modest at $53.8 million in 1965. The figure represented just 3

Few aircraft have captured the public imagination as has the U-2, and even fewer have had so distinguished a history over so long a period. It is the only aircraft that the USAF ever reintroduced into production.

percent of sales, about what grocery stores were expected to do, and hardly the usurious rip-off of the American public that is often imputed to aerospace manufacturers.

Things were looking good for the future. Lockheed had won hotly contested competitions for the Air Force's large air lifter, the C-5A Galaxy, and the Army's attack helicopter, a revolutionary design that would be designated the AH-56A Cheyenne. The lure of the commercial airliner was still strong, and the work already done on the C-141 and the C-5 studies combined with the advent of the new high-bypass turbofan engines so that design studies could begin on a 250-seat wide-body transport to be used on U.S. domestic routes.

The company was also continuing its policy of diversification. The Lockheed Aircraft Service Company had started as a customer service desk in Burbank in 1937. It had grown to be a worldwide organization, operating more than twenty-five service centers on six continents. The corporation also diversified into shipbuilding, rocket motors, and other ventures, of which more later.

As might be expected, with this series of ongoing successes and glowing prospects, the personnel at Lockheed corporate headquarters were confident. The Gross brothers had created a vehicle that the rigorous management style of Dan Haughton, ably assisted by his faithful, industrious number two, Carl Kotchian, could steer into a profitable future.

It was indeed a powerful dynasty, made up of men of great and diverse talent. The visionary Robert Gross had died in 1961, and his more detail-and management-oriented brother Courtlandt succeeded him as chairman, retaining that office until 1967. Both men had absolute confidence in Haughton, a taskmaster who worked himself and everyone else endlessly, paying excruciating attention to every detail. Haughton was named president in 1961 and chairman and CEO in 1967, when Kotchian succeeded him as president and chief operating officer. Kotchian was a master salesman, both of ideas within the company and aircraft outside it.

Although these leaders had experienced some trying times, their track record had been remarkably consistent. Profits had been earned every year since 1948, with the sole exception of 1960, when the Electra wing failures caused a $43 million loss. But even the Electra program had been turned to good account for two reasons. The first was the absolute integrity with which Lockheed remedied the Electra's deficiency, and the second was the aircraft's subsequent military success as the Orion patrol and antisubmarine-warfare plane.

Unfortunately, disaster loomed ahead in many of the programs that were begun with such confidence. The troubles arose from a variety of sources, but the problems of the various programs were understandably interrelated, given that they all shared Lockheed's top corporate management philosophy and all had to draw water from the same financial well.

The scale of the difficulties Lockheed would encounter is easiest to understand if each program is dealt with individually. The source of their problems can be analyzed and their cumulative effects upon the Lockheed Corporation can then be measured.

The C-5

The success of the C-5 as a military aircraft has been demonstrated in every part of the world. Like other Lockheed transports, it has gained a great deal of its reputation in the execution of missions of compassion, but when it has been committed to combat, it has done superbly well.

Yet the C-5 program itself was an agony for Lockheed and for the government. There is plenty of blame to apportion for the trouble.

Despite disclaimers at the time and later, Lockheed was certainly too optimistic about the ease with which it could handle the project. The C-5 proved to be far more than a "scaled-up C-141." The Haughton management style, which reverberated down through the ranks, was a negative factor. At every level, supervisors could be found who followed Haughton's authoritarian practice; there was a tendency to insist that orders were to be followed exactly, even when feedback from the floor indicated other actions were necessary. The Lockheed reporting system was flawed in that reliance was placed in "catch-up" operations that caused optimistic reports to be rendered both internally and externally. It was perhaps not evident at the time, even to those at the source of the trouble, but the hard truths about many subjects—costs, schedules, changes, etc.—were sometimes blurred by waffled reporting, to the extent that no one knew the exact status of many critical areas of the program.

Nor was the Air Force immune from blame. The most critical error made by the Air Force was at the very beginning of the program. After a decision had been made to award the contract to Lockheed, the Air Force informed the company that the landing distances projected by Lockheed were inaccurate and provided its own estimates. To bring the aircraft performance up to the Air Force figures, Lockheed was forced to agree to a major redesign of the wing, and to guarantee the new performance figures. Lockheed objected, on the basis that it believed its figures to be correct, and because it could not, in the ten days the Air Force had allotted, redesign the wing and check the figures.

The Air Force was adamant—and was the customer. Lockheed agreed to redesign the wing, which started the process of increased weight and drag that would ultimately cause so much of the C-5A's problems.

The Air Force also gave the C-5A program far too much supervision. Change orders came in an endless flow, and the C-5 itself was laden with features (such as the elaborate landing gear designed to permit rough-field operation) that proved not to be useful under the actual conditions under which the aircraft would operate. And just as Lockheed reporting was flawed, so was that of the Air Force. In some instances, inferences to be made from the admittedly ambiguous Lockheed reports were further slanted in an effort to protect the Air Force point of view.

In short, both sides were often caught up in finger-pointing controversies when their mutual interests would have been better served by more intelligent, completely open cooperation.

The heart of the problem was contractual. Both Lockheed and the USAF had agreed to the contract; both hoped that it would be possible to execute. Yet the contract was an unfulfillable monstrosity that worked against the interest of the government and the contractor with almost equal ferocity. Few will be surprised to learn that it originated in the office of the Secretary of Defense.

The Would-be Magic Wand of Competition: Total Package Procurement

The intensity of all military competitions was heightened by the introduction of a new concept from Secretary McNamara's quantitatively oriented DOD procurement agencies. Called "Total Package Procurement" (TPP), the new concept required manufacturers to compete for an entire program, from research and development through production, all under a single contract. Standards were to be set for price, schedule, and performance, and it was made well known that the government did not intend to budge from the agreements.

TPP was a well-intentioned approach to consider a program in its entirety, prevent cost overruns, and insure that contractors met all contractual requirements. A clause stipulated that the contractor was responsible for the complete system performance, including engines, and was required to take action to correct any discrepancies. It should have been obvious that this was clearly beyond the bounds of any contractor's ability in a firm-fixed-price development/production contract, but it was nonetheless an integral part of the TPP concept. (Larry Kitchen later commented that TPP was essentially a firm-fixed-price development program.)

Robert H. Charles, who was appointed assistant secretary of the Air Force for installations and logistics by President Kennedy in 1963, was the principal creator of the TPP program. Charles had worked for McDonnell Aircraft for eighteen years, seven of them as vice president. There is some irony in the fact that his long experience on the contractor side imbued him with a passionate belief that military procurement needed drastic reform—he knew where bodies could be buried. A popular catchphrase of the time, "holding the contractor's feet to the fire," became a particularly apt description of TPP—unfortunately, no one realized that Total Package Procurement insured mutual immolation. TPP became a petri dish for the cultivation of adversarial relationships, rather than a medium for obtaining weapon systems at a reasonable cost on a timely basis. It carried an almost Orwellian Big Brother approach to an extreme, and failed to consider elements that should have been obvious, given the long and often dismal history of aircraft procurement. TPP failed to anticipate the effect of rapid inflation (inevitable in the Vietnam War era), the customary changes in Air Force requirements, and the ever popular "hobby-shopping" as Air Force advocates introduced new and often unnecessary elements into the program, each one requiring changes. Worse, it did not provide a ready mechanism for settling disputes in an equitable manner. The government could stick to its guns, and, if it so desired, could literally bankrupt a contractor.

In retrospect, there is no question that Lockheed (and probably its two competitors) was guilty of overoptimistic pricing. Given its excellent experience with the C-141, Lockheed expected the state-of-the-art C-5 to be a similar if larger program. Things were not that simple, for a variety of reasons, including the sheer size of the aircraft.

More significant, perhaps, was a general hardening of management arteries. Companies are much like human beings, and success tends to breed habit patterns that may work well in one instance, but when institutionalized, adversely affect performance. And companies change as they grow older; at Lockheed-Georgia, a climate of cronyism had begun to develop, one that was reflected in job assignments, promotions, and decision making. This is a perfectly normal business happenstance, but it did not make handling the myriad management and production problems of the C-5 any easier. These problems would persist until the arrival of new ideas and new concepts from managers schooled in Sunnyvale's LMSC methods.

TPP was designed to prevent the contractor from "getting well" on the change-order process, an almost routine event in previous competitions. Changes are inevitable, and the contractor is in a position to take advantage of the changes with higher prices. But when TPP tried to "level the playing field," it instead bulldozed a potential burial ground for Lockheed, as it would have for any contractor. (There are those who dispute the efficacy of a contractor using change orders to improve its business position, but most people agree that it is an influential factor in the defense business.)

On the surface, TPP seemed to give a hammer to the government with which to beat the contractor, and it was so used. No one in the Department of Defense saw that the government-contractor relationship was so intertwined that the government would feel any pain inflicted on the contractor, for the Air Force needed the C-5, and the long, costly competition had already shut out any alternate source.

The TPP concept also resulted in one of the great aviation ironies. The winner of the competition, Lockheed, would take tremendous financial losses in producing just eighty-one of the C-5As under the original contract. The loser, Boeing, would convert its effort into the design of the commercial 747 and then build more than a thousand of what became the most successful large passenger transport in history.

The competition for the C-5 contract had been a close one, and although each competitor thought its own product was the best, price proved to be critical. Lockheed bid $1.9 billion for the entire package, while Douglas bid $2 billion and Boeing $2.3 billion. The Air Force liked both the Lockheed and Boeing designs, but did not favor the Douglas entry. Lockheed was selected. Secretary McNamara ordered a comprehensive review of the bidding, and found no evidence of a Lockheed "buy-in." Courtlandt Gross, then chairman of the firm, later recalled that Lockheed had planned a profit margin of about 10 percent, an estimate in which Haughton concurred. Unaware of the coming economic and contractual turbulence, they had committed Lockheed to an eight-year program that involved the design of a very sophisticated airplane, and the first use of a complicated and potentially disastrous new contractual arrangement. It proved to be far easier to make the C-5 fly than to master the TPP process.

Lockheed's TPP contract for the C-5 called for the production of 5 aircraft followed by "Run A" of 53 production aircraft; if these were satisfactory, a "Run B" of 57 could be added on for a total of 115 aircraft. As the program developed, design changes called for by the Air Force, and inflation, resulted in a total cost of $5.2 billion even though Run B was reduced to 23 aircraft. The increase in cost and the parallel increase in unit price set Lockheed up to be the target for the media and Congress.

The agony of the cost overruns was exacerbated by the protests of an Air Force civil servant, Ernest Fitzgerald, who, in musical terms, first blew the whistle and then tooted his own horn. Attempts to mollify—or muzzle, according to your point of view—Fitzgerald were clumsily handled, and he emerged a folk hero, his name a synonym for bucking the military-industrial complex. All of Fitzgerald's efforts were dwarfed, however, by those of Senator William Proxmire and the media, who enjoyed a field day at Lockheed's expense.

Unfortunately, as accusations were hurled and hearings were held, no one recognized that the extreme rise in cost was in fact a lesser problem than the result of the contractual decisions made under TPP guidelines.

As happens with most aircraft during the design process, the C-5A experienced a growth in empty weight that impaired its performance, causing a drop in its range with a payload of one hundred thousand pounds to only 6,720 miles. Lockheed sought permission to regain the lost performance by using newly available engines of greater thrust, at a cost of about an additional $5 million. The Air Force refused, insisting that Lockheed undertake a massive weight-reduction program instead. It added a proviso: Lockheed could undertake the engine change at its own expense if it wished, but it still had to make the original weight stipulation. This was sheer lunacy on the part of the Air Force, in which an untried contractual concept was given precedence over prudent engineering and standard aviation practice.

The weight-reduction program involved, among many other things, the chemical milling of wing spars to reduce their weight. This costly and time-consuming process involved taping the mammoth wing spar, then dipping it in an acid bath, removing it, untaping, cleaning, retaping, and redipping. Each dip in the acid bath reduced weight by a fraction—but also reduced strength. The result was that the planned thirty-thousand-hour life span was cut to eight thousand hours, and even this shortened life was attainable only by limiting payload to fifty thousand pounds, except under emergency conditions. At the time, Lockheed engineers were not aware that the reduction in strength would be so great; they believed that they were removing only the safety margin that they had built into the initial calculations. As the situation developed, means were found to mitigate the problem not only by limiting the payload, but also by improved flight techniques using so-called active ailerons controlled by computers.

The math, if ugly, is fairly straightforward. The change to the more powerful engines would have cost $5 million, avoided the most drastic elements of the weight-reduction program, and provided a thirty-thousand-hour life. The drop from the thirty-thousand-hour life-span figure to eight thousand works out to be about a 73 percent reduction. If that same 73 percent figure is applied against the ultimate program cost of $5.2 billion, the result is a waste of $3.79 billion.

Total Package Procurement proved to be counterproductive on a co-lossal scale.

Yet TPP was a banner under which critics such as the *Washington Post* and Senator Proxmire rallied, somehow construing the method of contracting to be a malevolent conspiracy masterminded by the contractor to bilk the government of money, instead of a governmental choke collar on the contractor. The provisions for determining the price of Run B depended upon the cost of Run A. Critics claimed that Lockheed had deliberately inflated its initial costs so that it could cash in on Run B, even though there was no guarantee as to how many—if any—aircraft would actually be procured in the second increment. It should have been obvious that no contractor would have worked deliberately to achieve a certain loss of huge proportions on the first procurement in the hope of recovering on a second procurement, given that the terrible cost of the first run would prejudice the customer against an additional buy.

Unfortunately, logic did not have headline appeal, and Lockheed was made to appear a deliberate villain, when it was at most culpable of overoptimism and an inability to cope with the scale of the project and the rising price index. Lockheed had no choice but to contest the terms of the contract, and a lengthy and painful series of negotiations took place at Wright Field.

Production Dilemma

In contrast to the critics' contentions, the management at Lockheed-Georgia was fully involved in the struggle to build the C-5 as economically as possible. There was no point to building airplanes at a loss, as Dan Haughton constantly reminded them, and his continual oversight may well have exacerbated the problem. The pressure he exerted on Lockheed-Georgia management is reflected in the relatively rapid turnover of the top leaders. Dick Pulver was general manager (president) from 1959 to May of 1967, during the initial "ramp-up" to production. He was succeeded by Tom May, who served until February 1970. May was succeeded in turn by Robert Fuhrman, who served until November 1971, when future Lockheed chairman Larry Kitchen took over.

Furhman and Kitchen were not the first to join Lockheed-Georgia from LMSC. In 1965—in the very early days of the C-5A program—Roy Anderson, who later became chairman and chief executive officer, was sent to Georgia from LMSC to strengthen Georgia's financial and business management. Anderson, highly respected for his financial acumen, was instrumental in surfacing the emerging C-5 problems and recognizing the significance of their potential. But his time in Georgia was limited, as the growing financial problems at corporate headquarters resulted in his transfer to the corporate staff as assistant treasurer in 1968. He would play a critical role in negotiating the final settlement on the C-5A contract in 1971.

The rapid turnover reflected the anxiety over the C-5, but also portended another trend within the Lockheed Corporation, one that would have enormous impact on its future. Both Fuhrman and Kitchen were products of the Lockheed Missiles and Space Company. Both had proven their skills in the highly successful Fleet Ballistic Missile Program. When Fuhrman was selected to go to Georgia as company president, he asked Kitchen to accompany him as vice president of finance and administration, even though Kitchen's background was primarily technical. Beginning with Anderson's appearance in Georgia, LMSC would have an increasingly pervasive effect upon Lockheed's upper management.

In a recent interview, Kitchen recalled his dismay on his first visits to the C-5 production line after coming from the relatively ordered efficiency of the Fleet Ballistic Missile effort: "I'd go down and go through the fuselage. You know how big a C-5 is, and I could not see through the fuselage—it was jam-packed with people. Some would be making initial installations and some would be making changes; behind them would be another crew, ripping out what they had done and putting in another change."

Kitchen, a no-nonsense manager, analyzed the situation and realized that the engineering department was inundated with changes. Configuration control had been lost. Kitchen insisted on a stand-down, stopping production so that engineering could catch up and restore order. The stand-down was resisted both by the Air Force and by Lockheed corporate leaders, but he made it stick.

Fuhrman had also designated Kitchen to be the hatchet man, and he set to work paring down the workforce. When they arrived, there were over twenty thousand people and production chaos. When he left in 1975, ten thousand people were employed on a rational production line, a number consistent with the current workload. He had raised the operating profit of the Georgia plant to about 9 percent, and was then challenged by Carl Kotchian to get it to 11 percent. With his characteristic energy, Kitchen and his team were running a streamlined operation, now producing C-130s primarily, but still doing a great deal of modification work, up to a record 21 percent level.

There were a series of great triumphs, including "stretch" of the C-141 and the successful efforts to sell additional C-130s when it seemed that the line was about to be shut down. Kitchen also was able to retrieve the C-5A program by selling the Department of Defense on the modification program that provided a new wing and years of additional service life.

Kitchen regards the four years he served as president of the Georgia Company as the most rewarding of his career, even though he went on to hold the top position of the corporation. At Lockheed-Georgia, he imitated Haughton—a man he admires immensely—in one respect, by having staff meetings every morning at seven o'clock with a small number of key people. Unlike Haughton, who at times worked with his transmitter button locked down, Kitchen listened, running his meetings as a collegial team effort. Each day, problems would be surfaced and decisions would be made as the management style developed at LMSC was gradually applied. Kitchen carefully reviewed the organization chart at Georgia and cut down the number of levels of management, combining or eliminating organizations. He soon had the managerial trend lines going in the correct direction—overhead down, quality up, costs down, schedule on track.

The vast difference in management styles between LMSC and Lockheed Corporate or Lockheed-Georgia was illustrated in an incident that Kitchen still regards as a management coup: persuading Haughton not to visit so often.

It was Haughton's custom to fly down in his JetStar every Sunday morning to hold his own seven o'clock meeting, reviewing every aspect of the program. A classic micromanager, he knew the details of the programs as well as any of the Georgia managers, who were terrified by his domineering, taskmaster manner. They found themselves spending most of their time putting together "Haughton-proof" briefings for the Sunday inquisition. Kitchen told Haughton frankly that his visits were taking too much time away from his managers and were keeping them from getting their job done. Haughton called Kitchen a "smart-ass," and then reluctantly agreed to come only once every two weeks. Kitchen eventually persuaded him to make the visit monthly—and production picked up accordingly. All eighty-one C-5As were delivered by May 1973, amid a hurricane of controversy that would resonate for years.

With guidance from Haughton and Anderson, a Georgia team

led by corporate executive vice president William Rieke and including Kitchen, Dick Taylor, and others renegotiated the C-5A contract in 1970. The renegotiation created, in effect, a cost-plus-fixed-loss contract (the fixed loss being about $250 million) for the C-5A program. It was part of a global settlement with the DOD.

Kitchen's leadership created a totally new atmosphere of genuine teamwork at Lockheed-Georgia. One result of this was an improved productivity and quality control that resulted in an enormous saving (approximately $150 million) to the Air Force estimate to complete the remainder of the contract. A second result was a change in the Georgia corporate culture that was reflected in the modifications later done on the C-141, the rapid and cost-effective production of the C-5B, and the enduring C-130 production.

In retrospect, it is evident that if Total Package Procurement had focused on the needs of the service rather than on circumventing possible contractor inequities, the C-5As would not have needed to be rewinged. In addition, the C-5Bs could have been included in the initial production run at an advantageous price. Total Package Procurement was ultimately abandoned, even though its primary advocate, Robert Charles, insisted to the end that it was the correct way to do business.

The C-5 was but the starting point of Lockheed's time of trouble. As devastating as the losses were on the program, their most long-lasting and debilitating effects were on an intangible element: the credibility of Lockheed's leaders.

The AH-56A Cheyenne

The Vietnam War had a mixed effect upon defense contractors. On the one hand, it brought about increased procurements of existing weapon systems and the formulation of requirements for new weapons; on the other, it consumed so much of the defense budget that programs were always candidates for cancellation if they did not prove out quickly and economically.

The early success of helicopters in Vietnam had inspired the Army to hold the Advanced Aerial Fire Support System (AAFSS) competition to obtain a swift, heavily armored and armed battle helicopter. It too was to be a Total Package Procurement contract and it too would be impossible to fulfill.

Tough requirements were set—the helicopter was to have a top speed of 220 knots (253 mph), a ferry range of 2,100 miles, and the ability to hover out of ground effect at six thousand feet—a real challenge.

Of twelve companies that submitted entries, two were selected, Sikorsky, with its model S-66 and its long, distinguished history of helicopter development, and Lockheed, with its model CL-840.

Lockheed's helicopter history was limited, but adventuresome. The Lockheed CL-475 debuted in 1959 with typical Irv Culver innovations. Culver had built a radio-controlled model helicopter with a rigid rotor, and it served as a basis for a two-seat helicopter featuring a rigid rotor coupled to a gyroscope system. After initial difficulties, the piston-engine-powered CL-475 proved to be very easy to fly, and inspired two second-generation designs, the Models 186 and 286.

These continued the use of the rigid rotor, this time in combination with jet engines. While the CL-475 had been a simple design, without much aerodynamic refinement, the new design was a four-seat aircraft of very clean lines, and featuring retractable aluminum alloy landing skids. The gyroscope ring of the CL-475, which had been so conspicuous a departure from other helicopter designs, was now replaced by three weighted arms mounted above the three-blade rotor.

A series of five custom-built prototypes evolved from the original CL-475. Slightly modified, the new two-seat design was designated XH-51A, two examples of which were evaluated by both the Army and the Navy in 1962. Once again, the rigid rotor provided a very stable, easy-to-fly aircraft, one with a top speed of 174 mph.

To see just how much speed could be obtained from a rigid-rotor helicopter, the Army funded the modification of the second prototype into the XH-51A Compound, the designation referring to its incorporation of an additional jet engine for propulsion. A stub wing of seventeen-foot span was added, and a Pratt & Whitney J60 turbojet was placed on the left side of the fuselage. By June 29, 1967, the XH-51A Compound had reached 302.6 mph, a speed absolutely unheard of for helicopters.

NASA acquired a third Model 186, and used it as a research vehicle. Lockheed also built two Model 286s as a speculative venture. These five-seat aircraft were intended for commercial use and received FAA certification in 1966. Despite their high performance (top speed of 206 mph) they failed to gain civil orders.

Yet even this slim history provided the basis for the CL-840, subsequently designated the AH-56A Cheyenne. (The Army preferred

XH-51A compound helicopter featured a stub wing and a Pratt & Whitney J60
turbojet installed on the port side.

naming its aircraft after Indian tribes, a practice that in recent years
has seen some objections raised by Native Americans.) The Cheyenne
was unique; it was a "compound" helicopter with a pusher propeller
at the tail to provide thrust at high speed. It was very handsome, with
a long, slender fuselage and small wings of almost twenty-seven-foot
span. The purpose of the wings was to off-load the rotor during high-
speed flight; at zero lift, the rotor was used only for pitch and roll
control. Powered by a General Electric T-64 jet engine, the Cheyenne
had a four-blade rigid rotor with a diameter of fifty feet, five inches.
The crew of two sat in tandem, the pilot raised above the gunner-
copilot. The forward armament was installed in a stabilized platform
that could swivel through 360 degrees, and could be fitted with a 40-
mm Aeronutronic grenade launcher, a 30-mm Aeronutronic cannon
or a 7.62 mm minigun. There were six underwing attachment points
for TOW antitank missiles or 2.75-mm rocket pods. Aiming devices
were extremely sophisticated for the time, with an early helmet gun
sight and night-vision equipment.

Initial trials were promising, with the first flight occurring on

The AH-56A Cheyenne was one of the most advanced helicopters of its era, and featured a radical four-blade rigid main rotor, a derivative of engineer Irv Culver's thinking.

September 21, 1967. Stability problems were encountered, both at low altitudes and at high speeds.

Eventually, both the low-altitude and the high-speed instability were remedied. Lockheed continued to pursue the program, and considerable progress was made, although unit cost ultimately increased by almost 50 percent more than had originally been estimated. The program eventually succumbed to the general shortfall of defense money due to the Vietnam War, and a general mutual disenchantment between Lockheed and the Army. By August 1972, the program was terminated, and the potentially powerful Cheyenne was relegated to footnotes in history.

One of those footnotes was written by Willis Hawkins, who stoutly maintains that the program was stopped prematurely. He bases his argument on the difficulty that the Army encountered later when it once again sought an advanced attack helicopter. In Hawkins's math—and he is a very accurate engineer—the Army could have purchased more than 2,700 Cheyennes, with all problems solved, for the money it spent developing the new helicopter, the Hughes (later McDonnell Douglas) AH-64A Apache. He is careful to point out that the Cheyenne, despite its being designed twenty years before, was faster, carried more payload, and was much more agile than the Apache.

The Cheyenne was a $150 million strike two against Lockheed.

Lockheed Shipbuilding and Construction Company

This temporary loss of focus could probably be filed under the heading "It looked like a good idea at the time." The venerable Puget Sound Bridge and Dredging Company was sold to Lockheed in 1959. The company had a long and distinguished record of building ships that extended back to 1898; it was also an important factor in construction in the Pacific Northwest. The name was changed in 1965 to reflect the new ownership. Lockheed undertook to build and repair ships for the U.S. Navy, and made heavy capital investments in new machinery. Despite successful efforts in building forty-four ships, including icebreakers, submarine tenders, and landing ships, Lockheed was never able to integrate the shipyard operations into its overall plans, nor was it able to make the shipyards profitable. One factor was the relative cost of labor, which was much higher on the West Coast than in the South or the East. The drain from the shipyard coincided with other major shortfalls from the C-5A and Cheyenne programs, and the business was discontinued in 1987, to the general relief of everyone in the company.

Other Problem Areas

In 1960, Lockheed had entered the rocket-engine field and the Lockheed Propulsion Company was involved in the design of the SR75-LP-1 two-stage solid-propellant motor for the Boeing AGM-69A SRAM (Short-Range Attack Missile). This air-to-surface missile carried a 170-kiloton W69 nuclear warhead, and was for Strategic Air Command bombers what the MIRV was for missiles, a multiplier for the delivery system. The SRAMs were a stand-off attack against the primary Soviet defense installations, clearing a path for either free-fall bombs or air-launched cruise missiles.

The SRAM rocket motor proved to be difficult, and Lockheed had to make a claim for an additional $50 million under its contract to Boeing; this was ultimately settled for $20 million, the difference being absorbed by Lockheed as a loss. The SRAMs were operated successfully for a number of years, but had to be prematurely retired when the rocket motors proved to be unstable in storage.

Serious attempts at diversification brought Lockheed into the ship building business. It did very well until rising costs of West Coast labor made it impossible to compete with shipyards elsewhere.

Lockheed was now engaged with the Department of Defense in the dispute of over $500 million in the settlement of contracts on the C-5A, Cheyenne, SRAM, and ships. DOD played hardball; Lockheed wanted to negotiate the settlement of the Cheyenne, but pursue the C-5A arguments in court. The Defense Department refused. Lockheed had to negotiate a settlement for all the contracts or none.

In the end, Haughton and Anderson, who was now corporate controller, recognized that there was no alternative to a global settlement. Negotiations commenced under the Armed Services Procurement Regulations. The settlement, made with David Packard at the highest levels of the DOD, came in the last days of 1970—and was not a moment too early. Lockheed's precarious financial position worsened, and Lockheed's bankers were persuaded only with difficulty not to abandon ship.

This was a milestone in Anderson's career. It demonstrated his ability to win the confidence of the banks, and provided the groundwork for intense negotiations which were to come over the next several years as Lockheed fought to avoid bankruptcy and chart a course for the future.

The settlements had the following financial impact on Lockheed:

C-5A	$247 million
AH-56A	124 million
Ships	89 million
SRAM	24 million
Total	$484 million

These pretax losses adversely affected net earnings so that Lockheed incurred a net loss for 1970 of almost $86 million on sales of $2.5 billion. The settlement was the largest loss ever taken by a defense contractor, and if nothing else, should have driven a stake through the heart of the canard of a profit-mongering military-industrial complex.

During the long negotiations leading up to the settlement, and in the aftermath of the agreement, Lockheed was subject to a firestorm of criticism in Congress and the media. Dan Haughton, always a persuasive witness no matter how dire the circumstances, attempted to alleviate the situation by pointing to Lockheed's past and current accomplishments. He noted that since its founding, Lockheed had delivered more 33,000 military and civil aircraft and more than 1,600 missiles and spacecraft. (It must have galled Haughton not to be able to talk about the stunning achievements of LMSC, most of which were so classified as to be unknown to the Congress and the press.) He cited the records set by the F-104, U-2, SR-71, and other Lockheed aircraft. He touted the success of the C-130, C-141, and P-3C, noting that the composite record of these aircraft showed that they were within 1 percent of their target costs and schedules. The aircraft on which Lockheed had significant cost overrun problems (the C-5A and Cheyenne) were both products of the new Total Package Procurement system.

Despite security restrictions, LMSC offered him fertile ground for relating Lockheed's prowess. The Polaris had been delivered two and one-half years ahead of schedule with costs only 0.5 percent over target. He spoke of the laurels of the Agena satellite program, which had achieved a 92 percent success rate on its launches. The ongoing story of the spy satellites could not be told.

Lockheed's presentations were successful within Congress, even if they were flayed in the record and in the press, and would lay the groundwork for later talks when Lockheed's very existence was at stake. Its net worth in 1968 had been almost $371 million; by the end of 1970 this was reduced to $235 million, severely affecting its ability to borrow just when, for the first time, Lockheed desperately needed to borrow significant sums.

Lockheed's problems with military procurements were soon to be echoed by difficulties in the civilian marketplace.

The Sirens Sing Again

The siren song of commercial aircraft had been heard again in 1963, when the Federal Aviation Administration announced a phased competition for design studies of a supersonic transport. Boeing and Lockheed responded. Lockheed eventually had a portfolio of double-delta-wing Mach 3 designs.

The beautiful Lockheed L-2000 design was generally regarded by the airlines to be the most feasible concept, but the award went to Boeing on December 31, 1966. Ironically, Boeing's winning swing-wing design was subsequently modified to a configuration very similar to the Lockheed L-2000. The decision may have reflected the government's interest in apportioning contracts evenly, for Lockheed had just won the C-5 contest, while Douglas had won the contest for the Manned Orbiting Laboratory, an early space station concept.

As events transpired, the idea of a supersonic transport was abandoned by the FAA in the face of environmental pressures and the near certainty that a supersonic transport would not be profitable in the long run. The Anglo-French Concorde, a much smaller Mach 2 airplane, proved the point exactly. Only sixteen Concordes were built, and although they performed brilliantly, there was no hope of their ever being able to recover the total costs of research and development and production.

The loss of the SST competition freed up a considerable number of Lockheed engineers at a time when there was a growing interest in entering the jet airliner market. Lockheed-California design teams had prepared design studies for a large twin-engine antisubmarine-warfare aircraft as a logical follow-on to the Orion. This design did not come to fruition, for the Navy elected to stay with the Orion, but it did give Lockheed confidence in responding to an American Airlines requirement for a wide-bodied 250-seat airliner to use on domestic routes.

American's chief engineer, Franklin W. Kolk, generated the requirement, which called for a twin-engine aircraft that would operate over routes such as Los Angeles to Chicago (1,750 nautical miles) or Chicago to New York (640 nautical miles). Kolk was to have great influence on the ultimate competition between Lockheed and McDonnell Douglas, as did Robert Rummell, his counterpart at TWA. Rummell had worked for Lockheed in the past and was one of the few people with whom Howard Hughes dealt directly.

Kolk's initial requirement would grow over time to be modified by the needs of American and four other major airlines—United, TWA, Delta, and Eastern. Each airline involved its engineers in the process to create a set of specifications. Given the state of the art, it was inevitable that the two competing airframe companies, Lockheed and McDonnell Douglas, would evolve very similar aircraft, in terms of dimensions and performance. Only a professional could examine the two aircraft and determine that the L-1011 was clearly more advanced technically and was a bridge to the future, while the DC-10 was a more traditional aircraft, based heavily on past DC-8 and DC-9 practice. (Work was begun by Great Britain, France, and Germany on the Airbus Industrie A-300 wide-body transport in July 1967. It would have significantly different configuration. Great Britain would eventually withdraw from the consortium.)

The One Mistake

The executives who managed Lockheed for most of the past thirty years were products of LMSC. Some of them worked directly with Dan Haughton, and those who did admire him. However, all agree that Haughton did make at least one major error, one that he admitted to: he failed to take the steps necessary to purchase the Douglas Aircraft Company before McDonnell did so in April 1967.

The prospect of Lockheed's acquiring Douglas had been carefully reviewed by upper management. It was economically feasible, and the elimination of competition from the market would have made Lockheed a much stronger player against Boeing. It was recognized that Douglas had some inherent production problems reflected in the late deliveries of both DC-8 and DC-9 aircraft, and that their costs were reportedly out of control. These were felt to be manageable difficulties that Lockheed could turn around. One reason given for the decision not to buy was a desire to let Douglas go under and then pick it up for a bargain price. But according to many who were there at the time, Haughton declined to take action primarily because "Lockheed did not want to build aircraft someone else had designed." It was felt that the merger would create a situation in which Lockheed would concentrate on military aircraft while Douglas would be the lead on the commercial side. Thus corporate chauvinism, pure and simple, carried the seeds of disaster. It might not have been Haughton's only mistake, but it was a sufficiently grievous error.

Shifting Circumstances, Rubber Requirements

Lockheed found itself in competition with McDonnell Douglas, as the new firm was known, for an as-yet to be fully defined aircraft to fit a market niche between the 707/DC-8 and the 747. William M. Hannan was named project engineer for the Lockheed-California team.

The dominant factors for the original concept of the L-1011 were the number of passengers and the design range. American Airlines wanted high passenger capacity and a one-stop transcontinental range, for example, New York to Chicago and Chicago to Los Angeles. This could have been achieved with two engines. Other airlines wanted the same passenger load, but for long-distance flight over the oceans, three engines were required. Two engines were also considered inadequate for operation out of airports at high elevations (e.g., Denver) when outside air temperatures were high.

The advent of a new series of high-bypass engines (which had been brought about by the C-5 competition), the Pratt & Whitney JT9D, the General Electric CF6, and the Rolls-Royce RB.211, put another critical variable into the decision equation. The CF-6 was a development of the TF39 used in the C-5A, and the JT9D had been adopted by the Boeing 747. The Rolls-Royce RB.211 was a very advanced engine, but was not as far along in its development as either of the two other entries. (Engine designations are arcane; in this instance, RB stood for Rolls-Royce Barnoldswick, the original turbine-engine factory site, while 211 was the numerical sequence of the engine in the Rolls-Royce lineup.) Perhaps the most critical element was the fact that Lockheed needed help to fund development, and while neither Pratt & Whitney nor General Electric would offer any, Rolls-Royce did.

Every airline proudly advertises its choice of aircraft, extolling its virtues. Every manufacturer proudly lists the logos and colors of airlines that fly its equipment. One would never gather from these mutual expressions of admiration just how viciously the companies negotiate with each other to obtain every possible edge. The negotiations become fiercest when it is perceived that the other party is in some difficulty.

Relations between aircraft manufacturers and their suppliers—engine builders, equipment providers, service providers—are conducted in exactly the same manner. The result is that the selection of an aircraft such as the proposed Lockheed L-1011 TriStar and the McDonnell Douglas DC-10 becomes a series of small wars, complete with espionage, propaganda, disinformation, and bloody battles at the negotiating table, with no quarter asked or given. The spirit of combat is such that companies often ignore long-term advantages in the interest of satisfying short-term victories.

As events transpired, McDonnell Douglas entered the race for the wide-body transport a little later than Lockheed. Both the McDonnell Douglas and the Lockheed teams synthesized all of the available information, and both concluded that the new airliner would have to have three engines, rather than two.

This created an engine-placement problem, which in turn was affected by the dimensions of the engines being considered for use. The highly successful three-engine Boeing 727 had placed the third engine in the rear of the fuselage, using an S-shaped duct to run air from the intake, through the engine, and out the rear. This method was adopted by Lockheed. Although there were some problems associated with directing the airflow through the S-shaped duct, the installation was more streamlined and was easier to integrate with the fuselage structure.

McDonnell Douglas chose to place their engine ten feet up on the vertical surface, where no duct was required. (The need to be perceived as "different" probably mattered as well.) The position did require an extremely strong vertical surface, and that meant increased weight. More importantly, it reduced the size of the rudder. To gain engine-out control, the wing engines had to be moved inboard. Because of the wing sweep, this also moved them forward, and precluded the use of two forward passenger doors as had been done on the L-1011. The result was a less flexible interior configuration.

Airlines place great importance upon the choice of engines. A paramount consideration is cost, of course, but such factors as past experience with the manufacturer, fuel consumption, maintenance requirements, and commonality with other equipment all influence decisions. Lockheed was offering customers the choice of either General Electric or Rolls-Royce engines, but it clearly favored the latter, not least because of Rolls-Royce's offer of development assistance.

The RB.211 seemed to have been designed specifically for the L-1011, in terms of weight, power, and dimensions. Gerhard "Herman the German" Neumann, General Electric's combination superengineer and supersalesman, tried to convince Haughton to use the GE CF6. He argued that the Rolls-Royce was a "paper engine" and that the claims being made for it were impossible to accomplish within the proposed schedule. For his part, Haughton deemed the CF6 to be too long for placement in the rear fuselage; the L-1011 would have to be redesigned to accommodate it.

A complex, intense struggle ensued, in which the competition between airlines overlapped the competition between the aircraft and engine manufacturers. In a rational world, an agreement would have been reached in which all of the airlines would have selected one aircraft using one type of engine. This would have provided the airlines with the lowest-cost means of transportation, and the winning engine and aircraft companies with a viable product from which a profit might be made. Even the losing aircraft and engine manufacturers would have benefited, for they could have cut their losses and turned to other products.

It was not to be, for reasons of personal preference, brand loyalty, and, sad to say, greed, in which every company sought to gain the largest piece of the profit pie by squeezing every other company. American Airlines assumed that as the instigator of the competition, its decision on which aircraft and which engine to buy would be followed by the other airlines.

American also favored the Rolls-Royce engine, as did United, TWA, and Eastern. Delta preferred the GE engine, as did McDonnell Douglas. Lockheed interpreted American's preference for the Rolls-Royce as a strong sign that they also preferred Lockheed. Haughton did not know that Kolk, American's chief engineer and the "father" of the wide-body program, was disappointed that Lockheed had decided not to build a twin-engine aircraft and was now determined that American would buy the Douglas aircraft. It was not that the DC-10 was superior to the L-1011; most engineers, pilots, and passengers will confirm that the opposite was the case. Kolk, and American, melded

The Lockheed L-1011 was very much liked by its pilots and by passengers. Unfortunately, it entered the market against a formidable rival, the Douglas DC-10, at a time when rising labor costs and other factors made profitability impossible.

their disappointment with Lockheed and their confidence in Douglas into a decision to buy the DC-10.

Haughton's continued belief that Kolk favored the TriStar was fostered by American's entertainment of successively lower bids from Lockheed. In the hardball game of aircraft sales, American was using Lockheed merely as a foil to force the price of the DC-10 down, even though it never intended to buy the TriStar. So similar were the aircraft, and so intense was the bidding, that the price variant on a roughly $15 million airplane was only $200,000—just over 1 percent.

On February 19, 1968, Haughton sought to ice the deal by making a last-minute significant price concession to George Spater, American's president. To his mounting horror, he, and his chief finance man, Frank Frain, were kept waiting outside Spater's office for almost two hours before he was informed—by an American vice president, Donald J. Lloyd Jones—that American had just picked McDonnell Douglas. The purchase was for 25 aircraft and an option for 25 more. It was both a blow to Lockheed and an apparent calculated insult to Haughton, who was outraged.

His immediate reaction was to go to American's competitors and offer an even greater price reduction; he would sell the first L-1011s to the first buyer at $14.4 million, a price based on anger and desperation and not on practical economics.

The initial results were startling: Eastern and TWA made a joint announcement that they were buying L-1011s, equipped with Rolls-Royce engines, for an amount over $2 billion. Eastern's order was for 25 aircraft and 25 options, TWA's for 33 aircraft and 11 options. Delta soon followed suit, ordering 24 L-1011s, equipped with RB.211s, even though they still preferred GE engines. Northeast (which would merge with Delta in 1971) ordered 4.

The scope of Haughton's planning was illustrated by the arrangements he made to dampen American concerns about the purchase of foreign engines. A small British firm, Air Holdings, Ltd., normally acted as an airline sales agent for manufacturers. Haughton's connections allowed him to create an elaborate offset scheme by which he could announce the sale of 50 L-1011s to Air Holdings, Ltd., bringing total orders to 144. The order served to quiet congressional rumblings by showing that significant foreign money would flow to the United States to buy airframes, and thus offset the outward flow of funds to purchase engines. Every aspect of the deal was legitimate; funding was available and a down payment was made. Yet what Air Holdings was really buying was delivery positions on the production line, along with options to buy. It was set up to do exactly what Howard Hughes had done so profitably with the JetStar.

The situation was a heroic triumph for Haughton. He had turned what he regarded as American's perfidious dealings into a bonanza of sales, and to make it sweeter, isolated American, McDonnell Douglas, and General Electric in the process.

Yet the basic circumstances of the deal were bizarre. Most people believed that the market (generally estimated to require no more than 750 wide-body aircraft) could not support both the TriStar and the DC-10, nor could the combined L-1011/DC-10 production support more than one engine manufacturer. Everything now depended upon the decision by United Airlines, for if it opted for the L-1011, American would have to recant, cancel its DC-10 orders, and join the parade to Burbank even as GE and McDonnell Douglas folded their respective tents.

It was not to be. General Electric offered extraordinarily favorable financial terms to United so that it would select the CF6 engine for either the L-1011 or DC-10. Haughton told United that he would not redesign the TriStar to accept the General Electric engine, an effort that he estimated would cost $100 million. (Rolls-Royce provided a complete package—engine, fan airflow reverse, pod cowlings and related systems, noise-attenuation devices, etc. General Electric did not, and Boeing had spurned an attempt by Haughton to purchase the 747 GE installation package.) But more important than anything was Haughton's overoptimism. He felt strongly that United would see the folly of a divided market, accept the RB.211 engine, and choose the L-1011—case closed.

It was a catastrophic mistake, based in part on a sheepish approach by American's Spater to obtain backup positions on the L-1011 line if McDonnell Douglas exercised its option not to proceed with the DC-10. If American was now tilting to Lockheed, could United do otherwise?

Haughton should have perceived that United was now in a perfect position to dictate terms to both the aircraft and the engine manufacturers, and it proceeded to do so, whipsawing each company to drive prices down. The tactics worked so well that United could purchase either plane or either engine at essentially identical prices.

Lockheed was now administered a second dose of what it regarded as treacherous industrial behavior. Having maneuvered itself into the catbird seat, United, like American, did what it had planned to do all along: buy the McDonnell Douglas DC-10, based on its preference for products from the historic Douglas line. It announced that it would purchase 60 DC-10s with an option for 30 more. The market was now divided in a way that would insure that neither McDonnell Douglas nor Lockheed would reach a break-even point in their production, nor would the engine manufacturers have as large a market as they needed to make a profit at the reduced prices they had quoted.

And there were further troubles ahead.

Done In by a Seagull

The RB.211 was a highly sophisticated engine, using a three-stage low-pressure turbine (its competitors used two stages). It was built up of seven modules, each one easily changed for maintenance, and its design permitted the use of comparatively short rotating assemblies, which meant that overall engine dimensions were reduced. Its weak link was a single-stage eighty-nine-inch-diameter fan with twenty-five wide blades made of Hyfil (carbon-fiber composite), which greatly reduced weight, not only in the fan, but in other engine parts affected by the weight of the fan, primarily the fan bearings and their structural housings.

In 1969, the standard test for susceptibility to bird-strike damage was made. Three dead (but not frozen, as happened in a later test to another aircraft) chickens, designated "Boston Sea Gulls" by the FAA, were pneumatically fired into an operating RB.211. The Hyfil sustained the strike beautifully, but the bearing and housing failed and the fan departed the engine. Rolls had developed a backup solid titanium fan which was identical aerodynamically but was much heavier and required a new heavier housing and bearings, increasing total engine weight. (This fan did not even hiccup when exposed to the "Boston Sea Gull" test.) The economies implicit in a lighter engine vanished, and with it the RB.211's competitive edge. There were many other problems, including leaking seals and bearing problems, but these were typical of new engines and susceptible to engineering cures.

The TriStar Flies

While all of the difficult political games were being played, Lockheed's superb engineering created a very advanced aircraft, which was first flown on November 16, 1970. The pilot was H. B. Dees, assisted by copilot R. C. Cokeley and research and development engineer G. E. Fisher.

The aircraft flew very well, and throughout its history, flight crews, maintenance personnel, and passengers have lauded the L-1011 as perhaps the most user-friendly of the wide-body aircraft. The prototype L-1011 was retained by Lockheed as a development vehicle for improved models, of which there were three, the L-1011-100, -200, and -500. A total of 249 production Tristars were purchased new by eighteen airlines, while used L-1011s were used by a number of others. The Royal Air Force purchased 6 from British Airways and 3 from Pan American and converted them to tankers for in-flight refueling. (McDonnell Douglas would build 446 DC-10s over a twenty-year production span, proving that the market estimate for 750 aircraft was just about right.)

But in a soap-opera twist, the fate of the TriStar was not in the hands of its builders or its customers, but rather in those of its engine manufacturer, Rolls-Royce.

The engine on which Haughton had staked Lockheed's corporate life had a troubled development, having difficulty in delivering its

The graceful L-1011 TriStar became an economic disaster for Lockheed, one that could not be readily terminated because of commitments to customers.

required performance. These problems were eventually worked out, and the RB.211 did well in service. But before the engines could be proven effective, Rolls-Royce fell victim to the tremendous competitive pressures (applied primarily by General Electric, but reinforced by Lockheed) that drove engine sale prices down to the point that the venerable firm was losing money at a tremendous rate. In a bit of theater as dramatic as any seen before in the aircraft industry, Rolls-Royce declared itself bankrupt on February 4, 1971. As bad as this news was, it created the background for what can only be described as Haughton's greatest role, that of savior of the British aircraft-engine industry.

A Doleful Chronology

The complex Lockheed financial situation is best understood by a bare-bones presentation of the facts in chronological order. The following list is oversimplified, for the real-world situation was infinitely more complex, with politics, personalities, and company rivalries all impinging on events, but these items will serve as a schematic outline of what happened.

1969

MAY: Aware that the L-1011 program would constitute a drain on resources for a number of years, Lockheed arranged for a $400 million line of credit.

1970

JANUARY: Rolls-Royce, acknowledging a cash-flow problem, lays off 3,500 employees.

MARCH: Lockheed announces that it is in severe financial difficulty because of disagreements with the Air Force on the cost of the C-5A. Rolls-Royce dropped from stock index of *London Financial Times* because of financial problems.

APRIL: Rolls-Royce announces L-1011 engines will have titanium rather than Hyfil blades.

MAY: British Industrial Reorganization Corporation, a government agency, provides Rolls-Royce with $24 million in return for a 12 percent equity.

JULY: Lockheed dedicates a state-of-the-art $50 million plant at Palmdale to produce L-1011s.

AUGUST: McDonnell Douglas DC-10 makes first flight; L-1011 prototype is rolled out.

SEPTEMBER: Lockheed announces a $500 million credit arrangement with a twenty-four-bank consortium.

NOVEMBER: Rolls-Royce announces RB.211 development costs have risen from original estimate of $168 million to $324 million.
The L-1011 makes first flight at Palmdale.

1971

JANUARY: Rolls-Royce announces Hyfil blades have failed bird-impact tests.

FEBRUARY: Rolls-Royce declares bankruptcy.
Lockheed lays off 4,000 employees at Burbank and 2,000 at Palmdale; L-1011 production held in abeyance for ten months.
Haughton urges British government to sustain Rolls-Royce.
The newly formed "Rolls-Royce (1971)," owned by the government, is registered on London Stock Exchange.

MARCH: Secretary of the Treasury John Connally meets with British officials to discuss conditions for continuation of RB.211 and L-1011 projects.
Great Britain agrees to continue RB.211 project if U.S. government or U.S. banks guarantee that Lockheed will build the L-1011.

Lockheed agrees to pay as much as $120 million more for engines if British government continues RB.211 production.

APRIL: Lockheed meets with twenty-four creditor banks; Secretary Connally states that the banks will not be satisfied without a government loan guarantee. British prime minister Edward Heath says that unless a loan is guaranteed to Lockheed, the British government will not proceed with RB.211 program.

MAY: Treasury Secretary Connally announces that the White House will ask Congress to guarantee $250 million in bank loans to Lockheed, inasmuch as 24,000 jobs and $1.4 billion in investment are involved.
Lockheed agrees to pay $575 million for 555 engines.

AUGUST: President Richard Nixon signs the Emergency Loan Guarantee Act, Public Law 92–70.

SEPTEMBER: Emergency Loan Guarantee Board approves Lockheed application for government guarantee of $250 million. Lockheed is to pay a competitive interest rate, including 2 percent to the government as a guarantee fee.

The Other Side of the Street

Haughton was at his very best before Congress; he mesmerized the chairman of the House Banking Committee, the curmudgeon— but fellow Alabaman—Wright Patman, with Southern charm and his usual command of facts. He succeeded in persuading Congress to pass the Emergency Loan Guarantee Act over the most ardent opposition of Senator William Proxmire and an avalanche of arguments against the idea from General Electric. At the same time, Haughton, Kotchian, Anderson, and their trusted aides had been wooing the representatives of twenty-four banks and the airline customers to keep faith. Finally, on September 14, 1971, representatives of the banks, airlines, Rolls-Royce, the Emergency Loan Guarantee Board, and Lockheed met at the New York Federal Reserve Bank, there to sign documents to complete a $650 million financing package.

The loan guarantee was immediately characterized by the uninformed in the media as a colossal government handout to Lockheed. In fact, the loans were private commercial loans, and the government not only never had to put up any money, it earned $31 million in

Lockheed employees loyally supported their company in its struggle to stay afloat
during the crisis with Rolls-Royce and the L-1011 program.

guarantee fees. The risk to the taxpayer was always minimal. There
were many precedents for the federal guarantee—at the time it was
issued, the federal government was already guaranteeing and insuring
loans which totaled $137 billion.

During this time of trial, Brian M. Freeman was secretary to the
Emergency Loan Guarantee Board and financial counselor to the general counsel of the Treasury Department. He had come to Washington
from an appointment at the Harvard Business School to, in his words,
"avoid traditional work." He found himself plunged for more than
four years into the intricacies that occur when government intervenes
in (or for) business—a practice he disapproves of from an economic
and business perspective, but acknowledges as appropriate political
action. In the course of that time, he essentially managed not only the
Lockheed loan guarantee program, but also that of the Chrysler Corporation and the programs of direct and indirect financing to Conrail.

The author asked Freeman for his impression of Lockheed, its
principals and their principles, and the merits of its case. He responded
that Lockheed was, to a large degree, a victim of the guarantee program

because of the ongoing congressional frenzy over, and the previous bad publicity surrounding, cost overruns by defense contractors. In that regard, he maintains that there was significant doubt that Lockheed was the primary party at fault on the overruns, and that had it fought the battle in court it had a substantial potential for prevailing.

His view of Lockheed's management was extraordinarily positive. They were "honorable people, in some ways like Boy Scouts, who always dealt well with all parties in the guarantee program. They spent significant effort to be responsive, and that includes Haughton, Anderson, Marafino, et. al."

Freeman says that had he headed Lockheed, he might not have allowed the corporation to be abused by the Congress and the administration to the degree it was at times, because it was subject to greater scrutiny and different standards than other American corporations. At the time, however, the attitude of Lockheed's management was that "Lockheed was a significant beneficiary of government defense programs, and in that context, should do what the government wanted, even when the government was clearly wrong."

In regard to the foreign-payments scandal, Freeman stated that Lockheed was doing business exactly as the vast majority of other American companies were doing it in the foreign markets. He remarked further that if it had not been doing business in that manner, Lockheed's management might have been criticized for being seriously at fault. In fact, its activities were far less egregious than many others'. The rules changed midstream.

Freeman's views were known at the time internally. However, he could not make his comments publicly because he did not view that as his role. Moreover, any words would have been overridden by the almost universally bad press Lockheed was receiving. Yet it is interesting, and valuable, to get an objective view from the man who managed the government's loan guarantee program at the time.

Lockheed was saved—but its troubles were not over. Before going into the next series of problems, it is appropriate to briefly examine the actions of Dan Haughton in what many consider to be his finest hour.

Cold Fish for Breakfast

Haughton was always praised for his courtly Southern manners when negotiating. He was beloved in England, particularly by the rank-and-file Rolls-Royce personnel, who were always amazed at his ability to remember their names. His friendly attitude was not often found among the leaders at Rolls-Royce.

In an interview, Haughton recalled that he and several of his colleagues went to England in early February 1971, still exhausted from settling the Defense Department claims. The purpose of the trip was to review the status of the RB.211 program. They arrived at Heathrow at about 10:00 A.M. and were met by a Rolls-Royce representative who told them there was to be a luncheon in the Rolls-Royce hotel suite. Haughton and Frank Frain went directly to the meeting, suffering from jet lag. It was about 4:00 A.M. California time, but they had to toy with their sherry and a luncheon of cold salmon.

The group sat down, and before they had finished their lunch, Rolls-Royce announced that it was going into receivership. A principal consideration of the Rolls-Royce executives was an English law that made it a felony for directors of a firm to spend money they didn't have—and Rolls-Royce was clearly in that position.

Haughton was shocked, but retained his composure, and immediately went to work to rectify the situation. He began with a whirlwind series of meetings, working his way up the British government's chain of command. On February 3, 1971, the onetime coal-mining-camp brat received a call from the prime minister of England, Edward Heath. Haughton and Frain met with Heath, and did their best to persuade him that placing Rolls-Royce into receivership would have disastrous effects upon both Great Britain and the United States. They were not immediately successful—the decision had already been made, and Rolls-Royce went into receivership on February 4. Yet Haughton had made a favorable impression that would soon pay dividends.

Within ten days, Haughton was back in London, persuading the British to see what could be worked out between the British government, Rolls-Royce, and Lockheed. A long series of negotiations followed, culminating with a meeting at the British embassy in Washington. Haughton, Carl Kotchian, Roy Anderson, and a few other Lockheed personnel met with Lord Carrington and his British team. The agreement they reached saved Rolls-Royce and was a keystone for the subsequent Emergency Loan Guarantee Act.

Many of the Lockheed personnel who were in attendance at the meetings with the English representatives went on to top positions at Lockheed. They all give full credit to Dan Haughton for saving Rolls-Royce, and in doing so, saving Lockheed.

A Combination of Problems

In the thirteen-year period from 1960 through 1972, the Lockheed Corporation recorded over $26 billion in sales. In eight of those thirteen years, it made a total profit of $364 million. But losses in five critical years amounted to $209 million, so that the net profit over the period was $155 million. Thus thirteen years of high-risk, arduous effort and tremendous achievement attained a rate of return of about 0.6 percent. In this same period, the Missiles and Space Company accounted for 36 percent of total sales, and 128 percent of the consolidated after-tax net earnings. LMSC was a life preserver.

Despite all the problems, the L-1011 line was restarted, and by October 1971, 4,500 employees had been rehired. FAA Type Approval was received on April 12, 1972. Eastern Airlines began scheduled service with the TriStar on April 24. Unfortunately, production costs continued to escalate for a variety of reasons that included concurrent incorporation of new test engineering changes with earlier production activities, the refurbishing of early flight test aircraft to meet customer requirements, the acceleration of efforts to reduce delays in delivery, and the retraining of employees.

Production of the TriStar peaked at 41 in 1973, then declined to modest levels, ranging from 8 in 1978 to 24 in 1980. Despite the fact that stockholders' equity had fallen to a low of $26.5 million, Lockheed maintained an optimistic front as late as 1974, estimating a total sales of 350 L-1011 aircraft, with 260 being the estimated break-even point. By this time, it had invested more than $500 million in development costs, and hoped to achieve $2.7 billion in sales. The extended-range version of the aircraft, the L-1011-500, was expected to bring in an additional $1.8 billion in sales of 100 aircraft.

It should have happened, for the TriStar was an excellent aircraft, economical to operate, and preferred by most passengers to the other wide-body transports. But the desired sales did not materialize, and by 1981 it was clear that, painful as it was, the TriStar had to be phased out, at a cost of $730 million before any tax write-offs. Lockheed's equity had built up over the period, primarily from the activities of LMSC, but was now reduced to $141 million. Phasing out was not easy, for TriStar production was of course directly tied to Lockheed's financial strength, and the timing of the phasedown had to be geared to Lockheed's equity position.

Lockheed had lost $2.5 billion on the L-1011 program, an average loss of $10 million per airplane, excluding the cost of the money. The losses incurred by the TriStar soaked up earnings by other elements of the corporation, notably LMSC and Georgia, and naturally had a deleterious effect on corporate morale, for it destroyed the incentive program for executives. Yet the sense of family was so strong at Lockheed that few key people jumped ship, although many of them were wooed by outside firms.

Early in 1970 and 1971, when the significant losses from the defense programs were recognized and when the need for additional financing was so evident, Haughton, Kotchian, and Anderson were quietly seeking merger partners. On many a Sunday, when the corporate offices were largely deserted, meetings were held with key representatives of major corporations. But Lockheed's financial story was not impressive, and the bet on the future seemed too risky for the potential partners.

In 1973 and 1974, when L-1011 costs were growing and when it became obvious that financing was in jeopardy, the merger alternative reappeared at the suggestion of Arthur Young & Company, Lockheed's auditors. Haughton sent Roy Anderson to investigate the possibility of the Textron Corporation becoming a merger partner.

Haughton negotiated with the chairman of Textron, G. William Miller (later the U.S. secretary of the treasury), and the two men came very close to agreement. Textron was to have acquired about 50 percent of the company for about $50 million in shares, and another $50 million in convertible debentures, with Miller becoming chairman. Anderson recalls Haughton receiving a phone call from Miller in February 1975 declining the opportunity, almost certainly because of concerns over the fate of the L-1011, and the known difficulties with the Seattle shipyard. Negotiations and discussions had gone on for over a year without success. In retrospect, this was beneficial to the Lockheed shareholders.

The banks, exhausted with efforts to find a way to mitigate the financial risks they had undertaken with Lockheed credit, became parties to a new financial package which would extend financing, convert subordinated debentures to equity, and provide the foundation for a long-term financing agreement. There was light at the end of the tunnel. May of 1975 was a banner month—it was now apparent that Lockheed would remain independent. (Anderson's relief at the turn of events was reflected when he at last allowed future Vice Chairman Vince Marafino to turn in his five-year-old company car for a new one.)

Unfortunately, Textron's decision and the TriStar's difficulties were not the worst news of the decade for Lockheed.

The Time of Scandals

In 1975, the Northrop Company was being investigated for possible improprieties in the conduct of its foreign sales. Although any form of bribery was strictly illegal in the United States, it was a matter of common business practice in many areas of the world. Certain concessions had to be built into contracts to provide payment for intermediaries who were essential to secure the deal. The practice was widespread, and, when asked about it in a congressional hearing, Northrop's president, Tom Jones, made a remark to the effect that Northrop was not doing anything that Lockheed did not do. The effect of Jones's offhand comment upon the media and upon congressional investigators was electric: Lockheed became a new target.

Curiously, most members of Lockheed's upper management were not concerned, being convinced that Lockheed had not engaged in practices such as those Northrop was accused of. Their faith was soon shattered.

In June 1975, as the newly negotiated financing arrangements were being finalized with SEC filings, Lockheed management was faced with what turned out to be an impossible request.

Vincent N. Marafino, who ultimately became vice chairman of Lockheed, still winces as he recalls the incident. He learned that Lockheed executives were being asked by their independent auditor to sign a letter affirming that (1) all payments were made in accordance with official agreements and recorded in Lockheed's books; (2) no employee or official of any foreign government, or any director, officer, or employee of a customer was party to any of the agreements; and (3) no director, officer, or managerial employee of Lockheed or any of its subsidiaries had any knowledge of the disposition of payments made to consultants.

At the time, Marafino was certain that there would be no trouble meeting these requirements and cheerfully had appropriate letters made up. The full import of the situation was realized when Dan Haughton refused to allow his officers to sign them.

It was then revealed that contracts to some foreign countries were designed to have, as a part of their price, a series of payments to consultants who had helped facilitate the deal. These consultants, in turn, allegedly paid bribes to people in positions of responsibility. Among the more notorious of those who were alleged to have received the bribes were Japan's Yoshio Kodama, and Prince Bernhard of the Netherlands.

Vincent M. Marafino is regarded by his colleagues as a financial genius who expertly guided Lockheed through the darkest days of its troubles to the heights that it reached in the 1990s. He was a team player, highly regarded by every Lockheed corporate executive.

The bribery scandal, coming on top of the long series of difficulties with the C-5, the Cheyenne, and other projects, shocked Lockheed personnel to the core. It seemed that the scandal might be the last straw, jeopardizing Lockheed's financial position.

The scandal created an immense amount of damage, far beyond the actual dollar amounts involved. One would have expected so notorious an event to have involved millions of dollars; when the facts were known, a total of $750,000 had been placed "outside normal channels of financial accountability" between 1968 and 1975. Of this amount, only $290,000 had been disbursed as commissioned. In terms of the modern view of ethics, even $1 would have been wrong, but in terms of the huge dollar amounts of the contracts involved, the amount seems almost laughably small.

Haughton Takes the Fall

The sense of Lockheed family extended to Haughton, who was regarded as a stern, demanding, sometimes overly tough father figure, but one with a heart of gold. His subordinates admired his tender solicitude for his wife, who was ill and required his care. Kitchen, who candidly terms Haughton a micromanager with a tendency to intimidate his employees, nonetheless stands by him as a great leader. Roy Anderson, the absolute epitome of a gentleman, holds Haughton in equally high regard. When asked directly if Lockheed's problems at the time might not have stemmed from Haughton's hubris, Anderson replied, with a smile, that it was exuberance, and not hubris, that had precipitated the difficulties.

Yet the facts seem clear. Haughton ran a tight ship. He demanded and received absolute control. He was ably supported in this by Carl Kotchian, who to this day is unapologetic about conducting business as other companies did. As a result of Haughton's leadership, Lockheed, notwithstanding its enormous technical successes, became immersed in a series of financial and ethical problems that almost caused its demise. It was saved in large part by the pervasive sense of family, an apt term no matter how often used, and by a total change of management and management style to enable the firm to recover.

Wearied by events, and aware of his responsibilities, Haughton resigned as chairman of the board on February 13, 1976. Kotchian, as vice chairman and president, also resigned. The two men signed a poignant letter of farewell.

Lockheed now completely revised its board of directors, and carefully selected new top leaders whose integrity would be unquestioned. Yet this was but the start of a new era for Lockheed, one that would take it to the very top of the aerospace world. For the next two years, as its new management strove to reinstate Lockheed's reputation for integrity, the company had to suffer the slings and arrows of the media. Any report of a new difficulty in the aviation industry was inevitably linked in some manner to past Lockheed problems. The members of the Lockheed public relations staff tried valiantly to counter these reports, but it took years of effort, spectacular new achievements, and the demonstrated integrity of its new leaders to remove the odium of the preceding decade. Other troubles would arise in the form of attempted hostile takeovers, but the next twenty years would see the steady rise of the Lockheed Corporation to the very top of the industry, positioning it for what would be termed "the merger of equals" with the Martin Marietta Corporation. And the restless pace of events did not stop there; instead, the new Lockheed Martin combination would expand further, absorbing essential parts of Loral before announcing its intention to acquire Northrop Grumman.

CHAPTER 12

Changes in Management Style Allow Lockheed to Flourish

The cascading problems of the previous decade made it essential for Lockheed to re-create itself. It would not be sufficient to establish a "new image." The corporation had to redefine itself with the financial world, the Congress, the military, and (the most difficult task of all) the media. No one doubted that Lockheed made first-rate equipment; too many doubted the firm's integrity, for even Lockheed's own public relations department releases had equated the succession of troubles with Teapot Dome and Watergate. In many respects, the comparisons were unfair. Lockheed had done nothing illegal, but the payments scandal came as a climax to the widely publicized arguments with the Department of Defense, and the cumulative effect of the series of adverse stories had to be overcome.

The first order of the day was to select a new chairman of the board, one who had not risen from the ranks at Lockheed and also a person who had an impeccable national and international reputation. Not surprisingly, Lockheed turned to a man with an irreproachable record of financial probity, Robert W. Haack.

Haack shared the simple, basic American background and early work experience of many Lockheed employees. He had been born in Milwaukee in 1917, the son of a German father and Dutch mother who raised him in a very religious environment. While at Hope College, in Holland, Michigan, he worked part-time as a machinist for the Allis Chalmers Company. There he became a member of the United Automobile Workers, a CIO union that was heavily dominated by Communists—unusual for a man who would become a noted financier.

In 1940, he began working at an investment company, and with the exception of the war years, stayed there until 1964. A private pilot, he entered the navy in 1942, intent on flying training. Unfortunately, a physical condition associated with high-altitude flight caused him to be grounded. He did a tour in the Pacific in a ground job, picked up malaria and dengue fever, and was sent back to San Diego to convalesce. After recovering, he went to Maine to work with a torpedo squadron, and then was released to return to his position with Robert W. Baird & Company in Milwaukee. There, he had a long and successful career, enhanced by a record of outstanding public service that prompted his selection in 1963 as chairman of the board of the National Association of Securities Dealers. He moved to Washington, D.C., to head an association of about five thousand firms for three years and there undertook a badly needed series of reforms that greatly improved the public's position in trading over-the-counter securities. Recognition of his excellent work resulted in his appointment in 1967 to the prestigious and powerful position of the president of the New York Stock Exchange.

There, in 1970, he advocated the establishment of a schedule of competitive commissions rather than a standard set commission, a proposal that initially rocked the industry but subsequently proved to be extremely beneficial, reinforcing Haack's reputation for honesty. The daily routine of being a chief executive officer of a stock exchange had begun to wear on him, however, and he decided to leave. He had been approached by several companies to become a director, and, as he later remarked, at the age of fifty-five he felt due for a change. He became director of a number of companies, and in August 1972 Dan Haughton asked Haack to join Lockheed's board. Haughton had somewhat belatedly realized that Lockheed's board of directors needed to be reinvigorated with talent from the outside, and Haack was an ideal candidate.

Thus it was that on February 13, 1976, when Haughton and Kotchian resigned, Haack was the logical choice to be the new chairman of the board. (He later revealed the conditions under which he accepted the position. He said he would agree only "if it could be done gracefully, with Dan [Haughton]'s non-disapproval, and with the absolute, full unanimous support of the board.") As things transpired, Haughton, true to his reputation as a Southern gentleman, was very gracious about resigning. Carl Kotchian, however, resisted the idea, and Haack had to indicate that he would not assume his new position unless Kotchian also resigned before the issue was settled. Roy A. Anderson was selected as vice chairman, while Larry Kitchen was designated president and chief operating officer.

The change was terribly significant in many ways. All three men had established reputations for total honesty and integrity. Haack was to assume the role of "Mr. Outside," burnishing the company's reputation with the financial world and the media. Anderson and Kitchen both assumed "Mr. Inside" roles, salvaging the company's morale and repairing relations with the customers.

Haack conducted his effort with a calm, stalwart manner that restored confidence. He personally believed that Lockheed personnel were too much affected by the scandal, that they thought the firm to be more stigmatized than it actually was. Haack was a good businessman, and he knew that Lockheed's civil and military customers retained a high regard for the company, its products, and the way the company stood behind them. Perhaps more importantly, Haack recognized that Lockheed possessed a formidable depth of managerial talent. He had selected Anderson and Kitchen for the top jobs under him, but he was aware that LMSC, in particular, had parented a host of key managers who would serve the corporation well in the future.

Haack's role as chairman was eased because he held the fundamental belief that Lockheed had done nothing illegal, for there was no U.S. law at the time against making the sort of payments that had been made to persons in other countries. He toyed with the idea of going to court to prove his point, but then decided against it. His intimate knowledge of the stock market made him aware that if the court case went on for years, as it easily could, Lockheed's stock would suffer the entire time.

As a member of the board, he had long since been aware of the importance of the Lockheed sense of family. As chairman, the commitment and determination of his executives was driven home to him in short order, and he later often told the story of bringing a new member of the board, Wilson Newman, out to see Lockheed for the first time. It was a Saturday morning, and he said, "Wilson, I'm going to show you something you've never seen before . . . an executive parking lot in which there isn't a space to be had on Saturday morning." They rolled up to a parking lot jammed with cars, confirming his belief that his managers were passionate about reversing Lockheed's fortunes.

Perhaps even more important than a full executive parking lot was the fact that no top executive left during this time of trouble, despite the fact that there were no bonuses or stock options, while there was every prospect that the company would collapse, and with it, of course, their retirement dreams.

As chairman, Haack became more intimately acquainted with the depth of capability that the family possessed. Under his direction, a high-level strategy committee on public relations was set up, and large amounts were spent on corporate ads in major newspapers in the United States and around the world. The advertisements were convincing because they dealt with products of extraordinary performance, such as the SR-71, the space vehicles, the Trident missile, the TriStar, the S-3A Viking, the C-141, the C-130, the C-5, and the Canadian version of the Orion, the Canadair CP-140 Aurora. It was a portfolio of products of which any company could be proud. Ironically, given that Haack would look to it for leadership, LMSC was producing another family of products of perhaps even greater importance that could not be even hinted at because of their security classification.

Haack proved to be a convincing speaker, and he traversed the country talking about the "new Lockheed." One speech, given at the Commonwealth Club in San Francisco, was so successful that one of Lockheed's most vehement critics, the *Washington Post*, reprinted much of it under the headline "Lockheed Revisited."

As chairman, Haack pushed for a change in name on September 1, 1977, to the Lockheed Corporation, to reflect that aircraft and related services accounted for only 58 percent of sales—and to give impetus to the idea of a changed Lockheed. It was not long before Haack, who had accepted the position with the understanding that he would not remain long in office, began to feel that his inexperience in manufacturing operations obligated him to make way for someone else. He left on September 29, 1977, by which time he had calmed Lockheed's troubled waters, preparing the way not only for his immediate successors, but also for the following generations of leaders.

The board had been reconstituted so that ten of the seventeen members were outsiders, and a management succession committee was formed to ensure continuity.

A Beneficent Choice

An outside firm had been hired to develop a list of candidates for the position of chairman. The succession committee, with Haack as its head, whittled the list down to five leading candidates, and then to three. One of these was from a large Southern California company, and Haack had arrived at a handshake agreement with him—until the matter of compensation was discussed. The candidate promptly backed down. Another choice was the head of a large automotive firm from the Midwest. Haack posed a question: If the job were offered to him, how long it would take to "get his arms around this monster," meaning the gigantic, far-flung Lockheed Aircraft Corporation. When the executive replied "two to four weeks," he was quickly bundled off on a plane back east—Haack knew from personal experience that the job was much bigger than that.

Haack next conducted an informal interview with Roy Anderson, at the time chief financial officer. He then held a quick board meeting. When he returned from the meeting, he walked into Anderson's office and said, "You're it." It was undoubtedly the best choice he could have made.

Anderson recalls the day with a twinkle in his eye. He drove home, eager to share his news with his family. When he arrived, his eight-year-old son ran out to the car and triumphantly announced, "I'm president of my class." Anderson spent the evening focused on that, and delayed till the next morning telling his son about his own promotion.

Tried in the Fire

Roy Anderson was born in Ripon, California, on December 15, 1920, the fourth of six children of a farming family. His parents had been born in Sweden, and his father was a trained and capable carpenter with an insatiable yearning to farm. The family's income derived principally from the sale of milk and eggs, although his father supplemented this by building houses.

Upon graduation from high school in the midst of the Great Depression, he enrolled in a one-year business school. Then he worked as a steno clerk for an oil company in Stockton, California. He enlisted in the navy in February 1942 and was assigned to the Twelfth Naval District Intelligence Office. He was one of two men out of that facility selected to become a candidate for officer training in the V-12 program. Initially he was sent to Kansas State Teachers College in Pittsburg, Kansas, and then to Tulane University for sixteen months. His academic record qualified him to be sent to the Harvard Graduate School of Business for the midshipman-officers course.

After completing the schooling and a short term of sea duty, he left the service in April 1946 as an ensign in the U.S. Naval Reserve.

Anderson returned to California and entered, as so many of his subsequent LMSC colleagues would do, Stanford University. After graduating with a master's degree in business administration in March 1949, he decided to become a certified public accountant and went to work with a Palo Alto accounting firm. He had maintained his reserve status and was caught by the Korean War, being recalled to active duty in October 1950.

Once again his skills and his reputation were augmented by a bit of luck, and he was selected for the Naval Cost Inspection Service, which eventually led to an assignment at Westinghouse, in Sunnyvale. His performance there was such that Westinghouse offered him a job after he was released from duty in October 1952. Anderson had been contemplating returning to Stanford for a doctorate, but the Westinghouse offer was so good that he felt he could not refuse. He and his wife, Betty, whom he had married in June 1948, purchased a new three-bedroom home in Redwood City, California, for $10,450, a huge price for those days. They loved California, and when his career began to take off, he was offered promotions at Westinghouse's headquarters in Pittsburgh. After he turned down the third offer, he realized that he had to find another position, for then as now, refusal of promotion is poison in the corporate world. Just as he was mulling his alternatives, Lockheed's Missiles and Space Division began operations. Anderson joined Lockheed in October 1956, spent a brief period at Van Nuys, and then returned to Sunnyvale. He found that he fit in well with the Lockheed system and began to work with four men he admired tremendously, and who would influence his own management style: Herschel Brown, Stan Burriss, Gene Root, and Willis Hawkins. They, along with Hall Hibbard, had fostered a climate at LMSC that permitted bright young managers to do well. Anderson often commented later on the importance of these men. He said that Root was vital because of his vision and his recruitment of key personnel. Brown had a great ability to administer and control a burgeoning giant of a company laden with so many technical geniuses who demanded independence of action. Burriss's contribution was his ability to lead the Fleet Ballistic Missile program and establish such great credibility with not only the customer, but also with the corporation and its employees. Finally, he noted that Hawkins's aeronautical genius translated easily into leadership of the space programs.

Anderson's career prospered, first with the Standard Agena program, then with the classified programs of the Space Systems Division.

The Fire Heats Up

As a part of the emerging pattern of executive training, Anderson moved to Georgia in October 1965, as director of finance, just as the C-5 program was building up, and before the devastating impact of the new Total Package Procurement contract was realized. Lockheed had developed a program management system to correspond to that of the Air Force, and as a result, program managers were superimposed upon the normal Georgia functional organizations, resulting in an awkward dual line of reporting. This, in turn, caused reporting and analysis to become confused, and Anderson recalls that it was not until mid-1966 that he really began to understand what was happening—and what was wrong—with the C-5 program's design and production costs. He also recalls that it was then that his hair began to turn white, for he realized that an adversarial relationship had developed with the Air Force. Costs were rising, in part due to inflation, but also because of the inefficiencies that Larry Kitchen would subsequently uncover. The problems boiled over when the "safety valve" of the TPP contract, the purchase of a second run of aircraft with the price recalculated on the basis of the first run, was not totally fulfilled.

From the Frying Pan

By 1968, corporate management began to feel the burden of problems developing within major DOD programs and the L-1011 program. In September, Anderson was asked to return to Burbank as assistant treasurer, a corporate office. He was thus well positioned to learn of the problems that were about to fall upon Lockheed from every direction. He became the point man in the desperate survival efforts, which included settling the government's claims, negotiating successively higher lines of credit with the banks, and providing backup to Haughton and Kotchian in the salvage of Rolls-Royce and the L-1011 program. In all of these situations, many of which were distasteful in the extreme, Anderson so conducted himself as to win the respect, and even the affection, of the organizations with which he was negotiating. Thus, when Haughton and Kotchian left, he was a logical person to support the new chairman, Robert Haack. Anderson was much more knowledgeable about Lockheed's manufacturing operations than Haack, of course, but his background was primarily business and financial management. It made sense to pair him, as vice chairman, with Larry Kitchen as president as a part of the "new Lockheed" salvage team, for Kitchen (who came from a financial and operations background) had production experience both at LMSC and Georgia.

The Haack-Anderson-Kitchen trio proved to be a paradigm for Lockheed's management future. Haack allayed fears and planned the reorganization of the board and the company. Anderson would achieve success based on his business experience, leadership capabilities, and financial background. He was highly respected for his accurate financial forecasts, which took into consideration realistic costs, anticipated revenues, and the resultant cash flows. Anderson gives much credit to Vince Marafino and his staff for their constant support and for Marafino's ability to understand complex financial issues and present them with clarity to the financial community.

(It should be noted here that Marafino's relationship to Anderson is but one example of the hundreds of similar relationships that existed all through Lockheed, and that at once defined both the efficiency of the firm and its familial loyalty. Each of Lockheed's leaders developed a team of capable executives to support his efforts. Most of these executives operated in a loyal, supportive capacity to more than one of the leaders. Marafino's career in many ways is a metaphor for this phenomenon. He had all the qualities to be chairman himself, proven in his support of Haughton during the fight to save Rolls-Royce and to obtain and then repay the huge loans that Lockheed needed. At the same time, he was working with and for Anderson in these and other projects. He was equally essential to Larry Kitchen, Dan Tellep, and many others, all the way to the time of the Lockheed Martin merger, and beyond. Marafino is a symbol of both the quality and the depth of Lockheed's leadership. There were many people at Lockheed who performed similar roles, but space limitations preclude naming each one. Please understand, then, that when we speak of Anderson or Kitchen or Tellep, we are really speaking of their teams, which they would be the first to acknowledge were essential to their success.)

In Kitchen's case, he would lead his team using the best of Haughton's hard-nosed tactics, combined with a real sensitivity to personnel issues that made working for him far less intimidating.

A New COO

Kitchen left the Georgia Company in late 1975, and, as previously noted, was tapped to be president of the Lockheed Corporation on February 13, 1976. Kitchen later admitted freely that he had to make a major adjustment to his attitude. While in Georgia, he had felt that LMSC was getting a disproportionate share of corporate resources, particularly at a time when his own success was based in large part on unrelenting cuts to the Georgia workforce. And although his experience at Georgia had been extremely successful and satisfying, the hazards implicit in his new job as chief operating officer were daunting. The public relations disaster of the foreign-payments scandal was at its height. The Air Force was still unhappy about the costs of the C-5 contract, and the L-1011 program was not recovering from the twin setbacks of the RB. 211 problems and competition from McDonnell Douglas. Bob Haack had initiated a new Lockheed. Kitchen was anxious to join Roy Anderson in moving Lockheed forward.

Kitchen was born in 1923 in Fort Mill, South Carolina. The oldest of six children, he, like so many other future Lockheed executives, experienced the full pinch of the Depression years. Both his mother and father worked, but on different shifts, so there was always parental guidance. In January 1942 he joined the Marines, serving in maintenance in a fighter squadron in the South Pacific for twenty months. After the war, he took a low-paying civil service job with the U.S. Navy's Bureau of Aeronautics in Washington, just to remain associated with aviation. Despite his lack of a college education, over the next twelve years he advanced to the grade of GS-13, serving as chief of staff to the admiral in charge of fleet readiness.

When the Polaris program got under way, he exhibited the kind of risk-taking determination that would distinguish his career. He gave up his "safe" government position and joined Lockheed, at no increase in pay. There he benefited from the same associations of which

Anderson speaks so highly—Hawkins, Root, Brown, and Burriss. Kitchen later characterized them somewhat differently than Anderson, but with equal praise. He said: "Gene Root was the entrepreneur, the technical guy, and Herschel Brown was really a people-oriented guy, a very basic businessman, and so they really complemented each other. Stan Burriss was just an all-around type guy . . . tough to work for but always fair. . . . Burriss really groomed guys like me and Bob Furhman."

Given the responsibility for setting up the Polaris's logistic organization, Kitchen in the next nine years built up a large, functional group that served well for the fleet ballistic missiles that succeeded Polaris. After carefully training his replacement, he went to his boss, Bill Stevenson, and told him baldly that he wanted to move into Lockheed's rotational training program for high-potential executives. He laid out a management plan for his career, and in typical fashion told Stevenson that he did not want a pay increase, he just wanted a chance to prove himself. If he failed, he would expect to be fired.

Stevenson agreed. Kitchen was sent to a management course at the University of Pittsburgh, and then began the process of rotating through a series of managerial assignments that were six months or more in duration. These led directly to his assignment—and subsequent successes—at the Georgia plant, which, in turn, prepared him for a path to the very top.

Other Leaders in the Ranks

The success achieved by Anderson and Kitchen can be attributed to a fortunate management system that recognized talent, nurtured it, let it compete so that a process of natural selection took place, and then rewarded it with increasingly responsible positions. The competition was formidable, and there were many executives at Lockheed who could have done very well in the very top positions, but instead served out their careers as either presidents of one of the companies, or as vice presidents in the corporation. At the risk of being repetitive, the reason for this abundance of talent was the sense of Lockheed family. Many of those who remained when it was obvious that they were not going to be selected as chairman did so because they loved the company, and preferred having a less than number one job there to leaving to be chairman of a different—and no doubt less familial—firm.

Even as Anderson and Kitchen were settling into their new roles, other future stars were making themselves known. They included, among others, Robert Fuhrman, Dick Heppe, Bob Ormsby, Ben Rich, Daniel Tellep, Vance Coffman, Sam Araki, John McMahon, Kenneth Cannestra, James A. "Micky" Blackwell, Val Peline, Fred O'Green (whom Anderson characterizes as "the closest clone of Kelly Johnson"), James Plummer, and many more.

An Incredible Leap Forward

Given the unrelenting tide of difficult business situations, it is refreshing to look back at the purely technological world of air and space in which Lockheed achieved an utterly dominant position.

It is unfortunate that the deep black security in which most of LMSC's programs were so immersed prevents discussion of the many projects after Corona. The commanding lead the United States possesses in intelligence-gathering, meteorological, communication, and navigational satellites was not due entirely to Lockheed's efforts, but it is equally true that it would not have occurred if LMSC had not been involved. Thus, the achievements of engaging, learned leaders such as Sam Araki or dynamic executives like Val Peline can only be inferred from the fact that they attained very high level executive positions, have received many distinguished awards, and are highly regarded in the business community. It is a little disconcerting for the author of a history of Lockheed to confess that he has absolutely no idea what the projects were, how they exceeded Corona's capability, or what capabilities they had beyond intelligence-gathering, but that is the case. The Lockheed personnel interviewed for this book were so security-conscious that they were reluctant to discuss items that they knew had been declassified, for fear that some inadvertent disclosure might give away a secret in another area. One can only hope that within a reasonable passage of time, the great triumphs of LMSC, so fantastic in technology that they made the incredible achievements of the Corona project mundane enough to reveal, will be declassified so that their creators can receive the credit due them. In marked contrast, many of the further achievements of Kelly Johnson and his successors at the Skunk Works have been declassified and can be discussed freely.

These achievements are so remarkable for the degree of their technical ascendance over all competition that they will be dealt with in some detail, with a view of conveying just how advanced they were. The great spy plane, the SR-71, and the fantastic F-117A stealth fighter were incredible achievements, made possible only because Lockheed's management was willing to risk large sums of money on the technical genius resident in the Skunk Works. These programs, and their corresponding classified programs at LMSC, enabled the Lockheed Corporation to come roaring back from adversity.

There were many other elements of the corporation that contributed first to Lockheed's recovery and then to its rise to the peak of industrial power. There were also other difficulties encountered. Both of these facets of Lockheed's history will be dealt with in the next chapter. What follows is an attempt to highlight the extraordinary technological leaps that Lockheed made at the Skunk Works, to emphasize that these were not merely early advances that would be duplicated elsewhere in a matter of months. Instead, Lockheed engineering placed the firm many decades ahead of all other aircraft firms in the world. Never before, and never anywhere else, has such a dramatic leap been made. In simple aircraft terms, where there was a Wright biplane, a Curtiss had evolved soon after; the German Albatros was soon matched by the British Sopwith Camel; the Messerschmitt Bf 109 was equalled by the Spitfire; the MiG-15 and the F-86 were closely comparable—the list could go on. But never in aviation history have two aircraft emerged that were so many years in advance of all competition as the SR-71 and the F-117A. That Lockheed could follow these triumphs with the F-22 Raptor, which again outstrips all competition, simply confirms the resurgent engineering and fiscal health of the company.

There is another important element to record. Throughout the Skunk Works' existence, a basic question was implicit: Could it survive and operate without Kelly Johnson? When Johnson reached the age of sixty-five in 1975, he picked his own successor, Ben Rich. Ben proved, in spades, that not only could the Skunk Works survive and operate under his leadership, it would prosper.

Cold War Casualty

The end of the Cold War has been a wonderful circumstance for mankind, proving to be even more beneficial for the states of the former Soviet Union and its allies than it has been for the Western powers. The states that embraced Communism for that long dark period suffered terribly as all of the best and brightest were poured into military and space systems, while the consumer economy was virtually neglected. It may be that the end of the Cold War will permit a reversal of all of Communism's unseen and deadly legacies—rapidly diminishing life spans, terminally polluted waters, and a totally corrupt and misallocated economic system being just a few of them.

The fact remains, however, that for more than forty years the United States and its allies were directly confronted by the Soviet Union and the Warsaw Pact nations, whose armed forces had been built up to a fantastic extent with both conventional and nuclear weapons. The Communist powers had an enormous superiority in manpower, tanks, artillery, and aircraft. For much of the time, the tanks and artillery, at least, were qualitatively superior also, and in the later years, their aircraft reached at least parity if never superiority in quality.

More importantly, both the East and the West had massive nuclear forces on the alert, their targets determined, and awaiting only a signal to be unleashed. Both sides built an enormous number of delivery systems and warheads, so that the multiple effects of a true mutual exchange, including the residual radiation, would have almost certainly destroyed civilization on a worldwide scale. Whatever else the faults of the leadership of the Soviet Union, it was rational enough not to attempt to implement its first-strike doctrine. And, perhaps solely through good fortune, there were no freak accidents or incidents that triggered an exchange.

There has been one casualty of our victory in the Cold War, however, and that is the memory of the American public for just how deadly serious the threat was. With the advantage of our present insight into the utterly disastrous state that Communism brought the Soviet economy, we have had a tendency to denigrate the threat that the Soviet Union posed. The question is asked: If the enemy of so many years was unable to adequately feed, clothe, and house its people, how capable an opponent could it have been?

The answer, of course, is that the Soviet Union was enormously powerful, equipped by the later years of the Cold War with intercontinental ballistic missiles superior to our own in number, accuracy, throw weight, and hardening. It also had a small bomber force, capable, but a lesser threat than the hundreds of missiles that were aimed against us. Curiously, American leadership was able to handle the knowledge of the Soviet strength with some aplomb, for by that time our intelligence-gathering capability—in large measure courtesy of Lockheed—enabled us to gauge enemy intentions with a high degree of accuracy.

It was not so in the early days, when all we knew was that the

Soviet Union had developed nuclear and thermonuclear weapons far more swiftly than we thought possible, and had then gone on to score a dazzling series of space triumphs. Premier Nikita Khrushchev trumpeted both achievements in blustering speeches, warning darkly that Yury Gagarin was not the only cargo that the Soviet Union could place in space—it could also send thermonuclear weapons that could be directed to any place on earth. It was a bald threat and he meant every word of it.

The absolute lack of verifiable intelligence on Soviet capability had led to the fortunate combination of circumstances that, as previously noted, permitted Kelly Johnson and the Skunk Works to create the U-2. The U-2 was able to operate many years longer than anyone had planned, but when Gary Powers was shot down on May 1, 1960, overflights of the Soviet Union were canceled. A replacement was urgently required. As might be expected, the Skunk Works had been addressing the problem for many years, well before the U-2's first flight, but not always with viable solutions.

The Faded Suntan

Lockheed had been brought into a highly classified project to provide the airframe for a projected series of liquid-hydrogen-fueled engines to be built by the Garrett Company, based on the ideas of Randolph Samuel Rae, a British engineer who worked for the Summers Gyroscope Company in Santa Monica. The Garrett engines were deemed too complex, and Johnson put forward a proposal to build an aircraft using more conventional engines, but powered by liquid hydrogen. The task was assigned to Pratt & Whitney, while the Skunk Works was to provide the aircraft, under the code name Suntan and with the Lockheed designation CL-400. The aircraft was to be able to cruise at Mach 2.5 at one hundred thousand feet altitude for more than 2,500 miles. Johnson guaranteed first flight within eighteen months, if the by-now sacrosanct Skunk Works procedures were rigorously adhered to.

Yet by 1957, Johnson was convinced that the project should be dropped, for a number of reasons. The aircraft's range was deficient, and there was no apparent way to improve it. The logistical support of the aircraft with liquid hydrogen promised to be a nightmare. In-flight refueling was not possible, and the expense of establishing the

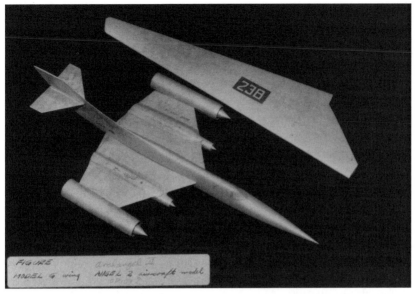

Some of the most interesting Lockheed projects never came to fruition. The Lockheed
CL-400 was intended to be a successor to the U-2. It was to have had engines
fueled with hydrogen. The almost complete prototype was scrapped when
the program was cancelled.

necessary ground support to refuel it at airfields around the world was
astronomical.

The program persisted for another two years, and $96 million in
unexpended funds were returned to the government when it was finally
killed at Johnson's insistence. The multimillion-dollar expenditure was
not a total loss, for it provided immense data on liquid-hydrogen systems that were later put to use on the Centaur rocket program. It gave
Pratt & Whitney practical experience in building a hydrogen-cycle
engine. And it also showed that the Skunk Works could develop and
build a large supersonic, high-altitude, long-range aircraft.

Steps toward the Blackbird

Two of the leading figures in the U-2 program, Richard Bissell and
Kelly Johnson, had as early as 1955 decided to explore a follow-on
aircraft that would seek to remedy the U-2's unexpected flaw—its easy
tracking by Soviet radar. A number of studies led to the conclusion
that the best design for an aircraft to overfly the Soviet Union with
impunity was a plane with a relatively low radar cross section that

would fly at very high speeds at very high altitudes. In other words, a Mach 3, ninety-thousand-foot-altitude aircraft with what would later come to be called stealth characteristics.

It thus transpired that the two most effective and longest-lived reconnaissance aircraft, both produced by the Skunk Works, would be aerodynamically antithetical. The U-2 was, as previously described, a lightly built subsonic aircraft, essentially a jet-powered sailplane. The new aircraft, which after many transformations would become the A-12 (and in a more sophisticated version, the SR-71), was a large, heavy, immensely strong aircraft designed to cruise in afterburner at Mach 3 for hours on end.

Johnson led his team through the usual long series of possible configurations that ranged from a slender paper-airplane-like arrow shape to configurations that looked much like the Convair B-58 Hustler. By April 21, 1958—two years and ten days before Gary Powers would be shot down—Johnson had drawn up a proposal for a Mach 3 aircraft that would cruise at ninety thousand feet and have a range of more than four thousand miles. As the U-2 had been dubbed "Angel," he used the code name Archangel. There were additional design studies, and Archangel II emerged as a large 135,000-pound aircraft powered by two Pratt & Whitney J58 turbojet engines and two seventy-five-inch ramjets. It was not favorably received by the Air Force because it required an exotic fuel for the ramjets.

The rejection was not disheartening—the desired performance was so great that Johnson expected to make a number of iterations before arriving at the solution. In the intervening months, Johnson's small project team slowly elucidated the formula for success, working from one design to the next, sometimes going back to incorporate features from an older design into a new one. Times have changed; today the work would be done on dozens of computers, with computer-aided design systems quickly working one iteration after another. Then it was done in classic style, with a few computers of laughable capacity by today's standards, but mostly with slide rules and calculators, and with every drawing requiring an engineer's hand on the drafting board. (Johnson referred to the slide rule he had used since his university days as "my Michigan computer.") Mercifully, at the time no one realized how painfully slow the process was.

Internal Lockheed tests hinted at what would be fully exploited in the future—wedge shapes had the effect of deflecting radar waves and reducing the radar signature. One model in the series, the A-7, incorporated this technique and also featured a later Blackbird signa-

Lockheed's Skunk Works set a standard never equaled by any other firm anywhere in the world with the introduction of the A-12. The Mach 3.0 single-seat aircraft was intended for use by the CIA.

ture note, vertical surfaces canted inward. Further design effort led to the A-11, an aircraft that superficially resembled the B-58, with an engine slung beneath each wing and a single vertical surface. The A-11 had excellent performance, and the designation persisted for many years in the myths surrounding the aircraft, in part because of a later reference to the type by Lyndon Johnson, who, for security reasons, was advised to use the earlier nomenclature. The A-11's comparatively high radar signature caused it to be rejected by the customer. To offset this, elements of the A-7 were introduced into the A-11 design to create the A-12.

Ben Rich recounts that he led a small six-man engineering team that included no aircraft designers at all through the endless iterations to arrive at the final configuration. They worked on a door stretched between two desks, laying out the information that was derived from the intensive wind-tunnel tests. From the data, the shape of the A-12 was derived. The long fuselage was given chines to obtain lift. To reduce the radar cross section, the engines were located in their mid-wing position, so that the shock wave at the design cruise speed of Mach 3.2 would just miss the inlets, and the outboard section of the wings were given a conical camber to relieve pressure. When they showed the proposed shape to Kelly Johnson he said, "That's it—you've got it."

Johnson appointed Dick Boehme as program manager, although it was a task he himself relished and never really relinquished. Once again, Richard Bissell and John Parangosky represented the CIA interest while Brigadier General Leo Geary acted for the Air Force. Bissell established an evaluation team headed by Dr. E. M. Land (of Polaroid fame) to monitor the program, which had received the code name Gusto.

It soon became evident that radar technology had remained far in advance of radar countermeasure technology. It was deemed impossible to create an aircraft that would be invisible—or almost so—to radar, and the design requirements were changed to recognize this. (Notwithstanding this, the resulting design was in fact the first stealth aircraft, as will be discussed below.) On August 28, Johnson was informed that Lockheed's latest design, the A-12, had been accepted, with the proviso that work be intensified on means to reduce further the radar signature.

The A-12 was a radical aircraft, with two large-diameter Pratt & Whitney J-58 engines midmounted on the modified delta wing. Distinctive all-moving vertical tail surfaces were placed above the engine nacelles and canted inward. It was to be able to fly at Mach 3.2 at altitudes approaching one hundred thousand feet over a range of 3,800 miles. At first glance, the most unusual element of the design appeared to be the elongated nose with its speedboatlike chines that gave it the appearance of a hooded cobra.

It was mutually agreed that the Skunk Works approach would prevail, and that the security measures that had worked so well for the U-2 were to be made even more stringent. Johnson set the first flight date just twenty months in the future. Project Gusto was terminated; the new project was code-named Oxcart. Although Lockheed was cautioned not to make large commitments of funds, it was granted a contract to build five A-12s for $96.6 million over the next twenty-four months.

Mountains to Climb

Few aircraft have so captured the imagination of the world as the Lockheed Blackbird, as the A-12/SR-71 series became known. The mystery surrounding its creation and employment, its starkly beautiful sculptural shape, and its absolute dominance in aircraft performance for more than thirty years has given the Blackbird a place unique in history as both an instrument of technology and as a universal cultural icon. Although many people are now familiar with its shape and sound, as rendered in a thousand television presentations, most are unaware that the task assigned Kelly Johnson and his small team would have been considered impossible by any other engineering establishment. In the more than three decades that have passed since the decision was made to proceed, no other country has been able to create an aircraft that exceeds the Blackbird's operational capability.

The scope of the problem was summarized in a July 1969 paper presented by Johnson to the American Institute of Aeronautics and Astronautics, detailing the problems and solutions of the YF-12A aircraft from his perspective. (The YF-12A was a proposed fighter version of the A-12, which first flew on August 7, 1963, and which, for our purposes here, was similar in most respects to the basic A-12.) His remarks give some dimension to the challenge he accepted from the CIA and the USAF, and to his remarkable optimism in promising to meet the challenge with the delivery of a flyable aircraft in twenty months. (In his early notes, Johnson apologized for selecting twenty rather than eighteen months for a delivery date, noting that Pratt & Whitney would require the additional time to produce a bypass version of the extremely sophisticated—and not yet flown—J58 engine. He was, for once, unduly optimistic.)

Johnson noted that it might have been expected that other advanced aircraft of the time, such as the North American XB-70 or X-15, would have provided an enormous amount of useful data to his team. The Oxcart project progressed so rapidly that it both surpassed and diverged from the XB-70 program. And because the X-15 was rocket-powered and conducted flights of very short duration, it did not encounter the problems of air-breathing power-plant inlet design or of extremely high steady state temperatures.

The power plants were initially left to Pratt & Whitney, for whom Johnson expressed the greatest admiration; later, his own team, led by the inimitable Ben Rich, would have to intervene. The engine would ultimately become one of the most sophisticated in the world, packaged in by far the most sophisticated nacelle.

In his paper, Johnson noted that the structural engineers were concerned about the anticipated high temperatures, ranging from 1,050 degrees Fahrenheit in the nacelle to 585 degrees at the nose and as low as 470 degrees at the tail. These had to be endured for a prolonged duration in the A-12. This led to a decision to use unconventional titanium alloys in a structure that had to be open for equipment installation, inspection, and maintenance.

Heat-resistant titanium was as strong as stainless steel, at approximately 50 percent of its weight. About 93 percent of the structural weight of the aircraft was titanium alloy, which had an ultimate strength of up to two hundred thousand pounds per square inch in later models. (The remaining 7 percent of structural weight was composed of Radar Absorbing Materials [RAM] to reduce the radar cross section. Asbestos and iron ferrites formed a large part of these materials.) Ultimately, the composite materials were used for the vertical fins instead of titanium, the first use of such materials for a major aircraft component.

Lockheed had experimented with titanium over the years, and sought to obtain a high strength-to-weight ratio at very low cost—an objective that proved impossible. In small applications, the difficulties inherent in using titanium were tractable; on a one-hundred-thousand-pound airframe, there were almost insuperable difficulties in forging, welding, riveting, or even drilling the material. Titanium was scarce and costly, and 80 percent of the initial deliveries of Beta B-120 titanium alloy from the manufacturer, the Titanium Metals Corporation, were rejected for contamination. It was not until the company officials were made aware of the intended use of the material that quality problems were solved.

Johnson's right-hand man and successor, Ben Rich, reaching back to his university courses, recalled that black paint could be a heat emitter as well as a heat absorber. A few quick calculations showed that using a softer alloy of titanium and painting it black would greatly ease construction difficulties. It was this discovery that led to the aircraft's natural nickname, Blackbird. Even though it ran counter to Johnson's fanatical obsession for reducing weight, the sixty pounds of paint required could reduce internal temperatures by as much as 86 degrees Fahrenheit. The paint had an additional advantage, for it contained tiny iron microspheres that dissipated electromagnetic radiation.

Temperature was a vital consideration in many other aspects of the design. At ordinary ground temperatures, the surface of the wing had corrugated ridges running chordwise (fore and aft); in flight, thermal expansion caused the aircraft to expand, the skin with it, stretching out the corrugated ridges into a relatively smooth surface. Standard readily procurable equipment such as electronic gear (particularly wires, plugs, and transducers) were not designed for sustained high temperatures. There were no hydraulic fluids or pumps that could operate at 600 degrees Fahrenheit continuously. (One hydraulic fluid product was offered to Johnson that did operate at 600 degrees; its drawback was that from room temperature up to 200 degrees it was just a white powder.) Grease that could sustain high temperatures had the characteristics of concrete at ordinary temperatures. Special heat exchangers had to be devised to reduce 1,300-degree-Fahrenheit bleed air from the engines down to a moderate 30 degrees Fahrenheit to cool the cockpit. No escape devices—parachute, drag chute, or ejector seat—had been designed that would take the range of temperatures that would be developed in the course of a flight. To counteract the inevitable thermal expansion and contraction of control-cable runs, they were made out of the same material used in watch springs, Elgiloy. The cockpit and the camera system had to be fitted with quartz glass panels that would provide clear vision in spite of the immense heat. Even such mundane matters as radomes, antennae, and access plates had to be redesigned to use new material and new construction techniques. One curious result of the extreme cycle of temperatures during the course of every flight was the annealing of the titanium, which made the Blackbird's outer skin stronger and stronger.

One of the most daunting aspects of the high-temperature flight regime was that there was no fuel available that could take the continuous high temperatures and not clog the engine fuel system. The A-12 carried eighty-five thousand pounds of fuel in five noninsulated wing and fuselage tanks, where in-flight temperatures would reach about 350 degrees, in part because fuel was used as a heat sink. The fuel, which was sometimes to be off-loaded from a KC-135 tanker at an ambient temperature of −60 degrees Fahrenheit, and then injected into the engines at high pressure and a temperature of 350 degrees Fahrenheit, was developed jointly by Ashland, Shell, Monsanto, and Pratt & Whitney. Called JP7, it was a safe, high-flash-point fuel that would not vaporize or blow up under the tremendous heat and pressure to which it would be subjected. It also contained chemicals that enhanced stealth characteristics by reducing the "shock diamonds" that formed in the exhaust at speed. Tankers had to be dedicated to carrying JP7 fuel, which ultimately had to be stocked in special fuel farms around the world. The low volatility of the JP7 was such that a lighted match would be extinguished if dropped into it. This was fortunate, as the Blackbird leaked like a sieve on the ground, fuel spilling through the structural gaps necessary to accommodate the thermal expansion of the metal at high speeds. When the metal expanded, there were no leaks. One side effect of a fuel tailored to the A-12/SR-71 requirements was that it was difficult to ignite at low temperatures and high altitudes by means of conventional ignition systems. Instead, a chemical ignition system using flash-sensitive tetraethyl borane was installed in case a restart was required either on the ground or in the air.

Rich's team created what he called a "smart fuel" system in which sensors placed in the tanks and fuel lines continuously sensed the fuel temperature, always routing the warmest fuel to the engine intakes while routing the coolest back into the tanks for warming. The landing gear retracted into wells, where the heat from the tires and brakes would be transferred by radiation cooling into the fuel tanks. Fuel was also used to maintain the center of gravity, being pumped fore or aft as required to trim for changes in speed.

The high temperatures had equally grave implications for the fuel pumps, the fuel lines, and the fuel-purging system. Johnson summarized the situation by remarking that "everything on the aircraft, from rivets and fluids up through materials and power plants, had to be invented from scratch." By the time the last Blackbird had rolled out (at a cost of about $17 million each), the Advanced Development Projects had manufactured 13 million separate titanium parts. Although the Skunk Works hated paperwork, the use of titanium on such a scale required that everything be recorded about each batch of material, from the mill pour right down to the direction of the grain of the metal in the sheet from which the part was made.

In a brilliant confirmation of the adage "Less is more," the number of design engineers in the Advanced Development Projects was considerably less than two hundred at the peak of the design effort. Among them were Ed Baldwin doing the design layout; Ed Martin acting as supervisor and working on systems; Dick Boehme, Ray McHenry, and Henry Combs on structures; Dave Robertson on the fuel system; Dan Zuck on the cockpit design (with expert assistance rendered by Lockheed's chief test pilot, Louis Schalk); aerodynamicists Dick Fuller and Burt O'Laughlin working at NASA's high-speed wind tunnel; Mervin Heal computing the weight; Lorne Cass figuring the loads; and Ben Rich (with young David Campbell) on thermodynamics and propulsion. It was a small but formidable team.

Engine Problems

Similar small teams were also used at Pratt & Whitney, whose chief designer, William Brown, worked well with Rich and his people. The huge J58 was a scaled-down, 80 percent version of the even larger

JT9 engine that had been developed for the XB-70. The engine had accumulated some seven hundred hours of running time before the Navy attack aircraft for which it had been intended was canceled. The original J58 produced twenty-six thousand tons of thrust using an afterburner, and was theoretically capable of propelling the attack plane at Mach 3 for a few seconds on a bomb run. By the time it had gone through the almost total revision required for incorporation in the Blackbird, the J58 was putting out 32,500 pounds of thrust. The analogy most preferred by Lockheed engineers was that the engines produced as much thrust as the four huge turbines of the *Queen Mary* ocean liner.

The Blackbird required much more of the engine than the attack plane would have. Instead of being used for a brief burst of power on takeoff and on a bomb run, the afterburners were required to operate for extended periods, gulping eight thousand gallons of fuel per hour. It is interesting to compare the demands made on the J58 with those made on other engines of the time. The best fighters during the period of the J58's conception were powered either by the Pratt & Whitney J57 or J75 engines. These engines could push the aircraft to speeds of Mach 2 for a maximum of fifteen minutes (normally for much less) and operate at a peak altitude of fifty-five thousand feet. In contrast, the J58 would be required to operate at speeds over Mach 3 on a continuous basis at altitudes up to one hundred thousand feet.

The extraordinary performance required of the J58 necessitated so many extensive changes to the basic engine that it was not ready on schedule, and the first examples of the Blackbird had to make do with the much smaller J75 engine for the early test work. The revision of the J58 involved the creation of what became known as a bleed bypass engine. The redesign effort was led by Robert Abernathy of Pratt & Whitney. The bleed bypass design, while complicated in both mechanical and electronic terms, avoided a number of major problems encountered at high Mach cruising speeds, including induced compressor stall, stress to the compressor blades as a result of the stall, unacceptably high temperatures, reduced thrust, and increased fuel consumption. Abernathy, Rich, and Johnson would work closely together to meet the extraordinary challenges to the highly classified J58 power plant.

The overall security requirements for the A-12 were so great that it was considered impossible to conduct flight operations out of Edwards Air Force Base, where most air force experimental flight tests were conducted. Ten air force bases that had been slated for closing were considered as alternates, but none proved to be acceptable. Some of the basing requirements were almost contradictory. The base had to be secure, and well away from civil and military airways, and yet it had to be easily accessible by air. Good weather all year round was an imperative, as was an eight-thousand-foot runway. The base had to be capable of accommodating large numbers of personnel, and have fuel facilities both for the Blackbird and for the conventional aircraft to support it.

The answer was to return to the secret Nevada base built for testing U-2s, and upgrade it to accommodate the new aircraft.

Almost simultaneously, a program began for selecting the personnel required to man the unit that would operate the A-12s. The Air Force, the CIA, and Kelly Johnson all helped develop the criteria. Pilot selection was rigorous. Candidates had to be between twenty-five and forty years of age, less than six feet tall, and less than 175 pounds. They had to be married, emotionally stable and extremely well motivated, have recent experience in high-performance aircraft, and be experts in aerial refueling. Equally high standards were set for all other personnel, from the commanding officer to the ground-crew men. Throughout the operation of the A-12 and its successor SR-71, the individuals selected to operate the aircraft were the best the Air Force and the CIA had to offer. As with the U-2 program, the officers selected were "sheep-dipped," that is, converted from military to ostensible civil status in a covert way that did not affect their careers in terms of seniority and rank.

First Flight

While all the multitudinous related tasks were being dealt with, production difficulties continued to frustrate Johnson, his Skunk Works team, and more importantly, the USAF and the CIA. The titanium proved even more difficult to work than had been thought, and material continued to be rejected for contamination. The planned production schedule began to slip, and Johnson told the CIA that Lockheed's difficulties with wing assembly and Pratt & Whitney's problems with the engines would result in a delay of three or four months in the schedule. He promptly received a rocket back from Richard Bissell: "I have learned of your expected additional delay in first flight from 30 August to 1 December 1961. This news is extremely shocking on top of our previous slippage from May to August and my understanding as of our meeting 19 December that the titanium extrusion problems were essentially overcome. I trust this is the last of such disappointments short of a severe earthquake in Burbank." (Unfortunately for Bissell and for Lockheed, he would be the victim, not of an earthquake, but of the abortive Bay of Pigs invasion of Cuba in April 1961. He had supported it, and when it failed, he had to leave. Lockheed lost a good dependable friend who had deflected many of Secretary McNamara's defense cuts.)

Such caustic comments from the usually unflappable Bissell indicated how important the A-12 was in CIA planning. The contemporary Soviet policy of expansion by encouraging revolutions in countries around the world had to be monitored and contained, and the A-12 was essential to that process.

The difficulties continued, particularly at Pratt & Whitney, where delays became so extreme that Johnson decided to adapt the A-12 to the J75 engine for preliminary test purposes. This was time-consuming and expensive in a program in which costs were already soaring out of sight, but it was a sensible fallback position.

The prototype A-12 was disassembled and moved by road to its test site in a caravan of trucks and a special trailer, arriving on February 28, 1962. There it was assembled, only to give immediate disappointment; the fuel-tank sealant had failed to adhere to the titanium, and the aircraft poured fuel on the ground. Repairs took more than a month. It was not until April 25 that test pilot Lou Schalk was to undertake high-speed taxi tests, with a planned momentary liftoff followed by an immediate landing on the runway. The taxi tests went off well, but as soon as Schalk lifted off, the aircraft wallowed erratically, oscillating laterally, longitudinally, and directionally. With total disaster only milliseconds away, it took all of Schalk's skills to establish control, chop the throttles, and land in a huge cloud of dust on the salt-lake bed, well off the runway. The low hop had reached no more than twenty feet in the air and touched down in little over a mile, rendering Schalk unable to make the traditional upbeat first-flight test report. The trouble turned out to be an improper fuel loading, which put the center of gravity too far aft; on subsequent flight tests, the airplane flew very well. This incredible lapse in oversight was the sort of inexplicable error that drives engineers and pilots crazy, but nevertheless lurks like a great white shark around every program.

The "official" first flight for CIA and USAF representatives took place on April 30, 1962, and went off smoothly. Eight days later, Schalk took the A-12 supersonic for the first time.

The A-12 was developed into the two-place SR-71A for use by the Air Force. The manufacture of the aircraft was as sophisticated as its engines and its aerodynamics.

The next five A-12s arrived by December 1962, and the tests were accelerated. These were all equipped with the J75 engines, including the fourth aircraft, a two-seater that was intended for training, and nicknamed the "Titanium Goose." While other aircraft were subsequently retrofitted with J58 engines, the "Goose" retained the J75s throughout its service. The first flight of an A-12 with two J58 engines installed occurred on January 15, 1963; an A-12 equipped with one J75 and one J58 had flown previously on October 5. The deliveries of J58 engines remained slow, and test flights revealed serious problems that hampered the A-12's attempts to reach its designed performance limits.

Other Versions

Despite the agonizing attenuation of the test program, the A-12's potential for growth was obvious, and both fighter-interceptor and bomber versions were studied, the AF-12 (later YF-12) and RB-12, respectively. The long-sought Department of Defense goal of com-

The YF-12A was intended to be
a long-range high-speed
interceptor. It was used to
set numerous speed and
altitude records.

monality would have been largely achieved, for the aircraft were almost identical except for the forward fuselage sections, which were modified to the suit the mission. The fighter version featured an advanced Hughes radar system, a full complement of missiles, and all the related fire-control system required. The bomber version carried a small but potent load of high-yield nuclear weapons. Three YF-12s would be built while the RB-12 remained on paper because it represented a budgetary threat to the Air Force's ill-fated B-70.

It is not surprising that with such a radically advanced aircraft, the testing process was fraught with incident. Of the fifteen A-12s and three YF-12s that were built, five A-12s and two YF-12s were lost in accidents, a daunting 39 percent loss rate. Two test pilots were killed. Kelly Johnson had to face the additional complications of accident investigation even as he attempted to surmount the complexities of production and test work. That he was able to prevail was a tribute not only to him, but also to his superiors, Hall Hibbard, Dan Haughton, and the Gross brothers. They recognized the great financial risk involved, but they allowed him to proceed, confident in his ability to ultimately deliver the aircraft that the country so desperately needed, and willing to risk huge sums to back that confidence.

Experience Builds

The utility of the U-2 had been demonstrated in the Cuban crisis, as was its vulnerability; on October 27, 1962, Major Rudolph

Anderson was shot down by an SA-2 missile. The tragic incident added urgency to the A-12's flight test program, and the Blackbird's performance envelope was pushed closer to the design requirements. Mach 3 had been reached by July 1963, and the design speed of Mach 3.2 was reached in November.

The existence of the aircraft was publicly revealed for the first time on February 29, 1964. President Lyndon Johnson had been the target of claims by Republicans that he was neglecting defense issues, and he responded by announcing the existence of the "A-11, which has been tested in sustained flights at more than 2,000 miles per hour and at altitudes in excess of 70,000 feet." Johnson went on to describe what was actually the YF-12 fighter version; his use of "A-11" has variously been described as an astute security measure or a simple misunderstanding of Kelly Johnson's inputs.

First Notice of the RS/SR-71

Less than five months later, President Johnson would make an announcement concerning the next version of the Blackbird, which was at the time designated RS(reconnaissance-strike)-71 by the Air Force. In his talk, he termed it the SR-71, and the designation was quickly adopted and SR came to stand for strategic reconnaissance. (Ben Rich delighted in recalling that the president's slip of the tongue required Lockheed to make changes on thirty-three thousand drawings.)

The USAF had chaffed at having to relinquish its traditional strategic reconnaissance role to the CIA in the A-12 program. It had not stinted on its assistance to the CIA, and had supported the Oxcart program fully, but the fact remained that it wished to have strategic reconnaissance within the province of the Strategic Air Command—a not unreasonable request.

Lockheed was eager to supply its needs, and Kelly Johnson did his usual inimitable series of presentations. On February 18, 1963, the Air Force authorized Lockheed to proceed to build six R-12s, with a contract for twenty-five more to follow. The program received the code name Senior Crown. The aircraft's R-12 designation was supplanted by SR-71, which will be used here because it is more familiar.

Kelly Johnson's ability to compartmentalize his various projects was amazing. Each version of the Blackbird—A-12, YF-12, F-12B, RB-12, R-12, M-12, M-21, SR-12, and RS-71/SR-71 among them—

The D-21 drone was developed to impart even greater immunity to enemy action than the Blackbird already possessed. The mother aircraft was designated M-21.

had its own security requirements, and its own specialist teams who knew only their parts of the project. There were also other major programs, such as Senior Bowl, which involved the design, construction, and test of the thirty-eight D-21 drone vehicles for unmanned strategic reconnaissance. Looking like a "baby" A-12, the D-21 (code-named Tagboard) had a range of 1,250 miles and a top speed of Mach 4 at ninety thousand feet. Powered by a Marquardt RJ43 ramjet, it was launched from specially built M-21 aircraft (an A-12 modified with a position for a launch control officer and the requisite dorsal pylon to mount the D-21). It was intended to overfly territory that was too dangerous or too sensitive for overflight by the piloted A-12s.

Tests proved the air-launch process to be too hazardous. On July 20, 1966, off Point Magu, California, a D-21 hit its launching aircraft immediately after its release at Mach 3.25. As might be expected, the M-21 broke up. Both M-21 crew members ejected, but the launch control officer, Ray Torick, drowned when his pressure suit filled with water. Johnson immediately decided that the launch technique was too hazardous to continue and recommended that it be stopped. The D-21 was subsequently modified for launch by two specially equipped Boeing B-52H aircraft of the 4200th Test Wing, operating out of Beale Air Force Base, California. At least four operational missions were flown; none was successful, one crashing in China, resulting in a heated diplomatic protest from Beijing. In the midst of these myriad efforts, Johnson was solving problems ranging from selecting engineers to getting the SR-71 ready for flight. In all of these programs and more, Johnson had to be able to maintain the secrecy, yet do an optimal job of sharing key information.

Senior Crown made perfect sense to the Air Force, but was a red flag to the budget police, who, reasonably enough, could not understand why the CIA operated an A-12 reconnaissance fleet and the Air Force operated an SR-71 fleet, each with virtually identical missions.

The principal difference in the two aircraft was the aft pressurized cockpit for a second crewman in the SR-71. Its SR-71 fuselage was stretched and equipment was rearranged to optimize the use of space and to accommodate the second crew member and 2,434 gallons of additional fuel.

All of the hard lessons learned in the A-12 program paid dividends as the SR-71 construction progressed smoothly, with Bob Gilliland making the first flight of the aircraft on December 22, 1964. The aircraft performed well, presaging a bright future in the Strategic Air Command, but because of politics and budgets, inevitably casting a long shadow over the A-12 program.

Blackbirds into Action

The performance of the YF-12s improved rapidly, and by May 1, 1965, the, air force was willing to attempt to set a number of international records. (For obvious security reasons, the CIA never used their aircraft to set records.) Two YF-12As were employed in the attempts, and the results amazed the world. In short order, the YF-12As established an absolute altitude record of 80,258 feet, and three speed records including the 15/25-kilometer closed-course record of 2,070.102 mph. It was an incredible performance, and should have resulted in orders for as many as two hundred aircraft in the fighter, reconnaissance, and bomber categories. Alas, it was not to be, for reasons of politics and bureaucratic timidity.

Despite these records, there were still serious concerns about the performance of the J58 engine. In a jet engine, it is desirable that the airflow enter the intake nacelles in a smooth manner, then stream back through the engine with a minimum of turbulence. Early jets were relatively slow, and the distance air had to flow from the simple open nacelles to the engine was short. As speeds increased, and the length of the ducting from intake to engine increased, controlling the flow became more of a challenge. A supersonic jet creates a shock wave that must be slowed to subsonic speeds before air can be admitted to the engine. In the A-12, airflow into the engine was modulated by a Hamilton Standard hydromechanical spike. The spike was programmed to move a total distance of twenty-six inches fore or aft as required. It operated in concert with a series of bypass doors, bleed ports, suck-in doors, tertiary doors, and ejector flaps to customize the flow of air through the engine and keep its volume constant as speed progressed from engine start to Mach 3.2. Once through the engine, the air had to be accelerated again to the same speed at which the aircraft was traveling, by means of the ejector system and the afterburners. The process of adjustment took an immense amount of test time before the proper synchronization of inlet-spike movement and engine-door opening and closing sequences was effected. In the meantime, the pilots had to contend with the hazard of a mismatch between the inlet spike and the engine's requirement for airflow. A mismatch would cause an "upstart," a violent "backfire" of the normal shock wave of inlet air. The aircraft tended to swing its nose sharply to the disturbed engine, although this was later countered by the Digital Automatic Flight and Inlet Control System (DAFICS). During early tests, the pilot would have to manually open the bypass doors and reset the spike to get the air flowing smoothly again. These troubles were most often encountered in the Mach 2.4 to 2.8 speed range (not where you wish to induce violent movement of the aircraft). Rich, who was responsible for intake design, decided that the fault lay with the Hamilton Standard spike, the movable cone used to match the shock wave with the inlet. He obtained an electrically powered actuator for the spike from the Garrett Corporation, and the problems were solved overnight. When all of the airflow devices were finally fine-tuned, the aircraft gained in thrust and reduced drag, so that speed went up and fuel consumption went down.

After his retirement, Rich used to give talks to young, new Lockheed engineers on the SR-71, and in particular its power plant. Always engaging, head nodding and arms flailing to indicate a punch line, he was given to jokes that would now be deemed slightly politically incorrect. Yet his manner enabled Rich to describe the remarkable power-plant conception in very human terms. He kept the audience laughing even as he discussed the intricate engineering details derived from his thousands of hours of wind-tunnel study. He relished questions, the more arcane the better. When asked why the nacelles of the Blackbird were round, rather than square as on so many supersonic fighters, he replied: "Because it's a pressure vessel. You don't see too many square pressure cookers." And then he would explain how, at speed, the process of metering the airflow by the spike-and-door combination created a situation in which 54 percent of the engine's thrust was being exerted by the pressure differential in the forward nacelle pressing against the round after-portion of the center body, the spike. Twenty-nine percent was produced by the ejector system and only 17 percent by the basic J58 engine itself. Rich would joke that the inlet was really pulling the engine, and characterized the engine-nacelle combination as a "supercharged ramjet."

Rich's innovations and other improvements in the aircraft's performance made it possible to declare it operational in November 1965. (Ironically, during the same month, the Bureau of the Budget fired its first shot across the bows of the A-12 and the SR-71. The accountants could tell precisely how much the two programs cost, but had no idea of the value of the information generated by Blackbird overflights.)

It happened that the A-12 was ready for deployment just as urgent requirements surfaced. The CIA called for the employment of the A-12 over China, and shortly thereafter the Department of Defense sought it for reconnaissance over North Vietnam. Plans were drawn up for an operation called Black Shield that called for A-12s to operate out of Kadena Air Base in Okinawa on a temporary basis at first, followed by a permanent deployment. The Oxcart detachment would be named the 1129th Special Activities Squadron, and given the affectionate nickname "the Road Runners."

By 1966, the A-12 had reached relative maturity and was meeting most of its specified requirements. Its sister ship, the YF-12, was demonstrating its ability to fire missiles at the speed of Mach 3.2 and bring down Boeing QB-47 drone aircraft. Yet no steps were taken to deploy the aircraft, because Secretary of Defense Robert McNamara denied permission. He was becoming increasingly committed to fighting a ground war in Southeast Asia, and refused to make use of air power to its fullest extent because he did not wish to antagonize Red China. In his judgment, the use of the A-12 was somehow more risky than the continued use of the U-2, although the latter was far more vulnerable to enemy surface-to-air missiles. In consequence, the funding for the A-12 was reduced. As the perceived threat of Soviet bombers had diminished, the YF-12 program was canceled.

Yet even McNamara could not ignore the continuing buildup of North Vietnamese capability. By May 1967, the surface-to-air defenses around Hanoi had reached a point at which a U-2 would almost certainly be shot down, and an agreement was reached to use the

A-12 over North Vietnam. The first mission was flown out of Kadena on May 31, and in a three-hour and thirty-nine-minute flight, photos were obtained of more than one-third of North Vietnam's 190 surface-to-air missile sites. Six more missions were flown by August 15, and while some radar activity was observed, no surface-to-air missiles were launched at the Blackbirds.

The Blackbird performed well over Vietnam and North Korea. Communist opposition increased, and missiles were launched on several occasions. Only one A-12 sustained damage, picking up one piece of shrapnel on the October 30, 1967, sortie over North Vietnam. The aircraft was used over North Korea in the aftermath of the seizure of the USS *Pueblo* on January 2, 1968.

The last operational flight of the A-12 was made on May 8, 1968, on a mission over North Korea. The Black Shield unit was brought back to the United States and the remaining Oxcart aircraft were stored in a hangar for more than two decades before seven of them were finally given to museums and an Air National Guard unit for display. (Of the three YF-12s, one was converted to an SR-71C, one was given to the Air Force Museum, and one crashed.) Under the cooperative hands of the CIA, the Air Force, and Lockheed, the A-12 became an incredibly capable weapon system with a potential active service life of thirty years or more. Political mismanagement inhibited its use and grounded it prematurely.

The Air Force and the SR-71

The question immediately rises as to why the Air Force simply did not take the A-12 into service, instead of opting for the SR-71. The answer is the Air Force requirement, which called for an aircraft with greater range, larger payload, and the need for a "back-seater," a reconnaissance systems officer (RSO), to obtain the maximum yield from the aircraft's equipment. The fuselage was lengthened slightly to accommodate an additional fuel tank, and the chines were enlarged.

As previously noted, on December 22, 1964, the first flight took place, but the first operational aircraft was a trainer version known as the SR-71B, which was delivered to Beale Air Force Base on January 7, 1966. The SR-71B had an elevated second cockpit for the instructor pilot.

The production of the SR-71 was difficult because of the high turnover of the workforce. The learning curve did not drop as forecast, and mistakes were made. Yet by December 1967, all thirty-one of the SR-71s had been delivered to the Ninth Strategic Reconnaissance Wing (SRW) at Beale. Two squadrons, the 1st and the 99th, whose histories go back to operations with General Pershing's 1913 efforts against Mexico, operated the Blackbirds. (The 9th SRW had replaced the 4200th SRW on June 25, 1966.)

Despite the A-12 experience, the high performance and sophistication of the SR-71 led to a series of accidents and incidents, only one of which resulted in a fatality. Nonetheless, unlike the CIA's somewhat tentative use of the A-12, SAC began employing the "Sled" (as the SR-71 was called by its pilots) extensively, and by the end of 1969 had flown more than one hundred operational missions. The Vietnam War made exceptional demands upon the aircraft. It was also used intensively from its base at RAF Mildenhall in the United Kingdom. Missions included surveillance of the Middle East, including Libya, Lebanon, and Yemen. Special assistance was rendered to Israel during the Yom Kippur War. In Southeast Asia many flights were made over North Vietnam, where the cameras could return photos of cargo on the decks and in the holds of ships in the harbor. A typical flight over North Korea lasted only seven minutes, but, reportedly, there were hundreds of much longer flights over Red China.

The usefulness of the SR-71 went beyond the military to the diplomatic tables. During the Yom Kippur War, Henry Kissinger asked that the SR-71 make reconnaissance flights over the battle area. Under U.S. pressure, Israeli premier Golda Meir had said that her troops had halted. To her embarrassment, Kissinger was able to lay two Blackbird photos in front of her, taken on successive days, which showed the advance was continuing.

Everything thus conspired to make the SR-71 legendary almost instantly. It was top secret; it flew higher, faster, and farther than any aircraft in history; and it covered enemy territory with impunity, apparently invulnerable to surface-to-air missile attacks, and certainly unapproachable even by interceptors as advanced as the Soviet MiG-25. As sophisticated as it was, it flew from relatively primitive forward operating locations, bases without the usual infrastructure, without difficulty. It also broke its sister ship A-12's records, establishing an altitude record for sustained level flight of 85,069 feet, a record for speed in a straight line of 2,193.17 mph, and a speed over a one-thousand-kilometer closed circuit of 2,092.294 mph. Many other records were set, all unbroken to this date.

Yet it was expensive to operate the SR-71, and by 1989, budget concerns and a shift in leadership clearly spelled the end of the program. The man considered certain to be the next Air Force chief of staff, General Jerome F. "Jerry" O'Malley, was killed in April 1985 when the North American T-39 Sabreliner in which he was being flown to a speaking engagement crashed. As Major O'Malley, he had flown the first operational flight of the SR-71 on March 21, 1968, and he was a strong supporter of the aircraft. The man who became chief of staff in his place on July 1, 1986, General Larry D. Welch, was opposed to the SR-71 as being too expensive to operate at thirty-eight thousand dollars per hour at a time when defense spending was on the decline. The aircraft was officially retired on January 26, 1990, to much official and unofficial disapproval. It had served well. The SR-71s logged a combined total of 53,490 hours of flight time, of which 11,675 had been spent at Mach 3 plus. They had flown 3,551 operational sorties for a total of 17,294 hours, during which more than a thousand surface-to-air missiles had been fired at them. All missed. Twelve SR-71s were lost, but only one crewman was killed, a tribute to the ejection seats and life-support systems.

When the Air Force retired the SR-71 in 1990, a decision was made to give one example to the Smithsonian Institution's National Air & Space Museum. The aircraft set a new transcontinental speed record, traversing 2,404 statute miles in sixty-seven minutes, fifty-four seconds, a remarkable flight for a museum piece.

Besides its combat capability, the Blackbird was also an excellent research aircraft. The National Aeronautics and Space Administration operated both YF-12 and SR-71 aircraft for experimental work, having obtained two SR-71As and the sole SR-71B trainer as supersonic test platforms. NASA's use of the SR-71 sustained it operationally until the Congress provided the Air Force $100 million in the fiscal year 1995 defense budget to bring three SR-71s back to operational use. On June 28, 1995, after extensive refurbishment, the first SR-71 was returned to the 9th SRW for its new tour of duty and to the general acclaim of the service and the public.

A Look Back at Kelly

In reviewing the A-12 and SR-71, Kelly Johnson's efforts in masterminding the design of the multiple models of the aircraft, developing the technology to use titanium on such a scale, and coordinating test and production efforts have been noted. Less obvious, but equally important, was his overall supervision of the selection and installation of the sophisticated systems intended for the aircraft. These were often as advanced state-of-the-art as the aircraft and engines, and required an incredible capacity to understand the many disciplines involved. Just a brief survey of a few of the more sophisticated systems will underline the breadth and depth of Johnson's genius. They included ultrasophisticated fire-control systems like that incorporating the Hughes AN/ASG-18 radar and Hughes GAR-9 rocket; advanced systems for launching air-to-air missiles at Mach 3.2; radical rotary bomb bays for dropping nuclear weapons; the Astro-Inertial Navigation System for navigation; sophisticated thirty-thousand-dollar pressure suits for the crew members; terminal radar for the use of air-to-ground missiles; the "Mach 3.2 aircraft carrier" for the D-21; ramjet engines for the latter project; modifications to the D-21 to mate with the B-52H; advance guidance systems; the advanced synthetic aperture radar system; advanced systems for NASA, including a version of the SR-71A equipped with an external burning "scramjet"—a supersonic combustion ramjet engine; exotic cameras; electronic intelligence-gathering systems; data links for air-to-ground and air-to-satellite operation; early efforts at global positioning systems (GPS); and many more. He was not responsible for the design of all these varied items by any means, but he was responsible for knowing exactly what effect each of them would have on the carrier aircraft, and he executed his responsibilities fully.

The Midlife Crisis

The CIA approved the Oxcart project in 1960; the Air Force retired the SR-71 in 1990, albeit temporarily. The midpoint of this tumultuous thirty-year period of design, development, construction, and operation of the SR-71 was 1975—the year in which Kelly Johnson retired from his post as senior vice president at Lockheed, and, of course, as the head of the Advanced Development Projects—the Skunk Works.

In Kelly's forty-two years at Lockheed, he had designed, or substantially contributed to the design of, forty Lockheed aircraft. He was showered with honors, including two Collier Trophies, aviation's most prestigious award. The first was in 1959, for his work in designing the F-104; the second was in 1965, for his work on the YF-12A. In the pantheon of American aviation luminaries, he undoubtedly ranks with

**The two greatest reconnaissance aircraft in history shown together: U-2 and SR-71.
Both were products of Lockheed's Skunk Works.**

leaders such as John Northrop, Donald Douglas, Glenn Martin, Reuben Fleet, James McDonnell, and Edward Wells. All of Johnson's colleagues have commented on Johnson's intuitive ability and on his willingness to back his opinions with a bet—usually a quarter—and they all admit that they paid him far more quarters than they received.

But being almost always correct had a downside as well. There is no question that Kelly's experience and knowledge gradually imparted a degree of hubris to him, so that he was not always politic in dealing with his customers. This might have been fine if his customers did not also have egos. Kelly did not recognize that in dealing with three- and four-star generals, and their civilian equivalents, his manner had to be adjusted from that used for dealing with his subordinates. He had become high-handed, telling customers what they needed, rather than listening to hear what they wanted. Over time, an adverse reaction set in, and it became difficult for Kelly to sell his ideas to the military, even when he was absolutely right. The result was that Lockheed was frozen out of the fighter business, and contracts that could have been won by exhibiting a little more flexibility were lost, just at a time when there were fewer contracts available to bid for.

His retirement did not mean that he cut all relations with

Lockheed. He continued as a member of the board of directors, and he was provided an office at the Skunk Works. There he would continue to work, both an asset and a problem for the man who now ran the Advanced Development Project office—Ben Rich.

Ben R. Rich: The Perfect New Broom

Perhaps the greatest testimony to Ben Rich's engineering and leadership ability is that Kelly Johnson selected him as a successor in spite of their almost totally opposite approaches to human relations. Former colleagues recall that when Johnson walked (hurtled is probably a better descriptive term) down a hallway, others in the passage had a tendency to freeze up against the wall, West Point cadet style, rather than to say hello. Johnson did not come to other people's offices to chitchat or pass the time of day, and if you were summoned to see him, you knew that you either had a problem or were about to get one. With Rich it was just the opposite. He was hail-fellow-well-met, and his coworkers fondly recall that his passage down an office hallway was marked by sequential peals of laughter, his own leading the lot, as he improved on his current joke at each cubbyhole. The personality differences were echoed in their physical presence; Johnson, as noted, was a big bull of a man, who seemed to fill up a room when he entered. Rich was short, slender, and had an ingratiatingly diffident manner that did not conceal his shrewd assessment of every situation.

Rich described himself as "ebullient, energetic, a perennial schmoozer and a cheerleader with an endless supply of one-liners and farmer's daughter jokes." More important, he was approachable; he liked people, and he was acutely conscious of the need to give the customer what he wanted. This basic understanding was a refreshing change to the Air Force and consequently to Lockheed. Rich also understood his own talents and his limitations. He did not consider himself a genius in Kelly Johnson's class, and told his colleagues that although he was going to continue adhering to Kelly's work rules and methods, he was not going to make every decision. Instead, he was going to give them tasks to accomplish and delegate both the responsibility and the authority to do so.

Yet, in his own way, Rich was undeniably also a genius. He was a tremendously capable engineer who made great contributions to the power-plant installation on the F-104, U-2, and SR-71, and would

Although possessed of a totally different personality than the man he replaced—Kelly Johnson—Ben Rich was a leader and a brilliant engineer who filled Johnson's shoes better than anyone else could have.

have the vision and the courage to go on to achieve one of the most dramatic breakthroughs in aviation history, the creation of the F-117A stealth fighter.

Ben Rich's family background differed markedly from that of most of his colleagues. His father, Isidore Rich, had superintended a hardwood lumber mill in Manila. He married Annie, a beautiful young French girl who lived in Alexandria, Egypt, after years of romance by correspondence. Ben was born and raised in the Philippines under his father's stern tutelage, which he later recognized had prepared him for working for Kelly Johnson.

The family, worried by the Japanese threat, had returned to Los Angeles just before World War II began. Father and son worked in machine shops during the war, with Ben not entering college until after V-J Day. He graduated from the University of California at Berkeley in 1949 with a degree in mechanical engineering, and went on to get a master's degree in aerothermodynamics at UCLA. It was a happy choice, as it netted Ben both a bride, Faye Mayer, and a shot at a job with Lockheed, where he was soon selected for a temporary job with Kelly at Building 82—the Advanced Development Projects building. He would stay with ADP for thirty-six years, becoming in his own time as synonymous with the Skunk Works as Kelly had been in his. And just as Kelly would have his great Collier Trophy defining moments in the sun, so would Ben.

His first success, however, was in the minor key. He convinced General David C. Jones, then chief of staff and later two-term chairman of the Joint Chiefs of Staff, that the U-2 production line had to be restarted. Jones agreed, and an improved version, called the TR-1 to get away from the U-2's spy-plane notoriety, entered production. Thirty-seven would be built, and they would ultimately be designated U-2R (or U-2RT for the two-seat version). They have served nobly around the world, including action in the Gulf War, and stand as another example of the Skunk Works' ability to deliver, service, and maintain unique aircraft unapproached by those of any other country. The Soviet Union attempted to build its own U-2–type aircraft, and failed utterly.

The Approach to Stealth

It was noted earlier that the initial design requirements for what became the Blackbird specified an invulnerability to radar detection. Although this was not fully achieved in the A-12 or the SR-71, it is worth repeating that the Blackbird was the first stealth aircraft. In 1962, it had a very low radar signature compared with its contemporaries such as the B-52, actually approximating that of the B-1B of two decades later. For comparison purposes, the radar cross section (RCS) of the B-52 is estimated at 1,076 square feet, while that of the B-1B is only 11 square feet. Generally, low radar signatures derive about 65 percent from the shape and 35 percent from radar-absorbent coatings.

Despite its low RCS, the SR-71 was tracked by enemy radar, and missiles and aircraft attempted interception. What was desired was an aircraft that would absolutely defy detection, and therefore be unavailable as a target for any type of interception. Intelligence reports revealed that the Soviet Union's radar was rapidly improving, and the prospects for success by low-level penetrators like the B-1B were diminishing. It thus became the goal of the Defense Advanced Research Projects Agency (DARPA) to elicit from industry an aircraft that would be so invisible to radar that either it would not be detected at all, or if detected, it would not be able to be targeted by either missiles or interceptors. Under the code name Have Blue, in 1973 five companies with recent experience designing fighters were asked to bid on the unclassified project. As in the case of the U-2, Lockheed was not asked to participate, but instead, invited itself to the party. This time, instead of Johnson's brusque insistence on the validity of his ideas, Rich went to work with charm and guile, revealing to DARPA how advanced Lockheed's previous stealth effort was, and agreeing to compete without any government funds. Rich knew that he held two trump cards, and Lockheed, the outsider, won the bid.

Experience and Exotic Mathematics

At the time of the Have Blue competition, Lockheed already had more experience in creating aircraft with a low-radar cross section than any other manufacturer, but it was a breakthrough insight into a set of mathematical formulas that would give it the key to ultimate success.

The insight came through the efforts of Denys Overholser, a mathematician and radar specialist. He had been doing some light reading in a paper called "Method of Edge Waves in the Physical Theory of Diffraction," authored by Pyotr Ufimtsev, the chief scientist at the Moscow Institute of Radio Engineering. The paper was abstruse in the extreme, and indecipherable to a layman. Published in 1966 in the Soviet Union, it had only recently been translated by the Foreign Technology Division at Wright Patterson Air Force Base. Overholser worked with a retired Lockheed mathematician, Bill Schroeder, to develop a computer program they named ECHO I; it was to be called the "Rosetta Stone" of stealth.

Schroeder had investigated the century-old work of Scottish mathematician James Clerk Maxwell, and the elaboration on it done by Arnold Johannes Sommerfeld, a German electromagnetics expert. Their calculations predicted the manner in which a given geometric configuration would scatter (or reflect) electromagnetic radiation. Ufimtsev had developed a simpler approach that concentrated on electromagnetic currents at the edges of geometric shapes. It was Schroeder who saw that the shape of an aircraft could be reduced to a finite set of two-dimensional surfaces that could be analyzed by the formulas of the three mathematicians they had studied. This was the stroke of genius, the recognition that by "faceting," a three-dimensional aircraft could be created out of a collection of flat panels, rather than by the usual French-curve shapes of the past.

Schroeder postulated that if triangular panels were used to form a vehicle surface, the number of individual radar reflection calculations could be reduced to a figure that contemporary computers could manage. The next step was to angle each flat surface at an angle of thirty degrees, in other words, in such a manner that any incoming radar beam would be reflected away from, rather than back to, its source. The question that remained was whether an aircraft so fashioned would also fly.

In his memoirs and in speeches, Ben Rich used to like to pretend that he did not understand Overholser's and Schroeder's calculations when they were initially explained to him. The fact was that he understood enough to know that if Overholser were correct, Lockheed had a product that would yield billions of dollars in sales over the next few decades. Ben was both blessed and cursed by Kelly Johnson, who came in twice a week on a consulting basis and, while much more approachable, was still free with his opinions. He warned Rich that he should not attempt such a high-risk venture as his first project—his reputation would be riding on it. More importantly, Lockheed was still immured in its financial troubles, and its chairman, Bob Haack, would have to think long and hard about funding a costly project that might not prove out. Notwithstanding this, Rich was convinced that Overholser's approach would work, and if so, that it would be invaluable. As events transpired, company president Larry Kitchen and vice chairman Roy Anderson both saw the potential merit in the idea and supported Rich's request for funds. By scraping the financial cupboard almost bare, they managed to provide Rich with the $10 million he needed, at a time when Lockheed finances were near their lowest ebb. This showed remarkable insight and courage on the part of upper management, just recovering from the long siege of anti-Lockheed publicity. They took grave risks when utter conservatism was a safer choice; and they did so because they knew Lockheed needed to begin selling aircraft to the government again, and because they had faith in Rich and the Skunk Works.

In a superheated five-week period, Overholser used ECHO I to solve for the radar cross section of the shape Schroeder had envisioned, and to predict how such a faceted aircraft shape would appear on radar. The concept was validated when an idealized aircraft model (nicknamed the "Hopeless Diamond") was tested and found to have a lower radar cross section than any previously tested shape.

(Lockheed did not intend to rely solely on shape for stealth; it would also make liberal use of radar-absorbent materials [RAM], which absorbed, rather than reflected, incoming radar energy.)

Models of the proposed Have Blue design were tested, and in April 1976 Lockheed was awarded the contract for a project that was immediately catapulted to beyond top secret to a compartmentalized status of "special access required" (SAR). Only a few people were made aware of the scope of the entire program. Northrop was also awarded a contract to build two Tacit Blue aircraft. These would assume an entirely different, whalelike shape, and be kept secret for longer than either the Have Blue aircraft or the F-117A fighter that resulted from them. The Tacit Blue was designed as a reconnaissance vehicle, and while it flew successfully and made some contributions to the Northrop B-2 stealth bomber, it did not have the impact or the importance of Have Blue.

Rich, the Supersalesman

During the early days of the project, extensive tests of full-size models of the Lockheed and Northrop concepts had been run at the Air Force's Ratscat Backscatter Measurement Range at White Sands, New Mexico. A pole-mounted thirty-eight-foot-span wooden version of the Hopeless Diamond had the approximate radar signature of a golf ball. In other words, an incoming aircraft the *shape* of the Hopeless Diamond (as we'll see, the size did not matter) would have no more reflectivity to an enemy radar set than a Titleist Professional. For all practical purposes, this meant that the aircraft, moving at near sonic speeds, would be impossible for any radar to acquire and track.

In the course of the testing, some false data were introduced that indicated that instead of a golf-ball-size RCS the Hopeless Diamond had the RCS of an ordinary marble. This gave Rich a new shtick; he bought some marble-size ball bearings, and when he would visit in the Pentagon he would roll the ball bearings on a general's desk and say, "Here's the observability of your airplane on radar." It was corny, and mildly incorrect—but it got the Air Force's attention, so much so that a contract was awarded to begin work on what became the F-117A one month before the Have Blue's first flight.

Rich's longtime friend, mentor, and pet annoyance, Kelly Johnson, did not just look over his shoulder at the stealth project, but forcibly expressed his opinion with a well-aimed kick to Rich's rear, insisting that so ugly an airplane would never fly. To Rich's immense satisfaction, he won a quarter bet from Johnson over which aircraft would have the lowest RCS—the D-21 drone or the new diamond-shaped aircraft. Models of both aircraft were placed in a test chamber, and the Hopeless Diamond was stealthier than the drone by an order of magnitude. Rich then showed Johnson that the numbers revealed in the test corresponded exactly to Overholser's computations. Johnson's intuition had failed him at the edge of the computer age. He simply could not believe Overholser's assertion that the amount of radar energy returned to a sender is independent of the target's size— that a bomber, a fighter, or a light plane of the same shape would have an identical radar cross section. In time, Johnson became a reluctant convert, accepting the new concepts on stealth, but still clinging to his contention that the ugly diamond shape could not be made to fly.

Despite his stature, he was human. It may have rankled Johnson that Rich had not only passed his first test, securing a production contract by leading his team to the successful creation of a radically new aircraft, the Have Blue, but had also ingratiated himself with the Air Force, repairing damage that Johnson had done.

More importantly for the future, Rich had proven himself to the old-timers at the Skunk Works who had doubted his ability to fill Kelly's shoes. With the exception of their fear of, and fascination with, Johnson, most of the individual members of the Skunk Works team had always had what today would be called "an attitude." They had always been irreverent, questioning, supremely confident in their own capabilities, and eager to puncture any inflated ego that happened to cross their path. Sherman Mullin, who succeeded Rich as head of the Skunk Works in 1991, recalls walking through a strangely quiet engineering section and thinking, "The insubordination level isn't high enough today."

And while his team followed Rich's lead willingly enough, he was acutely conscious that he was on trial. His successful sale of Have Blue to Lockheed's management and the Air Force gave him the stature needed to ensure that the production contract would be well executed.

Lockheed received a contract to build two prototypes. These were to be two-thirds-scale aircraft each powered by two of the time-proven General Electric J85 engines. Ed Baldwin, who had been so important on the layout and the structure of the U-2, designed the aircraft. It had an ugly industrial appearance that was completely unlike anything Lockheed had done in the past with its history of glorious Constellations and glamorous SR-71s. The new airplane looked like a giant lawn dart, with a fuselage twice as long as the wings.

The unconventional shape required a quadruple-redundant computer-operated fly-by-wire system that continuously corrected for its inherent instability, the quality that imparted a maneuverability essential for a successful fighter.

Rich's team approached the Have Blue aircraft in their usual comprehensive style, attending to a multitude of problems never before contemplated in what was now called a Very Low Observable (VLO) aircraft. The engine inlets had to have screens yet permit an ample flow of air. The jet exhausts had to be arranged to present a minimum infrared signature and inhibit radar reflection from the face of the turbine. No flaps, speed brakes, or high-lift devices were fitted to the modified delta wings. Elevons, a combination of ailerons and elevators that dated back to the days of the Northrop flying wings, were used in combination with two all-movable, inward-canted vertical fins, similar in concept to those of the SR-71. A movable, two-position tail surface, called the "platypus," was used to offset angles of attack (the angle between the wing chord and the flight path) of greater than twelve degrees.

Although government bureaucracy intruded more and more on the Skunk Works' operation, Rich's team worked with its customary drive to produce the two prototypes for a bargain $43 million.

The first airplane, designated HB 1001 (and also known as the XST-1 for experimental stealth technology), was flown to its test site inside a Lockheed C-5A on November 16, 1977, for a flight test program under the direction of Dick Miller. On December 1, Lockheed test pilot Bill Park made the first flight, just twenty months after contract award. Wearing a dazzle camouflage scheme reminiscent of World War I ships to disguise its shape, the HB 1001 was intended only as a flight-test vehicle, with no intensive attention given to its stealth characteristics. The number two aircraft, HB 1002, after extensive ground-testing of models, would be refined to test its VLO characteristics and painted an anonymous gray.

To facilitate construction and in keeping with Skunk Works practice, Rich had authorized the maximum use of off-the-shelf equipment, including a Northrop F-5 undercarriage, a General Dynamics F-16 fly-by-wire system and side-stick controller, and the two GE J85 engines from a Rockwell T-2B Buckeye trainer.

After five months of successful, if sometimes exciting, flight test, HB 1001 damaged its landing gear when dropped from a height of seven feet, touching down too hard on a landing attempt. Park made a successful go-around, but the gear was jammed in a half-retracted position. In an amazingly brave and skillful display of flying technique, he attempted to get the gear down and locked by bouncing down hard on the extended gear—no easy task given the touchy stability of the Have Blue aircraft. The gear stayed half-extended. After a climb back to ten thousand feet, an engine failed and he elected to bail out. Severely injured during the ejection process, he had to give up flying, but stayed on as Lockheed's director of flight operations. (Park had probably used up his quota of luck; on July 9, 1964, he had suffered a complete hydraulic failure in an A-12 as he came in to land. He ejected safely.)

The second aircraft, XST-2, aka HB 1002, was modified to incorporate lessons learned with the first prototype and was flown on July 20, 1978, by Lieutenant Colonel Norman "Ken" Dyson. It flew fifty-two times over the next year, validating Lockheed's VLO design, and ensuring that a follow-on contract would be awarded for a fighter. On what proved to be its final flight, the HB 1002 caught fire; Dyson was able to eject safely.

The two crashes did not discourage the Air Force. General Robert Dixon, a man who did so much to revitalize the Tactical Air Command, personally told Rich that Lockheed would receive a fixed-price contract for five full-scale development (FSD) and fifteen production aircraft. The program was named Senior Trend, and the stealth fighter was under way.

The Black Jet

By an unusual twist of fate, then brigadier general Larry D. Welch, a future chief of staff and the man who would later terminate the SR-71 program, was the principal Air Force contact for the proposed stealth fighter, which would be designated the F-117A. (The F-117 was first painted gray, then in camouflage, then gray again, and finally in jet black. During test operations, to avoid a security compromise, it came to be called the "Black Jet," and this became its nickname.)

Welch became the program's strongest advocate, keeping Assistant Secretary of Defense William Perry fully informed of its progress. But the Air Force's contractual terms were rigorous. The F-117A had to meet or exceed the stealth characteristics of the wooden mock-up, as well as meet all of its specified performance requirements—and the first fighter had to be test-flown within twenty-two months of the contract. It was a challenge worthy of the Skunk Works.

Rich had faith in the stealth concept, and pushed Lockheed to back experiments in the discipline. The first of these was the Have Blue test aircraft.

Rich designated Norman Nelson (who would head the Skunk Works from 1984 to 1986) as program manager. Nelson selected veterans from the Have Blue program to assist him, including a successor, Alan Brown, who was the group's "low observables" expert, and thus in a position to call the shots on some decisions. The Skunk Works' challenge was to produce a fighter-bomber aircraft that would be invulnerable to enemy detection. This meant a suppression of its radar and infrared signatures and making the aircraft difficult to see by means of camouflage, and by elimination of engine smoke trails and, more difficult, contrails. The aircraft sound had to be reduced to a minimum, and its electromagnetic emissions from onboard equipment eliminated. Each situation called for a different approach.

The basic shape and materials used in its construction were the principal methods of avoiding both the radar and infrared signatures. The modern General Electric F404 engine selected for use did not have a smoke problem, and contrails could be avoided by carefully selecting altitude and weather conditions. Passive electromagnetic emissions were largely eliminated by not incorporating an onboard radar, while other signals were minimized by use of special antennae.

The F-117A's configuration, although more conventional in some ways than that of the Have Blue aircraft, was still strikingly unusual. The triangular fuselage sat on the 67.5-degree swept wings like the turret of the Civil War *Monitor* stuck on its hull. Instead of inward-canted vertical surfaces, it adopted a swept-back V design, canted outward.

Construction was for the most part entirely conventional aluminum, except that the external surfaces were covered with plates of radar-absorbent material attached by an epoxy adhesive or, when needed, by sprayed-on RAM material. The cockpit was conventional with the exception of the gold film coatings that were incorporated in the canopy glass. (If there was no way to reflect the radar energy, the pilot's head would have dwarfed the entire aircraft on the radar screen.) As on the Have Blue aircraft, the engine intakes were covered with grids to reflect incoming radar energy, and the engines were exhausted through a wide "platypus"-style duct. The latter proved to be a tremendous design hazard for months, cracking under stress, until General Electric solved the problem.

The formulas that Overholser and Schroeder had incorporated int ECHO I were demanding in the extreme, and required that the aircraft be built with excruciating attention to detail and to finish. Even the slightest deviation from the tight finish work—a gear door cracked open, a few screws not tightened flush—and the airplane was suddenly visible on the radar screen. Maintenance workers had to add a new concern to their already demanding tasks—having to make sure that all access plates were exactly in place and that the RAM material was not abraded by a maintenance stand.

Rich understood very well that, despite its designation as a fighter, the F-117A's mission was to make a stealthy attack and drop precision-guided munitions on hard-to-reach targets. Although quite maneuverable, it was not going to mix it up in dogfights, nor was it going to be required to do close support work. This enabled Rich's team to make some compromises on speed, range, and maneuverability in favor of stealth characteristics. It was typical of Ben Rich that he did not attempt to force his decisions on the individual members of his team; as a result, he has been called "a perfect manager—he was there for the tough calls, and emergencies."

Unfortunately, Rich was himself suffering from a series of emergencies. His wife, Faye, who had long been unwell, passed away on August 18, 1980. It was a devastating blow to Rich, who was able to sustain himself only by throwing himself even more relentlessly into his work.

First Flight

Just eighteen months after the production contract had been signed, Ben Rich got a significant fifty-fifth birthday present. On June 18, 1981, Harold "Hal" Farley Jr. took off in the number one F-117A.

The aircraft flew fairly well, but exhibited directional-stability and control problems that led to a 15 percent increase in the size of the vertical fins. More aircraft were ordered, bringing the total to fifty-nine aircraft, for a total program value of more than $4 billion to Lockheed. It was a sweet victory for Rich; he was now unquestionably his own man, in charge of the Skunk Works in spirit as well as in fact.

The F-117As were built at an excruciatingly slow—read expensive—rate of about eight aircraft per year (Rich terms this "building aircraft by the season"), with the last delivery on July 12, 1990. Notwithstanding the slow rate, the Skunk Works' discipline was such that a good learning curve was achieved, and program profits were excellent. By the end of 1984, twenty-one Nighthawks had been delivered to the Tactical Air Command.

Many things happened during this period, including the two years between March 1984 and August 1986, when Rich was tasked to serve as president of the Lockheed Advanced Aeronautics Company. During his absence, he was succeeded for three months by veteran Dick Heppe (who would retire as president of the Lockheed California Company) and then by Norm Nelson.

The iron security that had been maintained during the test and production of the F-117A was continued through its operational deployment. During this same period of extreme security, the Skunk Works was growing in size, reaching 7,500 employees, and being progressively infiltrated by one bureaucratic functionary after another. Organizations that would have driven Kelly Johnson to drink or to murder now beset the Skunk Works, including the Environmental Protection Agency, the Equal Employment Opportunity Commission, the Occupational Safety and Health Administration and others. Many of these agencies' requirements were diametrically opposed to traditional Skunk Work needs for security and for specialized skills. The net effect of these agencies—especially the tons of paperwork they required—was to significantly change the nature of the Skunk Works over time. The law of the land made it impossible to run ADP as Kelly Johnson had run it. The national importance of Skunk Works products did not matter: execution of the bureaucratic regulations did. Organizational changes would also affect how the Skunk Works was run, but no matter what outside influence there was, there remained, to use their own term, a band of Skunks to carry on its mission.

Like the SR-71A, excellent security was maintained on the F-117A stealth fighter.
When it was finally revealed to the public, many people found it difficult to
believe that the angular aircraft could really fly.

Operational Use

The security on the F-117A was so complete that few people in the
USAF besides the actual operators knew of its existence. As the five
full-scale development (FSD) aircraft (nicknamed "Scorpions" by the
ground crew) began to enter test during 1981–82, the military unit to
use the production aircraft had to be established. The 4450th Tactical
Group, under the command of Colonel James S. Allen, moved to an
airfield at Tonopah Test Range, about thirty-two miles southeast of
the tiny Nevada town of Tonopah. Training began at once, and the
initial operational capability (IOC) came on October 28, 1983. The
arduous training was conducted entirely at night, to preserve secrecy.
The aircraft, contrary to reports, was not difficult to fly—it was *never*
called the "Wobblin' Goblin" by anyone but imaginative reporters.
Like any modern jet fighter, it was demanding, and so were the new
precision-guided munitions with which it was equipped. The unit also
had Vought A7D aircraft for training and as a security cover. These
were later replaced by Northrop T-38 trainers.

New tactics had to be devised, for the F-117A's mission was

unlike any other in aviation history. It was to be able to fly, alone, against the heaviest enemy defenses and with true surgical strikes destroy "high-value assets," that is, the enemy's leadership, command and control systems, communication and transportation centers, and other key elements.

On October 5, 1989, the 37th Tactical Fighter Wing (TFW) took over from the deactivated 4450th, with three squadrons of F-117As—the 415th, 416th, and 417th. The wing launched the F-117A's combat debut two months later in Operation Just Cause. Six F-117s were sent on the mission that so evolved that only two were required to drop bombs, on a field near the barracks of Panamanian Defense Force troops at Rio Hato. The two carried out their mission, which was intended to "stun, disorient and confuse" the opposition, but opponents of defense spending seized upon the "miss" as grounds to criticize. The aircraft was given its first public demonstration at Nellis Air Force Base, Nevada, on April 21, 1990—many were disappointed that the multifaceted F-117A did not look at all like the Testor Corporation's sleek, smoothly rounded "F-19 Stealth Fighter" plastic model, which had sold by the thousands.

Owning the Night

The Nighthawks, as they had become known, next demonstrated their legs in an amazing transfer from Tonopah to the King Khalid Air Base in Khamis Mushayt, Saudi Arabia, in preparation for combat against the invader of Kuwait, Saddam Hussein. Departing on August 19, 1990, twenty-one Nighthawks (including three spares) of the 37th had flown first to Langley Air Force Base in Virginia, and eighteen had then made the approximately fifteen-hour flight nonstop to Saudi Arabia, refueling from KC-10 tankers several times en route. They were reinforced by another eighteen F-117s on December 4. The Saudi Arabian base (which seemed much like the home base at Tonopah in terms of climate and geography) was nine hundred nautical miles from Baghdad, which meant that every mission would also require at least three aerial refuelings. It did not matter; Ben Rich's gamble would pay off a million times over in the pyrotechnic-filled skies over Baghdad.

Led by Colonel Alton C. "Al" Whitley Jr., the 37th TFW wrote a new chapter in air warfare beginning in the early morning of January 17, 1991, when Major Gregory Feest dropped a laser-guided weapon on an Iraqi radar center. (Feest had dropped the first bomb in Panama,

The F-117A proved itself for all time in Operation Desert Storm, where it broke the back of enemy defenses in the first hours of the war.

as well.) The Nighthawks were the only aircraft sent over Baghdad, and they penetrated a seemingly impassable flak and missile barrage without any casualties, and without even taking any hits. There is no indication that Iraqi radar ever tracked one of the F-117As at any time.

The results were spectacular, and broadcast to the world in almost real time. The F-117As took on the toughest jobs first, knocking out thirty-seven high-value targets, including the air-defense headquarters with its heavily redundant air-defense infrastructure. Although the Nighthawks mounted less than 3 percent of the total sorties flown on the first day of the war, they took out more than 30 percent of the targets. In 1,271 combat sorties during forty-three days of incessant combat, they made 1,669 hits on pinpoint targets, including high-value assets like the Osirak nuclear facility. They did their task so well that within days they had run out of the more important strategic targets for which they were designed, and were assigned to lesser but still worthy tasks such as destroying bridges or supply depots.

As sophisticated as the aircraft was, its highly motivated maintenance teams kept its mission-capable rate to just below 86 percent, even better than the peacetime average of 82 percent.

Saddam Hussein had expected the American public to fall victim

The pilots who flew the F-117A through the dense flak over Baghdad were amazed that none had sustained damage. They were received as heroes when they returned to the United States.

to the Vietnam syndrome and demand the recall of its troops. The exultation felt at the televised results of the Nighthawk's bombing extinguished any possibility of this. When victory came after forty-three days of air action and one hundred hours of ground combat, the American public decided that it liked winning wars this way—cleanly, quickly, with few U.S. casualties. The concept was soon taken a step further: *future* wars should be won in a similar manner, quickly, with few U.S. casualties—and with an amazing corollary: with few enemy casualties, as well. The only way to accomplish this is with stealth aircraft and precision-guided munitions—and in this, Ben Rich's F-117A had shown the way.

The Nighthawk's success in combat was even more pleasing to Rich than his receipt of the Collier Trophy for the aircraft in 1989, or for the many accolades he had received since. The fact that the aircraft flew continuously without incurring any casualties was even more important to him than the fact that it completely fulfilled is promise of eluding radar and delivering precision munitions.

The Reward for Winning

It might have been expected that the great success of the F-117 in the Gulf War might have gained further orders. The U.S. Navy was badly in need of a stealth aircraft, its A-12 project having failed, and Lockheed made proposals for an F-117N navalized version of the Nighthawk, but to no avail. Great Britain expressed an initial low level of interest and then backed away. And even the USAF declined further purchases, citing the expense of operating the F-117 as one reason, the same rationale it had used against the SR-71. In fact, the real reason underlying the refusal of both services to purchase F-117s was that it threatened procurement of new systems, the F/A-18E for the navy, and Lockheed's own F-22 for the Air Force.

The F-22 Raptor

As advanced as the F-22 Raptor is aerodynamically, its greatest importance is as the harbinger of an entirely new era in warfare. The overwhelming victory in the Persian Gulf War, with all its importance for the victory in the cold war, heralded this new age, in which control of information—and denial of information to the enemy—is the key to winning. The F-22 is the first product of the revolution in computing capability and in onboard electronics. The Raptor's incredible combination of speed, stealth, and agility gives it a dominance over every fighter in the world, including the longtime U.S. standards, the McDonnell Douglas F-15 and the Northrop Grumman F-14. (Agility goes beyond traditional maneuverability—it speaks to an aircraft's ability to move about its flight envelope quickly from one point to another, changing the magnitude and direction of the velocity vector in the shortest interval of time.) Its lethality is immeasurably enhanced by its enormous computing power, which will allow it to exchange information at an incredible rate with satellite, airborne, and ground stations.

The program that ultimately led to this twenty-first-century fighter began in 1981, when the requirement for an Advance Tactical Fighter (ATF) was formally identified by the USAF. It speaks volumes for current planning and programming techniques that the initial operational capability will not be achieved until after the turn of the century. The USAF wanted to minimize risk by allowing ample time for technologies to be integrated and proven before being committed to production.

Ben Rich's successor at the Skunk Works, Sherm Mullin, was the Lockheed program manager for what was the ATF. The Air Force had presented Lockheed and other competitors with a new and unwelcome situation in the ATF program. The Air Force asked that Lockheed cost-share 50 percent of the development program's $1.8 billion projected cost. Kitchen immediately protested that no company could undertake to invest almost a billion dollars in a competition that it might lose. It was essentially betting the company on the possibility of a win. Conversations with General Larry Skantze, then commanding Air Force Systems Command, revealed that the Air Force's position was firm: development costs had to be shared. Kitchen then proposed teaming with other firms, to spread the risk. The Air Force was against this, for fear it would diminish competition.

In the end, however, Kitchen's viewpoint prevailed, and from 1986, Mullin led the industry team composed of Lockheed, Boeing, and General Dynamics in a head-to-head competition with a team composed of Northrop and McDonnell Douglas. Both competing teams worked closely with Pratt & Whitney and General Electric, who were simultaneously conducting a competition for an engine to power the ATF.

Mullin's team defined the ATF in revolutionary terms. It was intended to be the definitive fighter aircraft in the world for most of the twenty-first century. It was to have a first-look, first-shoot, first-kill capability against any conceivable threat, with a tremendous emphasis on beyond-visual-range capability. The Air Force issued stringent low-observable requirements, and these were incorporated into the thinking. The ATF was to have the capability to cruise at supersonic speeds ("supercruise") without using the afterburner, and have extreme maneuverability at high speed. Lockheed selected vectored-thrust engines (in which a nozzle can be pointed in either up or down directions to direct thrust), while Northrop did not.

Balancing these requirements was not easy. Shaping the aircraft for stealth characteristics has an effect on potential speed, range, and especially, maneuverability. All software and avionics were to be extremely advanced, and all systems were to have high-reliability/low-maintenance characteristics. Somewhat optimistically, the aircraft was intended to weigh only fifty thousand pounds at takeoff gross weight and have a flyaway cost of only $35 million (in 1985 dollars).

To achieve these goals, Mullin's team had to assume that a wide

The Lockheed Martin F-22 will be the primary fighter of the twenty-first century. Shown here is the prototype Lockheed YF-22. Stealthy, but less angular than the F-117A, the YF-22 combines agility and supersonic cruise capability.

array of advanced technology currently under development would be available when needed. In 1987, the team decided that an extensive redesign was required, and after three months of ever more intensive effort, the configuration of the ATF was finally decided upon. His team would use a blended wing and body design with internal weapons bays and sufficient internal fuel for long-duration missions. The wing was a modified diamond shape, which provided great structural strength and high fuel volume. Its large area enhanced maneuverability and reduced both takeoff and landing distances. The wing was equipped with full-chord leading-edge flaps, ailerons, and flaperons. The large vertical tails, not all-moving as on the SR-71 and the F-117A, but equipped with large rudders, were canted outward, and the horizontal tails were all movable. The engines had two-dimensional, convergent-divergent exhaust nozzles with pitch axis thrust vectoring, twenty degrees up or down. Pitch-only thrust vectoring permitted smaller horizontal tails saving four hundred pounds in weight, and facilitated their differential use for high roll rates. The use of composites in 35 percent of the structure resulted in a 25 percent weight reduction over an all-aluminum aircraft.

The F-22 resembles the F-117A most in its front quadrant, where stealth is most important. The design team was able to depart from the strictly flat plate philosophy of the Black Jet because it now had access to a Cray computer, which could handle the thousandfold ad-

The advent of forward-firing heat-seeking missiles makes it necessary for an air
superiority fighter to have stealth characteristics and advanced armament.
The YF-22 pointed the way for both.

ditional calculations required to determine the stealth characteristics
of curved surfaces.

The YF-22 faced stiff competition from the Northrop–
McDonnell Douglas team, which produced the YF-23. The YF-23's
stealth characteristics derived from the same philosophical and mathematical base as the Northrop B-2 stealth bomber. The Northrop–
McDonnell Douglas team chose not to use thrust vectoring, and this
may have made the aircraft slightly less agile than the YF-22. The test
results are classified, but it is probable that the YF-23 was slightly faster.

As a result of the two competitions, airframe and engine, the Air
Force announced the selection of the Lockheed YF-22/Pratt & Whitney F119 engine combination as the winner. The Raptor had not been,
strictly speaking, a Skunk Works project, because of the potential size
of the production program, and the requirement for sharing information with the other team members. Nonetheless, the Skunk Works
provided many of the engineers, the methods, and the spirit that
moved the company to yet another high point.

The Lockheed system of moving high-potential managers now
proved itself again. Sherm Mullin assumed the leadership of the Skunk
Works in 1991, while a relative newcomer, clearly on the fast track,
and also assumed responsibility for the F-22.

Micky Blackwell caught the eye of a tough taskmaster, Ken Cannestra, at the Georgia plant. Cannestra liked him because, although a
Southerner, he was not one of the old guard, whose cronyism had
caused him problems. Blackwell was an excellent engineer, capable of

No nation in the world presently has the capability to field a fighter with the Raptor's prowess.

motivating people to get the job done. Cannestra brought him along swiftly, giving him more responsibility, and Blackwell was soon vice president of engineering. There he did a stellar job, revamping the organization, bringing in new blood—a difficult task at any organization—yet building teamwork at the same time. His expertise was so evident that when the budding F-22 program got into some difficulties, he was sent to California to bring, as Cannestra puts it "more engineering flair" to the California organization. He worked closely with Sherm Mullin. When the latter was promoted to head the Skunk Works (and subsequently induced to spend two additional years there before retiring) Blackwell took over the F-22 program.

Under the perennially reorganized Lockheed system, Cannestra was now serving as the Aeronautics Group president and president of the Georgia Company. Cannestra, very much in love with his new life in Atlanta and determined to retire there, brought Blackwell back to become president of the Georgia Company. He was thus positioned well to assume further responsibilities when the Lockheed Martin merger took place.

Those future responsibilities would include guiding the F-22 program through the many congressional hurdles to achieve funding, even with all of the problems implicit in bringing such a radical new combination of aircraft, engine, and equipment to production status. Significant progress was recorded on September 7, 1997, when Paul Metz took the first production F-22A into the air for the first time.

But even as the F-22 program proceeds, the essential task of winning the competition for the proposed new Joint Strike Fighter will have to be mastered. Similar challenges were to be found in every aspect of Lockheed's business, which had altered so dramatically for the better in just twenty years that it was obvious that the company was poised at the beginning of a new era.

The following chapter will deal with the full measure of that change, charting the company's remarkable rebound from 1975 to 1995, and, in the process, highlighting the amazing diversity of the company's components and their products.

CHAPTER 13

The Rebound:
1975 to 1995

In 1975, the term "survival of the fittest" had a dismaying ring to the leaders of Lockheed, for the company was hardly fit, having suffered grievous wounds over the past dozen years. Despite a repeatedly demonstrated technological mastery, it still had to face immense difficulties in terms of customer relations, public perception, and finances. The resignation of incumbent officers offered little comfort to shareholders, whose stock fell from over $13.00 to $3.75 a share on the New York Stock Exchange.

Despite deep-seated problems, the men and women of Lockheed persevered, clinging to Bob Gross's concept of family even as they underwent agonizing changes and reorganizations that affected almost every employee. Over the next twenty years, the new company leaders sailed a variety of courses, tacking with the business winds and even occasionally changing goals. Strategic planning efforts convinced them that Lockheed, in addition to its traditional strengths in aeronautics and defense business, should adopt objectives in the once foreign fields of space, systems integration, information systems, and other commercial systems. As totally unforeseen events transpired, these objectives would have to be modified.

One constant factor among the new leaders was a determination to remold the company so that it remained strong in defense sectors, but became competitive in nondefense markets. The tactics they used were at once conservative and daring. They diversified into new markets and sought to capitalize on new developments in a daring manner, but if things did not work out, they quickly cut their losses and pulled back. Other aircraft companies had proved how risky diversification could be, as with Boeing and its urban transportation systems or Grumman with its private planes and canoes. But almost all of Lockheed's new ventures were in high-technology fields.

By 1995, Lockheed had not only survived, but conclusively proved itself to be among the fittest of all aerospace companies. It now stood poised upon the brink of new business undertakings on a scale far beyond anything even their most adventuresome planners had ever dreamed of. It is instructive to review Lockheed's adept changes over the twenty-year period in which it revolutionized its relative standing in the industry. It is no coincidence that the twenty years were also characterized by the emergence of many of its top managers from the ranks of the Lockheed Missiles and Space Company.

The events of this fruitful two-decade period may be conveniently aligned into five-year segments in order to make the phenomenal growth that accompanied the changes in course more easily understood.

1975–1979

Despite 1975 being a year of trial whose events led, in February 1976, to the resignation of the chairman, Daniel J. Haughton, and the vice chairman, A. Carl Kotchian, Lockheed nonetheless recorded more than $3 billion in sales for the second consecutive year. The 1975 earnings were almost double those of 1974, but at $45.3 million, still remained at a low 1.5 percent of sales. Additional evidence of financial stress was revealed in the stockholders' equity, which had fallen to the dangerously low level of $75 million, making Lockheed vulnerable to a takeover.

The old guard and the new. From the left, old-guard members Daniel Haughton and Carl Kotchian, then the new guard: Larry Kitchen, Roy Anderson, and Robert B. Ormsby, Jr.

Haughton's successors in the newly named Office of the Chief Executive recognized their difficulties. These included the quadruple onus of the foreign-payments scandal, the continuing losses stemming from the L-1011 TriStar program, the huge long-term debt of more than $800 million, and the alienation of a principal customer, the United States Air Force. As noted, the new chairman, Robert W. Haack, would remain with Lockheed only briefly, to be succeeded in early 1977 by Roy A. Anderson as chairman and chief executive officer. Lawrence O. Kitchen remained corporate president and chief operating officer. The choice of Anderson as chairman would be a turning point for Lockheed. The company would be on a new course providing the foundation for its successes over the next twenty years.

Anderson's great success derived from his credibility both within

The United States Navy has found the Lockheed S-3 Viking to be extraordinarily adaptable. First flown on January 21, 1972, the twin-jet carrier-based patrol plane also does electronic countermeasures work.

and without the company. His leadership and knowledge enabled Lockheed to achieve financial survival during the trouble-filled years of the late 1960s and the first half of the 1970s. It was trust in Anderson that led two major banks, Bank of America and Bankers Trust, to provide Lockheed with the backing to pursue its strategic objectives.

Despite the vicissitudes of the previous decade, Anderson and his management team had much to work with. Company loyalty had kept almost all of the essential managers and workers on board during the difficult years. With the exception of the L-1011, almost all of the Lockheed programs were profitable, including such consistent money-makers as the "black" satellite programs, the fleet ballistic missiles, the P-3, CP-140, and S-3A antisubmarine-warfare aircraft, and the C-130 transport. The funded backlog exceeded $4 billion, and there were new programs on the horizon that promised much. One of these promises was illusory—the revitalization of the TriStar program by the launch of the shortened L-1011-500 in 1976. Undertaken on the strength of six firm orders and an option for three more aircraft by British Airways, it animated the TriStar program only briefly. In contrast, deliveries of the unsung but versatile SA-3 Viking hit their peak, with fifty accepted by the navy in 1975 and forty-four in 1976.

The Viking program forecast the future in many ways. Realizing that it lacked carrier-based aircraft experience, Lockheed elected to team with the LTV Corporation and the Univac Federal Systems Division of Sperry Rand, which specialized in antisubmarine-warfare systems. Many more team efforts would follow. Lockheed and its partners won the competition and an order for 187 aircraft. The first Viking flew on January 21, 1972, with the last delivery being made in August 1978. The aircraft was continuously updated over the years, and provided an unexpected bonus when its advanced electronic suite was adopted for incorporation into the P-3 aircraft selected by Canada for long-range maritime patrol work. The $697 million contract for what became the CP-140 Aurora aircraft was at the time the largest single export sale in Lockheed history. Eighteen Auroras were delivered between May 1980 and March 1981.

Anderson and Kitchen, backed up by Vincent N. Marafino, senior vice president, finance, and another LMSC alumnus, proved to be so formidable a combination that they were able to pronounce 1977 as "truly a year of regeneration." Sales had exceeded $3 billion for the fourth consecutive year, and profits had risen to $55 million. Long-term debt had been reduced to $417 million, and the U.S. loan guarantee was ended with a $31 million profit to the government. One major result of the improved situation was an increase in stockholder equity to $219 million. The situation was noted by the New York Stock Exchange, where Lockheed stock hit an unaccustomed high of just over $19.

The new management had not yet been able to alter the mix of Lockheed's business significantly. It remained, as in the past, heavily dependent upon the U.S. government, from which it derived 62 percent of its sales. Sales of aircraft and related services for domestic customers—$266 million—had dwindled to only 8 percent of total sales. Foreign customers provided 30 percent of Lockheed's business, with $1.03 billion in sales. The product mix was also unchanged. Aircraft and related services amounted to 58 percent of sales, while missiles, electronics, and space earned 36 percent. Other sources, including shipbuilding, accounted for the remaining 6 percent.

Anderson and Kitchen both saw the situation as a challenge. To capitalize on its expertise and transfer it to nondefense sectors, Lockheed had to follow a tough path, denying dividends to stockholders even while plowing money into research and development and new facilities. (Dividends on common stock were not resumed until the second quarter of 1984.) This took courage of a high order for the top management. Their confidence was based upon the belief that Lockheed's strengths were transferable to other industries. This philosophy was later well expressed by the dean of Lockheed engineers, Willis M. Hawkins, who said: "The wealth of technology essential to major aerospace systems inevitably becomes a warehouse of talent for many seemingly unrelated tasks. A robot responding to the delicate motions of a human hand does not suggest a fly-by-wire plane, but the control technologies are very similar." In a parallel comment, Hawkins stated, "Searching for debris in space and creating a pure atmosphere in which to assemble optics for the Hubble Space Telescope may seem remote from the task of monitoring and correcting man-made damage to our environment, but the technologies match and they are a part of Lockheed's talent, historically nurtured by the company's commitment to research and development."

Both Anderson and Kitchen knew intuitively that there were vast new fields opening to which Lockheed could apply its talents. It was their task, along with their management team, to find them, even as they mastered the never-routine details of operating a huge company. Early in his tenure Anderson focused on strategic issues and set in motion a planning team to consider options for diversification and growth. However, outstanding debt, limited equity, and a common stock that did not yet reflect its value in the marketplace inhibited execution of their plans.

Nonetheless, important strides were made. The cities of Burbank, Glendale, and Pasadena agreed to pay Lockheed $51 million for the Hollywood-Burbank Airport, infusing capital and easing a management burden. The Trident missile was deployed on schedule in October 1979, following the most successful development flight test program in the twenty-five years of the fleet ballistic missile program. Orders were on hand for 146 Trident missiles, and the A-3 Polaris and C-3 Poseidon missiles were still being serviced and supported.

The Space Systems Division continued to generate profits on "black" programs of which the public, the stockholders, and most of Lockheed's management were (and in most instances, still are) totally unaware. Other, more visible, space contracts were picked up. The company was hard at work on SEASAT-A, an ocean survey satellite, and it played an important role in the launch of the Viking spacecraft that landed on Mars, building the shrouds that protected the spacecraft during launch.

Within the depths of the ocean, Lockheed pursued a contract for ocean thermal energy conversion (OTEC), an appealing way of deriving energy from ocean surface layers heated by the sun. The heat was used to vaporize a working fluid so that a turbine was driven to generate electricity. And, where man had contaminated the environment with an oil spill, Lockheed was ready with its "Clean Sweep" unit to scoop up the oil. More than a hundred of these devices were sold to nations all over the world.

Both OTEC and Clean Sweep typified LMSC's initiative to diversify, but both were unsuccessful because they did not couple a financially sound plan to the technology. Had Lockheed captured the worldwide market for a Clean Sweep–like device, the work would not have employed more than one hundred people. Lockheed management saw that to maintain stable employment levels at LMSC, it needed to be involved in large-scale projects. The trio of Anderson, Kitchen, and Marafino began an intensive campaign to make sure technology and finances were matched.

There were hundreds of other contracts, many for relatively small amounts. Some of these were developed into larger projects, some were merely completed and forgotten, and some clearly indicated directions in which Lockheed did not wish to go.

One of the most important challenges, scientifically, financially, and philosophically, came when LMSC was selected to build the Hubble Space Telescope, launched by the Space Shuttle in orbit more than three hundred miles above the earth's surface.

The Hubble would not be trouble-free, but as it was designed to be serviced in space, its troubles could be fixed and its capability enhanced. The Hubble's initial difficulties, in which a tiny flaw (produced and tested by a subcontractor, Perkin-Elmer) in the dimension of the lens obscured the optics, actually added to the drama of the great adventure, humanizing the great 43-foot-long space telescope. Looking back 14 billion light-years was difficult for the average layman to comprehend—astigmatism was not. When crews from the Space Shuttle conducted the repairs, the human-instrument interfaces were rightly heralded as space triumphs.

Lockheed's willingness to invest in research facilities often paid off in a surprising manner. A huge (535,000-cubic-foot) clean room had to be built for the Hubble, so that particles down to 0.5 microns (twenty-millionths of an inch) could be excluded as it was assembled and tested. Once built, the clean room (which was cleaner than any hospital's surgery by orders of magnitude) had other customers lining up to pay to use it, turning what had been a tool into a profit center.

LMSC was also deeply involved in the Space Telescope's launch vehicle, for it was making special tiles to shield the Space Shuttle from the heat of reentry, at the rate of five thousand per month. Another space first was the creation of a 105-foot-long flexible solar array wing. The device unfolded like an unending venetian blind, and was a prototype for similar arrays to be used on the space station.

During this period, the Missiles and Space Company, constantly exploiting its broad base of technology, entered the field of aeronautics in a modest way with a contract to develop a remotely piloted vehicle (RPV) for the U.S. Army. Called the Aquila (and later, TADARS), the RPV was intended to become a platform capable of performing many tactical missions. Although the contract was ultimately canceled, LMSC learned a great deal that could be applied to an increasingly important field, that of "uninhabited aerial vehicles" (UAV).

The Lockheed Electronics Company (LEC), which had not yet performed to expectations, secured a large production contract for the Mark 86 shipboard weapon control systems, to direct gun and missile firing on many of the newest surface-combat ships. LEC was never to acquire its own critical mass but served as the nucleus for a vast expansion when Sanders Associates, a first-rate electronics firm, was acquired in 1986. Lockheed proposed a "take-out bid" for Sanders, which was being pursued by Loral at the same time, and the firm subsequently became the core of a vastly expanded business. Roy Anderson was asked to survey the company and oversee its consolidation into the Lockheed fold.

All of these varied programs were straws in the wind showing the direction that Anderson and Kitchen had charted for Lockheed. They were also the vehicles by which new managers would prove themselves ready to advance further to positions of leadership within the firm.

On the aeronautic front, the usual Lockheed product line stalwarts kept the regeneration going for the remainder of the five-year period. The Hercules transports continued to sell, averaging about 36 per year, and almost 1,600 had been delivered by the end of 1979. The new C-5 wing modification was a welcome addition to the workload. A contract to modify all of the C-141s to the C-141B stretched configuration proceeded well, as did the CP-140 contract. The Japanese signed a licensing agreement for the production of forty-five P-3 aircraft, of which forty-two were to be built in Japan. The USAF came back for an improved version of the U-2, with contracts for two TR-1A aircraft and one ER-2 earth resources aircraft for the National Aeronautics and Space Administration. Twenty-four more TR-1As were later placed on contract. In a manner of interorganizational synergy that became increasingly familiar, LMSC worked on a Precision Location and Strike System (PLSS) for use with the TR-1As.

Lockheed's activities extend to many diverse areas, including development
and operation of airports. Lockheed Air Terminal, Inc. developed the
Trillium terminal, in Toronto.

Two often overlooked elements of the aeronautic group, the
Lockheed Aircraft Service (LAS) Company and the Lockheed Air Terminal (LAT) continued to contribute to the bottom line.

LAS had its roots in the facilities set up in England during World
War II to assemble and modify aircraft. Established in 1946 as a
wholly-owned subsidiary to service and modify Lockheed and other
aircraft, LAS began in 1958 to produce flight data recorders, and by
1979 had manufactured more than three thousand of them for airline
service. A far more important portion of its business was conducted
in the deepest secrecy, preparing "black" aircraft modifications for air
force aircraft, primarily special versions of the C-130 for the Special
Forces. It also managed service and maintenance facilities overseas.

The Lockheed Air Terminal supported commercial airlines with refueling and servicing at twenty-five airports in the United States and abroad. LAT and LAS were augmented in the Aerospace Support Group by contracts with several foreign governments, including Saudi Arabia, Greece, Iran, Taiwan, and others. Saudi Arabia proved to be an exceptionally valuable customer, with Lockheed selling its C-130s, then providing the training and maintenance necessary for their up-keep. Lockheed also was a substantial partner in the Saudi Arabian Ground Environment Program (GEP), which encompassed the radar systems used for defense and for traffic control.

The Agony of the TriStar

Despite these aeronautical successes, the L-1011 still hung like an albatross around Lockheed's neck. Although it held only slight promise for a future return, the program had to be continued to meet commitments to customers and suppliers, and brave statements were made in annual reports and in advertisements. It was truly a remarkable aircraft, with a very high in-service rate, averaging as high as 98.1 percent reliability. Already a technology leader, it was improved with the addition of its extended wing and active aileron controls, coupled to a new Flight Management System. However, even when things picked up, as when thirty firm orders were received in 1979, other problems intervened. Production costs went up when raw materials and parts were difficult to obtain, and skilled manpower was scarce. The relentless annual program losses were debilitating, ranging from $94 million in 1975 to $199 million in 1979, and totaling $646 million for the five-year period. Over that same period, Lockheed's net earnings from all other operations were less than half that amount—$264.4 million.

Timing the seemingly inevitable production shutdown for the L-1011 was crucial, for not only were customers with priced options involved, but also suppliers, the banks, the stock market, and, most important of all, the employees. Lockheed's management, particularly Anderson, Marafino, and Dick Taylor, the L-1011 program manager, continually weighed all of the factors, looking for a window of op-portunity when the line could be shut down at the lowest overall cost. During the entire process they hoped in vain for means to revive the program.

1980–1984

Lockheed sales had first broken the $1 billion level in 1959. It required seven years before they exceeded $2 billion and eight before reaching the $3 billion mark in 1974, where they remained until 1978. In 1979, the $4 billion level was breached, and in 1980, sales exceeded $5.3 billion—33 percent more than the previous year.

These were heady numbers—but profit in 1980 had dropped to $28 million, less than half that of 1979, in large part due to the $199 million lost on the TriStar program. A $28 million profit on more than $5.3 billion in sales and $2.5 billion in assets was, to put it kindly, trivial, and it had to be improved.

Despite this, by 1980 Lockheed was in an excellent position, one marked by the advent of a new, modernized logo, which reflected the high technology of the future, linked to the familiar winged star of the past. The company was the sole prime contractor for fleet ballistic missiles, for fixed-wing antisubmarine-warfare aircraft, and for all strategic-airlift aircraft. It dominated intelligence-gathering with the SR-71 and U-2 series aircraft and with the long line of surveillance satellites that were too secret for their names or even their project numbers to be revealed.

Thus it might have been easy for Anderson to be a little easy on himself, to milk the existing contracts for profits and pay out dividends to make stockholders more content. He chose not to do so. Instead, he remained committed to finding new products and to investing millions in research and development, and plant and equipment additions. These expenditures were difficult to explain to shareholders who wanted dividends paid, and promptly; it required both tact and courage to pursue this course. The steady adherence to both R and D expenditures and investment in new facilities would bear fruit over the next five years.

The course Lockheed followed laid the ground for important future work in antiballistic missile defenses with the Homing Overlay Experiment (HOE) contract for the Army, intended to see if incoming nuclear warheads could be destroyed by a "silver bullet" direct hit rather than by defensive nuclear warhead explosions. This successful experiment was coupled with leading-edge technology in optics and precision pointing and tracking systems developed in the Palo Alto Research Labs, and enabled Lockheed to be a major contractor when

The Homing Overlay Experiment demonstrated the ability to defend against incoming intercontinental ballistic missiles on June 10, 1984, at the Kwajalein Missile Range. A HOE interceptor missile destroyed an ICBM launched from Vandenberg Air Force Base, California.

the highly controversial Strategic Defense Initiative was announced by the Reagan administration.

Lockheed was also dealing with environmental issues, broadening the scope of its technology to include large-scale experiments with solar energy and in extracting energy and minerals from the ocean floor.

As a part of the wide technological net Anderson and Kitchen were casting, Lockheed enthusiastically embraced the computer revolution. Unlike some companies, in which a management intimidated by technology often paid only lip service to the advent of computers, Lockheed management saw to it that computers were used internally to a maximum degree. It also created the Computer-graphics Augmented Design and Manufacturing system (CADAM), which became the focal point for all activities involving development, design, manufacture, and assembly of products. CADAM would be continually refined and extended, and would be adopted by companies all over the world. Lockheed also emphasized software development for use internally and for sale. The sophisticated software for Lockheed's DIALOG information retrieval system made it into the largest on-line system in the world.

These two developments in particular demonstrate the technical and financial acumen of Lockheed's top management. Anderson and Kitchen would allow Lockheed to investigate such product lines, spend the necessary money to develop them, and raise them to a profitable status. And then, if it turned out that these lines no longer complemented Lockheed's main thrust, they would be sold—as CADAM and DIALOG ultimately were.

Under Anderson's leadership Lockheed created multiple product lines that were both closely focused and highly profitable. Not all initiatives succeeded, and over the next decade, management showed an even swifter disposition to cut costs when things were not going well.

Despite the rush of expansion and the new frontiers being explored, the issue of ethical management was not forgotten. Larry Kitchen relates a story of a later competition for an antisubmarine-warfare contract. Lockheed was proposing an advanced version of the Orion, called the P-7. In the course of the negotiations, Kitchen became aware that a Lockheed employee had come into possession of the competitor's proposal, which contained all the preliminary details of their entry's performance and pricing. Kitchen immediately called the Secretary of the Navy, and in a face-to-face meeting told him the whole story and offered to drop out of the competition. The Navy did not think Lockheed's possession of the document had contaminated the case, and the competitor's CEO agreed—and complimented Kitchen on his honesty. (The P-7 project was later canceled when it became apparent that it would be too costly and not a sufficient advance over the P-3.)

Cutting the Gordian Garrote

When the time was right, Anderson, Kitchen, and Marafino had the courage to bite the bullet on the L-1011. This was an extremely emotional issue, as Lockheed had always viewed itself as a prime supplier of premier airliners, and it was difficult to abandon the field. On December 7, 1981, Anderson, with the support of Kitchen and Marafino, decided to phase out L-1011 operations. Their decision was based on the depressed sales of wide-body transports in general (a downturn of 50 percent in 1981) and the gloomy projection that the L-1011 could not be produced at a profitable rate before 1986. The company had built up sufficient equity to absorb the onetime loss, and had reestablished its credit rating so that it would be feasible to borrow, if necessary. The number of workers laid off was reduced by the need to provide continued support and spare parts for customers operating the L-1011.

The program cancellation in late 1981 resulted in a net loss of $289 million for the year, but was a genuine epiphany for the corporation. Free at last from the continuing struggle with the TriStar, the company now clearly saw the way to the future with new technologies that would make it increasing powerful, with greater sales and greater profits. The change was duly noted in the stock market. Those who had invested at the 1975 low of $3.75 were happy to see the market hit a high of $84.25 in 1982. It was just the beginning of an upward spiral.

Both Anderson and Marafino were financial experts whose vision and energy matched the technological genius of the top Lockheed engineers, and whose efforts were equally necessary to the corporation's progress. They made decisions that resulted in long-term debt being reduced even as shareholder equity rose. The L-1011 losses had reduced equity to $105 million, but it rose sharply thereafter, adding more than one billion in equity in three years to reach $1.152 billion by 1984. It was a stunning fiscal achievement, one accompanied by the carefully planned change in a mix of business.

Lockheed continually reorganized over the years, and the phaseout of the TriStar permitted a restructuring of the corporation in 1981 into four groups. It also saw the first year in which aircraft and related services were not the primary source of sales by the company. In 1981, the Aircraft and Related Services Group had sales of $1.9 billion, or thirty-seven percent of total sales. The Missiles, Space and Electronics Group had moved to the forefront, with sales of $2.5 billion, a forty-seven percent share. The Aerospace Support Group fell sharply to twelve percent of sales, with $600 million in business, while the Shipbuilding and Other Group fell to $200 million and 4 percent of sales. There would be other changes of focus in the future, but the Missiles, Space and Electronics Group would compete with the Aeronautics Group to remain in the forefront of Lockheed's activities.

The Reagan Years

Like all defense contractors, Lockheed benefited from the huge defense spending of the early years of the Reagan administration. The conversion of the StarLifter fleet to the C-141B configuration was completed on a $450 million contract. The firm experienced considerable satisfaction in fixing the C-5A's wing problem with a $1.2

billion modification program that was finished on schedule and proved to be profitable.

Larry Kitchen took up residency in Washington for several months, to counter Boeing's effort to sell the military cargo version of the 747 in place of the C-5B. He launched a superlative campaign based on undeniable facts to show that the C-5B could serve the USAF better than the modified 747. Aided by Richard Cook, vice president of Lockheed's Washington office, and backed up by a stream of data from the Georgia Company, Kitchen visited numerous senators and representatives, as well as DOD and USAF officials. He told a convincing story, armed with factual charts and handouts, keeping Anderson informed all the while of his progress and frustrations. The final result was a $7 billion contract for fifty aircraft. These were delivered in a brilliant manner, on schedule and under budget, providing a healing contrast to the turmoil of the original C-5A contract.

The C-5Bs are a perfect illustration of the effect that managers trained at the Lockheed Missiles and Space Company came to have upon the aeronautical sector. Ken Cannestra came to Lockheed-Georgia in 1983 and became president in 1986. He was appalled that aircraft were being completed with fifteen or twenty "squawks," or defects, per airplane. The Georgia people tried to explain to him that airplanes were different than missiles, and that an average of only fifteen defects per aircraft was good work. Cannestra responded that on a missile, you could have only zero defects, because once launched, you couldn't bring it back for repairs. He then insisted that the Georgia aircraft goal also be zero defects, and promptly heard himself being referred to as "this quack from California."

He began a rigorous process of quality control called TQIP—Total Quality Improvement Program—in an attempt to bring aircraft quality control efforts to the level of those required for spacecraft. A case in point was the mating of the tail section of the C-5B to the fuselage. The bolts that secured the tail section in place had a large tolerance, and a range of shims were available to make the fit. The concept of a shim instead of a precision fit enraged Cannestra; he shut down the production line and had his engineers examine all the steps where errors could occur, and where a "lap error" or cumulative error could build up. Over the protests of the air force, the workforce, and Burbank, he kept the line shut down for fourteen days while the problems were sorted out. When the line was started again, the tail section would drop into place and be bolted in with no shims at all.

The Trident II missile, the sixth generation of Fleet Ballistic Missiles, began development, and although it encountered problems in its initial underwater launches, it proved to be the most reliable of all the fleet ballistic missile family. Its production should extend to the next century, providing a steady inflow of funds.

MILSTAR has been discussed in a previous chapter, but a second new line of business was an equally remarkable coup. LMSC beat out the incumbent contractor, Rockwell International, to secure the contract to manage all ground processing of the space shuttle fleet at the Kennedy Space Center in Florida. Lockheed also participated in the Air Force activation of Vandenberg Air Force Base for shuttle operations. The space shuttle ground-processing contracts had a potential $6 billion value, and positioned Lockheed for an even closer association with NASA.

Two contracts of lesser dollar value but of immense technological importance stemmed from the Strategic Defense Initiative (SDI), President Reagan's plan to defend against ICBM attack. (SDI) met with fierce opposition and was unfairly and pejoratively termed "Star Wars" by the media. The Defense Advanced Research Projects Agency (DARPA) awarded two contracts to Lockheed for the demonstration of space-laser programs. The intent was to develop the technologies necessary to make directed-energy antiballistic missile defense systems possible. One contract was for Talon Gold, an orbital acquisition, pointing, and tracking experiment. The second was for LODE, a classified ground-based experiment to develop and demonstrate beam control concepts for laser weapon systems. These programs, parallelling the the work on the army's Homing Overlay Experiment, placed Lockheed at the forefront of space weapons technology. (The HOE would demonstrate its capability on June 10, 1984, when it tracked and located an unarmed ballistic missile warhead 100 miles above the Pacific Ocean and destroyed it with a direct impact velocity of 20,000 mph.) And although SDI would run into media opposition and legislative trouble, Lockheed learned much that would assist it in later contracts.

The advent of extremely sophisticated systems posed a difficult problem to government agencies that were unable to pay the salaries necessary to attract workers with high-level skills. The result was a trend toward subcontracting highly specialized services to industry, and Lockheed's diversification efforts were enhanced by providing such services to both the military and NASA. And, despite apprehensions about the difficulty of transferring research, development, production, and managerial methods learned under government contracts to private industry, Lockheed found that in the realm of high technology, it could provide services not obtainable elsewhere to commercial companies. As an example, the Michigan Bell and New York Telephone companies entered into contracts with Lockheed for audio response equipment.

Earnings reached $344 million in 1984, the third consecutive record since the TriStar had been stopped. Anderson was pleased with the record earnings and sales. Earnings benefited by the decrease in interest expense as debt declined and interest rates decreased. They also felt confident that Lockheed's current ascendancy in space would be maintained, for the company had the edge over all competitors in four vital areas: thermal and attitude control, data management, communications, and tracking.

The Marine Systems Group continued to supply conventional ships with high-technology features such as the USS *Whidbey Island,* a new LSD-41 class of amphibious support ship, but was also breaking new ground investigating small waterplane-area twin-hull (SWATH) ships. The SWATH ships were extremely stable and versatile, able to perform as ferries, cutters, or oceanographic/hydrographic research vessels. The SWATH configuration would emerge again in the *Sea Shadow,* a stealth technology vehicle.

The *Sea Shadow* was a very advanced vessel, sponsored by DARPA. LMSC approached its design and construction as it did missiles and satellites, and the ship was built faster and at lower cost, and could be operated with a much smaller crew. In conventional shipbuilding, a frame is built, and equipment is jammed into it. With the LMSC philosophy, the ship is designed from the mission point of view and the ship's shell is molded to accommodate the required equipment.

The stealthy *Sea Shadow* worked well, but it apparently presented the Navy with some institutional problems and was rejected. Araki maintains that the *Sea Shadow* construction philosophy and techniques could be used to advantage throughout the Navy's construction program. When DARPA studied the construction of the new arsenal ship, the *Sea Shadow* was used as a paradigm.

A new organization, Lockheed Corporation International, was formed to seek new markets for established products abroad and to explore new product opportunities. And, building on the extensive efforts made in the past, Lockheed increased its investment in new plants and equipment and in research and development to the level of $900 million a year. The previous investments in these areas had per-

The stealthy *Sea Shadow* was not only a dramatic new shape for Navy ships, but featured radical new techniques in construction and in operation. Here it emerges from the secret housing in the Hughes Mining Barge.

mitted the development of opportunities in computer systems and software for both the military and civil markets. At the same time, the entire management team engaged in a massive effort to lower costs throughout the corporation. Lockheed leadership was determined to grow big—but not fat.

As a sad postscript to this period, the company was rocked by a stunning loss when Mr. and Mrs. Courtlandt Gross were savagely murdered on July 15, 1982. Their housekeeper was also killed in what appeared to be an interrupted burglary. Gross had been Lockheed's chairman from 1961 to 1967, and remained a member of the board until 1977. He had fostered the growth of the company, and was well liked and respected by his fellow Lockheedians.

1985–1989

Roy Anderson's career at Lockheed paralleled the blossoming of the space age. He joined Lockheed in October 1956, a year before *Sputnik*. Over the next twenty-nine years, he would contribute his all to the firm, and see its sales grow from $742 million to more than $9.5 billion. After retiring in December 1985, after a nine-year term

Roy Anderson was one of the
most widely admired Lockheed
executives. His friendly manner,
and his ability to orchestrate
large company efforts, made him
the linchpin of Lockheed's
spectacular recovery.

as chairman and CEO, he would remain on the board through 1990, and then become chairman, emeritus. He still provides insight and information to the firm.

Beyond these successes, Anderson's years of leadership and service as chairman set a course and confirmed a culture for Lockheed that served as an underlying basis for Lockheed that still lives on. His ability to identify leaders, his openness and accessibility, his patience and willingess to listen, his foresight and vision to see the value and potential in Lockheed's assets—employees, technologies, and products—and his unwavering dedication created a new Lockheed, one that its founders would have been proud of. Anderson was the right man at the right time, and in Marafino's words, "he was a role model for many, enormously capable and credible, and with a wit and personality that are unmatched. He was everyone's friend."

Kitchen succeeded Anderson as chairman of the board and chief executive officer, while Robert A. Fuhrman, one of Lockheed's stalwarts, was designated president and chief operating officer. Fuhrman, a technical genius, had been Kitchen's mentor at Georgia, and the two men worked well together.

Kitchen, who had been president for ten years, started his three-year term as chairman and CEO at a happy time; 1985 was the fourth consecutive year that Lockheed had reported record earnings, with net earnings up 17 percent, to $401 million. A less driven executive might

Larry Kitchen served as both president and chairman of Lockheed, and was instrumental in creating some of the most important deals in the company's history.

have been satisfied with the status quo, for Lockheed had no fewer than 250 space-related contracts, including those for the important MILSTAR and shuttle processing programs. More mature programs such as the Trident II, the Space Telescope, and the C-5B were going well, and under wraps was the highly classified venture, the F-117A stealth fighter.

But Kitchen was not inclined to accept the expenditure of almost $3 billion in research, development, and facility funds to run in place; he was interested in exotic fields that included space surveillance, military communication satellites, advanced defense electronic systems, large space-astronomy platforms, and advanced missile technology. These were being vigorously pursued by the Missiles and Space Group and the Electronic System Group. The aeronautic side was not neglected, with emerging programs that included the advanced tactical fighter, tactical airlift aircraft, reconnaissance planes, and the aerospace plane, which in time would receive the catchy but inappropriate label of "the Orient Express." The aerospace plane was intended to fly in space like the shuttle, but carry its fuel internally, and take off and land from conventional runways. It was too great a reach for Lockheed, but especially for the Congress, and was ultimately canceled.

All of these programs would be characterized by uncertainty, long lead times, and high development costs. In the following years, a new and disturbing element would emerge that would make Lockheed more cautious in accepting defense contracts. The Department of Defense, sensing the inevitable decline in appropriations, began to ask contractors to "cost-share" development contracts. They were also asked to absorb other added risks, and at the same time were refused the opportunity to gain commensurate rewards. In essence, the government told contractors, "If you are serious about getting business, you will have to invest in development programs, even though your costs will never be recovered if you are not selected as the competition winner." Like the ill-fated Total Package Procurement concept, the ostensible purpose was to "cut the fat" from contracts. The real result was to cut margins, sometimes to the vanishing point. The process was sobering, one that led contractors to team wherever possible, even though teaming carried implicit hazards of coordination and of sharing proprietary information.

During August 1986 Lockheed Corporate headquarters moved from the rather small and crowded building at Burbank to new quarters at Calabasas, California. Hawkins remembers, with some glee, that an unheralded advantage of this move was that the California Company was now separated by many miles from corporate headquarters, and CALAC presidents could now run the company without corporate talent surging through the swinging doors to "help."

The air force chose Lockheed as one of the two companies to compete in the first phase of the advanced tactical fighter (ATF), which in time would become the F-22. The ATF was an example of the fruit borne from significant R & D spending in previous years. Sherman Mullin, who would later head the Skunk Works, was in charge of the ATF program, and would do an incredible job in the face of extreme challenges and extraordinary competition. Mullin was supported by the beloved Ben Rich at the Skunk Works and by versatile Dick Heppe of the Lockheed California Company. As previously noted, James "Micky" Blackwell would share honors with Mullin in winning the F-22 competition.

In August, Lockheed augmented its Electronics Group with the acquisition of Sanders Associates, a New Hampshire firm that was expert in the electronic countermeasures used by all four armed services, and in computer graphics. Sanders had provided equipment installed in the Viking antisubmarine-warfare aircraft, and an excellent working relationship had developed. Part of Sanders's appeal was its management's uncompromising attitude toward technical excellence and leadership. The primary reason for the acquisition, however, was the perception that the defense electronics market was growing at a faster rate than the defense budget itself. Lockheed's strategy embraced payloads as well as platforms, and this acquisition was a significant step forward. In addition, Sanders's CalComp division manufactured computers, plotters, digitizers, and graphic display terminals, and thus fit neatly into Lockheed's rapidly expanding information system programs.

Larry Kitchen called Roy Anderson back from retirement to transition Sanders into Lockheed, and after five months Val Peline was selected as president of Sanders and Lockheed Electronics Company. Eventually Peline merged the existing Lockheed Electronics Company into Sanders. He threw himself into his usual hectic routine, and along with the Sanders team, made it into a profitable and successful acquisition, one which moved Lockheed into the vital defense electronics marketplace. Lockheed had come a long way from the days when it was merely a provider of platforms; it had embraced the electronics industry with both arms and would move to expand its market share.

Still, not all development efforts led to immediate success, sometimes for technical and sometimes for political reasons. The success with the Homing Overlay Experiment had resulted in a $493 million contract for the SDI program to validate the technology for the ERIS (Exoatmospheric Reentry vehicle Interceptor Subsystem). ERIS, although providing an immense amount of knowledge, would ultimately have to be put on hold as the SDI program itself was dismantled. In another contractor teaming effort, Lockheed was the prime contractor, with Hughes, IBM, and Honeywell as associates, to build a Boost Surveillance and Tracking System (BSTS). The system was to detect a ballistic missile attack by detecting the launch of enemy vehicles.

A New Era Begins

Larry Kitchen stepped down in 1988, after serving ten years as president and chief operating officer and three as chairman and chief executive officer. During these years, Lockheed had been reinvented, changing from a company dominated by aeronautical systems to one dominated by space, missiles, defense electronics, and computer activities. He was succeeded by Daniel M. Tellep as chairman and chief executive. Bob Fuhrman became vice chairman and chief operating officer, while Vince Marafino was named vice chairman and chief financial and administrative officer. As Lockheed grew, the financial considerations in large contracts became almost as complex as the engineering aspects, and Marafino's role became increasingly important.

Kitchen went out with a bang, for the last year of his stewardship was the best to date in the company's history, with net earnings of $624 million, including nearly $200 million from the sale of assets, and $10.4 billion in sales. The shareholders' equity, a scanty $75 million in 1975, had risen to just under $2.5 billion.

But there were major problems brewing. The fixed-price development contract for the P-7 antisubmarine-warfare aircraft was in trouble, and a hostile suitor began accumulating large blocks of Lockheed stock.

The new chairman, Tellep, had a quiet, reserved persona that belied his inner fire; he was determined to make Lockheed the best company in the industry. A graduate of the University of California at Berkeley, he earned his bachelor's and master's degrees in mechanical engineering in 1954 and 1955, respectively. He began his career at Lockheed in 1955 as a principal scientist for the very productive X-17 missile reentry flight experiments, a remarkably responsible position for a twenty-four-year-old newcomer. Being on the cutting edge of missile reentry systems, a new discipline that was just coming into enormous demand by the Department of Defense, stood him in good stead, and he was quickly promoted to manage other programs dealing with this field of expertise. He worked on Fleet Ballistic Missile programs for over twenty years, learning much about program management from the typically strong leadership of the Missile Systems Division. He rose to the position of vice president of LMSC's Advanced System Division in 1975, became president of LMSC in 1984, and was named president of the Missiles and Space Systems Group in 1986.

His achievements at LMSC clearly forecast his future success as chairman. In his first year as president of LMSC in 1984, sales increased by almost $700 million to $3.4 billion, representing 41 percent of Lockheed's total sales. In his last full year as head of LMSC, sales had increased to $4.6 billion. Perhaps more important, he brought new kinds of business to LMSC, including the critical C³I (Command, Control, Communications and Intelligence) programs in which, unbeknownst to any but the most prescient, the future of warfare lay.

Tellep soon put his own imprint as chairman on Lockheed by introducing a general restructuring in April 1989, one that took into account an expected 2 to 5 percent annual decline in defense spending.

Tellep's appraisal of the business balance showed that in the future, at least 50 percent of sales would come from space and missiles, 30 percent from commercial and foreign sales and only 20 percent from aeronautical systems. Four major aircraft production programs, including the C-5, TR-1, F-117 and P3, had been phased out. Lockheed's airplane business was in difficulty and presented a severe challenge.

The new structure called for a Missiles and Space Systems Group (MSSG), an Aeronautical Systems Group (ASG), an Electronic Systems Group (ESG), and a totally new division, the Technology Services Group (TSG). Each would be given a new role in the corporation.

In an unusual departure from Lockheed's strong tradition of promoting only longtime company personnel whenever possible, Tellep and the board of directors selected a relative newcomer, John N. McMahon, to become group president of Missiles and Space Systems and president of the Lockheed Missiles and Space Company. McMahon had enjoyed a brilliant career with the Central Intelligence Agency, where, in 1982, he was appointed by President Reagan to become deputy director. In the CIA, he had often interfaced with Lockheed products, most notably the U-2 and the CORONA project. (As previously noted, he escorted Gary Powers during the clandestine exchange for the Soviet agent Abel.) In a recent interview, he stated that he had always been determined not to enter industry after his retirement from the CIA, but rather to establish a firm of his own. Despite the wealth of talent within LMSC, Tellep had been impressed by McMahon over the years, and persuaded him to join Lockheed in 1986 as vice president, plans and programs, at the Missiles and Space Systems Group. McMahon's persona is totally unlike the standard image of a CIA executive; open and courteous, with a great sense of humor, he has an avuncular quality which masked his hard-driving management style.

The Aeronautical Systems Group, headed since 1988 by Ken Cannestra, was realigned to create the Lockheed Aeronautical Systems Group. Relocated to Marietta, Georgia, from Burbank, it consisted of the Lockheed Aeronautical Systems Company in Marietta, the Lockheed Advanced Development Company (aka the Skunk Works) in Palmdale, and the Lockheed Aircraft Services Company in Ontario, California.

The new Technical Services Group, headed by Donald C. Jones, was a major move outside the bounds of previous Lockheed business experience. Jones had been a strong leader, and continued to demonstrate his prowess. More than half of TSG's work was for NASA,

John McMahon, long an
important figure in CIA
operations, became an effective
and popular leader at LMSC.

which repeatedly recognized Lockheed's efficiency in space shuttle processing with formal awards, including the coveted and rarely given NASA Excellence Award. The space shuttle processing contract and the refurbishment of Vandenberg Air Force Base to support Titan IV/Centaur launches constituted the bulk of TSG's effort, but environmental remedial programs were targeted to the tune of contracts valued at $5 billion over the next several years. In Toronto, TSG led as Lockheed became an equity partner and operator of the world's first privatized airport terminal, the Lester B. Pearson International Airport.

Because it was evident that new aircraft starts would be both fewer in number and separated by longer intervals, a decision was made to increase Lockheed's investment in commercial aircraft modification and repair centers. A new facility was built in Tucson, Arizona, to maintain older commercial aircraft such as the Boeing 707 and 727. (For some airline business diehards, there was a bitter irony in Lockheed's opening a repair facility for Boeing aircraft.). Another such facility, similar in scope and purpose, would be opened the following year at Norton Air Force Base, in San Bernardino, California, to repair 747s. These excursions into the field of airliner repair proved to be ill timed when a downturn in commercial airline operations took place, and both operations were ultimately phased out.

Val Peline led the Electronic Systems Group, which was engaged in the most rapidly changing competitive market that Lockheed faced. Peline had been a major figure in Lockheed's cost-cutting program, reducing his work force by 33 percent and electing to concentrate resources in a few major areas, particularly advanced avionics. ESG was particularly important in the F-22 competition. It provided the radar and missile warning capabilities, the cockpit control display systems, mission planning and automated test equipment—in essence the electronic heart of the fighter's combat capabilities.

As these new organizations were taking shape, the combined corporate sales declined in 1989 to $9.9 billion, and net revenues melted away to a mere $2 million. There were many reasons, but the most important were write-offs that had to be taken on fixed-price programs—the bane of a defense contractor. The tight pricing originally negotiated proved disastrous when the business base declined and higher production costs were encountered. The Aeronautical Systems Group had to absorb a $300 million write-off on the ill-starred P-7 antisubmarine-warfare aircraft program. At the same time, the advanced tactical fighter competition demanded a continued high level of investment.

In an effort to cut costs, Tellep made one of the most difficult, psychologically demanding decisions of his career when he authorized the movement of operations from Burbank to the more efficient facilities built for the L-1011 at Palmdale, as well as those at Rye Canyon, California, and Marietta, Georgia. News of this decision reverberated like thunder through the company—Lockheed leaving Burbank was like General Motors leaving Detroit. Many were horrified that the great tradition of immortal aircraft flying first from Burbank runways would come to an end. It was a terribly emotional issue at every level, and an enormous amount of attention had to be paid to worker concerns about the move.

Tellep went personally to the Burbank, Palmdale, and Rye Canyon facilities to explain the painful logic of the decision to the employees. In one huge hangar he met with some two thousand workers, their mood ranging between sadness and anger. Tellep's natural distress was relieved only slightly when, after one of his talks, a few employees approached him and said they understood that something had to be done.

Financially, it was an easy decision to make. There was no production going on at Burbank, where Lockheed owned the facilities and

Despite his quiet demeanor, Daniel M. Tellep proved himself to be a fighter when it became necessary to defend Lockheed against an unfriendly takeover attempt. As chairman of the board, Tellep used an expert team to lead Lockheed to its peak in the industry.

had to undertake their increasingly costly maintenance. In contrast, two-thirds of the facility in Marietta was owned by the government and only leased by Lockheed, greatly easing maintenance costs.

Ken Cannestra of Lockheed Aeronautical Systems Company originated the idea of moving aircraft production to Georgia, and sold Tellep on the concept. He recalls that many protested the move, but about eight hundred employees transferred, and fortunately, almost all of them fell in love with the Atlanta area. Cannestra, lean and fit, proved to be exactly what Lockheed-Georgia needed to move it from the days of Haughton's autocracy to a plant capable of manufacturing the most advanced fighter in the world.

1990–1995

Tellep's reticence belied his strong control of the company over the seven years of his tenure as chairman, a period that saw the end of the Cold War, with all its adverse consequences for defense business. Lockheed had to transition its space activities from a Cold War status in which it monitored existing treaties and verified national capabilities to a situation in which space had a primary value in gathering and controlling information. President Bush and Secretary of Defense Richard Cheney made an almost immediate cut of $50 billion in defense spending. First John McMahon and then Sam Araki led Lockheed's response at LMSC, cutting back proportionately more than the defense cuts, and reinventing LMSC to compete for civilian business. As will be shown, this included moving aggressively to the Iridium satellite system, remote sensing, and commercial arrangements with firms in the former Soviet Union, including the previously mentioned relationship with Khrunichev and Energia.

Baptism of Fire

In 1990, Tellep had to endure what he termed his "baptism of fire," the first of two attempts at a hostile takeover by a Texas investor. In the process, Tellep traded his reserve for a heroic gunfighter image, ready to shoot it out at the board of directors corral. He rallied the employees and the shareholders to fight sharp, no-holds-barred battles against a man they regarded as a predator.

The wealthy Dallas investor, billionaire Harold C. Simmons, operated under the name of his company, NL Industries, which owned less than 19 percent of Lockheed stock. Simmons had a reputation both as a raider and as a man whose tactics could revitalize moribund companies. Lockheed assumed that his intention was to acquire control and then terminate the company's pension plan, using the resulting $1.5 billion surplus to reduce the cost of acquisition. This of course struck at the heart of the Lockheed family, and Tellep, Marafino, and the rest of Lockheed's top management were determined to prevent Simmons's taking control.

It was not easy. Simmons maintained initially that he was just an interested investor. In time, his aides let it be known that his intent was to retain Lockheed's core businesses and sell off all nondefense ventures, thus reversing the strategy that Tellep was pursuing. In early 1990, Simmons struck. He sought out disgruntled investors, filed a lawsuit, and demanded six seats on the Lockheed board. He began a proxy fight, saying that he intended to file his own slate of fifteen directors for the Lockheed board. Some institutional investors wavered, and for a time it looked as if he might win. But Tellep traveled across the country incessantly to rally investors to his side. Vince Marafino, the financial architect of so many of Lockheed's major decisions, and the board of directors worked ceaselessly with Tellep, as did Lockheed's new vice president of investor relations, Walt Skowronski. One of their major gambits was the creation of an employee stock ownership plan that had the effect of making a takeover less attractive.

Tellep, Marafino, and the entire management team had genuine concerns that Simmons might succeed in taking over Lockheed, and a polling firm showed that the vote might be precariously close. For a number of months the management worked seven days a week, dividing time between running the company and fighting the proxy battle. Lockheed's board of directors was deeply involved, and special meetings and telephone conferences kept its members apprised of developments on a weekly basis.

To cut down on the time Simmons had to solicit votes, Tellep advanced the date of the annual stockholders' meeting by five weeks, to March 29, 1990. He asked Anderson and Kitchen to help keep the employees informed. When the results of the voting were officially announced at the subsequent April 16 meeting, Tellep and his board had won a clear victory, with Simmons getting less than 37 percent of the vote.

Simmons was hurt, for he had bought in at a high price. A year later, he began the takeover process again, this time demanding three seats on Lockheed's board of directors. (Some maintained that his actions were not so much a genuine takeover attempt as they were a ploy to bolster Lockheed's stock prices so that he could bail out without too great a loss.) He had clearly underestimated the Lockheed management, which was now battle-hardened and in the fight to win. A genuine crusader in the cause of the Lockheed family, Tellep was certain that Simmons intended to loot the pension fund and would probably sell off the company in pieces. To prevent Simmons's gaining control, he had prepared well, leading a corporation-wide cost-cutting exercise. He pared down the workforce from 82,500 to 73,000, and transferred expensive California work to Georgia. Sales were maintained at just under $10 billion and net earnings were $335 million. Wall Street gauged the future for Lockheed and found it positive, sending the stock up 9 points to top out at 41 by the time of the annual stockholders' meeting.

It was too much for Simmons, who ended his proxy fight by selling 12 million of his 12.5 million shares, and taking a $42 million loss. This was a time when one issue—the potential takeover of Lockheed—touched all employees. The sense of family mentioned earlier was never stronger, and during the two years of proxy battles, one could sense a palpable cohesiveness throughout the corporation. With the exception of a handful of employees, no one wanted to lose Lockheed to a Texas raider.

The victory was sweet for Tellep and his team. He had been responsible for many highly successful programs, and he had guided a major company to great successes, but these were less personal triumphs. The fight with Simmons had reached him at a visceral level, and he had enjoyed the brutally hard but exhilarating challenge of outthinking and outworking his formidable opponent.

The tough two years of the Simmons fight had been offset by other, very productive developments. Lockheed's tradition of funding research and development combined with an aggressive sales and marketing program to win contract after contract. In 1990, production programs were complemented by no less than 625 customer-funded R & D contracts, with a total value of $3.8 billion. The Strategic Defense Initiative's Boost Surveillance and Tracking System, which was still in the competitive stage, had evolved into the Air Force's Advanced Warning System (AWS), later called SBIRS, which had a potential value of $7 billion over twenty years. An entire suite of national security space programs had evolved, led by the MILSTAR satellite program, which offered so much promise for the future in terms of both science and economics, and which would lead to a later commercial venture.

Each program was still charged with drama, and none more so than ERIS, which offered promise of an antiballistic missile defense. ERIS intercepted a dummy ICBM warhead on its first flight, an event described as a "bullet hitting a bullet."

And as new programs came into being, old programs flourished. Incredibly, given the short time in which it had been conceived and the pressures under which it had been born, the fleet ballistic missile program celebrated its thirty-fifth anniversary by continuing to be a smashing success. The creation of the Polaris system and its subsequent deployment has been called a miracle of technical and management judgment by the government, under William F. Raborn and Levering Smith, and by Lockheed, led by Burriss, Fuhrman, and Hawkins. The other ballistic missile systems lived up to the Polaris example, and the Navy happily made the maximum incentive awards for these highly classified programs.

In other areas, the integration of Sanders was going well, and that company was providing an advanced electronic suite for Lockheed's single most important future project, the F-22, which had a potential of $30 billion in sales over the next twenty years. And, like the fable of the salt mill and the sea, the "black" programs continued to generate revenue in an endless stream.

There were huge achievements and new contracts on the civil side, as well. On April 25, 1990, the Hubble Space Telescope was deployed at long last from the Space Shuttle *Discoverer*. Although difficulties were encountered with the Perkin-Elmer mirror, NASA considered Lockheed's work so efficient that it awarded 97 percent of the maximum fee possible. Contracts were received for work on Space Station *Freedom*, and the first studies were undertaken on NASA's proposed "Mission to Planet Earth Program" and on the "Space Exploration Initiative," the latter calling for manned bases on the moon and Mars by the year 2020. Large contracts were also won for computer integration work in the nondefense government sector.

The year 1991 had a triple distinction: the final victory over Simmons, winning the F-22 competition against a very tough competitor, and the magnificent showing made by Lockheed products during the Gulf War. The intelligence-gathering, meteorological, and communications satellites to which Lockheed had contributed so much were not only indispensable, they forecast the future. The most compelling television broadcasts in history showed how the bombing of Baghdad had been spearheaded by individual flights of Lockheed F-117As, weaving their way through a seemingly impenetrable hail of fire. Less visible, but equally important, were the contributions of the C-5s, C-141s, and C-130s. No less than nine types of Lockheed aircraft operated in the theater, including U-2s, TR-1As, SA-3s, Italian Air Force F-104s, and Royal Air Force L-1011 tankers. One would like to think that the Gross brothers, Kelly Johnson, and all the other Lockheed greats who had taken their last flight were looking down on this remarkable and satisfying showing.

Once Simmons's second takeover attempt was squelched, Tellep explored other possibilities for expansion.

A Call from Fort Worth

The dissolution of the Soviet Union had a traumatic psychological effect upon the defense industry that exceeded the actual financial effects of the reductions in defense spending. Companies that had already experienced some difficulties, or did not feel they had the resources to develop new product lines, elected to leave the industry, turning their resources to other tasks.

One such company was General Dynamics, then headed by former Apollo astronaut William Anders. The firm's history went back to 1923, when Reuben Fleet formed Consolidated Aircraft Corporation. A World War II merger with Vultee Aircraft led to the formation of Consolidated Vultee (Convair), which in 1953 became one of five divisions of the General Dynamics Corporation.

The board of General Dynamics gave approval to Anders's stated intent of increasing the value of the company's stock. He accomplished the task in virtuoso manner, in part by doing essentially what an outside raider might have done: ruthlessly breaking up the company and selling its components. Traditionalists decried the passing of another great aviation name, but Anders was simply reading the writing on the Department of Defense wall.

Cannestra remembers a call from Gordon England, who was managing General Dynamic's Fort Worth operation, where the F-16 fighter was built. England flew into Georgia in his own airplane and proposed that Lockheed purchase the General Dynamics operation. Cannestra called a group together to analyze the situation. He found it promising and recommended to Tellep that the deal be made.

The chairman initially had some reservations. In the not too distant past, he had seriously contemplated selling off Lockheed's aeronautic interests to generate cash and more closely focus the company's business. Now, the F-22 program was coming along, and he was concerned that the management in Georgia might be stretched too thin. On the other hand, General Dynamics was already a partner in the F-22 team, and the purchase would give Lockheed a two-thirds interest in the program. Cannestra had noted that GD's managerial and production methods were very much like Lockheed's, which mitigated concern about integrating the two workforces.

Tellep soon saw that the F-16 program was, in his terms, a "good franchise," in that there were an excellent product, an ongoing production line, some six hundred back orders for the aircraft, and, most important, the requirement to service and maintain the thousands of F-16s already in the field. The decision marked Lockheed's return to a premier position in the fighter market, with the F-16, F-117A, and F-22 in its portfolio. Cannestra has remarked that within six months, the Fort Worth Division was operating as if it had always been a part of Lockheed. The acquisition of General Dynamics' tactical military aircraft business at Fort Worth, concluded on February 28, 1993, for

The decline in defense spending dictated that some firms merge. Lockheed acquired General Dynamic's fighter interests at Fort Worth, including the fabled F-16 Fighting Falcon.

$1.52 billion, also influenced Tellep's thinking. The defense industry was shrinking, but as it did so, more manufacturers were bailing out. If Lockheed went against the trend, and instead sought to expand within the industry, it could very well succeed and become one of the few—but powerful—survivors. The Fort Worth Division raised Lockheed's total sales to about $13 billion, and raised the formerly declining aeronautical core business to a robust $6.5 billion.

Expanding Interests—and Improving with Use

Lockheed's growth in size was in fact exceeded by its growth in capability. The corporation had reached a critical mass in which the component companies complemented one another's strengths in almost every program. Every technology, even something as exotic as stealth, improves with use. Lockheed's experience was now so broad-based that it could bid with confidence upon virtually any sophisticated contract, military or civil, and, even more important, create products for which there was as yet no known demand. As a case in point, a Lockheed scientific team at the Lockheed Research Laboratories in Palo Alto created an integrated robotic X-ray inspection system for use on the F-22 production line. The team was able to do so only because Lockheed had within its own internal system the capability to integrate the required optics, computer software, charge-coupled semiconductor devices, robotics, material sciences, and artificial intelligence.

The year 1993 proved the validity of Lockheed's basic strategy, with sales of $13.1 billion and a record profit of $844 million from programs, with net earnings of $422 million. The mix of business had changed again, to a ratio of 64 percent U.S. defense contracts, 23 percent nondefense, and 13 percent foreign military. The most important commercial development was progress on the IRIDIUM venture with Motorola to place sixty-six commercial satellites in orbit.

Positioned by Strategy

Lockheed had moved from near-bankruptcy in the early 1970s to a position of genuine strength. A combination of proven products (such as the C-130, the Trident II, and the MILSTAR satellite) was complemented by future sources of income like the F-22 and commercial telecommunications. In the twenty-year journey, extensive experiments had been made in diversified industries, but in the long run, defense and civil government contracts proved to be the company's strong suit.

Tellep recalls that he was often asked by employees if management had a strategic plan, and he would shock them by responding, "No." He would then go on to explain that Lockheed did not develop a once-a-year, five-hundred-page strategic plan; instead, strategic planning had to be done on a daily or weekly basis because of the rapid and dramatic changes taking place in the industry. He then fine-tuned a traditional Lockheed five-point strategy that he referred to as a "guide star" or points on a compass.

While the concepts behind the five-point strategy were very complex, both on technical and financial grounds, they were expressed as follows:

1. Focus on core business—this was the technical and financial engine of the corporation.

2. Maintain premier technology—by which Lockheed was distinguished from its competitors.

3. Enter related new markets to develop a more balanced business base.

4. Capitalize on acquisitions that enhance Lockheed's technical and financial strength.

5. Reduce costs/improve competitiveness—always an imperative.

Of these five points, number 4, "capitalize on acquisitions that enhance Lockheed's technical and financial strength," would soon assume an importance that overshadowed all others. In 1994, Dan Tellep would begin crafting the agreements that led first to "the merger of equals" with Martin Marietta, and subsequently to further acquisitions. It also set an industry pattern that is still being played out.

To pursue the "merger of equals" was a difficult decision for Tellep and Marafino. It meant the end of an era, and the beginning of a new Lockheed as Lockheed Martin. It would require the blending together of two cultures and two workforces into one. It would be difficult, because of size alone, to maintain the sense of family and comradeship that was a Lockheed tradition.

And, while much has been written about the Lockheed Martin merger and credit has been given to many for masterminding it, the fact remains that the merger was initiated by Lockheed and Dan Tellep. It was the product of an evolving strategic plan that recognized existing market realities and expectations. Revolutionary consolidation was necessary to ensure preservation of critical defense assets and to insure the growth and prosperity for Lockheed shareholders and employees.

The Devil Is in the Details

In the very early stages of the merger planning, Tellep had outlined the probability of the consolidation of Lockheed and Martin Marietta's four space operations into two. Vance D. Coffman's task was to conduct the detailed studies and the planning.

In many ways, a merger is just another form of program management: there are milestones to achieve, each with a measurable financial consequence. But whereas a program is often emotionally neutral, the prospective merger was not. Although the top management wanted to ease the pain at every level, the merger would result in factories being closed, people losing jobs, and families being forced to move. It was not an easy task.

Coffman, who had been handpicked by Fritz Oder and then selected for the corporate office by Tellep, knew the meaning of hard work: his first job—at the age of eight—was plowing an Iowa cornfield for twenty-five cents an hour. After picking up a bachelor of science degree in aeronautical engineering from Iowa State University, he entered into some hardball negotiations with Lockheed's recruiting teams. Coffman was attracted to Lockheed because it had a graduate study program at Stanford. Lockheed was interested in Coffman because of his grades and reputation, but had a policy that students in the Stanford graduate study program had to put in two years of work first. After a number of interviews, Coffman laid down his ultimatum: either he entered the graduate study program immediately, or he was going elsewhere. Lockheed finally acceded to his request, and he spent the next six and one-half years working nearly full-time for the company, while picking up master's and doctoral degrees in aeronautics and astronautics at Stanford.

The superheated pace characterized his progress at LMSC, where he was quickly recognized as both a brilliant engineer and a talented manager—a combination of skills so rare in the industry that swift promotion was assured.

Coffman's detail-oriented personality was perfect for his systems manager role in "black" satellite programs. His coworkers found him to be easy to deal with, and in an industry that was based on clandestine and sometimes cloak-and-dagger activities, they liked his guileless, direct approach to management problems. These would stand him in good stead in the turbulent years ahead, when he was tasked to stage-manage some of the most important aspects of the Lockheed Martin merger.

CHAPTER 14

The Merger of Equals

Lockheed officials regarded the end of the Cold War with mixed feelings. They were delighted that their company had done so much to win the bloodless victory over the Soviet Union, but recognized that the fall of the Berlin Wall also symbolized the fall of the market structure upon which the very existence of Lockheed had been based.

Lockheed was not alone, of course. The entire defense industry was now in an apparently irreversible decline. In constant dollars (i.e., discounting for inflation) the defense budget was down about two-thirds from its 1980s peak. In terms of defense spending as a percentage of gross national product, the budgets were below pre–World War II levels. The massive decline left behind the remnants of the massive military buildup of the cold war. There was a huge, closely interrelated infrastructure of the most modern facilities, staffed by the most highly trained and skilled workforce in history. The efforts of the past four decades had pushed technology beyond the limits of the layman's imagination; since the end of World War II, humankind had gone to the moon, and its machines had gone far beyond, even leaving the solar system. *Sputnik's* repetitive but intimidating beeping had been the genesis for an intricate system of satellites used for intelligence gathering, meteorology, communications, and navigation. Entire satellite systems were dedicated to environmental use, monitoring the atmosphere and the oceans in a way that was inconceivable even twenty years before. Many sciences benefited, some as basic as agriculture; instead of the massive mutual destruction so long feared, the Cold War had inadvertently generated genuine means to improve the lot of people the world over.

The challenge to the defense industry now was to make decisions on retaining the capabilities that the Cold War had spawned and converting them to civilian use. There was an absolute imperative to preserve U.S. technological leadership, for competitors were coming on strong in both Europe and Asia. Many of these were heavily subsidized by their governments, which often gave them a price advantage that could be overcome only by superior performance and service.

In conference with their top executives, Dan Tellep and Vince Marafino had decided that Lockheed would make one or more acquisitions to bolster existing lines of business, and help create a more balanced portfolio. They did not wish to grow simply for the sake of size, and they certainly wanted to avoid the example of General Dynamics and simply sell off parts of the company. Such a process might benefit shareholders in the short term, but Lockheed managers had a strong sense of loyalty to their employees as well as to their customers. Over the long term, everyone would benefit by a policy of expansion that also explored alternatives to the defense industry whenever possible. Tellep and his associates felt that the path to ultimate survival was to attain a position where Lockheed would be a principal player in defense contracts—no matter who else had to leave the industry.

For many of the leaders who had grown up with LMSC, there was a particularly poignant sense of change. LMSC had seemed almost immune to postwar budget cuts initially, but eventually was caught up in the tide. After developing and producing six successive generations of fleet ballistic missile systems, there was to be no follow-on to the D5 Trident system. In space, their very success in building satellites with increased reliability and longevity meant that the once robust classified space business would shrink, and have little prospect of future growth.

Lockheed devised a set of criteria to determine if a company was desirable for acquisition. The criteria included a compatible management style, complementary products, good prospects for the future, and, not least, a willingness to be acquired. After the bitter Simmons experience, Lockheed did not intend to embark upon a hostile takeover of its own.

The work was done in secret, involving members of senior management and with the help of Morgan Stanley & Company as advisers. Eventually, no less than twenty three-ring binders were created, dossiers on a large number of firms, some of which were assessed much more intensely than others. A discouraging pattern had emerged. Most companies did not meet the criteria, and discrete inquiries of two that did were disappointing.

Of the two companies that matched Lockheed's criteria for acquisition, Hughes was the preferred candidate because of its complementary classified space business, its growing position in commercial telecommunication satellites, and its excellent technology. The management at LMSC, including both John McMahon and Sam Araki, expressed a strong preference for doing business with Hughes.

Tellep called Mike Armstrong, CEO at Hughes, and suggested that they explore ways in which they might put their two space businesses together. From the outset, Lockheed realized that it would be impossible to acquire all of Hughes because of the size of the enterprise and its value in the marketplace. In addition, their stock had begun to advance in price because of positive news about DirecTV, its direct broadcast television venture.

After months of study, in which every conceivable means of engagement was considered, from joint venture to simple teaming arrangements, it seemed evident that there was no viable way to define a relationship. Tellep later commented that it was "like looking at a shiny new car in a showroom, wanting it intensely, and ultimately realizing that despite the desire, you were not going to be able to get it."

Tellep then tried to interest Joe Gorman, the CEO of TRW. Gorman simply did not wish to do business, and did not even communicate Lockheed's interest in TRW to his colleagues until after the announcement of the Lockheed-Martin Marietta merger. It was disappointing to Lockheed and to many at TRW, for Lockheed-TRW would have been an outstanding combination.

At the end of one all-morning session on Saturday, March 19, 1994, Tellep indicated that although it had been a good meeting, no progress toward a decision had been made. When the meeting ended inconclusively, and most of the staff had left the room, the two men from Morgan Stanley, Jim Styne and Jon Ayers, asked if they could see just Tellep and Marafino. The bankers said they would like to try a fresh idea: a merger of equals with Martin Marietta.

Lockheed had worked with Martin Marietta in 1993 in a joint effort to acquire the missiles and aerostructures businesses of LTV, Lockheed being interested in the aircraft side and Martin Marietta the missile side. The managers of the two companies found that they had a lot in common, including the fact that both had a disciplined approach to acquisition. The exercise established a large measure of mutual trust.

The LTV deal had not worked out, but it was obvious that the two corporate cultures were compatible, and Tellep got along well with Norm Augustine, Martin Marietta's CEO. The shift in Lockheed's mind-set from "acquire" to "merge" made all the difference. Tellep summarized his thoughts by saying, "This is a marriage made in heaven," and so it would prove to be. After a brief discussion, Tellep commented that the cultures were compatible, and there was a good match of products, with only a few areas of competition. Overall, it sounded interesting. Tellep recognized that both companies had, for some time, been on parallel paths, both being proactive but disciplined in their search for acquisitions.

He picked up the phone and called. Augustine was not in, but soon called back. When he did, he expressed interest and asked for time to discuss it with a few key advisers.

Augustine called back again the following Monday and noted that Martin Marietta was planning a meeting with its key managers in Phoenix in the near future. Augustine suggested that Tellep bring a team to Phoenix to discuss the matter, which would be kept completely secret as a matter of course.

Throughout these developments, Tellep leaned heavily on Marafino's advice, as had his predecessors. Vince Marafino had for a long time played a pivotal role at Lockheed, having the unique distinction of serving as the company's chief financial officer (CFO) under three chairmen: Anderson, Kitchen, and Tellep. With Anderson, Marafino helped steer the company through the stresses of the L-1011 program and was instrumental in the decision to terminate the effort. During Kitchen's three-year tenure as chairman, Marafino helped pull off the acquisition of Sanders, greatly enhancing the electronics capability of the corporation. With Tellep, Marafino's final years with the company continued to involve high-stakes issues, including the proxy battles against Simmons, the acquisition of General Dynamics' fighter division, and now, the merger with Martin Marietta. With each chairman, Marafino served in a far broader capacity than implied by his title. His financial skills earned him the reputation of being one of the finest CFOs in the industry. In addition, his ability to think strategically and to see the organization from all vantage points made him an invaluable addition to the executive suite. Seen by some as a tough-minded manager, those who worked with him closely came to know him as a person totally dedicated to the best interest of the company and possessed of a delightful sense of humor.

Martin Marietta

Lockheed's potential partner in the merger had an equally long, distinguished history. Founded in 1912 by Glenn L. Martin, who had designed, built, and flown his own aircraft three years before at the age of twenty-three, the firm had followed a pattern of meeting changing business needs by changing its corporate status, just as the early Lockheed (Loughead) Aircraft Manufacturing Company had done. Aircraft were designed and built on the basis of the latest available information and were flown at air shows. Also like the Lockheed brothers, Glenn had an eye for talent. Over the years some of the most famous names in aviation would get their start with Martin, including such stellar figures as Charles Day, Charles Willard, Larry Bell, Eric Springer, James "Dutch" Kindleberger, Donald Douglas, and James McDonnell, to name but a few.

There had been remarkable similarities in the two companies over the years. Both had major failures in the commercial aircraft market before leaving the arena; both had been successful in missiles and space efforts; both had attempted diversification and achieved mixed results; both had to battle hostile takeover attempts; and both pursued acquisitions vigorously.

In 1993, Martin Marietta had sales of $9.4 billion, a negotiated backlog of $16.7 billion, and net income of $450.3 million, and em-

When further mergers were seen to be necessary, Lockheed turned to Martin Marietta, a firm founded by Glenn L. Martin.

ployed 94,000 people. The corresponding figures for Lockheed for the same year were as follows: sales, $13 billion; negotiated backlog, $28.9 billion; net income, $422 million; and employees, 83,500.

The Merger Is On

O nce the merger had been agreed upon in principle, an intense series of negotiations in the deepest secrecy was necessary to bring the deal off. Vince Marafino recalls that during the long, hard weeks in which all of the myriad details necessary for a merger of such a magnitude were worked out, there was only one instance when there was overt doubt about its being executed. This occurred during a briefing by Tellep of about twenty of the top managers at Lockheed, when Val Peline voiced his doubts about the wisdom of the merger. He was his usual articulate self and made his points well. It happened that Tellep and Marafino were called away from the discussion for an hour to meet with NASA administrator Daniel Goldin. Before leaving the Goldin meeting, Tellep asked the group to prepare a top-level summary of the positives as well as the negatives with the intent of establishing a group consensus of whether or not to proceed.

They came back in about an hour, and Tellep polled the

managers to see how they felt about the merger. To his surprise, they were unanimously for it—even Peline had been won over. From that point on, the issue was never in doubt.

The Twenty-first-Century Corporation

It soon developed that if the Lockheed–Martin Marietta merger was not made in heaven, it was certainly made in Wall Street, for everything that could have posed a major problem was resolved with an almost preternatural ease. The desirability of the merger from a business standpoint became immediately apparent, for although the two firms competed in some areas, their product lines were for the most part complementary, and both firms had activities in defense and non-defense areas. Even the launch vehicle field, where it seemed that the new Lockheed venture with the Proton launcher might compete with the Titan, was not an issue—the product lines meshed smoothly.

In short, the merger provided a single, stronger entity with which to compete for international business. At the same time, it was evident that there were large savings to be made in reduction of overhead, the consolidation of efforts from several plants to a smaller number, and, inevitably, a reduction in the total number in the workforce. The personnel cutbacks would be the most difficult to deal with, for they involved the human equation, and would demand the finest in human-relation skills.

Other social factors—those that stemmed from individual egos or corporate amour propre—were resolved more easily. Lockheed had already considered moving its headquarters to the East Coast, where the majority of its business was generated, so general location was not an issue. To ensure that the merger was perceived as one of equals, it was initially decided that a new building would be found so that both companies would move into a totally new environment. In time the Lockheed board objected to the expense of a new building; Martin Marietta already owned its handsome headquarters in Bethesda, Maryland, so a compromise was made. Lockheed's corporate staff would in fact move into the Martin Marietta headquarters building, but all of Martin Marietta's people would move out of their present offices and new offices would be assigned to the new combined management team. The idea was to make everyone feel that it was a new—and equal—beginning.

What could have been a major problem—who would be the first

chairman and chief executive officer of the firm—was resolved in an equally painless manner. Tellep was senior to Augustine by four years, and had already been contemplating retirement. An agreement was made that Tellep would be chairman and CEO for the first year of the merger, then retire first as CEO and a year later as chairman. Augustine was happy with this arrangement, and would surprise everyone in 1997, when he announced his own pending retirement. Marafino, who was planning to retire within a year, indicated no interest in taking a permanent position in the new company.

The very name of the company could have been an issue. It was decided to use the alphabet as the key, and to drop Marietta from the merged company's name. The alternative "Martin Lockheed" did not ring a bell, and as one investment banker participating in the negotiations noted, it would ultimately come down to "Marty Lockheed," which sounded like something out of a high school yearbook.

An intensive study was made to get the right logo. Historically, both companies had used a star in their respective logos, although both logos had changed over the years. The proposed logo that gained consensus managed to capture the new company perfectly, with two vectors joined to create a futuristic image suggesting a star.

Both companies had agreed that every effort should be made to conclude the merger arrangements within a year, and that the operation should work seamlessly and effortlessly on the first day the new company began business. They recognized that the new company would be so large that neither company's previous organizational structure would serve. They decided to group activities into four sectors: Aeronautics, Electronics, Information & Technology Services, and Space & Strategic Missiles. Later, a fifth, Energy & Environment, was added. These sectors would be located in the Bethesda headquarters. It was agreed that the Lockheed Martin corporate headquarters would be neither a holding company nor an operating company. Instead, its top managers would stay closely involved with each sector, and would see to it that each sector leader had what was termed a "dual vision," by which he would seek to maximize his efforts for both his individual sector and the corporation as a whole.

A new twenty-four-person board of directors was established, with representation divided evenly between Martin Marietta and Lockheed. Board committees were created to handle such matters as ethics, compensation, and finance. Again, the members of each committee came in about equal numbers from each firm.

Equal attention was paid to the organization and leadership of the corporate staff and each of the sectors. Selection of the key management positions was made by Tellep, Augustine, and their key advisers. The goal was to divide leadership positions between the two companies on a fifty-fifty basis. When a decision was made as to who would lead a staff function or a particular unit, that person was tasked to get with his opposite number from the other company and decide on structure and staffing. As it worked out, the division of leadership positions and key staffing worked out almost exactly fifty-fifty.

The personalities of the two chief executives played a part in the progress of the merger. Tellep was from a hands-on operating background, and was very interested in every detail, especially those dealing with integration and consolidation. Though Augustine was involved in numerous outside activities and committed to a heavy speaking schedule, he participated in critical decisions. The pair became good friends and worked effectively together in something of a Mr. Inside and Mr. Outside relationship. They presented an authentic, collegial relationship to the organization and continually stressed that the merger was one of equal partners. The fact that the management succession plan had been announced in advance defused potential tensions and provided a stabilizing influence in a time of monumental change.

An executive council was formed consisting of Tellep, his counterpart at Martin Marietta, Norman R. Augustine, Marafino, Tom Young, and Marcus C. Bennett. Decisions were made as to who would lead each of the four sectors. These were perhaps the most hotly contested positions, for it was from their ranks that the future corporate leaders would come. The division came nearly evenly, as the following were named president and chief operating officers of their respective sectors:

AERONAUTICS: James A. "Micky" Blackwell (Lockheed)
ELECTRONICS: Thomas A. Corcoran (Martin Marietta)
INFORMATION & TECHNOLOGY SERVICES: Peter B. Teets
  (Martin Marietta)
SPACE & STRATEGIC MISSILES: Vance D. Coffman (Lockheed)

When the personnel decks had been cleared away, a myriad of details remained. These related to such mundane issues as operating policies, the conformance of the two separate accounting and computer systems, the combination of personnel/benefits, and all such similar mechanisms of a sophisticated firm. In addition, dozens of other task forces were formed to address specific integration issues. Each of the sector presidents was charged with the task of preparing consolidation and cost reduction plans for their sector.

An Analysis of the Merger

In 1992, Tellep and Augustine had attended a meeting in the Pentagon at which they were briefed by members of the secretary of defense's staff. The thrust of the briefing was the necessary downsizing of the defense industry. Charts were produced to indicate that although there were five manufacturers of tactical aircraft, future defense budgets would support only two. In the space launch vehicle business, there were three competitors; again, the future would support only two. Of the five manufacturers of spacecraft, only two could be supported in the future. It was an ominous briefing, one that indicated two alternatives: leave the industry or merge to get a larger share of the diminished pie. These considerations were weighed heavily by both Tellep and Augustine.

A Triple Crown Winner

Both leaders were subsequently careful to emphasize that their new venture was to be a "merger of equals," a term they defined as "a strategic combination of two similarly sized, usually complementary business entities." It was established early and often that both companies conceded each other's possession of "premier technology," a term that describes their capability to operate in the vanguard of science, undertaking the most demanding tasks of defense, space exploration, and advanced electronics.

Both were major players in the defense market, with each company having just over 60 percent of its sales to the DOD. Curiously, the two companies' most complementary skills were in areas that could be exploited for the nondefense market—these included information systems, energy programs, government services, environmental programs, and the commercial side of both space and electronics. Given the anticipated continued decline in defense spending, this was of vital importance.

Both companies had experienced the agonies of attempted hostile

Norman R. Augustine and Daniel
M. Tellep orchestrated the
merger of two industry giants,
Lockheed and Martin Marietta,
into the formidable Lockheed
Martin Corporation. Tellep
described the "merger of equals"
as "a marriage made in heaven."

takeovers, and both were determined to make the merger as painless
and as positive as possible.

The financial strength of the new company was both obvious and
immense. Initially, the combined sales were expected to exceed $23
billion and the combined backlog to exceed $43 billion. The total
assets of Lockheed Martin exceeded $17 billion, while the shareholders' equity had reached $6.4 billion. A close analysis of the two organizations indicated that current Lockheed shareholders should receive
1.63 shares of stock in Lockheed Martin for each share of Lockheed
stock, while Martin Marietta shareholders would get shares in the new
company on a one-for-one basis. There were two additional important
financial factors to the deal: no additional debt was required, and the
merger would be accounted for as a pooling of interests.

In the press conference announcing the merger, Tellep made
three points. The first of these was that both Lockheed and Martin
Marietta had achieved comparable positions of leadership in their industry. The second was that the merger would lead to more value to
the shareholders, the customers, and the employees (a phenomenon
that Augustine referred to as "the Triple Crown"). The third was that

with its highly diversified advance technology, Lockheed Martin would be very competitive in the global marketplace.

Wall Street accepted the merger with enthusiasm. On announcement, Lockheed stock increased from $66 to $78.75 a share, a 19 percent increase. Martin Marietta stock increased 5 percent, from $48.25 to $50.875.

The industry was stunned by the sheer audacity of the merger— who could manage such a giant? And, as might be expected, alarms were sounded about the effect upon defense procurement and on the possibility of antitrust problems. The Defense Department had in fact invited industry consolidation, and looked upon the Lockheed Martin merger with some satisfaction. Lockheed had given an example of the possibilities of improving performance under defense contracts on the F-16 program. In 1987, under General Dynamic's management, 280 F-16s had rolled off the assembly line. By 1994, the demand for F-16s had reduced production to only 50 per year, less than 20 percent of the previous rate. Yet the Lockheed team had adopted new manufacturing techniques, including the Lean Manufacturing Initiative adapted from the Toyota automobile company practice, and was able to reverse the usual situation of having higher unit costs when production rates are lowered. It succeeded to the extent that it could offer new F-16s to the air force at a firm unit price of $20 million each, a good harbinger of the future.

A great deal of effort was placed into providing the necessary information to satisfy the requirements of the Hart-Scott-Rodino Act over the course of time, and all questions regarding the antitrust aspects of the merger were resolved with only minor adjustments. A less obvious but more important problem was that of confidentiality among the many teams presently competing for contracts. Lockheed belonged to some teams and Martin Marietta to others, and there was concern that the new firm of Lockheed Martin might have an unfair advantage. The agreements arrived at in the process of examining the antitrust aspects of the merger solved these difficulties.

Hardheaded reporters were particularly interested in first defining what savings might be possible, and second, asking what benefits would accrue to the government (and hence the public) from them. Some savings were obvious and immediate: there would be only one headquarters, one computer system, one information system. Other savings were less obvious, but Augustine had a favorite illustration, saying that it was better to have three factories working at full capacity than six working at half capacity. Both Tellep and Augustine were candid that there would be further downsizing of the organization to achieve economies. They pointed out that this would have occurred even if there had not been a merger, and the greater good of a larger number of employees would be secured by having a larger, viable company, one that would begin adding jobs as it grew.

In interview after interview, top officials of the new firm made it clear that the primary concerns about the merger—loss of jobs, reduction in competition, possible decrease in innovation—were the direct result of the downsizing of the defense industry, not of the merger itself. They stressed that the merger was a reaction to the reduction in the defense industry, and an attempt to ameliorate its worst effects. Even though absolutely accurate, these were difficult points for the public to understand, coming as they did from a new corporate giant, the likes of which the world had never before seen.

The merger was officially consummated on March 16, 1995, and, as hoped and predicted, the new company was operating as an entity on that date. Given the enormous scope of the new firm, the fact that it was operating at all was almost a miracle. Within the four major sectors there were almost fifty major operating companies. In addition, there were five major subsidiaries or firms in which Lockheed Martin held large investments.

Despite the complexity and diversity of the operation, the new firm was very successful in obtaining new contracts, winning more than 60 percent of the competitive bids it pursued. In hard dollar terms, in 1995 net earnings reached $682 million, and cash from operating activities, the lifeblood of an expanding company, was almost twice that, at $1.3 billion. Sales had remained steady at just under $23 billion, while the negotiated backlog declined slightly to $41 billion.

The shareholders were more encouraged by the performance of the new Lockheed Martin stock, which increased in value by 95 percent during 1995. Shareholders of both companies could look back only a few years to remember a period when both firms' stock prices were pitifully low for long periods of time.

The press and the government were watching Lockheed Martin's consolidation efforts to see if the gains Tellep and Augustine had promised would be forthcoming. By the end of the 1995, the company was able to announce that about $5 billion in savings would be made in the first five years after the merger, and that subsequent savings would amount to about $1.8 billion per year.

The success of the Lockheed–Martin Marietta merger to a large measure resulted from Dan Tellep's insistence from the beginning on three elements. These were (1) consolidation and cost savings must be an indispensable result, (2) a schedule and program must be put in place to provide operation as a single company on the day of closing, and (3) consolidations must be definitized and action plans initiated no later than three months after closing.

During the latter days of 1994, when the proposed merger was being defended by Lockheed and Martin Marietta executives, the term "synergy" was often used as a reason to merge, the argument being that the two firms combined could operate synergistically in a way they could not do as competitors. The practical results of that synergy may be illustrated by a single example, the VentureStar, which is described below. The key technologies required for such an advanced design were provided in almost equal measure from the old Lockheed and Martin Marietta heritage firms. Neither firm could have won the bid alone, and teaming might not have produced the same results as the consolidated efforts of the new Lockheed Martin company.

Overall, Tellep and Augustine had reason to be pleased with the results of their efforts, but they knew that there was more to be done.

More Mergers Under Way

In January 1996, Lockheed Martin stunned the world with the announcement of a strategic combination with the Loral Corporation. It seemed impossible that the firm would undertake another major expansion so soon, but the merger was proceeding well, and the acquisition of some elements of Loral played an important part in strengthening Lockheed Martin's position in the industry. The deal was quite involved, but had a total estimated value of $9.4 billion. In brief, Lockheed Martin acquired the defense electronics, systems integration, and certain other businesses of Loral for about $9.1 billion, including $2.1 billion in assumed debt. Of this amount, $7 billion was paid directly to Loral shareholders through a tender offer of $38 per share of Loral common stock. A newly formed company, Loral Space & Communications, issued one share of stock for each share of Loral common stock previously held. Lockheed Martin also made a $344 million investment in Loral Space, equivalent to about a 20 percent share of the company.

Another Giant Step

On July 3, 1997, a joint announcement was made on the proposed union of two of the largest firms in the aerospace industry—firms whose names were composed of four of the great pioneering aviation companies. Their respective boards of directors had approved a proposal that Lockheed Martin and Northrop Grumman be joined in what was termed a strategic combination with estimated 1997 revenues of $37 billion and nearly 230,000 employees. Northrop Grumman shareholders were to receive 1.1923 shares of Lockheed Martin common stock for each share of their stock. While the larger firm would be called Lockheed Martin, it was noted that the names Northrop and Grumman would endure within the corporation.

It would be a shame if they did not, for the United States has depended upon a series of superb aircraft from the two companies over the years, including the Grumman fighters (Wildcat, Hellcat, Tomcat, and others) and the Northrop Black Widow and B-2 stealth bomber.

The chairman of Northrop Grumman, Kent Kresa, had brought his firm to its strong position in the industry through a series of mergers and on the strength of its engineering. Given the size of Lockheed Martin and its principal rival, Boeing, it was a logical step to seek to improve its relative status. Kresa would become vice chairman of Lockheed Martin and serve on its board.

The proposed merger was seen as the logical next step in the overall consolidation of the defense industry, but was greeted by some concern over the antitrust implications of the deal. Lockheed Martin has expressed confidence that the combination will be approved. In March 1998 the government sought to stop the merger.

The growth of Lockheed Martin was paralleled by the expansion of its longtime rival, Boeing. On July 25, 1997, the McDonnell Douglas Corporation voted to approve a proposed merger with the Boeing Company. The new company dwarfed even Lockheed, with its combined 1995 revenues of $43.8 billion, combined backlog of $130.3 billion, and more than 200,000 employees.

When all mergers are approved, the defense industry will have three principal domestic companies in competition: Lockheed Martin, Boeing, and Raytheon. Some foreign officials have already expressed concern that these companies, individually or in concert, may be so powerful that they will be able to drive European aerospace rivals out of business. Ironically, European companies are using Lockheed Martin as a model for their own consolidations even as Lockheed Martin forges stronge alliances with foreign firms.

1996 Results and Products for the Future

The motto *E Pluribus Unum* (From Many, One) applies to Lockheed Martin almost as well as it does to the United States. The new firm is far more than the simple consolidation of Lockheed and Martin Marietta, with their subsequent acquisitions. Before the proposed Northrop Grumman combination, Lockheed Martin officially counted seventeen "heritage firms" as a part of its corporate background. A more detailed analysis of the company genealogy shows that it extends to more than sixty organizations, ranging from giants such as Ford Aerospace, Vought, RCA, and Sanders to lesser-known firms. Each contributed to the Lockheed Martin gene pool with ideas, traditions, and methods.

The new corporation employed almost 200,000 people by the end of 1996, and their combined efforts resulted in Lockheed Martin being chosen as one of the one hundred best-managed corporations by *Industry Week*. It was not an accident, but rather the result of assiduous planning and tight control.

In 1996, its first full year of operation, Lockheed Martin enjoyed $26.9 billion in sales, up $4 billion. Earnings per common share almost doubled, from $3.05 to $6.04, and the year-end stock price increased 16 percent to reach $91.50 per share. Backlog had risen to more than $50 billion, an encouraging figure that Augustine translated into a management goad: it meant that $1 million in new business had to be added *every four minutes* just to sustain the revenues.

The rise in share price was an external appreciation of internal actions, for management had moved swiftly in its efforts to consolidate and acquire new business. The consolidation efforts were at once the most necessary and the most painful. Lockheed Martin had immediately closed a number of unneeded facilities, but managed to keep the number of jobs eliminated down to 1,600, less than 1 percent of the workforce. Each job lost was painful to the individuals concerned, but given the scale of the operation, the total was smaller than had previously been estimated. Those who were laid off were given severance packages, job-relocation assistance, and other support.

The relatively small number of jobs lost was due in part to

Lockheed Martin's ability to offer positions elsewhere within the firm as a result of winning new competitions. In 1996, the company won 68 percent of the programs upon which it bid, a truly remarkable effort. Among these new programs were many that promised much for the future.

VentureStar

Selected by NASA to build a demonstrator for a completely reusable launch vehicle, Lockheed responded with a company organization suitable to the task. A select team from all parts of the firm was established to work as a "virtual company," one whose members did not have to concern themselves with traditional organizational boundaries.

The X-33 Reusuable Launch Vehicle Demonstrator is a half-scale suborbital flight vehicle demonstrator for the VentureStar, the world's first single-stage to-orbit (SSTO) vehicle. The primary goal of VentureStar is to reduce the cost of launching payloads to low earth orbit to one thousand dollars per pound, as compared to an estimated ten thousand dollars per pound on the Space Shuttle. The VentureStar will serve as a prototype for a future commercial fleet of SSTO Reusable Launch Vehicles (RLVs) to replace the space shuttle and many of the current expendable launch vehicles, which all date back to *mid-1950s* technology. The production vehicle will be 127 feet long, will weigh close to 1.8 million pounds at the time of its vertical takeoff, and will have the capability to place payloads weighing up to forty thousand pounds in orbit.

The current program will cost more than $1 billion through the year 2000, and will result in the subscale demonstrator vehicle, the X-33, making its first flight in 1999.

The VentureStar uses a lifting body configuration powered by linear aerospike engines fed by liquid oxygen and liquid hydrogen propellants. The aerospike engine is designed for high performance, minimum weight, and long life, and is adaptable to thrust vector control in both pitch and roll.

As advanced as the VentureStar is, its engineering derives from a long history of projects at both Lockheed and Martin Marietta, many of which addressed individual elements of the RLV challenge in other applications. The advanced engineering required for the VentureStar resulted in its becoming the very first nonclassified Skunk Works proj-

One of the many projects of Lockheed Martin is the VentureStar, a reusable single-stage-to-orbit (SSTO) launch vehicle that is intended to open new commercial markets by lowering the cost of getting into space.

ect, an event that has had a fundamental effect upon both the Skunk Works and Lockheed Martin as a whole.

The VentureStar is complemented by Lockheed Martin's selection to compete for the evolved expendable launch vehicle (EELV) program, intended to develop a family of expendable launch vehicles to replace Delta, Atlas, and Titan space launch vehicles.

The Joint Strike Fighter

Called by some the most important military aircraft program of the twenty-first century, the Joint Strike Fighter (JSF) is being developed to replace several different types of tactical aircraft in the U.S. Air Force, U.S. Navy, and U.S. Marine Corps, and in Great Britain's Royal Navy. Lockheed Martin received one of two concept demonstration contracts for the next-generation aircraft. An initial total requirement for three thousand aircraft is predicted to rise to a level of

Teaming with other companies, Lockheed Martin is also an entrant in the important Joint Strike Fighter competition, which may impact the F-22 program.

five thousand by midcentury. The Skunk Works will also have responsibility for designing and building the JSF prototypes.

Boeing, the company that now bids to be Lockheed Martin's primary competitor for almost all defense contracts, was the other winner. In a manner similar to the Advanced Tactical Fighter competition that resulted in the F-22, both companies will build two flying concept-demonstrator aircraft to demonstrate three configurations of the proposed fighter.

The basic concept behind the JSF is to provide an affordable family of multiservice aircraft by engineering commonality and modularity into the design. Commonality has been attempted before, and multiuse aircraft such as the McDonnell Douglas F-4 Phantom II have been successful. The JSF is the first aircraft to incorporate such very different mission modes in one basic design. One version will have to have the short-takeoff, vertical-landing, hover, and transition characteristics of today's McDonnell Douglas AV-8B, while another version will have the range and load-carrying characteristics of the Lockheed Martin F-16 or McDonnell Douglas F/A-18 aircraft.

The first delivery of an operational aircraft is planned for fiscal year 2008; in the meantime, Lockheed Martin finds itself in the unenviable position of competing against itself for limited defense budget funds with the F-22 and the JSF.

In addition to these major programs, there are a host of new ventures such as the Joint Air-to-Surface-Standoff Missile (JASSM) and a new attack submarine to complement the long list of standard

Lockheed Martin products. The latter include not only workhorses like the F-16 and C-130 aircraft, but a whole portfolio of programs in the Electronics, Information Services, and Energy & Environment Sectors.

A New Leader Emerges

Each merger and acquisition brought with it not only new programs and skills, but new personnel to fill the increasingly demanding top positions of Lockheed Martin. In recent years, it has not been unusual for an expanding company to look outside its ranks to find a chief executive. Lockheed Martin has proceeded counter to this trend, and, given the wealth of managerial talent available to it, will continue to do so.

Such is the case with Dr. Vance D. Coffman, who has never worked anywhere else than Lockheed. Identified by Dan Tellep as a prime candidate to succeed him as chairman, Coffman was carefully tutored and mentored. He had done very well at LMSC, and Tellep brought him up to headquarters to gain experience. There he demonstrated what Marafino has called "the capacity to grow." He quickly learned his new duties to the point that he was able to return to LMSC as president during the interval prior to the merger.

Coffman, naturally enough, had to view the merger with mixed emotions. Since he had already been placed in contention for the top job at Lockheed, the merger appeared to muddy the water, for in the Lockheed Martin Corporation, his rank and seniority would probably entitle him only to a position as president of a sector. Like many others, Coffman put aside his personal concerns, recognized that the merger was the best thing for Lockheed, and pressed forward with it.

As the merger progressed, Coffman was presented with one of the most difficult tasks. There was excess capacity at LMSC's California facility, and this meant that the older, higher-cost facilities in East Windsor, New Jersey, and Valley Forge, Pennsylvania, had to be closed. Both plants had recently benefited by a heavy investment in equipment, and both were operating at full capacity. They were of immense importance to their respective communities, and, naturally, their strong, loyal workforces did not wish to lose their jobs.

Coffman studied the situation with his usual attention to detail and came to the inescapable conclusion that the cost savings involved in closing the two plants and combining their operations in the

Vance D. Coffman, president and
vice chairman of Lockheed
Martin, proved his abilities at
LMSC, and during the process
of the merger.

Sunnyvale facility were too large to forgo. He took it upon himself personally to give the bad news to the two plants, and saw to it that the most essential employees received attractive packages to induce them to move west.

Doing an excellent job of human relations in an almost impossible task, Coffman softened his usual business persona and managed to convince the former Martin Marietta workforce that the closings had to be made, but that every effort would be taken to reduce hardships to an absolute minimum.

As a result, pioneering companies that built the first satellites at the dawn of the space age have joined forces in the Lockheed Martin merger to blaze a new trail for the twenty-first century. Consolidation in Sunnyvale, California has brought with it investment in the most innovative and technologically advanced production facilities in the industry. The centerpiece: a 65-million-dollar Commercial Satellite Center for the production and testing of spacecraft that are setting new standards for power and performance. Gleaming white, ultra-clean, and covering an area the size of two football fields under fifty-foot high ceilings, this "factory of the future" features co-located test facilities to dramatically reduce satellite cost and time to market.

Today, Lockheed Martin Missiles and Space builds on a legacy of more than 700 satellites successfully launched and orbited. The company is engaged in the design and production of 19 different types of spacecraft and satellites. They range in size from the 600-pound Lunar Prospecter spacecraft, placed in orbit around the moon in January 1998, to military systems such as the 10,000-pound MILSTAR communication satellite in geosynchronous Earth orbit. Between its commercial, NASA and government customers, Lockheed Martin Missiles and Space manages over two dozen separate spacecraft contracts with a long-term value of 2.5 billion dollars.

Coffman had done his job so well that by January 1996 he was advanced to the position of executive vice president and chief operating officer of the Lockheed Martin Corporation, being succeeded by Melvin Brashears at the Space & Strategic Missiles Sector. In 1997, when Augustine retired, Coffman was selected to become vice chairman and chief executive officer. One year later he became Chairman of the Lockheed Martin Board of Directors.

A Look Back to the Future

The history of the Lockheed Company in all its many guises is inspiring. From Allan and Malcolm Lockheed's early efforts, to the vision that gave Robert Gross the courage to secure forty thousand dollars to invest in the Lockheed name, to the dazzling successes of Lockheed products in World War II and the Cold War, to the incredible series of modern mergers, the firm has performed in a sterling manner. Somehow, despite its astronomical growth in size, Lockheed managed to hold on to its sense of family, and to transfer this to its new, larger entity as Lockheed Martin.

It has been able to do so only because of the people of Lockheed, who have worked so long, so loyally, and with such unselfish patriotism. It did not matter if there was peace or war, prosperity or depression, good times or bad, the people of Lockheed not only endured but, continuing to create, they prevailed. From their ranks sprang the great and necessary leaders to handle change. The people of Lockheed Martin will carry on in the tradition of Robert Gross, who said, decades earlier, "Look ahead, where the horizons are absolutely unlimited." Lockheed Martin is now poised to look beyond the horizons, into a future that is utterly boundless.

On July 16, 1998, as this book was going to press, Lockheed Martin announced the termination of the proposed merger. Lockheed Martin had been surprised at the strong opposition to the merger by the Department of Justice and the Department of Defense. The Department of Defense had, since 1993, urged consolidation of defense contractors in the post–Cold War environment. Lockheed Martin's Chairman and CEO, Vance Coffman, stated that "Continuing the litigation at this point is simply not in the best interest of Lockheed Martin's customers, shareholders or employees."

Some Notable Lockheed Aircraft Flights

Date	Pilot	Plane	Event	Result
Apr. 1928	Capt. George Hubert Wilkins, Lt. Ben Eielson	Vega	Flew 2,200 mi across top of world from Point Barrow, AK, to Spitsbergen	20.5 hr flying time (one stop)
Apr. 1928	Arthur Goebel and Harry Tucker	Vega	New York to Los Angeles	23 hr, 45 min (one stop); 24 hr, 20 min elapsed time
June 1928	Lee Schoenhair	Vega	San Diego, CA, to Harrisburg, PA	15 hr, 10 min nonstop; average speed 158 mph
Aug. 1928	Arthur Goebel and Harry Tucker	Vega	Los Angeles to New York	18 hr, 58 min nonstop; average speed 142 mph
Sep. 1928	Robert W. Cantwell	Vega	Class C winner, transcontinental derby, New York to Los Angeles, National Air Races	

Date	Pilot	Plane	Event	Result
Oct. 1928	Capt. C. B. D. Collyer, Harry Tucker	Vega	New York to Los Angeles	24 hr, 51 min nonstop
Dec. 1928	Capt. George Hubert Wilkins, Lt. Ben Eielson	Vega	First exploratory flight over Antarctic, 1,200 mi	9.5 hr
Feb. 1929	Capt. Frank Hawks, Oscar Grubb	Air Express	Los Angeles to New York	18 hr, 21 min, 59 sec nonstop
Apr. 1929	Anscel Eckman	Vega Seaplane	First nonstop flight, Seattle to Juneau, AK	
May 1929	Lt. Herbert Fahy	Vega	Solo endurance record	36 hr, 56 min, 36 sec
June 1929	Capt. Frank Hawks	Air Express	Round-trip flight, New York to Los Angeles, and return to New York	East to west, 19 hr, 10 min, 32 sec; west to east, 17 hr, 38 min, 17 sec nonstop; one stop in Los Angeles
Aug. 1929	Roscoe Turner	Air Express	Los Angeles to New York with full payload	18 hr, 55 min, including three stops
Aug. 1929	Henry Brown	Air Express	Nonstop Los Angeles-to-Cleveland Derby winner	13 hr, 15 min, 7 sec; 154.091 mph
Nov. 1929	Amelia Earhart	Vega	Speed record for women	Average speed 184.17 mph; fastest mile 197.8 mph
Feb. 1930	Col. and Mrs. Charles A. Lindbergh	Sirius	Glendale, CA, to Long Island, NY	14 hr, 23 min, 27 sec nonstop
May 1930	Roscoe Turner	Air Express	New York to Los Angeles	18 hr, 43 min, 34 sec
June 1930	W. S. Brock, E. F. Schlee	Vega	Jacksonville, FL, to San Diego, CA, and return	31 hr, 57 min
June 1930	Amelia Earhart	Vega	International speed record for women, 100 km	174.897 mph with no payload; 171.438 mph with 1,102 lb payload (500 kg)
Aug. 1930	Capt. Frank Hawks	Air Express	Solo record, Los Angeles to New York	12 hr, 25 min, 3 sec
Aug. 1930	Wiley Post	Vega	Nonstop Los Angeles-to-Chicago Derby winner	9 hr, 9 min, 4 sec 192.326 mph

Date	Pilot	Plane	Event	Result
Nov. 1930	Capt. Roy W. Ammel	Sirius	New York to Panama Canal Zone	24 hr, 35 min
Dec. 1930	Ruth Nichols	Vega	First transcontinental flight by a woman, Mineola, NY, to Burbank, CA	16 hr, 59 min, 30 sec
Dec. 1930	Ruth Nichols	Vega	First transcontinental flight by a woman, Los Angeles to New York	13 hr, 21 min
Feb. 1931	Glen Kidston	Vega	London to Paris	72 min
Mar. 1931	Ruth Nichols	Vega	American altitude record for women	28,743 ft
Mar. 1931	Vance Breese	Altair	San Francisco to Los Angeles	1 hr, 30 min, 40 sec, with an average speed of 235 mph
Apr. 1931	Ruth Nichols	Vega	International speed record for women	210.636 mph
July 1931	Wiley Post and Harold Gatty	Vega	First around-the-world flight of 15,474 mi	8 days, 15 hr, 51 min
July 1931	Capt. George Endress and Capt. Alexander Magyar	Sirius	Newfoundland to Hungary, 3,600 mi	26 hr nonstop
July–Aug. 1931	Col. and Mrs. Charles A. Lindbergh	Sirius	Washington, D.C., across Bering Sea to Tokyo	
Oct. 1931	Ruth Nichols	Vega	International distance record for women, Oakland, CA, to Louisville, KY	1,977.6 mi
Feb. 1932	Ruth Nichols	Vega	Unofficial world altitude record for Diesel-powered airplane	19,928 ft
May 1932	Amelia Earhart	Vega	First solo flight across the Atlantic by a woman, Newfoundland to Ireland	15 hr, 18 min
July 1932	James Mattern and Bennett Griffin	Vega	Fastest Atlantic crossing, Newfoundland to Berlin	17 hr, 30 min

Date	Pilot	Plane	Event	Result
July 1932	Amelia Earhart	Vega	Transcontinental record for women, Los Angeles to Newark, NJ	17 hr, 59 min
Aug. 1932	Amelia Earhart	Vega	International distance record for women, Los Angeles to Newark, NJ; first nonstop transcontinental flight by a woman	2,447.8 mi in 19 hr, 5 min
July–Dec. 1932	Col. and Mrs. Charles A. Lindbergh	Sirius	29,000-mi survey flight	29,000 mi
July 1933	Wiley Post	Vega	Record around-the-world flight of 15,596 mi	7 days, 18 hr, 49.5 min
Oct.–Nov. 1934	Charles Kingsford Smith and Capt. P. G. Taylor	Altair	7,365 mi flight from Brisbane, Australia, to Oakland, CA	54 hr, 49 min
Feb.–Apr. 1934	Laura Ingalls	Air Express	First woman over Andes; longest flight by a woman; first solo flight around South America; first flight by a woman from North to South America	16,897 mile flight
Jan. 1935	Amelia Earhart	Vega	First solo flight by a woman from Honolulu to Oakland	2,408 mi 18 hr, 16 min
Sep. 1935	Laura Ingalls	Orion	New nonstop transcontinental record for women, Burbank, CA, to Newark, NJ	13 hr, 34 min
Feb. 1935	Wiley Post	Vega	Unofficial altitude record	Approximately 55,000 ft
Apr. 1936	James H. Doolittle	Electra	Set speed record over Chicago & Southern Airline route from Chicago to New Orleans	5 hr, 55 min

Date	Pilot	Plane	Event	Result
Nov. 1936	Max Aitken, Marshall Headle, Brian Allen, and Ray Buckminster	Electra Junior	Set record from Las Vegas NV, to Burbank, CA	1 hr, 2 min Average speed of 256 mph
May 1937	Dick Merrill and John Lambie	Electra	New York to Northweald, England, for coronation of King George VI	20 hr, 48 min
May 1937	Dick Merrill and John Lambie	Electra	Southampton, England, to Squantum, MA, return flight from coronation	24 hr, 55 min
July 1938	Howard Hughes	Super Electra	Record around-the-world flight	3 days, 19 hr, 9 min
Feb. 1939	Benjamin Kelsey	XP-38	Unofficial 2,460-mi transcontinental speed record, March Field, CA, to Mitchel Field, NY	7 hr, 43 min Average speed of 356 mph
Sep. 1946	Cmdrs. Thomas Davies, Eugene Rankin, and Walter Reid, and Lt. Cmdr. Roy Tabeling	P2V-1	Distance record of 11,235.6 mi from Perth, Australia, to Port Columbus, OH	55 hr, 17 min
Jan. 1946	Col. William Councill	P-80A	Nonstop transcontinental speed record from Long Beach, CA, to New York	4 hr, 13 min, 26 sec Average speed of 580.93 mph over a distance of 2,453.8 mi
Apr. 1946	Capt. Martin Smith	P-80A	Speed record from New York to Washington, D.C.	20 min, 15 sec
June 1946	Lt. Henry Johnson	P-80A	1,000-km speed record	426.97 mph
Aug. 1946	Col. Leon Gray	FP-80A	Bendix Trophy Race winner, Jet Division	4 hr, 8 min, 18 sec 494.779 mph
Sep. 1946	Lt. W. J. Reilly	P-80A	Weatherhead Jet Speed Dash	578.360 mph
Sep. 1946	Maj. Gus Lundquist	P-80A	Thompson Trophy Race winner, Jet Division	515.853 mph
June 1947	Col. Albert Boyd	P-80R	Absolute world speed record	623.608 mph

Date	Pilot	Plane	Event	Result
Sep. 1947	Capt. Bernor	FP-80A	Allison Trophy Race winner	494.277 mph
Sep. 1947	Anthony LeVier	P-38L	Sohio Trophy Race winner	360.866 mph
Sep. 1947	Col. Leon Gray	FP-80A	Bendix Trophy Race winner, Jet Division	4 hr, 2 min, 34 sec 507.255 mph
Sep. 1947	Lt. Col. R. L. Petit	P-80A	Thompson Trophy Race winner, Jet Division	500.704 mph
May 1958	Maj. Howard Johnson	YF-104A	World altitude record	91,249 ft
May 1958	Capt. Walter Irwin	YF-104A	Speed record over 15/25 km course	1,404.19 mph
Dec. 1958	unknown	F-104A	Three time-to-climb records	3,000 m (9,842 ft) 41.35 sec; 15,000 m (49,212 ft) 131.1 sec; 25,000 m (82,020 ft) 266.03 sec
May 1958	Capt. Walter Irwin	F-104A	Absolute world speed record	1,404.09 mph
Dec. 1959	unknown	F-104C	World altitude record	103,389 ft (31,513 m)
May 1964	Jacqueline Cochran	TF-104G	Women's speed record over 15/25 km course	1,429.3 mph
June 1964	Jacqueline Cochran	TF-104G	Women's speed record over 100-km course	1,303 mph
June 1964	Jacqueline Cochran	TF-104G	Women's speed record over 500-km course	1,127 mph
May 1965	Col. Robert Stephens	YF-12A	Absolute world speed record	2,070.115 mph
Apr. 1971	Maj. Thomas Estes and Maj. Dewain Vick	SR-71	Sustained horizontal flight with in-flight refueling	15,000 mi
July 1976	Capt. Robert Helt and Maj. Larry Elliot	SR-71	Height in sustained horizontal flight	85,069 ft
July 1976	Capt. Eldon Joersz and Maj. George Morgan Jr.	SR-71	Speed in a straight line	2,193 mph
July 1976	Maj. Adolphus Bledsoe and Maj. John Fuller	SR-71	Speed over a 1,000-km closed circuit	2,092 mph

Date	Pilot	Plane	Event	Result
Sep. 1976	Maj. James Sullivan and Maj. Noel Widdifield	SR-71	Beale AFB to RAE Farnborough nonstop with in-flight refueling	1 hr, 55 min, 42 sec 3,490 mi
Sep. 1976	Capt. Harold Adams and Maj. William Machorek	SR-71	London to Los Angeles nonstop with in-flight refueling	1,487 mph 5,645 mi
Oct. 1977	Darryl Greenamyer	F-104RB	Low-altitude 3-km speed record for Class C.1, Group III aircraft	988.26 mph

Aircraft and Fleet Ballistic Missile Characteristics

Basic Model No.	Aircraft Name	Span ft-in.	Length ft-in.	Gross Weight lb	Empty Weight lb	Wing Area sq-ft	Service Ceiling ft	Range mi	Cruise Speed mph	Max Speed mph	Remarks
A	Design Only										Details unknown
B	Design Only										"
C	Design Only										"
D	Design Only										"
E	Design Only										"
G	Float Plane	46-0/36-0	30-0	2,200	1,616				51	63	First Lockheed (Loughead) airplane
F-1	Flying Boat	74-0/48-0	35-0	7,300	4,200			510	70	84	Biplane flying boat
F-1A	Land Plane	75-0/48-0	35-0	Similar to F-1							Conversion of F-1 to land plane
HS-2L	Flying Boat	74-0/64-0	39-0	6,432						85	Curtiss design, license-built for U.S. Navy
S-1	Sport Plane	28-0/24-0	20-0	825	375		12,000			70	8-hour endurance
1	Vega	41-0	27-8	3,470	1,650	275	15,000	900	118	138	
2	Vega	41-0	27-6	3,853	2,565	275	19,000	725	165	155	
3	Air Express	41-0	27-6	4,375	2,533	288	17,250	750	135	185	
4	Explorer	48-6	27-6	9,008	3,075	313		5,500		165	
5	Vega	41-0	27-8	4,033						170	
6	Model number not used										Possible design study
7	Explorer Special	48-6	27-6	3,433	3,075	313				165	Similar to Explorer, but with some design changes
8	Sirius	42-10	27-6	4,600	4,289	294	26,100	975	150	175	
8E-F	Altair	40-10	27-4	4,895	3,235	293	23,800	580	175	230	
9	Orion	41-10	28-4	5,800	3,420	294	22,000	750	175	225	
DL-1	Vega	41-0	27-6	4,270						178	Metal Vega fuselage built by Detroit Aircraft
DL-2	Sirius	42-10	27-10	5,170	2,958	294	18,000	870	145	175	Metal Sirius fuselage built by Detroit Aircraft
XP-900	As Air Corps YP-24	42-9.5	28-9	4,360	3,010	292	25,000	556	215	235	Detroit Aircraft project
10	Electra	55-0	38-7	10,300	6,454	458	19,400	810	190	202	8-passenger transport

Basic Model No.	Aircraft Name	Span ft-in.	Length ft-in.	Gross Weight lb	Empty Weight lb	Wing Area sq-ft	Service Ceiling ft	Range mi	Cruise Speed mph	Max Speed mph	Remarks
10	XFM-2 Multiplace Fighter										Design study only, none built
10	XC-35		38-7	10,300	7,940	458	31,500		214	236	
11	Design Study										6-passenger transport with Menasco Unitwin engine
11	Altair 8G	40-10	27-4	Similar to Model 8E							Altair flying test bed for Menasco Unitwin engine
12	Electra Junior	49-6	36-4	8,400	5,765	352	22,900	800	213	225	6-passenger transport
13	Model number not used										
14	Super Electra	65-6	44-4	17,500	10,300	551	24,300	1,500	215	247	Data for Model 14H
14	Hudson Bomber	65-6	44-4	17,500	11,630	551	25,000	1,960	220	246	Data for Hudson I
15	Design Study										Vega-built navy patrol bomber
15	PV-1 Harpoon	65-6	51-9	34,000	20,197	551	26,300	1,360	170	322	Model 10 derivative, not built
16	Design Study										
17	Model number not used										
18	Lodestar	65-6	49-10	19,200						218	
19	Design Study										Model 14 derivative, not built
20	Design Study										Model 14 derivative, not built
21	Ventura			See Model 37							Initial model designation for Ventura bomber
22	P-38 Lightning	52-0	37-10	17,500	12,800	328	44,000	450	290	414	Data for P-38L
22	XP-58 Chain Lightning	70-0	49-5	39,192	31,624	600	38,200	1,250	283	436	Allison V-3420 engines
23	XP-49	52-0	40-1	22,000	15,464	327	37,500	680	372	406	Continental XIV-1430 engines
24	Proposed navy version of P-38										None built
25	Model number not used										

No.	Name / Description										Remarks
26	P2V Neptune	104-0	78-3	72,000	39,900	1,000	26,000	3,195	207	353	Data for P2V-5
27	Proposed twin-engine transport using canard surfaces								353		None built
28	Model number not used										
29	Proposed twin-engine attack bomber										None built
30	Proposed twin-engine attack bomber using canard surfaces										None built
31	Proposed export derivative of Model 29 attack bomber										None built
32	Proposed military reconnaissance version of Model 18										None built
33	Little Dipper	25-0	17-6	725	425	104	16,000	210	90	100	
34	Big Dipper	31-0	22-2	1,450	935		16,000	305	119	136	Two-place pusher aircraft designed for private flying
35	Military Trainer	29-9	25-5.75	1,930	1,362	148	16,000		129	134	Design purchased from North American Aviation
36	Model number not used										
37	Ventura	65-6	51-5	26,000	17,233	551	25,000	925	272	312	Military version of the Lodestar
38	Model number not used										
39	Model number not used										
40	Aerial Target	23-0	14-3.5		848		10,000			160	Pilotless design, 5 built
41	Aerial Target proposal										Pilotless design, none built
42	Aerial Target proposal										Pilotless design, none built
43	Unknown										
44	Excalibur										4-engine transport, None built
45	Proposed radio control vehicle										None built
46-48	Unknown										
49	Constellation	123-0	95-2	86,250	55,345	1,650	25,000	2,290	275	329	Data for original model Constellation
50	Proposed liaison aircraft										None built
51	XB-30 Bomber										Model 49 Constellation derivative, none built
52	Proposed single-engine fighter										None built
53-59	Unknown										
60	Proposed twin-engine crew trainer										None built

Basic Model No.	Aircraft Name	Span ft-in.	Length ft-in.	Gross Weight lb	Empty Weight lb	Wing Area sq-ft	Service Ceiling ft	Range mi	Cruise Speed mph	Max Speed mph	Remarks
61	Proposed twin-engine crew trainer										None built
62	Proposed twin-engine crew trainer										None built
63-70	Unknown										Applications unknown
71-73	Model numbers opened for Lockheed-Georgia										
74	Unknown										
75	Saturn	74-0	51-6	16,000						228	Feeder line passenger airplane
76-79	Model numbers opened for Lockheed-Georgia										Applications unknown
80	P-80 Shooting Star	38-10.5	34-6	14,000	7,920	238	45,000	780	410	558	Data for P-80A
80	T-33	38-10.5	37-9	15,061	8,365	235	48,000	1,025	455	600	
80	F-94	37-4	44-6	24,184	12,708	233	51,400	805	493	640	Data for F-94C
80	T2V	42-10	38-6.5	16,800	11,965	240	40,000	970		580	
81	XFV-1	30-10.11	36-10.2	16,221	11,599	246	43,300		410	580	Vertical takeoff and landing aircraft
82	C-130	132-6	97-8	175,000	76,780	1,745	42,900	2,745	355	386	Data for C-130H
83	F-104 Starfighter	21-9	54-8	29,038	18,218	196	58,000	1,080	510	1,146	Data for F-104G
84	W2V-1										Navy contract canceled
85	P-3 Orion	99-8	116-10	142,000	61,491	1,300	28,300	1,550	378	473	Data for P-3C
86	XH-51A	35-0 (rotor dia.)	42-1	4,100	2,640			350	160	174	Experimental attack helicopter
87	AH-56 Cheyenne	50-5 (rotor dia.)	54-7	25,880	12,215	1,300	25,000	1,225	247	253	Attack helicopter
88	Electra (turboprop)	99-0	104-6	113,000	57,400	1,300	28,400	2,200	373	448	
89	XR60-1 Constitution	189-1.25	156-1	184,000	114,575	3,610	27,600	6,300	269	303	
90	XF-90	40-0	56-2	31,060	18,050	345	39,000	1,050	473	668	
91	Supersonic transport design										None built
92	Proposed civil helicopter										
93	L-1011 Tristar	155-4	178-8	430,000	234,275	3,456	42,000	2,880	495	545	Data for L-1011-1
94	S-3 Viking	68-8	53-4	52,539	26,650	598	35,000	2,000	403	518	

Aircraft specifications (continued):

No.	Name	Span ft-in	Length ft-in	Gross wt lb	Empty wt lb	Wing area sq ft	Ceiling ft	Range mi	Cruise mph	Max speed	Notes
95-98	Unknown / Interceptor Project										USAF contract canceled
99	X-27 Lancer	28-8	56-4	32,500	17,250	311				1,450	Project canceled, none built
	CL-475	32-0 (rotor dia.)		2,000	1,625					90	Prototype rigid rotor research helicopter vehicle
	U-2	80-2	49-8	24,150	14,250	600	70,000	3,000		430	
	U-2R (TR-1)	103-0	62-10.5		24,750	1,000	70,000	2,995	504	547	
	JetStar II	54-5	60-5	44,500	2,024	543	43,000	550	130	167	Light utility transport
	LASA-60	39-4	28-1	3,752	4,995	210	23,100	600	390	463	
	XV-4 Hummingbird	27-1	33-9.5	12,580		104					Experimental VTOL aircraft
	C-141 Starlifter	160-0	145-0	323,100	136,900	3,228	51,700	4,155	478	565	Data for C-141A
	QT-2/X-26B Q-Star	57-1	30-10	2,182	1,576	180	18,500	350	75	115	
	YO-3A	57-0	29-4	3,800	3,129	205	14,000		110	138	
	C-5 Galaxy	222-8.5	247-9.5	837,000	374,000	6,200	35,750	3,435	518	571	Data for C-5B
	SR-71	55-7	107-5	170,000		913		690		2,250	
	F-117A	43-4	65-11	52,500		900			Mach .9		
	F-22A	44-6	62-1	29,500						Mach 2	
	X-33	68-0	63-0	273,000			60 mi			Mach 15+	Successor to the space shuttle

Missile Name	Weight lb	Length ft-in	Diameter in	Range nautical mi	Propulsion	Warhead
Polaris A1	28,000	28-6	54	1,200	Two-stage rocket	Single
Polaris A2	32,500	31-0	54	1,500	Two-stage rocket	Single
Polaris A3	35,700	32-4	54	2,500	Two-stage rocket	MRV*
Poseidon C3	64,400	34-0	74	2,500	Three-stage rocket	MIRV+
Trident 1 (C4)	71,000	34-0	74	4,000	Three-stage rocket	MIRV
Trident II D-5	130,000	44-6	83	6,000	Three-stage rocket	MIRV

*Multiple reentry vehicle

+Multiple independently-targeted reentry vehicle

Lockheed Corporation Subsidiaries, Affiliates, Divisions, and Groups

Many organizations, with their acronyms, have existed within Lockheed over the years. Over time, the same acronyms were sometimes applied to later and different organizations. Some organizations apparently were not given acronyms, or at least those acronyms have not been found in the author's research. The following list has most, but undoubtedly not all, of the many companies that were part and parcel of Lockheed life. They give some idea of the scope of the company, and also the impossibility of recording every event of eighty-five years of history in a single volume.

Subsidiaries	Organizational Title
d-Access Graphics, Inc.	ACCESS
d-AGT Holdings, Inc.	AGT
f-CALCOMP A.B.	CAAB
f-CALCOMP A/S	CALAS
f-CALCOMP Australia PTY. Ltd.	CAPL
f-CALCOMP B.V.	CALBV
f-CALCOMP Canada Ltd.	CALCAN
f-CALCOMP Espana S.A.	CCESPANA
f-CALCOMP Europe B.V.	CEBV
f-CALCOMP Europe Ltd.	CALEL
d-CALCOMP European Management Corporation	CEMCO
f-CALCOMP Foreign Sales Corporation	CFSC
f-CALCOMP Ges.m.b.h.	CGESmbH
f-CALCOMP GmbH	CCGmbH
f-CALCOMP Graphics Peripherals Ltd.	CGPL
f-CALCOMP Graphics Peripherals (China) Ltd.	CGPL CHINA
d-CALCOMP Inc.	CALCOMP
f-CALCOMP Japan Procurement KK	CJPKK
f-CALCOMP LIMITED	CALLIM
d-CALCOMP Pacific, Inc.	CPI
f-CALCOMP S.A.	CALCOSA
f-CALCOMP S.p.A.	CASPA
d-CALCOMP Technology and Procurement, Inc.	CTPI
d-California Computer Products, Inc.	CCPI
d-CSL Leasing Corporation	CSL
d-DATACOM Municipal Systems of Pennsylvania, Inc.	DMSP
f-FORJOHN Ltd.	FORJOHN

d-domestic
f-foreign

Subsidiaries	Organizational Title
f-FORMTEK Europe, N.V.	FENV
d-FORMTEK , Inc.	FORMTEK
d-FORMTEK International, Inc.	FORMTEK INTL
d-LFC Credit Corp.	LFCCC
d-Lockheed Aeromod Center, Inc.	LACI
d-Lockheed Aeronautical Systems Employment Services Company, Inc.	LASES
d-Lockheed Aeronautical Systems Support Company	LASS
d-Lockheed Aeroparts, Inc.	LAPI
f-Lockheed Aircraft (Australia) PTY. Ltd.	LAUS
d-Lockheed Aircraft, Inc.	LAI
f-Lockheed Aircraft International Ltd.	LAIL
d-Lockheed Aircraft Service International	LASI
f-Lockheed B.V.	LBV
f-Lockheed Canada Inc.	LCAN
d-Lockheed Commercial Aircraft Center, Inc.	LCAC
d-Lockheed Commercial Electronics Company	LCEC
d-Lockheed Commercial Space Company Inc.	LCSC
d-Lockheed Engineering & Sciences Company (Lockheed Martin Engineering & Sciences)	LESC
d-Lockheed Environmental Systems & Technologies Company (Lockheed Martin Environmental Systems & Technologies)	LESAT
d-Lockheed Foreign Enterprise Company, Inc.	LFEC
f-Lockheed Foreign Sales Corporation	LFSC
d-Lockheed Fort Rucker, Inc.	LFRI
d-Lockheed Fort Worth International Corporation	LFWIC
d-Lockheed-Hellas S.A.	LHSA
d-Lockheed Ho-Chin Incorporated	LHCI
d-Lockheed Idaho Technologies Company (Lockheed Martin Idaho Technologies)	LITCO

Subsidiaries	Organizational Title
f-Lockheed Information Management Services Canada Inc.	LIMSCA
f-Lockheed Information Management Services (UK) Ltd.	LIMS (UK)
d-Lockheed Information Technology Company	LITC
d-Lockheed Integrated Solutions Company	LISC
f-Lockheed International G.m.b.H.	LIGmbH
f-Lockheed International Ltd. Taiwan	LILT
d-Lockheed International Service and Investment Corporation	LISIC
d-Lockheed International Services, Inc.	LISI
d-Lockheed Investment Corporation	LIC
d-Lockheed Martin Finance Corporation	LMFC
d-Lockheed Martin IMS Corporation	LM IMS
f-Lockheed Martin International Ltd.	LMIL
f-Lockheed Martin International S.A.	LMISA
d-Lockheed Materials Processing Company	LMPC
d-Lockheed Mercator Information Company, Inc.	LMICI
f-Lockheed Middle-East Services	LMS
d-Lockheed Missiles & Space Company, Inc. (Lockhed Martin Missiles & Space)	LMSC
d-Lockheed Mortgage Corporation	LMC
d-Lockheed Nevada Company	LNC
d-Lockheed of Turkey, Inc.	LOTI
d-Lockheed Sanders, Inc. (Sanders, a Lockheed Martin Company)	SANDERS
d-Lockheed Services Company, Inc.	LSC
d-Lockheed Shipbuilding Company	LSC
d-Lockheed Space Operations Company (Lockheed Martin Space Operations)	LSOC
d-Lockheed Support Systems, Inc. (Lockheed Martin Logistics Management)	LSSI

Subsidiaries	Organizational Title
d-Lockheed Systems Company, Inc.	LSCI
d-Lockheed Technical Enterprises Corporation	LTEC
d-Lockheed Technical Operations Company, Inc. (Lockheed Martin Technical Operations)	LTOC
d-Lockheed Technical Services Company, Inc.	LTSC
f-Lockheed Technical Services (Malaysia) S.B.	LTSM
d-Lockheed Transport Systems, Inc.	LTSI
d-Lockheed-Vance, Inc.	LVI
d-Lockheed Worldwide Support Systems, Inc.	LWSS
f-Mountaingate Data Systems GmbH	MDS GmbH
d-Mountaingate Data Systems, Inc. (CA)	MOUNTAINGATE
d-Mountaingate Data Systems, Inc. (NV)	MDS
f-Mountaingate Data Systems Ireland, Ltd.	MDS Ireland
f-Mountaingate Data Systems U.K., Ltd.	MDS UK
d-Murdock Engineering Company	MURDOCK
f-NS CALCOMP Corporation	NSCC
f-N.V. CALCOMP S.A.	NVCALSA
d-Quality International Services, Inc.	QISI
d-Sanders Associates International, Inc.	SAII
d-Sanders Development Corporation	SDC
d-Star Reconveyance Corporation	SRC
d-Tristar Parts, Ltd.	TPL

Inactive Subsidiaries and Affiliates

d-CALCOMP International, Inc.	CII
d-Colby Crane & Manufacturing, Inc. (capitalization)	COLBY
f-General Dynamics Kabushiki Kaisha	GDKK
f-Guam Air Terminal Corporation (capitalization)	GATC
d-Puget Sound Bridge & Dry Dock Company, Inc. (no capitalization)	PUGET
d-Vega Aircraft Company (no capitalization, w/ assets)	VEGA

Affiliates	Organizational Title
f-Aeroplex of Central Europe	ACE
f-Airport Group Canada Inc.	AGI CAN
f-Airport Group International GmbH	AGI GmbH
d-Airport Group International, Inc.	AGI INC
d-Airport Group International, Ltd.	AGI LTD
d-Airport Group New York, Inc.	AGI NY
f-Airport Group United Kingdom Ltd.	AGI UK
f-Airod Sendirian Berhad	AIROD
d-Arnold W. Thompson Corporation	AWT
d-California Airport Partnerships, Inc.	CAPI
f-Guangzhou Aircraft Maintenance Engineering Company, Ltd.	GAMECO
f-Gulf Technology Systems Group	GULFTECH
f-Hellenic Business Development & Investment Company, S.A.	HBDIC
d-International Launch Services (formerly Lockheed Khrunichev Energia)	ILS
f-LAH Ltd.	LAH
f-Letlock Saudi Arabia Company Ltd.	LETLOCK
f-Lockheed Air Terminal S.A.	LATSA
f-Lockheed Investment Holding Company A.S. (Lockheed Yatirim Holdings A.S.)	LIHCAS
f-Pacific Aerospace Corporation Ltd.	PAC
d-Space Imaging, Inc.	SII
d-Thompson Consultants International, Inc.	TCO
f-Tusas Aerospace Industries, Inc.	TUSAS

Limited Liability Company

d-Airport Group International Holdings, L.L.C.	AGI LLC

d-domestic
f-foreign

Partnership Corporation	Organizational Title
d-Vought Corporation	VOUGHT

Nonprofit Corporation

d-Lockheed Leadership Fund	LLF

Divisions

Lockheed Advanced Development Company (Lockheed Martin Skunk Works)	LADC
Lockheed Aeronautical Systems Company (Lockheed Martin Aeronautical Systems)	LASC
Lockheed Aircraft Service Company (Lockheed Martin Aircraft Services)	LAS
Lockheed Fort Worth Company (Lockheed Martin Tactical Aircraft Systems)	LFWC
Lockheed Properties Division	LPD

Former Subsidiaries and Affiliates

Commercial Steel Fabricators, Inc.
    100% owned by Puget Sound
        Bridge & Drydock
    Incorporated 1911—
        Washington
    Dissolved June 30, 1961

Lockheed Electronics Company
(LEC)
(Formerly Stavid Engineering,
Inc.)
    100% owned by Lockheed
        Aircraft Corporation
    Incorporated August 27,
    1959—Delaware
    Merged with LAC August 29,
        1961

Colby Crane & Manufacturing,
Inc.
(Formerly Colby Steel &
Manufacturing, Inc.)
    100% owned by Puget Sound
        Bridge & Drydock
    Incorporated September 28,
        1949—Washington
    Dissolved August 3, 1962
    (NOTE: Eagle Manufacturing
        Company, formerly a
        subsidiary of Colby Steel
        & Manufacturing, Inc.,
        merged with that
        company as of December
        23, 1960).

d-domestic
f-foreign

Former Subsidiaries and Affiliates

Lockheed Aircraft Service, Inc.
  100% owned by Lockheed
    Aircraft Corporation
  Incorporated November 29,
    1946—California
  Merged with LAC May 7,
    1962

Lockheed Aircraft Service–New
York, Inc.
(Formerly LASI—
name changed in 1959)
  Owned by Lockheed Aircraft
    Service, Inc.
  Incorporated August 2, 1948—
    New York
  Merged into LAS, Inc., May
    7, 1962

Lockheed Propulsion Company
(Formerly Grand Central Rocket
Co.)
  100% owned by Lockheed
    Aircraft Corporation as of
    August 30, 1961
  Incorporated May 21, 1957—
    California
  Merged with LAC February
    4, 1963

Aviones Lockheed–Kaiser S.A.
  50% owned by LAISA
  Incorporated April 1, 1960—
    Argentina
  Transferred to IKA September
    29, 1963

Industria Latinoamericana de
Accesorios S.A.
  Affiliate of LAISA

Incorporated March 16,
1964—Argentina
LAISA sold all its equity
  interest to
IKA-Renault S.A.I.C.F., an
  Argentine company,
June 12, 1968

Transportation Systems, Inc.
  50% owned by Lockheed
    Aircraft Corporation
  Incorporated March 3, 1961—
    Georgia
  LAC's interest transferred to
    Lykes Corporation
March 26, 1969

Lockheed Azcarate, S.A.
  72.323% by LAISA; 27.766%
    by LAC
  Incorporated December 10,
    1958—Mexico
  Dissolved January 12, 1970

Compania Impulsora de
Industrias Mexicanas, S.A.
  Incorporated August 14,
    1961—Mexico
  Sold August 31, 1970

Ventura Manufacturing
Company
  100% owned by Lockheed
    Aircraft Corporation
  Incorporated March 26,
    1968—Texas
  Sold April 1, 1971

Comet, S.A.
  70.016% owned by LAISA;
    12.672% owned by LSA;
  17.312% owned by "others"

Former Subsidiaries and Affiliates

Incorporated November 22,
1963—Mexico
Sold June 24, 1971

Network Finance Ltd.
(Formerly Hooker Finance
Company Ltd.)
10.4% owned by LAI, Inc.
Incorporated June 6, 1951—
Australia
Sold July 15, 1971

Nihon Lockheed Monorail K.K.
8.33% owned by LAIL
Incorporated May 4, 1961
Dissolved

Aviquipo Domestic International
Sales Corporation
100% owned by Aviquipo,
Inc.
Incorporated April 28, 1975—
Nevada
Dissolved December 19, 1975

Lockheed Domestic
International Sales Corporation
100% owned by LAC
Incorporated April 28, 1975—
Nevada
Dissolved December 19, 1975

Lockheed Western Sales
Corporation
100% owned by LAC
Incorporated January 31,
1974—Nevada
Dissolved December 19, 1975

Lockheed International Limited
Taiwan
100% owned by LAIL

Incorporated April 10, 1974
Dissolved September 16,
1976

Aviquipo, Inc.
100% owned by Lockheed
Corporation
Incorporated October 27,
1933—New York
Dissolved August 21, 1978

Estalsa, S.A.
8.33% owned by LAI
Incorporated December 31,
1965
Dissolved December 2, 1976

Lockheed Asian Export
Company
Lockheed Corporation—no
shares issued
Incorporated February 24,
1978
Dissolved March 5, 1979

Aeronautica Macchi S.p.A.
20% owned by Lockheed
Corporation
Incorporated 1912
(Lockheed Aircraft Company
interest acquired
November 27, 1959, n/o
LAISA and transferred
n/o LAC June 28, 1967)
Sold February 22, 1979

Aviaco Traders Limited
100% owned by Lockheed
Corporation
Incorporated November 5,
1969
Dissolved October 31, 1979

Former Subsidiaries and Affiliates

Lockheed Petroleum Services, Ltd.
  100% owned by LPS, Inc.
  Incorporated August 11, 1969—Vancouver, B.C. (a British Columbia corporation)
  Sold December 20, 1979

Lockheed Petroleum Services, Inc.
  100% owned by Lockheed Corporation
  Incorporated May 8, 1978—California
  Sold December 20, 1979

Lockheed Petroleum Services (U.K.) Limited
  a subsidiary of LPS Ltd.
  Incorporated January 9, 1976—United Kingdom
  Sold December 20, 1979

Lockheed Equipamentos e Servicios Ltda.
  a subsidiary of LPS Ltd.
  Incorporated November 21, 1975—Brazil
  Sold December 20, 1979

Lockheed Aircraft Nederland B.V. (formerly N.V.)
  100% owned by Lockheed Corporation—Holland
  Dissolved February 14, 1980

Lockheed (Africa and Mid-East) S.A.
  100% owned by Lockheed Corporation

Formerly Lockheed Aircraft (Mid-East) S.A.—name changed September 13, 1978
  Incorporated June 29, 1971—Switzerland
  Merged into Lockheed Aircraft (Europe) S.A. December 19, 1980 (LAESA became Lockheed Corporation International S.A. as of January 13, 1981)

Lockheed S.A. de C.V.
  100% owned by Lockheed Corporation
  Incorporated September 22, 1958—Mexico
  Acquired by LAC November 3, 1968
  Liquidated January 12, 1983

Alaska State Fueling Facilities Corporation (ASFFC)
  Incorporated April 30, 1981—Alaska
  Dissolved February 18, 1983

LFC Credit Corporation (New York)
  Merged into Lockheed Finance Corporation July 23, 1982

Airarms Incorporated
  100% owned by Lockheed Aircraft Company
  Incorporated April 27, 1940

Former Subsidiaries and Affiliates

Acquired by LAC August 31, 1942
Dissolved August 19, 1983

Lockheed Systems S.A.
Incorporated December 12, 1974—Switzerland
Dissolved August 22, 1983

Lockheed Properties, Inc.
100% owned by Lockheed Corporation
Incorporated August 24, 1970
Merged into Lockheed Corporation August 29, 1983

Lockheed Aircraft International, S.A.
100% owned by Lockheed Corporation
Incorporated August 28, 1959
Dissolved August 16, 1983

LDS Corporation
100% owned by Lockheed Corporation
Incorporated March 19, 1984
Merged into Datacom Systems Corporation May 17, 1984

Los Angeles Fueling Facilities Corporation (LAFFC)
Lockheed Air Terminal, Inc.—no shares issued
Incorporated December 21, 1981—California
Dissolved June 12, 1984

San Francisco Fueling Facilities Corporation (SFFFC)
Lockheed Air Terminal, Inc.—no shares issued
Incorporated July 2, 1981—California
Dissolved June 12, 1984

Tricities Protective Services, Inc. (TPSI)—
100% owned by Lockheed Air Terminal, Inc.
Incorporated April 26, 1982—California
Dissolved June 12, 1984

Honolulu Fueling Facilities Corporation (HFFC)
4.6% owned by Lockheed Air Terminal, Inc.
Incorporated August 25, 1979—Hawaii
LAT returned stock in 1984

Portland Fueling Facilities Corporation (PFFC)
10% owned by Lockheed Air Terminal, Inc.
Incorporated November 18, 1971—Oregon
Stock returned in 1984

Reno Fueling Facilites Corporation (RFFC)
Lockheed Air Terminal—no shares held
Incorporated December 28, 1979—Nevada
No LAT investment—closed 1984

Former Subsidiaries and Affiliates

Lockheed Technology S.A. (LTSA)
    Incorporated December 12, 1974—Switzerland
    Dissolved July 14, 1984

Oklahoma Fueling Facilities Corporation (OFFC)
    100% owned by Lockheed Air Terminal, Inc.
    Incorporated August 8, 1980—Oklahoma
    Dissolved December 12, 1985

Ocean Minerals, Inc. (OMI)
    39.71% owned by Lockheed Missiles & Space Company
    Incorporated November 4, 1977—Delaware
    Renewed February 29, 1984—Delaware
    Dissolved December 12, 1985

Lockheed Domestic International Sales Corp. II (LDISC II)
    100% owned by Lockheed Corporation
    Incorporated August 4, 1983—Nevada
    Dissolved December 18, 1985

Datacom Municipal Systems of Ohio, Inc. (DMSO)
    100% owned by Datacom Systems Corporation
    Incorporated August 10, 1982—Ohio
    Dissolved December 27, 1985

Lockheed Overseas Capital N.V. (LOCNV)
    100% owned by Lockheed Corporation
    Incorporated June 15, 1979—Netherlands Antilles
    Dissolved December 29, 1985

Datacom Municipal Systems of Texas, Inc. (DMST)
    100% owned by Datacom Systems Corporation
    Incorporated March 28, 1983—Texas
    Dissolved December 30, 1985

Lockheed Aircraft International, Inc. (LAI)
    100% owned by Lockheed Corporation
    Incorporated November 22, 1943—California
    Dissolved January 28, 1986

Panel Lock Homes (Phil) Inc. (PHIL)
    34% owned by Lockheed Corporation
    Incorporated October 10, 1967—Philippines
    Lockheed acquired shares from Lockheed Aircraft International, A.G. September 24, 1976
    All stock disposed of April 9, 1986

CTL Corporation (CTL)
    50% owned by Lockheed Corporation

Former Subsidiaries and Affiliates

Incorporated May 17, 1978—
Cayman Islands
Dissolved March 31, 1986

Pontifex Acquisition
Corporation (PONTIFEX)
100% owned by Lockheed
Corporation
Incorporated July 7, 1986—
Delaware
Merged into Sanders
Associates October 6,
1986

Coventry Business Systems, Inc.
100% owned by Datacom
Systems Corporation
Incorporated January 15,
1979—New York
Dissolved November 19,
1986

Sanders Securities Corporation
(SSECCO)
100% owned by Sanders
Associates, Inc.
Incorporated December 12,
1984—Massachusetts
Merged into Sanders
Associates December 1,
1986

Calcomp S.A. de C.V. (CSACV)
49% owned by Sanders
Associates
Incorporated May 1980—
Mexico
Sold during FY 1986 to
private party

Arizona Fueling Facilities
Corporation (AFFC)
Affiliate of Lockheed Air
Terminal, Inc.
Incorporated January 23,
1979—Arizona
Stock returned in 1986

Utah Fueling Facilities
Corporation (UFFC)
Lockheed Air Terminal, Inc.—
no shares
Incorporated August 28,
1980—Utah
Dissolved in 1986

Martemis Systems AG
(MARTEMIS)
100% owned by Metier
Management Systems
Holding BV
Incorporated 1982—
Switzerland
Liquidated December 31,
1986

Macrodata Corporation
100% owned by Datacom
Systems Corporation
Incorporated June 29, 1983—
California
Dissolved June, 1987

Datacom Collections Systems
Corporation (DCSC)
100% owned by Datacom
Systems Corporation
Incorporated April 7, 1971—
New York
Dissolved July 28, 1987

Former Subsidiaries and Affiliates

Brophy & Associates, Inc.
(BROPHY)
  100% owned by Datacom
    Systems Corporation
  Incorporated May 5, 1982—
    Delaware
  Dissolved August 19, 1987

Dicon N.V. (DICONNV)
  100% owned by Metier
    Management Systems Int'l
    N.V.
  Incorporated 1982—
    Netherlands Antilles
  Liquidated August 28, 1987

Metier Management Systems
International N.V.
  100% owned by Metier, Inc.
  Incorporated April 19, 1982
  Liquidated August 28, 1987

Lockheed Sait Electronics S.A.
(LSE)
  50% owned by Lockheed
    Corporation
  Incorporated June 14, 1973—
    Belgium
  Liquidated October 20, 1987

Datacom Consultants, Inc.
(DCI)
  100% owned by Datacom
    Systems Corporation
  Incorporated August 30, 1979
  Dissolved June 24, 1988

Dialog Information Services,
Inc. (DIALOG)
  100% owned by Lockheed
    Corporation

Incorporated August 25,
  1980—California
Sold to Knight-Ridder
  Information Services, Inc.,
  August 31, 1988

Sanders International Sales
Corporation (SISCO)
  100% owned by Sanders
    Associates, Inc.
  Incorporated March 22,
    1982—Delaware
  Dissolved September 13,
    1988

S.A. Sales Corporation (SASCO)
  Incorporated May 19, 1982—
    Delaware
  Dissolved September 13,
    1988

Terak Corporation (TERAK)
  100% owned by CalComp
    Inc.
  Incorporated December
    1978—Delaware
  Dissolved November 15,
    1988

Lockheed Aircraft International,
A.G. (LAIAG)
  100% owned by Lockheed
    Corporation
  Incorporated July 8, 1960—
    Switzerland
  Liquidated December 2, 1988

Lockheed Canada Inc. (LCAN)
  100% owned by Lockheed
    Corporation

Former Subsidiaries and Affiliates

Incorporated September 9,
1939—Canada
Amalgamated with Sanders
Canada Inc. and ceased to
exist on December 25,
1988

Sanders Canada Inc. (SACI)
100% owned by Lockheed
Corporation
Incorporated April 11, 1985—
Canada
Amalgamated with Lockheed
Canada Inc. and ceased to
exist on December 25,
1988

Image Resource Corporation
(IMAGE)
100% owned by CalComp
Inc.
Incorporated January 15,
1971—California
Dissolved January 5, 1989

Getex Inc. (GETEX)
Lockheed Corporation—no
shares issued
Incorporated November 19,
1982—Georgia
Dissolved April 25, 1989

Artemis Middle East E.C.
100% owned by Metier Inc.
Incorporated March 1,
1983—Bahrain
Liquidated May 22, 1989

Lockheed Dataplan, Inc. (LDI)
100% owned by Lockheed
Corporation

Incorporated June 10, 1974—
California
Sold to Jeppesen Sanderson,
Inc., December 4, 1989

Memrykord Limited
(MEMRYKORD)
91% owned by Lockheed
DataPlan, Inc.
9% owned by Lockheed
Corporation
Incorporated July 15, 1977—
England
Sold to TM Holdings, Inc.,
December 4, 1989

Austcad Pty. Ltd. (AUSTCAD)
10% owned by CADAM
Inc.
Acquired August 18, 1986
(Australia)
Sold to IBM January 5, 1990

CADAM Inc. (CADAM)
100% owned by Lockheed
Corporation
Incorporated July 23,
1981—California
Sold to IBM January 5, 1990

Cadam Deutschland GmbH
(CDGmbH)
100% owned by CADAM
Inc.
Formed December 11, 1986—
Germany
Sold to IBM January 5, 1990

CADAM France SARL (CFS)
5% owned by CADAM Inc.

Former Subsidiaries and Affiliates

Formed December 16, 1985—
France
Sold to IBM January 5, 1990

CADAM International B.V.
(CIBV)
100% owned by CADAM
Inc.
Formed October 17, 1986—
the Netherlands
Sold to IBM January 5, 1990

CADAM Pacific Limited (CPL)
100% owned by CADAM
Inc.
Formed October 3, 1986—
Hong Kong
Sold to IBM January 5, 1990

CADAM Systems Company
(CSC)
50% owned by CADAM Inc.
Incorporated April 2, 1984—
Japan
Sold to IBM January 5,
1990

Artemis Management Systems
Holdings Limited
100% owned by Metier Inc.
Incorporated May 29,
1981—Hong Kong
Acquired by Lockheed
Corporation May 20,
1985
Sold to Lucas Industries, Inc.,
March 30, 1990

Artemis Management Systems
Pty. Limited

100% owned by Artemis
Management Systems
Holdings Ltd.
Incorporated August 12,
1981—Australia
Acquired by Lockheed
Corporation May 20,
1985
Sold to Lucas Industries, Inc.,
March 30, 1990

Dicon A.G. (DICONAG)
100% owned by Dicon
Holding Netherlands B.V
Incorporated October 26,
1982—Switzerland
Acquired by Lockheed
Corporation May 20,
1985
Sold to Lucas Industries, Inc.,
March 30, 1990

Dicon Holding Netherlands
B.V. (DICONBV)
100% owned by Dicon N.V.
Incorporated June 5, 1981—
the Netherlands
Acquired by Lockheed
Corporation May 20,
1985
Sold to Lucas Industries, Inc.,
March 30, 1990

Metier, Inc. (METIER)
100% owned by Lockheed
Corporation
Incorporated June 7, 1985—
California
Sold to Lucas Industries, Inc.,
March 30, 1990

Former Subsidiaries and Affiliates

Metier Management Systems
Benelux B.V.
  100% owned by Metier
    Management Systems
    Holding BV
  Incorporated August 27,
    1982—the Netherlands
  Acquired by Lockheed
    Corporation May 20,
    1985
  Sold to Lucas Industries, Inc.,
    March 30, 1990
Metier Management Systems
Deutschland GmbH
  100% owned by Metier
    Management Systems
    Holding BV
  Incorporated—West
    Germany
  Acquired by Lockheed
    Corporation May 20,
    1985
  Sold to Lucas Industries, Inc.,
    March 30, 1990
Metier Management Systems
France S.A.R.L.
  100% owned by Metier
    Management Systems
    Holding BV
  Incorporated June 8, 1978—
    France
  Acquired by Lockheed
    Corporation May 20,
    1985
  Sold to Lucas Industries, Inc.,
    March 30, 1990
Metier Management Systems
Holding B.V.

100% owned by Metier, Inc.
Incorporated 1983—the
  Netherlands
Acquired by Lockheed
  Corporation May 20,
  1985
Sold to Lucas Industries, Inc.,
  March 30, 1990

Metier Management Systems,
Inc.
  100% owned by Metier, Inc.
  Incorporated June 8, 1978—
    Delaware
  Acquired by Lockheed
    Corporation May 20,
    1985
  Sold to Lucas Industries, Inc.,
    March 30, 1990

Metier Management Systems
International Limited
  100% owned by Artemis
    Management Systems
    Holdings Ltd.
  Incorporated December 31,
    1981—Hong Kong
  Acquired by Lockheed
    Corporation May 20,
    1985
  Sold to Lucas Industries, Inc.,
    March 30, 1990

Metier Management Systems
Italia S.R.L.
  100% owned by Metier
    Management Systems
    Holding BV
  Incorporated July 4,
    1984—Italy

Former Subsidiaries and Affiliates

Acquired by Lockheed Corporation May 20, 1985
Sold to Lucas Industries, Inc., March 30, 1990

Metier Management Systems Limited
100% owned by Metier Management Systems Int'l Ltd.
Incorporated June 25, 1981—Japan
Acquired by Lockheed Corporation May 20, 1985
Sold to Lucas Industries, Inc., March 30, 1990

Metier Management Systems Limited
100% owned by Metier Systems, Ltd.
Incorporated December 6, 1976—England
Acquired by Lockheed Corporation May 20, 1985
Sold to Lucas Industries, Inc., March 30, 1990

Metier Management Systems Pte. Ltd.
100% owned by Artemis Management Systems Holdings Ltd.
Incorporated March 17, 1981—Singapore
Acquired by Lockheed

Corporation May 20, 1985
Sold to Lucas Industries, Inc., March 30, 1990

Metier Management Systems (R.S.A.) (Proprietary) Limited
100% owned by Metier Management Systems Holding BV
Incorporated 1984—South Africa
Acquired by Lockheed Corporation May 20, 1985
Sold to Lucas Industries, Inc., March 30, 1990

Metier Management Systems Scandinavia A/S
100% owned by Metier Management Systems Holding BV
Incorporated June 28, 1982—Norway
Acquired by Lockheed Corporation May 20, 1985
Sold to Lucas Industries, Inc., March 30, 1990

Metier Management Systems Sweden Aktiebolag
100% owned by Metier Management Systems Holding BV
Incorporated November, 1984—Sweden

Former Subsidiaries and Affiliates

Acquired by Lockheed
Corporation May 20,
1985
Sold to Lucas Industries, Inc.,
March 30, 1990

Metier Systems, Ltd.
100% owned by Metier, Inc.
Incorporated June 24,
1985—Delaware
Sold to Lucas Industries, Inc.,
March 30, 1990

Avicom International, Inc.
(AVICOM)
Incorporated November 16,
1979—California
Acquired by Lockheed Air
Terminal, Inc., May 29,
1985
Sold to Hughes Aircraft June
13, 1990

Avicom International, Inc. S.A.
(AVICOM SA)
Incorporated March 20,
1984—Mexico
Acquired by Lockheed Air
Terminal, Inc., May 29,
1985
Sold to Hughes Aircraft June
13, 1990

Lockheed Electronics Company,
Inc. (LEC)
Incorporated November 23,
1970—California
Merged into Lockheed
Sanders, Inc., July 1,
1990

High Point Realty Corporation
(HIPOINT)
Incorporated April 5,
1967—New Hampshire
Merged into Lockheed
Sanders, Inc., January 15,
1991

Hi-Tension Realty Corporation
(HITENSION)
Incorporated October 13,
1960—Delaware
Merged into Lockheed
Sanders, Inc., January 15,
1991

Lockheed Electronics
International Operations, Inc.
(LEIO)
100% owned by Lockheed
Sanders, Inc.
Incorporated August 9,
1979—New Jersey
Dissolved April 29, 1991

Lockheed Aircraft Service
Singapore Private Limited
(LASS)
100% owned by Lockheed
Corporation
Incorporated February 23,
1970—Singapore
Dissolved March 9, 1992

Transnational Housing
Company (TCH)
48% owned by Lockheed
Corporation
Incorporated August 23,
1977—Cayman Islands
Dissolved March 31, 1992

Former Subsidiaries and Affiliates

Lockport Marine (LOCKPORT)
100% owned by Lockheed
Corporation
Incorporated May 1, 1985—
Oregon
Dissolved April 27, 1992

Lockheed Systems & Services,
Inc. (LSASI)
100% owned by Lockheed
IMS
Incorporated September 26,
1991—Louisiana
Dissolved September 21,
1992

Analytyx Electronic Systems,
Inc. (ANALYTYX)
100% owned by Sanders
Associates, Inc.
Incorporated April 28,
1976—New Hampshire

Merged into Lockheed
Sanders, Inc., February
27, 1993

International Disarmament
Corporation (IDC)
33⅓% owned by Lockheed
Engineering & Sciences
Co.
Incorporated January 21,
1992—Delaware
Stock sold to B&W Energy
Investments October 14,
1994

Lockheed Employment Services,
Inc. (LESI)
Incorporated October 4,
1991—California
Sold to Lockheed Federal
Credit Union November
29, 1995

An Insight into a Few Important Lockheed Companies

Lockheed almost continuously adapted the framework of its organization to suit changing business needs. For example, we have seen how the establishment of the Lockheed Missile System Division in January 1954 grew rapidly into the Lockheed Missiles & Space Division in January 1959, and then, in June 1961, became the Lockheed Missiles & Space Company. In August 1971, the company was incorporated as LMSC, Incorporated, and went on from there.

This phenomenon of growth and proliferation occurred as well on the aeronautic side and with those companies formed during Lockheed's periodic attempts to diversify and to garner a higher proportion of nondefense business reach. Lockheed also formed or acquired many companies whose business complemented those of the parent corporation. Many of these companies had long, distinguished, and profitable histories, but space limitations preclude more than a brief summary description here. In many instances their leaders and workers had been part of the original Lockheed firm, and they never felt any loss of identity. In the case of acquisitions, it sometimes took a considerable period of time before members of the acquired organization felt that they were true members of the Lockheed family.

The following list gives some insight into the depth and breadth of Lockheed activities beyond those of making air- and spacecraft.

Lockheed Aircraft Service Corporation (Now Lockheed Martin Aeronautics International) From a small depot set up in Amsterdam in 1938 to furnish European operators of Lockheed equipment with a handy service and maintenance base, the pressures of war caused the Lockheed Aircraft Service Corporation to grow into a worldwide organization. In the same year, a base had been set up in Great Britain, near Liverpool, to reassemble Hudson bombers. A similar reassembly unit was established in Australia in 1939. When war came, further bases were established at Abbotsfinch and Renfrew in Scotland, and at Langford Lodge, near Belfast in Ireland, and a corresponding establishment was created in Dallas, Texas.

The expansion of effort led to the formation of the Lockheed Overseas Corporation, headed by the productive Lockheed salesman Carl Squier. When the war ended, these organizations were invaluable for forming the Lockheed Aircraft Service Company (LASC) in 1946.

LASC was the first of its type to be established by an aircraft manufacturing company. Its main lines of business included aircraft maintenance and modification; building aircraft systems trainers for a wide variety of aircraft, including the F-117A and the SR-71; technology transfer and training to foreign companies; technical field service (to include the operation of airports and bombing and gunnery ranges as well as the service and modification of aircraft and missiles); and the manufacture of flight data recorders and associated equipment. In the course of its more than five-decade history, it has processed nearly two hundred thousand aircraft of every major manufacturer. While much of the work was routine, all of it was important, particularly the maintenance of presidential aircraft. Some of the modifications performed were exotic, including the installation of the Gerard P. Kuiper Airborne Observatory on NASA's C-141 transport.

In recent years, the corporation has been at the leading edge of technology in the design, systems integration, and modification of exotic aircraft for intelligence, reconnaissance, and special operations. With headquarters at the Ontario (California) International Airport, LASC has a number of other Lockheed subsidiaries reporting to it, including Lockheed Aircraft Service International (LASI). A number of joint ventures with foreign countries, including China and Hungary, made LASC into a global operation before its merger with the Skunk Works.

Lockheed Air Terminal In 1940, Lockheed purchased the Union Air Terminal from United Air Lines for $1.5 million, with Cyril Chappellet being named president of the new company. At that time the airport was the major terminal for airlines in Southern California. Lockheed's ownership of the property facilitated its rapid expansion during the wartime years. The lessons learned at Burbank permitted the operation to expand to services including fueling at twenty-five additional airports in the United States, Panama, and Guam. As previously noted, after years of successful operation, the airport was sold in 1978 to the Hollywood-Burbank Airport Authority for $51 million. Memories of the airport linger, however; contemporary environmental concerns reach back to the more innocent days of industry when the disposition of fuels, paints, and other substances was not given the attention that it is today. The result is a series of legal disputes about the responsibility for cleaning up some of the environmental problems in the area.

Lockheed Engineering and Management Services Company (LEMSCO) (Later the Lockheed Engineering and Sciences Company and now Lockheed Martin Space Operations) Organized on the last day of 1979, LEMSCO absorbed several previous Lockheed entities into a new organization designed to provide government agencies, including NASA, with a variety of engineering, scientific, computer-related, and management services. The company derived from an earlier effort by a small team from Stavid Engineering, before it too became part of Lockheed. As time passed and technology progressed, the organization became increasingly sophisticated as it handled all space shuttle ground processing operations.

Lockheed Electronics Company (LEC) (Now the Lockheed Martin Electronics Sector) Lockheed started small with the 1959 acquisition of Stavid Engineering, a small electronics firm in Plainfield, New Jersey, merging the firm into the Lockheed Electronics and Avionics Division. The company was a leader in its field, producing a broad product line of radar and radar-based weapon control systems, air traffic control systems, computer components, and other electronic devices. Its diversification efforts led it to contracts in both commercial areas as mundane as building computing registers for oil delivery trucks, and exotic fields like tape recorders for satellites on NASA's deep space missions. In its later years, the company's most notable success was the Mark 86 shipboard fire-control system for the U.S. Navy.

Recognizing the need to attain a more prominent position in the electronics field, Lockheed acquired the Sanders Corporation in August 1986 to create Lockheed Sanders, Inc. The firm is now called Sanders, a Lockheed Martin Company.

Sanders had been founded in 1951 as Sanders Associates by eleven associates from the Raytheon Corporation. Within ten years it had become one of the nation's top one hundred defense contractors. The company built a reputation for technical excellence and pioneered in the field of electronic countermeasure systems. It became noted during the Vietnam War for its ability to react quickly to new requirements. During Desert Storm, more than two thousand Allied tactical aircraft were protected by Sanders-built systems.

Sanders built the electronic warfare suite for the F-22 fighter and has recently secured contracts for the next generation of electronic countermeasures equipment. Its president since 1988, Dr. John R. Kreick, is recognized internationally for his contributions to electronics countermeasures and for his management skills.

Lockheed Shipbuilding and Construction Company Lockheed's involvement with shipbuilding was briefly described in the text. The company had its origins with the establishment in 1889 as the Seattle division of the San Francisco Bridge Company. Founded to help repair the devastation of a fire that leveled Seattle's downtown area, the company branched into shipbuilding, launching its first ship in 1898. By 1899, the firm had changed its name to the Puget Sound Bridge and Dredging Company. Over the next sixty years it would establish an enviable reputation, building 146 ships and building major civilian and military installations. Lockheed acquired the firm in 1959, and changed its name to the Lockheed Shipbuilding and Construction Company in 1965. Despite successful completion of many projects, the combination of high labor rates and a technology that diverged from the main thrust of Lockheed's endeavors caused the company to discontinue operations in 1987.

A List of Lockheed
Test Pilots

All test pilots carry the cloak of glamour with them, but Lockheed test pilots occupy a special niche in aviation history. Their fame is extraordinary because they had the most extraordinary aircraft to fly. Lockheed products went far beyond "pushing the envelope"—they extended the envelope to entirely new frontiers. No other company had such an exotic series of aircraft to test, beginning with the Vega, and extending down through the P-38, P-80, F-104, U-2, SR-71, F-117, F-22, and, almost certainly, beyond.

Among the many Lockheed test pilots are some true giants, men to whom this entire book could have been devoted, and who either have or will have books written about them personally. It is impossible to choose the most capable from the long list, but the all-time all-stars include such experts as Eddie Bellante, Milo Burchan, Jimmy Mattern, Marshal Headle, Tony LeVier, Fish Salmon, Avery Black, Stan Beltz,

Jim Eastham, Dave Ferguson, Don Segner, Darryl Greenameyer, Bill Park, Sammy Mason, Vern Peterson, Lou Schalk, Joe Towle and more.

The list that follows includes most Lockheed test pilots and the planes with which they were closely associated.

Pilot	Major Aircraft Tested
Harvey Adams	C-130, B-47
Lloyd Adsit	C-130
Bob Akers	C-130
Jesse Allen	C-130, C-5, C-141
Harland Armitage	C-130, C-5, L-1011
Ken Armstrong	C-130, B-47
Olin Bankhead	C-130 (died in HTTB crash)
Eddie Bellante	Vega
Stan Beltz	YC-130
Avery Black	Super Constellation, P2V-7, WV-2, RC-121
Homer Blalock	C-130, C-5, C-141
Vance Breese	Altair, P-38 (contract test pilot)
Jim Brown III	F-117A
Milo Burcham	P-38, XP-80 (died in YP-80 crash)
Jim Buttram	C-130, JetStar
Herb Catlin	various
John Christensen	S-3A
Ernie Claypool	P-80 (died in P-80 accident)
Dick Clinton	C-130
Jack Clower	C-130, JetStar
O. J. Copeland	C-130
Ray Crandall	U2
Hank Dees	C-130, C-141, C-5
D. K. Dishew	C-130
Fred Dorr	C-130
Raleigh Drennon	C-130, JetStar
R. E. Dunai	C-130
Jack Dunn	C-130, C-5, JetStar
Bernie Dvorscak	C-130, C-5, C-141, Hummingbird
Jim Eastham	YF-12, SR-71
Ralph Evans	C-130, B-47
Jack Everett	C-130
Harold Farley Jr.	F-117A
Herb Faye	various
Dave Ferguson	F-117A, YF-22A

Pilot	Major Aircraft Tested
Jack Francis	C-130
W. N. Frazier	C-130
Joe Garrett	C-130, B-47
Bob Gilliland	F-104, SR-71
Kevin Gootee	C-130
Ray Goudey	XF-104, JetStar, U-2
Glen Gray	C-130, C-5, C-141
Mike Green	C-130
Darryl Greenameyer	SR-71
Kenny Grubbs	MB-334, P-3
Frank Hadden	C-130, C-5, C-141
Ivan Handley	C-130, B-47
Barret Hanley	C-130, C-5
Art Hansen	C-130, JetStar, B-47
Lloyd Harris	C-130, B-47
Al Head	C-130
Marshall Headle	Electra, Electra Jr., Super Electra, P-38
Walt Hensleigh	C-130, C-5, C-141
Les Hewitt	C-130, JetStar, B-47
Bob Hill	C-130, C-5, JetStar
Skip Holm	F-117A
Carl Hughes	C-130, C-5, C-141, B-47
J. L. Jenkins	C-130
Harold Johnson	various
Rick Johnstone	C-130, C-5
Billy Jones	C-130
Dave Kerzie	L-1011
Warren Lee	C-130, JetStar, B-47
R. E. Lemke	C-130
Tony LeVier	P-38, P-80, XF-90, F-94, F-104
Ted Limmer	C-130, C-5, C-141
Allan Loughead	Early Curtiss Pusher, F-1 Flying Boat
Bret Luedke	MB-334, F-22
Bob Luther	C-130, JetStar, B-47
Chuck Mahoy	C-130, JetStar
Bud Martin	C-130, Model 33 (Little Dipper)
Sammy Mason	Cheyenne
Robert Massey	various
Jimmy Mattern	P-38
Bob Matye	U-2

Pilot	Major Aircraft Tested
John McClure	C-130
George McEntire	various
"Slim" Menafee	various
Paul Metz	F-22
Don Mills	C-130, B-47
George Mitchell	C-130 (died in HTTB crash)
Don Moor	L-1011
Ralph Moore	C-5
Tom Morgenfeld	F-117A, YF-22A
Billy Morrell	C-130
"Red" Mulvahill	various
S. B. Murray	C-130
J. M. Myers	C-130
Joe Ozier	various
Bill Park	F-104, A-12, YF-12, Have Blue
Swede Parker	P-38
Lloyd Parsons	C-130, JetStar
Alfonso Persley	C-130, B-47
Art Peterson	F-104
Jeff Perterson	C-130
Vern Peterson	C-130, C-141, C-5, JetStar, B-47
Wiley Post	Vega (contract test pilot)
Frank Powers	U-2
Bob Price	C-130
Hank Price	C-130, C-5, C-141
Hal Quamme	C-130, Hummingbird
Bob Riedenauer	U-2, SR-71, F-117A
Wayne Roberts	C-130, P-3
Kenny Rooke	C-130
Rob Rowe	U-2
Herman Salmon	C-121, P-80, F-104
Don Segner	Cheyenne
Lyle Schaefer	C-130, P-3
Lou Schalk	A-12, F-104
Dick Schieber	JetStar
Bob Schumacher	U-2
Ralph Scott	C-130, B-47, JetStar
Carl Setili	JetStar
Jim Siberell	C-130, B-47
Robert Sieker	U-2 (died in U-2 accident)

Pilot	Major Aircraft Tested
Wendal Stultz	C-130
Leo Sullivan	C-130, C-5, C-141
Jim Thomas	F-117A
R. L. Thomas	C-130
William Thomas	various
Mick Thornstenson	C-130
Jim Towery	C-130, JetStar
Joe Towle	P-38
Roscoe Turner	Vega, Air Express (contract test pilot)
Ralph Virden	P-38 (died in YP-38 crash)
Vann Warren	C-130, JetStar
Bill Weaver	SR-71, L-1011
H. L. Webber	C-130
Ken Weir	S-3A, U-2, F-104, A-4S
Jim White	P-38, YP-80
Gene Whitton	C-130, C-141, B-47
Dick Wigton	JetStar
Roy Wimmer	YC-130
Roy Winter	various
Don Wright	C-130, JetStar, B-47
Ed Wycoff	C-130, JetStar, B-47

Bibliography

· · ·

Books

Days of Trial and Triumph: A Pictorial History of Lockheed. Burbank, Calif.: Lockheed Aircraft Corporation, 1969.

The Lockheed Star Chronicles. Vol. 1: 1934–1945. Palmdale, Calif.: Lockheed Employees Recreation Club/Lockheed Martin Skunk Works Star, 1996.

Days of Trial and Triumph. Burbank, Calif.: Corporate Publications, 1982.

Dateline Lockheed. Burbank, Calif.: Lockheed Corporate Communications, 1982.

Allen, Richard Sanders. *Revolution in the Sky.* New York: Orion Books, 1988.

Revolution in the Sky. Brattleboro, Vt.: Stephen Greene Press, 1967.

The Northrop Story. Atglen, Pa.: Schiffer Publishing, 1993.

Blay, Roy, ed. *Lockheed Horizons.* Issue 12. Burbank, Calif.: Lockheed Corporation, 1983.

Bodie, Warren. *The Lockheed P-38 Lightning.* Hiawassee, Ga.: Widewing Publications, 1991.

Bright, Charles D. *The Jet Makers.* Lawrence, Kans.: Regents Press of Kansas, 1978.

Craven, Wesley Frank, and James Lea Cate, eds. *The Army Air Forces in World War II.* 7 vols. Chicago: University of Chicago Press, 1948–58.

Davies, R. E. G. *Airlines of the United States Since 1914.* Washington, D.C.: Smithsonian Institution Press, 1982.

———. *Delta: An Airline and Its Aircraft.* Miami: Paladwr Press, 1990.

Francillon, Rene, J. *Lockheed Aircraft Since 1913.* London: Putnam & Company, 1983.

———. *McDonnell Douglas Aircraft Since 1920.* London: Putnam & Company, 1979.

Gunston, Bill. *World Encyclopedia of Aircraft Manufacturers.* Northamptonshire, England: Patrick Stephens, 1993.

Hawkins, Willis M. *Maintaining Aerospace Leadership.* New York: The Wings Club, 1983.

Holley, Irving Brinton, Jr., *Buying Aircraft: Materiel Procurement for the Army Air Forces.* Washington, D.C.: U.S. Government Printing Office, 1964.

Johnson, Clarence L., with Maggie Smith. *Kelly.* Washington, D.C.: Smithsonian Institution Press, 1985.

Kelsey, Benjamin S. *The Dragon's Teeth.* Washington, D.C.: Smithsonian Institution Press, 1982.

LeVier, Tony. *Pilot.* New York: Harper & Brothers, 1954.

Lewis, David W., and Wesley Phillips Newton. *Delta: The History of an Aircraft.* Athens, Ga.: University of Georgia Press, 1979.

Loftin, Laurence K., Jr. *Quest for Performance: The Evolution of Modern Aircraft.* Washington, D.C.: National Aeronautics and Space Administration, 1985.

Miller, Jay. *Lockheed's Skunk Works: The First Fifty Years.* Arlington, Tex.: Aerofax, Inc., 1993.

The X Planes, X-1 to X-29. Marine on St. Croix, Minn.: Specialty Press, 1983.

Newhouse, John. *The Sporty Game.* New York: Alfred A. Knopf, 1982.

Rich, Ben R., and Leo Janos. *Skunk Works: A Personal Memoir of My Years at Lockheed.* Boston: Little, Brown, and Co., 1994.

Sterling, Robert J. *From the Captain to the Colonel.* New York: Dial Press, 1980.

———. *Howard Hughes' Airline: An Informal History of TWA.* New York: St. Martin's Press, 1983.

Stinton, Darrol. *The Design of the Airplane.* New York: van Nostrand Reinhold Company, 1983.

Wagner, Ray. *American Combat Planes.* Garden City, N.Y.: 1982. Doubleday & Company, 1982.

Yenne, Bill. *Lockheed.* Greenwich, Conn.: Crescent Books, 1987.

Articles from American Aviation Historical Society Journal

Allen, Richard Sanders. "Barrel-Nosed Cigars." Vol. 9, no. 1 (1962), p. 39 (Lockheed Air Express).

———. "The Lockheed Sirius." Vol. 10, no. 4, (1965), pp. 266–80.

Armody, Francis J. "We Got Ours at Night (The Story of the Lockheed F-94 Starfire in Combat)." Vol. 27, no. 2, pp. 148–50.

Barr, Louis. "The Lockheed Constellation (A History) Part I." Vol. 28, no. 3/4 (1983), pp. 190–205.

———. "The Lockheed Constellation (A History) Part II." Vol 29, no. 1 (1984), pp. 44–55.

Bennett, William. "Medal of Honor Aircraft." [Major Charles J. Loring flying F-80B.] Vol. 19, no. 2 (1974), pp. 150–51.

Betts, Ed. "The Original Connies." Part I. Vol. 36, no. 2 (1991), pp. 114–23.

———. "The Original Connies." Part II. Vol. 36, no. 3 (1991), pp. 210–22.

———. "The Original Connies." Part III. Vol. 36, no. 4 (1991), pp. 290–305.

Emmert, Thomas M., and William T. Larkins. "Electra Junior, Lockheed's Model 12." Vol. 19, no. 4 (1974), pp. 307–19.

———. "Lockheed's Model 10 Electra." Vol. 23, no. 2 (1978), pp. 141–53.

———. "Super Electra: Lockheed's Model 14." Vol. 21, no. 2 (1976), pp. 101–11.

Galbraith, David. "The Aircraft History of Northwest Airlines." Vol. 21, no. 4 (1976), pp. 241–56.

Jarman, Lloyd. "Floats on Post-Rogers Lockheed." Vol. 37, no. 1 (1992), pp. 38–40.

Johnson, Chalmers A. "A Survey of Lockheed Orion History." Vol. 1, no. 1 (1956), pp. 4–6.

————. "Thirty Years of Lockheed Vegas." Vol. 2, no. 1 (1957), pp. 1–35.

Kohn, Gregory C. "The 'Century of Progress' Story." Vol. 3, no. 3 (1958), pp. 172–76. [Jimmy Mattern's attempted round-the-world flight.]

————. "The Story of Lockheed Vega-NR-469M." Vol. 3, no. 4 (1958), pp. 214–226.

"Lockheed L-188 Electra Production List." Vol. 7, no. 4 (1962), p. 284.

Mikesh, Robert C. "Lockheed C-121A Constellations in USAF and Civilian Service." Vol. 25, no. 1 (1980), pp. 10–18.

Ruotsala, James A. "Lockheed Vegas in Southeastern Alaska." Vol. 25, no. 1 (1980), pp. 2–9.

Scott, Denham. "Where Are They Now?—Allan Lockheed." Vol. 14, no. 1, pp. 59–60.

Smalley, L. S. "Civilian Lockheed-Vega 'Ventura' Modifications." Vol. 1, no. 2 (1956), pp. 41–42.

Smith, P. B. "Final Report of the Procurement, Inspection, Testing, and Acceptance of the Lockheed XP-58 Airplanes." Vol. 27, no. 2 (1982), pp. 120–35.

Wilson, Kenneth D. "Lloyd C. Stearman, 1898–1975." Vol. 36, no. 2 (1991), pp. 82–93.

Wright, Jay E. "The Lockheed Q-Star." Vol. 39, no. 3 (1994), p. 234.

Other Periodicals

Buzzetti, C. J., and W. L. Howland. "Measurement of Maneuvering Loads in Flight (P-38)." *Journal of the Aeronautics Sciences.* Vol. 12, no. 6 (April 1945), pp. 195–202.

Johnson, Clarence L. "Development of the Lockheed P-80A Jet Fighter Airplane." *Journal of the Aeronautics Sciences.* Vol. 14, no. 12 (December 1947), pp. 659–79.

————. "The Design of High-Speed Military Airplanes." *Journal of the Aeronautics Sciences.* Vol. 8, no. 12 (October 1941), pp. 467–74.

Lee, John G. "Air-Cooled vs. Liquid-Cooled Aircraft." *Journal of the Aeronautics Sciences.* Vol. 8, no. 6 (April 1941), pp. 219–29.

Lockheed Corporation. "Lockheed Today." Vol. 1, no. 10 (June 1992).

"Lockheed Air Express." *Aviation,* 14 May 1928, pp. 1370–72.

Scott, Denham. "The Lockheed Story." *Southern California Industrial News.* Issues of 1 May 1967 through 23 December 1968 (complete). [Scott was an early Lockheed employee and worked on the Vega airplanes.]

Stack, John. "Compressible Flows in Aeronautics." *Journal of the Aeronautics Sciences.* Vol. 12, no. 2 (April 1945), pp. 127–48.

Wright, T. P. "Speed—and Airplane Possibilities." *Journal of the Aeronautics Sciences.* Vol, 4, no. 3 (January 1937), pp. 89–99.

Oral History

Interviews by W. D. Perreault

R. A. Anderson, February 12, 1982.

Herschel J. Brown, February, 12, 1982.

J. E. Canaday, February 3, 1982.

Cyril Chappellet, February 12, 1982.

Harvey Christen, February 4, 1982.

F. A. (Al) Cleveland, date uncertain, probably early 1982.

R. Donaldson, February 11, 1982.

Frank Frain, February 11, 1982.

C. S. Gross, May 18, 1978.

D. J. Haughton, January 11, 12, 19, 1982, and April 5, 1982.

R. W. Haack, April 13, 1982.

M. C. Haddon, February 5, 1982.

W. M. Hawkins, February 1–2, 1982.

H. L. Hibbard, February 2, 1982.

J. K. Hull, February 8, 1982.

F. S. Jacques, February 4, 1982.

V. A. Johnson, May 7 and 8, 1982.

L. O. Kitchen, January 27, 1982.

A. C. Kotchian, February 10, 1982.

A. W. LeVier, January 26, 1982.

A. G. Meyer, February 23, 1982.

R. I. Mitchell, February 26, 1982.

Erik Nelson, April 13, 1982.

R. J. Osborn, February 9, 1982.

G. E. Rice, March 25, 1982.

L. E. Root, February 19, 1982.

L. Sullivan, May 28, 1982.

Anthony Stadlman, March 31, 1982.

C. S. Wagner, February 24, 1982.

W. R. Wilson, April 1, 1982.

Index

· · ·